Microsoft® Official Academic Course

Installing and Configuring Windows Server® 2012 Exam 70-410

Craig Zacker

Credits

VP & PUBLISHER	Don Fowley
EXECUTIVE EDITOR	John Kane
DIRECTOR OF SALES	Mitchell Beaton
EXECUTIVE MARKETING MANAGER	Chris Ruel
MICROSOFT PRODUCT MANAGER	Gene R. Longo of Microsoft Learning
TECHNICAL EDITORS	Jeff T. Parker
	Kenneth Hess
EDITORIAL PROGRAM ASSISTANT	Jennifer Lartz
ASSISTANT MARKETING MANAGER	Debbie Martin
SENIOR PRODUCTION MANAGER	Janis Soo
ASSOCIATE PRODUCTION MANAGER	Joel Balbin
CREATIVE DIRECTOR	Harry Nolan
COVER DESIGNER	Georgina Smith
SENIOR PRODUCT DESIGNER	Thomas Kulesa
CONTENT EDITOR	Wendy Ashenberg
PRODUCTION EDITOR	Eugenia Lee
TECHNOLOGY AND MEDIA	Tom Kulesa/Wendy Ashenberg

This book was set in Garamond by Aptara, Inc. and printed and bound by Bind-Rite Robbinsville. The covers were printed by Bind-Rite Robbinsville.

ISBN 978-1-118-51107-7

Printed in the United States of America

10 9 8 7 6 5 4 3 2 1

Foreword from the Publisher

Wiley's publishing vision for the Microsoft Official Academic Course series is to provide students and instructors with the skills and knowledge they need to use Microsoft technology effectively in all aspects of their personal and professional lives. Quality instruction is required to help both educators and students get the most from Microsoft's software tools and to become more productive. Thus, our mission is to make our instructional programs trusted educational companions for life.

To accomplish this mission, Wiley and Microsoft have partnered to develop the highest-quality educational programs for information workers, IT professionals, and developers. Materials created by this partnership carry the brand name "Microsoft Official Academic Course," assuring instructors and students alike that the content of these textbooks is fully endorsed by Microsoft and that they provide the highest-quality information and instruction on Microsoft products. The Microsoft Official Academic Course textbooks are "Official" in still one more way—they are the officially sanctioned courseware for Microsoft IT Academy members.

The Microsoft Official Academic Course series focuses on *workforce development*. These programs are aimed at those students seeking to enter the workforce, change jobs, or embark on new careers as information workers, IT professionals, and developers. Microsoft Official Academic Course programs address their needs by emphasizing authentic workplace scenarios with an abundance of projects, exercises, cases, and assessments.

The Microsoft Official Academic Courses are mapped to Microsoft's extensive research and job-task analysis, the same research and analysis used to create the Microsoft Certified Solutions Associate (MCSA) exam. The textbooks focus on real skills for real jobs. As students work through the projects and exercises in the textbooks and labs, they enhance their level of knowledge and their ability to apply the latest Microsoft technology to everyday tasks. These students also gain resume-building credentials that can assist them in finding a job, keeping their current job, or furthering their education.

The concept of life-long learning is today an utmost necessity. Job roles, and even whole job categories, are changing so quickly that none of us can stay competitive and productive without continuously updating our skills and capabilities. The Microsoft Official Academic Course offerings, and their focus on Microsoft certification exam preparation, provide a means for people to acquire and effectively update their skills and knowledge. Wiley supports students in this endeavor through the development and distribution of these courses as Microsoft's official academic publisher.

Today educational publishing requires attention to providing quality print and robust electronic content. By integrating Microsoft Official Academic Course products, MOAC Labs Online, and Microsoft certifications, we are better able to deliver efficient learning solutions for students and teachers alike.

Joseph Heider

General Manager and Senior Vice President

Preface

Welcome to the Microsoft Official Academic Course (MOAC) program for becoming a Microsoft Certified Solutions Associate for Windows Server 2012. MOAC represents the collaboration between Microsoft Learning and John Wiley & Sons, Inc. Microsoft and Wiley teamed up to produce a series of textbooks that deliver compelling and innovative teaching solutions to instructors and superior learning experiences for students. Infused and informed by in-depth knowledge from the creators of Windows Server 2012, and crafted by a publisher known worldwide for the pedagogical quality of its products, these textbooks maximize skills transfer in minimum time. Students are challenged to reach their potential by using their new technical skills as highly productive members of the workforce.

Because this knowledgebase comes directly from Microsoft, the architect of Windows Server 2012 and creator of the Microsoft Certified Solutions Associate exams, you are sure to receive the topical coverage that is most relevant to students' personal and professional success. Microsoft's direct participation not only assures you that MOAC textbook content is accurate and current, it also means that students will receive the best instruction possible to enable their success on certification exams and in the workplace.

■ The Microsoft Official Academic Course Program

The Microsoft Official Academic Course series is a complete program for instructors and institutions to prepare and deliver great courses on Microsoft software technologies. With MOAC, we recognize that because of the rapid pace of change in the technology and curriculum developed by Microsoft, there is an ongoing set of needs beyond classroom instruction tools for an instructor to be ready to teach the course. The MOAC program endeavors to provide solutions for all these needs in a systematic manner in order to ensure a successful and rewarding course experience for both instructor and student, including technical and curriculum training for instructor readiness with new software releases; the software itself for student use at home for building hands-on skills, assessment, and validation of skill development; and a great set of tools for delivering instruction in the classroom and lab. All are important to the smooth delivery of an interesting course on Microsoft software, and all are provided with the MOAC program. We think about the model below as a gauge for ensuring that we completely support you in your goal of teaching a great course. As you evaluate your instructional materials options, you may wish to use the model for comparison purposes with available products.

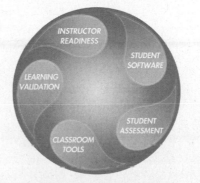

■ Textbook Organization

This textbook is organized in nineteen lessons, with each lesson corresponding to a particular exam objective for the 70-410 Installing and Configuring Windows Server 2012 exam. This MOAC textbook covers all the learning objectives for the 70-410 certification exam, which is the first exam needed in order to obtain a Microsoft Certified Solutions Associate (MCSA) certification. The exam objectives are highlighted throughout the textbook.

■ Pedagogical Features

Many pedagogical features have been developed specifically for Microsoft Official Academic Course programs.

Presenting the extensive procedural information and technical concepts woven throughout the textbook raises challenges for the student and instructor alike. The Illustrated Book Tour that follows provides a guide to the rich features contributing to Microsoft Official Academic Course program's pedagogical plan. Following is a list of key features in each lesson designed to prepare students for success on the certification exams and in the workplace:

- Each lesson begins with an overview of the skills covered in the lesson. More than a standard list of learning objectives, the overview correlates skills to the certification exam objective.

- Illustrations: Screen images provide visual feedback as students work through the exercises. The images reinforce key concepts, provide visual clues about the steps, and allow students to check their progress.

- Key Terms: Important technical vocabulary is listed at the beginning of the lesson. When these terms are used later in the lesson, they appear in bold italic type and are defined.

- Engaging point-of-use reader aids, located throughout the lessons, tell students why this topic is relevant (*The Bottom Line*), provide students with helpful hints (*Take Note*), or show cross-references to where content is covered in greater detail (*X Ref*). Reader aids also provide additional relevant or background information that adds value to the lesson.

- Certification Ready features throughout the text signal students where a specific certification objective is covered. They provide students with a chance to check their understanding of that particular exam objective and, if necessary, review the section of the lesson where it is covered. In addition, some Certification Ready sidebars will provide more general information that will assist with your exam preparation.

- Using Windows PowerShell: *Windows PowerShell* is a Windows command-line shell that can be utilized with many Windows Server 2012 functions. The Using Windows PowerShell sidebar provides Windows PowerShell-based alternatives to graphical user interface (GUI) functions or procedures. These sidebars begin with a brief description of what the Windows PowerShell commands can do, and they contain any parameters needed to perform the task at hand. When needed, explanations are provided for the functions of individual parameters.

- Knowledge Assessments provide lesson-ending activities that test students' comprehension and retention of the material taught, presented using some of the question types that they'll see on the certification exam.

- An important supplement to this textbook is the accompanying lab work. Labs are available via a Lab Manual and also by MOAC Labs Online. MOAC Labs Online provides students with the ability to work on the actual software simply by connecting through their Internet Explorer web browser. Either way, the labs use real-world scenarios to help students learn workplace skills associated with installing and configuring Windows Server 2012.

▪ Lesson Features

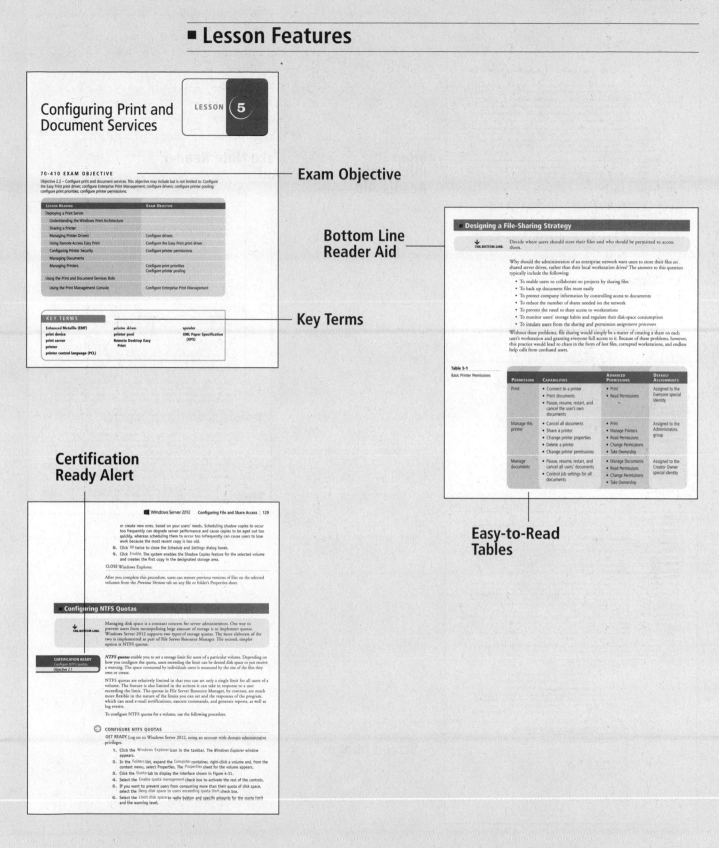

Exam Objective

Bottom Line Reader Aid

Key Terms

Certification Ready Alert

Easy-to-Read Tables

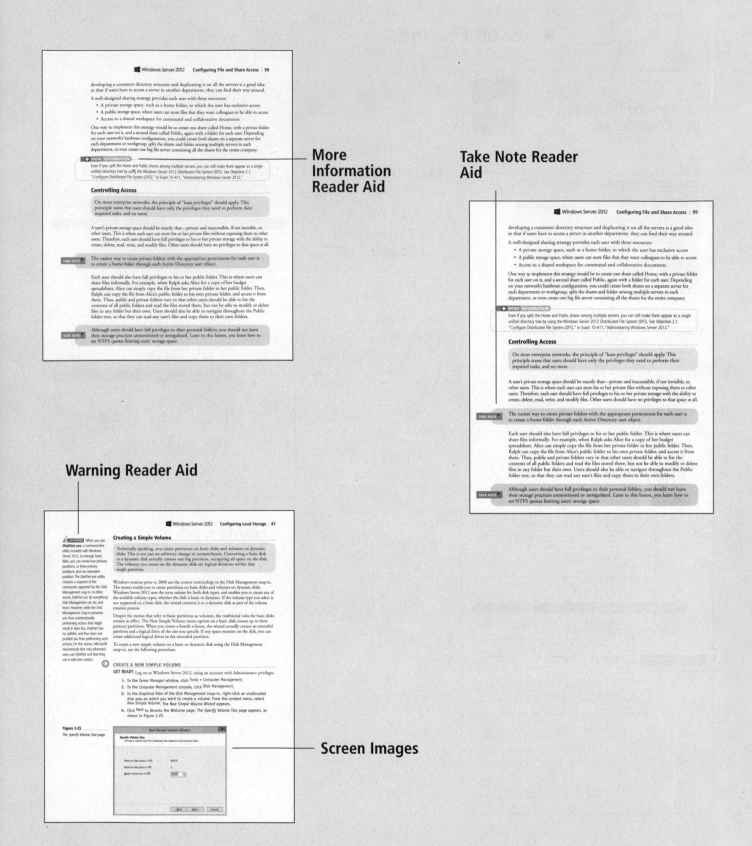

More Information Reader Aid

Take Note Reader Aid

Warning Reader Aid

Screen Images

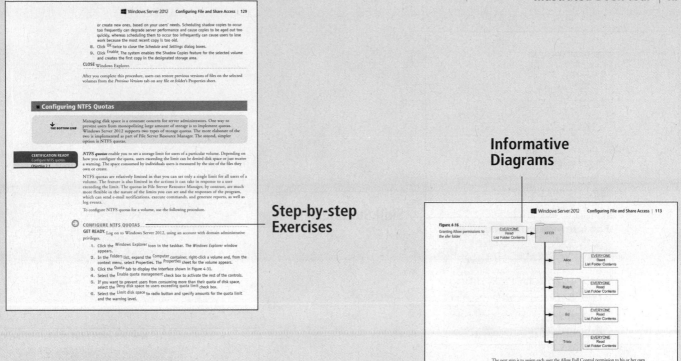

Informative Diagrams

Step-by-step Exercises

X Ref Reader Aid

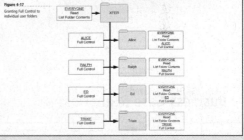

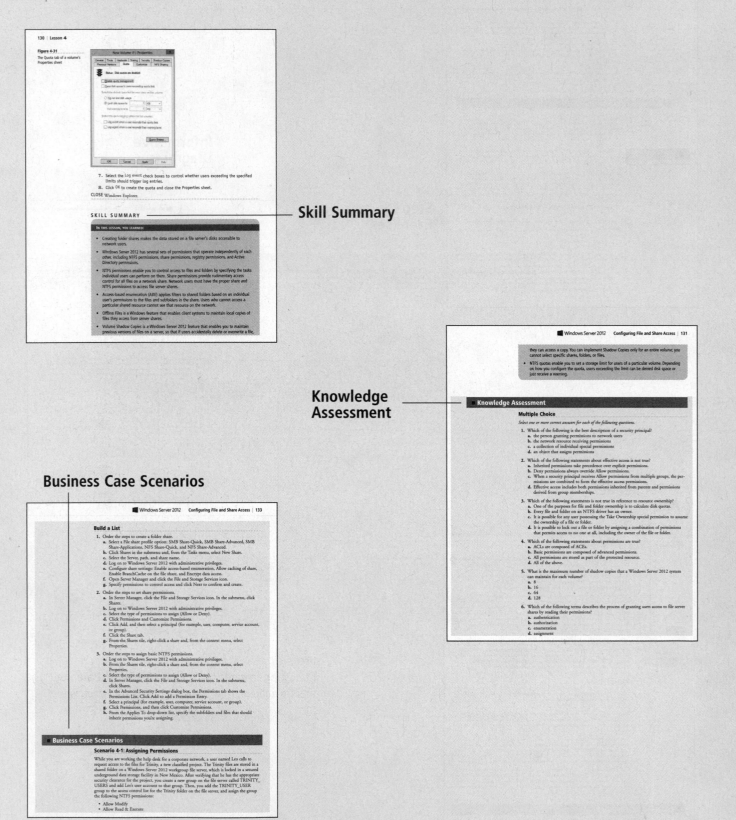

Skill Summary

Knowledge Assessment

Business Case Scenarios

Conventions and Features Used in This Book

This book uses particular fonts, symbols, and heading conventions to highlight important information or to call your attention to special steps. For more information about the features in each lesson, refer to the Illustrated Book Tour section.

CONVENTION	MEANING
↓ THE BOTTOM LINE	This feature provides a brief summary of the material to be covered in the section that follows.
CERTIFICATION READY	This feature signals the point in the text where a specific certification objective is covered. It provides you with a chance to check your understanding of that particular MCSA objective and, if necessary, review the section of the lesson where it is covered. In addition, some Certification Ready sidebars will provide more general information that will assist with your exam preparation.
TAKE NOTE* ✚ MORE INFORMATION	Reader aids appear in shaded boxes found in your text. *Take Note* and *More Information* provide helpful hints related to particular tasks or topics.
USING WINDOWS POWERSHELL	The Using Windows PowerShell sidebar provides Windows PowerShell-based alternatives to graphical user interface (GUI) functions or procedures.
⚠ WARNING	*Warning* points out instances when error or misuse could cause damage to the computer or network.
X REF	These *X Ref* notes provide pointers to information discussed elsewhere in the textbook or describe interesting features of Windows Server that are not directly addressed in the current topic or exercise.
A *shared printer* can be used by many individuals on a network.	Key terms appear in bold italic.
cd\windows\system32	Commands that are to be typed are shown in a special font.
Click Install Now.	Any button on the screen you are supposed to click on or select will appear in blue.

Instructor Support Program

The Microsoft Official Academic Course programs are accompanied by a rich array of resources that incorporate the extensive textbook visuals to form a pedagogically cohesive package. These resources provide all the materials instructors need to deploy and deliver their courses. Resource information available at www.wiley.com/college/microsoft includes:

- **DreamSpark Premium** is designed to provide the easiest and most inexpensive developer tools, products, and technologies available to faculty and students in labs, classrooms, and on student PCs. A free 3-year membership is available to qualified MOAC adopters.

  Note: Windows Server 2012 can be downloaded from DreamSpark Premium for use in this course.

- The **Instructor's Guide** contains solutions to all the textbook exercises as well as chapter summaries and lecture notes. The Instructor's Guide and Syllabi for various term lengths are available from the Instructor's Book Companion site.

- The **Test Bank** contains hundreds of questions organized by lesson in multiple-choice, best answer, build list, and essay formats and is available to download from the Instructor's Book Companion site. A complete answer key is provided.

- **PowerPoint Presentations.** A complete set of PowerPoint presentations is available on the Instructor's Book Companion site to enhance classroom presentations. Tailored to the text's topical coverage, these presentations are designed to convey key Windows Server 2012 concepts addressed in the text.

- **Available Textbook Figures.** All figures from the text are on the Instructor's Book Companion site. By using these visuals in class discussions, you can help focus students' attention on key elements of Windows Server and help them understand how to use it effectively in the workplace.

- **MOAC Labs Online.** MOAC Labs Online is a cloud-based environment that enables students to conduct exercises using real Microsoft products. These are not simulations but instead are live virtual machines where faculty and students can perform any activities they would on a local machine. MOAC Labs Online relieves the need for local setup, configuration, and most troubleshooting tasks. This represents an opportunity to lower costs, eliminate the hassle of lab setup, and support and improve student access and portability. Contact your Wiley rep about including MOAC Labs Online with your course offering.

- **Lab Answer Keys.** Answer keys for review questions found in the lab manuals and MOAC Labs Online are available on the Instructor's Book Companion site.

- **Lab Worksheets.** The review questions found in the lab manuals and MOAC Labs Online are gathered in Microsoft Word documents for students to use. These are available on the Instructor's Book Companion site.

- **Sharing with Fellow Faculty Members.** When it comes to improving the classroom experience, there is no better source of ideas and inspiration than your colleagues teaching the same material. The Wiley Faculty Network connects teachers with technology, facilitates the exchange of best practices, and helps to enhance instructional efficiency and effectiveness. Wiley Faculty Network activities include technology training and tutorials, virtual seminars, peer to peer exchanges of experiences and ideas, personal consulting, and sharing of resources. For details visit www.WhereFacultyConnect.com.

Wiley Faculty Network

DREAMSPARK PREMIUM—FREE 3-YEAR MEMBERSHIP AVAILABLE TO QUALIFIED ADOPTERS!

DreamSpark Premium is designed to provide the easiest and most inexpensive way for universities to make the latest Microsoft developer tools, products, and technologies available in labs, classrooms, and on student PCs. DreamSpark Premium is an annual membership program for departments teaching Science, Technology, Engineering, and Mathematics (STEM) courses. The membership provides a complete solution to keep academic labs, faculty, and students on the leading edge of technology.

Software available through the DreamSpark Premium program is provided at no charge to adopting departments through the Wiley and Microsoft publishing partnership.

Contact your Wiley rep for details.

For more information about the DreamSpark Premium program, go to Microsoft's DreamSpark website.

Note: Windows Server 2012 can be downloaded from DreamSpark Premium for use in this course.

■ Important Web Addresses and Phone Numbers

To locate the Wiley Global Education Rep in your area, go to http://www.wiley.com/college and click on the *"Who's My Rep?"* link at the top of the page, or call the MOAC Toll Free Number: 1 + (888) 764-7001 (U.S. & Canada only).

To learn more about becoming a Microsoft Certified Solutions Associate and exam availability, visit Microsoft's Training & Certification website.

Student Support Program

Book Companion Website (www.wiley.com/college/microsoft)

The students' book companion site for the MOAC series includes any resources, exercise files, and web links that will be used in conjunction with this course.

Wiley E-Text: Powered by VitalSource

Wiley E-Texts: Powered by VitalSource are innovative, electronic versions of printed textbooks. Students can buy Wiley E-Texts for around 40% off the U.S. price of the printed text and get the added value of permanence and portability. Wiley E-Texts provide students with numerous additional benefits that are not available with other e-text solutions.

Wiley E-Texts are NOT subscriptions; students download the Wiley E-Text to their computer desktops. Students own the content they buy to keep for as long as they want. Once a Wiley E-Text is downloaded to the computer desktop, students have instant access to all of the content without being online. Students can also print the sections they prefer to read in hard copy. Students also have access to fully integrated resources within their Wiley E-Text. From highlighting their e-text to taking and sharing notes, students can easily personalize their Wiley E-Text as they are reading or following along in class.

Microsoft Windows Server Software

Windows Server 2012 software is available through a DreamSpark student membership. DreamSpark is a Microsoft Program that provides students with free access to Microsoft software for learning, teaching, and research purposes. Students can download full versions of Windows Server 2012 and other types of software at no cost by visiting Microsoft's DreamSpark website.

▪ Microsoft Certification

Microsoft Certification has many benefits and enables you to keep your skills relevant, applicable, and competitive. In addition, Microsoft Certification is an industry standard that is recognized worldwide—which helps open doors to potential job opportunities. After you earn your Microsoft Certification, you have access to a number of benefits, which can be found on the Microsoft Certified Professional member site.

Microsoft Learning has reinvented the Microsoft Certification Program by building cloud-related skills validation into the industry's most recognized certification program. Microsoft Certified Solutions Expert (MCSE) and Microsoft Certified Solutions Developer (MCSD) are Microsoft's flagship certifications for professionals who want to lead their IT organization's journey to the cloud. These certifications recognize IT professionals with broad and deep skill sets across Microsoft solutions. The Microsoft Certified Solutions Associate (MCSA) is the certification for aspiring IT professionals and is also the prerequisite certification necessary to earn an MCSE. These new certifications integrate cloud-related and on-premise skills validation in order to support organizations and recognize individuals who have the skills required to be productive using Microsoft technologies.

On-premise or in the cloud, Microsoft training and certification empowers technology professionals to expand their skills and gain knowledge directly from the source. Securing these essential skills will allow you to grow your career and make yourself indispensable as the industry shifts to the cloud. Cloud computing ultimately enables IT to focus on more mission-critical activities, raising the bar of required expertise for IT professionals and developers. These reinvented certifications test on a deeper set of skills that map to real-world business context. Rather than testing only on a feature of a technology, Microsoft Certifications now validate more advanced skills and a deeper understanding of the platform.

Microsoft Certified Solutions Associate (MCSA)

The Microsoft Certified Solutions Associate (MCSA) certification is for students preparing to get their first jobs in Microsoft technology. Whether in the cloud or on-premise, this certification validates the core platform skills needed in an IT environment. The MCSA certifications are a requirement to achieve Microsoft's flagship Microsoft Certified Solutions Expert (MCSE) and Microsoft Certified Solutions Developer (MCSD) certifications.

The MCSA Windows Server 2012 certification shows that you have the primary set of Windows Server skills that are relevant across multiple solution areas in a business environment. The MCSA Windows Server 2012 certification is a prerequisite for earning the MCSE Server Infrastructure certification, the MCSE Desktop Infrastructure certification, or the MCSE Private Cloud certification.

Exam 70-410, Installing and Configuring Windows Server 2012, is part one of a series of three exams that validate the skills and knowledge necessary to implement a core Windows Server 2012 Infrastructure into an existing enterprise environment. This exam will validate the initial implementation and configuration of the Windows Server 2012 core services, such as Active Directory and the networking services. This exam along with the remaining two exams will collectively validate the skills and knowledge necessary for implementing, managing, maintaining, and provisioning services and infrastructure in a Windows Server 2012 environment.

If you are a student new to IT who may not yet be ready for MCSA, the Microsoft Technology Associate (MTA) certification is an optional starting point that may be available through your school.

You can learn more about the MCSA certification at the Microsoft Training & Certification website.

Preparing to Take an Exam

Unless you are a very experienced user, you will need to use test preparation materials to prepare to complete the test correctly and within the time allowed. The Microsoft Official Academic Course series is designed to prepare you with a strong knowledge of all exam topics, and with some additional review and practice on your own, you should feel confident in your ability to pass the appropriate exam.

After you decide which exam to take, review the list of objectives for the exam. You can easily identify tasks that are included in the objective list by locating the exam objective overview at the start of each lesson and the Certification Ready sidebars in the margin of the lessons in this book.

To register for the 70-410 exam, visit Microsoft Training & Certifications Registration webpage for directions on how to register with Prometric, the company that delivers the MCSA exams. Keep in mind these important items about the testing procedure:

- **What to expect.** Microsoft Certification testing labs typically have multiple workstations, which may or may not be occupied by other candidates. Test center administrators strive to provide a quiet and comfortable environment for all test takers.

- **Plan to arrive early.** It is recommended that you arrive at the test center at least 30 minutes before the test is scheduled to begin.

- **Bring your identification.** To take your exam, you must bring the identification (ID) that was specified when you registered for the exam. If you are unclear about which forms of ID are required, contact the exam sponsor identified in your registration information. Although requirements vary, you typically must show two valid forms of ID, one with a photo, both with your signature.

- **Leave personal items at home.** The only item allowed into the testing area is your identification, so leave any backpacks, laptops, briefcases, and other personal items at home. If you have items that cannot be left behind (such as purses), the testing center might have small lockers available for use.

- **Nondisclosure agreement.** At the testing center, Microsoft requires that you accept the terms of a nondisclosure agreement (NDA) and complete a brief demographic survey before taking your certification exam.

Craig Zacker is an instructor, writer, editor, and networker whose computing experience began in the days of teletypes and paper tape. After making the move from minicomputers to PCs, he worked as a network administrator and PC support technician while operating a freelance desktop publishing business. After earning a Master's Degree in English and American Literature from New York University, Craig worked extensively on the integration of Microsoft Windows operating systems into existing internetworks, supported fleets of Windows workstations, and was employed as a technical writer, content provider, and webmaster for the online services group of a large software company. Since devoting himself to writing and editing full-time, Craig has authored or contributed to dozens of books on operating systems, networking topics, and PC hardware. He has also published articles with top industry publications, developed online training courses for the various firms, and authored the following Microsoft Official Academic Course (MOAC), Academic Learning Series (ALS), and Self-Paced Training Kit titles:

MOAC: Windows Server 2008, Enterprise Administrator (Exam 70-647)

MOAC: Windows 7 Configuration (Exam 70-680)

MOAC: Windows Server Administrator (Exam 70-646)

MOAC: Configuring Windows Server 2008 Application Services (Exam 70-643)

MOAC: Configuring Microsoft Windows Vista (Exam 70-620)

MOAC: Implementing & Administering Security in a Windows Server 2003 Network (Exam 70-299)

MOAC: Managing & Maintaining a Microsoft Windows Server 2003 Environment (Exam 70-290)

ALS: Network+ Certification, Second, Third, and Fourth Editions

ALS: Planning & Maintaining a Windows Server 2003 Network Infrastructure (Exam 70-293)

ALS: Microsoft Windows 2000 Network Infrastructure Administration, Second Edition (2002)

MCSE Self-Paced Training Kit (Exam 70-293): Planning & Maintaining a Microsoft Windows Server 2003 Network Infrastructure (2003)

MCSA/MCSE Self-Paced Training Kit: Microsoft Windows 2000 Network Infrastructure Administration, Exam 70-216, Second Edition (2002)

MC SA Training Kit: Managing a Windows 2000 Network Environment (2002)

Network+ Certification Training Kit, First and Second Editions (2001)

Network+ Certification Readiness Review (2001)

Acknowledgments

We thank the MOAC faculty and instructors who have assisted us in building the Microsoft Official Academic Course courseware. These elite educators have acted as our sounding board on key pedagogical and design decisions leading to the development of the MOAC courseware for future Information Technology workers. They have provided invaluable advice in the service of quality instructional materials, and we truly appreciate their dedication to technology education.

Brian Bridson, Baker College of Flint

David Chaulk, Baker College Online

Ron Handlon, Remington College—Tampa Campus

Katherine James, Seneca College of Applied Arts & Technology

Wen Liu, ITT Educational Services

Zeshan Sattar, Pearson in Practice

Jared Spencer, Westwood College Online

David Vallerga, MTI College

Bonny Willy, Ivy Tech State College

We also thank Microsoft Learning's Lutz Ziob, Don Field, Tim Sneath, Moorthy Uppaluri, Keith Loeber, Rob Linsky, Anne Hamilton, Shelby Grieve, Christine Yoshida, Gene Longo, Mike Mulcare, Paul Schmitt, Martin DelRe, Colin Klein, Julia Stasio, and Josh Barnhill for their encouragement and support in making the Microsoft Official Academic Course programs the finest academic materials for mastering the newest Microsoft technologies for both students and instructors.

Brief Contents

Contents

Lesson 11: Deploying and Configuring the DHCP Service 298

Lesson 12: Deploying and Configuring the DNS Service 333

Lesson 19: Configuring Windows Firewall   550

Installing Servers

70-410 EXAM OBJECTIVE

Objective 1.1 – Install servers. This objective may include but is not limited to: Plan for a server installation; plan for server roles; plan for a server upgrade; install Server Core; optimize resource utilization by using Features on Demand; migrate roles from previous versions of Windows Server.

LESSON HEADING	EXAM OBJECTIVE
Selecting a Windows Server 2012 Edition	Plan for a server installation
Supporting Server Roles	Plan for server roles
Supporting Server Virtualization	
Server Licensing	
Installing Windows Server 2012	
System Requirements	
Performing a Clean Installation	
Installing Third-Party Drivers	
Working with Installation Partitions	
Choosing Installation Options	
Using Server Core	Install Server Core
Using the Minimal Server Interface	
Using Features on Demand	Optimize resource utilization by using Features on Demand
Upgrading Servers	Plan for a server upgrade
Upgrade Paths	
Preparing to Upgrade	
Performing an Upgrade Installation	
Migrating Roles	Migrate roles from previous versions of Windows Server
Installing Windows Server Migration Tools	
Using Migration Guides	

KEY TERMS

cmdlets	**Server Core**	**Windows PowerShell**
physical operating system environment (POSE)	**virtual operating system environment (VOSE)**	**WinSxS**

■ Selecting a Windows Server 2012 Edition

↓ **THE BOTTOM LINE**   Microsoft releases all its operating systems in multiple editions, which provides consumers with various price points and feature sets.

When planning a server deployment, you should choose the operating system edition based on multiple factors, including the following:

- The roles you intend the servers to perform
- The virtualization strategy you intent to implement
- The licensing strategy you plan to use

Compared with Windows Server 2008, Microsoft has simplified the process of selecting a Windows Server 2012 edition by reducing the available products. As with Windows Server 2008 R2, Windows Server 2012 requires a 64-bit processor architecture. All 32-bit versions have been eliminated, and for the first time since the Windows NT Server 4.0 release, no build will be released supporting Itanium processors. This leaves Windows Server 2012 with the following core editions:

- **Windows Server 2012 Datacenter:** This edition is designed for large and powerful servers with up to 64 processors and fault-tolerance features such as hot add processor support. As a result, this edition is available only through the Microsoft volume-licensing program and from original equipment manufacturers (OEMs), bundled with a server.
- **Windows Server 2012 Standard:** This edition includes the full set of Windows Server 2012 features, varying from the Datacenter edition only by the number of virtual machine instances permitted by the license.
- **Windows Server 2012 Essentials:** This edition includes nearly all the features in the Standard and Datacenter editions, except for Server Core, Hyper-V, and Active Directory Federation Services. This edition is limited to one physical or virtual server instance and a maximum of 25 users.
- **Windows Server 2012 Foundation:** This reduced version of the operating system is designed for small businesses that require only basic server features such as file and print services and application support. This edition includes no virtualization rights and is limited to 15 users.

CERTIFICATION READY
Plan for a server installation.
Objective 1.1

These various editions are priced commensurate with their capabilities. Obviously, your goal is to purchase the most inexpensive edition that provides all your needs. The following sections examine the primary differences between the Windows Server 2012 editions.

Supporting Server Roles

Windows Server 2012 includes predefined combinations of services called *roles* that implement common server functions.

Computers running the Windows Server 2012 operating system can perform a wide variety of tasks, using both the software included with the product and third-party applications. The activities Windows Server 2012 performs for network clients are known as roles. After you install the Windows Server 2012 operating system, you can use Server Manager or *Windows PowerShell* to assign one or more roles to that computer.

The roles included with Windows Server 2012 fall into three basic categories:

- **Directory services** store, organize, and supply information about a network and its resources.
- **Infrastructure services** provide support services for network clients.
- **Application services** provide communications services, operating environments, or programming interfaces for specific applications.

Table 1-1 lists the roles that Microsoft supplies with Windows Server 2012.

Table 1-1

Windows Server 2012 Server Roles

DIRECTORY SERVICES	INFRASTRUCTURE SERVICES	APPLICATION SERVICES
Active Directory Certificate Services implements certification authorities (CAs) and other services that facilitate the creation and management of the public key certificates used by the identity and access control elements of the Windows Server 2012 security infrastructure.	**DHCP (Dynamic Host Configuration Protocol) Server** provides network clients with dynamically assigned IP addresses and other TCP/IP configuration settings, such as subnet masks, default gateway addresses, and Domain Name System (DNS) server addresses.	**Application Server** provides an integrated environment for deploying and running server-based business applications designed within (or expressly for) the organization, such as those requiring the services provided by Internet Information Services (IIS), Microsoft .NET Framework 2.0 and 3.0, COM+, ASP .NET, Message Queuing, or Windows Communication Foundation (WCF).
Active Directory Domain Services (AD DS) configure the server to function as an Active Directory domain controller, which stores and manages a distributed database of network resources and application-specific information.	**DNS Server** provides name-to-address and address-to-name resolution services for AD DS and Internet clients. The Windows Server 2012 DNS server implementation also supports dynamic DNS and DHCP integration.	**Fax Server** enables you to manage fax devices and clients to send and receive faxes over the network.
Active Directory Federation Services create a single sign-on environment by implementing trust relationships that enable users on one network to access applications on other networks without providing a secondary set of logon credentials.	**Hyper-V** provides a hypervisor-based environment in which administrators can create virtual machines, each of which provides an isolated instance of the operating system environment.	**File and Storage Services** install tools and services that enhance Windows Server 2012's basic ability to provide network clients with access to files stored on server drives, including Distributed File System (DFS), DFS Replication, Storage Manager for Storage Area Networks (SANs), fast file searching, and file services for UNIX clients.

(continued)

Table 1-1

(continued)

DIRECTORY SERVICES	INFRASTRUCTURE SERVICES	APPLICATION SERVICES
Active Directory Lightweight Directory Services (AD LDS) implement a Lightweight Directory Access Protocol (LDAP) directory service that provides support for directory-enabled applications without incurring the extensive overhead of AD DS.	**Network Policy and Access Services (NPAS)** implement services such as Network Policy Server (NPS), Health Registration Authority (HRA), and Host Credential Authorization Protocol (HCAP), which enforce security policies for network users.	**Print and Document Services** provides clients with access to printers attached to the server or to the network, as well as centralized network printer and print server management, and printer deployment using Group Policy. Document services enable you to route images from network-attached scanners to users.
Active Directory Rights Management Services (AD RMS) make up a client/server system that uses certificates and licensing to implement persistent usage policies, which can control access to information, no matter where a user moves it.	**Remote Access** provides remote users with access to network resources by using DirectAccess and VPNs, as well as LAN and NAT routing services.	**Remote Desktop Services** enable clients on the network or on the Internet to access server-based applications remotely or the entire Windows desktop by using server resources.
	Volume Activation Services automate the management of Microsoft host keys and Key Management System (KMS) hosts.	**Web Server (IIS)** installs Internet Information Services (IIS) 7.5, which enables the organization to publish websites and web-based applications for use by intranet, extranet, and/or Internet clients.
	Windows Deployment Services (WDS) enable you to install Windows operating systems remotely on computers throughout the enterprise.	
	Windows Server Update Services (WSUS) automate the process of disseminating operating-system updates to Windows computers throughout the enterprise.	

Some Windows Server 2012 editions include all these roles, whereas others include only some of them. Selecting the appropriate edition of Windows Server has always been a matter of anticipating the roles that the computer must perform. At one time, this was a relatively simple process. You planned your server deployments by deciding which ones would be domain controllers, which ones would be web servers, and so forth. After you made these decisions, you were done, because server roles were largely static.

With the increased focus on virtualization in Windows Server 2012, however, more administrators must consider not only what roles servers must perform at the time of the deployment, but also what roles they will perform in the future.

By using virtualized servers, you can modify your network's server strategy at will to accommodate changing workloads and business requirements, or to adapt to unforeseen circumstances. Therefore, the process of anticipating the roles servers will perform must account for the potential expansion of your business, as well as possible emergency needs.

Table 1-2 lists the roles included with the various Windows Server 2012 editions.

Table 1-2

Roles Included in Windows Server 2012 Editions

ROLE	DATACENTER	STANDARD	FOUNDATION	ESSENTIALS
Active Directory Certificate Services	Yes	Yes	Limited to CA creation	Limited to CA creation
Active Directory Domain Services	Yes	Yes	Forest and domain root only	No
Active Directory Federation Services	Yes	Yes	No	No
Active Directory Lightweight Directory Services	Yes	Yes	Yes	No
Active Directory Rights Management Services	Yes	Yes	Yes	No
Application Server	Yes	Yes	Yes	Yes
DHCP Server	Yes	Yes	Yes	Yes
DNS Server	Yes	Yes	Yes	Yes
Fax Server	Yes	Yes	Yes	Yes
File and Storage Services	Yes	Yes	Yes (DFS limited)	Yes (DFS limited)
Hyper-V	Yes	Yes	No	No
Network Policy and Access Services	Yes	Yes	Yes (Limited connections)	
Print and Document Services	Yes	Yes	Yes	Yes
Remote Access	Yes	Yes	Yes	No
Remote Desktop Services	Yes	Yes	Yes (Limited connections)	Yes (Limited connections)
Volume Activation Services	Yes	Yes	Yes	No
Web Server (IIS)	Yes	Yes	Yes	Yes
Windows Deployment Services	Yes	Yes	Yes	Yes
Windows Server Update Services	Yes	Yes	Yes	Yes

Supporting Server Virtualization

The Windows Server 2012 Datacenter and Standard editions both include support for Hyper-V, but they vary in the number of virtual machines permitted by their licenses.

Each running instance of the Windows Server 2012 operating system is classified as being in a ***physical operating system environment (POSE)*** or a ***virtual operating system environment (VOSE)***. A POSE is a physical computer with its own hardware, and a VOSE is a virtual machine running on a Hyper-V server with virtualized hardware. When you purchase a Windows Server 2012 license, you can perform a POSE installation of the operating system, as always. After installing the Hyper-V role, you can then create virtual machines (VMs) and perform VOSE installations on them. The number of VOSE installations permitted by your license depends on the edition you purchased, as shown in Table 1-3.

Table 1-3

Physical and Virtual Instances Supported by Windows Server 2012 Editions

EDITION	POSE INSTANCES	VOSE INSTANCES
Datacenter	1	Unlimited
Standard	1	2
Foundation	1	0
Essentials	1 (POSE or VOSE)	1 (POSE or VOSE)

Server Licensing

Microsoft provides several different sales channels for Windows Server 2012 licenses, and not all editions are available through all the channels. Licensing Windows Server 2012 includes purchasing licenses for both servers and clients, and each one has many options.

TAKE NOTE *

The limitations specified in Table 1-3 are those of the license, not the software. For example, you can create more than four VMs on a copy of Windows Server 2012 Enterprise, but you must purchase additional licenses to do so.

If you are already involved in a licensing agreement with Microsoft, you should be aware of the server editions available to you through that agreement. If you are not, you should investigate the licensing options available to you before you select a server edition.

Table 1-4 lists the sales channels through which you can purchase each Windows Server 2012 edition.

Table 1-4

Windows Server Sales Channel Availability, by Edition

	RETAIL	VOLUME LICENSING	ORIGINAL EQUIPMENT MANUFACTURER
Datacenter	No	Yes	Yes
Standard	Yes	Yes	Yes
Foundation	No	No	Yes
Essentials	Yes	Yes	Yes

The licensing structure for Windows Server 2012 is considerably simpler than it has been in previous versions of the operating system. The licenses you need to purchase for a given server installation are affected by the following criteria:

- **Processors**—Both the Datacenter and the Standard edition come with a license that supports up to two physical processors. To run either one on a computer with more than two processors, you must purchase additional licenses.
- **Virtual instances**—The Standard edition license supports one physical instance and as many as two virtual operating system instances on a Hyper-V installation. If you want to create more than two virtual machines running Windows Server 2012 Standard, you must purchase additional licenses at the rate of two virtual instances per license. The Datacenter edition supports an unlimited number of virtual instances. The Essentials license enables you to install the operating system on one physical computer or one virtual machine, but not both. The Foundation license includes no virtual instances.
- **Clients**—The Foundation license supports up to 15 users and the Essentials edition up to 25 users. For the Standard and Datacenter editions, you must purchase client access licenses (CALs).

Installing Windows Server 2012

THE BOTTOM LINE

A clean installation is the simplest way to deploy Windows Server 2012 on a bare metal computer—that is, a computer with no operating system installed—or a computer with a partition that you are willing to reformat (losing all the data on the partition in the process).

If a computer is brand new and has no operating system installed on it, it cannot start until you supply a boot disk, such as a Windows Server 2012 installation disk. During installation, you select the disk partition on which you want to install the operating system, and the Setup program copies the operating system files there.

System Requirements

Choosing the correct hardware for a server requires an understanding of the tasks it will perform.

As of this writing, the minimum system requirements for all editions of Windows Server 2012 are as follows:

- 1.4 GHz 64-bit processor
- 512 MB RAM
- 32 GB disk space
- DVD or USB flash drive
- Super VGA (800x600) or higher resolution monitor

Having 32 GB of available disk space should be considered an absolute minimum. The system partition needs extra space if you install the system over a network or your computer has more than 16 GB of RAM installed. The additional disk space is required for paging, hibernation, and dump files. In practice, you are unlikely to come across a computer with

32 GB RAM and only 32 GB disk space. If you do, free more disk space or invest in additional storage hardware.

Not until you have decided how you will deploy your applications and what roles an application server will perform should you begin selecting the hardware that goes into the computer. Suppose that your organization decides to deploy an application suite such as Microsoft Office on all company workstations. If you decide to install the applications on each individual workstation, each computer must have sufficient memory and processor speed to run them efficiently. The application servers on the network then has to perform only relatively simple roles, such as file and print services, which do not require enormous amounts of server resources.

By contrast, if you decide to deploy the applications using Remote Desktop Services, you can use workstations with a minimal hardware configuration, because the servers take most of the burden. In this case, you need a more powerful application server in terms of processor and memory, or perhaps even several servers sharing the client load.

Server roles can also dictate requirements for specific subsystems within the server computers, as in the following examples:

- Servers hosting complex applications might require more memory and faster processors.
- File servers can benefit from disk arrays and hard drives with higher speeds and larger caches, or even a high performance drive interface, such as SCSI (Small Computer System Interface, pronounced "scuzzy").
- Web servers receiving large amounts of traffic might need higher-end network adapters or multiple adapters to connect to different subnets.
- Streaming media servers require sufficient hardware in all subsystems, because any performance bottleneck in the server can interrupt the client's media experience.

Enterprises with extensive server requirements might want to consider specialized server hardware, such as a storage area network, network attached storage, or a server cluster.

As part of Microsoft's increased emphasis on virtualization and cloud computing in its server products, the company has increased the maximum hardware configurations significantly for Windows Server 2012. Table 1-5 lists these maximums.

Table 1-5

Maximum Hardware Configurations in Windows Server Versions

	WINDOWS SERVER 2012	WINDOWS SERVER 2008 R2
Logical Processors	640	256
RAM	4 terabytes	2 terabytes
Failover cluster nodes	63	16

Performing a Clean Installation

A clean installation can be the basis for a new server, or the initial phase of a server migration.

To perform a clean installation of Windows Server 2012, use the following procedure.

➔ **PERFORM A CLEAN INSTALLATION**

GET READY. Prepare the computer for the Windows Server 2012 installation by making sure that all its external peripheral devices are connected and powered on.

1. Turn on the computer and insert the Windows Server 2012 installation disk into the DVD drive.
2. Press any key to boot from the DVD (if necessary). A progress indicator screen appears as Windows is loading files.

➕ **MORE INFORMATION**

The device that a PC uses to boot is specified in its system (or BIOS) settings. In some cases, you might have to modify these settings to enable the computer to boot from the Windows Server 2012 DVD. If you are not familiar with the operation of a particular computer, watch the screen carefully as the system starts and look for an instruction specifying what key to press to access the system settings.

The computer loads the Windows graphical interface and the Windows Setup page appears, as shown in Figure 1-1.

Figure 1-1

The Windows Setup page

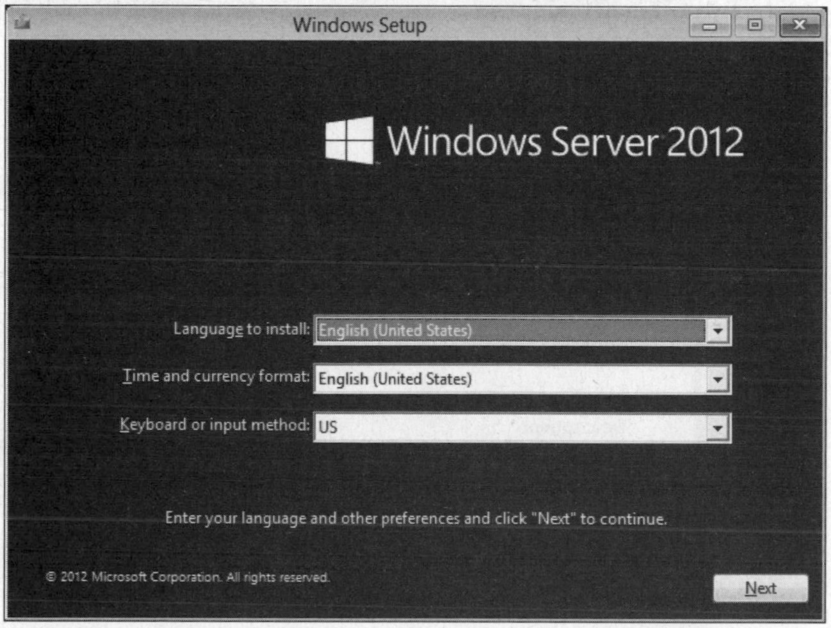

3. By using the drop-down lists provided, select the appropriate language to install, time and currency format, and keyboard or input method, and then click Next. The Windows Setup page appears, as shown in Figure 1-2.
4. Click Install Now. The Windows Setup Wizard appears, displaying the *Select the operating system you want to install* page, as shown in Figure 1-3.
5. Select the operating system edition and installation option you want to install and click Next. The *License Terms* page appears.

6. Select the I accept the license terms check box and click Next. The *Which type of
   installation do you want?* page appears, as shown in Figure 1-4.

Figure 1-4

The *Which type of installation do you want?* page

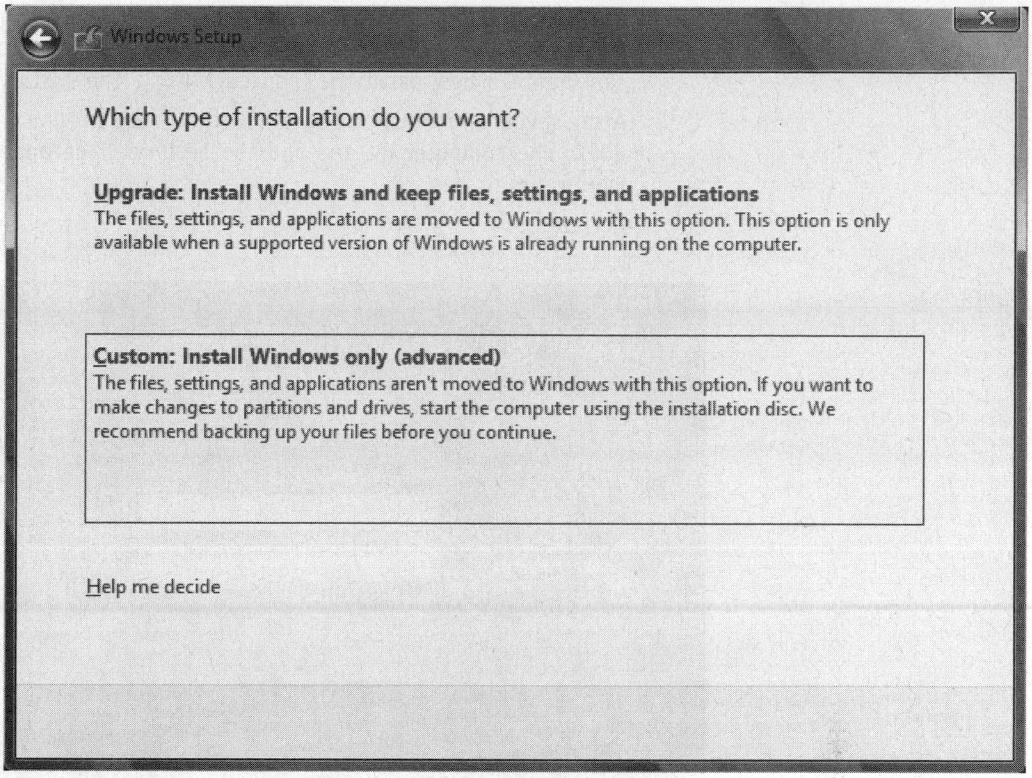

Windows Setup

Which type of installation do you want?

Upgrade: Install Windows and keep files, settings, and applications
The files, settings, and applications are moved to Windows with this option. This option is only available when a supported version of Windows is already running on the computer.

Custom: Install Windows only (advanced)
The files, settings, and applications aren't moved to Windows with this option. If you want to make changes to partitions and drives, start the computer using the installation disc. We recommend backing up your files before you continue.

Help me decide

7. Because you are performing a clean installation and not an upgrade, click the Custom: Install Windows Only (advanced) option. The *Where do you want to install Windows?* page appears, as shown in Figure 1-5.

Figure 1-5

The *Where do you want to install Windows?* page

Windows Setup

Where do you want to install Windows?

Name	Total size	Free space	Type
Drive 0 Unallocated Space	40.0 GB	40.0 GB	

✦ Refresh   Drive options (advanced)
💿 Load driver

Next

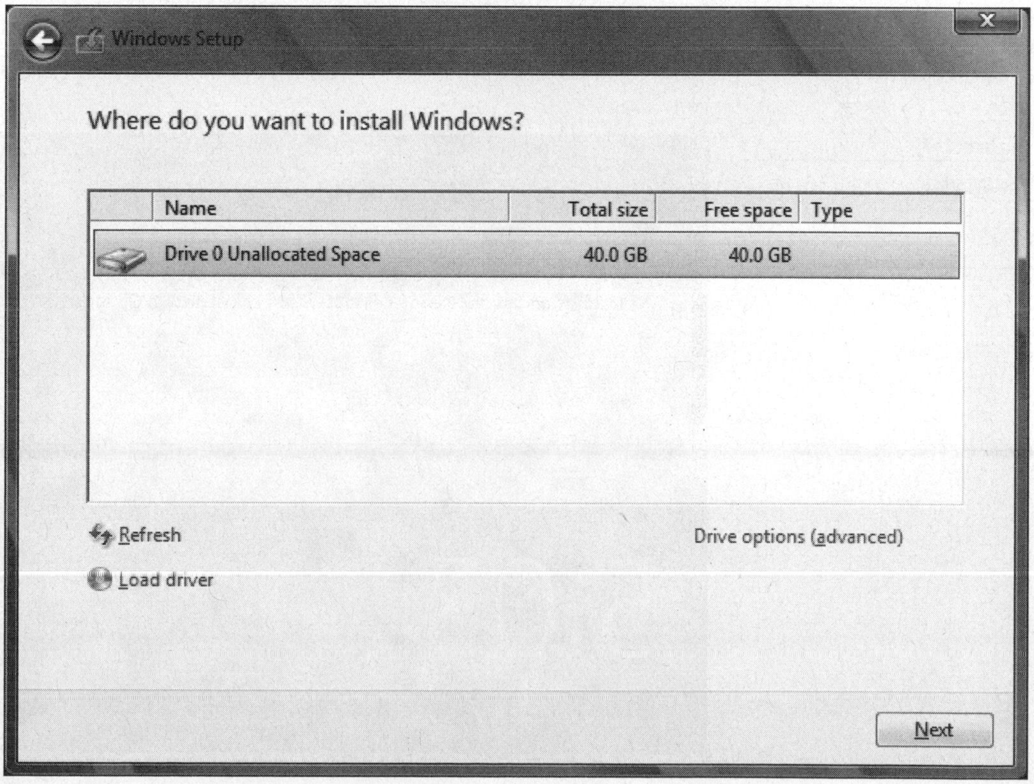

8. From the list provided, select the partition on which you want to install Windows Server 2012, or select an area of unallocated disk space where the Setup program can create a new partition. Then click Next. The *Installing Windows* page appears.

9. After several minutes, during which the Setup program installs Windows Server 2012, the computer restarts and the *Settings* page appears, as shown in Figure 1-6.

Figure 1-6

The Settings page

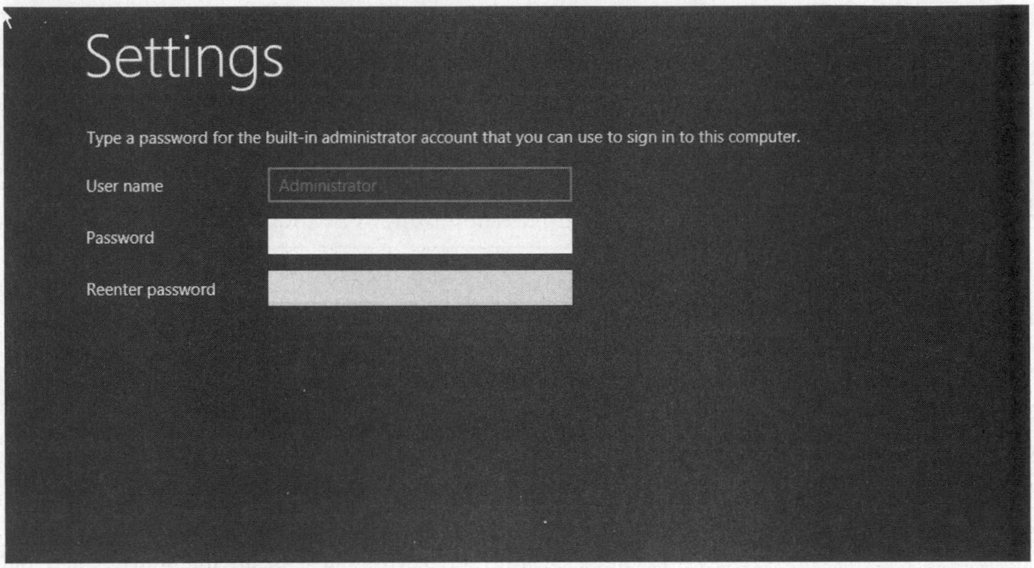

10. In the Password and Reenter Password text boxes, type the password to be associated with the Administrator account and press *Enter*. The system finalizes the installation and the Windows sign-on screen appears, as shown in Figure 1-7.

Figure 1-7

The Windows sign-on screen

Press Ctrl+Alt+Delete to sign in.

5:03
Tuesday, June 19

Installing Third-Party Drivers

In some cases, it might be necessary to install a driver supplied by a hardware manufacturer before the disks in the computer appear in the setup program.

During the Windows Server 2012 installation procedure, the Setup program enables you to select the partition or area of unallocated disk space where you want to install the operating system. The *Where do you want to install Windows?* page lists the partitions on all the computer's disk drives that the Setup program can detect with its default drivers. In most cases, all the computer's drives should appear in the list; if they do not, it is probably because Windows does not include a driver for the computer's drive controller.

If the computer's hard drives are connected to a third-party controller, rather than the one integrated into most motherboards, the list of partitions might appear empty, and you have to supply a driver for the Setup program to see the drives. Check the controller manufacturer's website for a driver supporting Windows Server 2012, or another recent version of Windows Server.

To install the driver, use the following procedure.

⊙ **INSTALL A THIRD-PARTY DISK DRIVER**

GET READY. If during a Windows Server 2012 installation no disk partitions or unallocated space appear on the *Where do you want to install Windows?* page, you must install the appropriate driver for your disk controller using the following procedure before the installation can continue.

1. On the *Where do you want to install Windows?* page, click the Load Driver button. A Load Driver message box appears, as shown in Figure 1-8.

Figure 1-8

The Load Driver message box

> **Load driver**
>
> To install the device driver for your drive, insert the installation media containing the driver files, and then click OK.
>
> Note: The installation media can be a CD, DVD, or USB flash drive.
>
> [Browse] [OK] [Cancel]

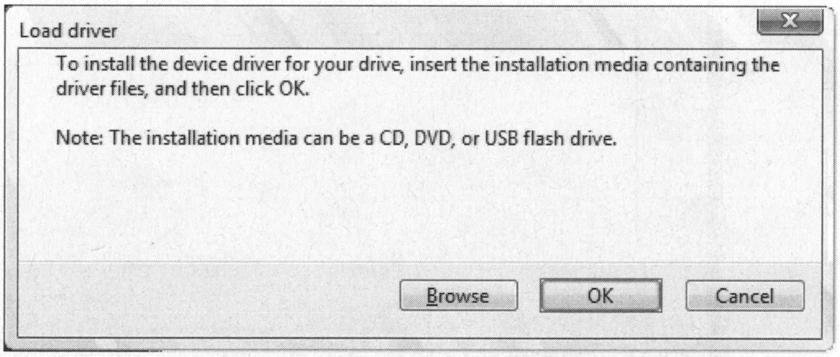

2. Insert the storage medium containing the driver into the computer. You can supply drivers on a CD, DVD, floppy disk, or USB flash drive.
3. Click OK if the driver is in the root directory of the storage medium, or Browse if you need to locate the driver in the directory structure of the disk. A list of the drivers found on the disk appears on the *Select the driver to install* page.
4. Select one of the drivers in the list and click Next.
5. When the driver loads, the partitions and unallocated space on the associated disks appear in the list on the *Where do you want to install Windows?* page.
6. Select the partition or area of unallocated space where you want to install Windows Server 2012 and then continue with the rest of the installation procedure, as covered earlier in this lesson.

Working with Installation Partitions

> In addition to installing disk drivers, the *Where do you want to install Windows?* page enables you to create, manage, and delete the partitions on your disks.

Clicking the *Drive options (advanced)* button on the page causes four additional buttons to appear, as shown in Figure 1-9. These buttons have the following functions:

- **Delete** removes an existing partition from a disk, permanently erasing all its data. You might want to delete partitions to consolidate unallocated disk space, enabling you to create a new, larger partition.

- **Extend** enables you to make an existing partition larger, as long as unallocated space is available immediately following the selected partition on the disk.

- **Format** enables you to format an existing partition on a disk, thereby erasing all its data. You do not need to format any new partitions you create for the install, but you might want to format an existing partition to eliminate unwanted files before installing Windows Server 2012 on it.

- **New** creates a new partition of a user-specified size in the selected area of unallocated space.

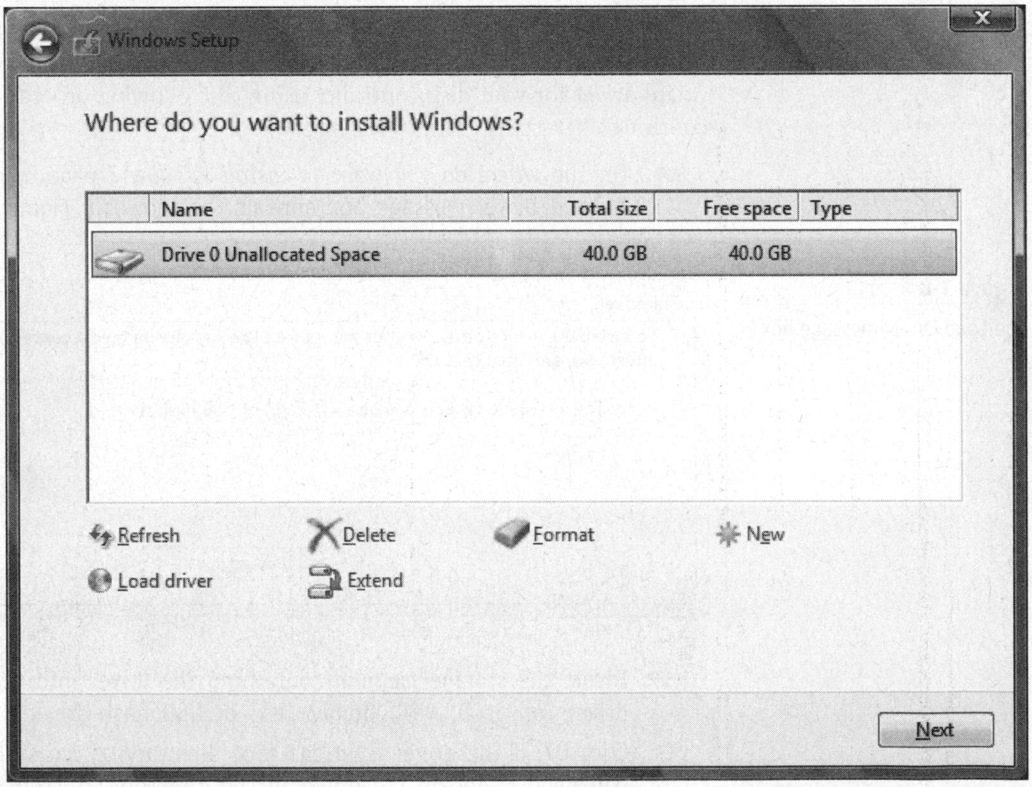

Figure 1-9

Additional buttons on the
*Where do you want to install
Windows?* page

Where do you want to install Windows?

Name	Total size	Free space	Type
Drive 0 Unallocated Space	40.0 GB	40.0 GB	

Refresh   Delete   Format   New
Load driver   Extend

Next

■ Choosing Installation Options

> **THE BOTTOM LINE**
>
> Many enterprise networks today use servers dedicated to a particular role. When a server is performing a single role, does it really make sense to have so many other processes running on the server that contribute little to that role?

Many IT administrators today are so accustomed to graphical user interfaces (GUIs) that they are unaware that there was ever any other way to operate a computer. When the first version of Windows NT Server appeared in 1993, many complained about wasting server resources on graphical displays and other elements that they deemed unnecessary. Up until that time, server displays were usually minimal, character-based, monochrome affairs. In fact, many servers had no display hardware at all, relying instead on text-based remote administration tools, such as Telnet.

Using Server Core

Windows Server 2012 includes an installation option that addresses those old complaints about wasting server resources on graphical displays.

TAKE NOTE *

Server Core is not a separate product or edition. It is an installation option included with the Windows Server 2012 Standard, Enterprise, and Datacenter editions.

When you select the Windows *Server Core* installation option, you get a stripped-down version of the operating system. There is no Start menu, no desktop Explorer shell, no Microsoft Management Console, and virtually no graphical applications. All you see when you start the computer is a single window with a command prompt, as shown in Figure 1-10.

The advantages of running servers using Server Core are several:

- **Hardware resource conservation:** Server Core eliminates some of the most memory- and processor-intensive elements of the Windows Server 2012 operating system, thus devoting more of the system hardware to running essential services.

Figure 1-10

The default Server Core interface

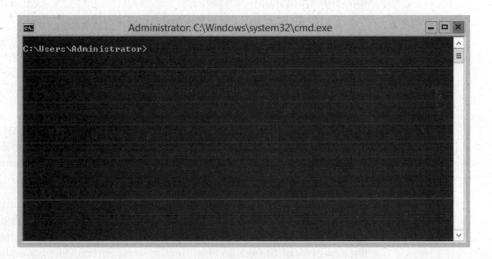

- **Reduced disk space:** Server Core requires less disk space for the installed operating system elements, as well as less swap space, which maximizes the utilization of the server's storage resources.
- **Reduced patch frequency:** Windows Server 2012's graphical elements are among the most frequently patched features, so running Server Core reduces the number of patches that you must apply. Fewer patches also mean fewer server restarts and less downtime.
- **Reduced attack surface:** The less software there is running on the computer, the fewer entrances are available for attackers to exploit. Server Core reduces the potential openings presented by the operating system, increasing its overall security.

When Microsoft first introduced the Server Core installation option in Windows Server 2008, the idea was intriguing, but few administrators took advantage of it. The main reason for this was that most server administrators were not sufficiently conversant with the command-line interface to manage a Windows server without a GUI.

In Windows Server 2008 and Windows Server 2008 R2, the decision to install the operating system via the Server Core option was irrevocable. After you installed the operating system using Server Core, in no way could you get the GUI back except to perform a complete reinstallation. That has all changed in Windows Server 2012. You can now switch a server from the Server Core option to the Server with a GUI option, and back again, at will, using Windows PowerShell commands.

+ MORE INFORMATION

For more information on converting from Server Core to Server with a GUI and back again, refer to Lesson 2, "Configuring Servers."

This ability means that you can install Windows Server 2012 using the Server with a GUI option, if you want to, configure the server using the familiar graphical tools, and then switch the server to Server Core, to take advantage of the benefits listed earlier.

SERVER CORE DEFAULTS

In Windows Server 2012, Microsoft is attempting to fundamentally modify the way administrators work with their servers. Server Core is now the default installation option because in the new way of managing servers, you should rarely, if ever, have to work at the server console, either physically or remotely.

Windows Server has long been capable of remote administration, but this capability has been a piecemeal affair. Some Microsoft Management Console (MMC) snap-ins enabled administrators to connect to remote servers, and Windows PowerShell 2.0 provided some remote capabilities from the command line, but Windows Server 2012, for the first time, includes comprehensive remote administration tools that virtually eliminate the need to work at the server console.

The new Server Manager application in Windows Server 2012 enables you to add servers from all over the enterprise and create server groups to facilitate the configuration of multiple systems simultaneously. The new Windows PowerShell 3.0 environment increases the number of available commands—known as *cmdlets*—from 230 to more than 2,430.

With tools like these, it is possible for you to install your servers using the Server Core option, execute a few commands to join each server to an AD DS domain, and then never touch the server console again. You can perform all subsequent administration tasks, including deployment of roles and features, by using Server Manager and Windows PowerShell from a remote workstation.

SERVER CORE CAPABILITIES

In addition to omitting most of the graphical interface, a Server Core installation omits some of the server roles found in a Server with a GUI installation. However, the Server Core option in Windows Server 2012 includes 13 of the 19 roles, plus support for SQL Server 2012, as opposed to only 10 roles in Windows Server 2008 R2 and 9 in Windows Server 2008.

Table 1-6 lists the roles and features that are available and not available in a Windows Server 2012 Server Core installation.

Table 1-6

Windows Server 2012 Server
Core Roles

ROLES AVAILABLE IN SERVER CORE INSTALLATION	ROLES NOT AVAILABLE IN SERVER CORE INSTALLATION
Active Directory Certificate Services	Active Directory Federation Services
Active Directory Domain Services	Application Server
Active Directory Lightweight Directory Services	Fax Server
Active Directory Rights Management Services	Network Policy and Access Services
DHCP Server	Remote Desktop Services: • Remote Desktop Gateway • Remote Desktop Session Host • Remote Desktop Web Access
DNS Server	Volume Activation Services
File and Storage Services	Windows Deployment Services
Hyper-V	
Print and Document Services	
Remote Desktop Services: • Remote Desktop Connection Broker • Remote Desktop Licensing • Remote Desktop Virtualization Host	
Remote Access	
Web Server (IIS)	
Windows Server Update Services	

Using the Minimal Server Interface

If the advantages of Server Core sound tempting but you do not want to give up certain traditional server administration tools, Windows Server 2012 provides a compromise called the Minimal Server Interface.

The Minimal Server Interface setting removes some of the most hardware-intensive elements from the graphical interface. These elements include Internet Explorer and the components that make up the Windows shell, including the desktop, Windows Explorer, and the Modern application interface. Also omitted are the Control Panel applets implemented as shell extensions, including the following:

- Programs and Features
- Network and Sharing Center
- Devices and Printers Center
- Display
- Firewall
- Windows Update
- Fonts
- Storage Spaces

Left in the Minimal Server Interface are the Server Manager and MMC applications, as well as Device Manager and the entire Windows PowerShell interface. This provides you with most of the tools you need to manage local and remote servers

TAKE NOTE *

The omission of Internet Explorer in the Minimal Server Interface affects the performance of some MMC snap-ins. For example, the Group Policy Management snap-in relies on Hypertext Markup Language (HTML) for some of its displays, and those displays do not function in the Minimal Server Interface.

To configure a Windows Server 2012 Server with a GUI installation to use the Minimal Server Interface, complete the following procedure.

CONFIGURE THE MINIMAL SERVER INTERFACE

GET READY. Log on to the server running Windows Server 2012 using an account with administrative privileges. The Server Manager window appears.

1. Click Manage > Remove Roles and Features. The Remove Roles and Features Wizard appears, showing the *Before You Begin* page.
2. Click Next. The *Server Selection* page appears.
3. In the Server Pool list, select the server you want to modify and click Next. The *Remove Server Roles* page appears.
4. Click Next. The *Remove Features* page appears.
5. Scroll down the Features list and expand the User Interfaces and Infrastructure feature, as shown in Figure 1-11.

Figure 1-11

The User Interfaces and Infrastructure feature in the Remove Roles and Features Wizard

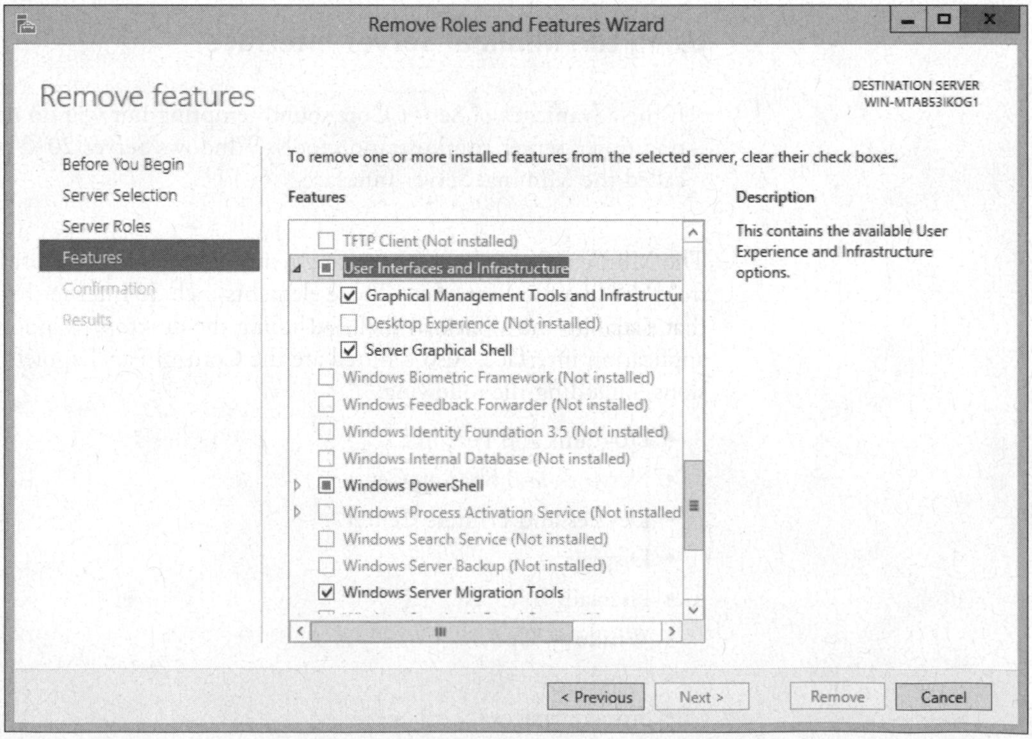

TAKE NOTE *

Removing the Graphical
Management Tools and
Infrastructure package
as well as the Server
Graphical Shell converts
the computer to the
Server Core installation
option.

6. Clear the Server Graphical Shell check box and click Next. The *Confirm Removal Selections* page appears.

7. Click Remove. The *Removal Progress* page appears.

8. When the removal is complete, click Close.

9. Restart the server.

Using Features on Demand

During a Windows Server 2012 installation, the Setup program copies the files for all operating system components from the installation medium to a directory called *WinSxS,* the side-by-side component store. This enables you to activate any features included with Windows Server 2012 without having to supply an installation medium.

The drawback of this arrangement is that the WinSxS directory occupies a significant amount of disk space, much of which is, in many cases, devoted to data that will never be used.

CERTIFICATION READY
Optimize resource
utilization by using
Features on Demand.
Objective 1.1

With the increasing use of virtual machines to distribute server roles, enterprise networks often have more copies of the server operating system than ever before, and therefore more wasted disk space. Also, the advanced storage technologies often used by today's server infrastructures, such as storage area networks (SANs) and solid state drives (SSDs), are making that disk space more expensive.

Features on Demand, new to Windows Server 2012, is a third state for operating system features that enables administrators to conserve disk space by removing specific features not only from operation, but also from the WinSxS directory.

This state is intended for features that you do not intend to install on a particular server. If, for example, you want to disable the Server Graphical Shell feature in Windows Server 2012 to prevent Internet Explorer, Windows Explorer, and the desktop shell from running, and you want to remove the files that provide those features from the disk completely, you can do so with Features on Demand. By removing all the disk files for all your unused features on all your virtual machines, the accumulated savings in disk space can be substantial.

Features on Demand provide a third installation state for each feature in Windows Server 2012. In previous versions of the operating system, you could enable or disable features. Windows Server 2012 provides the following three states:

- Enabled
- Disabled
- Disabled with payload removed

To implement this third state, you must use the Windows PowerShell `Uninstall-WindowsFeature` cmdlet, which now supports a new `Remove` flag. Thus, the Windows PowerShell command to disable the Server Graphical Shell and remove its source files from the WinSxS directory would be as follows:

```
Uninstall-WindowsFeature Server-Gui-Shell -Remove
```

Deleting the source files for a feature from the WinSxS folder does not make them irretrievably gone. If you try to enable that feature again, the system downloads it from Windows Update or, alternatively, retrieves it from an image file you specify using the `-Source` flag with the `Install-WindowsFeature` cmdlet. This enables you to retrieve the required files from a removable disk or from an image file on the local network. You can also use Group Policy to specify a list of installation sources.

TAKE NOTE*

This ability to retrieve source files for a feature from another location is the actual functionality to which the name Features on Demand is referring. Microsoft often uses this capability to reduce the size of updates downloaded from the Internet. After the user installs the update, the program downloads the additional files required and completes the installation.

■ Upgrading Servers

THE BOTTOM LINE

An in-place upgrade is the most complicated form of Windows Server 2012 installation. It is also the lengthiest and the most likely to cause problems during its execution. Whenever possible, Microsoft recommends that administrators perform a clean installation, or migrate required applications and settings instead.

During an in-place upgrade, the Setup program creates a new Windows folder and installs the Windows Server 2012 operating system files into it. This is only half of the process, however. The program must then migrate the applications, files, and settings from the old OS. This calls for a variety of procedures, such as importing the user profiles, copying all pertinent settings from the old registry to the new one, locating applications and data files, and updating device drivers with new versions.

CERTIFICATION READY
Plan for a server
upgrade.
Objective 1.1

While in-place upgrades often proceed smoothly, the complexity of the upgrade process and the large number of variables involved means that many things can potentially go wrong. To minimize the risks involved, you must to take the upgrade process seriously, prepare the system beforehand, and have the ability to troubleshoot any problems that might arise. The following sections discuss these subjects in detail.

Upgrade Paths

Upgrade paths for Windows Server 2012 are quite limited. In fact, they are easier to specify when you can perform an upgrade than when you cannot.

If you have a 64-bit computer running Windows Server 2008 or Windows Server 2008 R2, you can upgrade it to Windows Server 2012 as long as you use the same (or a lower) operating system edition.

Windows Server 2012 does not support the following:

- Upgrades from Windows Server versions prior to Windows Server 2008
- Upgrades from Windows workstation operating systems
- Cross-edition upgrades, such as Windows Server 2008 Standard Edition to Windows Server 2012 Datacenter Edition
- Cross-platform upgrades, such as 32-bit Windows Server 2008 to 64-bit Windows Server 2012
- Upgrades from any Itanium edition
- Cross-language upgrades, such as from Windows Server 2008, U.S. English, to Windows Server 2012, French

In any of these cases, the Windows Setup program does not permit the upgrade to proceed.

Preparing to Upgrade

> Before you begin an in-place upgrade to Windows Server 2012, you should perform a number of preliminary procedures to ensure that the process goes smoothly and that server data is protected.

Consider the following before you perform any upgrade to Windows Server 2012:

- **Check hardware compatibility.** Make sure that the server meets the minimum hardware requirements for Windows Server 2012.

- **Check disk space.** Make sure that sufficient free disk space is on the partition where the old operating system is installed. During the upgrade procedure, sufficient disk space is needed to hold both operating systems simultaneously. After the upgrade is complete, you can remove the old files, freeing up some additional space.

- **Confirm that software is signed.** All kernel-mode software on the server, including device drivers, must be digitally signed, or the upgrade will not proceed. If you cannot locate a software update for any signed application or driver, you must uninstall the application or driver before you proceed with the installation.

- **Check application compatibility.** The Setup program displays a Compatibility Report page that can point out possible application compatibility problems. You can sometimes solve these problems by updating or upgrading the applications. Create an inventory of the software products installed on the server and check the manufacturers' websites for updates, availability of upgrades, and announcements regarding support for Windows Server 2012. In an enterprise environment, you should test all applications for Windows Server 2012 compatibility, no matter what the manufacturer says, before you perform any operating system upgrades.

- **Ensure computer functionality.** Make sure that Windows Server 2008 or Windows Server 2008 R2 is running properly on the computer before you begin the upgrade process. Check the Event Viewer console for warnings and errors. You must start an in-place upgrade from within the existing operating system, so you cannot count on Windows Server 2012 to correct any problems that prevent the computer from starting or running the Setup program.

- **Perform a full backup.** Before you perform any upgrade procedure, you should back up the entire system, or at the very least the essential data files. Removable hard drives make this a simple process, even if the computer does not have a suitable backup device.

- **Purchase Windows Server 2012.** Be sure to purchase the appropriate Windows Server 2012 edition for the upgrade, and have the installation disk and product key handy.

Performing an Upgrade Installation

> Windows Server 2012 permits you to perform an upgrade installation only after you have met the prerequisites described in the previous section.

To perform a Windows Server 2012 upgrade installation from Windows Server 2008 or Windows Server 2008 R2, use the following procedure.

➔ PERFORM AN UPGRADE INSTALLATION

GET READY. Start the server and log on using an account with administrative privileges.

1. Insert the Windows Server 2012 installation disk into the DVD drive and start the Setup program. The Windows Setup window appears.

2. Click Install Now. The Windows Setup Wizard appears, displaying the *Select the operating system you want to install* page.

3. Select the operating system edition and installation option you want to install and click Next. The *License Terms* page appears.

4. Select the I accept the license terms check box and click Next. *The Which type of installation do you want?* page appears.

5. Click the Upgrade: Install Windows and keep files, settings, and applications option. The *Compatibility report (saved to your desktop)* page appears, as shown in Figure 1-12.

Figure 1-12

The Compatibility Report page

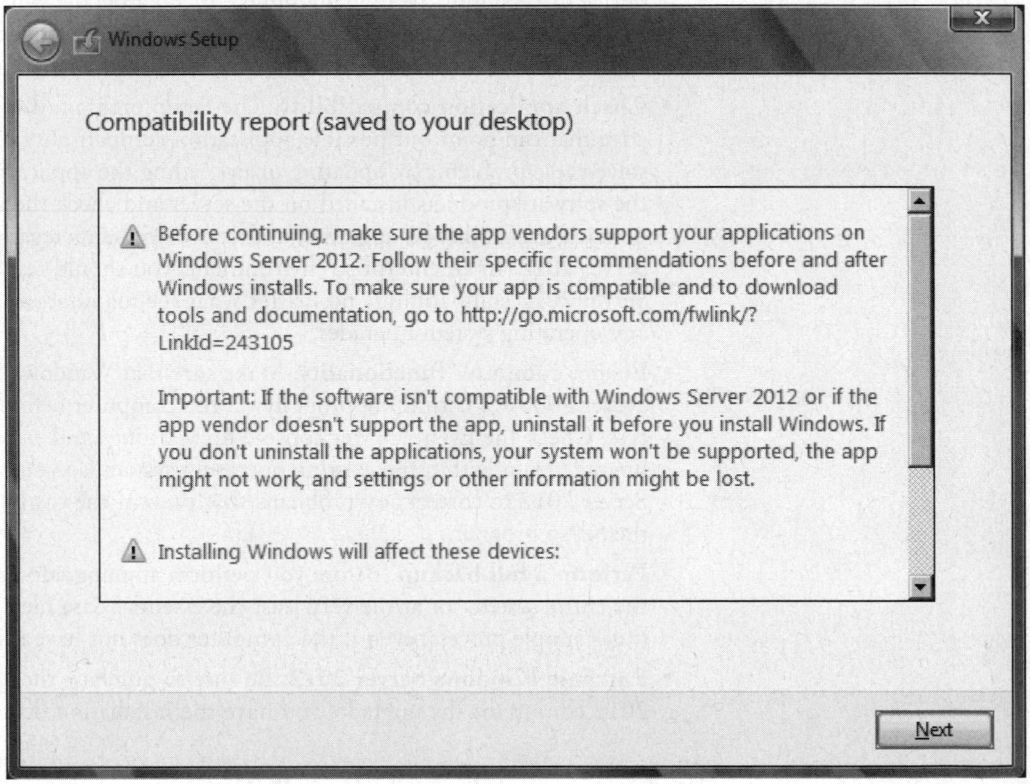

6. Note the compatibility information provided by the Setup program and click Next. The *Upgrading Windows* page appears, as shown in Figure 1-13.

Figure 1-13

The Upgrading Windows page

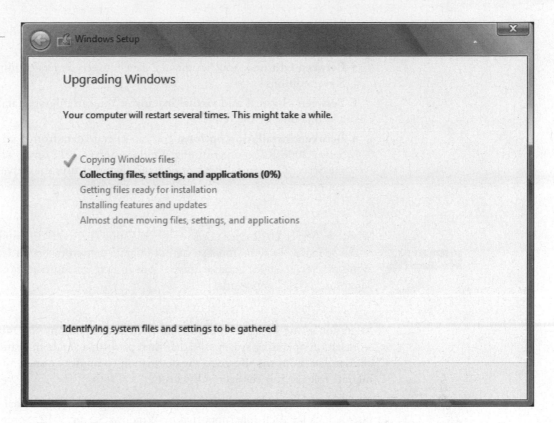

After several minutes, during which the Setup program upgrades Windows Server 2008 or Windows Server 2008 R2 to Windows Server 2012 and restarts the computer several times, the system finalizes the installation and the Windows sign-on screen appears.

TAKE NOTE*

In some cases, you might have to close the Setup program to update, upgrade, or uninstall an incompatible application.

During the upgrade process, when the system restarts, the boot menu provides an option to roll back to the previous operating system version. However, after the upgrade is complete, this option is no longer available; uninstalling Windows Server 2012 and reverting to the old operating system version is not possible.

■ Migrating Roles

↓
THE BOTTOM LINE

Migration is the preferred method of replacing an existing server with one running Windows Server 2012. Unlike an in-place upgrade, a migration copies vital information from an existing server to a clean Windows Server 2012 installation.

During a migration, virtually all the restrictions listed earlier concerning upgrades do not apply. By using the Windows Server Migration Tools and migration guides supplied with Windows Server 2012, you can migrate data between servers under any of the following conditions:

CERTIFICATION READY
Migrate roles from previous versions of Windows Server.
Objective 1.1

- **Between versions:** You can migrate data from any Windows Server version since Windows Server 2003 SP2 to Windows Server 2012. This includes migrations from one server running Windows Server 2012 to another.

- **Between platforms:** You can migrate data from an x86- or x64-based server to an x64-based server running Windows Server 2012.
- **Between editions:** You can migrate data between servers running different Windows Server editions.
- **Between physical and virtual instances:** You can migrate data from a physical server to a virtual one, or the reverse.
- **Between installation options:** You can migrate data from a server running Windows Server 2008 R2 to one running Windows Server 2012, even when one server is using the Server Core installation option and the other uses the Server Core with a GUI option.

TAKE NOTE * Windows Server 2012 does not support migrations between different language versions of the operating system. You also cannot migrate data from Server Core installations of Windows Server 2008, because Server Code in that version does not include support for Microsoft .NET Framework.

Migration at the server level is different from any migrations you might have performed on workstation operating systems. Rather than perform a single migration procedure that copies all user data from the source to the destination computer at once, in a server migration you migrate roles or role services individually.

Windows Server 2012 includes a collection of migration guides that provide individualized instructions for each role supported by Windows Server 2012. Some roles require the use of the Windows Server Migration Tools; others do not.

Installing Windows Server Migration Tools

Windows Server Migration Tools is a Windows Server 2012 feature that consists of Windows PowerShell cmdlets and help files that enable administrators to migrate certain roles between servers.

Before you can use the migration tools, however, you must install the Windows Server Migration Tools feature on the destination server running Windows Server 2012, and then copy the appropriate version of the tools to the source server.

Windows Server Migration Tools is a standard feature that you install on Windows Server 2012 using the Add Roles and Features Wizard in Server Manager, as shown in Figure 1-14, or the `Install-WindowsFeature` Windows PowerShell cmdlet.

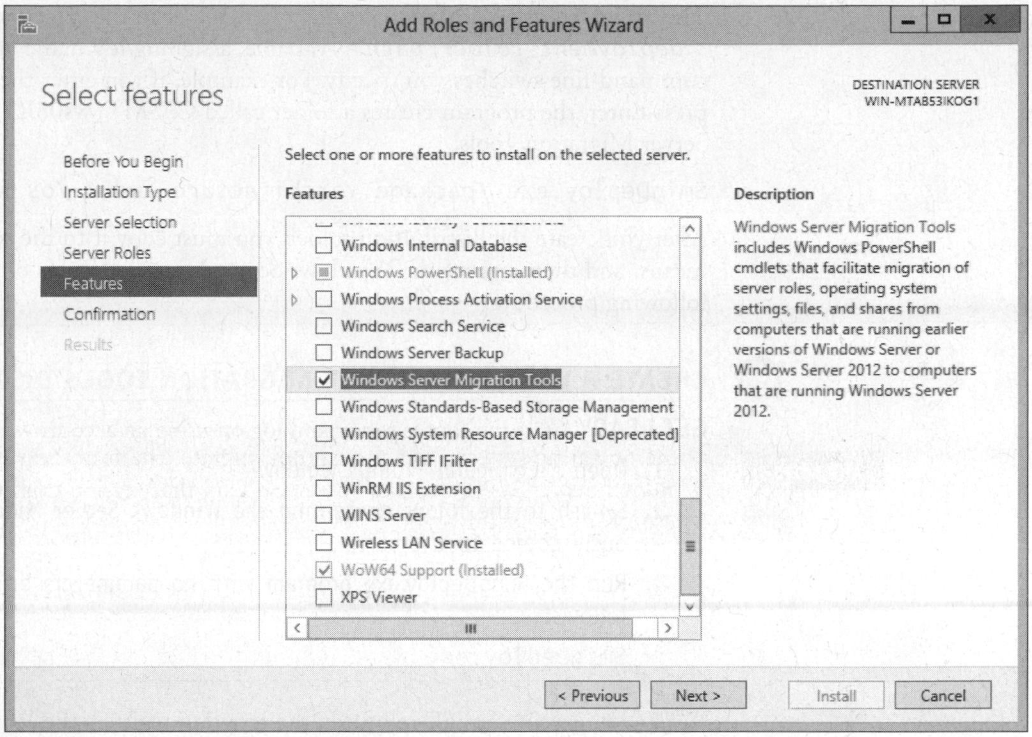

Figure 1-14

The Select Features page of the
Add Roles and Features Wizard

USING WINDOWS POWERSHELL

To install the Windows Server Migration Tools feature using Windows PowerShell, use the following syntax:

```
Install-WindowsFeature Migration [-ComputerName <computer_name>]
```

After you install the Windows Server Migration Tools feature on the destination server, you must create a distribution folder containing the tools for the source server. This distribution folder must contain the appropriate files for the platform and the operating system version of the source server.

To create the distribution folder on a server running Windows Server 2012 with the Windows Server Migration Tools feature already installed, use the following procedure.

CREATE A WINDOWS SERVER MIGRATION TOOLS DISTRIBUTION FOLDER

GET READY. Start the destination server running Windows Server 2012 and log on using an account with administrative privileges.

1. Open a Command Prompt window.
2. Switch to the directory containing the Windows Server Migration Tools files by typing the following command and pressing Enter:

   ```
   cd\windows\system32\ServerMigrationTools
   ```
3. Run the SmigDeploy.exe program with the appropriate command line switches for the platform and operating system version of the source server, using the following syntax:

   ```
   SmigDeploy.exe /package /architecture [x86|amd64] /os
   [WS08|WS08R2|WS03] /path <deployment_folder_path>
   ```

The SmigDeploy.exe program creates a new folder in the directory you specify for the <*deployment_folder_path*> variable, assigning it a name and location based on the command-line switches you specify. For example, if you enter the following command and press Enter, the program creates a folder called C:\SMT_ws08R2_amd64 containing the Server Migration Tools.

```
SmigDeploy.exe /package /architecture amd64 /os WS08R2 /path C:\
```

After you create the distribution folder, you must copy it to the source server by any standard means, and then register the Windows Server Migration Tools on the source server using the following procedure.

 **CREATE A WINDOWS SERVER MIGRATION TOOLS DISTRIBUTION FOLDER**

GET READY. Start the source server and log on using an account with administrative privileges.

1. Open a Command Prompt window.
2. Switch to the folder containing the Windows Server Migration Tools that you previously copied to the server.
3. Run the SmigDeploy.exe program with no parameters on the command line, as follows:

```
SmigDeploy.exe
```

When you execute SmigDeploy.exe, the program registers the Windows Server Migration Tools on the source server and opens a Windows PowerShell window in which you can use those tools, as shown in Figure 1-15.

Figure 1-15

Registering Windows Server Migration Tools

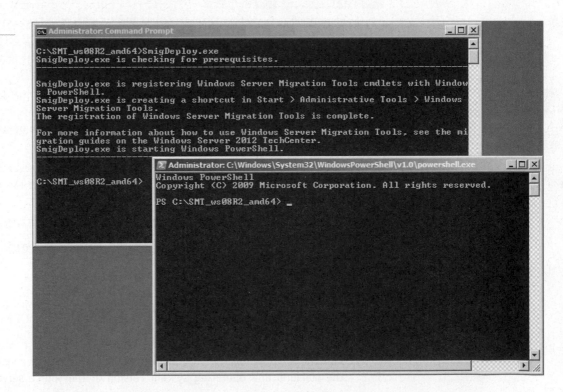

To use the migration tools in a new Windows PowerShell session, you must open a Windows PowerShell window with elevated user rights and then add the appropriate snap-in, using the following syntax:

```
Add-PSSnapin Microsoft.Windows.ServerManager.Migration
```

Using Migration Guides

> After you install the Windows Server Migration Tools on both the source and the destination servers, you can proceed to migrate data between the two.

By using the migration tools, you can migrate certain roles, features, shares, operating system settings, and other data from the source server to the destination server running Windows Server 2012. Some roles require the use of the migration tools while others do not, having their own internal communication capabilities.

For example, the Print and Document Services role includes a Printer Migration Wizard (and a command-line tool called Printbrm.exe) that enables you to export printers on a source server to a file and import the file on the destination server. Roles that do not have capabilities like this rely on the Windows Server Migration Tools.

Migrating all the Windows Server roles does not involve any one procedure, whether the roles have their own migration tools or not. Instead, Microsoft provides detailed migration guides for individual roles, and sometimes for individual role services within a role.

➕ **MORE INFORMATION**

Up-to-date migration guides are available at the Windows Server Migration Portal in the Windows Server 2012 TechCenter, from Microsoft's TechNet website.

A typical migration guide contains elements such as the following:

- **Compatibility notes:** Lists or tables containing specific circumstances in which the guide procedures apply, and circumstances in which they do not apply. These include notes regarding migrations between different operating systems, platforms, and installation options.

- **Guide contents:** A list of the sections appearing in the migration guide

- **Migration overview:** A high-level list of the procedures required to complete the migration, linked to the instructions for the procedures themselves.

- **Migration requirements:** A list of the software, permissions, and other elements needed to complete the migration, as well as the estimated amount of time required.

- **Pre-migration tasks:** Detailed instructions for procedures you must complete before beginning the actual migration, including installation of required software and backup of existing data.

- **Migration procedures:** Detailed instructions for the individual procedures you must perform to complete the migration.

- **Post-migration procedures:** Instructions for removing or disabling a role from the source server or restoring the systems to their previous states.

SKILL SUMMARY

IN THIS LESSON, YOU LEARNED:

- Microsoft releases all its operating systems in multiple editions, which provides consumers with various price points and feature sets.

- Windows Server 2012 includes predefined combinations of services called roles that implement common server functions.

- A clean installation is the simplest way to deploy Windows Server 2012 on a bare metal computer or a computer with a partition that you are willing to reformat (losing all the data on the partition in the process).

- Many enterprise networks today use servers dedicated to a particular role. When a server is performing a single role, does it really make sense to have so many other processes running on the server that contribute little to that role?

- When you select the Windows Server Core installation option, you get a stripped-down version of the operating system.

- If the advantages of Server Core sound tempting but you do not want to give up certain traditional server administration tools, Windows Server 2012 provides a compromise called the Minimal Server Interface.

- The Minimal Server Interface is a setting that removes some of the most hardware-intensive elements from the graphical interface.

- An in-place upgrade is the most complicated form of Windows Server 2012 installation. It is also the lengthiest and the most likely to cause problems during its execution. Whenever possible, Microsoft recommends that administrators perform a clean installation, or migrate required applications and settings instead.

- Migration is the preferred method of replacing an existing server with one running Windows Server 2012. Unlike an in-place upgrade, a migration copies vital information from an existing server to a clean Windows Server 2012 installation.

- Windows Server Migration Tools is a Windows Server 2012 feature that consists of Windows PowerShell cmdlets and help files that enable administrators to migrate certain roles between servers.

■ Knowledge Assessment

Multiple Choice

Select one or more correct answers for each of the following questions.

1. Which of the following roles implement what can be classified as infrastructure services? (Choose all that apply)?
   a. DNS
   b. Web Server (IIS)
   c. DHCP
   d. Remote Desktop Services

2. Which of the following is a valid upgrade path to Windows Server 2012?
   a. Windows Server 2003 Standard to Windows Server 2012 Standard
   b. Windows Server 2008 Standard to Windows Server 2012 Standard
   c. Windows Server 2008 R2 32-bit to Windows Server 2012 64-bit
   d. Windows 7 Ultimate to Windows Server 2012 Essentials

3. Which feature must you add to a Windows Server 2012 Server Core installation to convert it to the Minimal Server Interface?
   a. Graphical Management Tools and Infrastructure
   b. Server Graphical Shell
   c. Windows PowerShell
   d. Microsoft Management Console

4. What is the name of the directory where Windows stores all of the operating system modules it might need to install at a later time?
   a. Windows
   b. System32
   c. Bin
   d. WinSxS

5. Which of the following are valid reasons why administrators might want to install their Windows Server 2012 servers using the Server Core option? (Choose all that apply)
   a. A Server Core installation can be converted to the full GUI without reinstalling the operating system.
   b. The PowerShell 3.0 interface in Windows Server 2012 includes more than 10 times as many cmdlets as PowerShell 2.0.
   c. The new Server Manager in Windows Server 2012 makes it far easier to administer servers remotely.
   d. A Windows Server 2012 Server Core license costs significantly less than a full GUI license.

6. Windows Server 2012 requires what processor architecture?
   a. 64-bit processor only
   b. 32-bit processor and 64-bit processor
   c. Any processor provided it is physical, not virtual
   d. Minimum dual–core processor

7. What are the minimum system memory requirements to run all editions of Windows Server 2012?
   a. 256 MB RAM
   b. 512 MB RAM
   c. 2 GB RAM
   d. 4 GB RAM

8. What is the default installation of installing Windows Server 2012?
   a. Server Core
   b. Startup GUI
   c. PowerShell
   d. There is no default.

9. What Windows Server 2012 role would you install to provide network resources to remote users?
   a. Network Policy and Access Services
   b. Remote Access
   c. Windows Deployment Services
   d. Web Server (IIS)

10. What Windows Server 2012 role enforces security policies for network users?
   a. Network Policy and Access Services
   b. Remote Access
   c. Active Directory Rights Management Services
   d. Remote Desktop Services

Best Answer

Choose the letter that corresponds to the best answer. More than one answer choice may achieve the goal. Select the BEST answer.

1. You are deciding which Windows Server 2012 edition is right for your needs: a Remote Access server. You are eager to create a virtual machine (VM) on which you can install a virtual operating system environment (VOSE). You foresee needing only one VOSE. What Windows Server 2012 edition is best?
   a. Windows Server 2012 Datacenter edition
   b. Windows Server 2012 Standard edition
   c. Windows Server 2012 Foundation edition
   d. Windows Server 2012 Essentials edition

2. Your company wants to upgrade to Windows Server 2012. Considering the present environment of mostly Windows Server 2008 R2 servers, what is the best path to upgrade to Windows Server 2012?
   a. Perform an in-place upgrade of a Windows Server 2008 R2 machine
   b. Create a virtual instance of Windows Server 2012
   c. Perform a clean installation of Windows Server 2012
   d. Perform an in-place upgrade of the current lowest Windows Server edition

3. You are tempted by the advantages of Server Core, but you do not want to give up certain traditional server administration tools. What is the best option made available by Windows Server 2012 as a compromise?
   a. Use the Minimal Server Interface
   b. Use PowerShell
   c. Use cmdlets
   d. Use the full graphical user interface (GUI)

4. What is the purpose of Microsoft releasing multiple editions of Windows Server 2012?
   a. To better secure a server by eliminating unnecessary features
   b. To accommodate needs of different companies
   c. To offer various feature sets and at different price points
   d. To complement available 32-bit server editions

5. Active Directory Rights Management Services (AD RMS) are available on which Windows Server 2012 edition?
   a. Windows Server 2012 Datacenter edition
   b. Windows Server 2012 Datacenter and Standard editions
   c. Windows Server 2012 Datacenter, Standard, and Foundation editions
   d. All Windows Server 2012 editions

Build a List

1. Order the steps to install Windows Server 2012.
   a. Select the appropriate language, time and currency format, and so on
   b. After accepting the license terms, select the type of installation
   c. Boot up the computer with the Windows Server 2012 DVD
   d. Select whether a clean installation or an upgrade
   e. Enter the password associated with the new Administrator account
   f. Select a partition on which to install or create a new partition

2. Order the steps to create and register a Windows Server Migration Tools Distribution Folder, ending with the use of the migration tools in a new PowerShell session.
   a. Start the destination server and log on with administrative privileges
   b. Copy the distribution folder to the source server

    c. Run the SmigDeploy.exe program with the appropriate command-line switches for the platform and operating system version of the source server, using the following syntax:

```
SmigDeploy.exe /package
 /architecture [x86|amd64]
 /os [WS08|WS08R2|WS03]
 /path <deployment_folder_path>
```

    d. Type: `Add-PSSnapin Microsoft.Windows.ServerManager.Migration`

    e. At a command prompt on the destination server's folder, type: `SmigDeploy.exe`

3. Order the steps to upgrade to Windows Server 2012.
    a. Migrate services and applications
    b. Perform an in-place upgrade on Windows Server 2003 servers
    c. Install a clean instance of Windows Server 2012.
    d. Check hardware and application compatibility and disk space
    e. Perform a full backup

▪ Business Case Scenarios

Scenario 1-1: Preparing for an Upgrade to Windows Server 2012

Walk through the steps an administrator needs to do to prepare for an upgrade to Windows Server 2012.

Scenario 1-2: Switching to GUI Installation

A server is running the Server Core installation of Windows Server 2012. What would you do if you desired the GUI installation?

2 LESSON

Configuring Servers

70-410 EXAM OBJECTIVE

Objective 1.2 – Configure servers. This objective may include but is not limited to: Configure Server Core; delegate administration; add and remove features in offline images; deploy roles on remote servers; convert Server Core to/from full GUI; configure services; configure NIC teaming.

LESSON HEADING	EXAM OBJECTIVE
Completing Post-Installation Tasks	
Using GUI Tools	
Using Command-Line Tools	Configure Server Core
Converting Between GUI and Server Core	Convert Server Core to/from full GUI
Configuring NIC Teaming	Configure NIC teaming
Using Roles, Features, and Services	
Using Server Manager	
Adding Roles and Features	Deploy roles on remote servers
Deploying Roles to VHDs	Add and remove features in offline images
Configuring Services	Configure services
Delegating Server Administration	Delegate administration

KEY TERMS

NIC teaming
role group

■ Completing Post-Installation Tasks

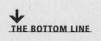

As part of the new emphasis on cloud-based services in Windows networking, Windows Server 2012 contains various tools that have been overhauled to facilitate remote server management capabilities.

With the new Server Manager, for example, you can fully manage Windows servers without ever having to interact directly with the server console, either physically or remotely. However, immediately after the operating system installation, you might have to perform some tasks that require direct access to the server console. These tasks might include the following:

- Configuring the network connection
- Setting the time zone
- Renaming the computer
- Joining a domain
- Enabling Remote Desktop
- Configuring Windows Update settings

Using GUI Tools

> In Windows Server 2012, the Properties tile in Server Manager provides the same functionality as the Initial Configuration Tasks window in previous versions.

To complete any or all post-installation configuration tasks on a GUI Windows Server 2012 installation, use the following procedure.

⊙ CONFIGURE A GUI INSTALLATION

GET READY. Log on to the server running Windows Server 2012 using an account with administrative privileges. The *Server Manager* window appears.

1. In the left pane, click the Local Server icon. The Properties tile for the server appears, as shown in Figure 2-1.

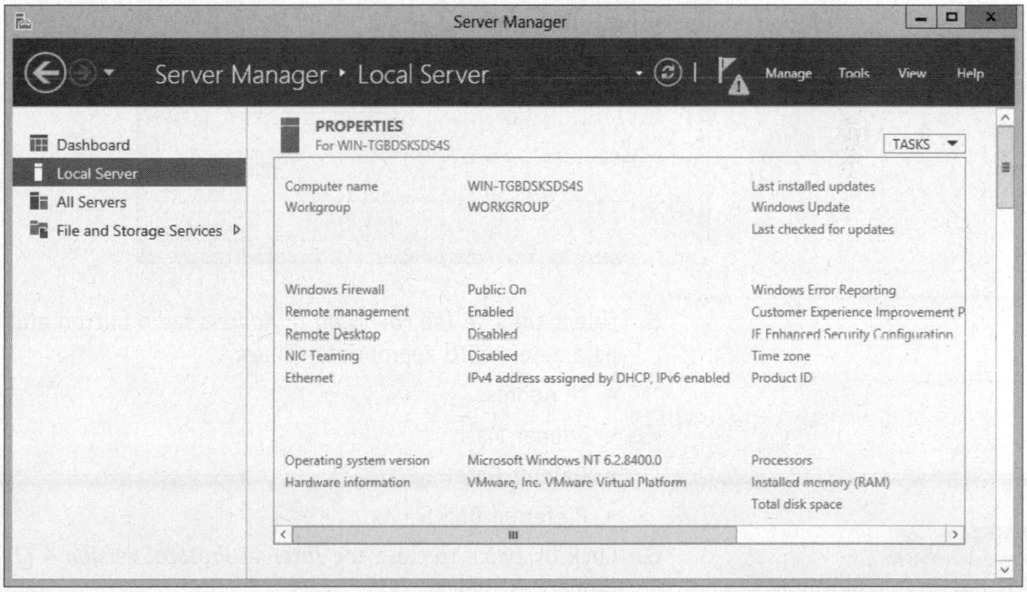

Figure 2-1

The Properties tile of the local server in Server Manager

2. In the Properties tile, the Ethernet entry specifies the status of the computer's network interface. If the network has an active Dynamic Host Configuration Protocol (DHCPv4) server, the server has already retrieved an IPv4 address and other settings and configured the interface. If the network has no DHCP server, or if you must configure the computer with a static IPv4 address, click the Ethernet hyperlink. The Network Connections window appears, as shown in Figure 2-2.

Figure 2-2

The Network Connections window

3. Right-click the Ethernet connection and, from the context menu, select Properties. The *Ethernet Properties* sheet appears.

4. Select the *Internet Protocol Version 4 (TCP/IPv4)* component and click Properties. The *Internet Protocol Version 4 (TCP/IPv4) Properties* sheet appears, as shown in Figure 2-3.

Figure 2-3

The *Internet Protocol Version 4 (TCP/IPv4) Properties* sheet

```
Internet Protocol Version 4 (TCP/IPv4) Properties      ?   X

General

You can get IP settings assigned automatically if your network supports
this capability. Otherwise, you need to ask your network administrator
for the appropriate IP settings.

  ○ Obtain an IP address automatically
  ● Use the following IP address:
     IP address:              [   .   .   .   ]
     Subnet mask:            [   .   .   .   ]
     Default gateway:        [   .   .   .   ]

  ○ Obtain DNS server address automatically
  ● Use the following DNS server addresses:
     Preferred DNS server:   [   .   .   .   ]
     Alternate DNS server:   [   .   .   .   ]

  ☐ Validate settings upon exit             [ Advanced... ]

                                    [  OK  ]  [ Cancel ]
```

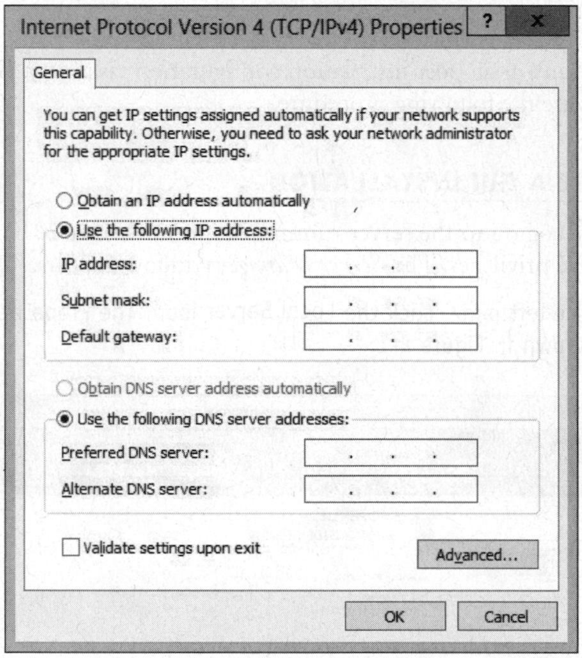

5. Select the *Use The Following IP Address* radio button and configure the following parameters with appropriate values:
   - IP Address
   - Subnet Mask
   - Default Gateway
   - Preferred DNS Server

6. Click OK twice to close the *Internet Protocol Version 4 (TCP/IPv4)* and *Ethernet* Properties sheets.

7. Accurate computer clock time is essential for Active Directory Domain Services (AD DS) communication. If the server is located in a time zone other than the default Pacific zone, click the Time Zone hyperlink to display the *Date and Time* dialog box.

8. Click Change Time Zone. The *Time Zone Settings* dialog box appears, as shown in Figure 2-4.

TAKE NOTE*

At this time, you might also want to configure NIC teaming. For more information, see "Configuring NIC Teaming," later in this lesson.

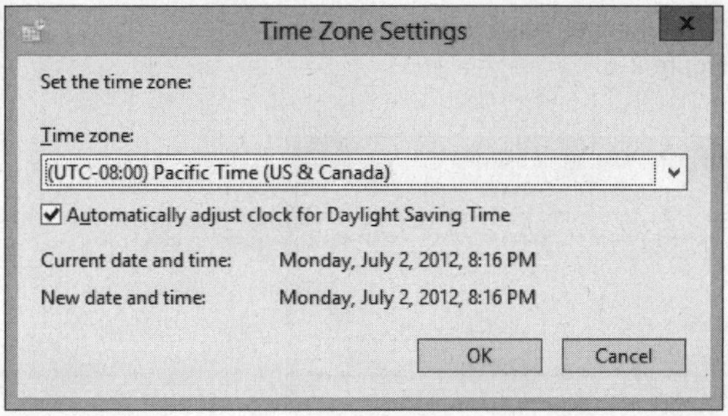

Figure 2-4

The *Time Zone Settings* dialog box

9. Select the appropriate Time Zone setting for the server's permanent location and click OK twice to close the dialog boxes.

10. By default, Windows Server 2012 does not allow Remote Desktop connections. To enable them, click the Remote Desktop hyperlink to open the Remote tab of the *System Properties* sheet, as shown in Figure 2-5.

Figure 2-5

The Remote tab of the *System Properties* sheet

11. Select the Allow remote connections to this computer radio button. A Remote Desktop Connection message box appears.

12. Click OK to enable the required firewall exception.

13. Click Select Users to grant users remote desktop permissions, if desired, and click OK.

14. Click OK to close the *System Properties* sheet.

15. In a manual operating system installation, the Windows Setup program assigns a unique name beginning with *WIN-* to the computer. To change the name of the computer and join it to a domain, click the Computer Name hyperlink to display the *System Properties* sheet.

16. Click Change. The *Computer Name/Domain Changes* dialog box appears, as shown in Figure 2-6.

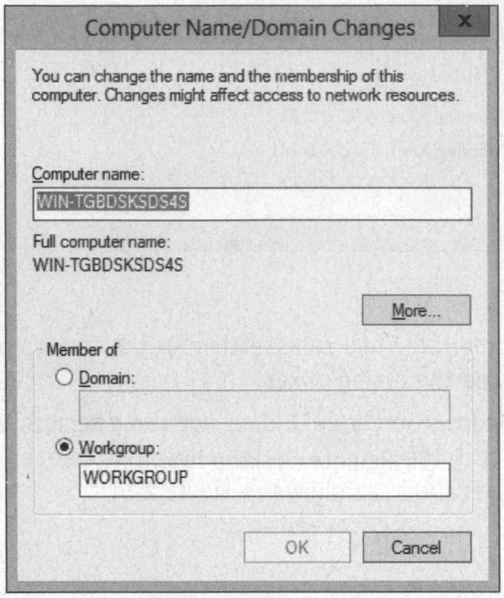

Figure 2-6

The *Computer Name/Domain Changes* dialog box

17. In the Computer Name field, type the new name for the computer.

18. Click the Domain radio button and type the name of the domain to which you want to join the computer.

19. Click OK. A *Windows Security* dialog box appears, as shown in Figure 2-7.

Figure 2-7

The *Windows Security* dialog box

20. In the User Name and Password fields, type the credentials for a domain account with the privileges needed to add a computer to the specified domain and click OK. A Welcome to the Domain message box appears, followed by a message box informing you that you must restart the computer.

21. Click OK twice to close the message boxes.

22. Close the *System Properties* sheet and restart the computer when you are prompted to do so.

If necessary, because of limited physical access to the server, you can confine this procedure to configuring the network connection and enabling Remote Desktop. Then, you can use Remote Desktop to connect to the server and configure everything else.

Using Command-Line Tools

> If you selected the Server Core option when installing Windows Server 2012, you can perform the same post-installation tasks from the command line.

CERTIFICATION READY
Configure Server Core.
Objective 1.2

At the very minimum, you need to rename the computer and join it to a domain. To perform these tasks, use the Netdom.exe command.

To rename a computer, run Netdom.exe with the following syntax, as shown in Figure 2-8:

```
netdom renamecomputer %ComputerName% /NewName: <NewComputerName>
```

Figure 2-8

Renaming a computer from the command line

To restart the computer as directed, use the following command:

```
shutdown /r
```

Then, to join the computer to a domain, use the following syntax:

```
netdom join %ComputerName% /domain:<DomainName>
/userd:<UserName> /passwordd:*
```

In this command, the asterisk (*) in the `/passwordd` parameter causes the program to prompt you for the password to the user account you specified.

These commands assume that a DHCP server has already configured the computer's TCP/IP client. If this is not the case, you must configure it manually before you can join a domain. To assign a static IP address to a computer using Server Core, use the Netsh.exe program or the Windows Management Instrumentation (WMI) access provided by Windows PowerShell.

Converting Between GUI and Server Core

> In Windows Server 2012, you can convert a computer installed with the full GUI option to Server Core and add the full GUI to a Server Core computer.

CERTIFICATION READY
Convert Server Core to/
from full GUI.
Objective 1.2

This is a major improvement in the usefulness of Server Core over the version in Windows Server 2008 R2, in which you can change the interface only by reinstalling the entire operating system. With this capability, you can install servers with the full GUI, use the graphical tools to perform the initial setup, and then convert them to Server Core to conserve system resources. If later it becomes necessary, it is possible to reinstall the GUI components.

To convert a full GUI installation of Windows Server 2012 to Server Core using Server Manager, use the following procedure.

➔ CONVERT A GUI SERVER TO SERVER CORE

GET READY. Log on to the server running Windows Server 2012 by using an account with administrative privileges. The Server Manager window appears.

1. From the Manage menu, select Remove Roles and Features. The Remove Roles and Features Wizard appears, displaying the *Before you begin* page.
2. Click Next. The *Select destination server* page appears.
3. Select the server you want to convert to Server Core and click Next. The *Remove Server Roles* page appears.
4. Click Next. The *Remove features* page appears.
5. Scroll down in the list and expand the User Interfaces and Infrastructure feature, as shown in Figure 2-9.

Figure 2-9

The *Remove features* page in Server Manager

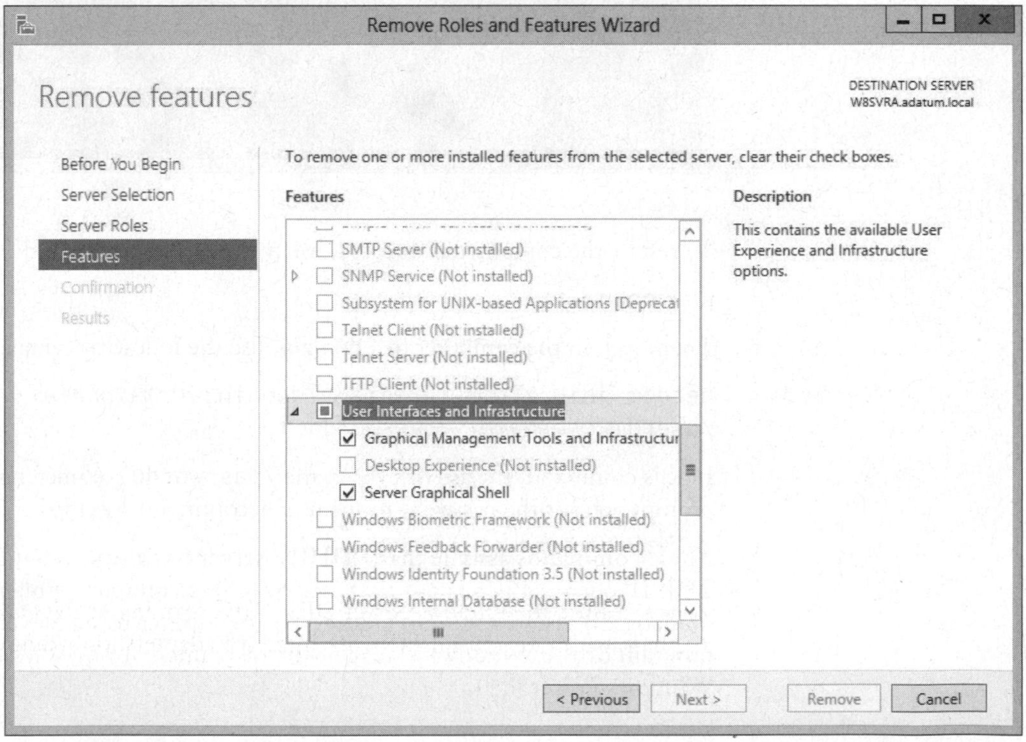

6. Clear the check boxes for the following components:
   - Graphical Management Tools and Infrastructure
   - Server Graphical Shell
7. The *Remove features that require Graphical Management Tools and Infrastructure* dialog box appears, as shown in Figure 2-10, with a list of dependent features that must be uninstalled. Click Remove Features.
8. Click Next. The *Confirm removal selections* page appears.

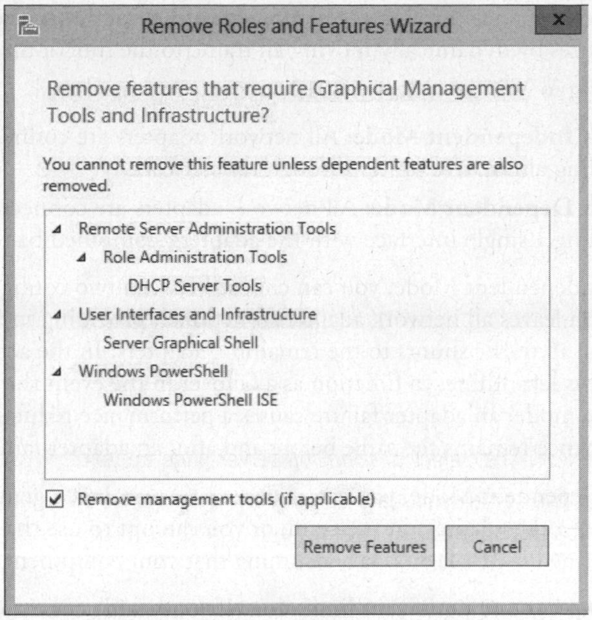

Figure 2-10

The *Remove features that require Graphical Management Tools and Infrastructure* dialog box

9. Select the Restart the destination server automatically if required check box and click Remove. The *Removal progress* page appears as the wizard uninstalls the feature.

10. Click Close. When the removal is completed, the computer restarts.

To add the full GUI to a Server Core computer, you must use Windows PowerShell to install the same features you removed in the previous procedure.

USING WINDOWS POWERSHELL

To convert a Windows Server 2012 Server Core installation to the full GUI option, use the following Windows PowerShell command:

```
Install-WindowsFeature
Server-Gui-Mgmt-Infra, Server-Gui-Shell -Restart
```

To convert a full GUI server installation to Server Core, use the following command:

```
Uninstall-WindowsFeature
Server-Gui-Mgmt-Infra, Server-Gui-Shell -Restart
```

Configuring NIC Teaming

A new feature in Windows Server 2012, NIC teaming enables administrators to combine the bandwidth of multiple network interface adapters, providing increased performance and fault tolerance.

CERTIFICATION READY
Configure NIC Teaming.
Objective 1.2

Virtualization enables you to separate vital network functions on different systems without having to purchase a separate physical computer for each one. However, one drawback of this practice is that a single server hosting multiple virtual machines is still a single point of failure for all of them. A single malfunctioning network adapter, a faulty switch, or even an unplugged cable can bring down a host server and all its VMs with it.

NIC teaming—also called bonding, balancing, and aggregation—is a technology that has been available for some time, but was always tied to specific hardware implementations. The NIC teaming capability in Windows Server 2012 is hardware independent and enables you to combine multiple physical network adapters into a single interface. The results can include increased performance through the combined throughput of the adapters and protection from adapter failures by dynamically moving all traffic to the functioning NICs.

NIC teaming in Windows Server 2012 supports two modes:

- **Switch Independent Mode:** All network adapters are connected to different switches, providing alternative routes through the network.
- **Switch Dependent Mode:** All network adapters are connected to the same switch, providing a single interface with the adapters' combined bandwidth.

In Switch Independent Mode, you can choose between two configurations. The active/active configuration leaves all network adapters functional, providing increased throughout. If one adapter fails, all traffic shunts to the remaining adapters. In the active/standby configuration, one adapter is left offline, to function as a failover in the event the active adapter fails. In active/active mode, an adapter failure causes a performance reduction; in active/standby mode, the performance remains the same before and after an adapter failure.

In Switch Dependent Mode, you can choose static teaming, a generic mode that balances traffic between the adapters in the team, or you can opt to use the Link Aggregation Control Protocol defined in IEEE 802.3ax, assuming that your equipment supports it.

NIC teaming has one significant limitation. If your traffic consists of large TCP sequences, such as a Hyper-V live migration, the system avoids using multiple adapters for those sequences to minimize the number of lost and out-of-order TCP segments. You therefore do not realize any performance increase for large file transfers using TCP.

You can create and manage NIC teams using Server Manager or Windows PowerShell. To create a NIC team using Server Manager, use the following procedure.

CREATE A NIC TEAM

GET READY. Log on to the server running Windows Server 2012 using an account with administrative privileges. The Server Manager window appears.

1. In the navigation pane, click the Local Server icon. The Local Server homepage appears.
2. In the Properties tile, click the *NIC Teaming* hyperlink. The *NIC Teaming* window appears, as shown in Figure 2-11.

Figure 2-11

The *NIC Teaming* window in Server Manager

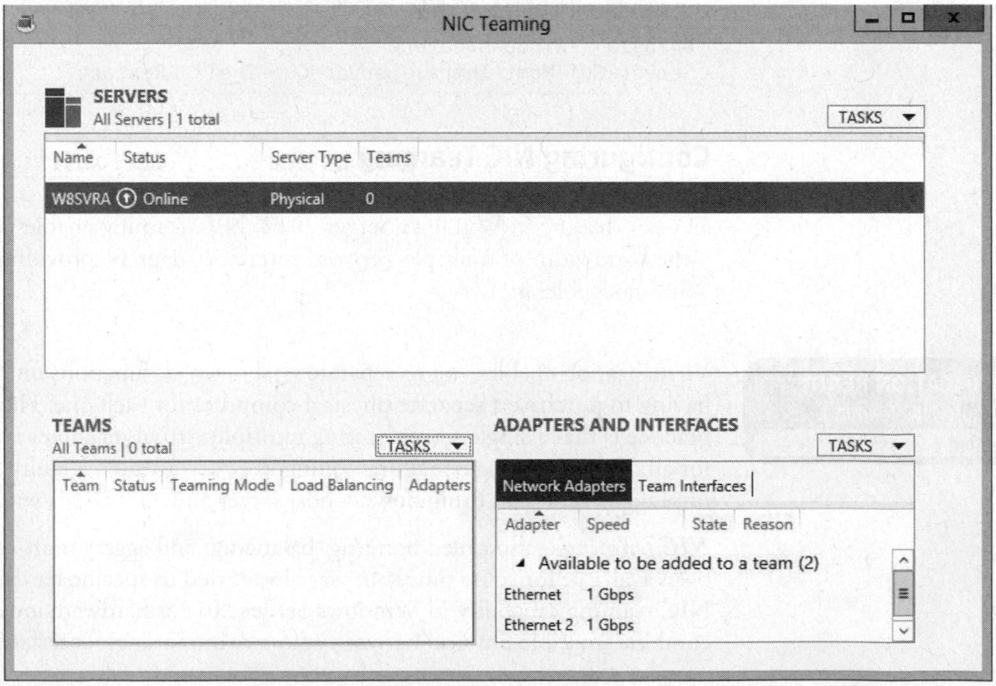

3. In the Teams tile, click the Tasks menu and select New Team. The *New team* page appears.
4. Click the Additional properties down arrow to expand the window, as shown in Figure 2-12.

Figure 2-12

The *New team* page in Server Manager

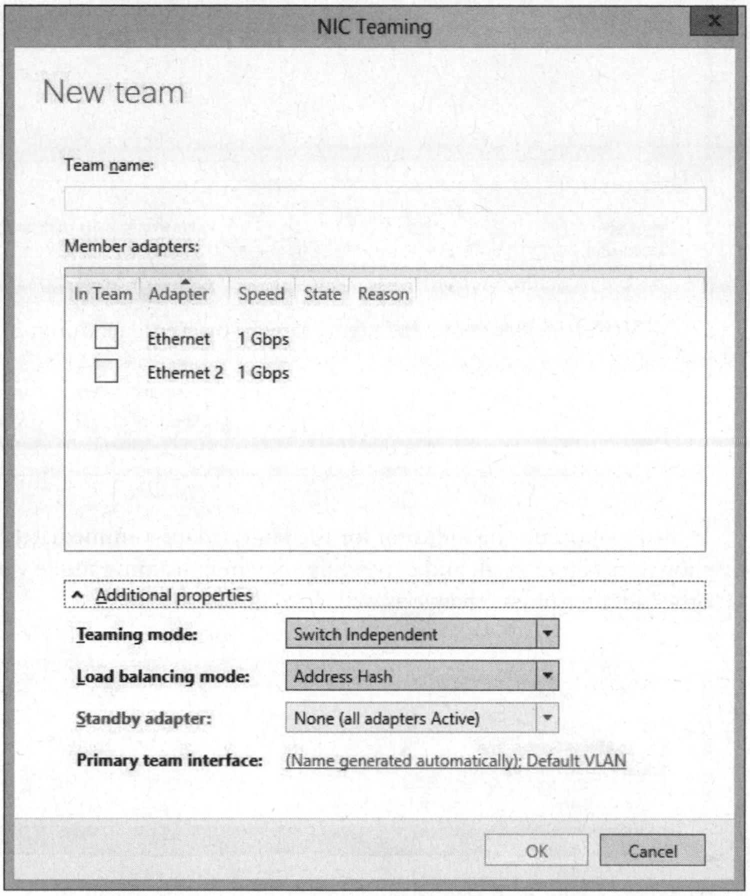

5. In the Team Name text box, type the name you want to assign to the team.
6. In the Member adapters box, select the network adapters you want to add to the team.
7. In the Teaming Mode drop-down list, select one of the following options:
   • Static Teaming
   • Switch Independent
   • LACP
8. In the Load balancing mode drop-down list, select one of the following options:
   • Address Hash
   • Hyper-V Port
9. If you selected Switch Independent for the Teaming mode value, from the Standby adapter drop-down list, select one of adapters you added to the team to function as the offline standby.
10. Click OK. The new team appears in the Teams tile, as shown in Figure 2-13.

After you create a NIC team, you can use the NIC Teaming window to monitor the status of the team and the team interface you created. The team itself and the individual adapters all have status indicators that inform you if an adapter goes offline.

Figure 2-13

A new NIC team in the *NIC Teaming* window in Server Manager

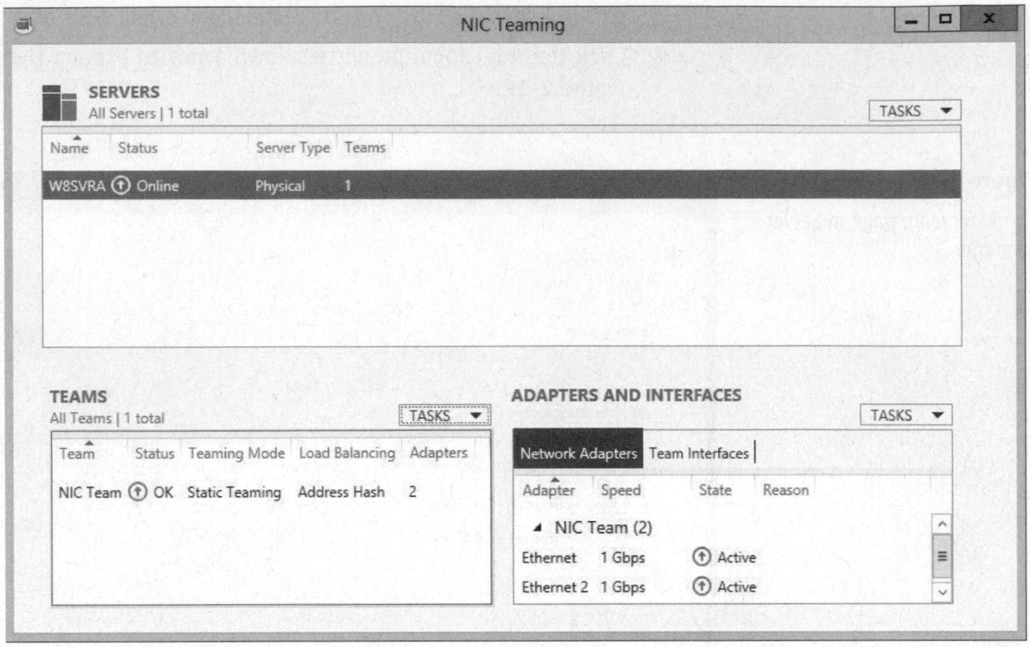

If this does occur, the indicator for the faulty adapter immediately switches to disconnected, as shown in Figure 2-14, and depending on which teaming mode you chose, the status of the other adapter might change as well.

Figure 2-14

A NIC team with a failed adapter

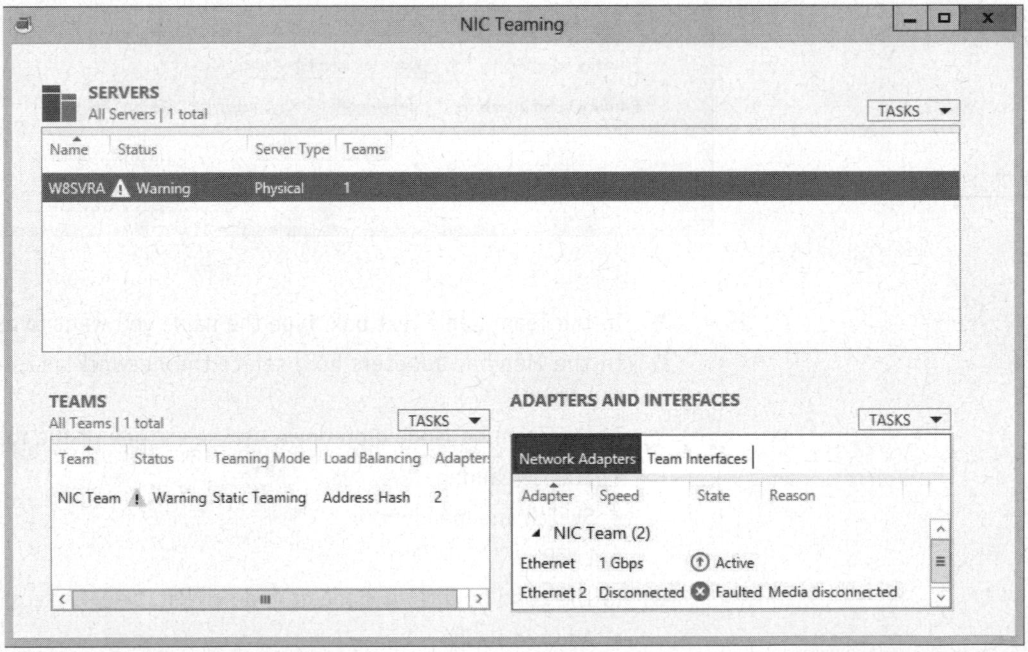

USING WINDOWS POWERSHELL

To manage NIC teaming with Windows PowerShell, you use the cmdlets in the NetLbfoTeam module. To create a new NIC team, you use the New-NetLbfoTeam cmdlet with the following basic syntax:

```
New-NetLbfoTeam -Name <team name> -TeamMembers <NIC1, NIC2,…>
[-TeamingMode LACP|Static|SwitchIndependent]
[-LoadBalancingAlgorithm TransportPorts|IPAddresses
|MACAddresses|HyperVPort]
```

■ Using Roles, Features, and Services

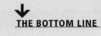

THE BOTTOM LINE   Configuring servers running Windows Server 2012 is initially a matter of deploying roles, features, and services.

For a list of the roles included with Windows Server 2012, refer to Table 1-1 in Lesson 1.

A role, as noted in Lesson 1, "Installing Servers," is a combination of components that implements a common server infrastructure, application, or directory service function. Roles can consist of applications, management tools, utilities, and other components, all devoted to a particular end.

Roles define the primary functions of a server. A server with the Web Server (IIS) role installed is referred to as a web server, no matter what other functions it might perform.

A feature is a smaller module, typically with a single purpose, such as a management tool, an extension to a service, or an optional infrastructure component. The object of packaging software components as features is to avoid consuming system resources for tools that not every system administrator will use or need.

Table 2-1 lists the features supplied with Windows Server 2012.

Table 2-1

Windows Server 2012 Features

FEATURE	DESCRIPTION
.NET Framework 3.5 Features	A software package containing code that provides solutions to a large number of common programming requirements, including user interface, database access, cryptographic security, and network communications routines. Software developers can use these routines, with their own code, to build Windows applications more easily.
.NET Framework 4.5 Features	A software package that provides programming tools for building and running applications for PCs, smart phones, and cloud systems.
Background Intelligent Transfer Service (BITS)	A service that enables client computers to transmit and receive files without using resources needed by other processes.
BitLocker Drive Encryption	A data-protection feature that encrypts entire hard disk volumes, allowing access to the volumes only after validating the integrity of the computer's boot components and confirming that no one has moved the drive to another computer.
BitLocker Network Unlock	A feature that implements a network-based key protector service for domain computers.
BranchCache	A technology that enables the computer to function as either a BranchCache content server or a hosted cache server at a branch office location.
Client for NFS	A client that enables the computer to access NFS shares on UNIX/Linux servers.
Data Center Bridging	A feature that provides hardware-based quality of service and reliability on networks using iSCSI and Fibre Channel over Ethernet.
Enhanced Storage	A technology that enables the operating system to access additional functions on Enhanced Storage hardware devices.
Failover Clustering	A technology that enables multiple servers to work together at performing the same tasks, to provide high availability for applications and services.

(continued)

Table 2-1

(continued)

FEATURE	DESCRIPTION
Group Policy Management	A tool that installs the Group Policy Management Console, a Microsoft Management Console snap-in that simplifies the process of deploying, managing, and troubleshooting Group Policy Objects (GPOs).
Ink and Handwriting Services	A feature that implements APIs that support the use of pen flicks and handwriting recognition in applications.
Internet Printing Client	A client technology that enables users to send print jobs to remote web server-based printers, using an Internet connection.
IP Address Management (IPAM) Server	A feature that provides a unified framework for IP address allocation and infrastructure servers such as DHCP and DNS.
Internet Storage Name Service (iSNS)	A technology that provides discovery services for clients accessing storage area networks running the Internet Small Computer System Interface (iSCSI), including registration, deregistration, and queries.
LPR (Line Printer Remote) Port Monitor	A feature that enables the computer to send print jobs to a UNIX computer with a compatible line printer daemon (LPD) implementation running on it.
Management OData IIS Extension	An infrastructure that provides a web-based service that supports Windows PowerShell cmdlets.
Media Foundation	A platform that provides the infrastructure required for server applications to work with media files.
Message Queuing	A technology that provides a variety of messaging services enabling applications to communicate, even when they run on different operating systems, use different types of networks, run at different times, or are temporarily offline.
Multipath I/O (MPIO)	A technology that provides multiple data paths to a single server storage device.
Network Load Balancing (NLB)	A feature that distributes incoming client traffic evenly among servers running the same application, enabling you to scale the application up or down by adding or removing servers as needed.
Peer Name Resolution Protocol (PNRP)	A name-resolution service that enables computers to register their peer names and associate them with their IPv6 addresses. Other computers on the network can then use the service to resolve a name into an address, enabling them to establish a connection to the named computer.
Quality Windows Audio Video Experience (qWave)	A feature that provides flow control and traffic prioritization services for applications that stream audio and video content over a network.
RAS Connection Manager Administration Kit (CMAK)	A tool kit that enables you to create customized service profiles for the Connection Manager client dialer application.
Remote Assistance	A feature that enables one user to provide technical support or training to another user at a remote computer by observing the remote user's desktop or by taking control of it.
Remote Differential Compression (RDC)	A synchronization algorithm that enables applications to conserve network bandwidth by determining what parts of a file have changed and transmitting only the modifications over the network.
Remote Server Administration Tools	A tool kit that enables administrators to access management tools on remote computers running Windows Server 2003 and Windows Server 2008.

Table 2-1

(continued)

Feature	Description
RPC Over HTTP Proxy	A component that enables objects to receive Remote Procedure Calls (RPC) messages using the Hypertext Transfer Protocol (HTTP), even if someone has moved the object to another server on the network.
Simple TCP/IP Services	A service that implements the Character Generator, Daytime, Discard, Echo, and Quote of the Day services, as defined in the TCP/IP standards.
SMTP (Simple Mail Transfer Protocol) Server	A server that provides communication between e-mail servers, and between e-mail clients and servers.
SNMP Service	A service that installs support for the Simple Network Management Protocol (SNMP), which enables network management applications to communicate with the agents for managed devices on the network.
Subsystem for UNIX-based Applications (Deprecated)	A technology that enables the server to compile and run UNIX-based applications.
Telnet Client	A client that enables the computer to connect to a Telnet server and access a command-line administration interface.
Telnet Server	A server that enables remote users running Telnet clients to connect to the computers and access a command-line administration interface.
TFTP (Trivial File Transfer Protocol) Client	A client that enables the computer to send files to and receive them from a TFTP server on the network, without needing authentication.
User Interfaces and Infrastructure	An infrastructure that provides the graphical interface that distinguishes a full GUI installation from Server Core.
Windows Biometric Framework	A framework that provides the software required to use fingerprint scanners for user authentication.
Windows Feedback Forwarder	A feature that enables the server to forward statistical information to Microsoft for development purposes.
Windows Identity Foundation 3.5	A set of .NET Framework classes superseded by .NET Framework 4.5.
Windows Internal Database	A database that implements a relational data store that other server roles and features can use.
Windows PowerShell	A command-line shell and scripting language that provides improved administration and automation capabilities.
Windows Process Activation Service (WAS)	An environment that generalizes the IIS process model by removing the dependency on HTTP, thus enabling WCF applications to use non-HTTP protocols. This feature is required to run the Web Server (IIS) role.
Windows Search Service	A service that enables client systems to perform fast file searches on servers.
Windows Server Backup	A feature that enables administrators to perform full or partial server backups at scheduled intervals.
Windows Server Migration Tools	A tool kit that provides role-specific tools for migrating data from earlier versions of Windows Server.

(continued)

Table 2-1

(continued)

Feature	Description
Windows Standards-based Storage Management	A feature that provides the server with access to storage devices conforming to the SMI-S standard.
Windows System Resource Manager (WSRM) (Deprecated)	A feature that enables administrators to allocate specific amounts of CPU and memory resources to specific applications, services, or processes.
Windows TIFF Filter	A filter that enables the server to perform optical character recognition (OCR) scans of TIFF graphic files.
WinRM IIS Extension	A technology that enables the server to receive management requests from clients using web services.
WINS Server	A server that provides NetBIOS name registration and resolution services for down-level Windows clients.
Wireless LAN Service	A service that implements the Wireless LAN (WLAN) AutoConfig service, which detects and configures wireless network adapters, and manages wireless networking profiles and connections.
WoW64 Support	A feature that enables the server to run 32-bit applications on Server Core installations.
XPS Viewer	A viewer that enables users to read and digitally sign XPS documents.

To install roles and features in Windows Server 2012, you can use the Add Roles and Features Wizard in Server Manager, the Server ManagerCmd.exe tool at the command line, or the `Add-WindowsFeature` cmdlet in Windows PowerShell.

TAKE NOTE *

Some members of the Windows Server development team have stated that their ultimate goal is to create a server operating system with a default configuration that consists of nothing more than the tools needed to add roles and features. Windows Server 2012 is a major step toward this goal, in that you can remove a great deal of the infrastructure you do not need from the server's memory and hard disks.

A service is a program that runs continuously in the background, typically providing server functions by listening for incoming requests from clients. Roles typically include a number of services, as do some features. After you install the roles or features that implement services, you can manage them as needed through Server Manager and command-line tools.

■ Using Server Manager

↓ **THE BOTTOM LINE**

The Server Manager tool in Windows Server 2012 is a completely new application that is the first and most obvious evidence of a major paradigm shift in Windows Server administration.

In previous version of Windows Server, an administrator wanting to install a role using graphical controls had to work at the server console by either physically sitting at the keyboard or connecting to it using Remote Desktop Services (formerly Terminal Services). By contrast, the Windows Server 2012 Server Manager can install roles and features to any server on the network, and even to multiple servers or groups of servers at once.

Adding Roles and Features

> The Server Manager program in Windows Server 2012 combines what used to be separate wizards for adding roles and features into one, the Add Roles and Features Wizard.

After you add multiple servers to the Server Manager interface, they are integrated into the Add Roles and Features Wizard, so you can deploy roles and features to any of your servers.

To install roles and features using Server Manager, use the following procedure.

CERTIFICATION READY
Deploy roles on remote servers.
Objective 1.2

⊙ INSTALL ROLES AND FEATURES USING SERVER MANAGER

GET READY. Log on to the server running Windows Server 2012 using an account with administrative privileges. The Server Manager window appears.

1. From the Manage menu, select Add Roles and Features. The Add Roles and Features Wizard appears, displaying the *Before you begin* page.

2. Click Next. The *Select Installation Type* page appears, as shown in Figure 2-15.

Figure 2-15

The *Select Installation Type* page in the Add Roles and Features Wizard

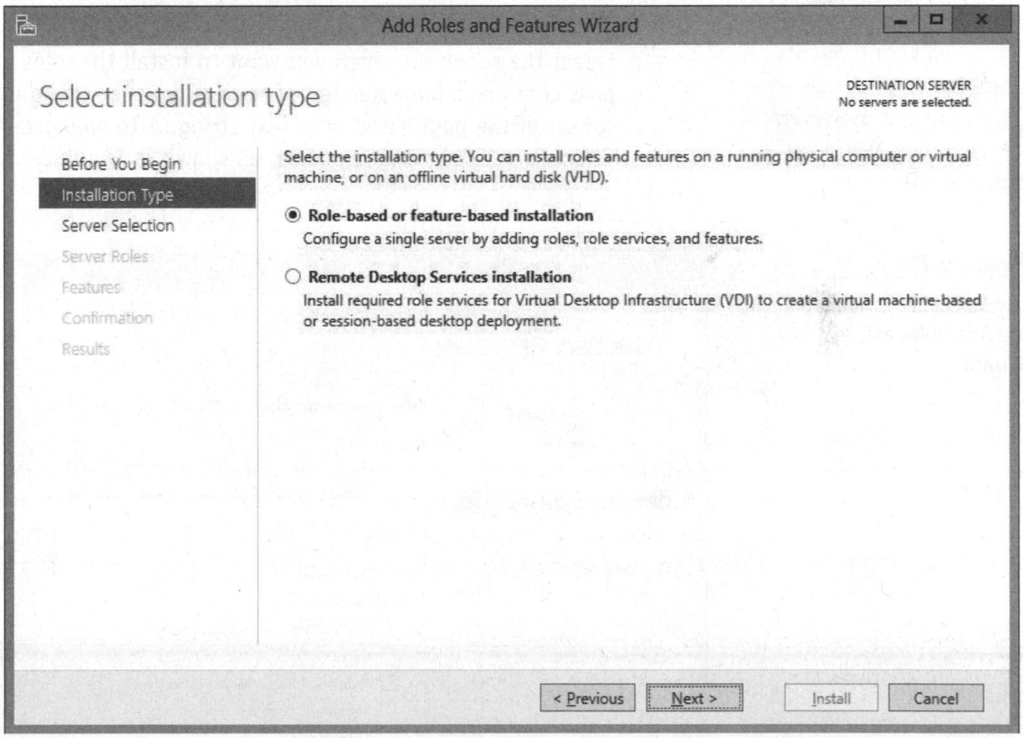

3. Leave the *Role-based or feature-based installation* radio button selected and click Next. The *Select destination server* page appears, as shown in Figure 2-16.

➕ **MORE INFORMATION**
The Remote Desktop Services (RDS) installation radio button provides a separate procedure that enables you to perform a distributed installation of the various RDS role services to different servers on the network.

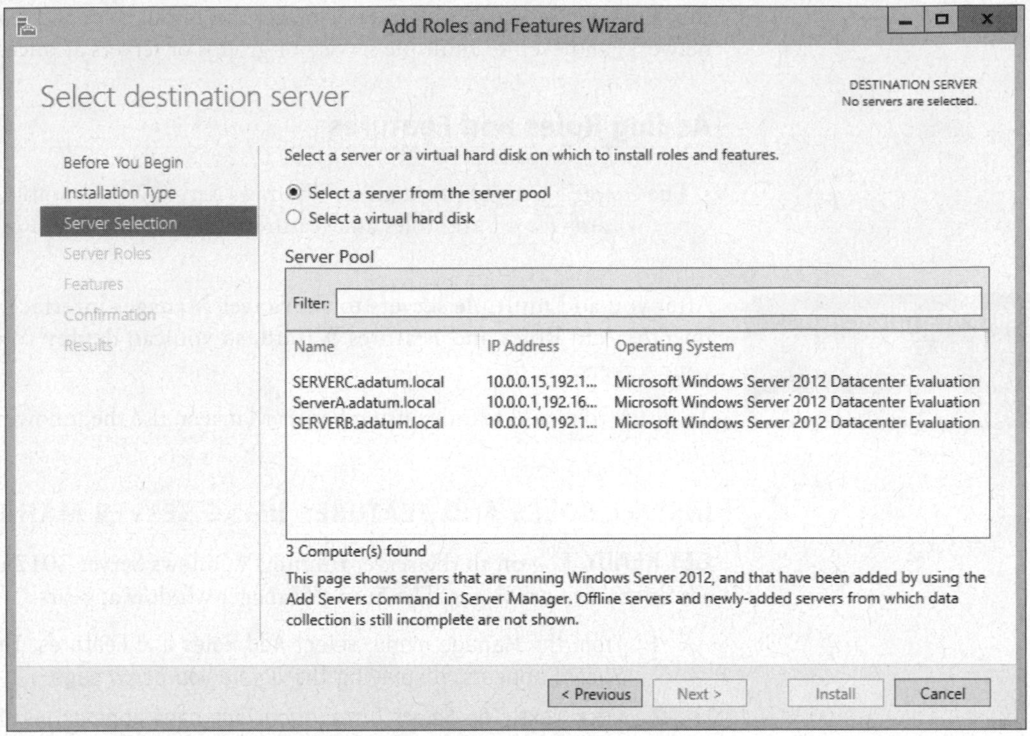

Figure 2-16

The *Select destination server* page in the Add Roles and Features Wizard

TAKE NOTE *

Although you can use the Add Roles and Features Wizard to install components to any server you have added to Server Manager, you cannot use it to install components to multiple servers at once. You can, however, do this using Windows PowerShell.

4. Select the server on which you want to install the roles and/or features. If the server pool contains a large number of servers, you can use the filter text box to display a subset of the pool based on a text string. After you select the server, click Next. The *Select Server Roles* page appears, as shown in Figure 2-17.

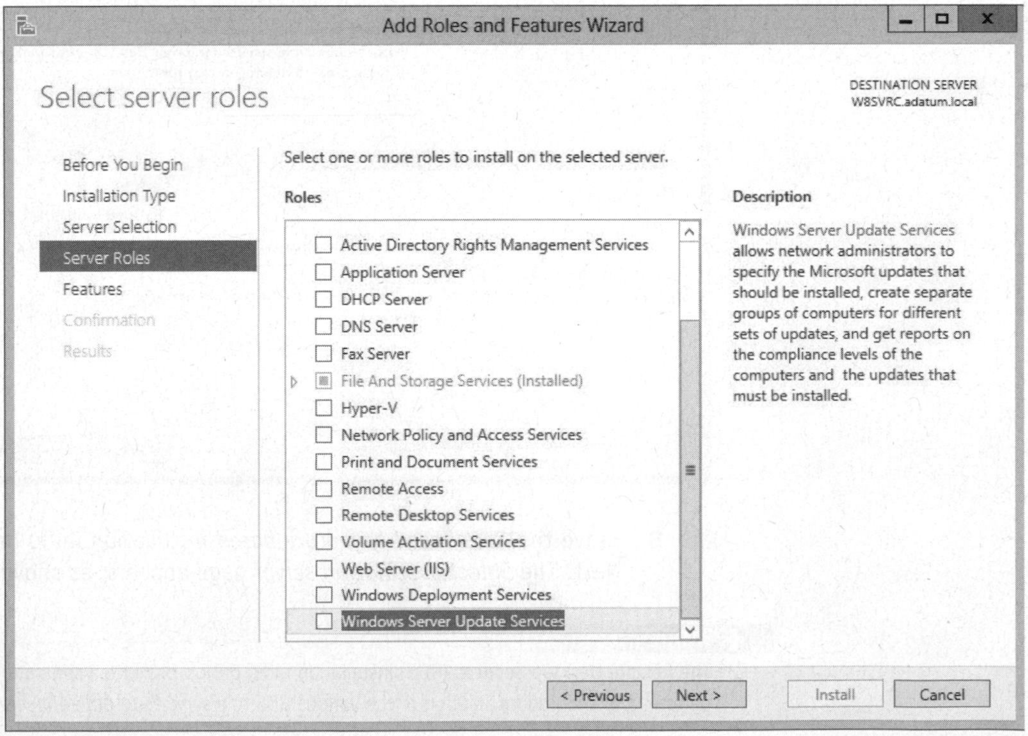

Figure 2-17

The *Select Server Roles* page in the Add Roles and Features Wizard

5. Select the role or roles you want to install on the selected server. If the roles you select have other roles or features as dependencies, an *Add features that are required* dialog box appears, as shown in Figure 2-18.

Figure 2-18

The *Add features that are required* dialog box in the Add Roles and Features Wizard

Add Roles and Features Wizard
Add features that are required for Windows Server Update Services?
You cannot install Windows Server Update Services unless the following role services or features are also installed.
.NET Framework 4.5 Features
ASP.NET 4.5
Remote Server Administration Tools
Role Administration Tools
Windows Server Update Services Tools
API and PowerShell cmdlets
Web Server (IIS)
Management Tools
IIS 6 Management Compatibility
Include management tools (if applicable)
Add Features
Cancel

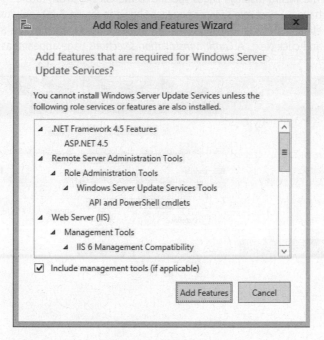

TAKE NOTE*

Unlike previous versions of Server Manager, the Windows Server 2012 version enables you to select all the roles and features for a particular server configuration at once, rather than make you run the wizard multiple times.

6. Click Add Features to accept the dependencies, and then click Next. The *Select features* page appears, as shown in Figure 2-19.

Figure 2-19

The *Select features* page in the Add Roles and Features Wizard

Add Roles and Features Wizard
Select features
DESTINATION SERVER
W8SVRA.adatum.local
Before You Begin
Installation Type
Server Selection
Server Roles
Features
Confirmation
Results
Select one or more features to install on the selected server.
Features
.NET Framework 3.5 Features
.NET Framework 4.5 Features (Installed)
Background Intelligent Transfer Service (BITS)
BitLocker Drive Encryption
BitLocker Network Unlock
BranchCache
Client for NFS
Data Center Bridging
Enhanced Storage
Failover Clustering
Group Policy Management (Installed)
Ink and Handwriting Services
Internet Printing Client
IP Address Management (IPAM) Server
Description
.NET Framework 3.5 combines the power of the .NET Framework 2.0 APIs with new technologies for building applications that offer appealing user interfaces, protect your customers' personal identity information, enable seamless and secure communication, and provide the ability to model a range of business processes.
< Previous
Next >
Install
Cancel

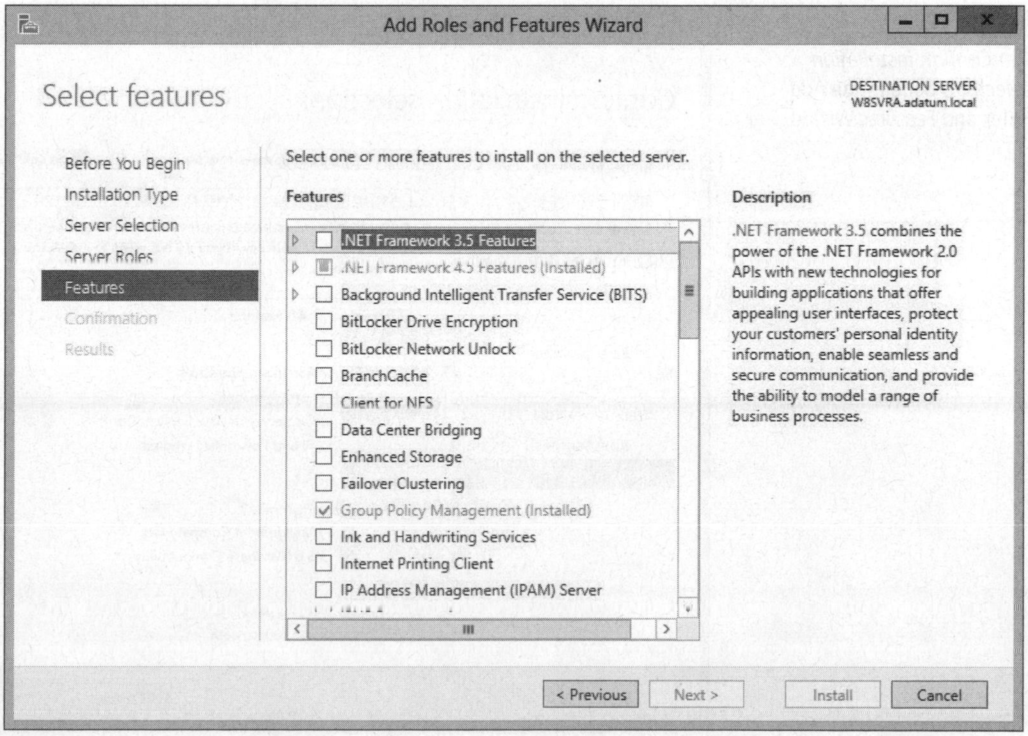

7. Select any features you want to install in the selected server and click Next. Dependencies also might appear for your feature selections.

8. The wizard displays pages specific to the roles and/or features you have chosen. Most roles have a *Select role services* page, as shown in Figure 2-20, on which you can select which elements of the role you want to install. Complete each of the role- or feature-specific pages and click Next. A *Confirm installation selections* page appears, as shown in Figure 2-21.

Figure 2-20

The *Select role services* page in the Add Roles and Features Wizard

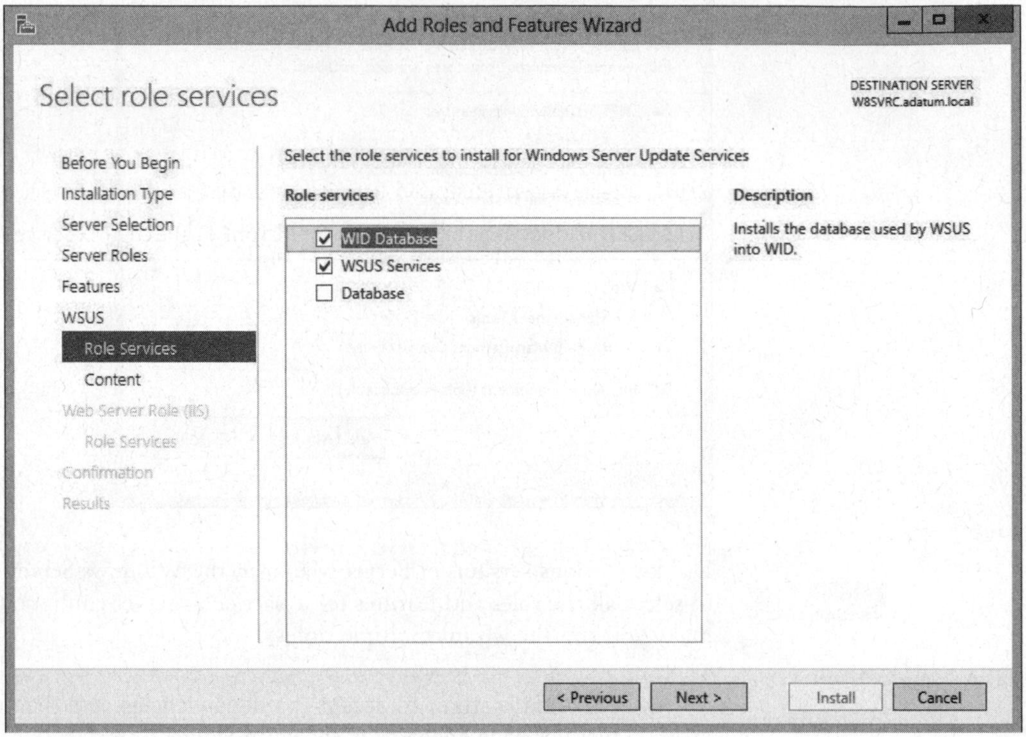

Figure 2-21

The *Confirm installation selections* page in the Add Roles and Features Wizard

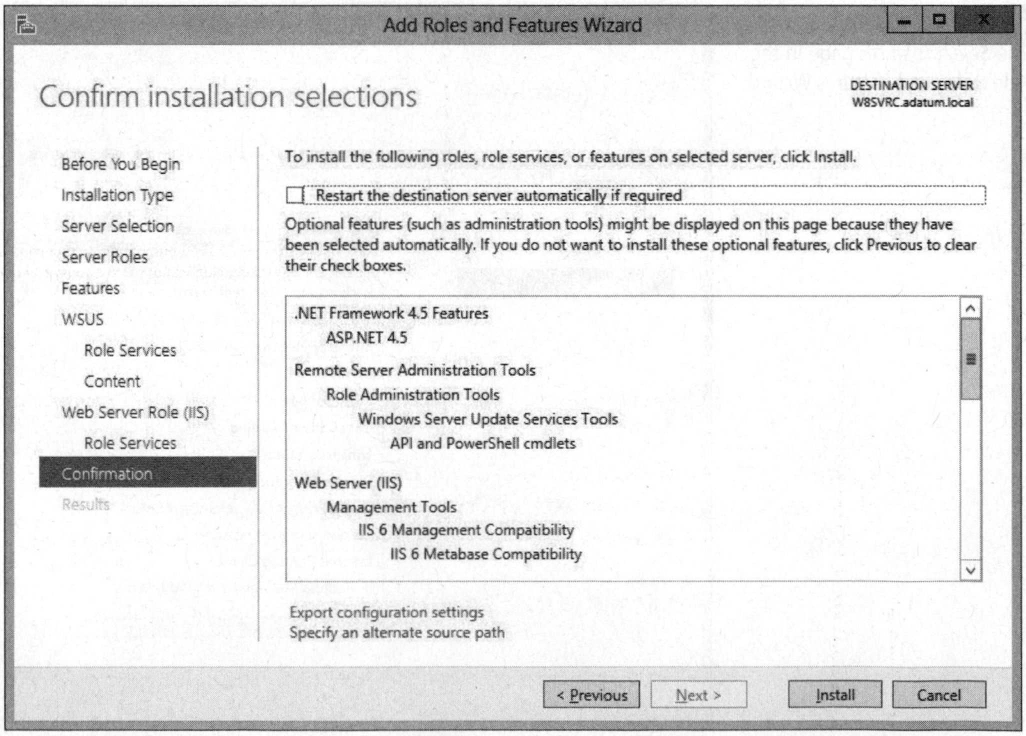

9. Select from the following optional functions, if desired:

- **Restart the destination server automatically if desired** causes the server to restart automatically when the installation completes, if the selected roles and features require it.

- **Export configuration settings** create an XML script documenting the procedures performed by the wizard, which you can use to install the same configuration on another server using Windows PowerShell.

- **Specify an alternate source path** specifies the location of an image file containing the software needed to install the selected roles and features

USING WINDOWS POWERSHELL

To use an exported configuration file to install roles and features on another computer running Windows Server 2012, use the following command in a Windows PowerShell session with elevated privileges:

```
Install-WindowsFeature –ConfigurationFilePath <ExportedConfig.xml>
```

10. Click Install. The *Installation progress* page appears, as shown in Figure 2-22. Depending on the roles and features installed, the wizard might display hyperlinks to the tools needed to perform required post-installation tasks. When the installation is completed, click Close to terminate the wizard.

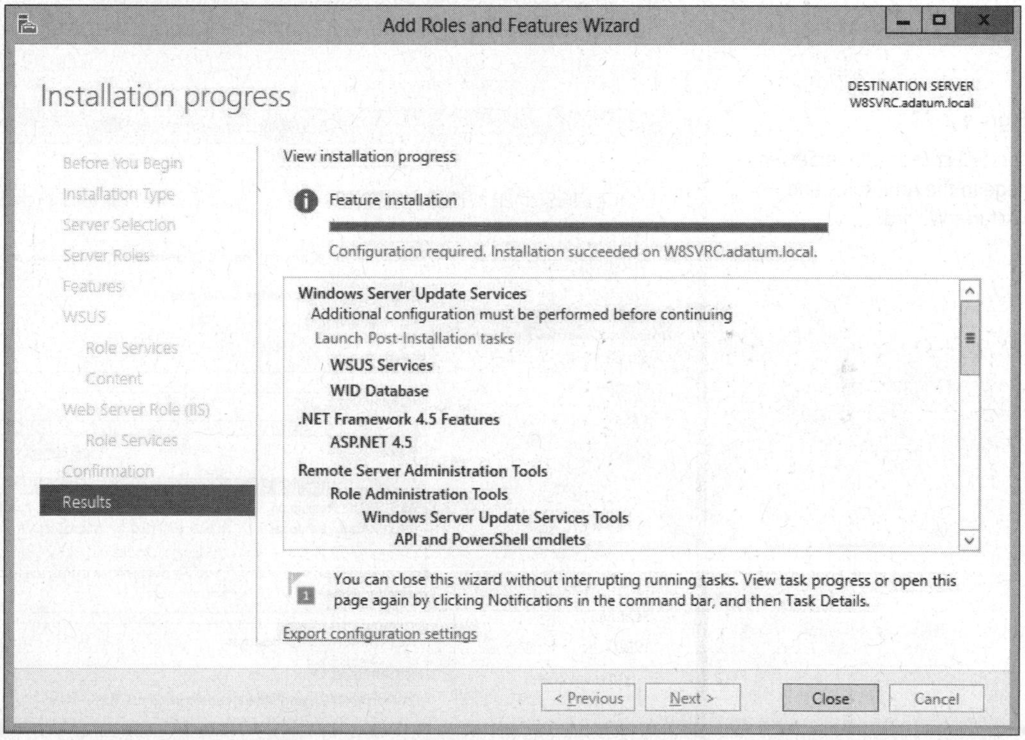

Figure 2-22

The *Installation progress* page in the Add Roles and Features Wizard

After you install roles on your servers, the roles appear as icons in the navigation pane. These icons actually represent *role groups*. Each role group contains all instances of that role found on any of your added servers. You can therefore administer the role across all servers on which you have installed it.

Deploying Roles to VHDs

In addition to installing roles and features to servers on the network, Server Manager also enables administrators to install them to virtual machines currently in an offline state.

In an enterprise virtualization strategy, administrators frequently maintain virtual machines (VMs) in an offline state. For example, you might have an offline web server VM stored on a backup host server, in case the computer hosting your main web server VMs should fail. Server Manager enables you to select a virtual hard disk (VHD) file and install or remove roles and features without having to start the VM.

CERTIFICATION READY
Add and remove features in offline images.
Objective 1.2

To install roles and/or features to an offline VHD file, use the following procedure.

INSTALL ROLES AND FEATURES TO AN OFFLINE VHD FILE

GET READY. Log on to the server running Windows Server 2012 using an account with administrative privileges. The Server Manager window appears.

1. From the Manage menu, select Add Roles and Features. The Add Roles and Features Wizard appears, displaying the *Before you begin* page.
2. Click Next. The *Select Installation Type* page appears.
3. Leave the *Role-based or feature-based installation* radio button selected and click Next. The *Select Destination Server* page appears.
4. Select the Select a virtual hard disk radio button.
5. A Virtual Hard Disk text box appears at the bottom of the page. In this text box, type in or browse to the location of the VHD file you want to modify.
6. In the Server Pool box, select the server that the wizard should use to mount the VHD file, as shown in Figure 2-23, and click Next. The *Select Server Roles* page appears.

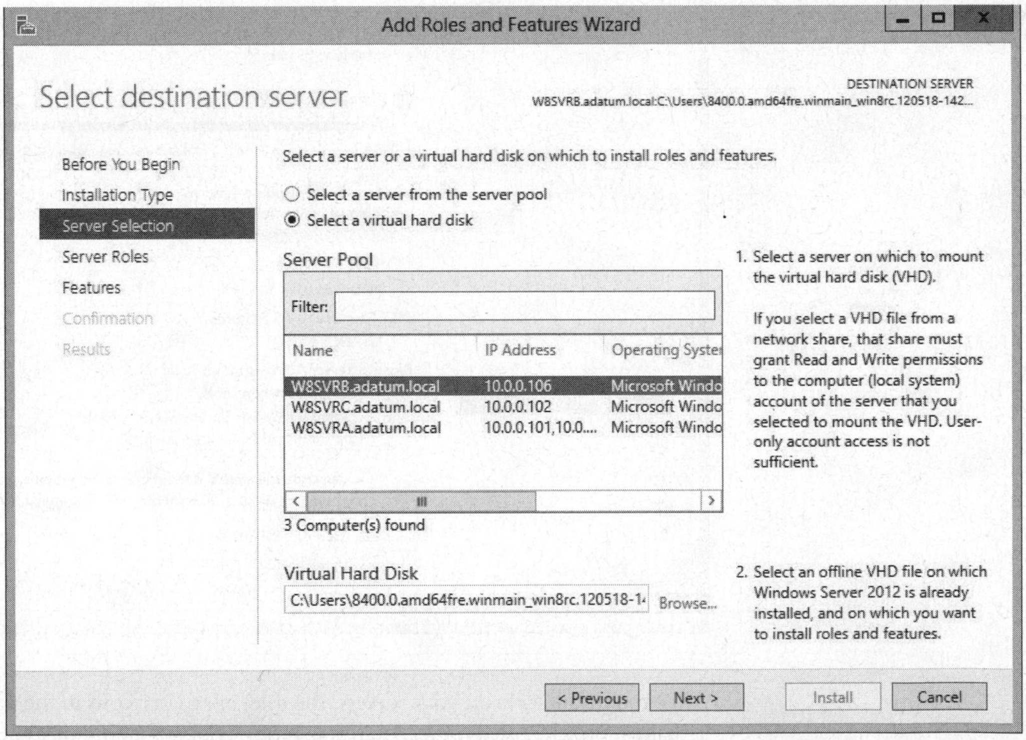

Figure 2-23
The *Select Destination Server* page in the Add Roles and Features Wizard

TAKE NOTE*
The wizard must mount the VHD file on the server you select, and look inside and determine which roles and features are already installed and which are available for installation. Mounting a VHD file makes it available only through the computer's file system; it is not the same as starting the virtual machine using the VHD.

7. Select the role or roles you want to install on the selected server, adding the required dependencies, if necessary, and click Next. The *Select features* page appears.

8. Select any features you want to install in the selected server and click Next. Dependencies also might appear for your feature selections.

9. The wizard then displays pages specific to the roles and/or features you have chosen, enabling you to select role services and configure other settings. Complete each of the role- or feature-specific pages and click Next. A *Confirmation* page appears.

10. Click Install. The *Installation progress* page appears.

11. When the installation is completed, click Close to dismount the VHD and terminate the wizard.

Configuring Services

> Most Windows Server roles and many features include *services*, programs that run continuously in the background, typically waiting for a client process to send a request to them. Server Manager provides access to services running on servers all over the network.

CERTIFICATION READY
Configure services.
Objective 1.2

When you first look at the Local Server homepage in Server Manager, one tile that you find there is the Services tile, as shown in Figure 2-24. This tile lists all the services installed on the server and specifies the operational status and their Start Types. When you right-click a service, the context menu provides controls that enable you to start, stop, restart, pause, and resume the service.

Figure 2-24

The Services tile in Server Manager

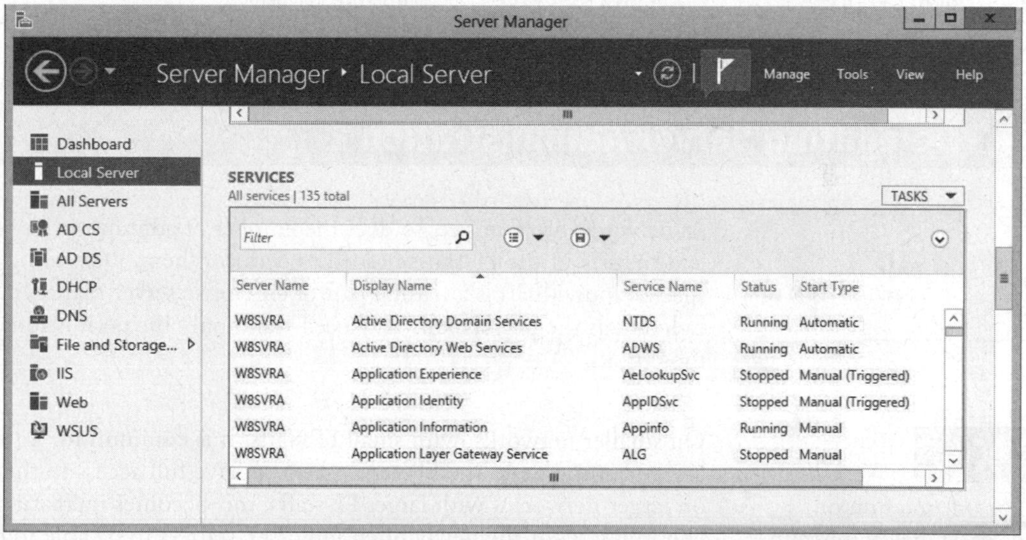

The Services tile in Server Manager is not unlike the traditional Services MMC snap-in found in previous versions of Windows Server. However, although you can start and stop a service in Server Manager, you cannot modify its Start Type, which specifies whether the service should start automatically with the operating system. For that, you must use the Services MMC snap in.

Another difference of the Services tile in Windows Server 2012 Server Manager is that it appears in many locations throughout Server Manager, displaying a list of services for a different context in each location. This is a good example of the organizational principle of the new

Server Manager. The same tools, repeated in many places, provide a consistent management interface to different sets of components.

For example, when you select the All Servers icon in the navigational pane, you see first the Servers tile, as usual, containing all the servers you have added to the Server Manager console. When you select some or all servers and scroll down to the Services tile, you see the same display as before, except that it now contains all services for all the computers you selected. This enables you to monitor the services on all servers at once.

In the same way, when you select one of the role group icons, you can select from the servers running that role and the Services tile will contain only the services associated with that role for the servers you selected.

To manipulate other server configuration settings, you must use the Services MMC snap-in as mentioned earlier. However, you can launch that, and many other snap-ins, by using Server Manager.

After selecting a server from the Servers pane in any group homepage, click the Tools menu to display a list of the server-specific utilities and MMC snap-ins, including the Services snap-in, directed at the selected server.

CERTIFICATION READY
Delegate administration.
Objective 1.2

REF

For information on delegating printer privileges, see "Configuring Printer Security" in Lesson 5, "Configuring Print and Document Services."

USING WINDOWS POWERSHELL

You can manage services using Windows PowerShell by using the following cmdlets:

- `Get-Service` lists the services installed on the system. Use this cmdlet to discover the names you should use to reference services in Windows PowerShell commands.
- `Start-Service` starts a stopped service.
- `Stop-Service` stops a running service.
- `Restart-Service` stops and starts a running service.
- `Set-Service` modifies a service's properties.

■ Delegating Server Administration

↓ THE BOTTOM LINE

As networks grow in size, so does the number of administrative tasks to perform regularly and the size of the IT staffs needed to perform them. Delegating administrative tasks to specific individuals is a natural part of enterprise server management, as is assigning those individuals the permissions they need—and only the permissions they need—to perform those tasks.

X REF

For information on delegating administrative control via Active Directory, see "Using OUs to Delegate Active Directory Management Tasks" in Lesson 15, "Creating and Managing Active Directory Groups and Organizational Units."

On smaller networks, with small IT staffs, it is common for task delegation to be informal, and for everyone in the IT department to have full access to the entire network. However, on larger networks, with larger IT staffs, this becomes increasingly impractical. For example, you might want the newly hired junior IT staffers to be able to create new user accounts, but you do not want them to be able to redesign your Active Directory tree or change the CEO's password.

Delegation, therefore, is the practice by which administrators grant other users a subset of the privileges that they themselves possess. As such, delegation is as much a matter of restricting permissions as it is of granting them. You want to provide individuals with the privileges they need, while protecting sensitive information and delicate infrastructure.

SKILL SUMMARY

IN THIS LESSON, YOU LEARNED:

- With the new Server Manager, you can fully manage Windows servers without ever having to interact directly with the server console, either physically or remotely.

- Immediately after the operating system installation, you might have to perform some tasks that require direct access to the server console.

- If you selected the Server Core option when installing Windows Server 2012, you can perform post-installation tasks from the command line.

- In Windows Server 2012, the Properties tile in Server Manager provides the same functionality as the Initial Configuration Tasks window in previous versions.

- In Windows Server 2012, you can convert a computer installed with the full GUI option to Server Core, and add the full GUI to a Server Core computer.

- A new feature in Windows Server 2012, NIC teaming enables administrators to combine the bandwidth of multiple network interface adapters, providing increased performance and fault tolerance.

- In addition to installing roles and features to servers on the network, Server Manager also enables administrators to install them to virtual machines currently in an offline state.

■ Knowledge Assessment

Multiple Choice

Select one or more correct answers for each of the following questions.

1. Which features must you remove from a full GUI installation of Windows Server 2012 to convert it to a Server Core installation? (Choose all that apply)
   a. Windows Management Instrumentation
   b. Graphical Management Tools and Infrastructure
   c. Desktop Experience
   d. Server Graphical Shell

2. Which of the following NIC teaming modes provides fault tolerance and bandwidth aggregation?
   a. Hyper-V live migration
   b. Switch Independent Mode
   c. Switch Dependent Mode
   d. Link Aggregation Control Protocol

3. Which of the following command-line tools do you use to join a computer to a domain?
   a. Net.exe
   b. Netsh.exe
   c. Netdom.exe
   d. Ipconfig.exe

4. Which of the following statements about Server Manager is not true?
   a. Server Manager can deploy roles to multiple servers at the same time.
   b. Server Manager can deploy roles to VHDs while they are offline.
   c. Server Manager can install roles and features at the same time.
   d. Server Manager can install roles and features to any Windows Server 2012 server on the network.

5. Which of the following operations can you not perform on a service using Server Manager? (Choose all that apply)
   a. Stop a running service
   b. Start a stopped service
   c. Disable a service
   d. Configure a service to start when the computer starts

6. Name the two methods to assign a static IP address to a computer using Server Core.
   a. Server Manager and the netdom.exe command
   b. The netdom.exe command and the IPv4 Properties sheet
   c. The IPv4 Properties sheet and the netsh.exe command
   d. The netsh.exe command and Windows Management Instrumentation (WMI) access provided by Windows PowerShell

7. Before you can deploy roles to multiple remote servers, what must be done?
   a. Perform an in-place upgrade to Windows Server 2012.
   b. Ensure the remote servers are patched sufficiently.
   c. Add the remote servers to the Server Manager interface.
   d. Perform a full backup

8. What utility allows you to install components to multiple servers at once?
   a. The Add Roles and Features Wizard only
   b. Both Add Roles and Features Wizard and Windows PowerShell
   c. Windows PowerShell only
   d. The Minimal Server Interface

9. What method is available to install roles and features on another Windows Server 2012 computer using Windows PowerShell?
   a. Use the `Install-WindowsFeature` command and an exported configuration file
   b. Use the `Install-WindowsRole` command and an exported configuration file
   c. Use Server Manager and the proper tile
   d. It is not possible using Windows PowerShell

10. What is the key principle to delegating server administrative tasks?
    a. Granting individuals the tasks they feel most comfortable doing
    b. Granting individuals only the permissions needed to do the delegated job
    c. Assign the delegated tasks to the person most likely to benefit
    d. Assigning enough permissions to do the delegated tasks as well as anticipated tasks

Best Answer

Choose the letter that corresponds to the best answer. More than one answer choice may achieve the goal. Select the BEST answer.

1. On a Windows Server 2012 server, you decide to change the interface. Select the best answer to convert a GUI server to Server Core.
   a. Reinstall the operating system and select Server Core upon installation
   b. Use Server Manager to start the Remove Roles and Features Wizard
   c. Use Server Manager to deselect the Server Graphical Shell option
   d. There is no option to downgrade from GUI to Server Core

2. Windows Server 2012 provides hardware-independent NIC teaming or bonding to enable better network performance and adapter fault-tolerance. However, in what scenario is the NIC teaming limited?
   a. During a Hyper-V live migration
   b. When network adapters connect to different switches
   c. When network traffic consists of large TCP sequences
   d. For multiple network adapters to function as one interface

3. As an administrator of a Windows Server 2012 network, you want to add a role to a few servers on the network. What is your best available option?
   a. Install a role at the target server's console
   b. Use Server Manager on the nearest Windows Server 2012
   c. Connect to the target server using Remote Desktop Services
   d. Using PowerShell, install the desired role to all target servers at once

4. What is the advantage of deploying roles to a virtual hard disk (VHD) file?
   a. Administrators can use Server Manager to modify VHD files
   b. An administrator can modify server roles to offline virtual machines (VMs) without starting the VM
   c. An administrator can modify server roles to offline VMs without connecting the VM to the network
   d. VHD files require fewer resources (for example, hard drive space)

5. What is the key benefit behind delegating server administration?
   a. In larger networks, delegation uses permissions to restrict access
   b. In smaller networks, delegation provides formalized synergy
   c. In larger networks, delegation improves prioritization of tasks
   d. In smaller networks, delegation creates employment opportunities

Build a List

1. You have finished a new installation. Order the steps to rename the computer and join it to a domain using the command prompt.
   a. Type `netdom join %ComputerName%`
      `/domain:<DomainName>`
      `/userd:<UserName> /passwordd:*`
   b. Restart the computer by typing `shutdown /r`
   c. Ensure DHCP has already configured the computers TCP/IP client
   d. Type `netdom renamecomputer %ComputerName%`
      `/NewName: <NewComputerName>`

2. Order the steps to install a role or feature using Server Manager.
   a. Select the destination server
   b. Choose the Select Installation Type (Role-based or Feature-based installation selected)
   c. Add required features or services the needed service depends upon
   d. Log on with administrative privileges and start Server Manager
   e. Select the server role
   f. From the Manage menu, select Add Roles and Features

3. Order the steps to install a role or feature to an offline VHD file.
   a. From the Manage menu, select Add Roles and Features
   b. Choose the Select Installation Type (Role-based or Feature-based installation selected)
   c. Log on with administrative privileges and start Server Manager
   d. For Destination server, select Virtual Hard Disk
   e. Close the wizard to dismount the VHD
   f. Type in or browse to the location of the VHD file you want to modify
   g. Select the role and required features

■ Business Case Scenarios

Scenario 2-1: Installing Roles with a Batch File

Mark Lee is an IT technician whose supervisor has assigned the task of configuring 20 new servers, which Mark is to ship to the company's branch offices around the country. He must configure each server to function as a file server with support for DFS and UNIX clients, a print server with support for Internet and UNIX printing, a fax server, and a secured, intranet Web/FTP server for domain users. Write a Windows PowerShell script that Mark can use to install all of the required software elements on a server.

Scenario 2-2: Deploying Roles to VHDs

You maintain several virtual machines (VMs) in an offline state. How do you proceed to add a particular role to one of those VMs?

Configuring Local Storage

70-410 EXAM OBJECTIVE

Objective 1.3 – Configure local storage. This objective may include but is not limited to: Design storage spaces; configure basic and dynamic disks; configure MBR and GPT disks; manage volumes; create and mount virtual hard disks (VHDs); configure storage pools and disk pools.

LESSON HEADING	EXAM OBJECTIVE
Planning Server Storage	
Determining the Number of Servers Needed	
Estimating Storage Requirements	
Selecting a Storage Technology	
Planning for Storage Fault Tolerance	
Using Storage Spaces	Design storage spaces
Understanding Windows Disk Settings	
Selecting a Partition Style	Configure MBR and GPT disks
Understanding Disk Types	Configure basic and dynamic disks
Understanding Volume Types	
Choosing a Volume Size	
Understanding File Systems	
Working with Disks	
Adding a New Physical Disk	
Creating and Mounting VHDs	Create and mount virtual hard disks (VHDs)
Creating a Storage Pool	Configure storage pools and disk pools
Creating Virtual Disks	
Creating a Simple Volume	
Creating a Striped, Spanned, Mirrored, or RAID-5 Volume	
Extending and Shrinking Volumes and Disks	Manage volumes

■ Planning Server Storage

THE BOTTOM LINE

A Windows server can conceivably perform its tasks using the same type of storage as a workstation—that is, one or more standard hard disks connected to a standard drive interface such as Serial ATA (SATA). However, a server's I/O burdens vary quite differently from those of a workstation, and file requests from dozens or hundreds of users can easily overwhelm a standard storage subsystem. Also, standard hard disks offer no fault tolerance and their scalability is limited.

A variety of storage technologies are better suited for server use. The process of designing a storage solution for a server depends on several factors, including the following:

- The amount of storage the server needs
- The number of users that will be accessing the server at the same time
- The sensitivity of the data to be stored on the server
- The importance of the data to the organization

The following sections examine these factors and the technologies you can choose when creating a plan for your network storage solutions.

Determining the Number of Servers Needed

When is one big file server preferable to several smaller ones?

One of the most frequently asked questions when planning a server deployment is whether using one big server or several smaller ones is better. In the past, you might have considered the advantages and disadvantages of using one server to perform several roles versus distributing the roles among several smaller servers. Today, however, the emphasis is on virtualization, which means that although you might have many virtual machines running different roles, they could all be running on a single large physical server.

If you are considering large physical servers or your organization's storage requirements are extremely large, you must also consider the inherent storage limitations of Windows Server 2012, as listed in Table 3-1.

Table 3-1

Windows Server 2012 Storage Limitations

ATTRIBUTE	LIMIT BASED ON THE ON-DISK FORMAT
Maximum size of a single file	2^{64}-1 bytes
Maximum size of a single volume	Format supports 2^{78} bytes with 16KB cluster size. Windows stack addressing allows 2^{64} bytes
Maximum number of files in a directory	2^{64}
Maximum number of directories in a volume	2^{64}
Maximum filename length	32K Unicode characters
Maximum path length	32K
Maximum size of any storage pool	4 petabytes
Maximum number of storage pools in a system	No limit
Maximum number of spaces in a storage pool	No limit

The number of sites your enterprise network encompasses and the technologies you use to provide network communication between those sites can also affect your plans. If, for example, your organization has branch offices scattered around the world and uses relatively expensive wide area networking (WAN) links to connect them, installing a server at each location would probably be more economical than to have all your users access a single server via WAN links.

Within each site, the number of servers you need can depend on how often your users work with the same resources and how much fault tolerance and high availability you want to build into the system. For example, if each department in your organization typically works with its own applications and documents and rarely needs access to those of other departments, deploying individual servers to each department might be preferable. If everyone in your organization works with the same set of resources, centralized servers might be a better choice.

Estimating Storage Requirements

The amount of storage space you need in a server depends on various factors, not just the initial requirements of your applications and users.

For an application server, start by allocating the amount of space needed for the application files themselves, plus any other space the application needs, as recommended by the developer. If users will store documents on the server, allocate a specific amount of space for each user the server will support. Then, factor in the potential growth of your organization and your network, both in terms of additional users and additional space required by each user, and of the application itself, in terms of data files and updates.

In addition to the space allocated to applications and individual users, you must also consider the storage requirements for the following server elements:

- **Operating system:** The size of the operating system installation depends on the roles and features you choose to install. A typical Windows Server 2012 installation with the File Services role needs just over 10 GB, but the system requirements recommend 40 GB.
- **Paging file:** The traditional formula for the size of the paging file—pagefile.sys—on a computer running Windows is 1½ times the amount of memory installed on the computer. However, this formula has now come into question, due to the large amounts

of memory in some servers and the increasing use of Hyper-V. Virtual machines require physical, not virtual, memory, so you do not need to count the memory allotted to your VMs when calculating your paging file size.

- **Memory dump:** When Windows Server 2012 experiences a serious malfunction, it offers to dump the contents of the system memory to a file, which technicians can use for diagnostic purposes. The maximum size for a memory dump file is the amount of memory installed in the computer plus 1 MB. However, blue screens are relatively rare on Windows servers these days, and unless you are troubleshooting a chronic problem with the aid of a technician who can make use of a memory dump, you probably do not need to reserve space for this purpose.

- **Log files:** Be sure to consider any applications that maintain their own logs, in addition to the operating system logs. You can configure the maximum log size for Windows event logs and for most application logs, and add those values to calculate the total log space required.

- **Shadow copies:** The Windows Server 2012 shadow copies feature automatically retains copies of files on a server volume in multiple versions from specific points in time. Shadow copies can use up to 10% of a volume, by default. However, Microsoft recommends enlarging this value for volumes containing frequently modified files.

- **Fault tolerance:** Fault-tolerance technologies, such as disk mirroring and disk parity, can profoundly affect disk consumption. Mirroring disks cuts the effective storage size in half, and parity can reduce it by as much as one third.

Selecting a Storage Technology

> Planning for server storage encompasses both hardware and software elements. You must decide how much storage space you need, as well as how much and what type of fault tolerance, and then select appropriate hardware to implement your decisions.

The following sections examine some of the storage technologies you can choose from when designing a server storage subsystem.

SELECTING A PHYSICAL DISK TECHNOLOGY

Most computers, including servers, use *direct-attached storage*—that is, the hard drives are located inside the computer case. For servers that require more storage space than a standard computer case can hold, or that have special availability requirements, a variety of external storage hardware options are available.

Of the many specifications that hard disk manufacturers provide for their products, the best gauge of the drive's performance is the rotational speed of the spindle that holds the platters. Typical desktop workstation hard drives have rotational speeds of 7,200 revolutions per minute (rpm). For a server, consider 10,000 as the minimum acceptable speed; many higher-end server drives run at 15,000 rpm, which is preferable but costly.

Just as important as the speed and capacity of the hard disks you select is the interface the disks use to connect to the computer. A server on an enterprise network often has to handle large numbers of disk I/O requests simultaneously, far more than a workstation drive with a single user ever would. For that reason, an interface that might be more than sufficient for a workstation, such as the ATA (Advanced Technology Attachment) interface that most workstation drives use, would perform poorly under a file server load.

ATA devices are limited to a maximum transmission speed of 133 MB/sec, which is relatively slow by server standards. The other big problem with ATA devices is that the cable can handle only a single command at any one time. If you have two drives connected to an ATA cable,

Hard drives using the ATA interface are commonly referred to as Integrated Drive Electronics (IDE) or Enhanced IDE (EIDE) drives.

a command sent to the first drive has to complete before the system can send a command to the second drive. For a server that must handle requests from many simultaneous users, this arrangement is inherently inefficient.

The newer Serial ATA (SATA) standards increase the maximum transmission speed to 600 MB/sec and addresses the ATA unitasking problem with a technology called Native Command Queuing (NCQ). NCQ enables a drive to optimize the order in which it processes commands, to minimize drive seek times. However, SATA supports only a single drive per channel and uses NCQ only when the computer has a motherboard and chipset that supports the Advanced Host Controller Interface (AHCI) standard. Computers that do not comply with this standard run the drives in "IDE emulation" mode, which disables their NCQ and hot-plugging capabilities. While SATA drives are more efficient than ATA and can be a viable solution for relatively low-volume servers, they are not suitable for large enterprise servers.

Small Computer System Interface (SCSI) is the traditional storage interface for enterprise servers. SCSI offers transmission rates up to 640 MB/sec, support for up to 16 devices on a single bus, and the capability to queue commands on each device. This enables multiple drives connected to one SCSI host adapter to process commands simultaneously and independently, which is an ideal environment for a high-volume server.

Many different SCSI standards exist, with different bus types, transmission speeds, and cable configurations. Most implementations available today use serial attached SCSI (SAS), which, like SATA, is a version of the original parallel standard adapted to use serial communications.

SAS and SCSI hard drives are usually quite a bit more expensive than those using any of the other disk interfaces, despite that the disk assemblies are virtually identical; only the electronics providing the interface are different. However, for most administrators of large enterprise networks, the enhanced performance of SAS and SCSI drives in a high-traffic environment is worth the added expense.

USING EXTERNAL DRIVE ARRAYS

High-capacity servers often store hard drives in a separate housing, called an ***external drive array***, which typically incorporates a disk controller, power supply, cooling fans, and cache memory into an independent unit. Drive arrays can connect to a computer via a disk interface, such as SCSI (Small Computer System Interface), IEEE 1394 (FireWire), external SATA (eSATA), or Universal Serial Bus (USB); or via a network interface, such as iSCSI or Fibre Channel.

Drive arrays enable a server to host more physical hard drives than a normal computer case can hold, and often include additional fault-tolerance features, such as hot-swappable drives, redundant power supplies, and hardware-based RAID. Obviously, the more features the array has, and the more drives it can hold, the higher the cost. Large arrays intended for enterprise networks can easily cost tens of thousands of dollars.

Drive arrays typically operate in one of the following configurations:

- ***Storage area network (SAN):*** This is a separate network dedicated solely to storage devices, such as drive arrays, magnetic tape autochangers, and optical jukeboxes (see Figure 3-1). SANs use a high-speed networking technology, such as iSCSI or Fibre Channel, to enable them to transmit large amounts of data very quickly. Therefore, a server connected to a SAN will have two separate network interfaces: one to the SAN and one to the standard local area network (LAN). A SAN provides block-based storage services to the computers connected to it, just as though the storage devices were installed inside the computer. The storage hardware on a SAN might provide additional capabilities, such as RAID, but the computer implements the file system used to store and protect data on the SAN devices.

TAKE NOTE *

With the introduction of the Serial ATA interface, the original ATA interface has been retroactively named Parallel ATA (PATA), in reference to the way in which these devices transmit data over 16 connections simultaneously.

Figure 3-1

A SAN is a separate network dedicated to file servers and external storage devices

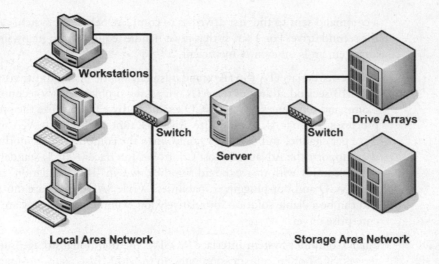

- *Network attached storage (NAS):* A NAS drive array varies from a SAN array primarily in its software. NAS devices are essentially dedicated file servers that provide file-based storage services directly to clients on the network. A NAS array connects to a standard LAN, using traditional Ethernet hardware (see Figure 3-2), and does not require a separate computer to implement the file system or function as a file server. In addition to the storage subsystem, the NAS device has its own processor and memory hardware, and runs its own operating system with a web interface for administrative access. The operating system is typically a stripped-down version of UNIX or Linux designed to provide only data storage, data access, and management functions. Most NAS devices support both the Server Message Block (SMB) protocol used by Windows clients and the Network File System (NFS) protocol used by most UNIX and Linux distributions.

Figure 3-2

A NAS device connects directly to the LAN and functions as a self-contained file server

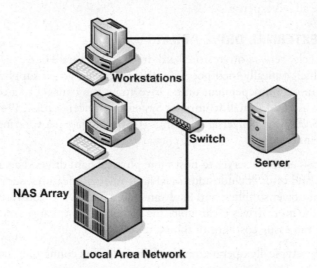

- *Just a Bunch of Disks (JBOD):* SAN and NAS arrays typically can concatenate multiple disks into a single addressable resource. No matter how many physical drives are mounted in the array, the array appears to operating systems and applications as though it is one large disk. By contrast, a JBOD array is just a housing for the drives. Each disk appears to the operating system as a separate resource, as though it was physically installed in the computer.

SANs and NAS devices are both technologies designed to provide scalability and fault tolerance to network data storage systems. A SAN is more complicated and more expensive to implement, but it can provide excellent performance due to its use of a separate network medium and virtually unlimited storage capacity.

> **+ MORE INFORMATION**
>
> Windows Server 2012 includes several SAN management features and tools, which are covered in Exam 70-412, "Configuring Advanced Windows Server 2012 Services."

Adding a NAS device to your network is a simple way to provide your users with additional storage and reduce the processing burden on your servers. Despite its almost plug-and-play convenience, however, NAS does have some significant drawbacks. Because the NAS array is a self-contained device with its own processing hardware and operating system, it has inherent limitations. NAS devices typically do not have upgradeable processors, memory, or network interfaces. If too many users or I/O requests overburden a NAS device, it can reach its performance limit, and you can do nothing except purchase another NAS device. By contrast, direct-attached storage and SANs both use standard computers to serve files, which you can upgrade in all the usual ways: by adding or replacing hardware, moving the drives to a more powerful computer, or adding another server to a cluster.

JBOD arrays are the simplest and therefore the least expensive of the three types. They are designed simply to provide a server with access to more hard disk drives than can fit in the computer case or be supported by the computer's power supply.

Planning for Storage Fault Tolerance

> How valuable is your data, and how much are you willing to spend to protect it from disaster?

Depending on the nature of your organization, fault tolerance for your servers might be a convenience or an absolute requirement. For some businesses, a server hard drive failure might mean a few hours of lost productivity. For an order-entry department, it could mean lost income. For a hospital records department, it could mean lost lives. Depending on where in this range your organization falls, you might consider using a fault-tolerance mechanism to make sure that your users always have access to their applications and data.

The essence of fault tolerance is immediate redundancy. If one copy of a file becomes unavailable due to a disk error or failure, another copy online can take its place almost immediately. Various fault-tolerance mechanisms provide this redundancy in different ways. Some create redundant blocks, redundant files, redundant volumes, redundant drives, and even redundant servers.

As with many computer technologies, fault tolerance is a tradeoff between performance and expense. The mechanisms that provide the most fault tolerance are usually the most expensive. And it is up to you and your organization to decide the value of continuous access to your data.

The following sections discuss some of the most common fault-tolerance mechanisms used by and for servers. You can implement all these technologies in several ways, through Windows Server 2012 or by third-party products.

USING DISK MIRRORING

Disk mirroring, in which the computer writes the same data to identical volumes on two different disks, is one of the simplest forms of fault tolerance to implement and manage, but it is also one of the more expensive solutions. By mirroring volumes, you are essentially paying twice as much for your storage space.

Little or no performance penalty is associated with mirroring volumes, as long as you use a hardware configuration that enables the two drives to write their data simultaneously. As discussed earlier in this lesson, SCSI, SAS, and SATA drives are suitable for disk mirroring, but parallel ATA drives are not, because two ATA drives on the same interface have to write their data sequentially, not simultaneously, thus slowing down the volume's performance substantially.

A variation on disk mirroring, called *disk duplexing*, uses duplicate host adapters as well as duplicate hard drives. Installing the drives on separate host adapters adds an extra measure of fault tolerance, enabling users to continue working if either a drive or a host adapter fails. Duplexing also enables the computer to mirror ATA drives effectively, because each disk is connected to a separate host adapter.

USING RAID

Redundant Array of Independent Disks (RAID) is a group of technologies that uses multiple disk drives in various configurations to store data, providing increased performance or fault tolerance, or both. Table 3-2 lists the standard RAID configurations.

Table 3-2

RAID Levels

RAID LEVEL	RAID FUNCTIONALITY	MINIMUM NUMBER OF DISKS REQUIRED	DESCRIPTION
RAID 0	Stripe set without parity	2	Implemented in Windows Server 2012 as a striped volume, RAID 0 provides no fault tolerance, but it does enhance performance, due to the parallel read/write operations that occur on all drives simultaneously. RAID 0 has no error-detection mechanism, so the failure of one disk causes the loss of all data on the volume.
RAID 1	Mirror set without parity	2	Implemented in Windows Server 2012 as a mirrored volume, a RAID 1 array provides increased read performance, as well as fault tolerance. The array can continue to serve files as long as one disk remains operational.
RAID 3	Byte-level stripe set with dedicated parity	3	Not implemented in Windows Server 2012, a RAID 3 array stripes data at the byte level across the disks, reserving one disk for parity information. A RAID 3 array can survive the loss of any one disk, but because every write to one of the data disks requires a write to the parity disk, the parity disk becomes a performance bottleneck.
RAID 4	Block-level stripe set with dedicated parity	3	Not implemented in Windows Server 2012, RAID 4 is identical in structure to RAID 3, except that a RAID 4 array uses larger, block-level stripes, which improves performance on the data disks. The parity disk can still be a performance bottleneck, however.
RAID 5	Stripe set with distributed parity	3	Implemented in Windows Server 2012, a RAID 5 volume stripes data and parity blocks across all disks, making sure that a block and its parity information are never stored on the same disk. Distributing the parity eliminates the performance bottleneck of the dedicated parity drive in RAID 3 and RAID 4, but the need to calculate the parity information still adds overhead to the system. A RAID 5 array can tolerate the loss of any one of its drives and rebuild the missing data when the drive is repaired or replaced.
RAID 6	Stripe set with dual distributed parity	4	Not implemented in Windows Server 2012, RAID 6 uses the same structure as RAID 5, except that it stripes two copies of the parity information with the data. This enables the array to survive the failure of two drives. When a RAID 5 array suffers a drive failure, the array is vulnerable to data loss until the failed drive is replaced and the missing data rebuilt, which in the case of a large volume can take a long time. On the other hand, a RAID 6 array remains protected against data loss, even while one failed drive is rebuilding.

➕ MORE INFORMATION

Understanding Parity

Parity is a mathematical algorithm that some disk storage technologies levels use to provide data redundancy in their disk write operations. To calculate the parity information for a drive array, the system takes the values for the same data bit at a specific location on each drive in the array and adds them together to determine whether the total is odd or even. The system then uses the resulting total to calculate a value for a parity bit corresponding to those data bits. The system then repeats the process for every bit location on the drives. If one drive is lost due to a hardware failure, the system can restore each lost data bit by calculating its value using the remaining data bits and the parity bit.

For example, in an array with five disks, suppose the first four disks have the values 1, 1, 0, and 1 for their first bit. The total of the four bits is 3, an odd number, so the system sets the first bit of the fifth disk, the parity disk, to 0, indicating an odd result for the total of the bits on the other four disks. Suppose then that one disk fails. If the parity disk fails, no actual data is lost, so data I/O can proceed normally. If one of the four data disks is lost, the total of the first bits in the remaining three disks will be either odd or even. If the total is even, because we know the parity bit is odd, the bit in the missing disk must have been a 1. If the total is odd, the bit in the missing disk must have been a 0. After the failed disk hardware is replaced, the disk controller can reconstruct the lost data.

RAID arrays that use parity provide the same fault tolerance as mirrored disks in that the array can survive the failure of any one drive, but they leave more storage space for data. While mirrored disks provide only half of their total storage capacity for data, the data storage capacity of a RAID array that uses single parity is the size of the disks multiplied by the number of disks in the array, minus one. For example, a RAID 5 array that uses five 200 GB disks has a data storage capacity of 800 GB.

One drawback of the parity system, however, is that the process of recalculating lost bits can degrade the array's performance temporarily. The process of reconstructing an entire drive also can be lengthy.

In addition to the RAID levels listed in Table 3-2 are hybrid RAID solutions, such as RAID 0+1, which is an array of striped drives mirrored on a duplicate array. Windows Server 2012 provides support for only RAID levels 0, 1, and 5 (although the operating system does not refer to RAID 0 and RAID 1 as such, calling them striping and mirroring, respectively). To implement these hybrid RAID solutions, or any standard RAID level other than 0, 1, or 5, you must install a third-party product.

Third-party products can implement RAID functions in software (as Windows Server 2012 does) or in hardware. Most third-party RAID implementations are hardware-based and can range from a host adapter card that you connect to your own drives to a complete array containing drives and a host adapter. Generally, hardware RAID implementations are more expensive than software implementations but provide better performance because a hardware RAID solution offloads the parity calculations and disk manipulation functions from the system processor to the RAID controller itself.

Using Storage Spaces

Windows Server 2012 includes a new disk virtualization technology called *Storage Spaces*, which enables a server to concatenate storage space from individual physical disks and allocate that space to create virtual disks of any size supported by the hardware.

This type of virtualization is a feature often found in SAN and NAS technologies, which require a substantial investment in specialized hardware and administrative skill. Storage Space provides similar capabilities, using standard direct-attached disk drives or simple external JBOD arrays.

Storage Spaces uses unallocated disk space on server drives to create storage pools. A ***storage pool*** can span multiple drives invisibly, providing an accumulated storage resource that you can expand or reduce as needed by adding disks to or removing them from the pool. By using the space in the pool, you can create ***virtual disks*** of any size.

Once created, a virtual disk behaves much like a physical disk, except that the actual bits might be stored on any number of physical drives in the system. Virtual disks can also provide fault tolerance by using the physical disks in the storage pool to hold mirrored or parity data.

Virtual disks can also be thinly provisioned, meaning that while you specify a maximum size for the disk, it starts out small and grows as you add data to it. You can therefore create a virtual disk with a maximum size that is larger than that of your storage space.

For example, if you plan to allocate a maximum of 10 TB for your database files, you can create a thin 10 TB virtual disk, even if you only have a 2 TB storage pool. The application using the disk will function normally, gradually adding data until the storage pool is nearly consumed, at which point the system notifies you to add more space to the pool. You can then install more physical storage and add it to the pool, gradually expanding it until it can support the entire 10 TB required by the disk.

After creating a virtual disk, you can create volumes on it, just as you would on a physical disk. Server Manager provides the tools needed to create and manage storage pools and virtual disks, as well as the capability to create volumes and file system shares, with some limitations.

■ Understanding Windows Disk Settings

 THE BOTTOM LINE   When preparing a disk for use, Windows Server 2012 servers often require different settings than workstations.

When you install Windows Server 2012 on a computer, the setup program automatically performs all preparation tasks for the primary hard disk in the system. However, when you install additional hard disk drives on a server, or when you want to use different settings from the system defaults, you must perform the following tasks manually:

- **Select a partitioning style:** Windows Server 2012 supports two hard disk partition styles: the master boot record (MBR) partition style and the GUID (globally unique identifier) partition table (GPT) partition style. You must choose one of these partition styles for a drive; you cannot use both.
- **Select a disk type:** Windows Server 2012 supports two disk types: basic and dynamic. You cannot use both types on the same disk drive, but you can mix disk types in the same computer.
- **Divide the disk into partitions or volumes:** Although many professionals use the terms *partition* and *volume* interchangeably, it is correct to refer to partitions on basic disks, and volumes on dynamic disks.
- **Format the partitions or volumes with a file system:** Windows Server 2012 supports the NTFS file system, the FAT file system (including the FAT16, FAT32, and exFAT variants), and the new ReFS file system.

The following sections examine the options for each of these tasks.

Selecting a Partition Style

> The term *partition style* refers to the method Windows operating systems use to organize partitions on the disk.

Servers running Windows Server 2012 computers can use either of the following hard disk partition styles:

- *Master Boot Record (MBR):* The MBR partition style has been around since before Windows and is still a common partition style for x86-based and x64-based computers.
- *GUID Partition Table (GPT):* GPT has existed since the late 1990s, but no x86 versions of Windows prior to Windows Server 2008 and Windows Vista supports it. Today, most operating systems support GPT, including Windows Server 2012.

MBR uses a partition table to point to the locations of the partitions on the disk. The MBR disk partitioning style supports volumes up to 2 TB in size, and up to either four primary partitions or three primary partitions and one extended partition on a single drive.

GPT varies from MBR in that partitions, rather than hidden sectors, store data critical to platform operation. GPT-partitioned disks also use redundant primary and backup partition tables for improved integrity. Although GPT specifications permit an unlimited number of partitions, the Windows implementation restricts partitions to 128 per disk. The GPT disk partitioning style supports volumes up to 18 exabytes (1 exabyte = 1 billion gigabytes, or 2^{60} bytes).

Unless the computer's architecture provides support for an Extensible Firmware Interface (EFI)–based boot partition, it is not possible to boot from a GPT disk. If this is the case, the system drive must be an MBR disk, and you can use GPT only on separate non-bootable disks used for data storage.

Before Windows Server 2008 and Windows Vista, all x86-based Windows computers used only the MBR partition style. Computers based on the x64 platform could use either the MBR or GPT partition style, as long as the GPT disk was not the boot disk.

Now that hard drives larger than 2 TB are readily available, the selection of a partition style is more critical than ever. When you initialize a physical disk using the traditional Disk Management snap-in, MBR is the default partition style, as it always has been. You can also use the snap-in to convert a disk between MBR and GPT partition styles, although you can do so only on disks that do not have partitions or volumes created on them.

When you use Server Manager to initialize a disk in Windows Server 2012, it uses the GPT partition style, whether the disk is physical or virtual. Server Manager has no controls supporting MBR, although it does display the partition style in the Disks tile.

Table 3-3 compares some of the characteristics of the MBR and GPT partition styles.

Table 3-3

MBR and GPT Partition Style Comparison

Master Boot Record (MBR)	GUID Partition Table (GPT)
Supports up to four primary partitions or three primary partitions and one extended partition, with unlimited logical drives on the extended partition	Supports up to 128 primary partitions
Supports volumes up to 2 terabytes	Supports volumes up to 18 exabytes
Hidden (unpartitioned) sectors store data critical to platform operation	Partitions store data critical to platform operation
Replication and cyclical redundancy checks (CRCs) are not features of MBR's partition table	Replication and CRC protection of the partition table provide increased reliability

Understanding Disk Types

Most personal computers use basic disks because they are easiest to manage. Advanced volume types require the use of dynamic disks.

A ***basic disk*** using the MBR partition style uses primary partitions, extended partitions, and logical drives to organize data. A primary partition appears to the operating system as though it is a physically separate disk and can host an operating system, in which case it is known as the active partition.

CERTIFICATION READY
Configure basic and dynamic disks.
Objective 1.3

During the operating system installation, the setup program creates a system partition and a boot partition. The system partition contains hardware-related files that the computer uses to start. The boot partition contains the operating system files, which are stored in the Windows file folder. In most cases, these two partitions are one and the same, the active primary partition that Windows uses when starting. The active partition tells the computer which system partition and operating system to use to start Windows.

When you work with basic MBR disks in Windows Server 2012, you can create three volumes that take the form of primary partitions. When you create the fourth volume, the system creates an extended partition, with a logical drive on it, of the size you specified. If the disk still has free space left, the system allocates it to the extended partition (see Figure 3-3), which you can use to create additional logical drives.

Figure 3-3
Primary and extended partitions on a basic disk using MBR

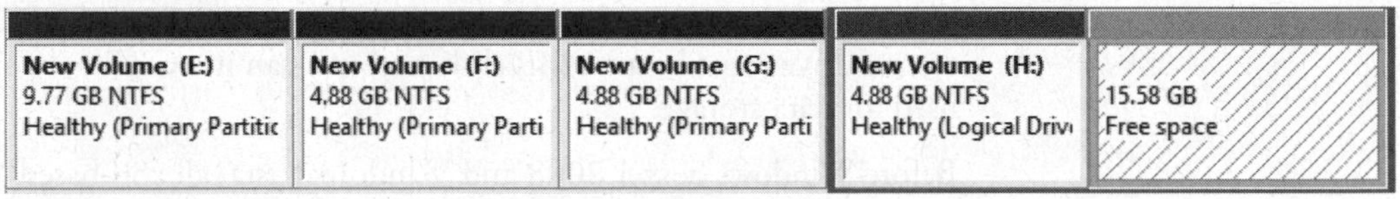
New Volume (E:)
9.77 GB NTFS
Healthy (Primary Partitic
New Volume (F:)
4.88 GB NTFS
Healthy (Primary Parti
New Volume (G:)
4.88 GB NTFS
Healthy (Primary Parti
New Volume (H:)
4.88 GB NTFS
Healthy (Logical Driv
15.58 GB
Free space

Table 3-4 compares some of the characteristics of primary and extended partitions.

Table 3-4
Primary and Extended Partition Comparison

PRIMARY PARTITIONS	EXTENDED PARTITIONS
A primary partition functions as though it is a physically separate disk and can host an operating system.	Extended partitions cannot host an operating system.
You can mark a primary partition as an active partition but can have only one active partition per hard disk. The system BIOS looks to the active partition for the boot files it uses to start the operating system.	You cannot mark an extended partition as an active partition.
On a basic disk using MBR, you can create up to four primary partitions, or three primary partitions and one extended partition.	A basic disk using MBR can contain only one extended partition, but unlimited logical drives.
You format each primary partition and assign a unique drive letter.	You do not format the extended partition itself, but the logical drives it contains. You assign a unique drive letter to each of the logical drives.

When you select the GPT partition style, the disk still appears as a basic disk, but you can create up to 128 volumes, each of which appears as a primary partition, as shown in Figure 3-4. GPT disks have no extended partitions or logical drives.

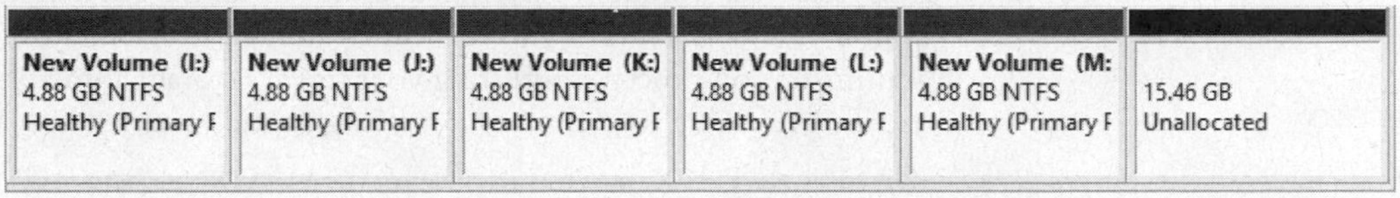

Figure 3-4

Primary partitions on a basic disk using GPT

New Volume (I:) 4.88 GB NTFS Healthy (Primary F	New Volume (J:) 4.88 GB NTFS Healthy (Primary F	New Volume (K:) 4.88 GB NTFS Healthy (Primary F	New Volume (L:) 4.88 GB NTFS Healthy (Primary F	New Volume (M: 4.88 GB NTFS Healthy (Primary F	15.46 GB Unallocated

The alternative to using a basic disk is to convert it to a ***dynamic disk***. Converting a basic disk to a dynamic disk creates a single partition that occupies the entire disk. You can then create an unlimited number of volumes out of the space in that partition. Dynamic disks support several different types of volumes, as described in the next section.

Understanding Volume Types

A dynamic disk can contain an unlimited number of volumes that function much like primary partitions on a basic disk, but you cannot mark an existing dynamic disk as active.

When you create a volume on a dynamic disk using the Disk Management snap-in in Windows Server 2012, you choose from the following five volume types:

- **Simple volume:** Consists of space from a single disk. After you create a simple volume, you can extend it to multiple disks to create a spanned or striped volume, as long as it is not a system volume or boot volume. You can also extend a simple volume into any adjacent unallocated space on the same disk or, with some limitations, shrink the volume by de-allocating any unused space in the volume.

- **Spanned volume:** Consists of space from 2 to 32 physical disks, all of which must be dynamic disks. A spanned volume is essentially a method for combining the space from multiple dynamic disks into a single large volume. Windows Server 2012 writes to the spanned volume by filling all the space on the first disk and then fills each additional disk in turn. You can extend a spanned volume at any time by adding disk space. Creating a spanned volume does not increase the disk's read/write performance, nor does it provide fault tolerance. In fact, if a single physical disk in the spanned volume fails, all data in the entire volume is lost.

- **Striped volume:** Consists of space from 2 to 32 physical disks, all of which must be dynamic disks. The difference between a striped volume and a spanned volume is that in a striped volume, the system writes data one stripe at a time to each successive disk in the volume. Striping provides improved performance because each disk drive in the array has time to seek the location of its next stripe while the other drives are writing. Striped volumes do not provide fault tolerance, however, and you cannot extend them after creation. If a single physical disk in the striped volume fails, all data in the entire volume is lost.

- **Mirrored volume:** Consists of an identical amount of space on two physical disks, both of which must be dynamic disks. The system performs all read/write operations on both disks simultaneously, so they contain duplicate copies of all data stored on the volume. If one of the disks fails, the other continues to provide access to the volume until the failed disk is repaired or replaced.

- **RAID-5 volume:** Consists of space on three or more physical disks, all of which must be dynamic. The system stripes data and parity information across all disks so that if one physical disk fails, the missing data can be re-created using the parity information on the other disks. RAID-5 volumes provide improved read performance, because of the disk striping, but write performance suffers due to the need for parity calculations.

Choosing a Volume Size

Although Windows Server 2012 can support volumes larger than 1 exabyte in size (and 1 exabyte equals 1 million TB), this does not mean that you should create volumes that big, even if you have a server with that much storage. To facilitate the maintenance and administration processes, splitting your server's storage into volumes of manageable size is usually preferable over creating a single, gigantic volume.

One common practice is to choose a volume size based on the capacity of your network backup solution. For example, if you perform network backups using tape drives with an 80 GB capacity, creating volumes that can fit onto a single tape can facilitate the backup process. Creating smaller volumes also speeds up the restore process if you have to recover a volume from a tape or other backup medium.

Another factor is the amount of downtime your business can tolerate. If one of your volumes suffers a file system error, and you do not have a fault-tolerance mechanism in place to keep the system running, you might have to bring it down so that you can run a disk repair utility. The larger the volume, the longer the repair process will take, and the longer your users will be without their files. For extremely large volumes, the repair process can take hours or even days.

Of course, erring in the other extreme is also possible. Splitting a 1 TB drive into 100 volumes of 10 GB, for example, would also be an administrative nightmare, in many different ways.

Understanding File Systems

To organize and store data or programs on a hard drive, you must install a file system, the underlying disk drive structure that enables you to store information on your computer. You install file systems by formatting a partition or volume on the hard disk.

In Windows Server 2012, five file system options are available: NTFS, FAT32, exFAT, FAT (also known as FAT16), and ReFS. NTFS and ReFS are the preferred file systems for a server; the main benefits are improved support for larger hard drives that FAT and better security in the form of encryption and permissions that restrict access by unauthorized users.

Because the FAT (File Allocation Table) file systems lack the security that NTFS provides, any user who gains access to your computer can read any file without restriction. FAT file systems also have disk size limitations: FAT32 cannot handle a partition greater than 32 GB, or a file greater than 4 GB. FAT cannot handle a hard disk greater than 4 GB, or a file greater than 2 GB. Because of these limitations, the only viable reason for using FAT16 or FAT32 is the need to dual boot the computer with a non-Windows operating system or a previous version of Windows that does not support NTFS, which is not a likely configuration for a server.

ReFS (Resilient File System) is a new file system debuting in Windows Server 2012 that offers practically unlimited file and directory sizes and increased resiliency that eliminates the need for error-checking tools, such as Chkdsk.exe. However, ReFS does not include support for NTFS features such as file compression, Encrypted File System (EFS), and disk quotas. ReFS disks also cannot be read by any operating systems older than Windows Server 2012 and Windows 8.

■ Working with Disks

Windows Server 2012 includes tools that enable you to manage disks graphically or from the command prompt.

All Windows Server 2012 installations include the File and Storage Services role, which causes Server Manager to display a submenu when you click the icon in the navigational pane (see Figure 3-5). This submenu provides access to homepages that enable you to manage volumes, disks, storage pools, shares, and iSCSI devices.

Figure 3-5

The File and Storage Services submenu in Server Manager

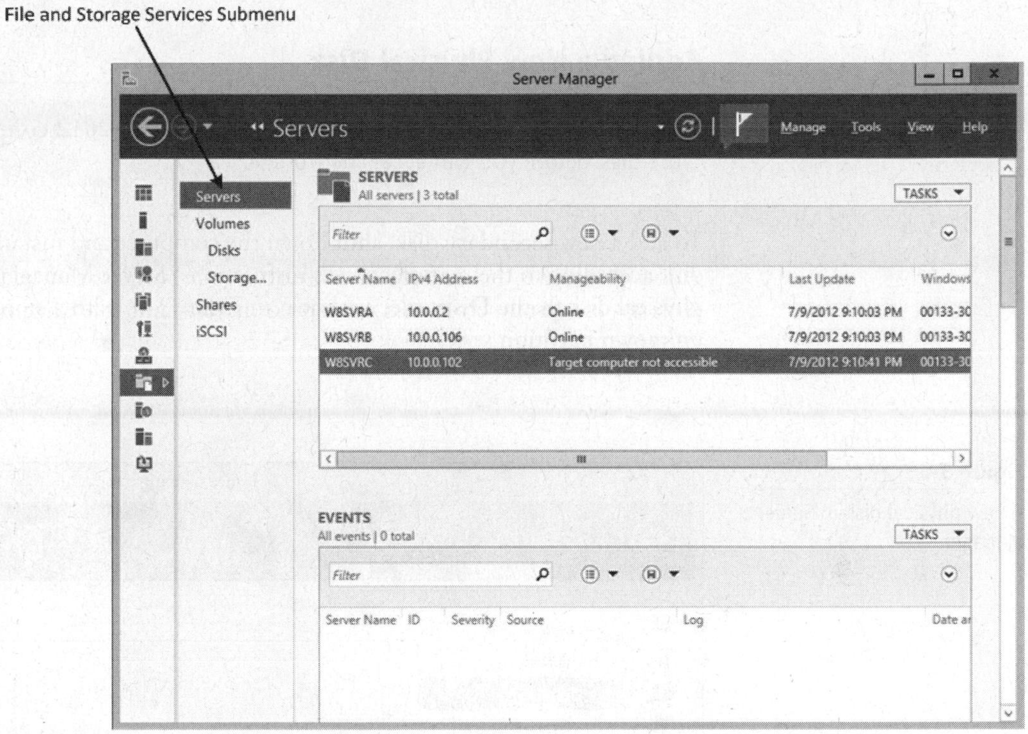

Server Manager is the only graphical tool that can manage storage pools and create virtual disks. It can also perform some—but not all—of the standard disk and volume management operations on physical disks. As with the other Server Manager homepages, the File and Storage Services pages also enable you to perform tasks on any servers you have added to the interface.

Disk Management is a Microsoft Management Console (MMC) snap-in that is the traditional tool for performing disk-related tasks, such as the following:

- Initializing disks
- Selecting a partition style
- Converting basic disks to dynamic disks
- Creating partitions and volumes
- Extending, shrinking, and deleting volumes
- Formatting partitions and volumes
- Assigning and changing driver letters and paths
- Examining and managing physical disk properties, such as disk quotas, folder sharing, and error checking

To access the Disk Management snap-in, you can open the Computer Management console in any of the following ways:

- In *Server Manager*, in the *Servers* tile, right-click the server you want to manage and, from the context menu, select *Computer Management*.

- From the *Administrative Tools* program group, select *Computer Management*.
- Open the *Run* dialog box and execute the *compmgmt.msc* file.

You can also open the Disk Management snap-in directly by running Diskmgmt.exe and manage disks and volumes from the command line by using the DiskPart.exe utility.

Adding a New Physical Disk

When you add a new hard disk to a Windows Server 2012 computer, you must initialize the disk before you can access its storage.

To add a new secondary disk, shut down the computer and install or attach the new physical disk according to the manufacturer's instructions. Server Manager displays a newly added physical disk in the Disks tile, as shown in Figure 3-6, with a status of Offline and an unknown partition style.

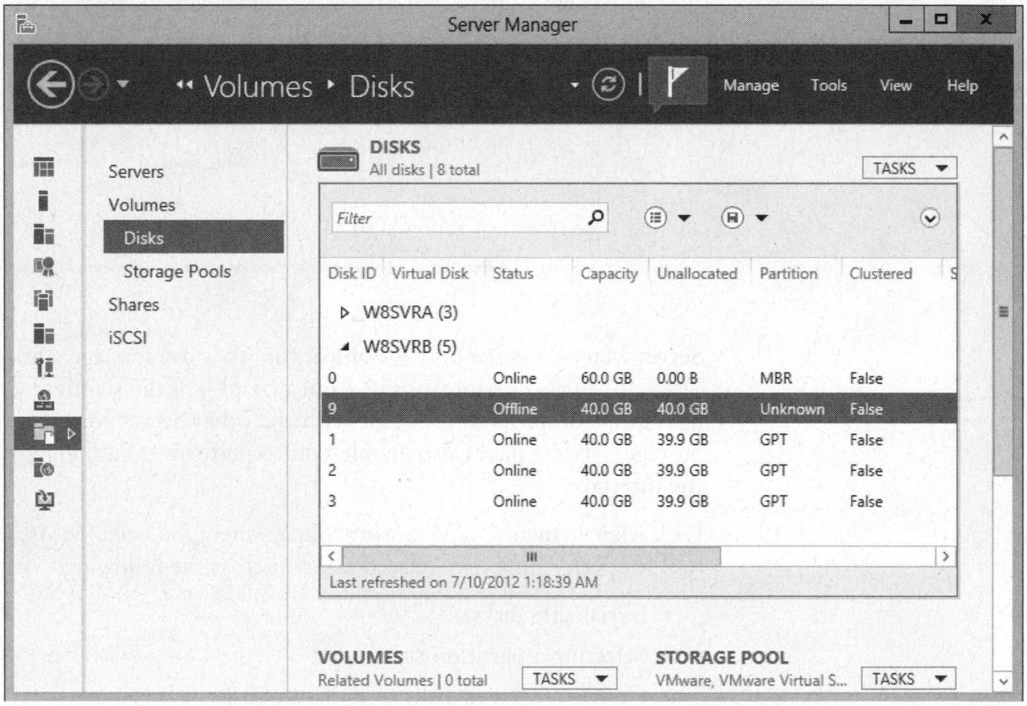

Figure 3-6

A new physical disk in Server Manager

To make the disk accessible, you must first bring it online by right-clicking it in the *Disks* tile and, from the context menu, selecting *Bring Online*. After you confirm your action and the disk status changes to Online, right-click it and select *Initialize*.

Unlike the Disk Management snap-in, Server Manager gives you no choice of the partition style for the disk. A *Task progress* window appears, as shown in Figure 3-7; when the process completes, you click *Close*, and the disk appears in the list with a partition style of GPT.

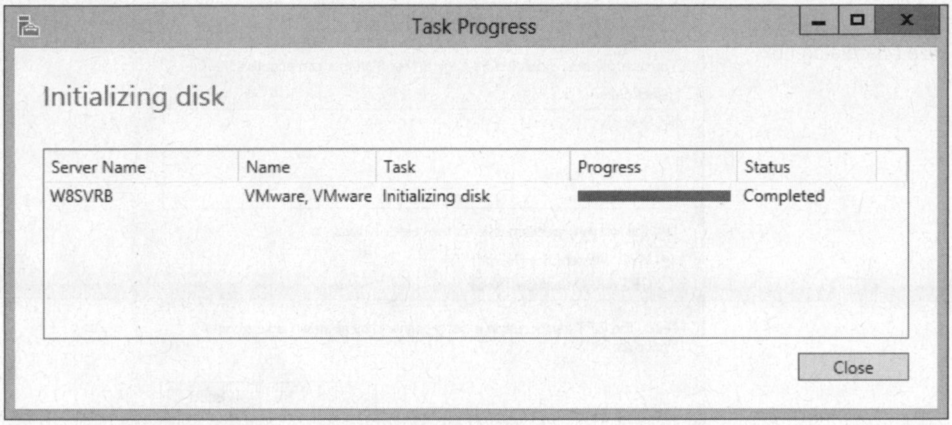

Figure 3-7

A Task progress window in Server Manager

Figure 3-7 content: Task Progress window

Server Name	Name	Task	Progress	Status
W8SVRB	VMware, VMware	Initializing disk		Completed

To initialize a new physical disk and choose a partition style using the Disk Management snap-in, use the following procedure.

ADD A NEW PHYSICAL DISK

GET READY. Log on to Windows Server 2012, using an account with Administrator privileges. The *Server Manager* window appears.

1. Click Tools > Computer Management to display the *Computer Management* console.
2. Click Disk Management. The Disk Management snap-in appears, as shown in Figure 3-8.

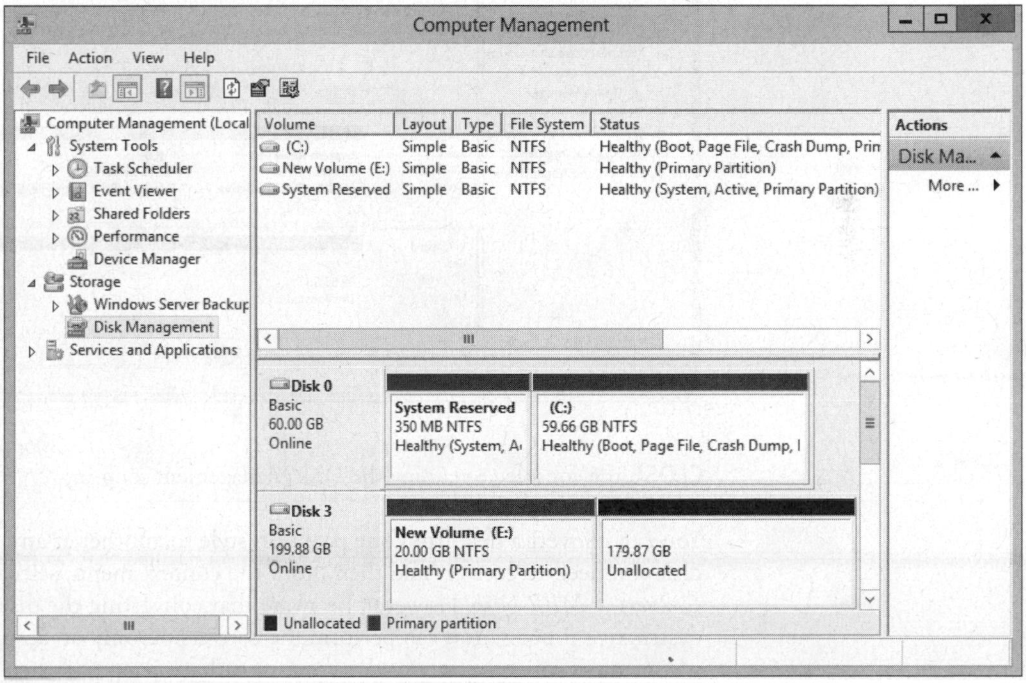

Figure 3-8

The Disk Management snap-in

3. Right-click the disk box and, from the context menu, select Online. The disk status switches to *Not Initialized*.
4. Right-click the disk box and, from the context menu, select Initialize Disk. The *Initialize Disk* dialog box appears, as shown in Figure 3-9.

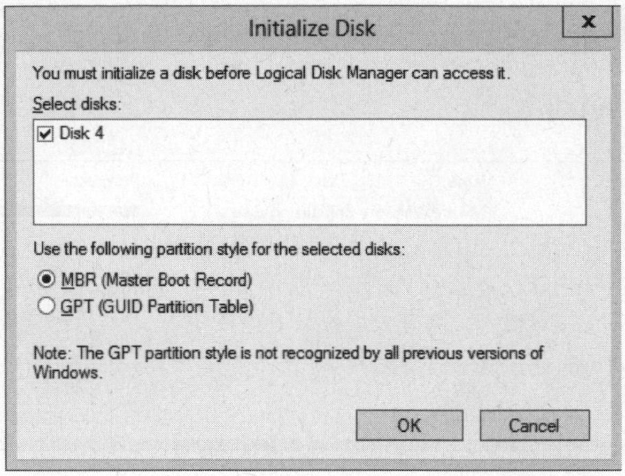

Figure 3-9

The *Initialize Disk* dialog box

5. In the Select disks box, verify that the check box for the new disk is selected.

6. For the Use the following partition style for the selected disks option, select either MBR (Master Boot Record) or GPT (GUID Partition Table) and click OK. The snap-in initializes the disk, causing its status to appear as Online, as shown in Figure 3-10.

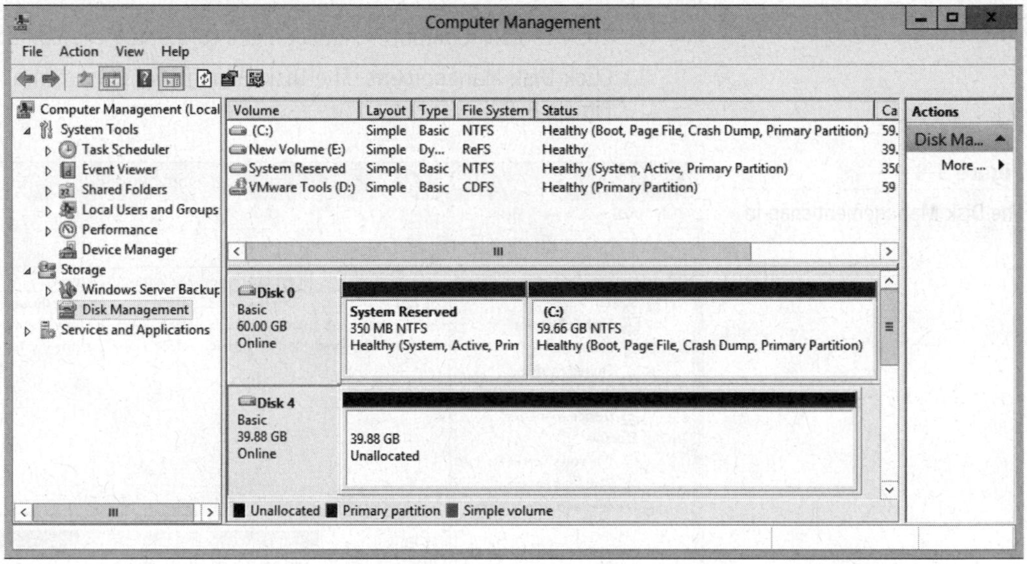

Figure 3-10

The Disk Management snap-in, with a newly initialized disk

CLOSE the console containing the Disk Management snap-in.

You can convert a disk from one partition style to another at any time by right-clicking the disk you need to convert and then, from the context menu, selecting *Convert to GPT Disk* or *Convert to MBR Disk*. However, be aware that converting the disk partition style is a destructive process. You can perform the conversion only on an unallocated disk, so if the disk you want to convert contains data, you must back it up and then delete all existing partitions or volumes before you begin the conversion.

Creating and Mounting VHDs

Hyper-V relies on the ***Virtual Hard Disk (VHD)*** format to store virtual disk data in files that can easily be transferred from one computer to another.

The Disk Management snap-in in Windows Server 2012 enables you to create VHD files and mount them on the computer. As soon as the VHDs are mounted, you can treat them just like physical disks and use them to store data. Dismounting a VHD packages the stored data in the file, so you can copy or move it as needed.

To create a VHD in Disk Management, use the following procedure.

CREATE A VHD

GET READY. Log on to Windows Server 2012, using an account with Administrator privileges. The *Server Manager* window appears.

1. Click Tools > Computer Management.
2. In the Computer Management console, click Disk Management. The Disk Management snap-in appears.
3. From the Action menu, select Create VHD. The *Create and Attach Virtual Hard Disk* dialog box appears, as shown in Figure 3-11.

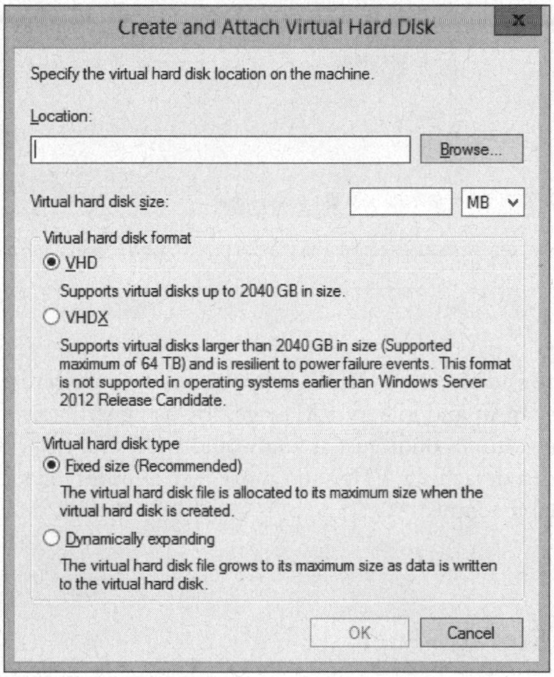

CERTIFICATION READY
Create and mount virtual hard disks (VHDs).
Objective 1.3

Figure 3-11

The *Create and Attach Virtual Hard Disk* dialog box

4. In the Location text box, specify the path and name for the file you want to create.
5. In the Virtual hard disk size text box, specify the maximum size of the disk you want to create.
6. Select one of the following virtual hard disk format options:
   - VHD: The original and more compatible format, which supports files up to 2,040 GB.
   - VHDX: A new version of the format that supports files up to 64 TB, but can be read only by computers running Windows Server 2012 and Windows 8.
7. Select one of the following virtual hard disk type options:
   - Fixed size allocates all disk space for the VHD file at once.
   - Dynamically expanding allocates disk space to the VHD file as you add data to the virtual hard disk.

8. Click OK. The system creates the VHD file and attaches it, so that it appears as a disk in the snap-in, as shown in Figure 3-12.

Figure 3-12

A newly created and attached VHD

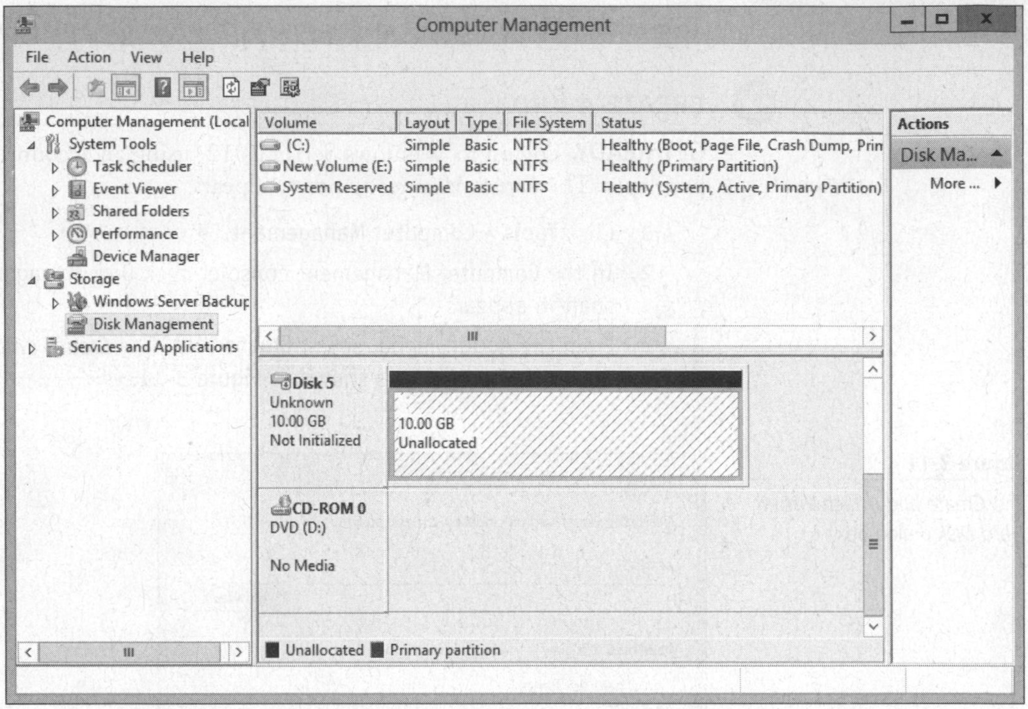

After you create and attach the VHD, it appears as an uninitialized disk in the Disk Management snap-in and in Server Manager. By using either tool, you can initialize the disk and create volumes on it, just as you would a physical disk. After storing data on the volumes, you can detach the VHD and move it to another location or mount it on a Hyper-V virtual machine.

Creating a Storage Pool

CERTIFICATION READY
Configure storage pools and disk pools.
Objective 1.3

After you install your physical disks, you can concatenate their space into a storage pool, from which you can create virtual disks of any size.

To create a storage pool via Server Manager, use the following procedure.

CREATE A STORAGE POOL

GET READY. Log on to Windows Server 2012, using an account with Administrator privileges.

1. In the *Server Manager* window, click the File and Storage Services icon and, in the submenu that appears, click Storage Pools. The *Storage Pools* homepage appears, as shown in Figure 3-13.

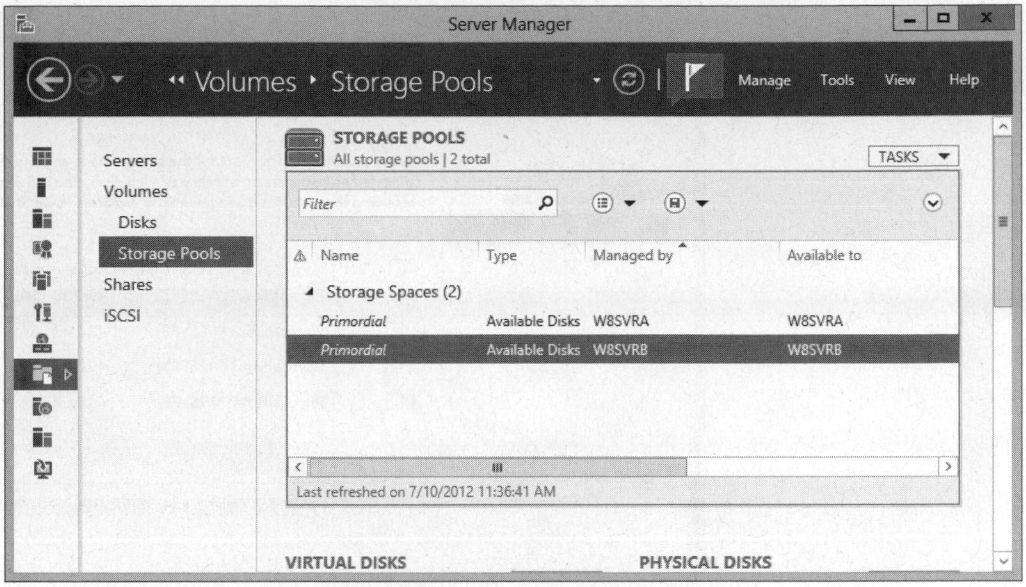

Figure 3-13

The *Storage Pools* homepage

2. In the *Storage Pools* tile, select the primordial space on the server where you want to create the pool and then, from the Tasks menu, select New Storage Pool. The *New Storage Pool Wizard* appears, displaying the *Before you begin* page.

3. Click Next. The *Specify a storage pool name and subsystem* page appears, as shown in Figure 3-14.

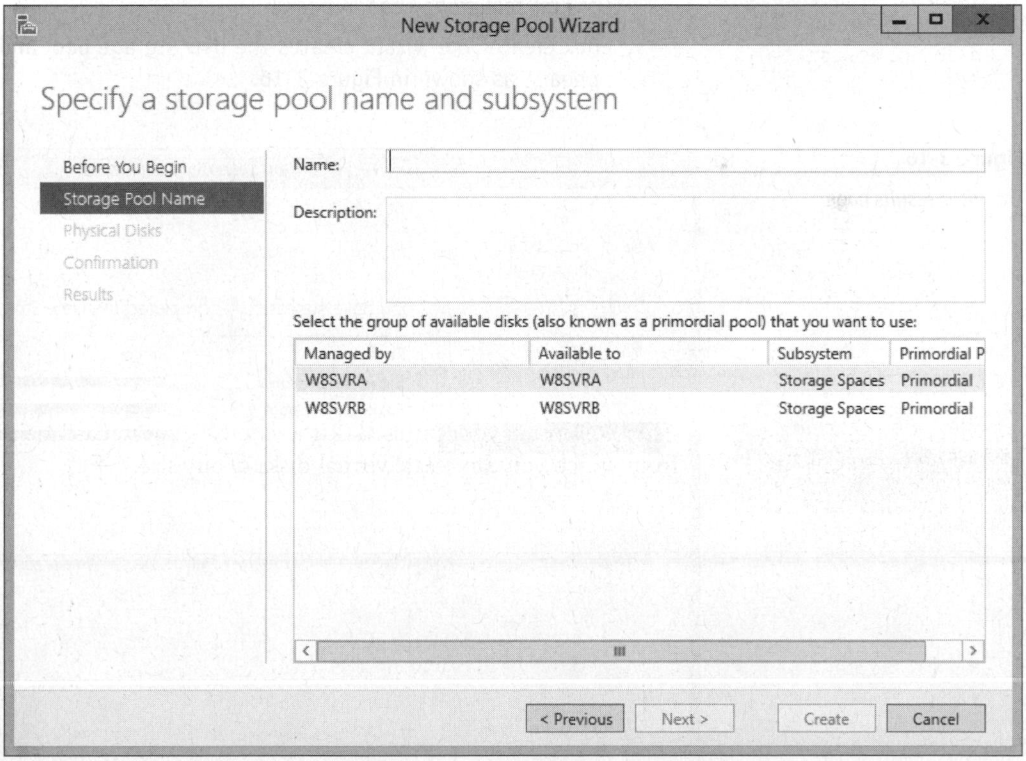

Figure 3-14

The *Specify a storage pool name and subsystem* page

4. In the Name text box, type the name you want to assign to the storage pool. Then, select the server on which you want to create the pool and click Next. The *Select physical disks for the storage pool* page appears, as shown in Figure 3-15.

Figure 3-15

The Select physical disks for the storage pool page

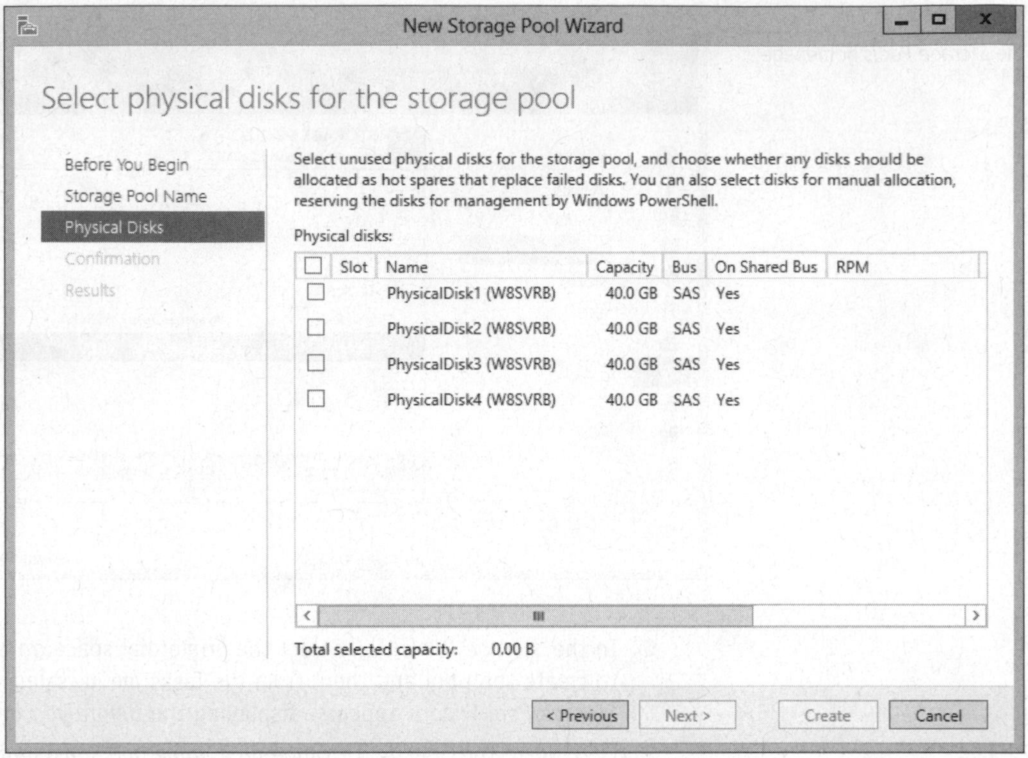

TAKE NOTE*

The wizard displays only the disks eligible for addition to the pool. Disks that already have partitions or volumes on them do not appear.

5. Select the check boxes for the disks you want to add to the pool and click Next. The *Confirm selections* page appears.
6. Click Create. The wizard creates the new storage pool and the *View results* page appears, as shown in Figure 3-16.

Figure 3-16

The *View results* page

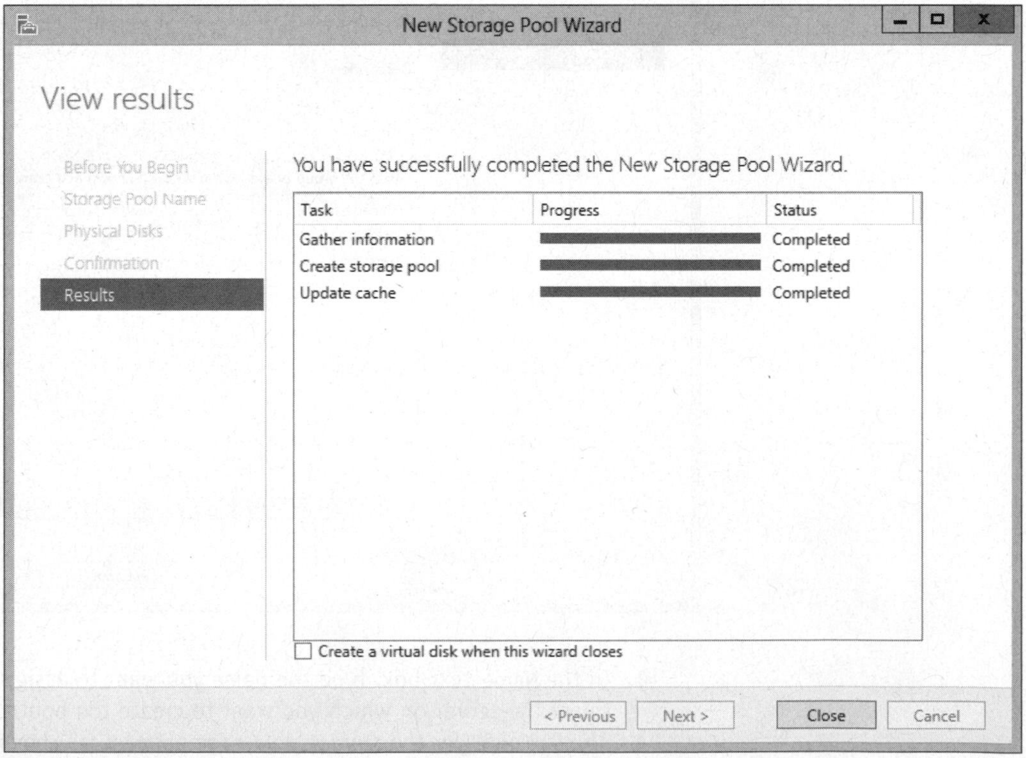

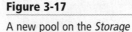

7. Click Close. The wizard closes, and the *Storage Pools* homepage lists the new pool, as shown in Figure 3-17.

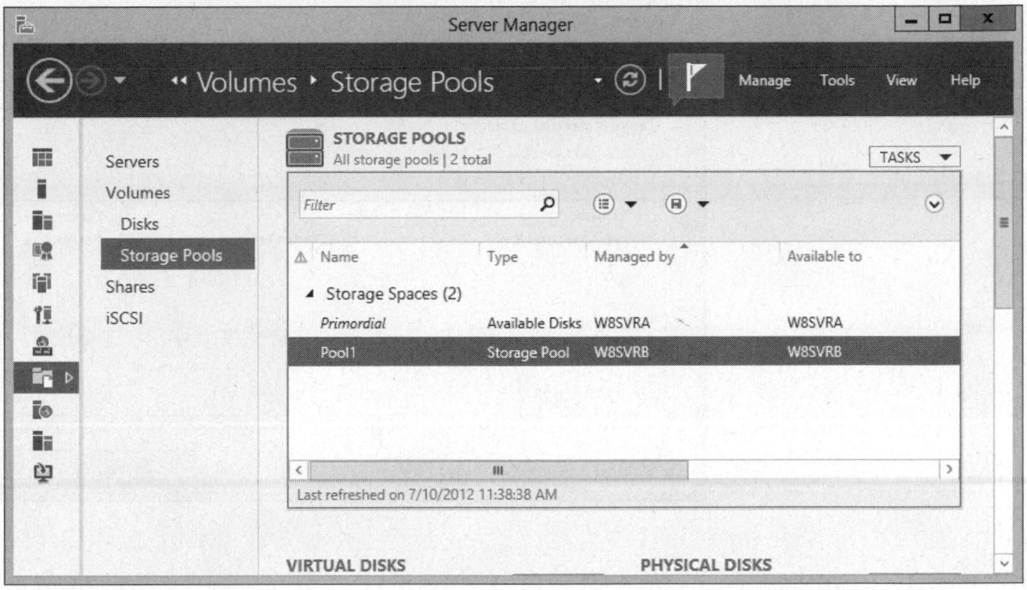

Figure 3-17

A new pool on the *Storage Pools* homepage

	Server Manager	
	◀◀ Volumes ▸ Storage Pools	Manage Tools View Help

STORAGE POOLS
All storage pools | 2 total

TASKS ▼

Filter

⚠	Name	Type	Managed by	Available to
	◢ Storage Spaces (2)			
	Primordial	Available Disks	W8SVRA	W8SVRA
	Pool1	Storage Pool	W8SVRB	W8SVRB

Last refreshed on 7/10/2012 11:38:38 AM

VIRTUAL DISKS   PHYSICAL DISKS

CLOSE the *Server Manager* window.

After you create a storage pool, you can modify its capacity by adding or removing physical disks. The *Tasks* menu in the *Physical Disks* tile on the *Storage Pools* homepage contains the following options:

- *Add Physical Disk* enables you to add a physical disk to the pool, as long as it is initialized and does not contain any volumes

- *Evict Disk* prepares a physical disk for removal from the storage pool by moving all data it contains to the other physical disks in the pool. This can cause the status of virtual disks using mirror or parity fault tolerance to revert to Warning, if the eviction causes the number of physical disks in the pool to fall below the minimum required

- *Remove Disk* removes the space provided by a physical disk from the storage pool. This option appears only if all data already has been evicted from the disk.

USING WINDOWS POWERSHELL

To create a new storage pool using Windows PowerShell, you use the New-StoragePool cmdlet with the following basic syntax:

```
New-StoragePool -FriendlyName <pool name>
-StorageSubSystemFriendlyName <subsystem name>
-PhysicalDisks <disk names>
```

To obtain the correct designations for the storage subsystem and the physical disks, use the Get-StorageSubsystem and Get-PhysicalDisk cmdlets.

For example the following command generates a list of all the physical disks in the system available for pooling and assigns it to the variable $disks:

```
$disks=(GetPhysicalDisk -CanPool $true)
```

The next command then creates a new storage pool, specifying the $disks variable to the -PhysicalDisks parameter. The results are shown in Figure 3-18.

```
New-StoragePool -FriendlyName Pool1
-StorageSubSystemFriendlyName "Storage Spaces on ServerC"
-PhysicalDisks $disks
```

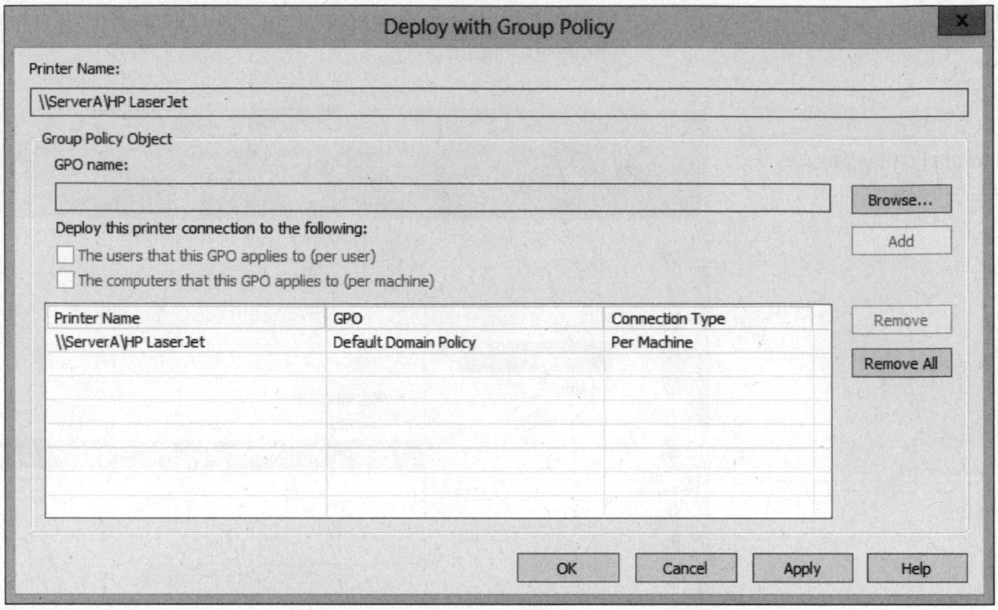

Figure 3-18

A new pool created using
Windows PowerShell

Creating Virtual Disks

After you create a storage pool, you can use the space to create as many virtual disks as you need.

To create a virtual disk using Server Manager, use the following procedure.

CREATE A VIRTUAL DISK

GET READY. Log on to Windows Server 2012, using an account with Administrator privileges.

1. In the *Server Manager* window, click the File and Storage Services icon and, in the submenu, click Storage Pools. The *Storage Pools* homepage appears.
2. Scroll down (if necessary) to expose the *Virtual Disks* tile and, from the Tasks menu, select New Virtual Disk. The *New Virtual Disk* menu appears, displaying the *Before you begin* page.
3. Click Next. The *Select the server and storage pool* page appears, as shown in Figure 3-19.
4. Select the pool in which you want to create a virtual disk and click Next. The *Specify the virtual disk name* page appears, as shown in Figure 3-20.

Figure 3-19

The *Select the server and storage pool* page

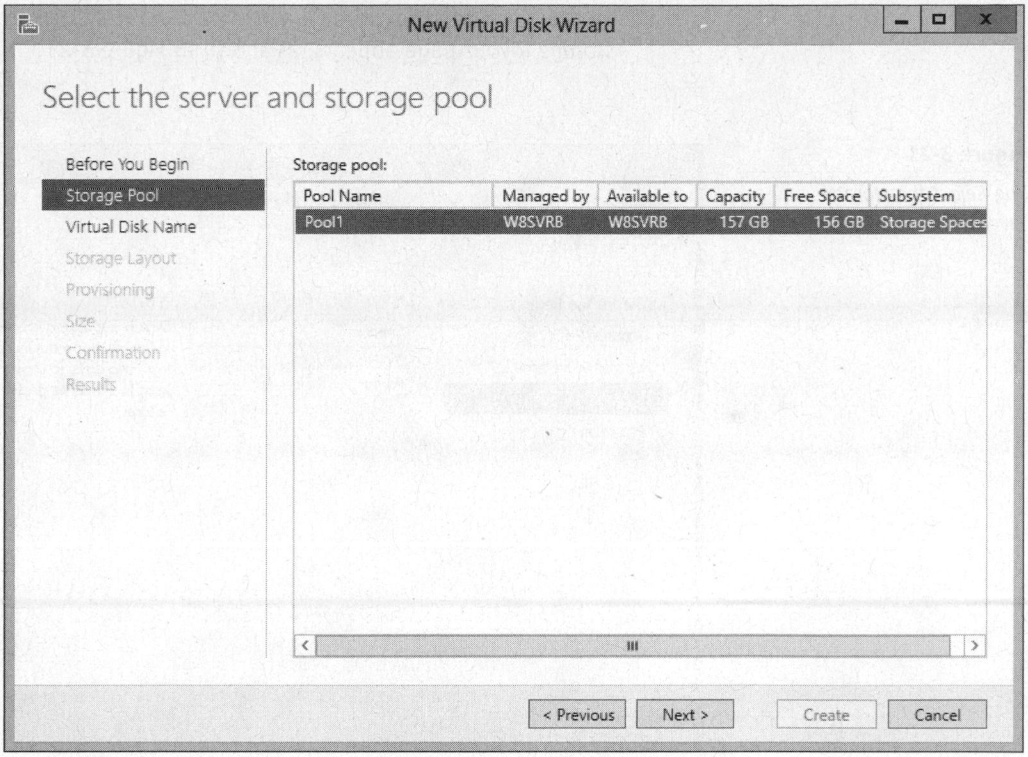

Figure 3-20

The *Specify the virtual disk name* page

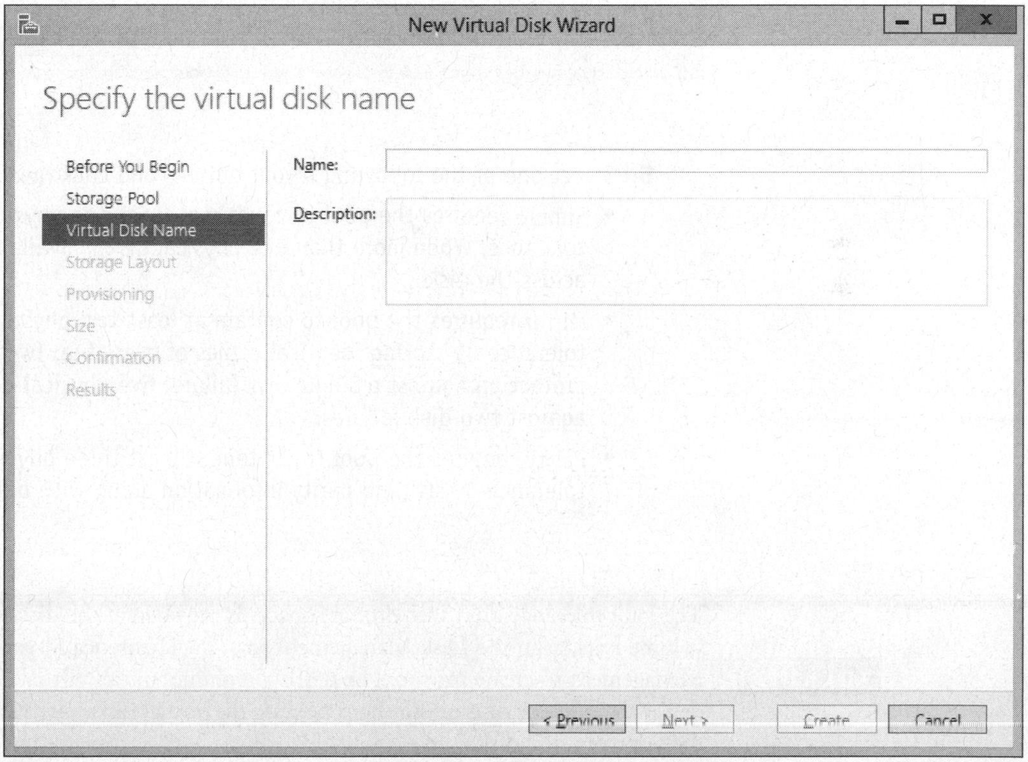

5. In the Name text box, type a name for the virtual disk and click Next. The *Select the storage layout* page appears, as shown in Figure 3-21.

New Virtual Disk Wizard

Select the storage layout

Before You Begin
Storage Pool
Virtual Disk Name
Storage Layout
Provisioning
Size
Confirmation
Results

Layout:
Simple
Mirror
Parity

Description:
Data is duplicated on two or three physical disks, increasing reliability, but reducing capacity. This storage layout requires at least two disks to protect you from a single disk failure, or at least five disks to protect you from two simultaneous disk failures.

< Previous   Next >   Create   Cancel

6. Select one of the following layout options and click Next:
- Simple requires the pool to contain at least one physical disk and provides no fault tolerance. When more than one physical disk is available, the system stripes data across the disks.
- Mirror requires the pool to contain at least two physical disks and provides fault tolerance by storing identical copies of every file. Two physical disks provide protection against a single disk failure; five physical disks provide protection against two disk failures.
- Parity requires the pool to contain at least three physical disks and provides fault tolerance by striping parity information along with data.

TAKE NOTE*

The fault tolerance built into Storage Spaces is provided at the disk level, not at the volume level, as in the Disk Management snap-in. Theoretically, you can use Disk Management to create mirrored or RAID-5 volumes out of virtual disks, but this would defeat the purpose of creating them because the virtual disks might very well be located on the same physical disk.

The *Specify the provisioning type* page appears, as shown in Figure 3-22.

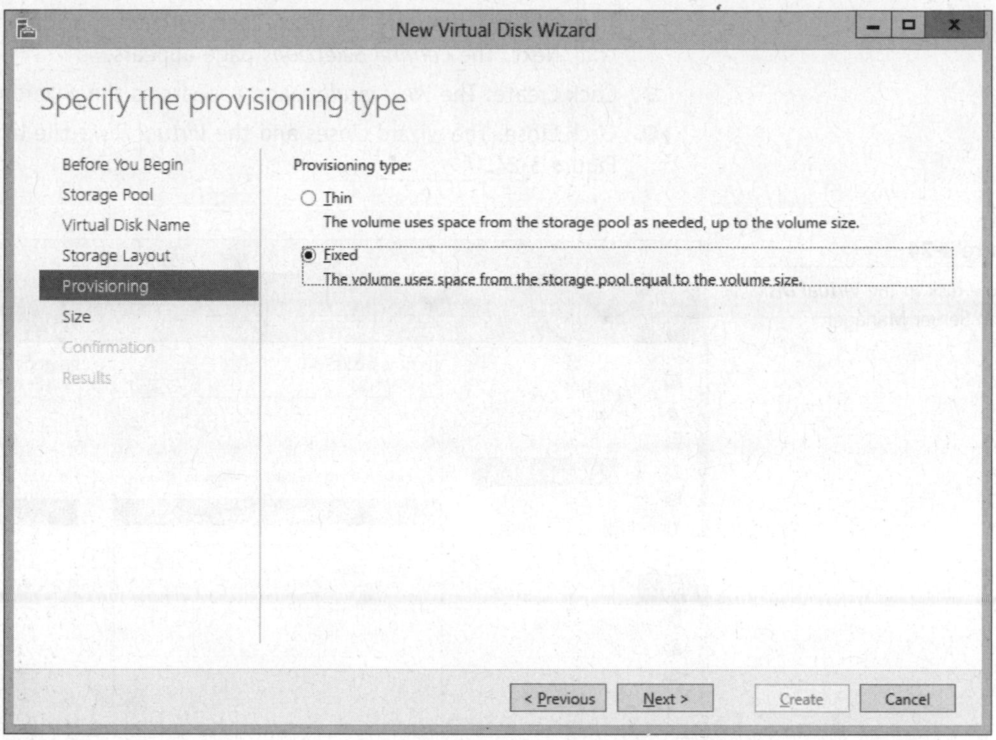

Figure 3-22

The *Specify the provisioning type* page

7. Select one of the following provisioning options and click Next:

- Thin: The system allocates space from the storage pool to the disk as needed, up to the maximum specified size.
- Fixed: The system allocates the maximum specified amount of space to the disk immediately on creating it.

The *Specify the size of the virtual disk* page appears, as shown in Figure 3-23.

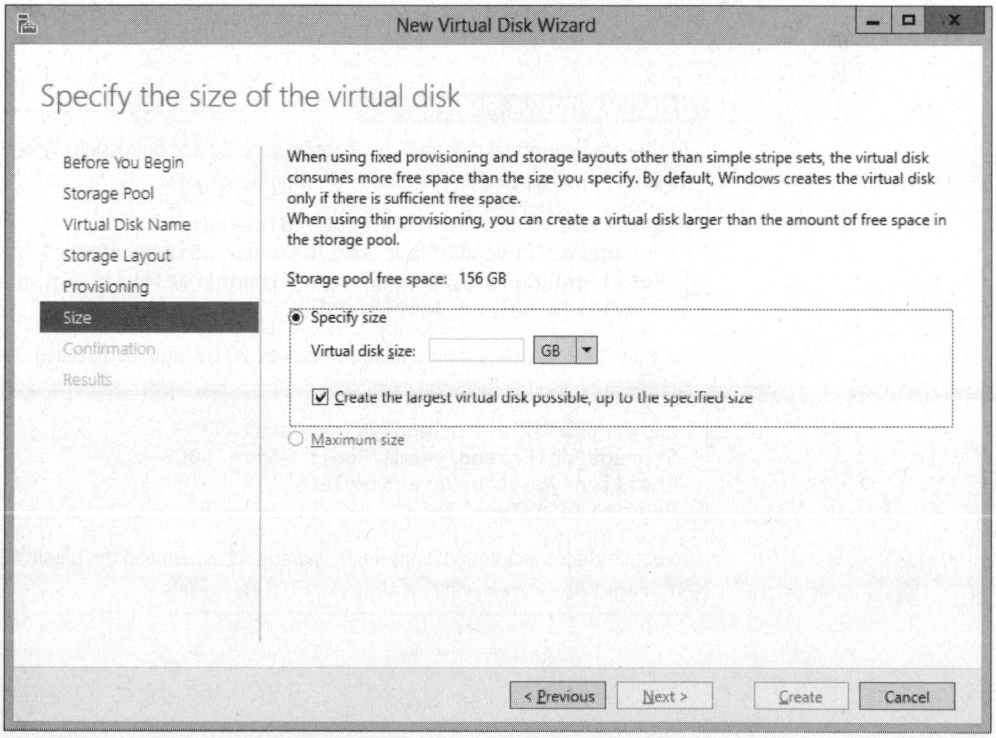

Figure 3-23

The *Specify the size of the virtual disk* page

8. In the Virtual disk size text box, specify the size of the disk you want to create and click Next. The *Confirm Selections* page appears.

9. Click Create. The *View results* page appears as the wizard creates the disk.

10. Click Close. The wizard closes and the *Virtual Disks* tile lists the new disk, as shown in Figure 3-24.

Figure 3-24

A new disk in the *Virtual Disks* tile in Server Manager

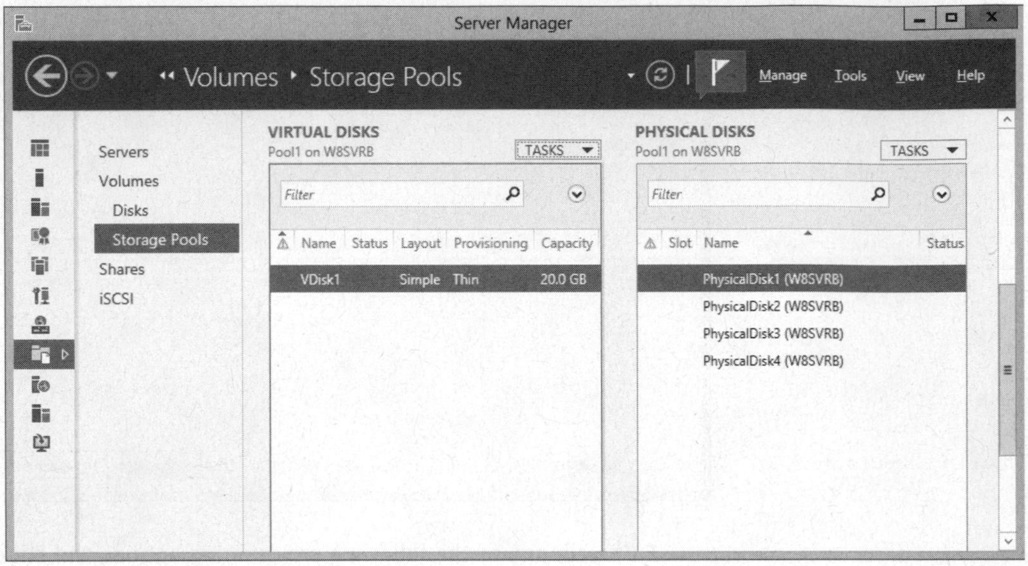

CLOSE the *Server Manager* window.

By default, the New Volume Wizard launches when you create a new virtual disk. At this point, the disk is a virtual equivalent to a newly installed physical disk. It contains nothing but unallocated space, and you must create at least one volume before you can store data on it.

USING WINDOWS POWERSHELL

To create a new virtual disk from the space on your storage pool using Windows PowerShell, you use the `New-VirtualDisk` cmdlet with the following basic syntax:

```
New-VirtualDisk –FriendlyName <disk name>
–StoragePoolFriendlyName <pool name> -Size <size>
[-ResiliencySettingName Simple|Mirror|Parity]
[-ProvisioningType Thin|Fixed]
```

For example, to create a simple, thinly provisioned 50 GB virtual disk called Data1 from the previously created storage pool, use the following example.

```
New-VirtualDisk –FriendlyName Data1
–StoragePoolFriendlyName Pool1 -Size 50GB
-ResiliencySettingName Simple
-ProvisioningType Thin
```

To obtain the correct designations for the storage subsystem and the physical disks, use the `Get-StorageSubsystem` and `Get-PhysicalDisk` cmdlets.

⚠️ **WARNING** When you use ***DiskPart.exe***, a command-line utility included with Windows Server 2012, to manage basic disks, you can create four primary partitions, or three primary partitions and one extended partition. The DiskPart.exe utility contains a superset of the commands supported by the Disk Management snap-in. In other words, DiskPart can do everything Disk Management can do, and more. However, while the Disk Management Snap-in prevents you from unintentionally performing actions that might result in data loss, DiskPart has no safeties, and thus does not prohibit you from performing such actions. For this reason, Microsoft recommends that only advanced users use DiskPart and that they use it with due caution.

Creating a Simple Volume

Technically speaking, you create partitions on basic disks and volumes on dynamic disks. This is not just an arbitrary change in nomenclature. Converting a basic disk to a dynamic disk actually creates one big partition, occupying all space on the disk. The volumes you create on the dynamic disk are logical divisions within that single partition.

Windows versions prior to 2008 use the correct terminology in the Disk Management snap-in. The menus enable you to create partitions on basic disks and volumes on dynamic disks. Windows Server 2012 uses the term *volume* for both disk types, and enables you to create any of the available volume types, whether the disk is basic or dynamic. If the volume type you select is not supported on a basic disk, the wizard converts it to a dynamic disk as part of the volume creation process.

Despite the menus that refer to basic partitions as volumes, the traditional rules for basic disks remain in effect. The New Simple Volume menu option on a basic disk creates up to three primary partitions. When you create a fourth volume, the wizard actually creates an extended partition and a logical drive of the size you specify. If any space remains on the disk, you can create additional logical drives in the extended partition.

To create a new simple volume on a basic or dynamic disk using the Disk Management snap-in, use the following procedure.

➡️ **CREATE A NEW SIMPLE VOLUME**

GET READY. Log on to Windows Server 2012, using an account with Administrator privileges.

1. In the *Server Manager* window, click Tools > Computer Management.
2. In the *Computer Management* console, click Disk Management.
3. In the *Graphical View* of the *Disk Management* snap-in, right-click an unallocated disk area on which you want to create a volume. From the context menu, select New Simple Volume. The *New Simple Volume Wizard* appears.
4. Click Next to dismiss the *Welcome* page. The *Specify Volume Size* page appears, as shown in Figure 3-25.

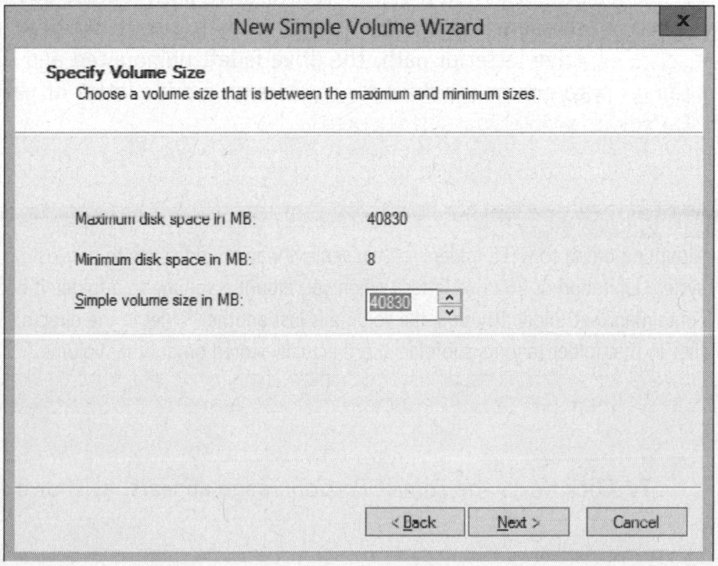

Figure 3-25

The *Specify Volume Size* page

New Simple Volume Wizard

Specify Volume Size
Choose a volume size that is between the maximum and minimum sizes.

Maximum disk space in MB: 40830

Minimum disk space in MB: 8

Simple volume size in MB: 40830

< Back   Next >   Cancel

5. Select the size for the new partition or volume, within the maximum and minimum limits stated on the page, using the Simple volume size in MB spin box, and then click Next. The *Assign Drive Letter or Path* page appears, as shown in Figure 3-26.

Figure 3-26

The *Assign Drive Letter or Path* page

New Simple Volume Wizard

Assign Drive Letter or Path
For easier access, you can assign a drive letter or drive path to your partition.

◉ Assign the following drive letter: E ▾

○ Mount in the following empty NTFS folder:
                                                   Browse...

○ Do not assign a drive letter or drive path

< Back   Next >   Cancel

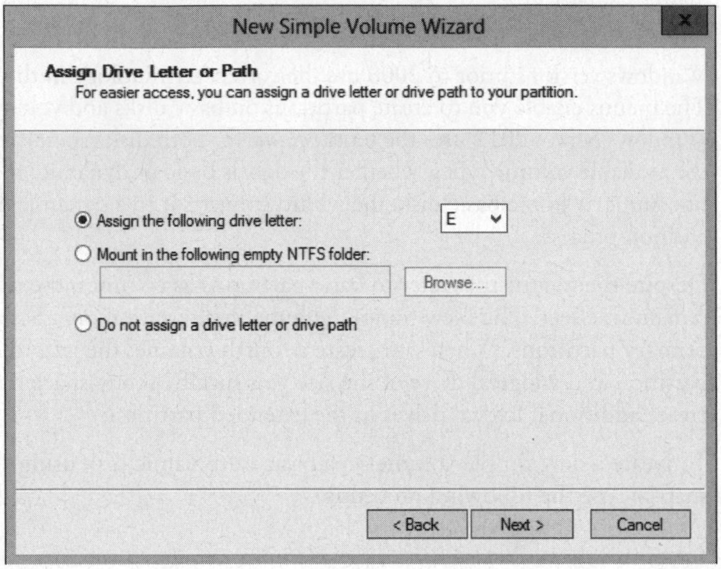

6. Configure one of the following options:
   • Assign the following drive letter: If you select this option, click the associated drop-down list for a list of available drive letters and select the letter you want to assign to the drive.
   • Mount in the following empty NTFS folder: If you select this option, either key the path to an existing NTFS folder or click Browse to search for or create a new folder. The folder you specify will list the entire contents of the new drive.
   • Do not assign a drive letter or drive path: Select this option if you want to create the partition but are not yet ready to use it. When you do not assign a volume a drive letter or path, the drive is left unmounted and inaccessible. When you want to mount the drive for use, assign a drive letter or path to it.

➕ **MORE INFORMATION**

Mounting drives to NTFS folders is a convenient way to add space to an existing drive or overcome the built-in system limitation of 26 drive letters. When you mount a volume to a folder, it becomes a logical part of the volume containing that folder. To users, the volume is just another folder in the directory tree. They are unaware that the files in that folder (and its subfolders) are actually stored on another volume.

7. Click Next. The *Format Partition* page appears, as shown in Figure 3-27.

Figure 3-27

The *Format Partition* page

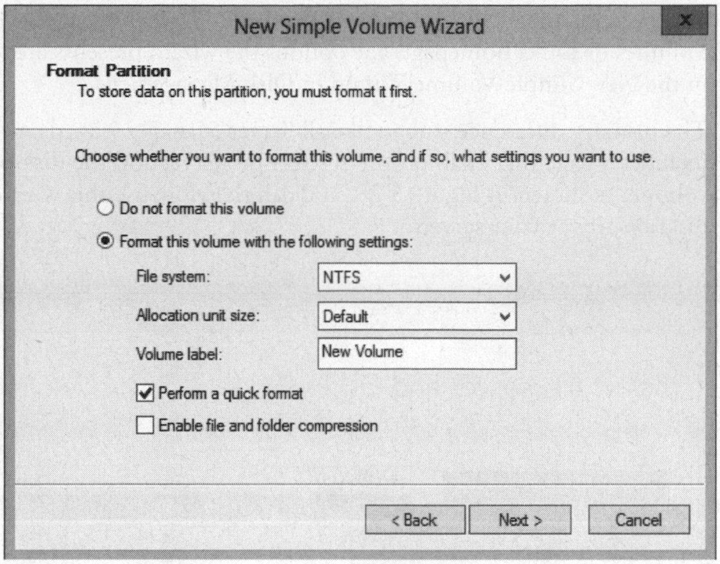

> **New Simple Volume Wizard** ☒
>
> **Format Partition**
>   To store data on this partition, you must format it first.
>
> _____
>
> Choose whether you want to format this volume, and if so, what settings you want to use.
>
> ○ Do not format this volume
> ◉ Format this volume with the following settings:
>
>   File system: [NTFS   ▾]
>   Allocation unit size: [Default   ▾]
>   Volume label: [New Volume   ]
>
>   ☑ Perform a quick format
>   ☐ Enable file and folder compression
>
>   [< Back] [Next >] [Cancel]

8. Specify whether the wizard should format the volume and, if so, how. If you do not want to format the volume at this time, select the Do not format this volume option. If you do want to format the volume, select the Format this volume with the following settings option, and then configure the following associated options:

   • File system: Select the desired file system. The options available depend on the size of the volume, and can include ReFS, NTFS, exFAT, FAT32, or FAT.

   • Allocation unit size: Specify the file system's cluster size. The cluster size signifies the basic unit of bytes in which the system allocates disk space. The system calculates the default allocation unit size based on the size of the volume. You can override this value by clicking the associated drop-down list and then selecting one of the values. For example, if your client uses consistently small files, you may want to set the allocation unit size to a smaller cluster size.

   • Volume label: Specify a name for the partition or volume. The default name is New Volume, but you can change the name to anything you want.

   • Perform a quick format: When you select this option, Windows formats the disk without checking for errors. This is a faster method with which to format the drive, but Microsoft does not recommend it. When you check for errors, the system looks for and marks bad sectors on the disk so that your clients will not use those areas.

   • Enable file and folder compression: Selecting this option turns on folder compression for the disk. This option is available only for volumes being formatted with the NTFS file system.

9. Click Next. The Completing the New Simple Volume Wizard page appears.

10. Review the settings to confirm your options, and then click Finish. The wizard creates the volume according to your specifications.

CLOSE the console containing the Disk Management snap-in.

After you create a simple volume, you can use the Disk Management snap-in to modify its properties by extending or shrinking it, as described later in this lesson.

This procedure can create volumes on physical or virtual disks. You can also create simple volumes by using a similar wizard in Server Manager.

When you launch the New Volume Wizard in Server Manager, which you can do from the Volumes or Disks homepage, the options the wizard presents are virtually identical to those in the New Simple Volume Wizard in Disk Management.

The primary difference is that, like all Server Manager wizards, the New Volume Wizard includes a page that enables you to select the server and the disk on which you want to create volume, as shown in Figure 3-28. You can therefore use this wizard to create volumes on any disk, on any of your servers.

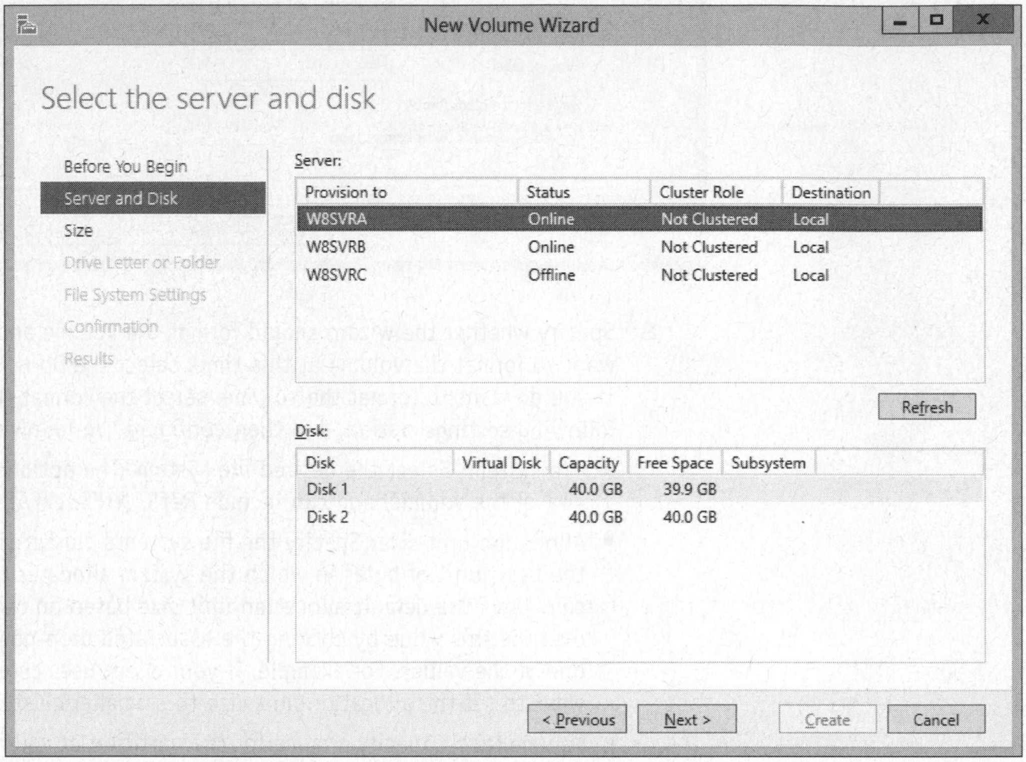

Figure 3-28

The *Select the server and disk* page in the New Volume Wizard in Server Manager

New Volume Wizard

Select the server and disk

- Before You Begin
- Server and Disk
- Size
- Drive Letter or Folder
- File System Settings
- Confirmation
- Results

Server:

Provision to	Status	Cluster Role	Destination
W8SVRA	Online	Not Clustered	Local
W8SVRB	Online	Not Clustered	Local
W8SVRC	Offline	Not Clustered	Local

Refresh

Disk:

Disk	Virtual Disk	Capacity	Free Space	Subsystem
Disk 1		40.0 GB	39.9 GB	
Disk 2		40.0 GB	40.0 GB	

< Previous   Next >   Create   Cancel

Creating a Striped, Spanned, Mirrored, or RAID-5 Volume

The procedure for creating a striped, spanned, mirrored, or RAID-5 volume is almost the same as that for creating a simple volume, except that the *Specify Volume Size* page is replaced by the *Select Disks* page.

To create a striped, spanned, mirrored, or RAID-5 volume, use the following procedure.

 CREATE A STRIPED, SPANNED, MIRRORED, OR RAID-5 VOLUME

GET READY. Log on to Windows Server 2012, using an account with Administrator privileges.

1. In the *Server Manager* window, click Tools > Computer Management.
2. In the *Computer Management* console, click Disk Management.
3. In the *Disk Management* snap-in, right-click an unallocated area on a disk and, from the context menu, select the command for the type of volume you want to create. A *New Volume Wizard* appears, named for your selected volume type.
4. Click Next to dismiss the *Welcome* page. The *Select Disks* page appears, as shown in Figure 3-29.

Figure 3-29

The *Select Disks* page

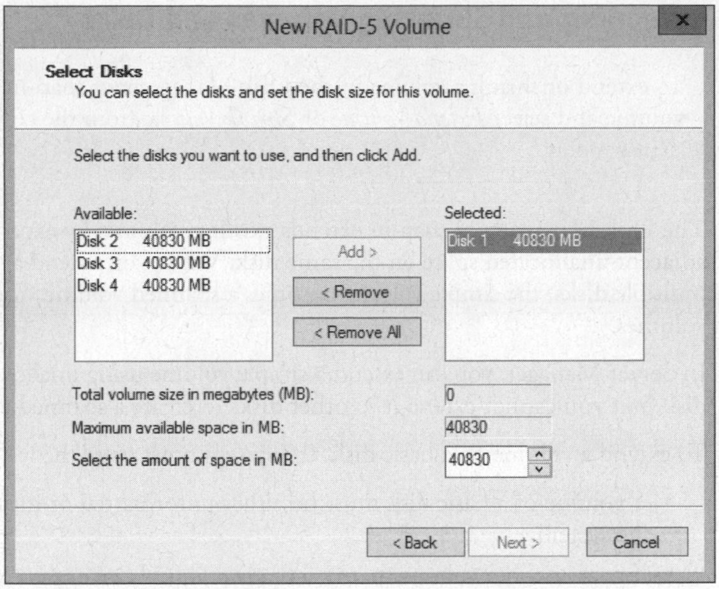

---

5. On the *Select Disks* page, select the disks you want to use for the new volume from the Available list box, and then click Add. The disks you chose are moved to the *Selected* list box, joining the original disk you selected when launching the wizard. For a striped, spanned, or mirrored volume, you must have at least two disks in the Selected list; for a RAID-5 volume, you must have at least three.

6. Specify the amount of space you want to use on each disk, using the Select the amount of space in MB spin box. Then click Next. The *Assign Drive Letter or Path* page appears.

   - If you are creating a spanned volume, you must click each disk in the Selected list and specify the amount of space to use on that disk. The default value for each disk is the size of the unallocated space on that disk.

   - If you are creating a striped, mirrored, or RAID-5 volume, you specify only one value, because such volumes require the same amount of space on each disk. The default value is the size of the unallocated space on the disk with the least amount of space free.

7. Specify whether you want to assign a drive letter or path, and then click Next. The *Format Partition* page appears.

8. Specify if or how you want to format the volume, and then click Next. The *Completing the New Simple Volume Wizard* page appears.

9. Review the settings to confirm your options, and then click Finish. If any of the disks you selected to create the volume are basic disks, a *Disk Management* message box appears, warning that the volume creation process will convert the basic disks to dynamic disks.

10. Click Yes. The wizard creates the volume according to your specifications.

CLOSE the Disk Management snap-in.

X REF

See the "Create a New Simple Volume" procedure, in the preceding section, for more information about the options on the *Assign Drive Letter or Path and Format Partition* pages.

The commands that appear in a disk's context menu depend on the number of disks installed in the computer and the presence of unallocated space on them. For example, at least two disks with unallocated space must be available to create a striped, spanned, or mirrored volume, and at least three disks must be available to create a RAID-5 volume.

Extending and Shrinking Volumes and Disks

> To extend or shrink a volume in the Disk Management snap-in, you simply right-click a volume and select *Extend Volume* or *Shrink Volume* from the context menu or from the *Action* menu.

The Disk Management snap-in extends existing volumes by expanding them into adjacent unallocated space on the same disk. When you extend a simple volume across multiple disks, the simple volume becomes a spanned volume. You cannot extend striped volumes.

In Server Manager, you can extend a simple volume using unallocated space on the same disk, but you cannot extend it to other disks to create a spanned volume.

To extend a volume on a basic disk, the system must meet the following requirements:

- A volume of a basic disk must be either unformatted or formatted with the NTFS file system.
- If you extend a volume that is actually a logical drive, the console first consumes the contiguous free space remaining in the extended partition. If you attempt to extend the logical drive beyond the confines of its extended partition, the extended partition expands to any unallocated space left on the disk.
- You can extend logical drives, boot volumes, or system volumes only into contiguous space, and only if the hard disk can be upgraded to a dynamic disk. The operating system enables you to extend other types of basic volumes into noncontiguous space but prompts you to convert the basic disk to a dynamic disk.

To extend a volume on a dynamic disk, the system must meet these requirements:

- When extending a simple volume, you can use only the available space on the same disk, if the volume is to remain simple.
- You can extend a simple volume across additional disks if it is not a system volume or a boot volume. However, after you expand a simple volume to another disk, it is no longer a simple volume; it becomes a spanned volume.
- You can extend a simple or spanned volume if it does not have a file system (a raw volume) or if you formatted it using the NTFS file system. (You cannot extend volumes using the FAT or FAT32 file systems.)
- You cannot extend mirrored or RAID-5 volumes, although you can add a mirror to an existing simple volume.

When shrinking volumes, the Disk Management snap-in frees up space at the end of the volume, relocating the existing volume's files, if necessary. The snap-in then converts that free space to new unallocated space on the disk. Server Manager cannot shrink volumes.

To shrink basic disk volumes and simple or spanned dynamic disk volumes, the system must meet the following requirements:

- The existing volume must not be full and must contain the specified amount of available free space for shrinking.
- The volume must not be a raw partition (one without a file system). Shrinking a raw partition that contains data might destroy the data.
- You can shrink a volume only if you formatted it using the NTFS file system. (You cannot shrink volumes using the FAT or FAT32 file systems.)

- You cannot shrink striped, mirrored, or RAID-5 volumes.
- You should always defragment a volume before you attempt to shrink it.

Physical disks, obviously, cannot be extended, but virtual disks can. In Server Manager, you can right-click a virtual disk and select *Extend Virtual Disk* from the context menu to display the Extend Virtual Disk dialog box, as shown in Figure 3-30.

Figure 3-30

The *Extend Virtual Disk* dialog box

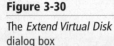

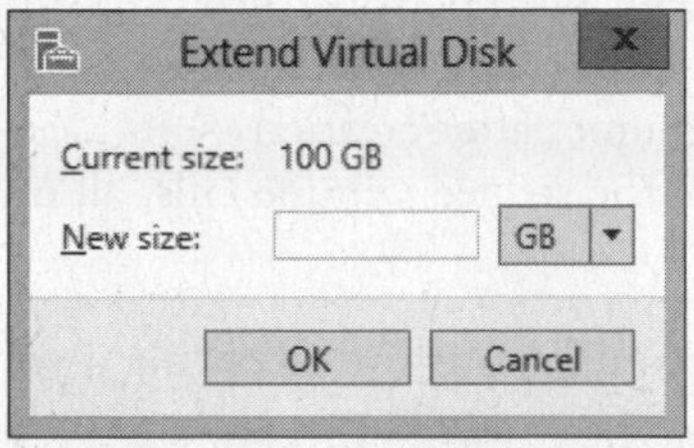

If you elected to use thin provisioning when you created the virtual disk, you can even extend its size beyond the storage pool's current capacity. To actually store that much data on the disk, however, you must first expand the pool to provide enough space.

SKILL SUMMARY

IN THIS LESSON, YOU LEARNED:

- Windows Server 2012 supports two hard disk partition types: MBR and GPT; two disk types: basic and dynamic; five volume types: simple, striped, spanned, mirrored, and RAID-5; and three file systems: ReFS, NTFS, and FAT.

- The Disk Management snap-in can initialize, partition, and format disks on the local machine. Server Manager can perform many of the same tasks for servers all over the network.

- A Windows server can conceivably perform its tasks using the same type of storage as a workstation. However, a server's I/O burdens are quite different from those of a workstation, and file requests from dozens or hundreds of users can easily overwhelm a standard storage subsystem. Standard hard disks also offer no fault tolerance and are limited in their scalability.

- Windows Server 2012 includes a new disk virtualization technology called Storage Spaces, which enables a server to concatenate storage space from individual physical disks and allocate it to create virtual disks of any size supported by the hardware.

- All Windows Server 2012 installations include the File and Storage Services role, which causes Server Manager to display a submenu when you click the icon in the navigational pane. This submenu provides access to homepages that enable you to manage volumes, disks, storage pools, shares, and iSCSI devices.

- The Disk Management snap-in in Windows Server 2012 enables you to create VHD files and mount them on the computer.

- After you install your physical disks, you can concatenate their space into a storage pool, from which you can create virtual disks of any size. After you create a storage pool, you can use the space to create as many virtual disks as you need.

Knowledge Assessment

Multiple Choice

Select one or more correct answers for each of the following questions.

1. Which of the following statements are true of striped volumes?
   a. Striped volumes provide enhanced performance over simple volumes.
   b. Striped volumes provide greater fault tolerance than simple volumes.
   c. You can extend striped volumes after creation.
   d. If a single physical disk in the striped volume fails, all of the data in the entire volume is lost.

2. Which of the following are requirements for extending a volume on a dynamic disk?
   a. If you want to extend a simple volume, you can use only the available space on the same disk, if the volume is to remain simple.
   b. The volume must have a file system before you can extend a simple or spanned volume.
   c. You can extend a simple or spanned volume if you formatted it using the FAT or FAT32 file systems.
   d. You can extend a simple volume across additional disks if it is not a system volume or a boot volume.

3. Which of the following are not true in reference to converting a basic disk to a dynamic disk?
   a. You cannot convert a basic disk to a dynamic disk if you need to dual boot the computer.
   b. You cannot convert drives with volumes that use an allocation unit size greater than 512 bytes.
   c. A boot partition or system partition on a basic disk cannot be extended into a striped or spanned volume, even if you convert the disk to a dynamic disk.
   d. The conversion will fail if the hard drive does not have at least 1 MB of free space at the end of the disk.

4. Which of the following Windows Server 2012 features enables users to access files that they have accidentally overwritten?
   a. Offline Files
   b. parity-based RAID
   c. Windows Installer 4.0
   d. Volume Shadow Copies

5. Which of the following RAID levels yields the largest percentage of usable disk space?
   a. RAID 0
   b. RAID 1
   c. RAID 5
   d. RAID 6

6. To use Shadow Copies, you must enable the feature at which of the following levels?
   a. the file level
   b. the folder level
   c. the volume level

7. Which of the following are not true about differences between network attached storage (NAS) devices and storage area network (SAN) devices?
   a. NAS devices provide a file system implementation; SAN devices do not .
   b. NAS devices must have their own processor and memory hardware; SAN devices do not require these components

    c. NAS devices require a specialized protocol, such as Fibre Channel or iSCSI; SAN devices use standard networking protocols.

    d. NAS devices must run their own operating system and typically provide a web interface for administrative access; SAN devices do not have to have either one.

8. Which of the following volume types supported by Windows Server 2012 do not provide fault tolerance? (Choose all that apply)

    a. Striped

    b. Spanned

    c. Mirrored

    d. RAID-5

9. A JBOD drive array is an alternative to which of the following?

    a. SAN

    b. SCSI

    c. RAID

    d. iSCSI

Best Answer

Choose the letter that corresponds to the best answer. More than one answer choice may achieve the goal. Select the BEST answer.

1. What scenario would an organization prefer centralized servers and storage to having individual servers and storage per department?

    a. Each department typically works with its own applications and documents, rarely needing access to other departments.

    b. Each department typically works with its own applications and documents, occasionally needing access to other departments.

    c. Everyone in the organization works with his or her own individual resources.

    d. Everyone in the organization works with the same set of resources.

2. Concerning storage solutions, select the disk configuration that offers the least expensive disk consumption.

    a. Just a Bunch of Disks (JBOD)

    b. Disk mirroring

    c. RAID 5

    d. RAID 3

3. Concerning storage solutions, select the disk configuration that offers the most protection in case of drive failure.

    a. RAID 0

    b. RAID 1

    c. RAID 5

    d. Large volume on a single drive

4. What is the next step after creating a virtual hard disk (VHD)?

    a. Mounting it either through Server Manager or the Disk Management snap-in

    b. Initializing the disk and creating volumes on it, just as you would a physical disk

    c. Using the VHD (creation of the VHD file readies the disk for storage)

    d. Mounting the VHD file to a Hyper-V virtual machine

5. What is a key advantage of Server Manager over the Disk Management snap-in?

    a. The Server Manager now offers disk-related functions from the navigational pane.

    b. Server Manager is more user-friendly.

c. The Disk Management snap-in enables you to create VHD files and mount them on the computer.

d. Server Manager can perform many of the same functions for servers all over the network.

Build a List

1. Order the steps to create and mount a VHD.
   a. Select the virtual hard disk format option (VHD or VHDX).
   b. Select one of the following VHD types (Fixed size or Dynamically expanding).
   c. Click OK for the system to create and attach the VHD file. The VHD appears as a disk in the Disk Management snap-in.
   d. Log on with administrative privileges and open Server Manager.
   e. Click Tools > Computer Management.
   f. Specify the Location path and name for the new VHD file, and then specify the maximum size of the disk.
   g. Click Disk Management, and then click Create VHD from the Action menu.

2. Order the steps to create a virtual disk.
   a. Log on with administrative privileges and open Server Manager.
   b. In the Virtual Disks tile, select New Virtual Disk from the Tasks menu.
   c. From their respective pages, select the pool in which you want to create a virtual disk and type a name for the virtual disk.
   d. Click Files and Storage Services > Storage Pools.
   e. From the Select the Storage Layout page, choose among Simple, Mirror, and Parity options.
   f. From the Specify the Provisioning Type, choose among Thin and Fixed options.
   g. Specify the virtual disk size, and then click Create to confirm.

3. Order the steps to create a storage pool. Not all steps will be used.
   a. Confirm selection and close the wizard.
   b. In the Storage Pools tile, select the primordial space on the server where you want to create the pool. From the Tasks menu, select New Storage Pool.
   c. Log on with administrative privileges and open Server Manager.
   d. In the New Storage Pool Wizard, specify a storage pool name and subsystem.
   e. Click Files and Storage Services > Storage Pools.
   f. Specify a name, server, and physical disks for the pool.

■ Business Case Scenario

Scenario 3-1: Planning Storage

On a new server running Windows Server 2012, Morris created a storage pool that consists of two physical drives holding 1 TB each. Then he created three simple virtual disks out of the space in the storage pool. Using the Disk Management snap-in, Morris then created a RAID-5 volume out of the three virtual disks.

With this in mind, answer the following questions:

1. In what way is Morris's storage plan ineffectual at providing fault tolerance?

2. Why will adding a third disk to the storage pool fail to improve the fault tolerance of the storage plan?

3. How can Morris modify the storage plan to make it fault tolerant?

Configuring File and Share Access

70-410 EXAM OBJECTIVE

Objective 2.1 – Configure file and share access. This objective may include but is not limited to: Create and configure shares; configure share permissions; configure offline files; configure NTFS permissions; configure access-based enumeration (ABE); configure Volume Shadow Copy Service (VSS); configure NTFS quotas.

LESSON HEADING	EXAM OBJECTIVE
Designing a File-Sharing Strategy	
Arranging Shares	
Controlling Access	
Mapping Drives	
Creating Folder Shares	Create and configure shares Configure access-based enumeration (ABE) Configure offline files
Assigning Permissions	
Understanding the Windows Permission Architecture	
Understanding Basic and Advanced Permissions	
Allowing and Denying Permissions	
Inheriting Permissions	
Understanding Effective Access	
Setting Share Permissions	Configure share permissions
Understanding NTFS Authorization	
Assigning Basic NTFS Permissions	Configure NTFS permissions
Assigning Advanced NTFS Permissions	
Understanding Resource Ownership	
Combining Share and NTFS Permissions	
Configuring Volume Shadow Copies	Configure Volume Shadow Copy Service (VSS)
Configuring NTFS Quotas	Configure NTFS quotas

KEY TERMS

access control entries (ACEs)	authorization	Offline Files
access control list (ACL)	basic permissions	security identifiers (SIDs)
access-based enumeration (ABE)	effective access	
advanced permissions	NTFS quotas	security principal

■ Designing a File-Sharing Strategy

↓
THE BOTTOM LINE

Decide where users should store their files and who should be permitted to access them.

Why should the administrators of an enterprise network want users to store their files on shared server drives, rather than their local workstation drives? The answers to this question typically include the following:

- To enable users to collaborate on projects by sharing files
- To back up document files more easily
- To protect company information by controlling access to documents
- To reduce the number of shares needed on the network
- To prevent the need to share access to workstations
- To monitor users' storage habits and regulate their disk-space consumption
- To insulate users from the sharing and permission assignment processes

Without these problems, file sharing would simply be a matter of creating a share on each user's workstation and granting everyone full access to it. Because of these problems, however, this practice would lead to chaos in the form of lost files, corrupted workstations, and endless help calls from confused users.

Server-based file shares should provide users with a simplified data storage solution that they can use to store their files, share files with other users, and easily locate the files shared by their colleagues. Behind the scenes, and unbeknown to users, you can use server-based storage tools to protect everyone's files, regulate access to sensitive data, and prevent users from abusing their storage privileges.

Arranging Shares

The first step in designing a file-sharing strategy is to decide how many shares to create and where to create them.

Simply installing a big hard drive in a server and giving everyone access to it would be as chaotic as sharing everyone's workstation drives. Depending on your organization's size, you might have one single file server or many servers scattered around the network.

For many large organizations, departmental or workgroup file servers are viable solutions. Each user has his or her "local" server, the directory layout of which becomes familiar. If you have separate file servers for the various departments or workgroups in your organization, developing a consistent directory structure and duplicating it on all the servers is a good idea so that if users have to access a server in another department, they can find their way around.

A well-designed sharing strategy provides each user with three resources:

- A private storage space, such as a home folder, to which the user has exclusive access
- A public storage space, where users can store files that they want colleagues to be able to access
- Access to a shared workspace for communal and collaborative documents

One way to implement this strategy would be to create one share called Home, with a private folder for each user on it, and a second share called Public, again with a folder for each user. Depending on your network's hardware configuration, you could create both shares on a separate server for each department or workgroup, split the shares and folder among multiple servers in each department, or even create one big file server containing all the shares for the entire company.

+ MORE INFORMATION

Even if you split the Home and Public shares among multiple servers, you can still make them appear as a single unified directory tree by using the Windows Server 2012 Distributed File System (DFS). See Objective 2.1, "Configure Distributed File System (DFS)," in Exam 70-411, "Administering Windows Server 2012."

Controlling Access

On most enterprise networks, the principle of "least privileges" should apply. This principle states that users should have only the privileges they need to perform their required tasks, and no more.

A user's private storage space should be exactly that—private and inaccessible, if not invisible, to other users. This is where each user can store his or her private files without exposing them to other users. Therefore, each user should have full privileges to his or her private storage with the ability to create, delete, read, write, and modify files. Other users should have no privileges to that space at all.

TAKE NOTE*

The easiest way to create private folders with the appropriate permissions for each user is to create a home folder through each Active Directory user object.

Each user should also have full privileges to his or her public folder. This is where users can share files informally. For example, when Ralph asks Alice for a copy of her budget spreadsheet, Alice can simply copy the file from her private folder to her public folder. Then, Ralph can copy the file from Alice's public folder to his own private folder, and access it from there. Thus, public and private folders vary in that other users should be able to list the contents of all public folders and read the files stored there, but not be able to modify or delete files in any folder but their own. Users should also be able to navigate throughout the Public folder tree, so that they can read any user's files and copy them to their own folders.

TAKE NOTE*

Although users should have full privileges to their personal folders, you should not leave their storage practices unmonitored or unregulated. Later in this lesson, you learn how to set NTFS quotas limiting users' storage space.

In the shared workspace for collaborative documents, users should have privileges based on their individual needs. Some users need read access only to certain files, whereas others might have to modify those files as well. You should limit the ability to create and delete files to managers or supervisors.

Administrators, of course, must have the privileges required to exercise full control over all users' private and public storage spaces, as well as the ability to modify permissions as needed.

Administrators typically use NTFS permissions to assign these privileges on a Windows Server 2012 file server. You have no compelling reason to use the FAT (File Allocation Table) file system in Windows Server 2012. NTFS provides not only the most granular user access control, but also other advanced storage features, including file encryption and compression. The new ReFS file system introduced in Windows Server 2012 lacks features such as encryption and compression, but it still supports the NTFS permission system.

To simplify the administration process, you should always assign permissions to security groups rather than to individuals. Assigning permissions to groups enables you to add new users or move them to other job assignments without modifying the permissions themselves. On a large Active Directory Domain Services (AD DS) network, you might also consider the standard practice of assigning the NTFS permissions to a domain local group, placing the user objects to receive the permissions in a global (or universal) group, and making the global group a member of a domain local group.

Except in special cases, explicitly denying NTFS permissions to users or groups usually is not necessary. Some administrators prefer to use this capability, however. When various administrators use different permission assignment techniques on the same network, it can become extremely difficult to track down the sources of certain effective permissions. Another way to simplify the administration process on an enterprise network is to establish specific permission assignment policies, so that everyone performs tasks the same way.

For more information on NTFS permission assignments, see "Assigning Permissions," later in this lesson.

Mapping Drives

After you create the folders for each user and assign permissions to the folders, you need to make sure that users can access their folders.

One way of doing this is to use the Folder Redirection settings in Group Policy to map each user's Documents folder to his or her home folder on the network share. This process is invisible to users, enabling them to work with their files without even knowing they are stored on a network drive.

Another way to provide users with easy and consistent access to their files is to map drive letters to each user's directories with logon scripts, so they can always find their files in the same place, using Windows Explorer. For example, you might consider mapping drive F: to a user's private home folder and drive G: to the user's Public folder. A third drive letter might point to the root of the Public share, so that the user can access other people's public folders.

Many users do not understand the fundamental concepts of network drive sharing and file management. Often, they just know that they store their files on the F: drive and are unaware that another user's F: drive might point to a different folder. However, consistent drive letter assignments on every workstation can simplify support for users experiencing problems storing or retrieving their files.

■ Creating Folder Shares

THE BOTTOM LINE

Sharing folders makes them accessible to network users.

After you configure the disks on a file server, you must create shares for network users to be able to access those disks. As noted in the planning discussions earlier in this lesson, you should have a sharing strategy in place by the time you are ready to actually create your shares. This strategy should consist of the following information:

CERTIFICATION READY
Create and configure shares.
Objective 2.1

- What folders you will share
- What names you will assign to the shares
- What permissions you will grant users to the shares
- What Offline Files settings you will use for the shares

If you are the Creator Owner of a folder, you can share it on a Windows Server 2012 computer by right-clicking the folder in any Windows Explorer window, selecting *Share with , Specific People* from the context menu, and following the instructions in the *File Sharing* dialog box, as shown in Figure 4-1.

Figure 4-1

The *File Sharing* dialog box

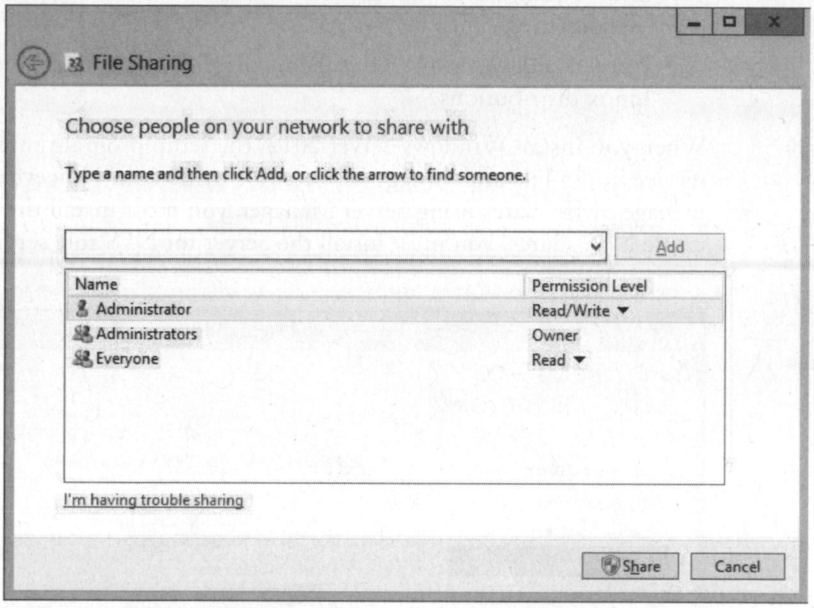

This method of creating shares provides a simplified interface that contains only limited control over elements such as share permissions. You can specify only that the share users receive Read or Read/Write permissions to the share. If you are not the Creator Owner of the folder, you can access the *Sharing* tab of the folder's Properties sheet instead. Clicking the *Share* button launches the same dialog box, and clicking the *Advanced Sharing* button displays the dialog box shown in Figure 4-2. Clicking the Permissions button in the Advanced Sharing dialog box provides greater control over share permissions through the standard interface shown in "Setting Share Permissions," later in this lesson.

Figure 4-2

The *Advanced Sharing* dialog box

TAKE NOTE* For network users to be able to see the shares you create on the file server, you must make sure that the Network Discovery and File Sharing settings are turned on in the Network and Sharing Center control panel.

However, to take control of the shares on all your disks on all your servers and exercise granular control over their properties, use the *File and Storage Services* homepage in Server Manager.

Windows Server 2012 supports two types of folder shares:

- *Server Message Blocks (SMB)* is the standard file-sharing protocol used by all versions of Windows.
- *Network File System (NFS)* is the standard file-sharing protocol used by most UNIX and Linux distributions.

When you install Windows Server 2012, the setup program installs the Storage Services role service in the File and Storage Services role by default. However, before you can create and manage SMB shares using Server Manager, you must install the File Server role service; to create NFS shares, you must install the Server for NFS role service, as shown in Figure 4-3.

Figure 4-3

Installing File and Storage Services role services

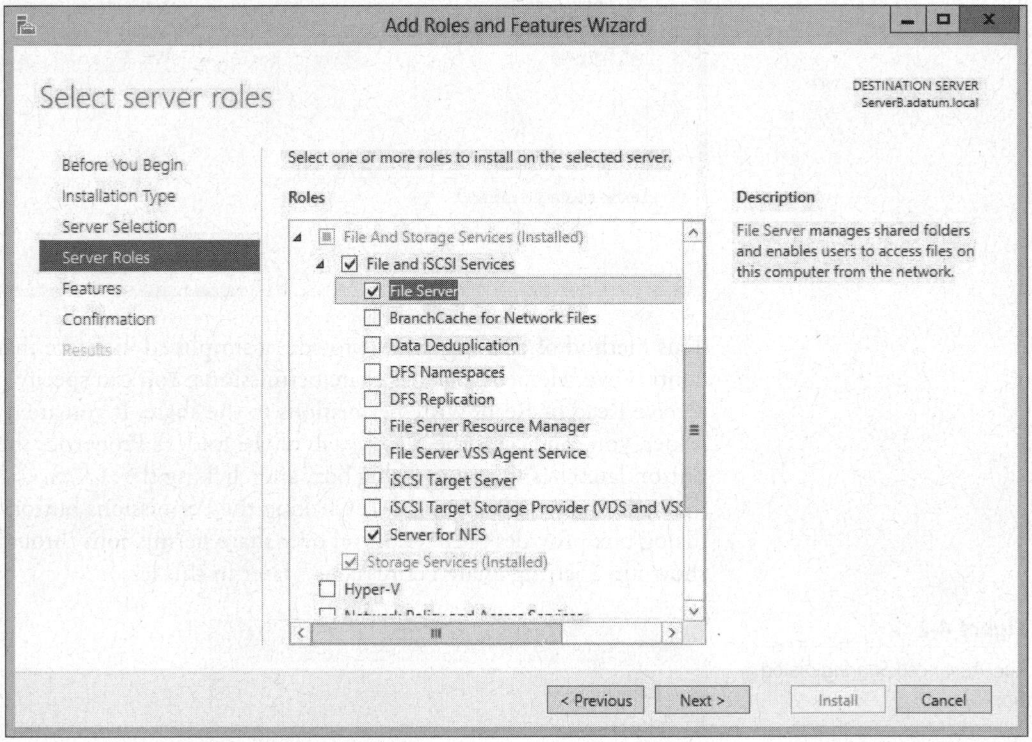

To create a folder share using Server Manager, use the following procedure.

CREATE A FOLDER SHARE

GET READY. Log on to Windows Server 2012, using an account with Administrator privileges. The Server Manager window appears.

1. Click the File and Storage Services icon and, in the submenu that appears, click Shares. The *Shares* homepage appears, as shown in Figure 4-4.
2. From the Tasks menu, select New Share. The *New Share Wizard* appears, displaying the *Select the profile for this share* page, as shown in Figure 4-5.

Figure 4-4

The Shares homepage

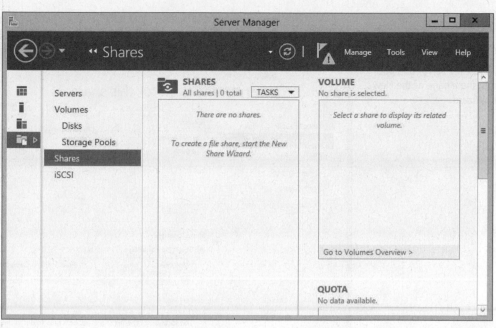

Figure 4-5

The *Select the profile for this share* page in the New Share Wizard

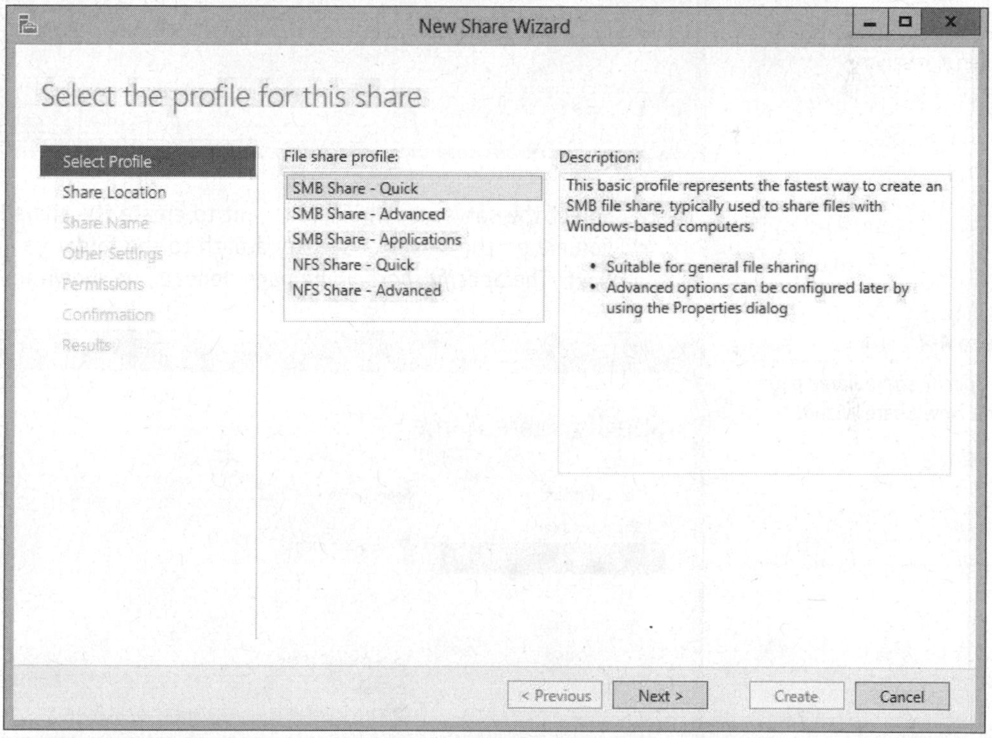

3. From the File share profile list, select one of the following options:
   - SMB Share–Quick provides basic SMB sharing with full share and NTFS permissions.
   - SMB Share–Advanced provides SMB sharing with full share and NTFS permissions and access to services provided by File Server Resource Manager.
   - SMB Share–Applications provides SMB sharing with settings suitable for Hyper-V and other applications.
   - NFS Share–Quick provides basic NFS sharing with authentication and permissions.
   - NFS Share–Advanced provides NFS sharing with authentication and permissions, plus access to services provided by File Server Resource Manager.

4. Click Next. The *Select the server and path for this share* page appears, as shown in Figure 4-6.

Figure 4-6

The *Select the server and path for this share* page of the New Share Wizard

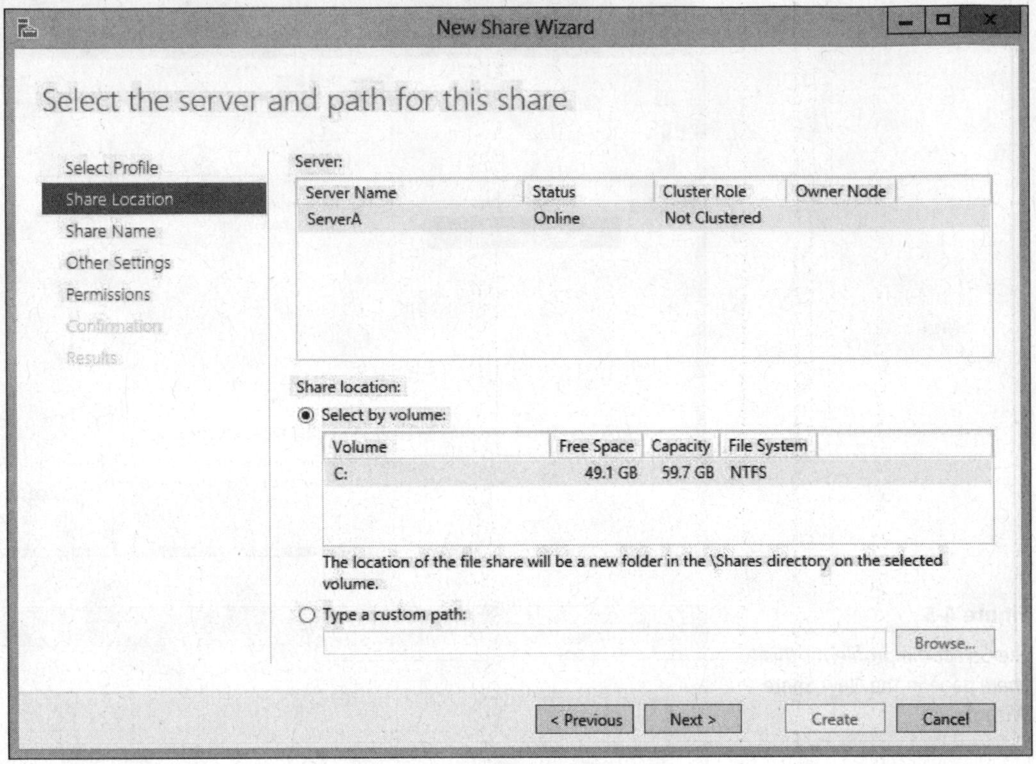

5. Select the server on which you want to create the share, and then either select a volume on the server or specify a path to the folder you want to share. Then click Next. The *Specify share name* page appears, as shown in Figure 4-7.

Figure 4-7

The *Specify share name* page of the New Share Wizard

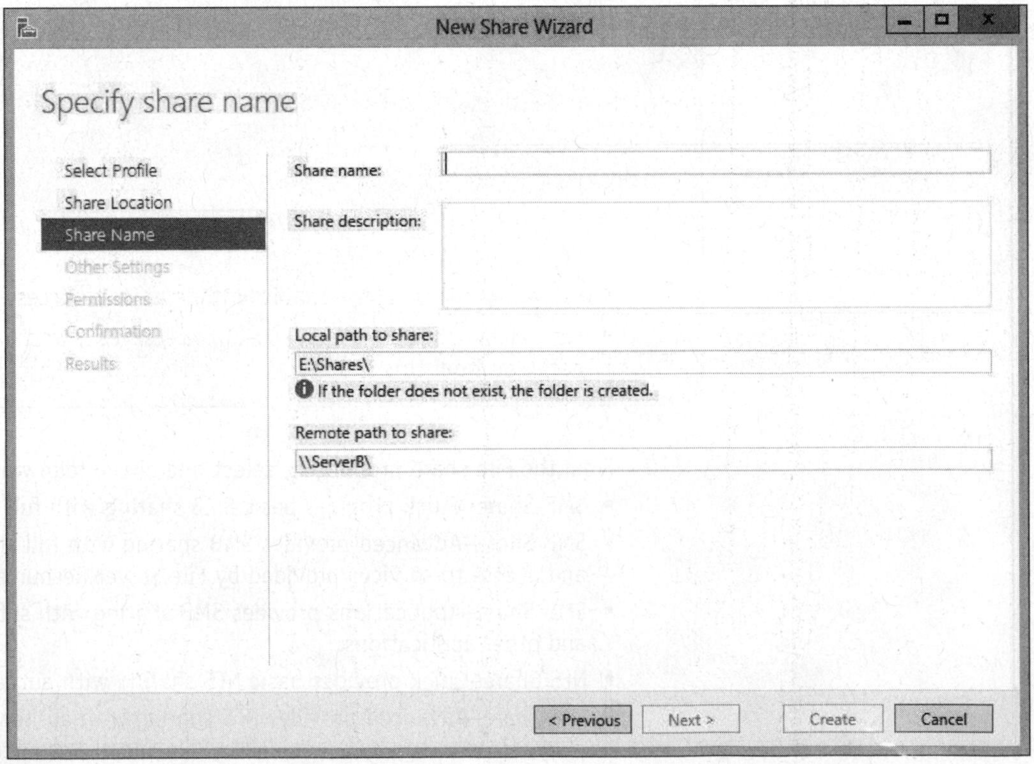

+ MORE INFORMATION

Selecting one of the NFS share profiles adds two pages to the wizard: *Specify authentication methods* and *Specify the share permissions*. Both of these pages provide access to functions implemented by the Server for NFS role service, as covered in Objective 2.1, "Configure Advanced File Services," in Exam 70-412, "Configuring Advanced Windows Server 2012 Services."

6. In the Share name text box, specify the name you want to assign to the share and click Next. The *Configure share settings* page appears, as shown in Figure 4-8.

Figure 4-8

The *Configure share settings* page of the New Share Wizard

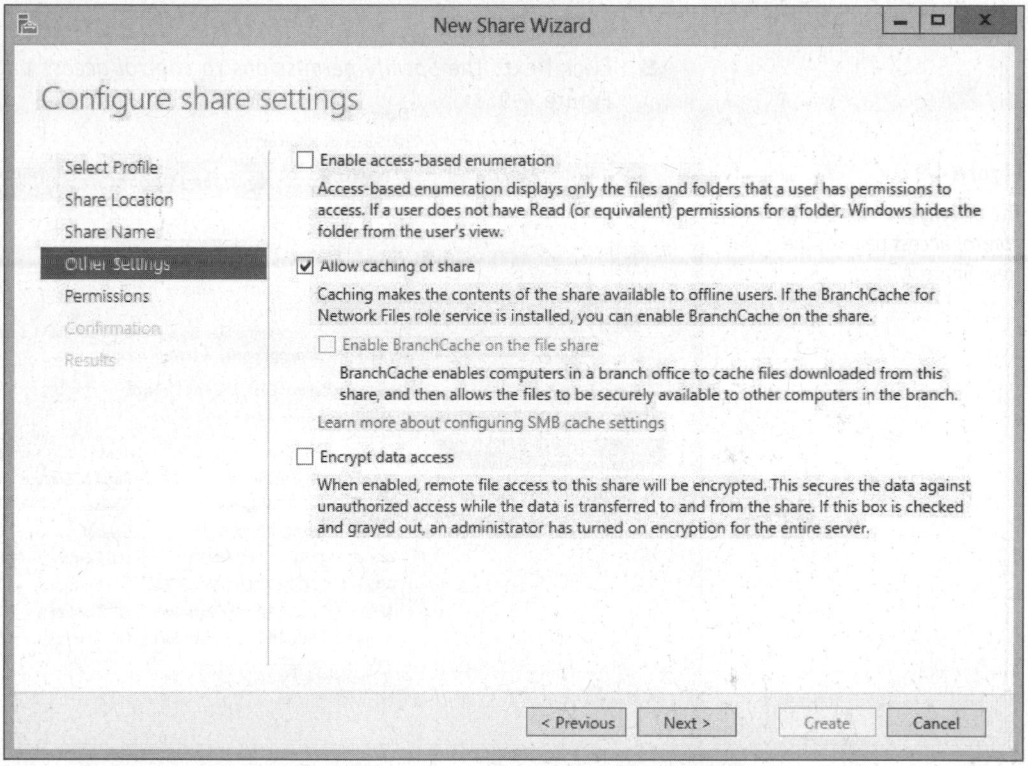

7. Select any or all of the following options:

- Enable access-based enumeration prevents users from seeing files and folders they do not have permission to access.
- Allow caching of share enables offline users to access the contents of the share.
- Enable BranchCache on the file share enables BranchCache servers to cache files accessed from this share.
- Encrypt data access causes the server to encrypt remote file access to this share.

CERTIFICATION READY
Configure access-based enumeration (ABE).
Objective 2.1

CERTIFICATION READY
Configure offline files.
Objective 2.1

TAKE NOTE*

***Access-based enumeration (ABE)**, a feature first introduced in Windows Server 2003 R2, applies filters to shared folders based on individual user's permissions to the files and subfolders in the share. Simply, users who cannot access a particular shared resource cannot see that resource on the network. This feature prevents users from searching through files and folders they cannot access. You can enable or disable ABE for shares at any time by opening the share's Properties sheet in the *Sharing and Storage Management* console and clicking *Advanced*, to display the same *Advanced* dialog box displayed by the *Provision a Shared Folder Wizard*.*

Offline Files, also known as client-side caching, is a Windows feature that enables client systems to maintain local copies of files they access from server shares. When a client selects the *Always available offline* option for a server-based file, folder, or share, the client system copies the selected data to the local drive and updates it regularly, so that the client user can always access it, even if the server is offline. To enable clients to use the Offline Files feature, the share must have the *Allow caching of share* check box selected. Windows Server 2012 and Windows 8 also have a new Always Offline mode for the Offline Files feature that causes clients to always use the cached copy of server files, providing better performance. To implement this mode, you must set the *Configure slow-link mode* Group Policy setting on the client to a value of 1 millisecond.

TAKE NOTE*

8. Click Next. The *Specify permissions to control access* page appears, as shown in Figure 4-9.

Figure 4-9

The *Specify permissions to control access* page of the New Share Wizard

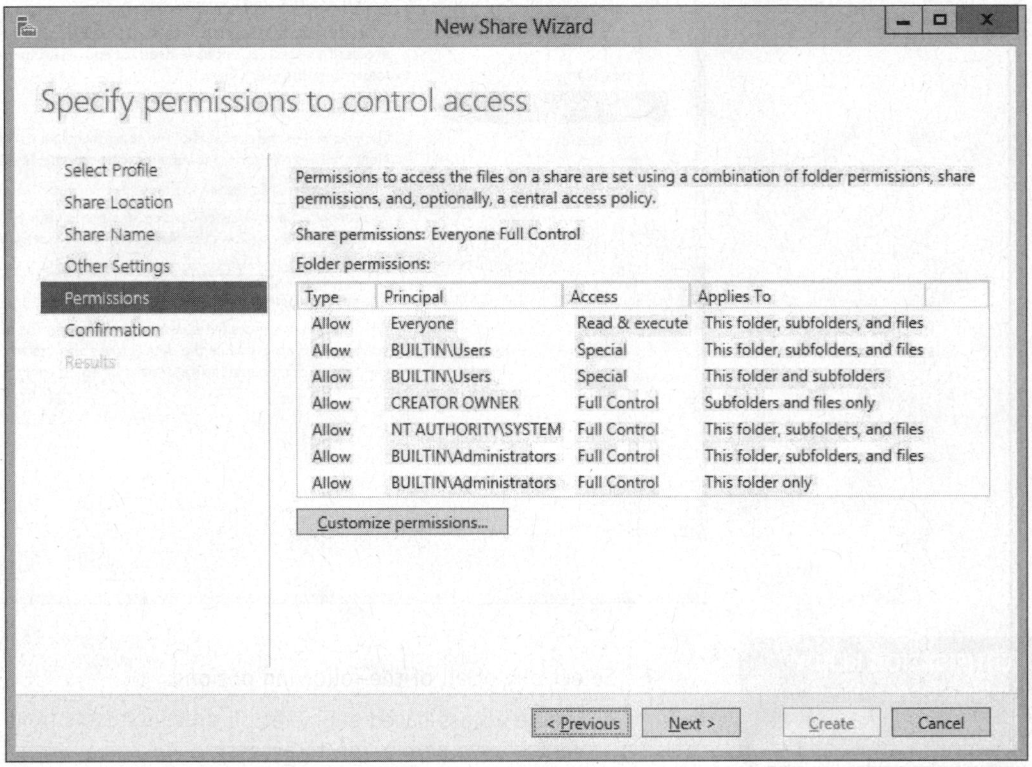

+ **MORE INFORMATION**

For more information on permissions, see "Assigning Permissions," later in this lesson. To set NTFS permissions, see "Assigning Basic NTFS permissions" and "Assigning Advanced NTFS permissions."

9. Modify the default share and NTFS permissions as needed and click Next. The *Confirm selections* page appears, as shown in Figure 4-10.

+ **MORE INFORMATION**

Selecting one of the Advanced share profiles adds two pages to the wizard: *Specify folder management properties* and *Apply a quota to a folder or volume*. Both these pages provide access to functions of the File Server Resource Manager application, as covered in Objective 2.2, "Configure File Server Resource Manager (FSRM)," in Exam 70-411, "Administering Windows Server 2012."

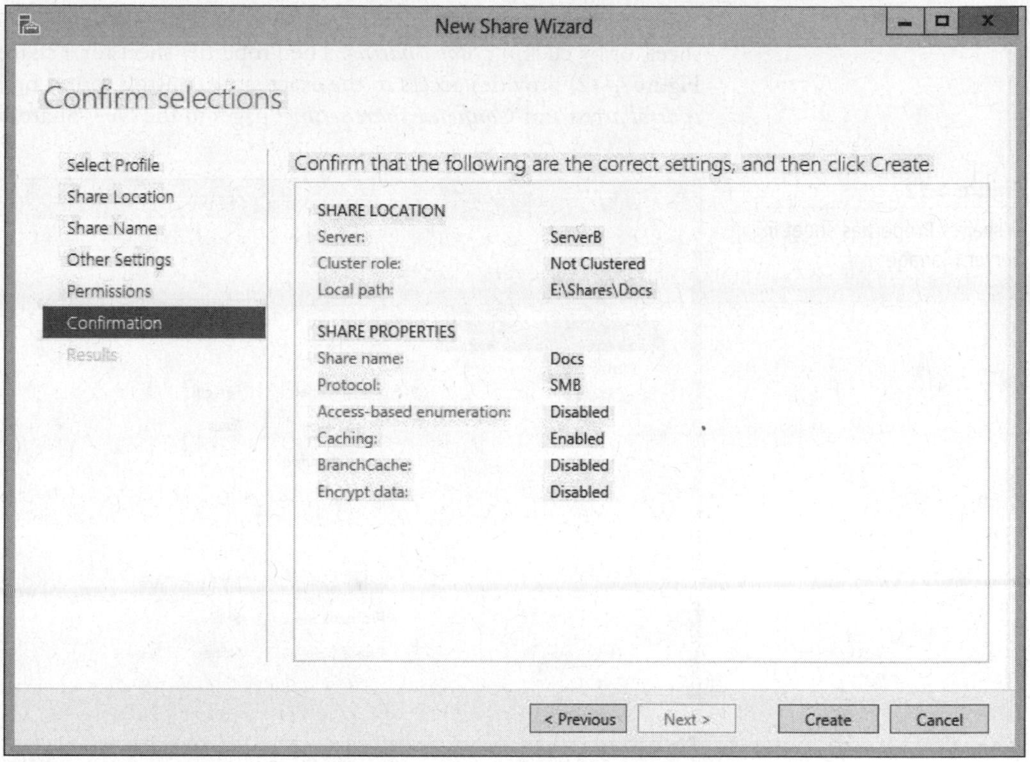

Figure 4-10

The *Confirm selections* page of the New Share Wizard

10. Click Create. The *View results* page appears as the wizard creates the share.

CLOSE the *New Share Wizard.*

After you create a share with the wizard, the new share appears in the *Shares* tile of the *Shares* homepage in Server Manager, as shown in Figure 4-11.

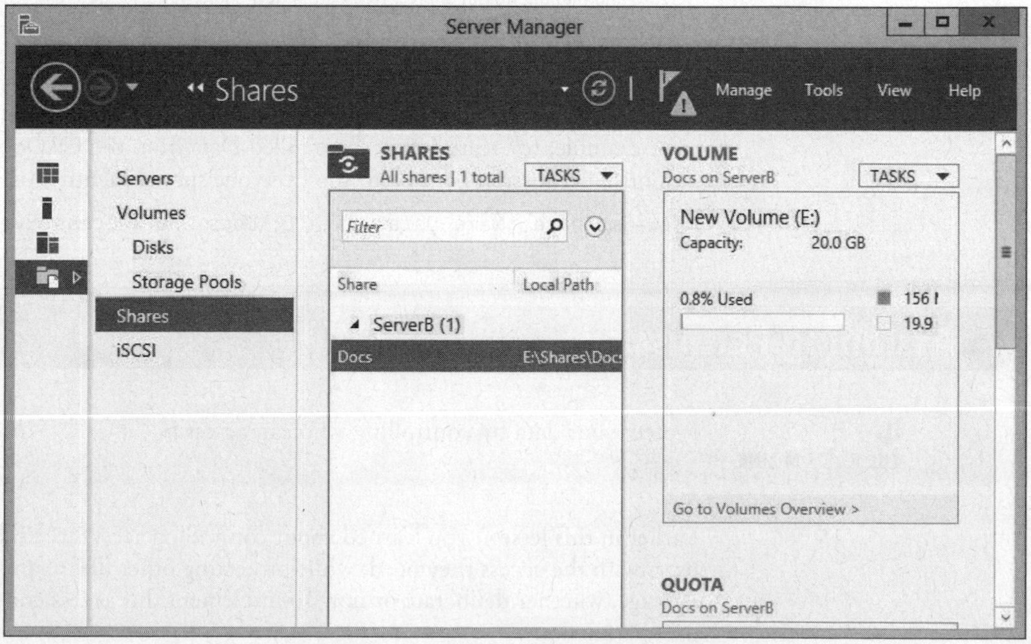

Figure 4-11

A new share on the *Shares* homepage in Server Manager

You can now use the tile to manage a share by right-clicking it and opening its Properties sheet, or by clicking *Stop Sharing*. The Properties sheet for a share in Server Manager (see Figure 4-12) provides access to the exact same controls found on the *Specify permissions to control access* and *Configure share settings* pages in the New Share Wizard.

Figure 4-12

A share's Properties sheet in Server Manager

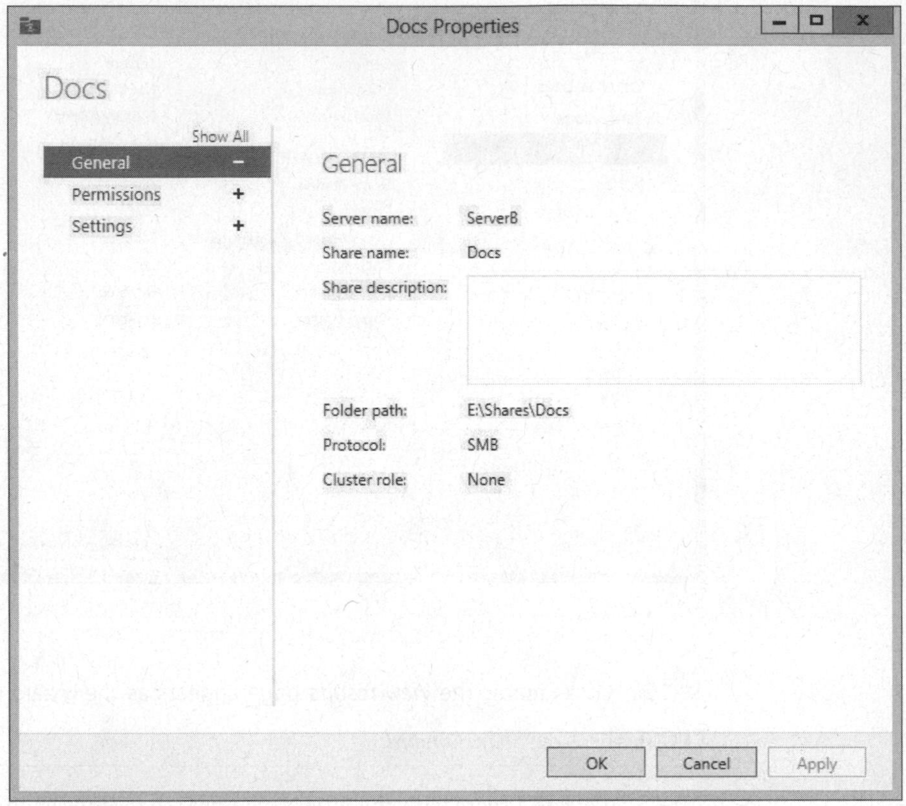

USING WINDOWS POWERSHELL

Windows Server 2012 includes a new Windows PowerShell module called **SmbShare**, which you can use to create and manage folder shares. To create a new share, you use the **New-SmbShare** cmdlet with the following basic syntax:

```
New-SmbShare –Name <share name> -Path <path name>
[-FullAccess <group>] [-ReadAccess <group>] [-NoAccess <group>]
```

For example, to create a new share called Data from the C:\Docs folder with the Allow Full Control permission granted to the Everyone special identity, use the following command:

```
New-SmbShare –Name Data -Path C:\Docs -FullAccess Everyone
```

■ Assigning Permissions

↓ **THE BOTTOM LINE**   Protect your data by controlling who can access it.

Earlier in this lesson, you learned about controlling access to a file server to provide network users with the access they need, while protecting other files against possible intrusion and damage, whether deliberate or not. To implement this access control, Windows Server 2012 uses permissions.

Permissions are privileges granted to specific system entities, such as users, groups, or computers, enabling them to perform a task or access a resource. For example, you can grant a specific user permission to read a file while denying that same user the permissions needed to modify or delete the file.

Windows Server 2012 has several sets of permissions that operate independently of each other. As a server administrator, you should be familiar with the operation of the following four permission systems:

- Share permissions control access to folders over a network. To access a file over a network, a user must have appropriate share permissions (and appropriate NTFS permissions, if the shared folder is on an NTFS volume).

- NTFS permissions control access to the files and folders stored on disk volumes formatted with the NTFS file system. To access a file, whether on the local system or over a network, a user must have the appropriate NTFS permissions.

- Registry permissions control access to specific parts of the Windows registry. An application that modifies registry settings or a user attempting to manually modify the registry must have the appropriate registry permissions.

- Active Directory permissions control access to specific parts of an AD DS hierarchy. Although file servers typically do not function as AD DS domain controllers, server administrators might use these permissions when servicing computers that are members of a domain.

All these permission systems operate independently of each other and sometimes combine to provide increased protection to a specific resource. For example, you might grant Ralph the NTFS permissions needed to access a spreadsheet stored on a file server volume. If Ralph sits down at the file server console and logs on as himself, he can access that spreadsheet. However, if Ralph is working at his own computer, he cannot access the spreadsheet until you create a share containing the file and grant Ralph the proper share permissions.

TAKE NOTE* While all these permissions systems are operating all the time, server administrators do not necessarily have to work with all of them regularly. In fact, many administrators never have to manually alter a Registry or Active Directory permission. However, many do work with NTFS and share permissions daily.

For network users to be able to access a shared folder on an NTFS drive, you must grant them both share permissions and NTFS permissions. As you saw earlier, you can grant these permissions as part of the share creation process, but you can also modify the permissions at any time afterward.

Understanding the Windows Permission Architecture

Permissions protect all files, folders, shares, registry keys, and AD DS objects.

To store the permissions, each element has an ***access control list (ACL)***. An ACL is a collection of individual permissions, in the form of ***access control entries (ACEs)***. Each ACE consists of a ***security principal*** (the name of the user, group, or computer granted the permissions) and the specific permissions assigned to that security principal. When you manage permissions in any of the Windows Server 2012 permission systems, you are actually creating and modifying the ACEs in an ACL.

It is important to understand that, in all Windows operating systems, permissions are stored as part of the protected element, not the security principal granted access. For example, when you grant a user the NTFS permissions needed to access a file, the ACE you create is stored in the file's ACL; it is not part of the user account. You can move the file to a different location, and its permissions go with it.

To manage permissions in Windows Server 2012, you use a tab in the protected element's Properties sheet, like the one shown in Figure 4-13, with the security principals listed at the top and the permissions associated with them at the bottom. Share permissions are typically found on a *Share Permissions* tab, and NTFS permissions are located on a *Security* tab. All Windows permission systems use the same basic interface, although the permissions themselves vary. Server Manager also provides access to NTFS and share permissions, using a slightly different interface.

Figure 4-13

The Security tab of a Properties sheet

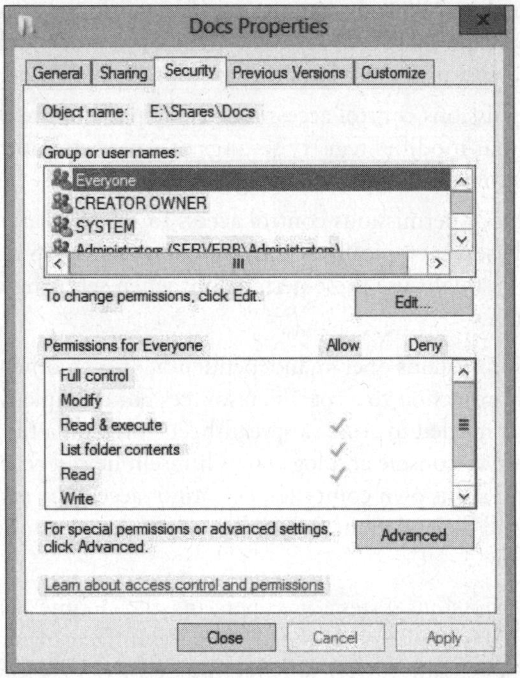

Understanding Basic and Advanced Permissions

The permissions protecting a particular system element are not like the keys to a lock, which provide either full access or no access at all. Permissions are designed to be granular, enabling you to grant specific degrees of access to security principals.

For example, you can use NTFS permissions to control not only who has access to a spreadsheet, but also the degree of access. You might grant Ralph permission to read and modify the spreadsheet, but Alice can only read it, and Ed cannot see it at all.

To provide this granularity, each Windows permission system has an assortment of permissions that you can assign to a security principal in any combination. Depending on the permission system you are working with, you might have dozens of different permissions available for a single system element.

If this is all starting to sound extremely complex, don't worry. Windows provides preconfigured permission combinations suitable for most common access control chores. When you open the Properties sheet for a system element and look at its *Security* tab, the NTFS permissions you see are called **basic permissions**. Basic permissions are actually combinations of **advanced permissions**, which provide the most granular control over the element.

CERTIFICATION READY
Prior to Windows Server 2012, basic permissions were known as standard permissions and advanced permissions were known as special permissions. Candidates for certification exams should be aware of these alternative terms.

For example, the NTFS permission system has 14 advanced permissions that you can assign to a folder or file. However, it also has 6 basic permissions that are various combinations of the 14 advanced permissions. In most cases, you work only with basic permissions. Many administrators rarely, if ever, work directly with advanced permissions.

If you do find it necessary to work with advanced permissions directly, Windows makes it possible. After you click the *Advanced* button on the *Security* tab of any Properties sheet, you access the ACEs for the selected system element directly through an *Advanced Security Settings* dialog box (see Figure 4-14). System Manager provides access to the same dialog box through a share's Properties sheet.

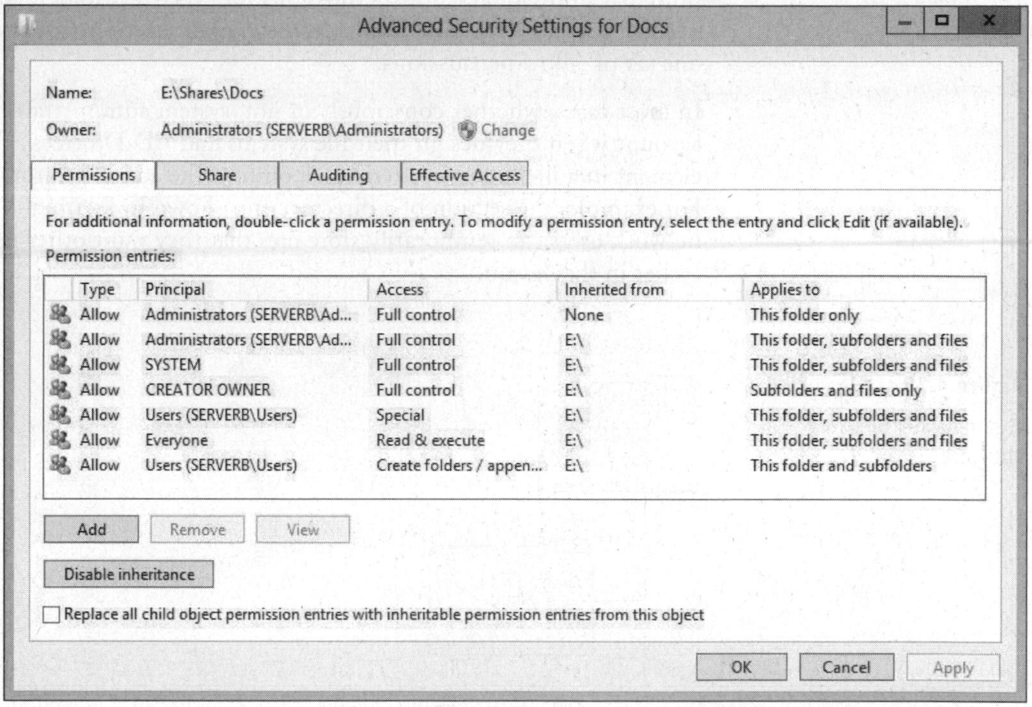

Figure 4-14

The *Advanced Security Settings* dialog box

Allowing and Denying Permissions

When you assign permissions to a system element, you are, in effect, creating a new ACE in the element's ACL.

ACEs come in two basic types: *Allow* and *Deny*. This makes approaching permission management tasks possible from two directions:

- **Additive:** Start with no permissions and then grant Allow permissions to individual security principals to provide them with the access they need.
- **Subtractive:** Start by granting all possible Allow permissions to individual security principals, providing them with full control over the system element, and then grant them Deny permissions for the access you do not want them to have.

Most administrators prefer the additive approach, because Windows, by default, attempts to limit access to important system elements. In a properly designed permission hierarchy, the use of Deny permissions is often not needed at all. Many administrators frown on their use, because combining Allow and Deny permissions in the same hierarchy can often make determining the effective permissions difficult for a specific system element.

Inheriting Permissions

The most important principle in permission management is that permissions tend to run downward through a hierarchy. This is called *permission inheritance*.

Permission inheritance means that parent elements pass their permissions down to their subordinate elements. For example, when you grant Alice Allow permissions to access the root of the D: drive, all the folders and subfolders on the D: drive inherit those permissions, and Alice can access them. The principle of inheritance simplifies the permission assignment process enormously. Without it, you would have to grant security principals individual Allow permissions for every file, folder, share, object, and key they need to access. With inheritance, you can grant access to an entire file system by creating one set of Allow permissions.

In most cases, whether consciously or not, system administrators take inheritance into account when they design their file systems and AD DS trees. The location of a system element in a hierarchy is often based on how the administrators plan to assign permissions. For example, the section of a directory tree shown in Figure 4-15 is intended to be where network users can temporarily store files that they want other users to access, as discussed earlier in this lesson.

Figure 4-15

A sample xfer directory structure

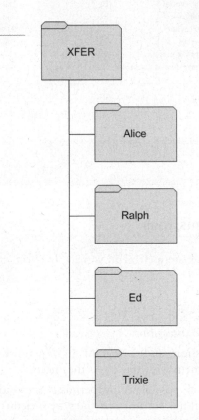

Because the administrator has assigned all users the Allow Read and Allow List Folder Contents standard permission to the xfer folder, as shown in Figure 4-16, everyone can read the files in the xfer directory. Because the assigned permissions run downward, all subfolders beneath xfer inherit those permissions, and all users can read the files in all the subfolders.

Figure 4-16

Granting Allow permissions to
the xfer folder

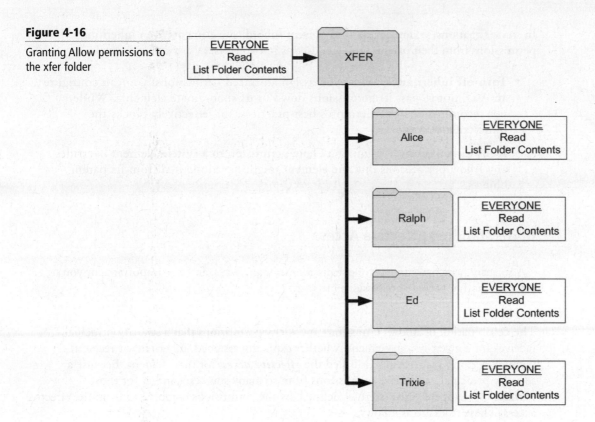

The next step is to assign each user the Allow Full Control permission to his or her own
subfolder, as shown in Figure 4-17. This enables each user to create, modify, and delete files in
his or her own folder, without compromising the security of other users' folders. Because the user
folders are at the bottom of the hierarchy, no subfolders inherit the Full Control permissions.

Figure 4-17

Granting Full Control to
individual user folders

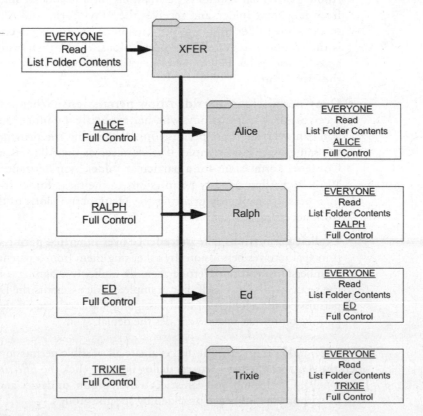

In some situations, you might want to prevent subordinate elements from inheriting permissions from their parents. You can do this in two ways:

- **Turn off inheritance:** When you assign advanced permissions, you can configure an ACE not to pass its permissions down to its subordinate elements. While not recommended by Microsoft's best practices, this effectively blocks the inheritance process.

- **Deny permissions:** Assigning a Deny permission to a system element overrides any Allow permissions that the element might have inherited from its parent objects.

Understanding Effective Access

A security principal can receive permissions in many ways, and it is important for you to understand how these permissions interact.

The combination of Allow permissions and Deny permissions that a security principal receives for a given system element, whether explicitly assigned, inherited, or received through a group membership, is called the *effective access* for that element. Because a security principal can receive permissions from so many sources, conflict for those permissions happens often, so rules define how the permissions combine to form the effective access. These rules are as follows:

- **Allow permissions are cumulative:** When a security principal receives Allow permissions from more than one source, the permissions are combined to form the effective access permissions. For example, if Alice receives the Allow Read and Allow List Folder Contents permissions for a particular folder by inheriting them from its parent folder, and receives the Allow Write and Allow Modify permissions to the same folder from a group membership, Alice's effective access for the folder is the combination of all four permissions. If you then explicitly grant Alice's user account the Allow Full Control permission, this fifth permission is combined with the other four.

- **Deny permissions override Allow permissions:** When a security principal receives Allow permissions, whether explicitly, by inheritance, or from a group, you can override those permissions by granting the principal Deny permissions of the same type. For example, if Alice receives the Allow Read and Allow List Folder Contents permissions for a particular folder by inheritance, and receives the Allow Write and Allow Modify permissions to the same folder from a group membership, explicitly granting the Deny permissions to that folder prevents her from accessing it in any way.

- **Explicit permissions take precedence over inherited permissions:** When a security principal receives permissions by inheriting them from a parent or from group memberships, you can override them by explicitly assigning contradicting permissions to the security principal itself. For example, if Alice inherits the Deny Full Access permission for a folder, explicitly assigning her user account the Allow Full Access permission to that folder overrides the denial.

Of course, rather than examine and evaluate all possible permission sources, you can just open the *Advanced Security Settings* dialog box and click the *Effective Access* tab, as shown in Figure 4-18. On this tab, you can select a user, group, or device and view its effective access, with or without the influence provided by specific groups.

Figure 4-18

The Effective Access tab of the Advanced Security Settings dialog box

Setting Share Permissions

On Windows Server 2012, shared folders have their own permission system, which is completely independent from the other Windows permission systems.

CERTIFICATION READY
Configure share permissions.
Objective 2.1

For network users to access shares on a file server, you must grant them the appropriate share permissions. By default, the Everyone special identity receives the Allow Full Control share permission to any new shares you create on a domain member server. On a standalone server, the Everyone special identity receives only the Allow Read share permission for new shares.

To modify the share permissions for an existing share via Windows Explorer, you open the Properties sheet for the shared folder, select the *Sharing* tab, and then click *Advanced Sharing and Permissions* to open the *Share Permissions* tab, as shown in Figure 4-19.

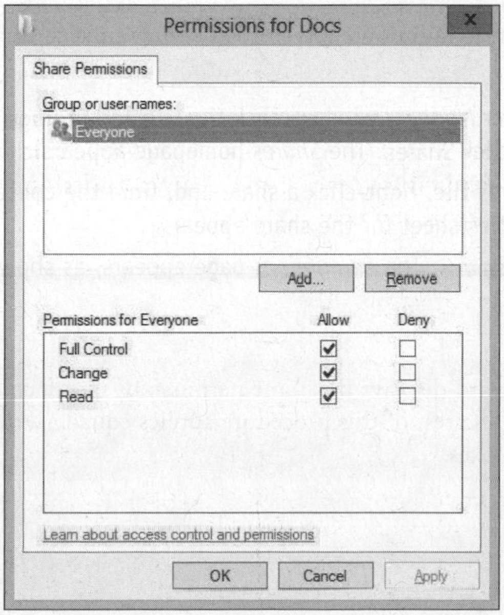

Figure 4-19

The Share Permissions tab for a shared folder

By using this interface, you can add security principals and allow or deny them the three share permissions listed in Table 4-1.

Table 4-1

Share Permissions and their functions

SHARE PERMISSION	ALLOWS OR DENIES SECURITY PRINCIPALS THE ABILITY TO:
Full Control	• Change file permissions • Take ownership of files • Perform all tasks allowed by the Change permission
Change	• Create folders • Add files to folders • Change data in files • Change file attributes • Delete folders and files • Perform all actions permitted by the Read permission
Read	• Display folder names, filenames, file data and attributes • Execute program files • Access other folders within the shared folder

 TAKE NOTE* The share permission system is relatively simple and has only three permissions. There is no distinction between basic and advanced permissions in this system.

To set share permissions via Server Manager while creating a share or modifying an existing one, use the following procedure.

⊙ **SET SHARE PERMISSIONS**

GET READY. Log on to Windows Server 2012, using an account with domain administrative privileges.

1. In the *Server Manager* window, click the File and Storage Services icon. In the submenu, click Shares. The *Shares* homepage appears.

2. In the *Shares* tile, right-click a share and, from the context menu, select Properties. The Properties sheet for the share appears.

3. Click Permissions. The *Permissions* page appears, as shown in Figure 4-20.

TAKE NOTE* The New Share Wizard displays this same permissions interface on its *Specify permissions to control access* page. The rest of this procedure applies equally well to that page and its subsequent dialog boxes.

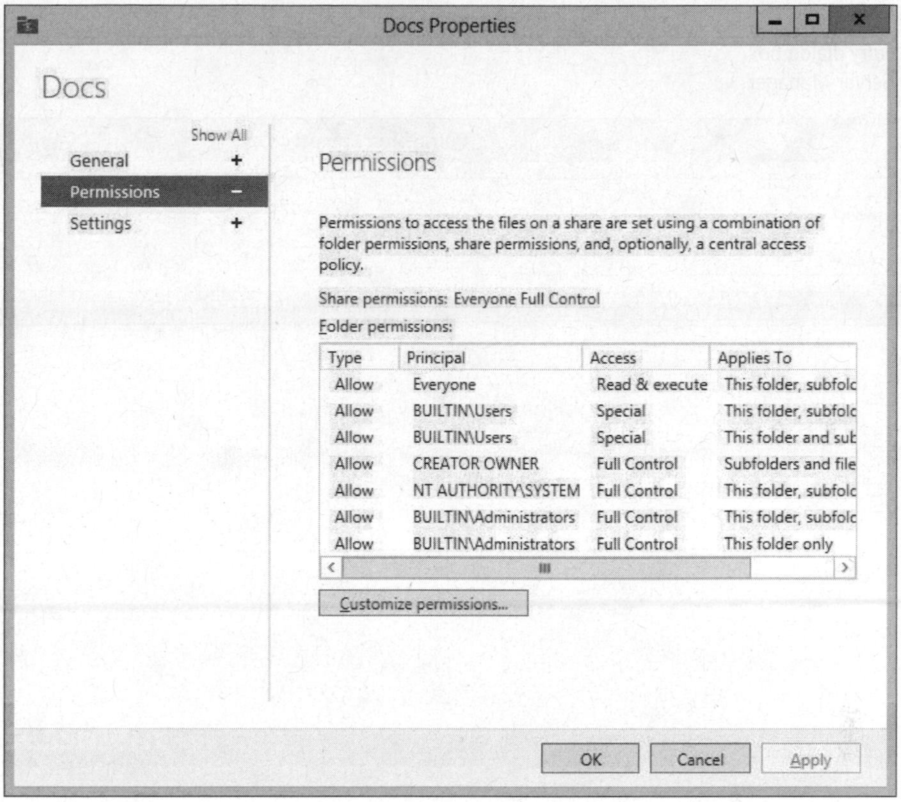

Figure 4-20

The Permissions page of a share's Properties sheet in Server Manager

Docs Properties

Docs

Show All

General   +

Permissions   −

Settings   +

Permissions

Permissions to access the files on a share are set using a combination of folder permissions, share permissions, and, optionally, a central access policy.

Share permissions: Everyone Full Control

Folder permissions:

Type	Principal	Access	Applies To
Allow	Everyone	Read & execute	This folder, subfolc
Allow	BUILTIN\Users	Special	This folder, subfolc
Allow	BUILTIN\Users	Special	This folder and sub
Allow	CREATOR OWNER	Full Control	Subfolders and file
Allow	NT AUTHORITY\SYSTEM	Full Control	This folder, subfolc
Allow	BUILTIN\Administrators	Full Control	This folder, subfolc
Allow	BUILTIN\Administrators	Full Control	This folder only

Customize permissions...

OK   Cancel   Apply

4. Click Customize Permissions. The *Advanced Security Settings* dialog box for the share appears.

5. Click the Share tab to display the interface shown in Figure 4-21.

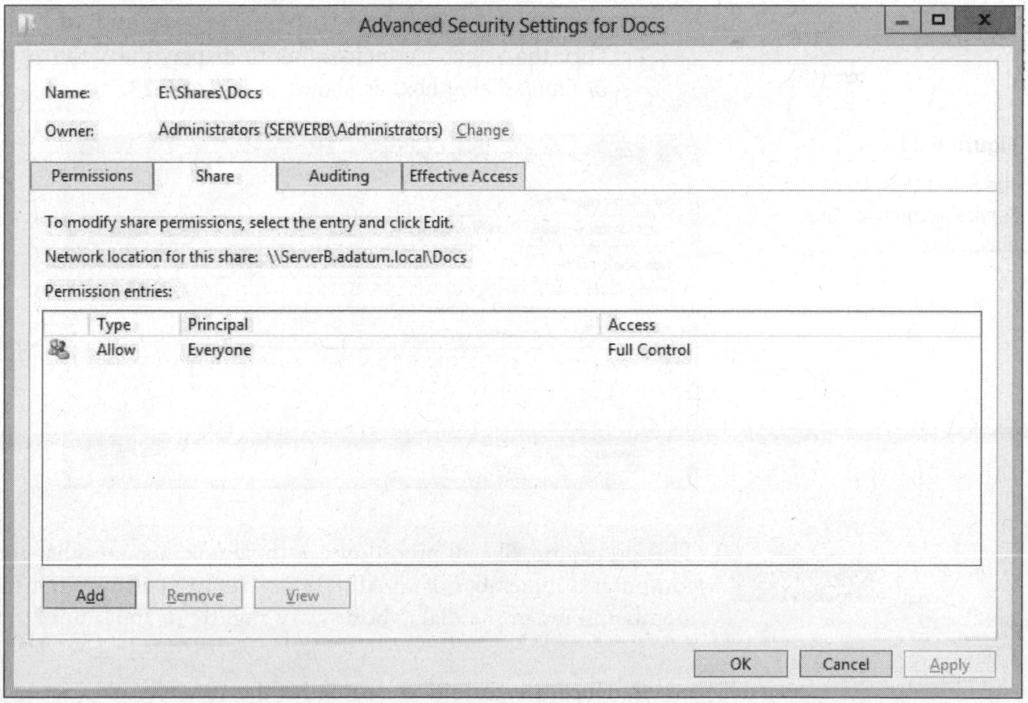

Figure 4-21

The Share tab of the Advanced Security Settings dialog box for a share in Server Manager

Advanced Security Settings for Docs

Name: E:\Shares\Docs

Owner: Administrators (SERVERB\Administrators) Change

| Permissions | Share | Auditing | Effective Access |

To modify share permissions, select the entry and click Edit.

Network location for this share: \\ServerB.adatum.local\Docs

Permission entries:

	Type	Principal	Access
👥	Allow	Everyone	Full Control

Add   Remove   View

OK   Cancel   Apply

6. Click Add. A *Permission Entry* dialog box for the share appears, as shown in Figure 4-22.

Figure 4-22

A *Permission Entry* dialog box
for a share in Server Manager

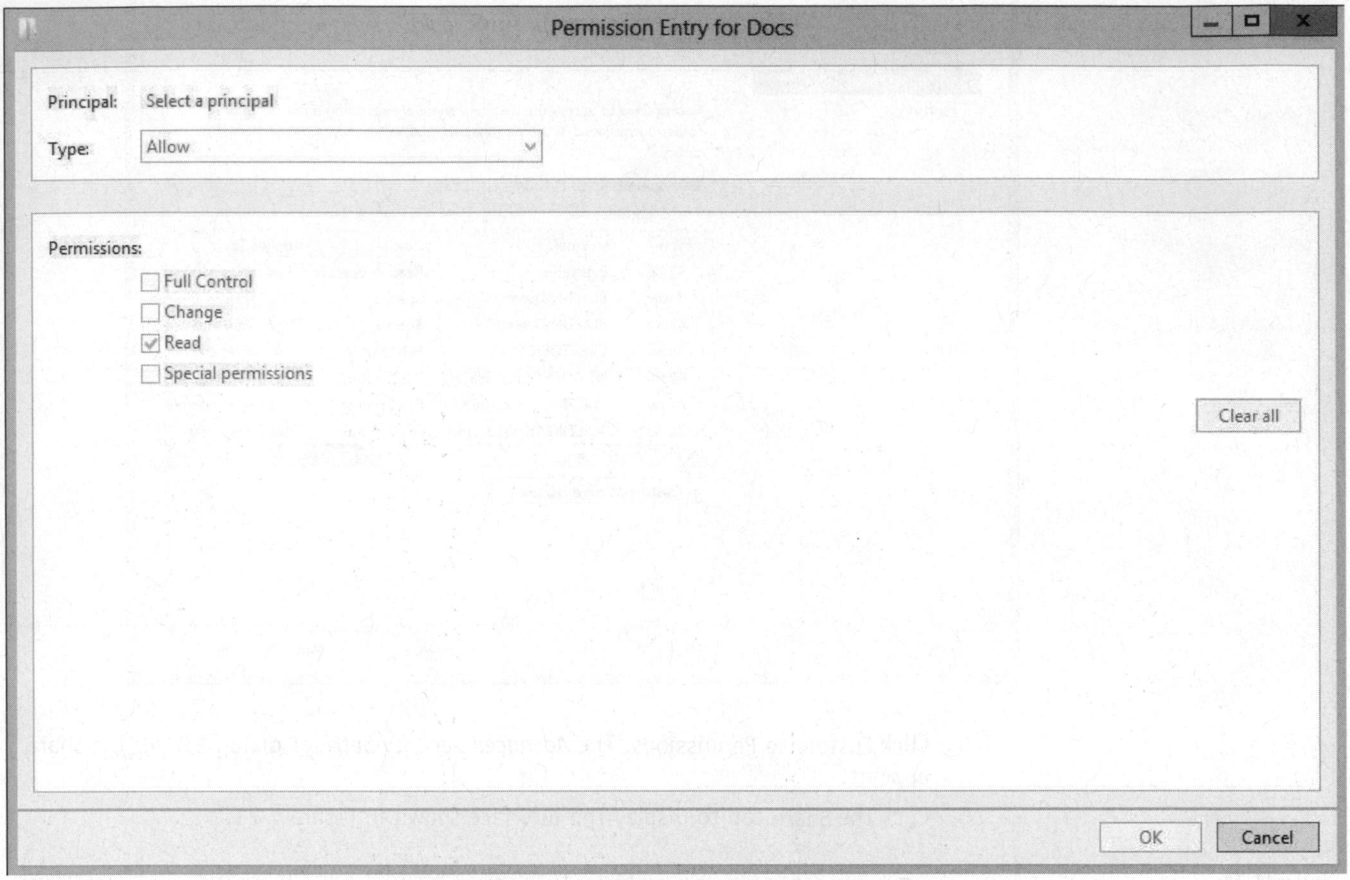

Permission Entry for Docs

Principal: Select a principal

Type: Allow

Permissions:

- ☐ Full Control
- ☐ Change
- ☑ Read
- ☐ Special permissions

Clear all

OK   Cancel

7. Click the Select a principal link to display the *Select User, Computer, Service Account, or Group* dialog box, as shown in Figure 4-23.

Figure 4-23

The Select User, Computer,
Service Account, or Group
dialog box

Select User, Computer, Service Account, or Group

Select this object type:

User, Group, or Built-in security principal   Object Types...

From this location:

adatum.local   Locations...

Enter the object name to select (examples):

Check Names

Advanced...   OK   Cancel

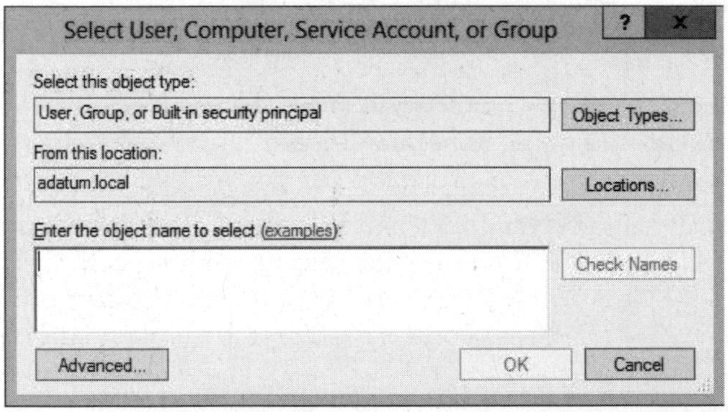

TAKE NOTE* This procedure, like all procedures in this book, assumes that the Windows Server 2012 computer is a member of an AD DS domain. On a computer that is not a domain member, some of the dialog boxes vary slightly in appearance.

8. Type the name of or search for the security principal to which you want to assign share permissions and click OK. The *Permission Entry* dialog box displays the security principal you specified.

9. Select the type of permissions you want to assign (Allow or Deny).

10. Select the check boxes for the permissions you want to assign and click OK. The *Advanced Security Settings* dialog box displays the new access control entry you just created, as shown in Figure 4-24.

Figure 4-24

A new share permission entry in a share's access control list

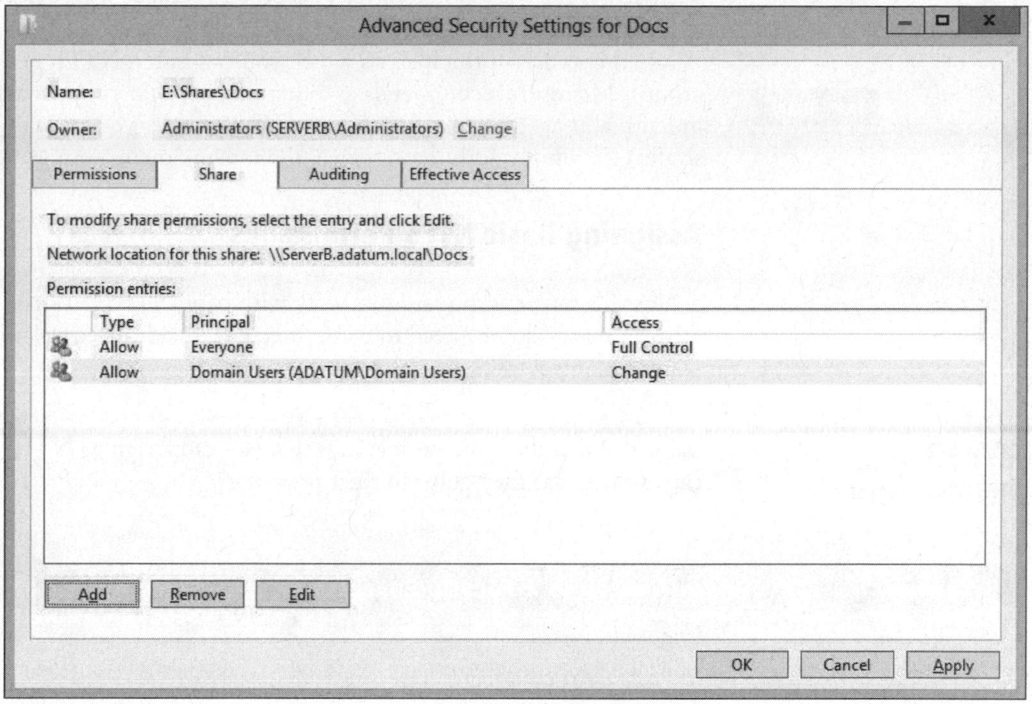

As discussed later in this lesson, many file server administrators simply leave the Allow Full Control share permission to the Everyone special identity in place, essentially bypassing the share permission system, and rely solely on NTFS permissions for granular file system protection.

TAKE NOTE*

11. Click OK to close the *Advanced Security Settings* dialog box.

12. Click OK to close the share's Properties sheet.

CLOSE the *Server Manager* window.

When assigning share permissions, you must be aware that they do not combine like NTFS permissions. If you grant Alice the Allow Read and Allow Change permissions to the shared C:\Documents\Alice folder and later deny her all three permissions to the shared C:\Documents folder, the Deny permissions prevent her from accessing any files through the C:\Documents share, including those in the C:\Documents\Alice folder. However, she can still access her files through the C:\Documents\Alice share because of the Allow permissions. In other words, the C:\Documents\Alice share does not inherit the Deny permissions from the C:\Documents share.

Understanding NTFS Authorization

Most Windows installations today use the NTFS and ReFS file systems, as opposed to FAT32. One main advantage of NTFS and ReFS is that they support permissions, which FAT32 does not. As described earlier in this lesson, every file and folder on an NTFS or ReFS drive has an ACL that consists of ACEs, each of which contains a security principal and the permissions assigned to that principal.

In the NTFS permission system, which ReFS also supports, the security principals involved are users and groups, which Windows refers to using *security identifiers (SIDs)*. When a user attempts to access an NTFS file or folder, the system reads the user's security access token, which contains the SIDs for the user's account and all groups to which the user belongs. The system then compares these SIDs to those stored in the file or folder's ACEs, to determine what access the user should have. This process is called *authorization*.

TAKE NOTE

While the security principals to which you can assign NTFS permissions can be users or groups, Microsoft recommends as a best practice that you not assign permissions to individual users, but to groups instead. This enables you to maintain your permission strategy by simply adding users to and removing them from groups.

Assigning Basic NTFS Permissions

Most file server administrators work with basic NTFS permissions almost exclusively because they do not need to work directly with advanced permissions for most common access-control tasks.

Table 4-2

NTFS Basic Permissions

Table 4-2 lists the basic permissions that you can assign to NTFS files or folders, and the capabilities that they grant to their possessors.

STANDARD PERMISSION	WHEN APPLIED TO A FOLDER, ENABLES A SECURITY PRINCIPAL TO:	WHEN APPLIED TO A FILE, ENABLES A SECURITY PRINCIPAL TO:
Full Control	• Modify the folder permissions • Take ownership of the folder • Delete subfolders and files contained in the folder • Perform all actions associated with all the other NTFS file permissions	• Modify the file permissions • Take ownership of the file • Perform all actions associated with all the other NTFS folder permissions
Modify	• Delete the folder • Perform all actions associated with the Write and the Read & Execute permissions	• Modify the file • Delete the file • Perform all actions associated with the Write and the Read & Execute permissions
Read and Execute	• Navigate through restricted folders to reach other files and folders • Perform all actions associated with the Read and List Folder Contents permissions	• Perform all actions associated with the Read permission • Run applications
List Folder Contents	• View the names of the files and subfolders contained in the folder	• Not applicable
Read	• See the files and subfolders contained in the folder • View the folder's ownership, permissions, and attributes	• Read the file contents • View the file's ownership, permissions, and attributes
Write	• Create new files and subfolders inside the folder • Modify the folder attributes • View the folder's ownership and permissions	• Overwrite the file • Modify the file attributes • View the file's ownership and permissions

To assign basic NTFS permissions to a shared folder, the options are essentially the same as with share permissions. You can open the folder's Properties sheet in Windows Explorer and select the *Security* tab, or you can open a share's Properties sheet in Server Manager, as in the following procedure.

 ASSIGN BASIC NTFS PERMISSIONS

GET READY. Log on to Windows Server 2012, using an account with domain administrative privileges. The Server Manager window appears.

1. Click the File and Storage Services icon and, in the submenu that appears, click Shares. The *Shares* homepage appears.

> **TAKE NOTE***
>
> NTFS permissions are not limited to shared folders. Every file and folder on an NTFS volume has permissions. Whereas this procedure describes the process of assigning permissions to a shared folder, you can open the Properties sheet for any folder in a Windows Explorer window, click the *Security* tab, and work with its NTFS permissions in the same way.

2. In the *Shares* tile, right-click a share and, from the context menu, select Properties. The Properties sheet for the share appears.

3. Click Permissions. The *Permissions* page appears.

> **TAKE NOTE***
>
> The *New Share Wizard* displays this same permissions interface on its *Specify permissions to control access* page. The rest of this procedure applies equally well to that page and its subsequent dialog boxes.

4. Click Customize Permissions. The *Advanced Security Settings* dialog box for the share appears, displaying the *Permissions* tab, as shown in Figure 4-25. This dialog box is as close as the Windows graphical interface can come to displaying the contents of an ACL. Each line in the *Permission Entries* list is essentially an ACE and includes the following information:

   • *Type* specifies whether the entry allows or denies the permission.

   • *Principal* specifies the name of the user, group, or device principal receiving the permission.

   • *Access* specifies the name of the permission assigned to the security principal. If the entry is used to assign multiple advanced permissions, the word *Special* appears in this field.

   • *Inherited From* specifies whether the permission is inherited and, if so, from where it is inherited.

   • *Applies To* specifies whether the permission is to be inherited by subordinate objects and, if so, by which ones.

Figure 4-25

The *Advanced Security Settings* dialog box for a share in Server Manager

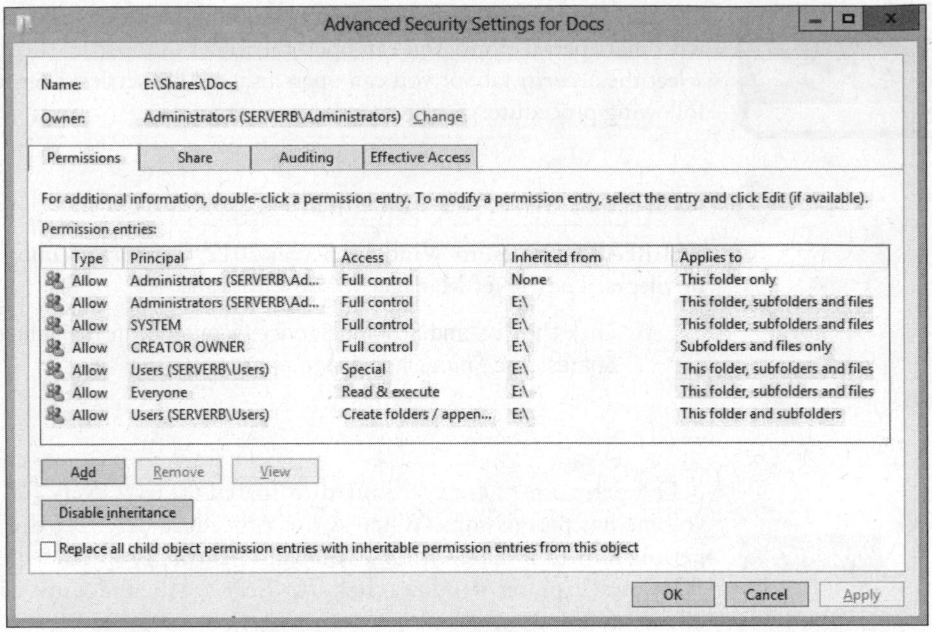

Figure 4-26

A *Permission Entry* dialog box for a share in Server Manager

5. Click Add. A *Permission Entry* dialog box for the share appears, as shown in Figure 4-26.

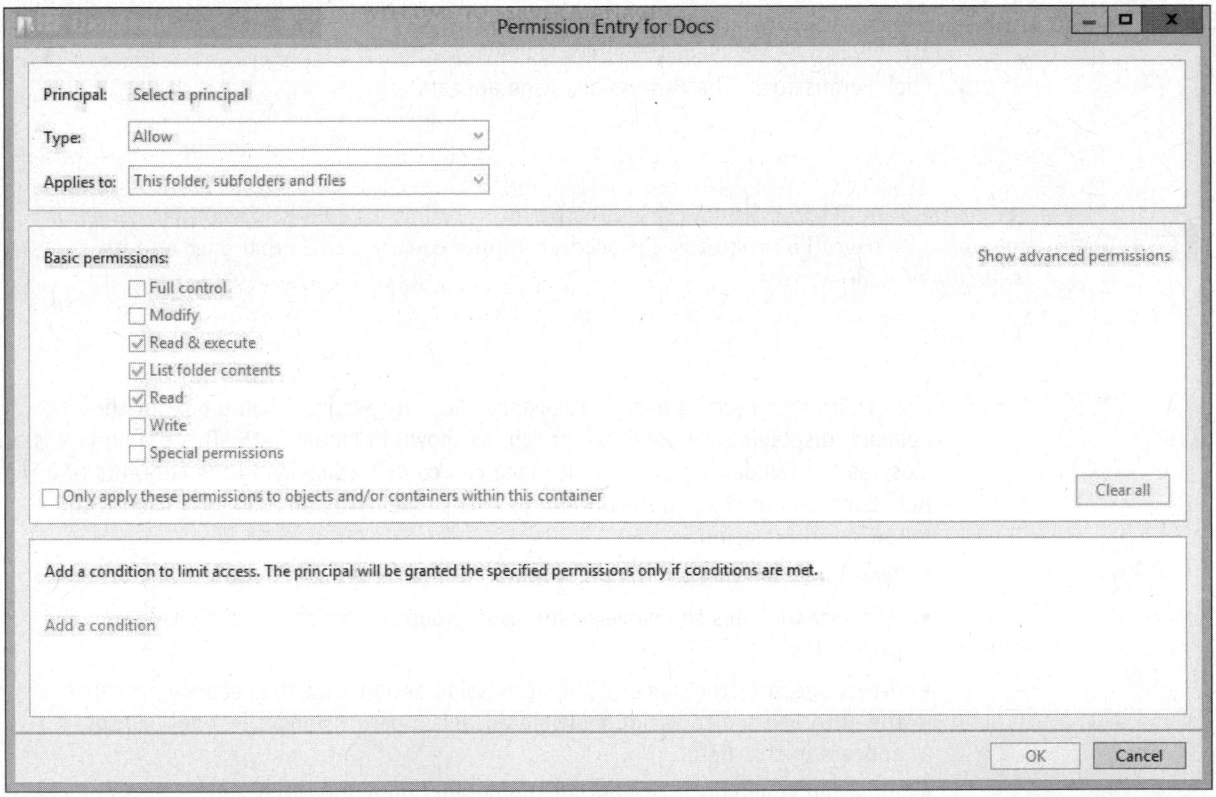

6. Click the Select a principal link to display the *Select User, Computer, Service Account, or Group* dialog box.

7. Type the name of or search for the security principal to which you want to assign share permissions and click OK. The *Permission Entry* dialog box displays the security principal you specified.

8. From the Type drop-down list, select the type of permissions you want to assign (Allow or Deny).

9. From the Applies to drop-down list, specify which subfolders and files should inherit the permissions you are assigning.

10. Select the check boxes for the basic permissions you want to assign and click OK. The *Advanced Security Settings* dialog box displays the new access control entry you just created.

➕ **MORE** INFORMATION

If you are using the File Classification Infrastructure capabilities in Windows Server 2012, you can use the *Add a condition to limit access* drop-down lists to assign permissions based on your classifications. For more information on FCI, see Objective 2.1, "Configure Advanced File Services," in Exam 70-412, "Configuring Advanced Windows Server 2012 Services."

11. Click OK to close the *Advanced Security Settings* dialog box.

TAKE NOTE *   Assigning permissions to a single folder takes only a moment, but for a folder with a large number of files and subfolders subordinate to it, the process can take a long time, because the system must modify the ACL of each folder and file.

12. Click OK to close the Properties sheet.

CLOSE the *Server Manager* window.

Assigning Advanced NTFS Permissions

In Windows Server 2012, the capability to manage advanced permissions is integrated into the same interface you use to manage basic permissions.

Figure 4-27

A *Permission Entry* dialog box displaying advanced permissions

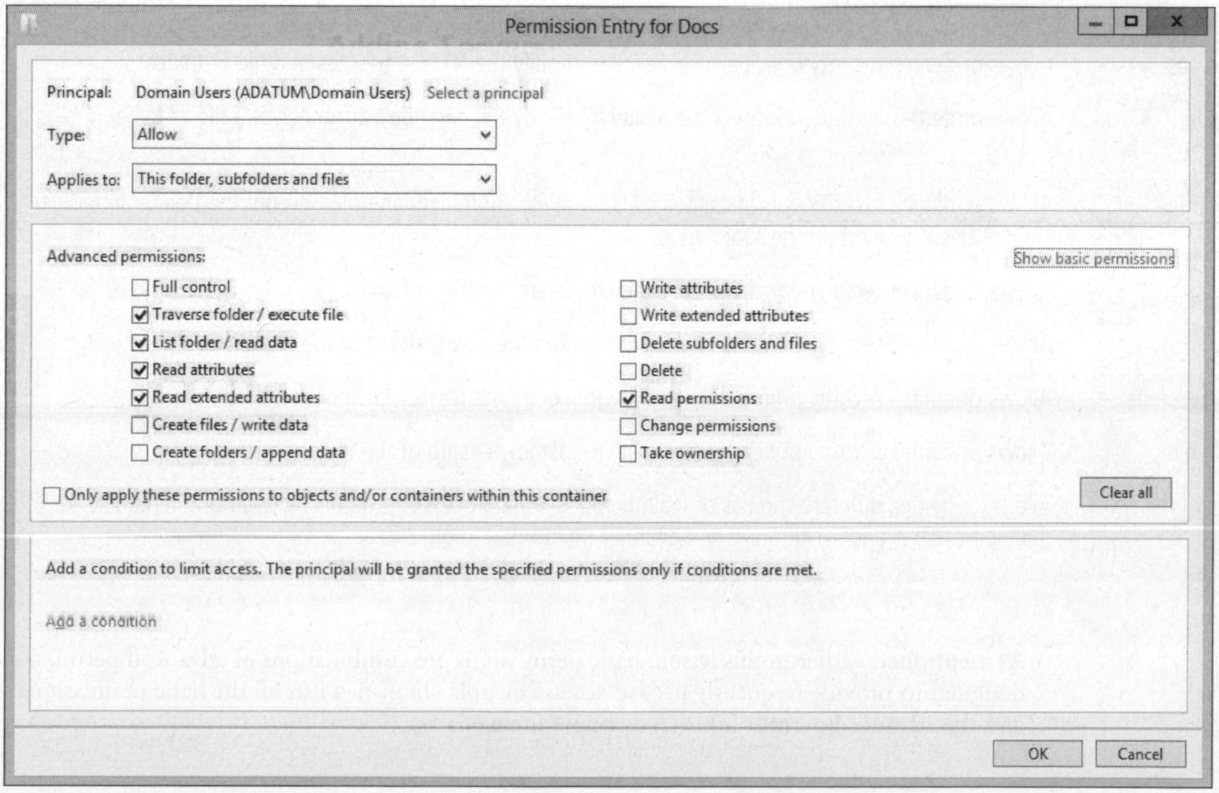

In the *Permission Entry* dialog box, clicking the *Show advanced permissions* link changes the list of basic permissions to a list of advanced permissions (see Figure 4-27). You can then assign advanced permissions in any combination, just as you would basic permissions.

Table 4-3

NTFS Advanced Permissions

Table 4-3 lists the NTFS advanced permissions that you can assign to files and folders, and the capabilities they grant to their possessors.

SPECIAL PERMISSION	FUNCTIONS
Traverse Folder/ Execute File	• The Traverse Folder permission allows or denies security principals the ability to move through folders that they do not have permission to access, so they can reach files or folders that they do have permission to access. This permission applies only to folders. • The Execute File permission allows or denies security principals the ability to run program files. This permission applies only to files.
List Folder/ Read Data	• The List Folder permission allows or denies security principals the ability to view the file and subfolder names within a folder. This permission applies only to folders. • The Read Data permission allows or denies security principals the ability to view the contents of a file. This permission applies only to files.
Read Attributes	Allows or denies security principals the ability to view the NTFS attributes of a file or folder.
Read Extended Attributes	Allows or denies security principals the ability to view the extended attributes of a file or folder.
Create Files/ Write Data	• The Create Files permission allows or denies security principals the ability to create files within the folder. This permission applies only to folders. • The Write Data permission allows or denies security principals the ability to modify the file and overwrite existing content. This permission applies only to files.
Create Folders/ Append Data	• The Create Folders permission allows or denies security principals the ability to create subfolders within a folder. This permission applies only to folders. • The Append Data permission allows or denies security principals the ability to add data to the end of the file but not to modify, delete, or overwrite existing data in the file. This permission applies only to files.
Write Attributes	Allows or denies security principals the ability to modify the NTFS attributes of a file or folder.
Write Extended Attributes	Allows or denies security principals the ability to modify the extended attributes of a file or folder.
Delete Subfolders and Files	Allows or denies security principals the ability to delete subfolders and files, even if the Delete permission has not been granted on the subfolder or file.
Delete	Allows or denies security principals the ability to delete the file or folder.
Read Permissions	Allows or denies security principals the ability to read the permissions for the file or folder.
Change Permissions	Allows or denies security principals the ability to modify the permissions for the file or folder.
Take Ownership	Allows or denies security principals the ability to take ownership of the file or folder.
Synchronize	Allows or denies different threads of multithreaded, multiprocessor programs to wait on the handle for the file or folder and synchronize with another thread that might signal it.

As mentioned earlier in this lesson, basic permissions are combinations of advanced permission designed to provide frequently needed access controls. Table 4-4 lists all the basic permissions and the advanced permissions that compose them.

Table 4-4

NTFS Basic Permissions and
their Advanced Permission
equivalents

BASIC PERMISSIONS	ADVANCED PERMISSIONS
Read	• List Folder/Read Data • Read Attributes • Read Extended Attributes • Read Permissions • Synchronize
Read and Execute	• List Folder/Read Data • Read Attributes • Read Extended Attributes • Read Permissions • Synchronize • Traverse Folder/Execute File
Modify	• Create Files/Write Data • Create Folders/Append Data • Delete • List Folder/Read Data • Read Attributes • Read Extended Attributes • Read Permissions • Synchronize • Write Attributes • Write Extended Attributes
Write	• Create Files/Write Data • Create Folders/Append Data • Read Permissions • Synchronize • Write Attributes • Write Extended Attributes
List Folder Contents	• List Folder/Read Data • Read Attributes • Read Extended Attributes • Read Permissions • Synchronize • Traverse Folder/Execute File
Full Control	• Change Permissions • Create Files/Write Data • Create Folders/Append Data • Delete • Delete Subfolders and Files • List Folder/Read Data • Read Attributes • Read Extended Attributes • Read Permissions • Synchronize • Take Ownership • Write Attributes • Write Extended Attributes

Understanding Resource Ownership

As you study the NTFS permission system, you might realize that it seems possible to lock out a file or folder—that is, assign a combination of permissions that permits access to no one at all, leaving the file or folder inaccessible. In fact, this is true.

A user with administrative privileges can revoke his or her own permissions, as well as everyone else's, preventing them from accessing a resource. However, the NTFS permissions system includes a "back door" that prevents these orphaned files and folders from remaining permanently inaccessible.

Every file and folder on an NTFS drive has an owner, and the owner always has the ability to modify the permissions for the file or folder, even if the owner has no permissions him- or herself. By default, the owner of a file or folder is the user account that created it. However, any account possessing the Take Ownership special permission (or the Full Control standard permission) can take ownership of the file or folder.

The Administrator user can take ownership of any file or folder, even those from which the previous owner has revoked all Administrator permissions. After the Administrator user takes ownership of a file or folder, he or she cannot assign ownership back to the previous owner. This prevents the Administrator account from accessing other users' files undetected.

The other purpose for file and folder ownership is to calculate disk quotas. When you set quotas specifying the maximum amount of disk space particular users can consume, Windows calculates a user's current disk consumption by adding the sizes of all the files and folders that the user owns.

To change the ownership of a file or folder, you must open the *Effective Access* tab of the *Advanced Security Settings* dialog box and select the *Change link by the Owner* setting.

Combining Share and NTFS Permissions

You must understand that the NTFS and share permission systems are completely separate from each other, and that for network users to access files on a shared NTFS drive, they must have both the correct NTFS and the correct share permissions.

The share and NTFS permissions assigned to a file or folder can conflict. For example, if a user has the NTFS Write and Modify permissions for a folder and lacks the share Change permission, that user cannot modify a file in that folder.

The simplest of the Windows permission systems is the share permission system, which provides only basic protection for shared network resources. Share permissions provide only three levels of access, compared to the far more complex system of NTFS permissions. Network administrators generally prefer to use either NTFS or share permissions, but not both.

TAKE NOTE * The Effective Access displayed in the *Advanced Security Settings* dialog box shows only the effective NTFS permissions, not the share permissions that might also constrain user access.

Share permissions provide limited protection, but this might be sufficient on some small networks. Share permissions might also be the only alternative on a computer with FAT32 drives, because the FAT file system does not have its own permission system.

On networks already possessing a well-planned system of NTFS permissions, share permissions are not really necessary. In this case, you can safely leave the Full Control share permission to Everyone, overriding the default Read permission, and allow the NTFS permissions to provide security. Adding share permissions to the mix would only complicate the administration process, without providing any additional security.

■ Configuring Volume Shadow Copies

THE BOTTOM LINE

Volume Shadow Copies is a Windows Server 2012 feature that enables you to maintain previous versions of files on a server, so that if users accidentally delete or overwrite a file, they can access a copy. You can implement shadow copies only for an entire volume; you cannot select specific shares, folders, or files.

To configure a Windows Server 2012 volume to create shadow copies, use the following procedure.

CONFIGURE SHADOW COPIES

GET READY. Log on to Windows Server 2012, using an account with domain administrative privileges.

CERTIFICATION READY
Configure Volume Shadow
Copy Service (VSS).
Objective 2.1

1. Click the Windows Explorer icon on the taskbar to display the *Windows Explorer* window.

2. In the Folders list, expand the Computer container, right-click a volume and, from the context menu, select Configure Shadow Copies. The *Shadow Copies* dialog box appears, as shown in Figure 4-28.

Figure 4-28

The Shadow Copies dialog box

```
┌─────────────────────────────────────────────────────────┐
│  Shadow Copies                                      [x]   │
├─────────────────────────────────────────────────────────┤
│ ┌─────────────┐                                           │
│ │Shadow Copies│                                           │
│ ├─────────────┴───────────────────────────────────────┐  │
│ │ Shadow copies allow users to view the contents of    │  │
│ │ shared folders as the contents existed at previous    │  │
│ │ points in time. For information on Shadow Copies,     │  │
│ │ click here.                                            │  │
│ │                                                        │  │
│ │ Select a volume:                                       │  │
│ │ ┌────────────────────────────────────────────────┐   │  │
│ │ │ Volume    Next Run Time  Shares   Used          │   │  │
│ │ │ \\?\Vol... Disabled       0                      │   │  │
│ │ │ C:\       Disabled       0                       │   │  │
│ │ │ E:\       Disabled       1                       │   │  │
│ │ │ F:\       Disabled       0                       │   │  │
│ │ └────────────────────────────────────────────────┘   │  │
│ │                                                        │  │
│ │  [  Enable  ]   [  Disable  ]      [ Settings... ]    │  │
│ │                                                        │  │
│ │ Shadow copies of selected volume                       │  │
│ │ ┌──────────────────────────┐                          │  │
│ │ │                          │    [  Create Now  ]       │  │
│ │ │                          │                           │  │
│ │ │                          │    [  Delete Now  ]       │  │
│ │ │                          │                           │  │
│ │ │                          │    [  Revert...   ]       │  │
│ │ └──────────────────────────┘                          │  │
│ │                                                        │  │
│ │                        [  OK  ]   [  Cancel  ]        │  │
│ └────────────────────────────────────────────────────┘  │
└─────────────────────────────────────────────────────────┘
```

3. In the Select a Volume box, choose the volume for which you want to enable shadow copies. By default, when you enable shadow copies for a volume, the system uses the following settings:

   • It stores the shadow copies on the selected volume.

   • It reserves a minimum of 300 MB of disk space for the shadow copies.

   • It creates shadow copies at 7:00 AM and 12:00 PM every weekday.

4. To modify the default parameters, click Settings. The *Settings* dialog box appears, as shown in Figure 4-29.

Figure 4-29

The *Settings* dialog box

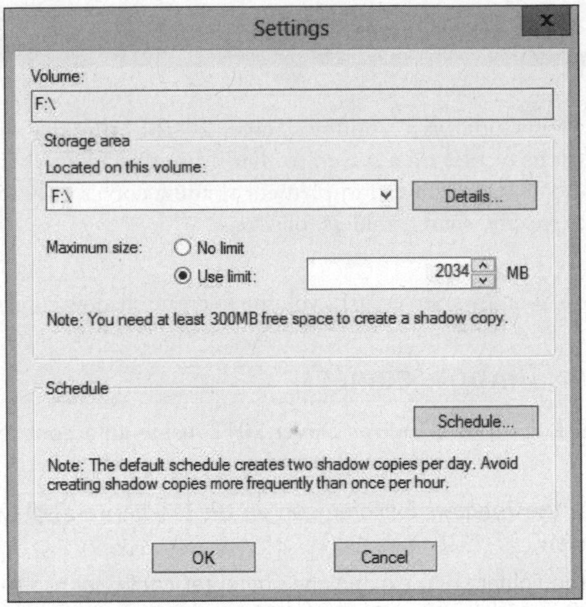

5. In the Storage Area box, specify the volume where you want to store the shadow copies. For a server operating with a high I/O load, such as a file server, Microsoft recommends that, for best performance, you create the Shadow Copies storage area on another volume, one that does not have Shadow Copies enabled. However, some third-party backup utilities require shadow copies to be stored on the same volume as the data.

6. Specify the Maximum Size for the storage area or choose the No Limit option. If the storage area fills up, the system begins deleting the oldest shadow copies, so if many large files are stored on the volume, increasing the size of the storage area can be beneficial. However, no matter how much space you allocate to the storage area, Windows Server 2012 supports a maximum of 64 shadow copies for each volume, after which the system begins deleting the oldest copies.

7. Click Schedule. The *Schedule* dialog box appears, as shown in Figure 4-30. By using the controls provided, you can modify the existing shadow copies tasks, delete them,

Figure 4-30

The *Schedule* dialog box

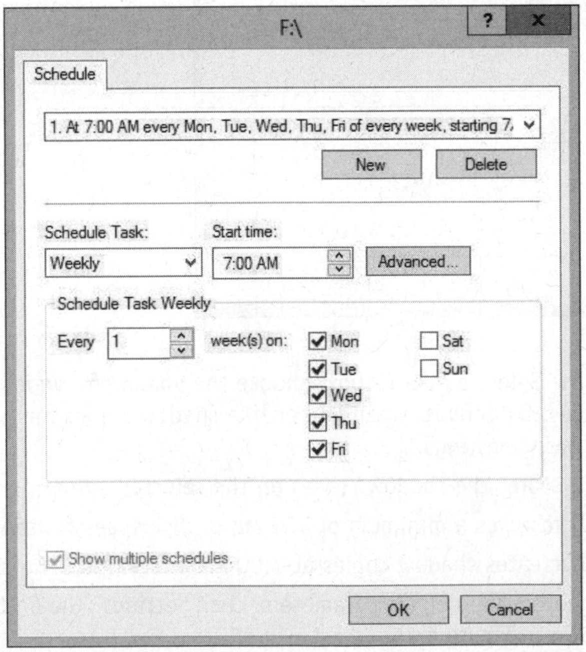

or create new ones, based on your users' needs. Scheduling shadow copies to occur too frequently can degrade server performance and cause copies to be aged out too quickly, whereas scheduling them to occur too infrequently can cause users to lose work because the most recent copy is too old.

8. Click OK twice to close the *Schedule* and *Settings* dialog boxes.

9. Click Enable. The system enables the Shadow Copies feature for the selected volume and creates the first copy in the designated storage area.

CLOSE Windows Explorer.

After you complete this procedure, users can restore previous versions of files on the selected volumes from the *Previous Versions* tab on any file or folder's Properties sheet.

■ Configuring NTFS Quotas

↓
THE BOTTOM LINE

Managing disk space is a constant concern for server administrators. One way to prevent users from monopolizing large amount of storage is to implement quotas. Windows Server 2012 supports two types of storage quotas. The more elaborate of the two is implemented as part of File Server Resource Manager. The second, simpler option is NTFS quotas.

CERTIFICATION READY
Configure NTFS quotas.
Objective 2.1

NTFS quotas enable you to set a storage limit for users of a particular volume. Depending on how you configure the quota, users exceeding the limit can be denied disk space or just receive a warning. The space consumed by individuals users is measured by the size of the files they own or create.

NTFS quotas are relatively limited in that you can set only a single limit for all users of a volume. The feature is also limited in the actions it can take in response to a user exceeding the limit. The quotas in File Server Resource Manager, by contrast, are much more flexible in the nature of the limits you can set and the responses of the program, which can send e-mail notifications, execute commands, and generate reports, as well as log events.

To configure NTFS quotas for a volume, use the following procedure.

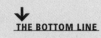 **CONFIGURE NTFS QUOTAS**

GET READY. Log on to Windows Server 2012, using an account with domain administrative privileges.

1. Click the Windows Explorer icon in the taskbar. The *Windows Explorer* window appears.

2. In the Folders list, expand the Computer container, right-click a volume and, from the context menu, select Properties. The Properties sheet for the volume appears.

3. Click the Quota tab to display the interface shown in Figure 4-31.

4. Select the Enable quota management check box to activate the rest of the controls.

5. If you want to prevent users from consuming more than their quota of disk space, select the Deny disk space to users exceeding quota limit check box.

6. Select the Limit disk space to radio button and specify amounts for the quota limit and the warning level.

Figure 4-31

The Quota tab of a volume's Properties sheet

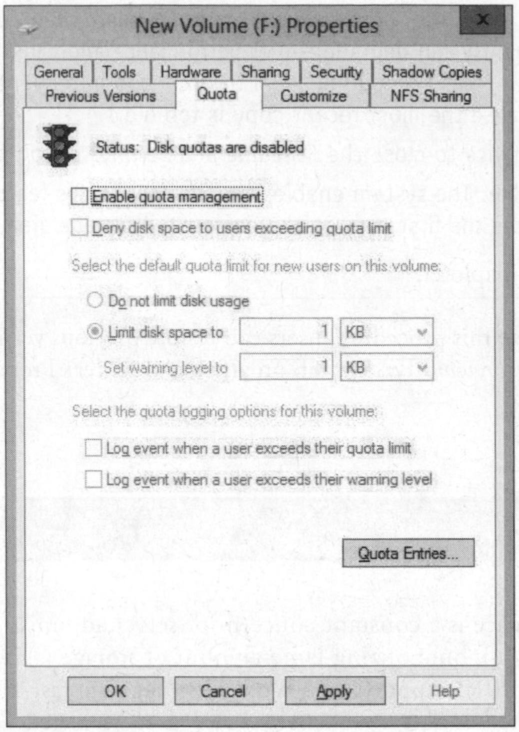

7. Select the Log event check boxes to control whether users exceeding the specified limits should trigger log entries.

8. Click OK to create the quota and close the Properties sheet.

CLOSE Windows Explorer.

SKILL SUMMARY

IN THIS LESSON, YOU LEARNED:

- Creating folder shares makes the data stored on a file server's disks accessible to network users.

- Windows Server 2012 has several sets of permissions that operate independently of each other, including NTFS permissions, share permissions, registry permissions, and Active Directory permissions.

- NTFS permissions enable you to control access to files and folders by specifying the tasks individual users can perform on them. Share permissions provide rudimentary access control for all files on a network share. Network users must have the proper share and NTFS permissions to access file server shares.

- Access-based enumeration (ABE) applies filters to shared folders based on an individual user's permissions to the files and subfolders in the share. Users who cannot access a particular shared resource cannot see that resource on the network.

- Offline Files is a Windows feature that enables client systems to maintain local copies of files they access from server shares.

- Volume Shadow Copies is a Windows Server 2012 feature that enables you to maintain previous versions of files on a server, so that if users accidentally delete or overwrite a file, they can access a copy. You can implement Shadow Copies only for an entire volume; you cannot select specific shares, folders, or files.

- NTFS quotas enable you to set a storage limit for users of a particular volume. Depending on how you configure the quota, users exceeding the limit can be denied disk space or just receive a warning.

Knowledge Assessment

Multiple Choice

Select one or more correct answers for each of the following questions.

1. Which of the following is the best description of a security principal?
   - a. the person granting permissions to network users
   - b. the network resource receiving permissions
   - c. a collection of individual special permissions
   - d. an object that assigns permissions

2. Which of the following statements about effective access is not true?
   - a. Inherited permissions take precedence over explicit permissions.
   - b. Deny permissions always override Allow permissions.
   - c. When a security principal receives Allow permissions from multiple groups, the permissions are combined to form the effective access permissions.
   - d. Effective access includes both permissions inherited from parents and permissions derived from group memberships.

3. Which of the following statements is not true in reference to resource ownership?
   - a. One of the purposes for file and folder ownership is to calculate disk quotas.
   - b. Every file and folder on an NTFS driver has an owner.
   - c. It is possible for any user possessing the Take Ownership special permission to assume the ownership of a file or folder.
   - d. It is possible to lock out a file or folder by assigning a combination of permissions that permits access to no one at all, including the owner of the file or folder.

4. Which of the following statements about permissions are true?
   - a. ACLs are composed of ACEs.
   - b. Basic permissions are composed of advanced permissions.
   - c. All permissions are stored as part of the protected resource.
   - d. All of the above.

5. What is the maximum number of shadow copies that a Windows Server 2012 system can maintain for each volume?
   - a. 8
   - b. 16
   - c. 64
   - d. 128

6. Which of the following terms describes the process of granting users access to file server shares by reading their permissions?
   - a. authentication
   - b. authorization
   - c. enumeration
   - d. assignment

7. Which of the following are tasks that you can perform using the quotas in File Server Resource Manager but you can't perform with NTFS quotas?
   a. Send an email message to an administrator when users exceed their limits.
   b. Specify different storage limits for each user.
   c. Prevent users from consuming any storage space on a volume beyond their allotted limit.
   d. Generate warnings to users when they approach their allotted storage limit.

8. In the NTFS permission system, combinations of advanced permissions are also known as _____ permissions.
   a. special
   b. basic
   c. share
   d. standard

Best Answer

Choose the letter that corresponds to the best answer. More than one answer choice may achieve the goal. Select the BEST answer.

1. What is a key reason for assigning permissions when configuring file and share access?
   a. Creates redundancy for file storage, providing a fault-tolerant file archive.
   b. Enables configuring offline files, improving performance.
   c. Improves data security, granting file and share access only to the users who need it.
   d. Assigns ownership to specific users, instilling responsibility and personal accountability.

2. You are deciding which file system to use. You need NTFS permission system support. You don't presently need encryption or compression, but might at a later date. What file system is your best choice?
   a. The traditional NTFS file system
   b. The new ReFS file system introduced in Windows Server 2012
   c. The FAT file system
   d. The NFS file system

3. If massive shares were split across multiple servers, what is the best way to make them appear as a single, unified directory tree?
   a. Windows Server 2012 Distributed File System
   b. Volume Shadow Copy Service
   c. Large volume split across multiple drives, attached to multiple servers
   d. Volumes created on a single Virtual Hard Disk (VHD)

4. Which of the following sets of permissions is responsible for controlling access to files and folders stored on a local disk volume?
   a. Share permissions
   b. NTFS permissions
   c. Registry permissions
   d. Active Directory permissions

5. Knowing how permissions can be cumulative or override each other is an important factor in understanding what?
   a. Permission inheritance
   b. Explicitly assigned permissions
   c. Permission precedence
   d. Effective access

Build a List

1. Order the steps to create a folder share.
    a. Select a File share profile option: SMB Share-Quick, SMB Share-Advanced, SMB Share-Applications, NFS Share-Quick, and NFS Share-Advanced.
    b. Click Shares in the submenu and, from the Tasks menu, select New Share.
    c. Select the Server, path, and share name.
    d. Log on to Windows Server 2012 with administrative privileges.
    e. Configure share settings: Enable access-based enumeration, Allow caching of share, Enable BranchCache on the file share, and Encrypt data access.
    f. Open Server Manager and click the File and Storage Services icon.
    g. Specify permissions to control access and click Next to confirm and create.

2. Order the steps to set share permissions.
    a. In Server Manager, click the File and Storage Services icon. In the submenu, click Shares.
    b. Log on to Windows Server 2012 with administrative privileges.
    c. Select the type of permissions to assign (Allow or Deny).
    d. Click Permissions and Customize Permissions.
    e. Click Add, and then select a principal (for example, user, computer, service account, or group).
    f. Click the Share tab.
    g. From the Shares tile, right-click a share and, from the context menu, select Properties.

3. Order the steps to assign basic NTFS permissions.
    a. Log on to Windows Server 2012 with administrative privileges.
    b. From the Shares tile, right-click a share and, from the context menu, select Properties.
    c. Select the type of permissions to assign (Allow or Deny).
    d. In Server Manager, click the File and Storage Services icon. In the submenu, click Shares.
    e. In the Advanced Security Settings dialog box, the Permissions tab shows the Permissions List. Click Add to add a Permission Entry.
    f. Select a principal (for example, user, computer, service account, or group).
    g. Click Permissions, and then click Customize Permissions.
    h. From the Applies To drop-down list, specify the subfolders and files that should inherit permissions you're assigning.

■ Business Case Scenarios

Scenario 4-1: Assigning Permissions

While you are working the help desk for a corporate network, a user named Leo calls to request access to the files for Trinity, a new classified project. The Trinity files are stored in a shared folder on a Windows Server 2012 workgroup file server, which is locked in a secured underground data storage facility in New Mexico. After verifying that he has the appropriate security clearance for the project, you create a new group on the file server called TRINITY_USERS and add Leo's user account to that group. Then, you add the TRINITY_USER group to the access control list for the Trinity folder on the file server, and assign the group the following NTFS permissions:

- Allow Modify
- Allow Read & Execute

- Allow List Folder Contents
- Allow Read
- Allow Write

Sometime later, Leo calls you to tell you that he is able to access the Trinity folder and read the files stored there, but he has been unable to save changes back to the server. What is the most likely cause of the problem?

Scenario 4-2: Accessing Orphaned Files

Libby, a new hire in the IT department, approaches you, her supervisor, ashen-faced. A few minutes earlier, the president of the company called the help desk and asked Libby to give his new assistant the permissions needed to access his personal budget spreadsheet. As she was attempting to assign the permissions, she accidentally deleted the BUDGET_USERS group from the spreadsheet's access control list. Libby is terrified because that group was the only entry in the file's ACL. Now, no one can access the spreadsheet file, not even the president or the Administrator account. Is there any way to gain access to the file, and if so, how?

Configuring Print and Document Services

70-410 EXAM OBJECTIVE

Objective 2.2 – Configure print and document services. This objective may include but is not limited to: Configure the Easy Print print driver; configure Enterprise Print Management; configure drivers; configure printer pooling; configure print priorities; configure printer permissions.

LESSON HEADING	EXAM OBJECTIVE
Deploying a Print Server	
Understanding the Windows Print Architecture	
Sharing a Printer	
Managing Printer Drivers	Configure drivers
Using Remote Access Easy Print	Configure the Easy Print print driver
Configuring Printer Security	Configure printer permissions
Managing Documents	
Managing Printers	Configure print priorities Configure printer pooling
Using the Print and Document Services Role	
Using the Print Management Console	Configure Enterprise Print Management

KEY TERMS

Enhanced Metafile (EMF)

print device

print server

printer

printer control language (PCL)

printer driver

printer pool

Remote Desktop Easy
  Print

spooler

XML Paper Specification
  (XPS)

■ Deploying a Print Server

↓ THE BOTTOM LINE Like the file-sharing functions discussed in previous lessons, print device sharing is one of the most basic applications for which local area networks were designed.

Installing, sharing, monitoring, and managing a single network print device is relatively simple, but when you are responsible for dozens or even hundreds of print devices on a large enterprise network, these tasks can be overwhelming.

Understanding the Windows Print Architecture

You need to understand the terms that Microsoft uses when referring to the various components of the network printing architecture.

Printing in Microsoft Windows typically involves these four components:

- A *print device* is the actual hardware that produces hard-copy documents on paper or other print media. Windows Server 2012 supports both *local print devices* directly attached to computer ports and *network interface print devices* connected to the network, either directly or through another computer.
- In Windows, a *printer* is the software interface through which a computer communicates with a print device. Windows Server 2012 supports numerous physical interfaces, including Universal Serial Bus (USB), IEEE 1394 (FireWire), parallel (LPT), serial (COM), Infrared Data Access (IrDA), Bluetooth ports, and network printing services such as lpr, Internet Printing Protocol (IPP), and standard TCP/IP ports.
- A *print server* is a computer (or standalone device) that receives print jobs from clients and sends them to print devices locally attached or connected to the network.
- A *printer driver* is a device driver that converts the print jobs generated by applications into an appropriate string of commands for a specific print device. Printer drivers are designed for specific print devices and provide applications with access to all a print device's features.

TAKE NOTE* *Printer* and *print device* are the most commonly misused terms of the Windows printing vocabulary. Obviously, many sources use *printer* to refer to the printing hardware. However, in Windows, printer and print device are not equivalents. For example, you can add a printer to a Windows Server 2012 computer without a physical print device being present. The computer can then host the printer, print server, and printer driver. These three components enable the computer to process the print jobs and store them in a print queue until the print device is available.

UNDERSTANDING WINDOWS PRINTING

These four components—print device, printer, print server, and printer driver—work together to process the print jobs produced by Windows applications and turn them into hard-copy documents, as shown in Figure 5-1.

Figure 5-1

The Windows print architecture

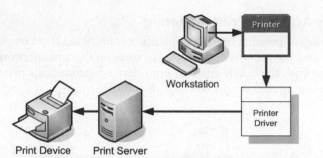

Before you can print documents in Windows, you must install at least one printer. To install a printer in Windows, you must do the following:

- Select the print device's specific manufacturer and model.
- Specify the port (or other interface) the computer will use to access the print device.
- Supply a printer driver specifically created for that print device.

When you print a document in an application, you select the destination printer for the print job.

The printer is associated with a printer driver that takes the commands generated by the application and converts them into a ***printer control language (PCL)***, a language understood by the printer. PCLs can be standardized, like the PostScript language, or they can be proprietary languages developed by the print device manufacturer.

The printer driver enables you to configure the print job to use the print device's various capabilities. These capabilities are typically incorporated into the printer's Properties sheet. For example, your word-processing application does not know if your print device is color, monochrome, or supports duplex printing; the printer driver provides support for print device features such as these.

After the printer processes a print job, it stores the job in a print queue, known as a ***spooler***. Depending on the arrangement of the printing components, the spooled jobs might be in a PCL format, ready to go to the print device, or in an interim format, in which case the printer driver must process the spooled jobs into the PCL format before sending them to the device. If other jobs are waiting to be printed, a new job might wait in the spooler for some time. When the server finally sends the job to the print device, the device reads the PCL commands and produces the hard-copy document.

TAKE NOTE *

The process of creating the required print elements is not necessarily a manual one. Some print device manufacturers supply a program that automatically creates and configures the required components.

WINDOWS PRINTING FLEXIBILITY

The flexibility of the Windows print architecture is manifested in the different ways that you can deploy the four printing components. A single computer can perform all the roles (except for the print device, of course), or you can distribute them across the network. The following sections describe four fundamental configurations that are the basis of most Windows printer deployments. You can scale these configurations up to accommodate a network of virtually any size.

Direct Printing

The simplest print architecture consists of one print device connected to one computer, also known as a *locally attached print device* (see Figure 5-2). When you connect a print device directly to a Windows Server 2012 computer and print from an application running on that system, the computer supplies the printer, printer driver, and print server functions.

Figure 5-2

A locally attached print device

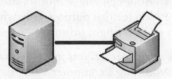

Locally Attached Printer Sharing

In addition to printing from an application running on that computer, you can also share the printer (and the print device) with other users on the same network. In this arrangement, the computer with the locally attached print device functions as a print server. Figure 5-3 shows the other computers on the network, the print clients.

Figure 5-3

Sharing a locally attached printer

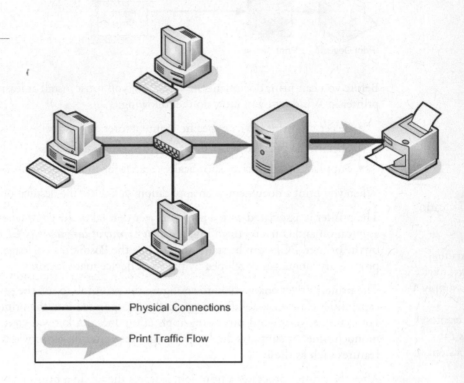

In the default Windows Server 2012 printer-sharing configuration, each client uses its own printer and printer driver. As before, the application running on the client computer sends the print job to the printer and the printer driver renders the job, based on the capabilities of the print device. In this arrangement, the printer driver creates a job file using one of two interim formats:

- *Enhanced Metafile (EMF)* is a standardized, highly portable print job format that is the default format used by the Windows 2000, Windows XP, and Windows Server 2003 print subsystems. The printer driver converts the application data into an EMF file, and the printer sends it to the print server, which stores it in the spooler. The spooler then uses the printer driver on the print server to render the job into the final PCL format understood by the print device.

- *XML Paper Specification (XPS)* is a new platform-independent document format first included with Windows Server 2008 and Windows Vista, in which print job files use a single XPS format for their entire journey to the print device, rather than be converted first to EMS and then to PCL.

The main advantage of this printing arrangement is that multiple users, located anywhere on the network, can send jobs to a single print device, connected to a computer functioning as a print server. The downside is that processing the print jobs for many users can impose a significant burden on the print server. Although any Windows computer can function as a print server, you should use a workstation for this purpose only when you have no more than a handful of print clients to support or a very light printing volume.

When you use a server computer as a print server, you must be aware of the system resources that the print server role requires. Dedicating a computer solely to print server duties is

TAKE NOTE✱

The format used depends on whether the client computer is running a newer XPS driver or an older driver that uses the EMF interim format.

necessary only when you have to support many print clients or a high volume of printing. In most cases, Windows servers that run the Print and Document Services role perform other functions as well. However, you must be judicious in your role assignments.

For example, one common practice is for a single server to function both as a print server and a file server. The usage patterns for these two roles complement each other in that they both tend to handle relatively brief transactions from clients. Running the Print and Document Services role on a domain controller is seldom a good idea, however, because network clients are constantly accessing the domain controller; their usage patterns are more conflicting than complementary.

Network-Attached Printing

The printing solutions discussed thus far involve print devices connected directly to a computer, using a USB or other port. However, you do not have to attach print devices to computers; instead, you can connect them directly to the network. Many print device models are equipped with network interface adapters, enabling you to attach a standard network cable. Some print devices have expansion slots into which you can install a network printer adapter purchased separately. Finally, for print devices with no networking capabilities, standalone network print servers are available, which connect to the network and enable you to attach one or more print devices. Print devices so equipped have their own IP addresses and typically an embedded web-based configuration interface.

With *network-attached print devices*, the primary deployment decision that you must make is to decide which computer will function as the print server. One simple, but often less than practical, option is to let each print client function as its own print server (see Figure 5-4). Each client processes and spools its own print jobs, connects to the print device using a TCP (Transmission Control Protocol) port, and sends the jobs directly to the device for printing.

Figure 5-4

A network-attached print device with multiple print servers

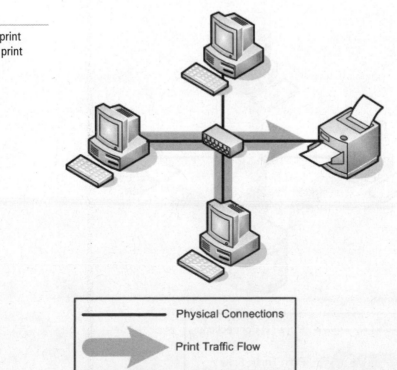

Even individual end users with no administrative assistance will find this arrangement simple to set up. However, the disadvantages are many, including the following:

- Users examining the print queue see only their own jobs.

- Users are oblivious of the other users accessing the print device. They have no way of knowing what other jobs have been sent to the print device, or how long it will be until the print device completes their jobs.

- Administrators have no way of centrally managing the print queue, because each client has its own print queue.

- Administrators cannot implement advanced printing features, such as printer pools or remote administration.

- Error messages appear only on the computer that originated the job the print device is currently processing.

- All print job processing is performed by the client computer, rather than be partially offloaded to an external print server.

For these reasons, this arrangement is suitable only for small workgroup networks that do not have dedicated administrators supporting them.

Network-Attached Printer Sharing

The other, far more popular, option for network-attached printing is to designate one computer as a print server and use it to service all print clients on the network. To do this, you install a printer on one computer, the print server, and configure it to access the print device directly through a TCP port. Then, you share the printer, just as you would a locally attached print device, and configure the clients to access the print share.

As you can see in Figure 5-5, the physical configuration is the same as in the previous arrangement, but the logical path the print jobs take on the way to the print device is different. Rather than go straight to the print device, the jobs go to the print server, which spools them and sends them to the print device in order.

Figure 5-5

A network-attached print device with a single shared print server

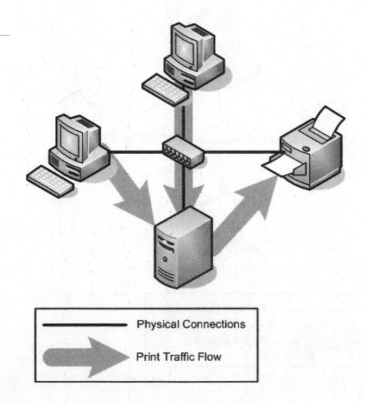

Physical Connections

Print Traffic Flow

With this arrangement, virtually all the disadvantages of the multiple print server arrangement become advantages:

- A single print queue stores all client jobs, so users and administrators can see a complete list of jobs waiting to be printed.
- Part of the job-rendering burden shifts to the print server, returning control of the client computer to the user more quickly.
- Administrators can manage all queued jobs from a remote location.
- Print error messages appear on all client computers.
- Administrators can implement printer pools and other advanced printing features.
- Administrators can manage security, auditing, monitoring, and logging functions from a central location.

Advanced Printing Configurations

You can use the four configurations described in the previous sections as building blocks to create printing solutions for their networks. You can use many possible variations to create a network printing architecture that supports your organization's needs. Some of the more advanced possibilities are as follows:

- You can connect a single printer to multiple print devices, creating a ***printer pool***. On a busy network with many print clients, the print server can distribute large numbers of incoming jobs among several identical print devices to provide more timely service and fault tolerance.
- You can connect multiple print devices that support different forms and paper sizes to a single print server, which can distribute jobs with different requirements to the appropriate print devices.
- You can connect multiple print servers to a single print device. By creating multiple print servers, you can configure different priorities, security settings, auditing, and monitoring parameters for different users. For example, you can create a high-priority print server for company executives, whereas junior users send their jobs to a lower-priority server. This ensures that the executives' jobs are printed first, even if the servers are both connected to the same print device.

Sharing a Printer

Using Windows Server 2012 as a print server can be simple or complex, depending on how many clients the server has to support and how much printing they do.

For a home or small business network, in which a handful of users need occasional access to the printer, no special preparation is necessary. However, if the computer must support heavy printer use, you might need the following hardware upgrades:

- **Additional system memory:** Processing print jobs requires system memory, just like any other application. If you plan to run heavy print traffic through a Windows Server 2012 server, in addition to other roles or applications, make sure that the computer has sufficient memory to support all its functions.
- **Additional disk space:** When a print device is busy, the print server spools additional incoming print jobs temporarily on a hard drive until the print device is free to receive them. Depending on the amount of print traffic and the types of print jobs, the print server might require a substantial amount of temporary storage for this purpose. Be sure also to plan for the extra storage space needed to support temporary print device outages. When a printer runs out of paper, ink, or toner, it remains idle until replenished, and the server must retain all incoming print jobs in the queue. This can cause the server to require even more storage space than normal.

• **Make the computer a dedicated print server:** In addition to memory and disk space, using Windows Server 2012 as a print server requires processor clock cycles, just like any other application. On a server handling heavy print traffic, other roles and applications are likely to experience substantial performance degradation. If you need a print server to handle heavy traffic, consider dedicating the computer to print server tasks only and deploying other roles and applications elsewhere.

On a Windows Server 2012 computer, you can share a printer as you are installing it or at any time afterward. On older printers, initiate the installation process by launching the *Add Printer Wizard* from the *Printers* control panel. However, most of the print devices on the market today use either a USB connection to a computer or an Ethernet connection to a network.

In the case of a USB-connected printer, you plug the print device into a USB port on the computer and turn on the device to initiate the installation process. Manual intervention is only required when Windows Server 2012 does not have a driver for the print device.

For network-attached print devices, an installation program supplied with the product locates the print device on the network, installs the correct drivers, creates a printer on the computer, and configures the printer with the proper IP address and other settings.

After you install the printer on the Windows Server 2012 computer that functions as your print server, you can share it with your network clients, using the following procedure.

SHARE A PRINTER

GET READY. Log on to Windows Server 2012 using a domain account with Administrator privileges.

1. Open the Control Panel and select Hardware> Devices and Printers. The *Devices and Printers* window appears, as shown in Figure 5-6.

Figure 5-6

The *Devices and Printers* window

2. Right-click the icon for the printer you want to share and, from the context menu, select Printer Properties. The printer's Properties sheet appears.

The context menu for every printer provides access to two Properties sheets. The *Printer Properties* menu item opens the Properties sheet for the printer and the Properties menu item opens the Properties sheet for the print device.

3. On the *Sharing* tab (see Figure 5-7), select the Share this printer check box. The *Share name* box shows the printer name. You can accept the default name or supply one of your own.

Figure 5-7

The Sharing tab of a printer's Properties sheet

4. Select one or both of the following optional check boxes:
   - Render print jobs on client computers minimizes the resource utilization on the print server by forcing the print clients to perform the bulk of the print processing.
   - List in the directory creates a new printer object in the Active Directory Domain Services (AD DS) database, enabling domain users to locate the printer by searching the directory. This option is available only when the computer is a member of an AD DS domain.
5. Click Additional Drivers to display the *Additional Drivers* dialog box. This dialog box enables you to load printer drivers for other Windows platforms, such as Itanium and x86. When you install the alternate drivers, the print server automatically supplies them to clients running those operating system versions.
6. Select any combination of the available check boxes and click OK. For each check box you selected, Windows Server 2012 displays a *Printer Drivers* dialog box.

7. In each *Printer Drivers* dialog box, key or browse to the location of the printer drivers for the selected operating system, and then click OK.

8. Click OK to close the *Additional Drivers* dialog box.

9. Click OK to close the Properties sheet for the printer. The printer icon in the *Printers* control panel now includes a symbol indicating that it is shared.

CLOSE the control panel.

At this point, the printer is available to clients on the network.

USING WINDOWS POWERSHELL

To share a printer with Windows PowerShell, use the `Set-Printer` cmdlet with the following syntax:

```
Set-Printer -Name "printer name" -Share $true|$false
-ShareName "share name"
```

For example, to share a printer called HP LaserJet and call the share HP, use the following command.

```
Set-Printer -Name "HP LaserJet" -Share $true
-ShareName "HP LaserJet"
```

Managing Printer Drivers

Printer driver components enable your computers to manage the capabilities of your print devices. When you install a printer on a server running Windows Server 2012, you install a driver that other Windows computers also can use.

Point and Print is the Windows function that enables clients to access the printers installed on print servers. A user on a workstation can select a printer on a server, and Windows automatically installs the driver that the client needs to process its own print jobs and send them to that printer.

The printer drivers you install on Windows Server 2012 are the same drivers that Windows workstations and other server versions use, with one stipulation. As a 64-bit platform, Windows Server 2012 uses 64-bit device drivers, which are suitable for other computers running 64-bit versions of Windows. If you have 32-bit Windows systems on your network, however, you must install a 32-bit driver on the server for those systems to use.

The *Additional Drivers* dialog box, accessible from the *Sharing* tab of a printer's Properties sheet, enables you to install drivers for other processor platforms. However, you must install those drivers from a computer running on the alternative platform.

In other words, to install a 32-bit driver for a printer on a server running Windows Server 2012, you must access the printer's Properties sheet from a computer running 32-bit version of Windows. You can do this by accessing the printer directly through the network using Windows Explorer, or by running the Print Management snap-in on the 32-bit system and using it to manage your Windows Server 2012 print server.

TAKE NOTE*

For the server to provide drivers supporting different platforms to client computers, you must make sure when installing the drivers for the same print device that they have the exact same name. For example, Windows Server 2012 treats *HP LaserJet 5200 PCL6* and *HP LaserJet 5200 PCL 6* as two completely different drivers. The names must be identical for the server to apply them properly.

Using Remote Access Easy Print

When a Remote Desktop Services client connects to a server, it runs applications using the server's processor(s) and memory. However, if that client wants to print a document from one of those applications, it wants the print job to go to the print device connected to the client computer.

Remote Desktop Easy Print is the component that enables Remote Desktop clients to print to their local print devices. Easy Print takes the form of a printer driver installed on the server, along with the Remote Desktop Session Host role service.

The Remote Desktop Easy Print driver appears in the Print Management snap-in automatically (see Figure 5-8), but it is not associated with a particular print device. Instead, the driver functions as a redirector, enabling the server to access the printers on the connected clients.

CERTIFICATION READY
Configure the Easy Print print driver.
Objective 2.2

Figure 5-8

The Remote Desktop Easy Print driver on a Remote Desktop Services server

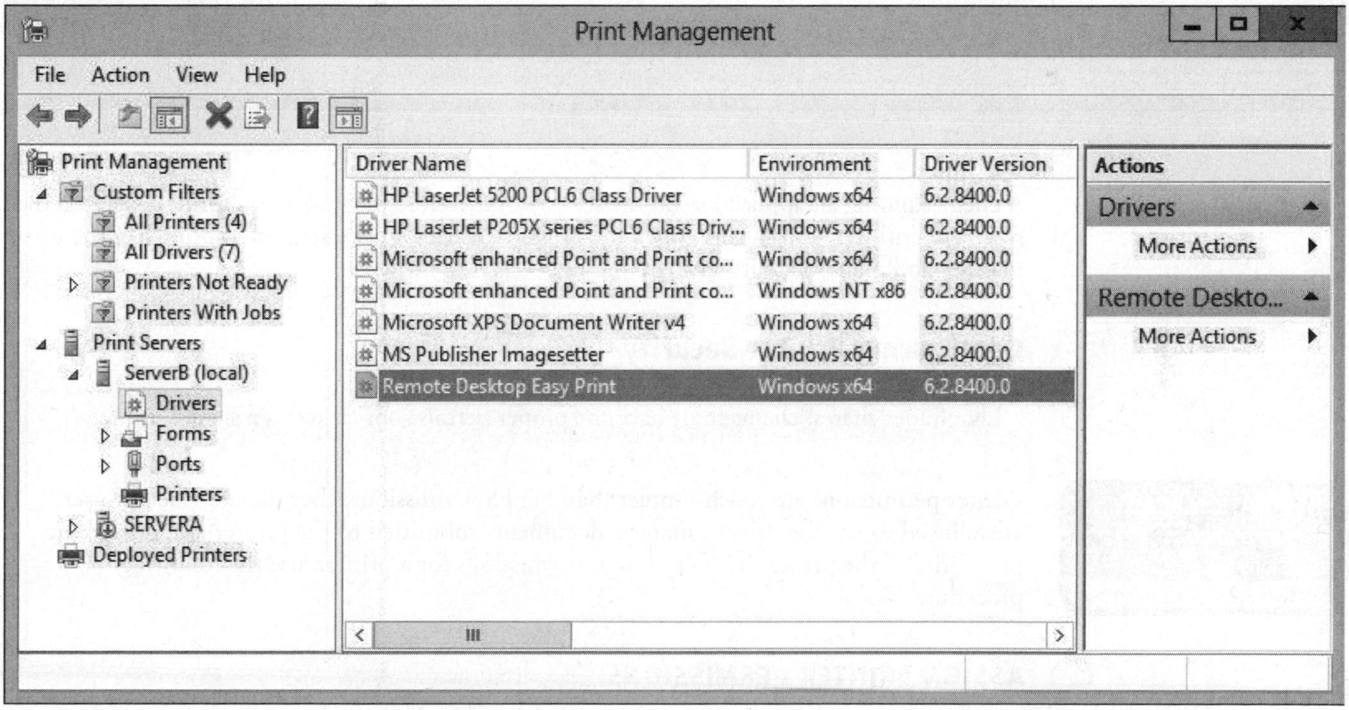

Easy Print requires no configuration other than the installation of the Remote Desktop Services role. However, as soon as it is operational, it provides the server administrator with additional access to the printers on the Remote Desktop clients.

When a Remote Desktop client connects to a server via the Remote Desktop Connection program or the RD Web Access site, the printers installed on the client system are redirected to the server and appear in the Print Management snap-in as redirected server printers, as shown in Figure 5-9.

Figure 5-9

Printers redirected by Easy
Print on a Remote Desktop
server

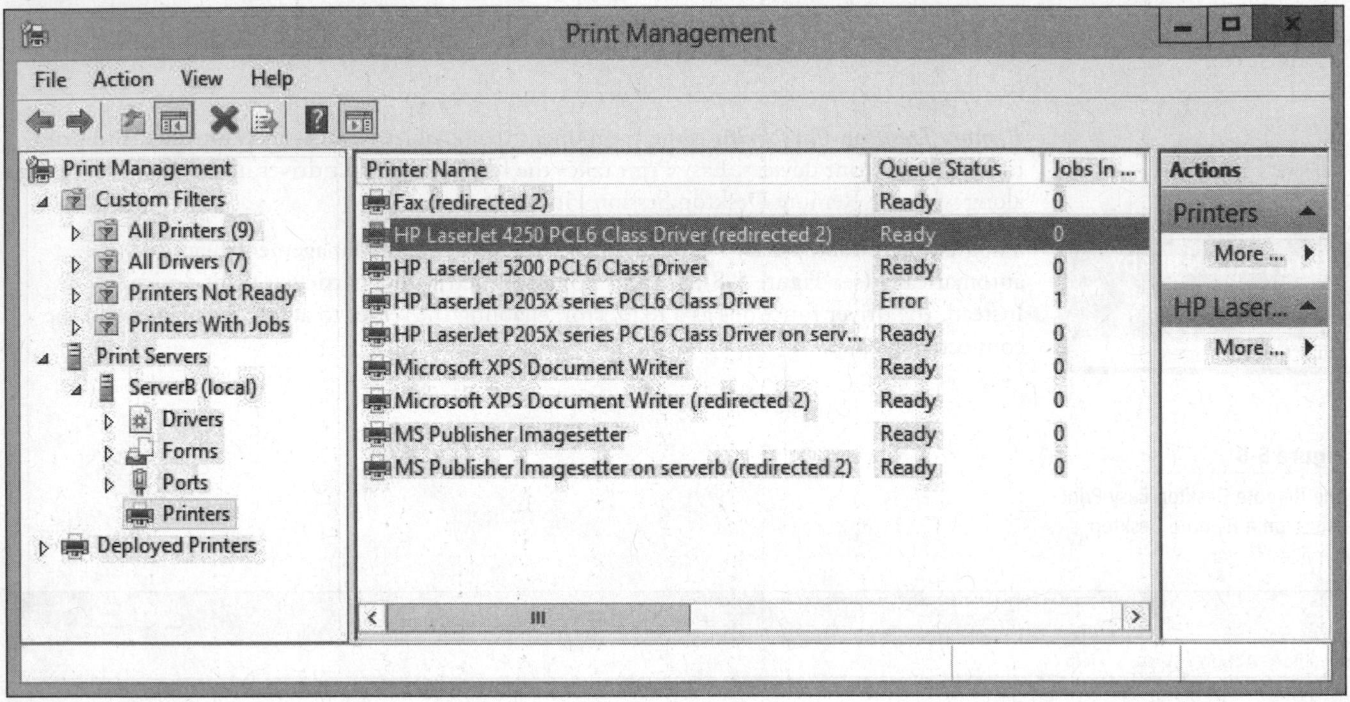

A client running an application on the server can therefore print to a local print device via the
redirected printer. You can also open the Properties sheet for the redirected printer in the usual
manner and manipulate its settings.

Configuring Printer Security

Like folder shares, clients must have the proper permissions to access a shared printer.

CERTIFICATION READY
Configure printer
permissions.
Objective 2.2

Printer permissions are much simpler than NTFS permissions; they dictate whether users
are allowed to use the printer, manage documents submitted to the printer, or manage the
properties of the printer itself. To assign permissions for a printer, use the following
procedure.

➔ ASSIGN PRINTER PERMISSIONS

GET READY. Log on to Windows Server 2012 using a domain account with Administrator
privileges.

1. Open the Control Panel and select Hardware> Devices and Printers. The *Devices and
   Printers* window appears.
2. Right-click one of the printer icons in the window and, from the context menu, select
   Printer Properties. The printer's Properties sheet appears.

   Click the Security tab, as shown in Figure 5-10. The top half of the display lists all
   the security principals now possessing permissions to the selected printer. The
   bottom half lists the permissions held by the selected security principal.

Figure 5-10

The Security tab of a printer's Properties sheet

HP LaserJet P205X series PCL6 Class Driver Properties

General | Sharing | Ports | Advanced | Color Management | Security | Device Settings

Group or user names:

- Everyone
- ALL APPLICATION PACKAGES
- CREATOR OWNER
- Administrator
- Administrators (SERVERB\Administrators)

Add...   Remove

Permissions for Everyone   Allow   Deny

Print	✓	☐
Manage this printer	☐	☐
Manage documents	☐	☐
Special permissions	☐	☐

For special permissions or advanced settings, click Advanced.   Advanced

Learn about access control and permissions

OK   Cancel   Apply

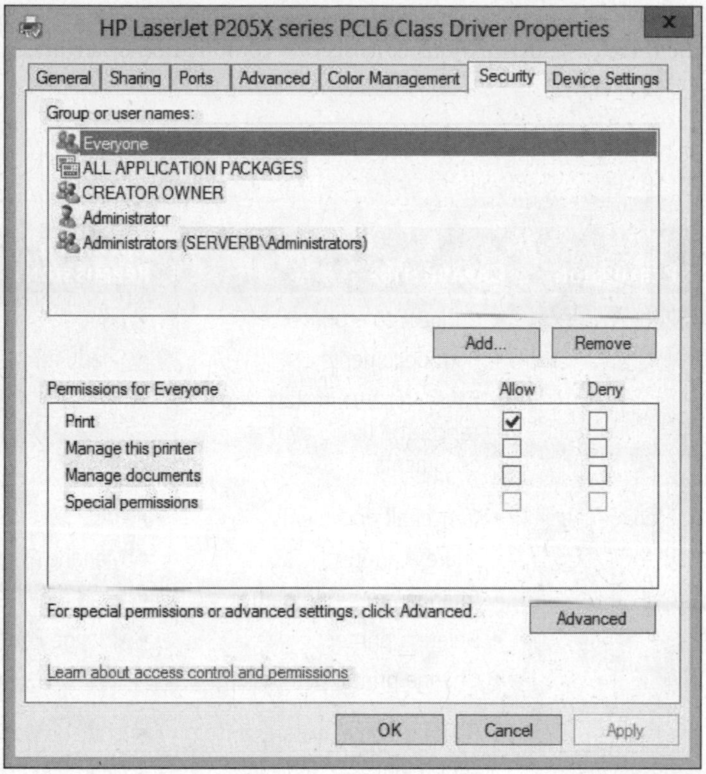

3. Click Add. The *Select Users, Computers, Service Accounts, or Groups* dialog box appears, as shown in Figure 5-11.

Figure 5-11

The *Select Users, Computers, Service Accounts, or Groups* dialog box

Select Users, Computers, Service Accounts, or Groups   ? X

Select this object type:

Users, Groups, or Built-in security principals   Object Types...

From this location:

adatum.local   Locations...

Enter the object names to select (examples):

Check Names

Advanced...   OK   Cancel

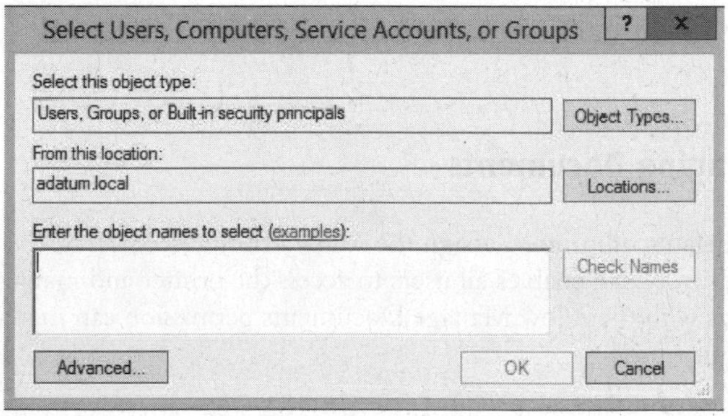

TAKE NOTE ✱

This procedure assumes that the Windows Server 2012 computer is a member of an Active Directory domain. When you assign printer permissions on a standalone server, you select local user and group accounts to be the security principals that receive the permissions.

4. In the Enter the object names to select text box, type a user or group name, and then click OK. The user or group appears in the *Group or user names* list of the printer's properties sheet.

5. Select the security principal you added, and then select or clear the check boxes in the bottom half of the properties sheet to Allow or Deny the user any of the basic permissions.

6. Click OK to close the Properties sheet.

CLOSE the control panel.

Like NTFS permissions, printer permissions come in two types: basic and advanced. Each of the three basic permissions consists of a combination of advanced permissions, as listed in Table 5-1.

Table 5-1

Basic Printer Permissions

Permission	Capabilities	Advanced Permissions	Default Assignments
Print	• Connect to a printer • Print documents • Pause, resume, restart, and cancel the user's own documents	• Print • Read Permissions	Assigned to the Everyone special identity
Manage this printer	• Cancel all documents • Share a printer • Change printer properties • Delete a printer • Change printer permissions	• Print • Manage Printers • Read Permissions • Change Permissions • Take Ownership	Assigned to the Administrators group
Manage documents	• Pause, resume, restart, and cancel all users' documents • Control job settings for all documents	• Manage Documents • Read Permissions • Change Permissions • Take Ownership	Assigned to the Creator Owner special identity

Managing Documents

By default, all printers assign the Allow Print permission to the Everyone special identity, which enables all users to access the printer and manage their own documents. Users with the Allow Manage Documents permission can manage any users' documents.

Managing documents refers to pausing, resuming, restarting, and cancelling documents currently waiting in a print queue. Windows Server 2012 provides a print queue window for every printer, which enables you to view the jobs currently waiting to be printed. To manage documents, use the following procedure.

 MANAGE DOCUMENTS

GET READY. Log on to Windows Server 2012 using any user account.

1. Open the Control Panel and select Hardware> Devices and Printers. The *Devices and Printers* window appears.

2. Right-click one of the printer icons and, from the context menu, select See what's printing. A print queue window named for the printer appears, as shown in Figure 5-12.

Figure 5-12

A Windows Server 2012 print queue window

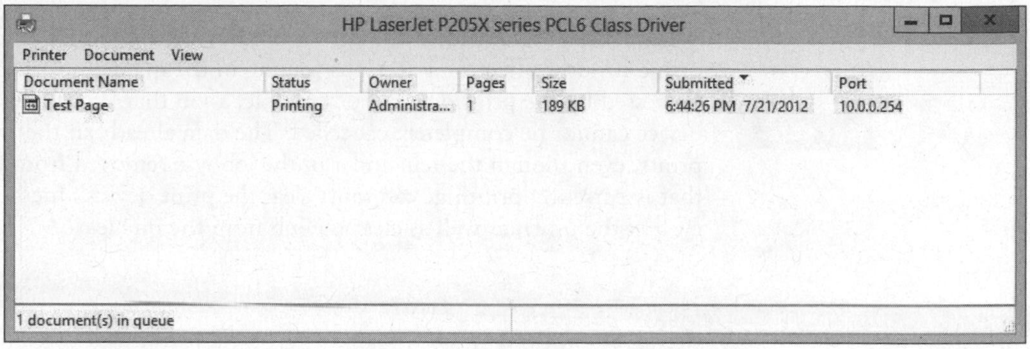

HP LaserJet P205X series PCL6 Class Driver						
Printer Document View						
Document Name	Status	Owner	Pages	Size	Submitted ▼	Port
▣ Test Page	Printing	Administra...	1	189 KB	6:44:26 PM 7/21/2012	10.0.0.254

1 document(s) in queue

3. Select a menu item to perform the associated function.

4. Close the print queue window.

CLOSE the control panel.

Table 5-2 lists the document management options available in the print queue window.

Table 5-2

Document Management Menu Commands

MENU ITEM	FUNCTION
Printer > Connect	Establishes a connection to a remote printer, enabling the computer to send print jobs to it
Printer > Set as default printer	Enables you to specify whether this should be the default printer for the computer
Printer > Printing preferences	Opens the Preferences dialog box supplied by the printer driver
Printer > Update driver	Enables you to supply an updated version of the printer driver
Printer > Pause Printing	Causes the print server to stop sending jobs to the print device until you restart it by selecting the same menu item again; all pending jobs remain in the queue
Printer > Cancel All Documents	Removes all pending jobs from the queue. In-progress jobs complete normally
Printer > Sharing	Opens the printer's Properties sheet and displays the *Sharing* tab
Printer > Use Printer Offline	Enables users to send jobs to the printer, where they remain unprocessed in the queue, until you select the same menu item again
Printer > Properties	Opens the Properties sheet for the printer
Document > Pause	Pauses the selected document, preventing the print server from sending the job to the print device
Document > Resume	Causes the print server to resume processing a selected document that was previously been paused
Document > Restart	Causes the print server to discard the current job and restart printing the selected document from the beginning
Document > Cancel	Causes the print server to remove the selected document from the queue
Document > Properties	Opens the Properties sheet for the selected job

TAKE NOTE

When managing documents, keep in mind that the commands accessible from the print queue window affect only the jobs waiting in the queue, not those currently being processed by the print device. For example, a job that is partially transmitted to the print device cannot be completely cancelled. The data already in the print device's memory prints, even though the remainder of the job was removed from the queue. To stop a job that is currently printing, you must clear the print device's memory (by resetting or power cycling the unit), as well as clear the job from the queue.

USING WINDOWS POWERSHELL

To manage queued documents with Windows PowerShell, you use cmdlets such as the following:

`Remove-PrintJob`

`Restart-PrintJob`

`Suspend-PrintJob`

`Resume-PrintJob`

Managing Printers

Users with the Allow Manage This Printer permission can go beyond manipulating queued documents; they can reconfigure the printer itself. Managing a printer refers to altering the operational parameters that affect all users and controlling access to the printer.

Generally, most software-based tasks that fall under the category of managing a printer are those you perform once while setting up the printer for the first time. Day-to-day printer management is more likely to involve physical maintenance, such as clearing print jams, reloading paper, and changing toner or ink cartridges. However, the following sections examine some of the printer manager's typical configuration tasks.

SETTING PRINTER PRIORITIES

In some cases, you might want to give certain users in your organization priority access to a print device so that when print traffic is heavy, their jobs are processed before those of other users. To do this, you must create multiple printers, associate them with the same print device, and then modify their priorities, as described in the following procedure.

CERTIFICATION READY
Configure print priorities.
Objective 2.2

➜ SET A PRINTER'S PRIORITY

GET READY. Log on to Windows Server 2012 using an account with the Manage This Printer permission.

1. Open the Control Panel and select Hardware> Devices and Printers. The *Devices and Printers* window appears.
2. Right-click one of the printer icons and then, from the context menu, select Printer Properties. The Properties sheet for the printer appears.
3. On the *Advanced* tab (see Figure 5-13), set the Priority spin box to a number representing the highest priority you want to set for the printer. Higher numbers represent higher priorities. The highest possible priority is 99.

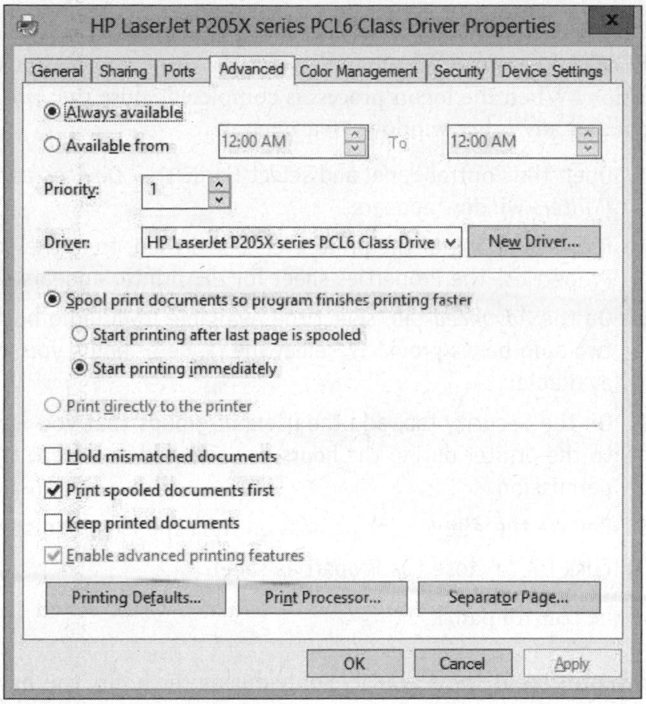

Figure 5-13

The Advanced tab of a printer's Properties sheet

HP LaserJet P205X series PCL6 Class Driver Properties   ✕

General | Sharing | Ports | Advanced | Color Management | Security | Device Settings

◉ Always available

○ Available from   12:00 AM   To   12:00 AM

Priority: 1

Driver: HP LaserJet P205X series PCL6 Class Drive ⌄   New Driver...

◉ Spool print documents so program finishes printing faster
  ○ Start printing after last page is spooled
  ◉ Start printing immediately
○ Print directly to the printer

☐ Hold mismatched documents
☑ Print spooled documents first
☐ Keep printed documents
☑ Enable advanced printing features

Printing Defaults...   Print Processor...   Separator Page...

OK   Cancel   Apply

> **TAKE NOTE***
>
> The values of the *Priority* spin box do not have any absolute significance; they are pertinent only in relation to each other. As long as one printer has a higher priority value than another, the server processes its print jobs first. In other words, it does not matter if the higher priority value is 9 or 99, as long as the lower priority value is less.

4. On the *Security* tab, add the users or groups that you want to provide with high-priority access to the printer and assign the Allow Print permission to them.

5. Revoke the Allow Print permission from the Everyone special identity.

6. Click OK to close the Properties sheet.

7. Create an identical printer, using the same printer driver and pointing to the same print device. Leave the Priority setting to its default value of 1 and leave the default permissions in place.

8. Rename the printers, specifying the priority assigned to each one.

CLOSE the control panel.

Inform the privileged users that they should send their jobs to the high-priority printer. All jobs sent to that printer are processed before those sent to the other, lower-priority printer.

SCHEDULING PRINTER ACCESS

Sometimes, you might want to limit certain users' access to a printer to specific times of the day or night. For example, your organization might have a color laser printer that the company's graphic designers use during business hours, but you permit other employees to use it after 5:00 PM. To do this, you associate multiple printers with a single print device, much as you did to set different printer priorities.

After creating two printers, both pointing to the same print device, you configure their scheduling using the following procedure.

⊙ SCHEDULE PRINTER ACCESS

GET READY. Log on to Windows Server 2012 using an account with the Manage Printer permission. When the logon process is completed, close the *Initial Configuration Tasks* window and any other windows that open.

1. Open the Control Panel and select Hardware> Devices and Printers. The *Devices and Printers* window appears.

2. Right-click one of the printer icons and then, from the context menu, select Printer Properties. The Properties sheet for the printer appears.

3. On the *Advanced* tab, select the Available from radio button and then, in the two spin boxes provided, select the range of hours you want the printer to be available.

4. On the Security tab, add the users or groups that you want to provide with access to the printer during the hours you selected and grant them the Allow Print permission.

5. Revoke the Allow Print permission from the Everyone special identity.

6. Click OK to close the Properties sheet.

CLOSE the control panel.

The two printers are now available only during the hours you have specified.

CREATING A PRINTER POOL

CERTIFICATION READY
Configure printer pooling.
Objective 2.2

As mentioned earlier, a printer pool increases the production capability of a single printer by connecting it to multiple print devices. When you create a printer pool, the print server sends each incoming job to the first print device it finds that is not busy. This effectively distributes the jobs among the available print devices, as shown in Figure 5-14, providing users with more rapid service.

Figure 5-14

Printer pooling shares print jobs among multiple print devices

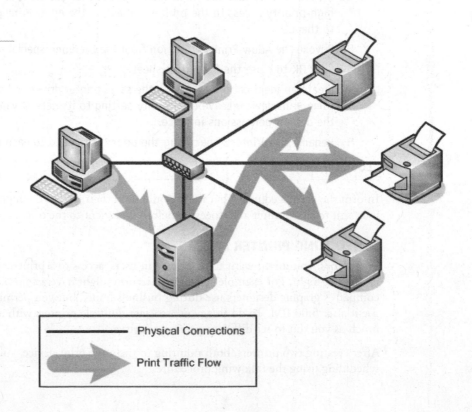

Physical Connections

Print Traffic Flow

To configure a printer pool, use the following procedure.

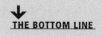 **CREATE A PRINTER POOL**

GET READY. Log on to Windows Server 2012 using an account with the Manage Printer permission. When the logon process is completed, close the Initial *Configuration Tasks* window and any other windows that open.

1. Open the Control Panel and select Hardware> Devices and Printers. The *Devices and Printers* window appears.

2. Right-click one of the printer icons and then, from the context menu, select Printer Properties. The Properties sheet for the printer appears.

3. On the Ports tab, select all ports to which the print devices are connected (see Figure 5-15).

Figure 5-15

The Ports tab of a printer's Properties sheet

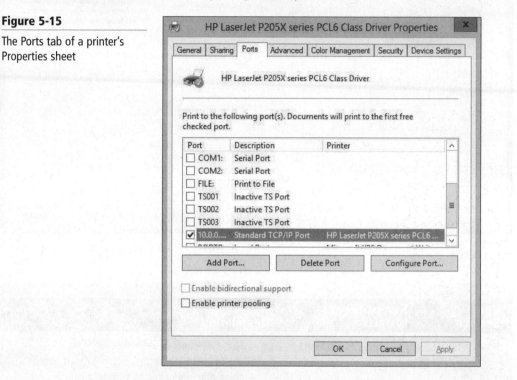

4. Select the Enable printer pooling check box, and then click OK.

CLOSE the control panel.

To create a printer pool, you must have at least two identical print devices, or at least print devices that use the same printer driver. The print devices must be in the same location, because you cannot tell which print device will process a given document. You must also connect all print devices in the pool to the same print server. If the print server is a Windows Server 2012 computer, you can connect the print devices to any viable ports.

■ Using the Print and Document Services Role

THE BOTTOM LINE

All printer sharing and management capabilities discussed in the previous sections are available on any Windows Server 2012 computer in its default installation configuration. However, installing the Print and Document Services role on the computer provides additional tools that are particularly useful to administrators involved with network printing on an enterprise scale.

When you install the Print and Document Services role using Server Manager's Add Roles and Features Wizard, a *Select role services* page appears, as shown in Figure 5-16, enabling you to select from the options listed in Table 5-3.

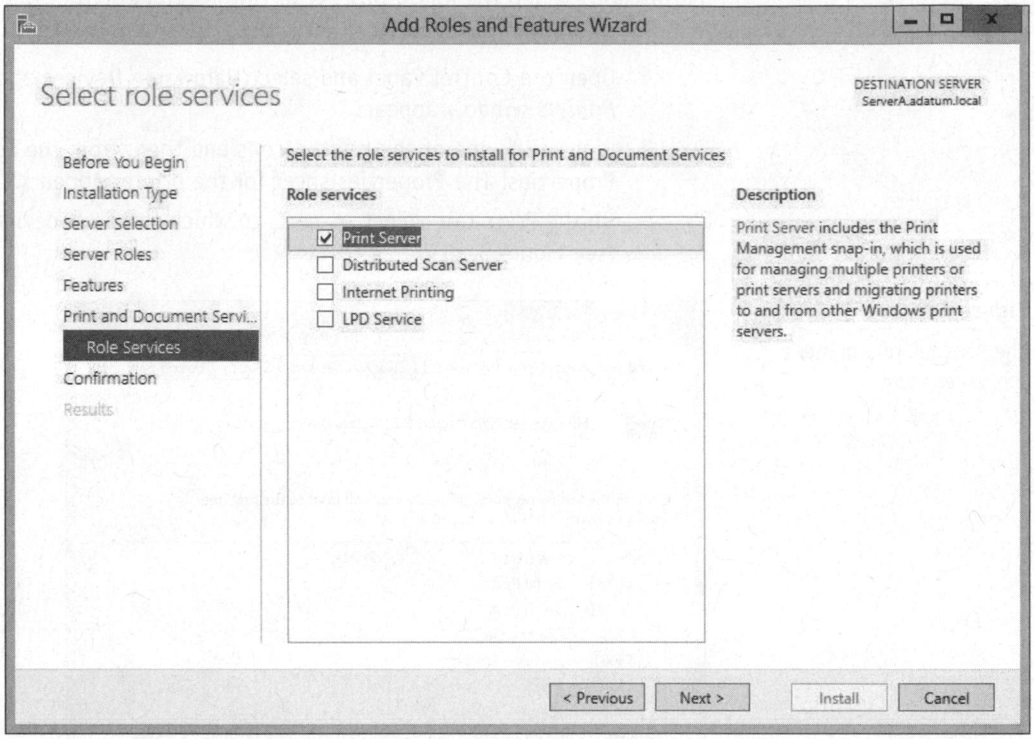

Figure 5-16

The *Select role services* page for the Print Services role

Table 5-3

Role Service Selections for the Print Services Role

ROLE SERVICE	SYSTEM SERVICES INSTALLED	DESCRIPTION
Print Server	Print Spooler (Spooler)	• Installs the Print Management console for Microsoft Management Console (MMC), which enables administrators to deploy, monitor, and manage printers throughout the enterprise. • Is the only required role service when you add the Print Services role.
Distributed Scan Server	Distributed Scan Server (ScanServer)	• Enables the computer to receive documents from network-based scanners and forward them to the appropriate users.
Internet Printing	• World Wide Web Publishing Service (w3svc) • IIS Admin Service (iisadmin)	• Creates a website that enables users on the Internet to send print jobs to shared Windows printers.
LPD Service	TCP/IP Print Server (LPDSVC)	• Enables UNIX clients running the LPR (line printer remote) program to send their print jobs to Windows printers.

To install the Internet Printing role service, you must also install the Web Server (IIS) role with certain specific role services. The *Add Roles and Features Wizard* enforces these dependencies by displaying an *Add features that are required for Internet Printing?* message box (see Figure 5-17) when you select the Internet Printing role service. Clicking *Add Features* causes the wizard to select the exact role services within Web Server (IIS) role that the Internet Printing service needs.

Figure 5-17

The *Add features that are required for Internet Printing?* message box

Figure 5-18

The Print Services node in Server Manager

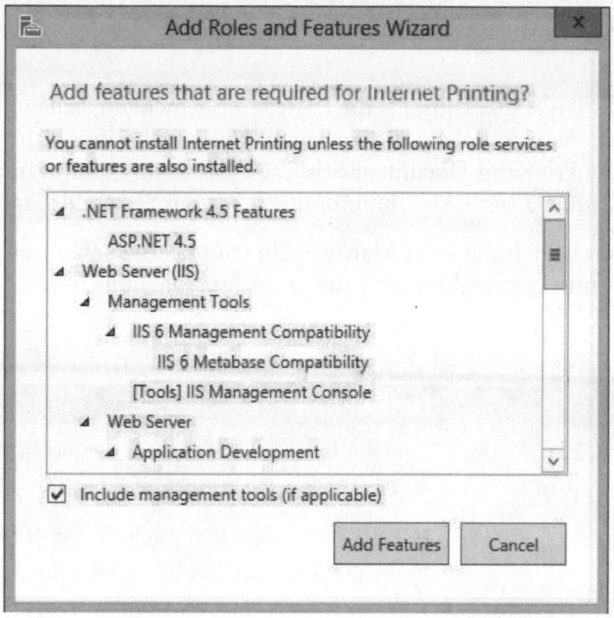

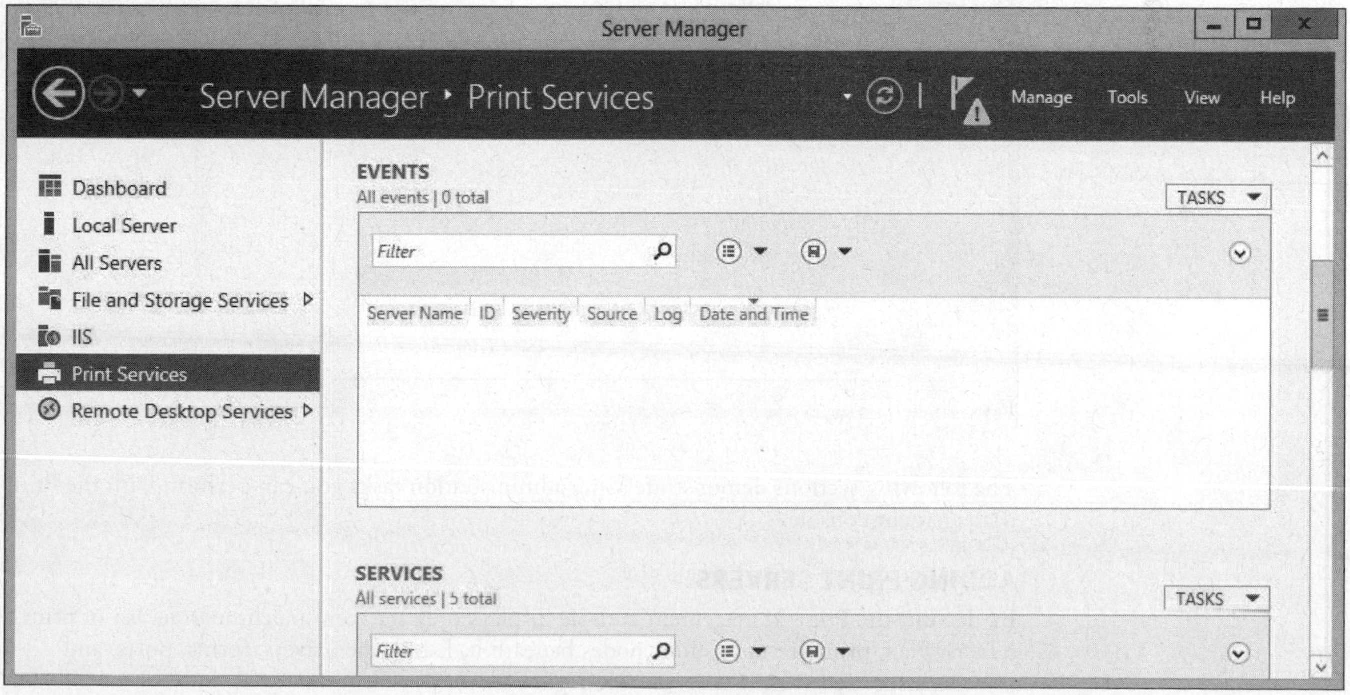

As always, Windows Server 2012 adds a new icon to the Server Manager navigation pane when you install a role. The Print Services homepage contains a filtered view of print-related event log entries, a status display for the role-related system services and role services, and performance counters, as shown in Figure 5-18.

Using the Print Management Console

The Print Management snap-in for MMC, an administrative tool, consolidates the controls for the printing components throughout the enterprise into a single console. With this tool, you can access the print queues and Properties sheets for all network printers in the enterprise, deploy printers to client computers via Group Policy, and create custom views that simplify the process of detecting print devices that need attention due to errors or depleted consumables.

Windows Server 2012 installs the Print Management console when you add the Print and Document Services role to the computer. You can also install the console without the role by adding the Print and Document Services Tools feature, found under *Remote Server Administration Tools > Role Administration Tools* in Server Manager.

CERTIFICATION READY
Configure Enterprise
Print Management.
Objective 2.2

When you launch the Print Management console, the default display, shown in Figure 5-19, includes in the scope (left) pane the nodes listed in Table 5-4.

Table 5-4

Print Management Nodes

NODE	DESCRIPTION
Custom Filters	Contains composite views of all printers hosted by the print servers listed in the console, regulated by customizable filters
Print Servers	Lists all print servers that you have added to the console, and all drivers, forms, ports, and printers for each print server
Deployed Printers	Lists all printers you have deployed with Group Policy through the console

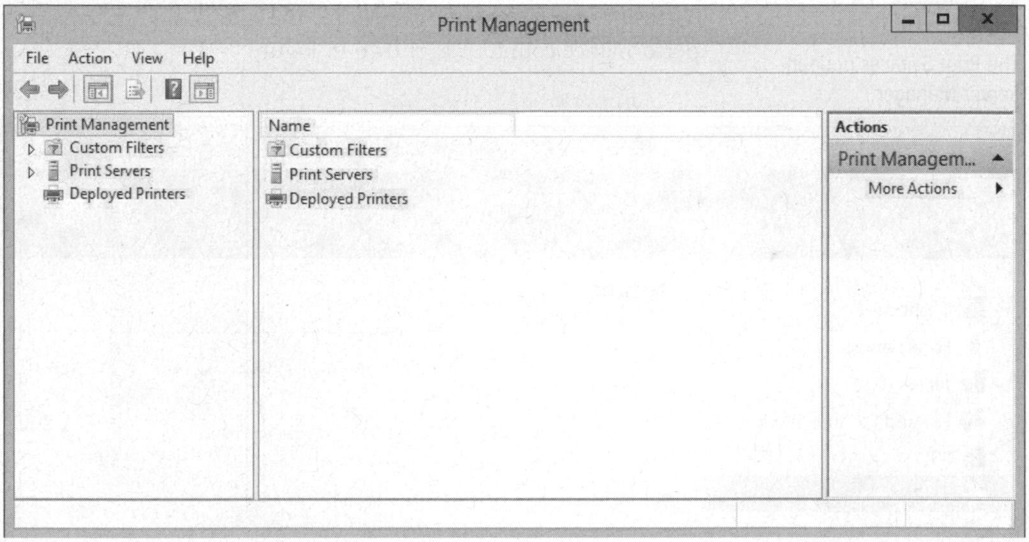

Figure 5-19

The Print Management console

The following sections demonstrate some administration tasks you can perform with the Print Management console.

ADDING PRINT SERVERS

By default, the Print Management console displays only the local machine in its list of print servers. Each print server has four nodes beneath it, listing the drivers, forms, ports, and printers associated with that server (see Figure 5-20).

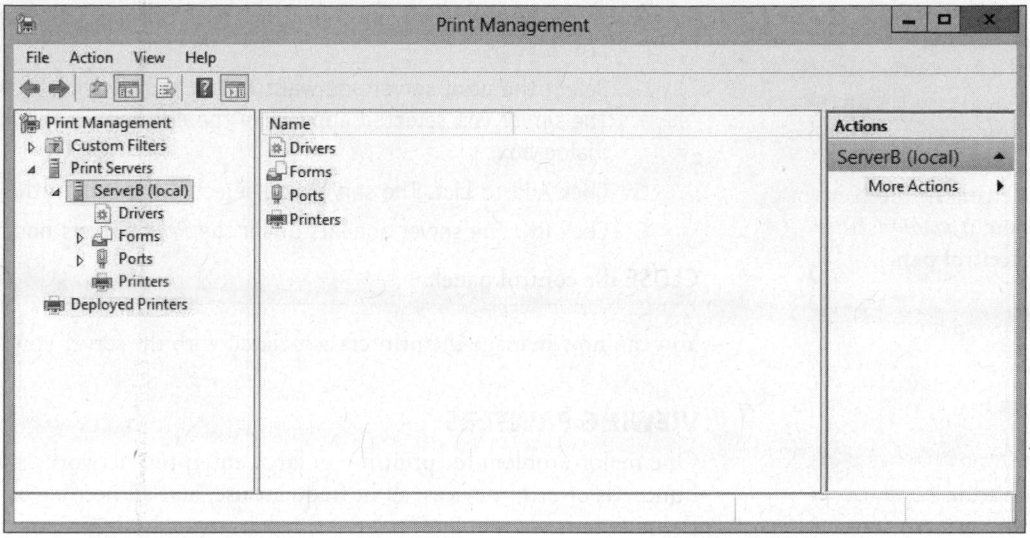

Figure 5-20

A print server displayed in the Print Management console

To manage other print servers and their printers, you must first add them to the console, using the following procedure.

ADD A PRINT SERVER

GET READY. Log on to Windows Server 2012 using a domain account with Administrator privileges.

1. In the *Server Manager* window, click Tools > Print Management. The *Print Management* console appears.
2. Right-click the Print Servers node and, from the context menu, click Add/Remove Servers. The *Add/Remove Servers* dialog box appears, as shown in Figure 5-21.

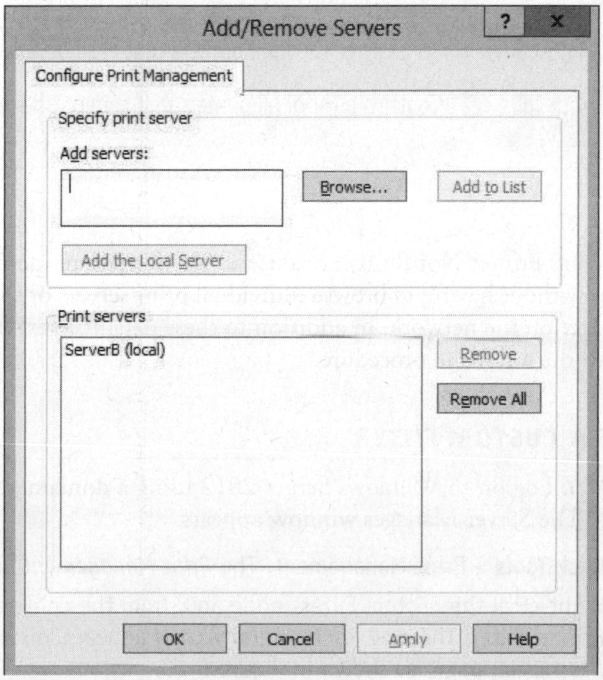

Figure 5-21

The *Add/Remove Servers* dialog box

TAKE NOTE*

To browse for print servers on the network, you must activate the *Network Discovery* setting in the Network and *Sharing Center* control panel.

3. In the *Specify Print Server* section, click Browse. The *Select Print Server* dialog box appears.

4. Select the print server you want to add to the console and click Select Server. The server you selected appears in the *Add servers* box in the *Add/Remove Servers* dialog box.

5. Click Add to List. The server you selected appears in the *Print Servers* list.

6. Click OK. The server appears under the *Print Servers* node.

CLOSE the control panel.

You can now manage the printers associated with the server you have added to the console.

VIEWING PRINTERS

One major problem for printing on large enterprise networks is keeping track of dozens or hundreds of print devices, all in frequent use, and all needing attention regularly. Whether the maintenance required is a major repair, replenishing ink or toner, or just filling the paper trays, print devices cannot get the attention they need until an administrator is aware of the problem.

The Print Management console provides many ways to view the printing components associated with the network's print servers. To create views, the console takes the complete list of printers and applies various filters to it, selecting which printers to display. Under the Custom Filters node are four default filters, as listed in Table 5-5.

Table 5-5

Default Filters

FILTER	DESCRIPTION
All Printers	Contains a list of all the printers hosted by all the print servers added to the console
All Drivers	Contains a list of all printer drivers installed on all print servers added to the console
Printers Not Ready	Contains a list of all printers that are not reporting a Ready status
Printers With Jobs	Contains a list of all printers that currently have jobs waiting in the print queue

Views such as Printer Not Ready are a useful way for you to identify printers that need attention, without having to browse individual print servers or search through a long list of every printer on the network. In addition to these defaults, you can create your own custom filters with the following procedure.

CREATE A CUSTOM FILTER

GET READY. Log on to Windows Server 2012 using a domain account with Administrator privileges. The Server Manager window appears.

1. Click Tools > Print Management. The *Print Management* console appears.

2. Right-click the Custom Filters node and, from the context menu, select Add New Printer Filter. The *New Printer Filter Wizard* appears, displaying the *Filter Name and Description* page, as shown in Figure 5-22.

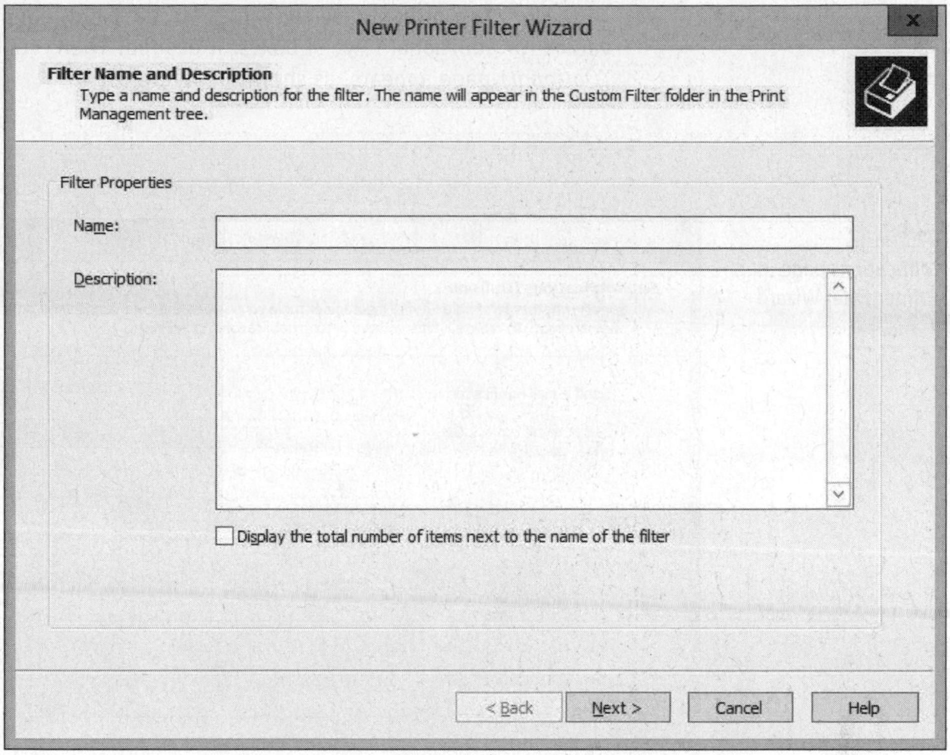

Figure 5-22

The *Filter Name and Description* page in the New Printer Filter Wizard

3. In the Name text box, type a name for the filter; optionally, add a description for the filter in the Description text box. If you want the number of printers in the filtered list to appear next to the filter name, select the Display the total number of items next to the name of the filter check box. Then click Next. The *Define a filter* page appears, as shown in Figure 5-23.

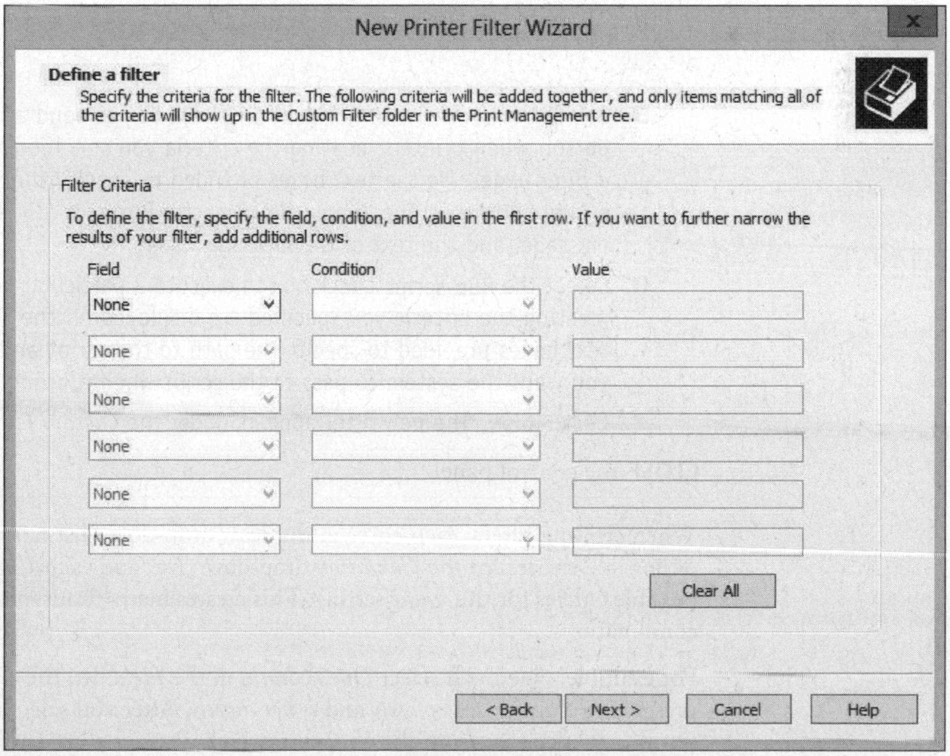

Figure 5-23

The *Define a filter* page in the New Printer Filter Wizard

4. In the top row of boxes, select values for the Field, Condition, and Value fields. Select values for additional rows of boxes, if desired. Then, click Next. The *Set Notifications (Optional)* page appears, as shown in Figure 5-24.

5. Select the Send e-mail notification check box to send a message to a specific person when printers meeting the criteria you specified are displayed on the *Define a filter* page. Use the text boxes provided to specify the sender's and recipient's e-mail addresses, the Simple Mail Transfer Protocol (SMTP) server that sends the message, and the text of the message itself.

6. Select the Run script check box to execute a particular script file when printers meeting the criteria you specified are displayed on the *Define a filter* page. Use the text boxes provided to specify the path to the script and any additional arguments you want the system to pass to the script when running it.

7. Click Finish. The new filter appears under the *Custom Filters* node.

CLOSE the control panel.

When creating filters, each entry in the *Field* drop-down list has its own collection of possible entries for the *Condition* drop-down list, and each *Condition* entry has its own possible entries for the *Value* setting. This creates many thousands of possible filter combinations.

For example, when you select *Queue Status* in the *Field* list, the *Condition* drop-down list presents two options: *is exactly* and *is not exactly*. After you select one of these Condition settings, you choose from the *Value* list, which displays all possible queue status messages that the print server can report, as shown in Figure 5-25.

Figure 5-25

Filter status values

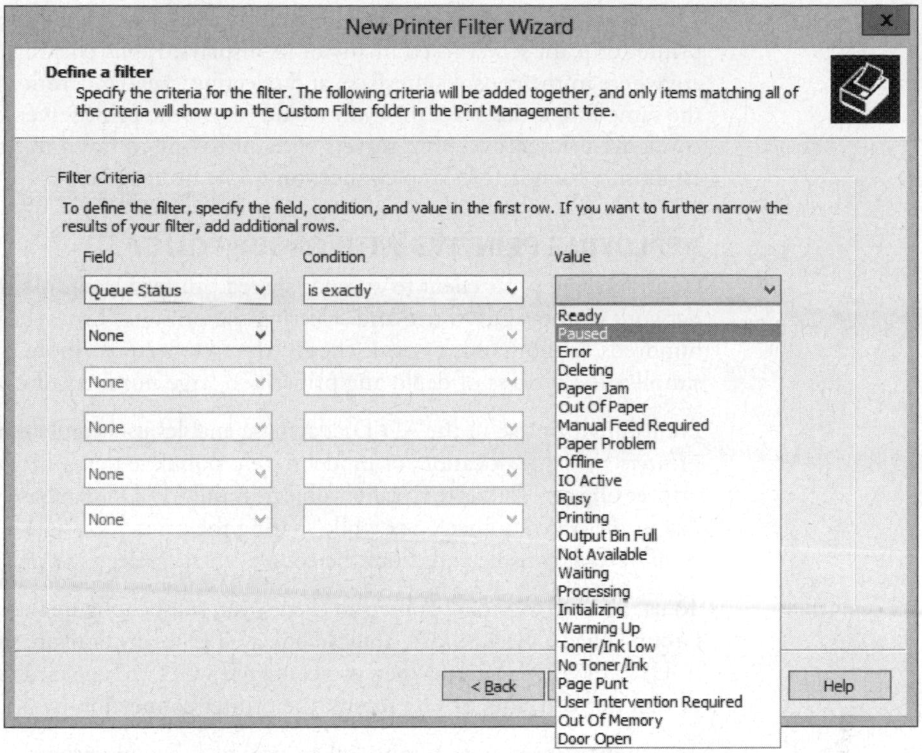

If you create a filter with the settings *Queue Status*, *is exactly*, and *Error*, the filter displays all printers currently reporting an error condition. You might find a filter like this useful for detecting printers reporting one specific condition, but many different status messages can indicate a print device stoppage. For a busy printer administrator, a better combination might be a filter with the settings *Queue Status*, *is not exactly*, and *Ready*. This way, the filter displays all printers with abnormal conditions that need administrative attention.

MANAGING PRINTERS AND PRINT SERVERS

After you use filtered views to isolate the printers you want to examine, selecting a printer displays its status, the number of jobs currently in its print queue, and the name of the print server hosting it. If you right-click the filter in the scope pane and, from the context menu, select *Show Extended View*, an additional pane appears containing the contents of the selected printer's queue (see Figure 5-26). You can manipulate the queued jobs just as you would from the print queue window on the print server console.

Figure 5-26

The Print Management console's extended view

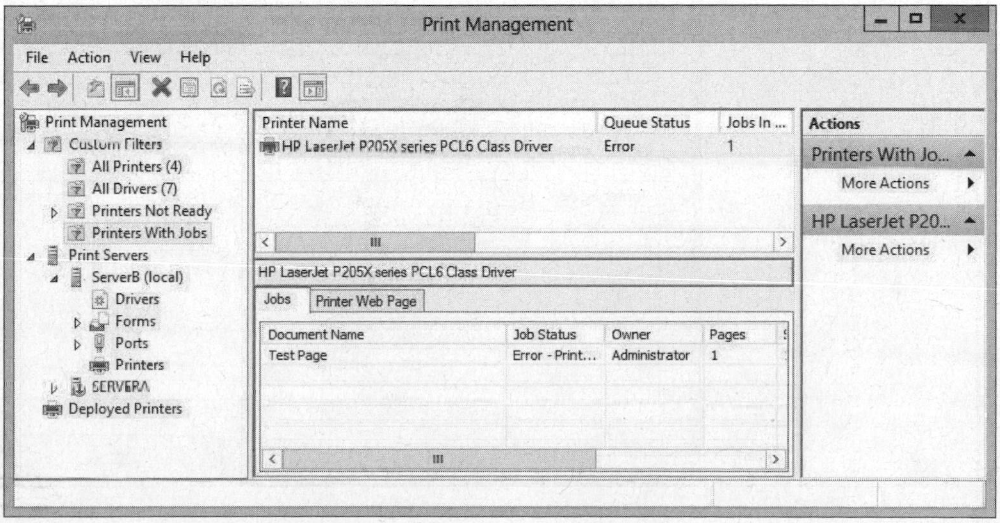

The Print Management console also enables you to access the configuration interface for any printer or print server listed in any of its displays. Right-clicking a printer or print server anywhere in the console interface, and selecting *Properties* from the context menu, displays the same Properties sheet that you would see on the print server computer itself. You can then configure printers and print servers without having to travel to the site of the print server or establish a Remote Desktop connection to the print server.

DEPLOYING PRINTERS WITH GROUP POLICY

Configuring a print client to access a shared printer is a simple matter of browsing the network or the AD DS tree and selecting the printer. However, when you have to configure hundreds or thousands of print clients, the task becomes more complicated. AD DS helps simplify the process of deploying printers to large numbers of clients.

Publishing printers in the AD DS database enables users and administrators to search for printers by name, location, or model (if you populate the *Location* and *Model* fields in the printer object). To create a printer object in the AD DS database, you can either select the *List in the directory* check box while sharing the printer, or right-click a printer in the *Print Management* console and, from the context menu, select *List in Directory*.

To use AD DS to deploy printers to clients, you must configure the appropriate policies in a Group Policy Object (GPO). You can link a GPO to any domain, site, or organizational unit (OU) in the AD DS tree. When you configure a GPO to deploy a printer, all users or computers in that domain, site, or OU receive the printer connection by default when they log on.

To deploy printers with Group Policy, use the following procedure.

➔ DEPLOY PRINTERS WITH GROUP POLICY

GET READY. Log on to Windows Server 2012, using a domain account with Administrator privileges. The Server Manager window appears.

1. Click Tools > Print Management. The *Print Management* console appears.
2. Right-click a printer in the console's scope pane and, from the context menu, select Deploy with Group Policy. The *Deploy with Group Policy* dialog box appears, as shown in Figure 5-27.

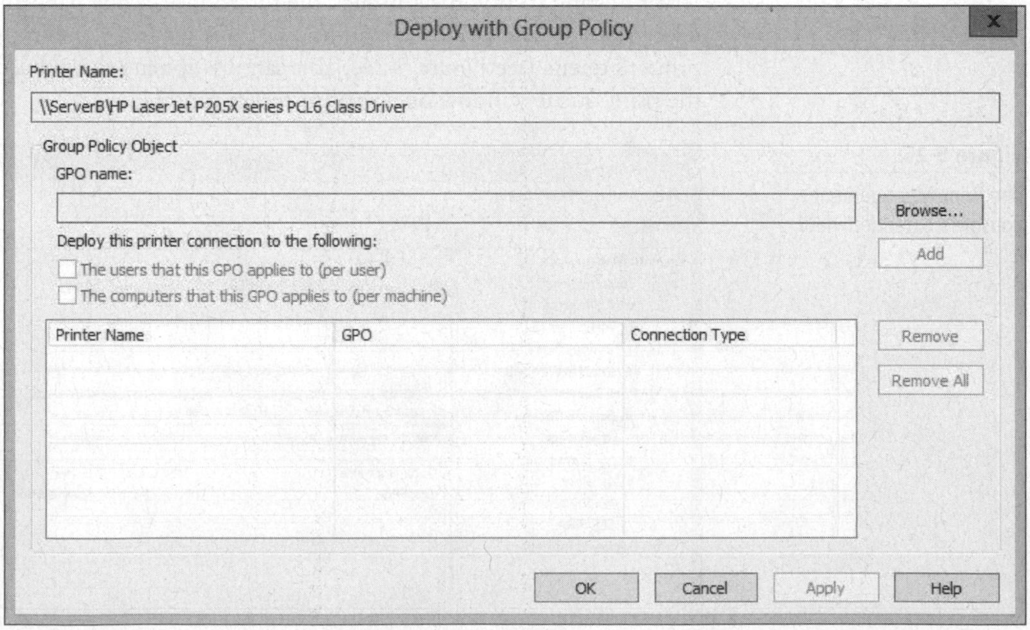

Figure 5-27

The *Deploy with Group Policy* dialog box

3. Click Browse. The *Browse for a Group Policy Object* dialog box appears, as shown in Figure 5-28.

4. Select the GPO you want to use to deploy the printer and click OK. The GPO you selected appears in the *GPO Name* field (see Figure 5-29).

5. Select the appropriate check box to select whether to deploy the printer to the users associated with the GPO, the computers, or both. Then click Add. The new printer/ GPO associations appear in the table (see Figure 5-30).

Figure 5-30

The *Deploy with Group Policy* dialog box with a printer/GPO association

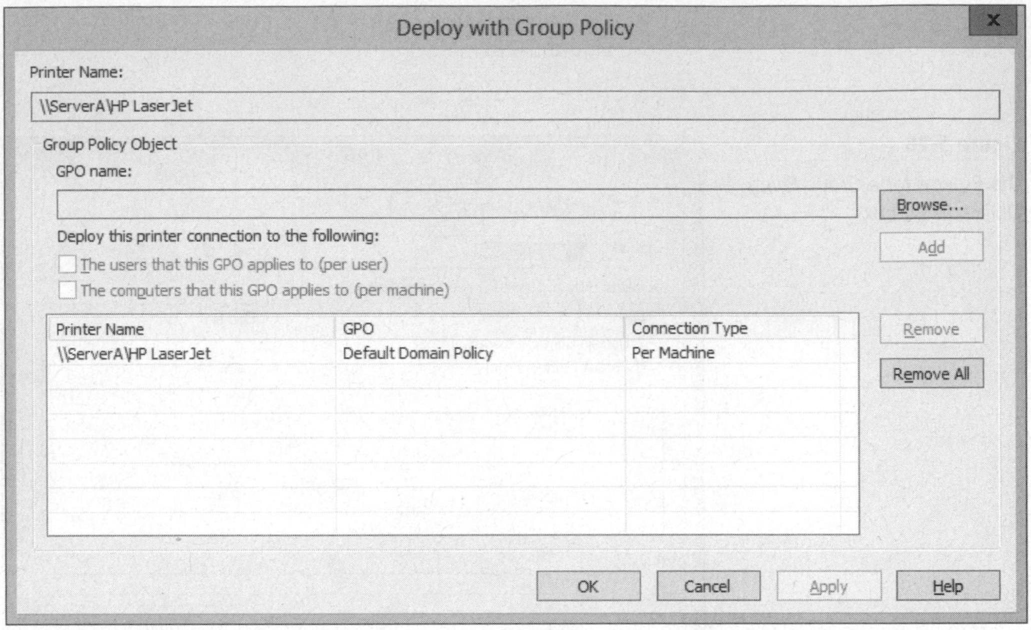

Deploying the printer to the users means that all users associated with the GPO will receive the printer connection, no matter what computer they use to log on. Deploying the printer to the computers means that all computers associated with the GPO will receive the printer connection, no matter who logs on to them.

6. Click OK. A *Print Management* message box appears, informing you that the operation has succeeded.

7. Click OK, then click OK again to close the *Deploy with Group Policy* dialog box.

CLOSE the control panel.

The next time any users running Windows Server 2008 or later and Windows Vista or later who are associated with the GPO refresh their policies or restart, they receive the new settings, and the printer appears in the *Printers* control panel.

TAKE NOTE* Clients running earlier versions of Windows, including Windows XP and Windows Server 2003, do not support automatic policy-based printer deployments. To enable the GPO to deploy printers on these computers, you must configure the systems to run a utility called PushPrinterConnections.exe. The most convenient way to do this is to configure the same GPO you used for the printer deployment to run the program from a user logon script or machine script.

SKILL SUMMARY

IN THIS LESSON, YOU LEARNED:

- Printing in Microsoft Windows typically involves the following four components: print device, printer, print server, and print driver.

- The printer driver enables you to configure the print job to use the various capabilities of the print device.

- The simplest form of print architecture consists of one print device connected to one computer, known as a locally attached print device. You can share this printer (and the print device) with other users on the same network.

- With network-attached print devices, your primary deployment decision is which computer will function as the print server.

- Remote Desktop Easy Print is a driver that enables Remote Desktop clients running applications on a server to redirect their print jobs back to their local print devices.

- Printer permissions are much simpler than NTFS permissions; they basically dictate whether users are allowed to merely use the printer, manage documents submitted to the printer, or manage the properties of the printer itself.

- The Print Management snap-in for MMC is an administrative tool that consolidates the controls for the printing components throughout the enterprise into a single console.

- To use Active Directory to deploy printers to clients, you must configure the appropriate policies in a Group Policy Object (GPO).

■ Knowledge Assessment

Multiple Choice

Select one or more correct answers for each of the following questions.

1. Which of the following terms describes the software interface through which a computer communicates with a print device?
   a. Printer
   b. Print server
   c. Printer driver
   d. Print Management snap-in

2. What printing configuration makes the computer with the locally attached print device function as a print server?
   a. Network-attached printer sharing
   b. Network-attached printing
   c. Locally attached printer sharing
   d. Direct printing

3. When planning for additional disk space for the print server spooler, consider extra storage for _____.
   a. overhead in case of several smaller print jobs
   b. the print server page file
   c. older, less efficient print drivers
   d. temporary print device outages

4. Can you install 32-bit print drivers on a Windows Server 2012 system?
   a. No, because Windows Server 2012 is a 64-bit platform.
   b. Yes, because Windows Server 2012 is a 64-bit platform, which comes with 32-bit support.
   c. No, but you can install the 32-bit driver through Server Manager.
   d. No, but you can install the 32-bit driver from a computer running a 32-bit version of Windows.

5. What is the purpose of the Remote Desktop Easy Print driver?
   a. Easy Print allows remote clients to print to local print devices via a print redirector.
   b. Easy Print allows administrators to configure printers for users connected remotely.
   c. Easy Print allows administrators to print to remote print devices via a print redirector.
   d. Easy Print allows remote configuration of all printers.

6. For a user to print, pause, resume, restart, and cancel his or her documents, the user must possess the basic _____ permission.
   a. Take Ownership
   b. Manage This Printer
   c. Basic Print
   d. Manage Documents

7. You are setting up a printer pool on a computer running Windows Server 2012. The printer pool contains three print devices, all identical. You open the Properties dialog box for the printer and select the Enable Printer Pooling option on the Ports tab. What must you do next?
   a. Configure the LPT1 port to support three printers.
   b. Select or create the ports mapped to the three printers
   c. On the Device Settings tab, configure the installable options to support two additional print devices.
   d. On the Advanced tab, configure the priority for each print device so that printing is distributed among the three print devices.

8. One of your print devices is not working properly, and you want to temporarily prevent users from sending jobs to the printer serving that device. What should you do?
   a. Stop sharing the printer
   b. Remove the printer from Active Directory
   c. Change the printer port
   d. Rename the share

9. You are administering a computer running Windows Server 2012 configured as a print server. Users in the Marketing group complain that they cannot print documents using a printer on the server. You view the permissions in the printer's properties. The Marketing group is allowed Manage Documents permission. Why can't the users print to the printer?
   a. The Everyone group must be granted the Manage Documents permission.
   b. The Administrators group must be granted the Manage Printers permission.
   c. The Marketing group must be granted the Print permission.
   d. The Marketing group must be granted the Manage Printers permission.

10. You are administering a print server running Windows Server 2012. You want to perform maintenance on a print device physically connected to the print server. There are several documents in the print queue. You want to prevent the documents from being printed to the printer, but you don't want users to have to resubmit the documents to the printer. What is the best way to do this?
    a. Open the printer's Properties dialog box, select the Sharing tab, and then select the Do Not Share This Printer option.
    b. Open the printer's Properties dialog box and select a port that is not associated with a print device
    c. Open the printer's queue window, select the first document, and then select Pause from the Document window
    d. Open the printer's queue window, and select the Pause Printing option from the Printer menu.

Best Answer

Choose the letter that corresponds to the best answer. More than one answer choice may achieve the goal. Select the BEST answer.

1. Which of the four fundamental printer configurations is the best printer deployment for a company of many users requiring the use of a few printers?
   a. Direct printing
   b. Locally attached printer sharing
   c. Network-attached printing
   d. Network-attached printer sharing

2. What key disadvantage exists for administrators in network-attached printing (local computer as print server)?
   a. The client computer performs the print job processing, rather than the external print server.
   b. Error messages appear only on the computer that originated the print job.
   c. There is no central way to manage the print queue, because each client has its own.
   d. Users can see only their own print queues.

3. Your responsibilities include managing documents, particularly those waiting in the print queue. How does Windows Server 2012 permit viewing these documents as an administrator?
   a. You can view documents across all print queues and print devices.
   b. You can view documents per print queue.
   c. You can view documents in the locally attached print device.
   d. You can view documents using only the associated PowerShell cmdlet.

4. What permission do users have by default regarding printer access and the ability to manage documents?
   a. By default, all printers assign the Allow Print permission to Everyone.
   b. By default, all printers do not assign permission to any user.
   c. By default, all users have the Allow Manage Documents permission.
   d. By default, all printers assign the Allow Print permission to Administrators.

5. What administrative tool consolidates the controls for the printing components throughout the enterprise into a single console?
   a. Server Manager
   b. Print Management snap-in for MMC
   c. Control Panel
   d. Remote Desktop Easy Print

Build a List

1. Order the steps to install a printer in Windows Server 2012. Not all steps will be used.
   a. Connect the print device before finishing the printer installation.
   b. Specify the port (or other interface) the computer will use to access the print device.
   c. Select the print device's specific manufacturer and model.
   d. Supply a printer driver specifically created for that print device.
   e. Load paper into the print device.

2. Order the steps to assign printer permissions.
   a. Click Add, and then select a principal (for example, user, computer, service account, or group) to add.
   b. Right-click one of the printer icons and, from the context window, select Printer Properties.

   c. Log on to Windows Server 2012 with administrative privileges.
   d. Open the Control Panel and select Hardware > Devices and Printers.
   e. Click the Security tab of the printer's Properties sheet.
   f. Select the type of permissions to assign (Allow or Deny).

3. Order steps to add a print server. Not all steps will be used.
   a. Select the print server you want to add to the console and click Select Server. The server you select appears in the Add servers box in the Add/Remove Servers dialog box.
   b. In the Server Manager window, click Tools > Print Management. The Print Management console appears.
   c. Log on to Windows Server 2012 with administrative privileges.
   d. Click Add to List. The server you select appears in the Print Servers list.
   e. In the Specify Print Server section, click Browse. The Select Print Server dialog box appears.

■ Business Case Scenarios

Scenario 5-1: Enhancing Print Performance

You are a desktop support technician for a law firm with a group of 10 legal secretaries who provide administrative support to the attorneys. The secretaries use a single, shared, high-speed laser printer connected to a dedicated Windows Server 2012 print server. They regularly print multiple copies of large documents, and although the laser printer is fast, it runs constantly. Sometimes, the secretaries have to wait 20 minutes or more after submitting a print job for their documents to reach the top of the queue. The office manager has offered to purchase additional printers for the department. However, the secretaries are accustomed to simply clicking the Print button, and don't like the idea of having to examine multiple print queues to determine which one has the fewest jobs before submitting a document. What can you do to provide the department with a printing solution that will enable the secretaries to utilize additional printers most efficiently?

Scenario 5-2: Troubleshooting Printer Delays

One of your small business clients has a print device connected to a server running Windows Server 2012. He has shared the printer so that the other network users can access it. Often, the other users print large documents that take a long time to print, but sometimes your client and other users have important documents that need to be printed before any long documents that are waiting in the printer queue. What would you suggest to this user?

Configuring Servers for Remote Management

70-410 EXAM OBJECTIVE

Objective 2.3 – Configure servers for remote management. This objective may include but is not limited to: Configure WinRM; configure down-level server management; configure servers for day-to-day management tasks; configure multi-server management; configure Server Core; configure Windows Firewall

LESSON HEADING	EXAM OBJECTIVE
Using Server Manager for Remote Management	
Adding Servers	Configure multi-server management
Calibrating Server Manager Performance	
Managing Windows Server 2012 Servers	Configure WinRM Configure Windows Firewall Configure Server Core
Managing Down-Level Servers	Configure down-level server management
Creating Server Groups	
Using Remote Server Administration Tools	
Using Windows PowerShell Web Access	
Installing Windows PowerShell Web Access	
Configuring the Windows PowerShell Web Access Gateway	
Creating Authorization Rules	
Working with Remote Servers	Configure servers for day-to-day management tasks

KEY TERMS

authorization rules

session configuration

Windows Remote Management (WinRM)

■ Using Server Manager for Remote Management

↓
THE BOTTOM LINE
Windows Server 2012 facilitates remote server management, so that you do not need to work at the server console. This capability conserves server resources that can be devoted to applications.

Since Windows Server 2003, Server Manager has been the primary server administration tool for Windows Server. The most obvious improvement to the Server Manager tool in Windows Server 2012 is the capability to perform administrative tasks on remote servers, as well as on the local system.

After you log on to a GUI installation of Windows Server 2012 with an administrative account, Server Manager loads automatically, displaying the Welcome tile, as shown in Figure 6-1.

Figure 6-1

The Welcome tile in Server Manager

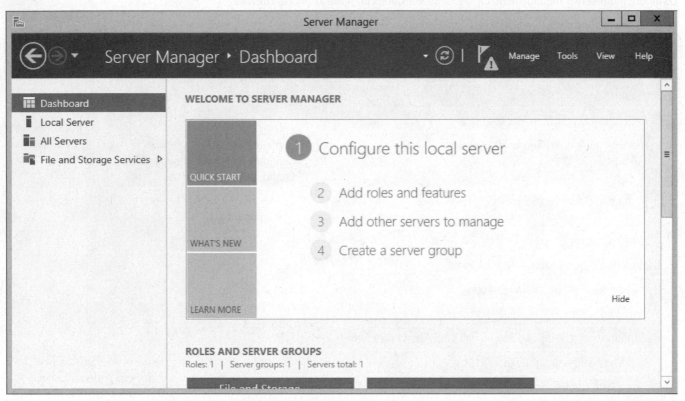

The Server Manager interface contains a navigation pane on the left with icons representing various views of server resources. Selecting an icon displays a homepage in the right pane, which contains tiles with information about the resource. The Dashboard page, which appears by default, contains, in addition to the Welcome tile, thumbnails that summarize the other views available in Server Manager, as shown in Figure 6-2. The other views include Local Server, All Servers, and server groups and role groups.

Figure 6-2

Dashboard thumbnails in
Server Manager

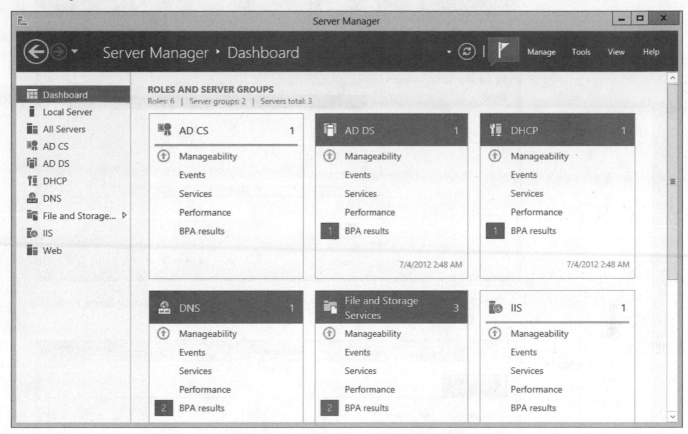

Adding Servers

> The primary difference between the Windows Server 2012 Server Manager and previous
> versions is the capability to add and manage multiple servers at once.

Although only the local server appears in Server Manager when you first run it, you can
add other servers, enabling you to manage them together. The servers you add can be
physical or virtual, and can run any version of Windows Server since Windows Server
2003. After you add servers to the interface, you can create groups containing collections
of servers, such as the servers at a particular location or those performing a particular
function. These groups appear in the navigation pane, enabling you to administer them as
a single entity.

To add servers in Server Manager, use the following procedure.

CERTIFICATION READY
Configure multi-server
management.
Objective 2.3

ADD SERVERS IN SERVER MANAGER

GET READY. Log on to the server running Windows Server 2012 using an account with
administrative privileges. The Server Manager window appears.

1. In the navigation pane, click the All Servers icon. The All Servers homepage appears,
as shown in Figure 6-3.

Figure 6-3

The All Servers homepage in Server Manager

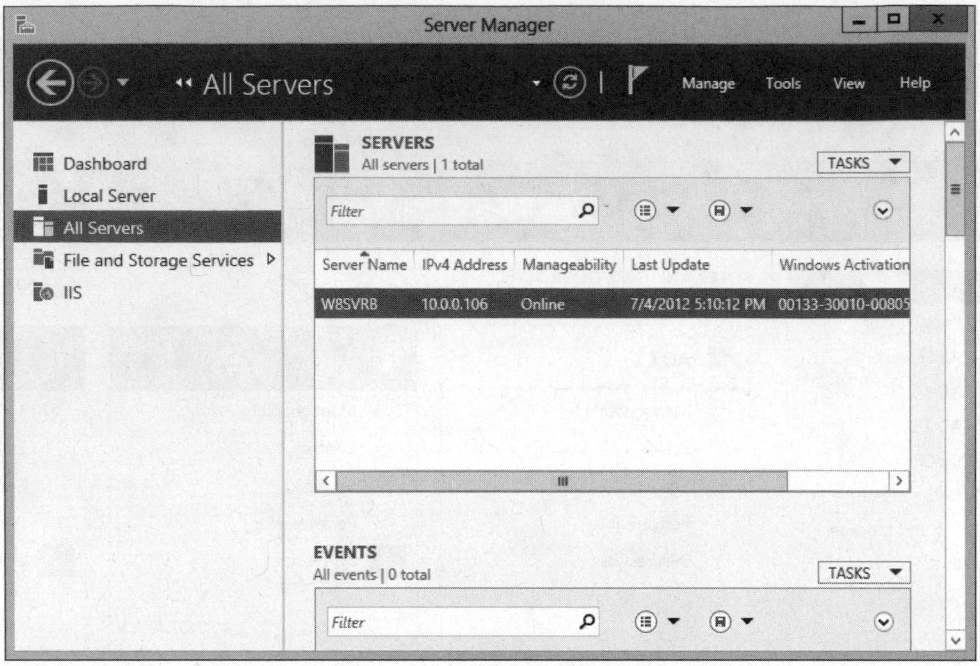

2. From the Manage menu, select Add Servers. The Add Servers dialog box appears, as shown in Figure 6-4.

Figure 6-4

The Add Servers dialog box in Server Manager

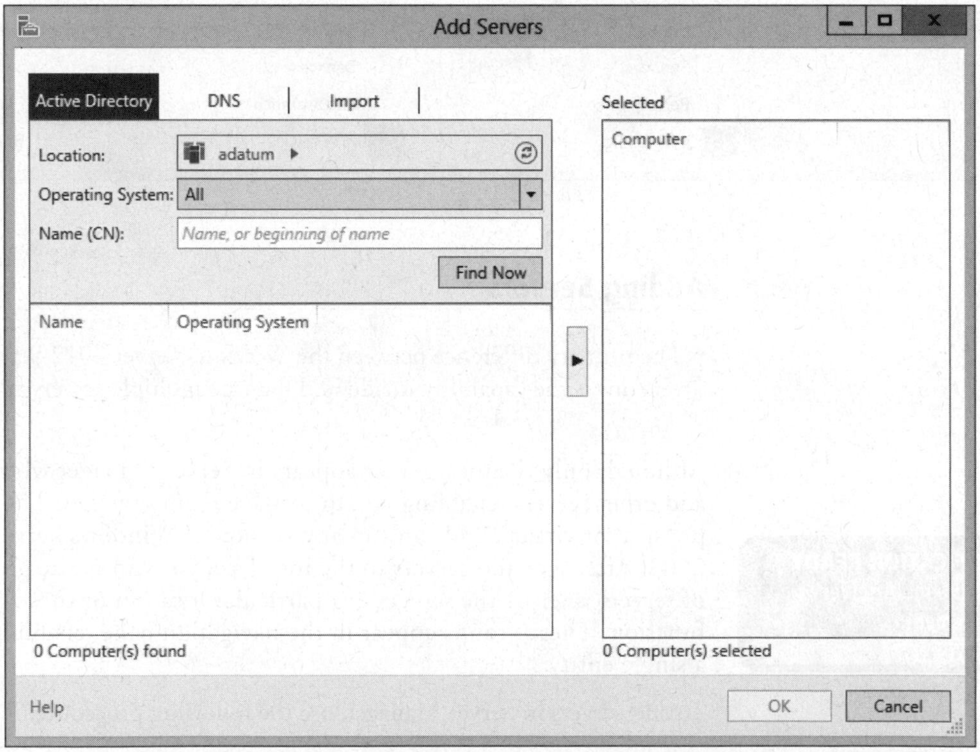

3. Select one of the following tabs to specify how you want to locate servers to add:

- **Active Directory** enables you to search for computers running specific operating systems in specific locations in the local Active Directory Domain Services (AD DS) domain.
- **DNS** enables you to search for servers in your configured Domain Name System (DNS) server.

  • **Import** enables you to supply a text file containing the names or IP addresses of
    the servers you want to add.

4. Initiate a search or upload a text file to display a list of available servers, as shown
   in Figure 6-5.

Figure 6-5

Searching for servers in Server
Manager

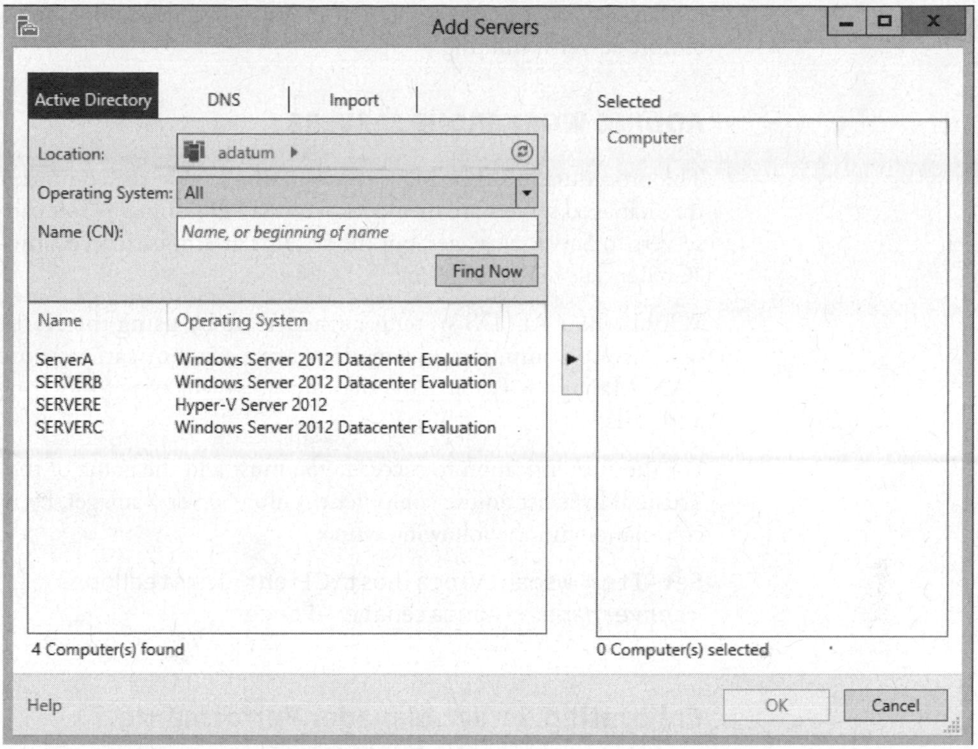

5. Select the servers you want to add and click the right arrow button to add them to
   the Selected list, as shown in Figure 6-6.

Figure 6-6

Selecting servers in Server
Manager

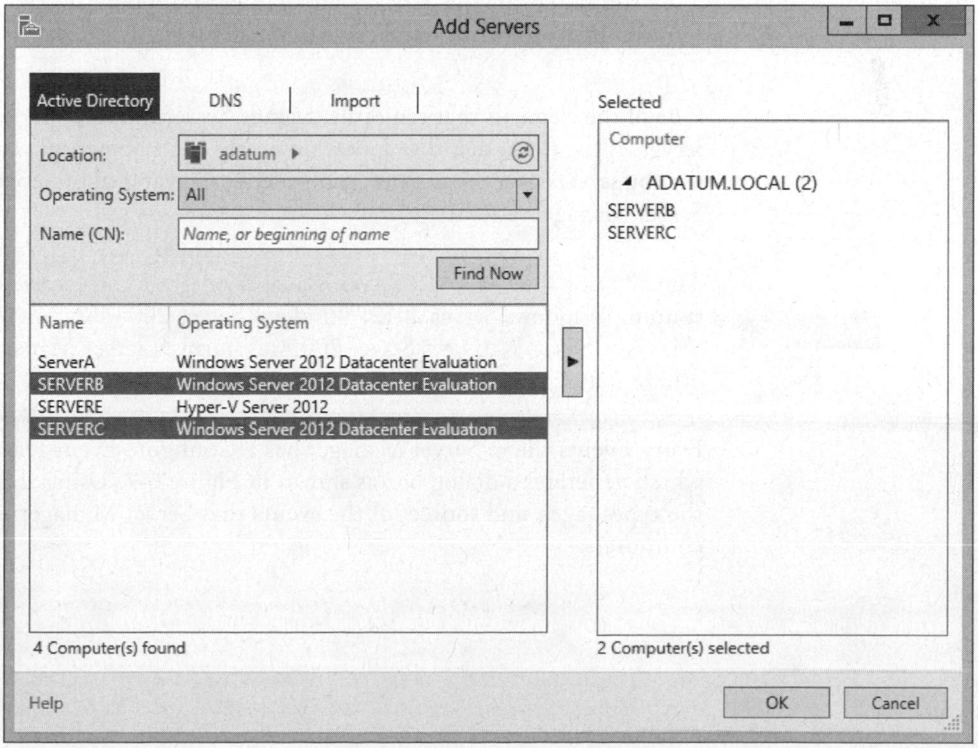

6. Click OK. The servers you selected are added to the All Servers homepage.

CLOSE the Server Manger console.

After you add remote servers to the Server Manager interface, they appear on the All Servers homepage. You can access them in various ways, depending on the Windows version the remote server is running.

ADDING WORKGROUP SERVERS

The procedure in the previous section assumes that the computer running Server Manager and the managed servers are members of an AD DS domain. You can usually add workgroup servers to Server Manager, but the system's attempts to access the remote servers fail with a "Credentials not valid" error.

Why is that? AD DS systems authenticate by using the Kerberos protocol, but Windows workgroup computers use an alternative authentication protocol called NTLM (NT LAN Manager). Essentially, the remote server tries to log on to the workgroup server and fails.

For the authentication to succeed, you must add the name of the workgroup server to the TrustedHosts list on the computer running Server Manager, by using a Windows PowerShell command with the following syntax:

```
Set-Item wsman:\localhost\Client\TrustedHosts
<servername> -Concatenate -Force
```

Calibrating Server Manager Performance

Server Manager has been tested with nearly 100 servers added to the interface. However, the tool's performance is based on a number of factors, including the hardware resources of the computer running Server Manager and the amount of data the remote servers are transmitting to Server Manager over the network.

One of the elements that can easily degrade Server Manager performance when you add many servers is the Event tiles that appear on nearly every homepage. Large numbers of event records sent by servers over the network can generate a great deal of network traffic, slowing down Server Manager refreshes.

TAKE NOTE*

The Windows Server 2012 Server Manager program can receive events from remote servers running Windows Server 2012, Windows Server 2008 R2, and Widows Server 2008. Servers running Windows Server 2003 can furnish Server Manager only with their online/offline status.

Every Events tile in Server Manager has a Configure Event Data option in the Tasks menu, which generates a dialog box as shown in Figure 6-7. Using this interface, you can specify the types, ages, and sources of the events that Server Manager pulls from the remote computers.

Figure 6-7

The Configure Event Data dialog box in Server Manager

```
┌──────────────────────────────────────────────────────────────┐
│ ▣                    Configure Event Data          [─][□][ X ] │
├──────────────────────────────────────────────────────────────┤
│                                                                │
│   These settings determine how Server Manager gathers event    │
│   data from servers in the server group that you are currently │
│   managing. Changes to defaults that significantly increase    │
│   the number of events in the Events tile can result in        │
│   delayed responses from Server Manager.                       │
│                                                                │
│   Show events with these severity levels                       │
│   ☑ Critical   ☑ Error   ☑ Warning   ☐ Informational          │
│                                                                │
│   Get events that have occured within the past  [ 24 hours ▼] │
│                                                                │
│   Get events from the following event log files [ Multiple  ▼]│
│                                                                │
│                                       [   OK   ] [  Cancel  ]  │
└──────────────────────────────────────────────────────────────┘
```

Although Microsoft has tested Server Manager with nearly 100 added servers, this is not a set limit. The resources of the computer running Server Manager and the network condition can result in performance degradation with fewer added servers or adequate performance with more than 100. For true enterprise class server management capabilities, however, Microsoft System Center 2012 provides a more comprehensive feature set with virtually unlimited expansion.

Managing Windows Server 2012 Servers

> After you add servers running Windows Server 2012 to Server Manager, you can immediately use the Add Roles and Features Wizard to install roles and features on any server you add.

You can also perform other administrative tasks, such as configure NIC teaming and restart the server, because Windows Remote Management (WinRM) is enabled by default on Windows Server 2012. **WinRM** is a Windows feature that enables administrators to execute management commands and scripts on remote computers, using a communications protocol called WS-Management Protocol.

CONFIGURING WINRM

WinRM enables you to manage a computer from a remote location using tools based on Windows Management Instrumentation (WMI) and Windows PowerShell. If the default WinRM setting has been modified, or if you want to change it manually, you can do so through the Server Manager interface.

CERTIFICATION READY
Configure WinRM.
Objective 2.3

On the Local Server homepage, the Properties tile contains a Remote management indicator that specifies the server's current WinRM status. To change the WinRM state, click the Remote management hyperlink to open the Configure Remote Management dialog box, as shown in Figure 6-8. Clearing the Enable remote management of this server from other computers check box disables WinRM, and selecting the check box enables it.

Figure 6-8

The Configure Remote
Management dialog box

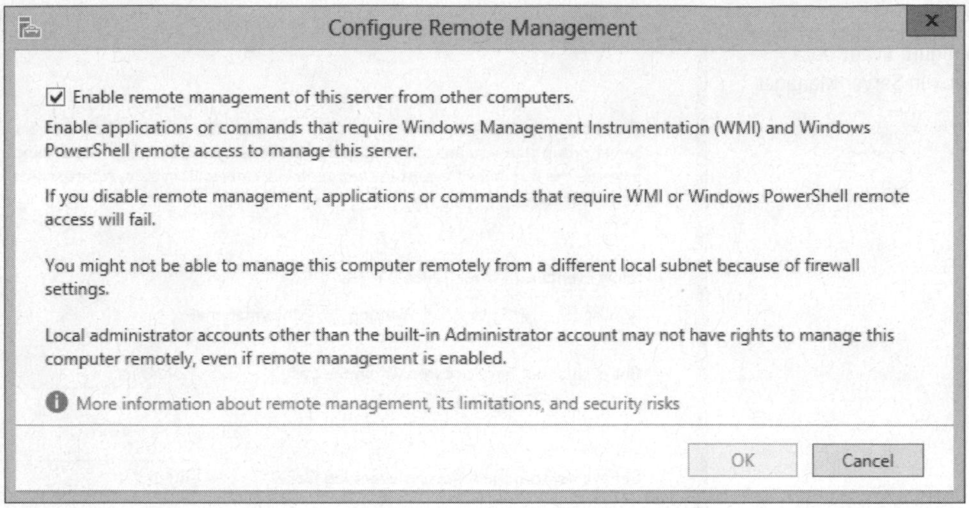

Configure Remote Management   [x]

☑ Enable remote management of this server from other computers.

Enable applications or commands that require Windows Management Instrumentation (WMI) and Windows
PowerShell remote access to manage this server.

If you disable remote management, applications or commands that require WMI or Windows PowerShell remote
access will fail.

You might not be able to manage this computer remotely from a different local subnet because of firewall
settings.

Local administrator accounts other than the built-in Administrator account may not have rights to manage this
computer remotely, even if remote management is enabled.

ⓘ More information about remote management, its limitations, and security risks

[OK]   [Cancel]

USING WINDOWS POWERSHELL

To manage WinRM from a Windows PowerShell session, as in the case of a computer with a Server Core
installation, use the following command:

```
Configure-SMRemoting.exe –Get|–Enable|–Disable
```

- **–Get** displays the current WinRM status.
- **–Enable** enables WinRM.
- **–Disable** disables WinRM.

CONFIGURING WINDOWS FIREWALL

However, if you attempt to launch Microsoft Management Console (MMC) snap-ins targeting
a remote server (such as the Computer Management console), you will receive an error because
of the default Windows Firewall settings on Windows Server 2012. MMC uses the Distributed
Component Object Model (DCOM) for remote management, rather than WinRM, and these
settings are not enabled by default.

To address this problem, you must enable the following inbound Windows Firewall rules on
the remote server you want to manage:

- COM+ Network Access (DCOM-In)
- Remote Event Log Management (NP-In)
- Remote Event Log Management (RPC)
- Remote Event Log Management (RPC-EPMAP)

To modify the firewall rules on the remote system, you can use one of the following
methods:

- Open the Windows Firewall with Advanced Security MMC snap-in on the remote
  server (if it is a Full GUI installation), as shown in Figure 6-9.
- Run the `Netsh AdvFirewall` command from an administrative command prompt.
- Use the NetSecurity module in Windows PowerShell.
- Create a Group Policy object containing the appropriate settings and apply it to the
  remote server.

Figure 6-9

The Windows Firewall with
Advanced Security MMC
snap-in

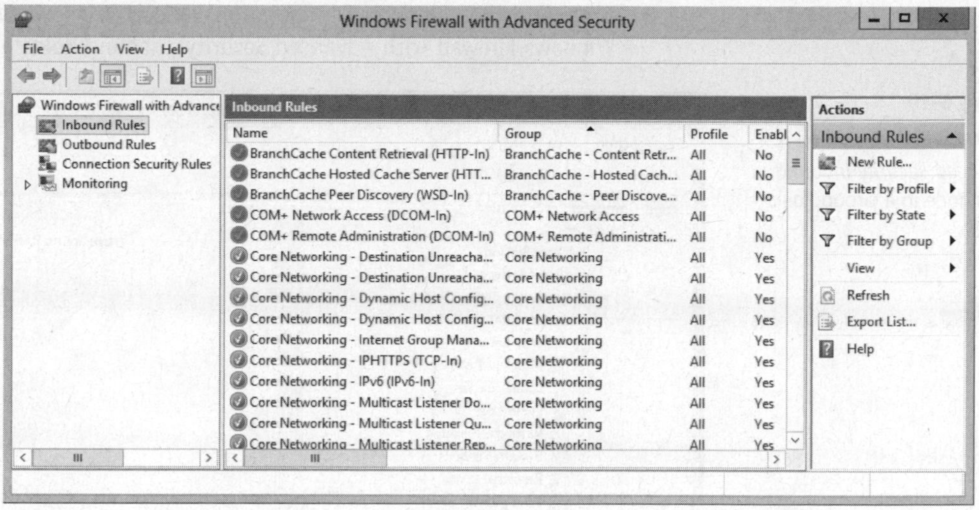

To configure the Windows Firewall rules required for remote server management using DCOM on a Server Core installation, you can use the following Windows PowerShell syntax:

```
Set-NetFirewallRule –name <rule name> –enabled True
```

To obtain the Windows PowerShell names for the preconfigured rules in Windows Firewall, you use the Get-NetFirewallRule command. Use the following resulting commands to enable the previous four rules:

```
Set-NetFirewallRule –name
ComPlusNetworkAccess-DCOM-In –enabled True

Set-NetFirewallRule –name
RemoteEventLogSvc-In-TCP –enabled True

Set-NetFirewallRule –name RemoteEventLogSvc-NP-In-TCP
–enabled True

Set-NetFirewallRule –name
RemoteEventLogSvc-RPCSS-In-TCP –enabled True
```

For remote management solutions, the Group Policy method provides distinct advantages. Not only does it enable you to configure the firewall on the remote system without accessing the server console directly, it also can configure the firewall on Server Core installations without working from the command line. Finally, and possibly most important for large networks, you can use Group Policy to configure the firewall on all servers you want to manage at once.

To configure Windows Firewall settings using Group Policy, use the following procedure. This procedure assumes that the server is a member of an AD DS domain and has the Group Policy Management feature installed.

⊙ CONFIGURE WINDOWS FIREWALL WITH GROUP POLICY

GET READY. Log on to the server running Windows Server 2012 using an account with administrative privileges. The Server Manager window appears.

1. Open the Group Policy Management console and create a new Group Policy object (GPO), giving it a name such as "Server Firewall Configuration."
2. Open the GPO you created using the Group Policy Management Editor.

➕ MORE INFORMATION

For more detailed information on creating GPOs and linking them to other objects, refer to Lesson 16, "Creating Group Policy Objects."

3. Browse to the Computer Configuration\Policies\Windows Settings\Security Settings\Windows Firewall with Advanced Security\Inbound Rules node, as shown in Figure 6-10.

Figure 6-10

The *Windows Firewall with Advanced Security Inbound Rules* node in a Group Policy object

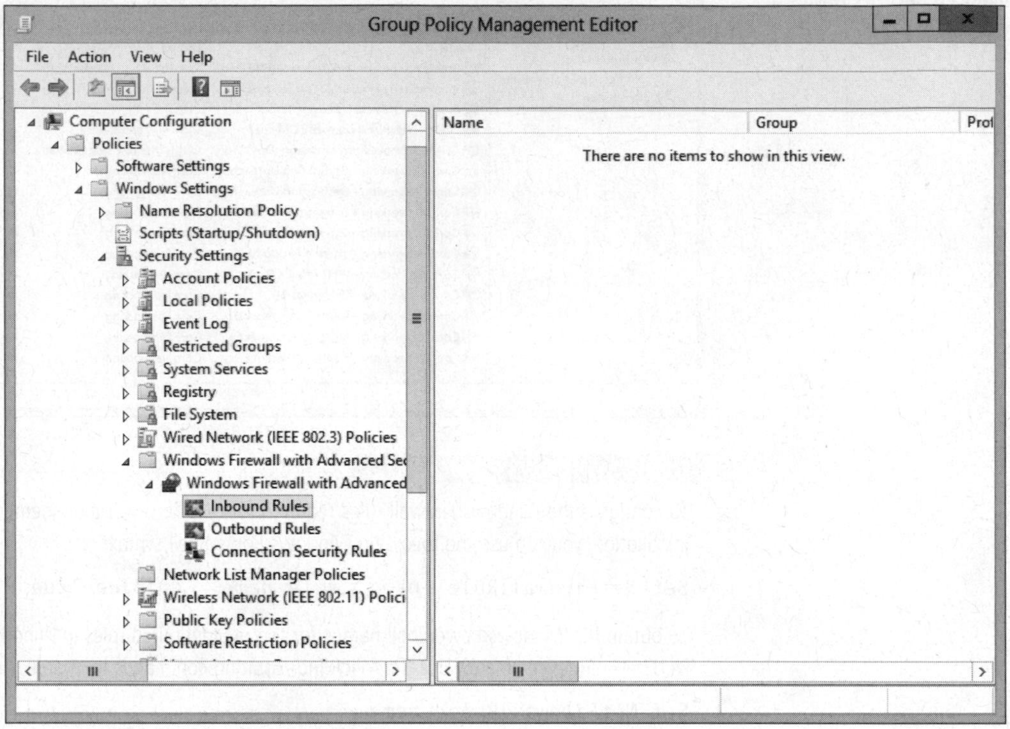

4. Right-click Inbound Rules and, from the context menu, select New Rule. The New Inbound Rule Wizard appears, displaying the Rule Type page, as shown in Figure 6-11.

Figure 6-11

The Rule Type page of the New Inbound Rule Wizard

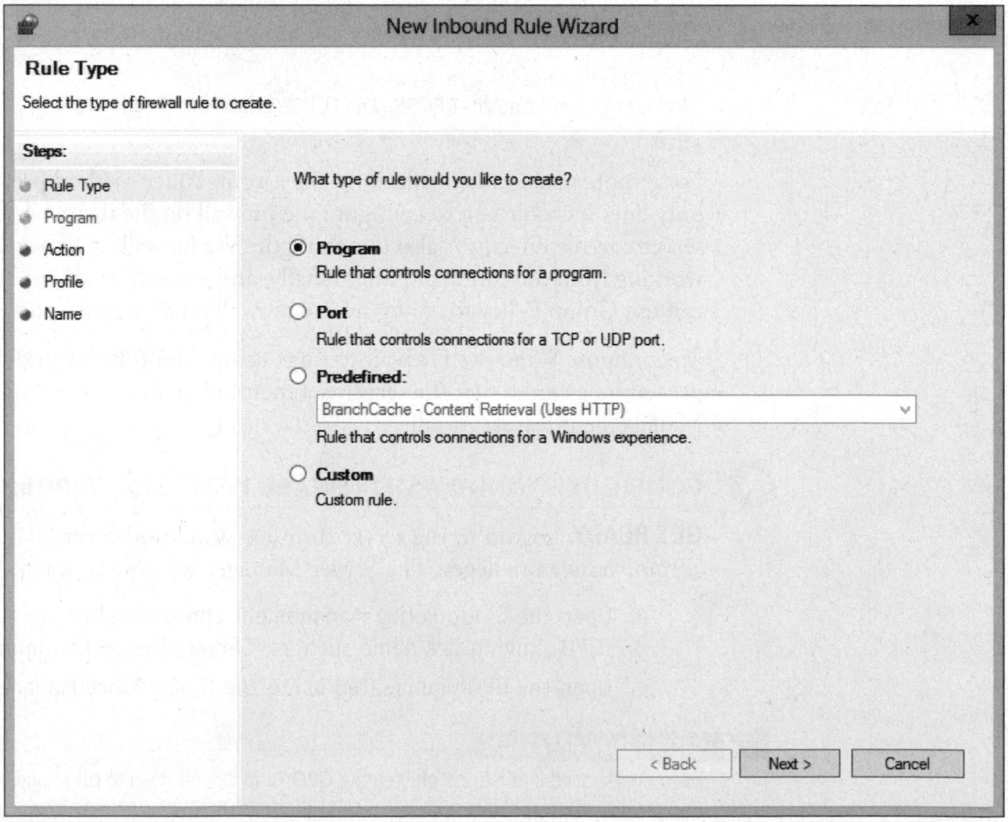

5. Select the Predefined option and, in the drop-down list, select COM+ Network Access and click Next. The Predefined Rules page appears, as shown in Figure 6-12.

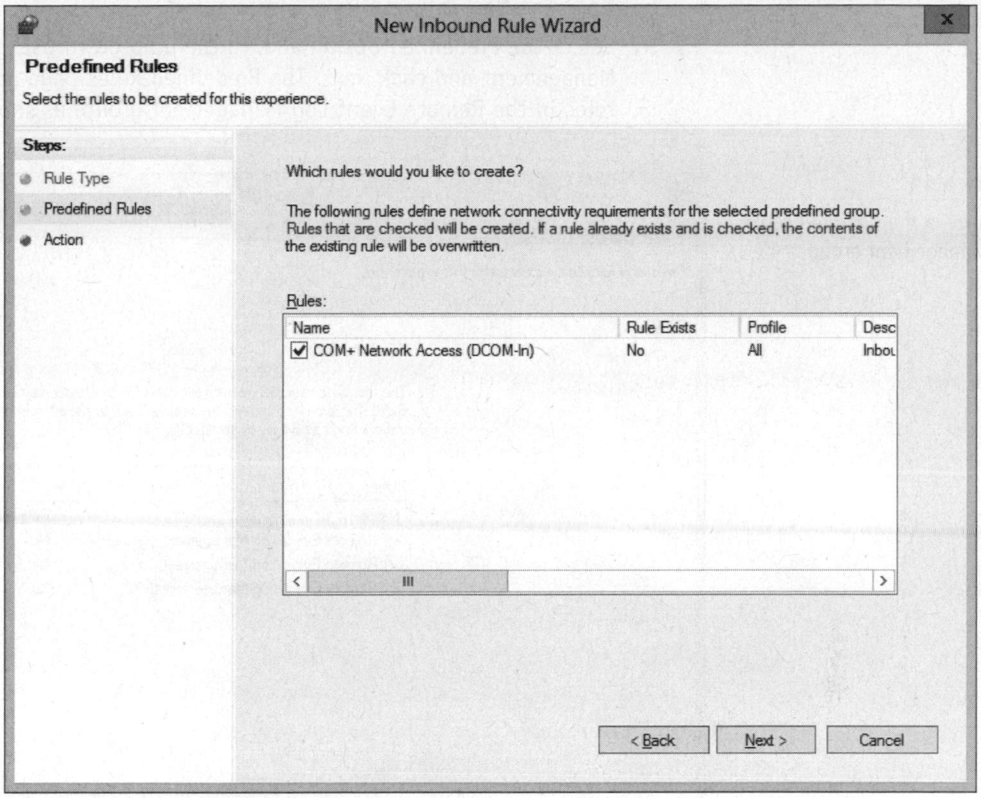

Figure 6-12

The Predefined Rules page of the New Inbound Rule Wizard

6. Click Next. The Action page appears, as shown in Figure 6-13.

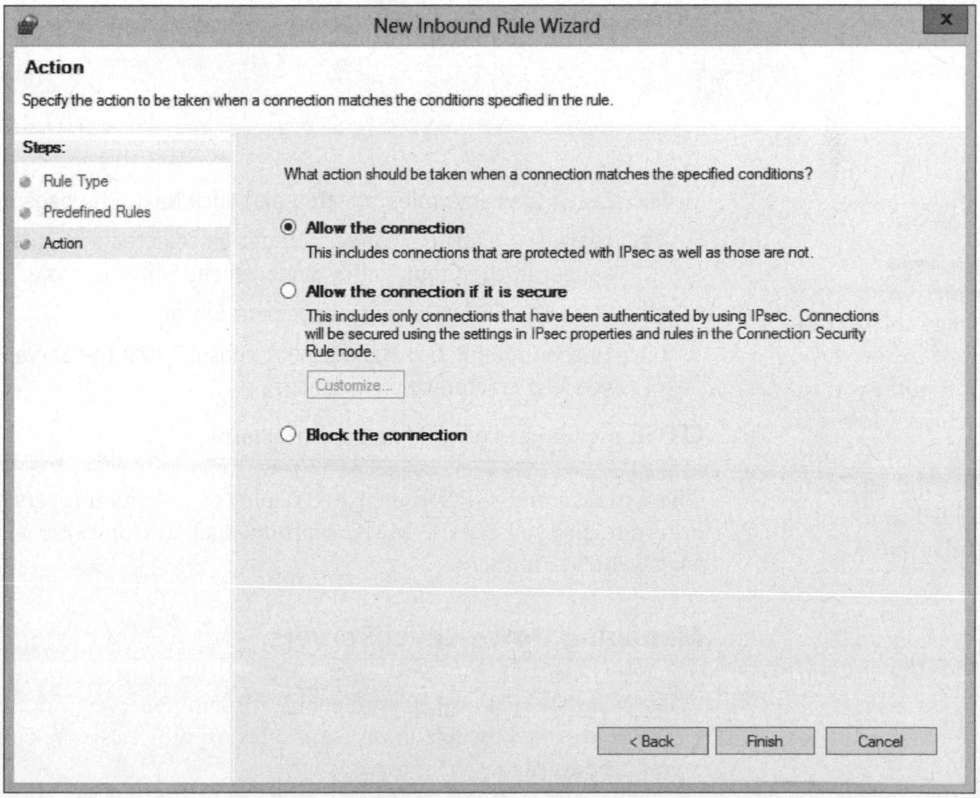

Figure 6-13

The Action page of the New Inbound Rule Wizard

7. Leave the Allow the connection option selected and click Finish. The rule appears in the Group Policy Management Editor console.

8. Open the New Inbound Rule Wizard again.

9. Select the Predefined option and, in the drop-down list, select Remote Event Log Management and click Next. The Predefined Rules page appears, displaying the three rules in the Remote Event Log Management group, as shown in Figure 6-14.

Figure 6-14

The rules in the Remote Event Log Management group

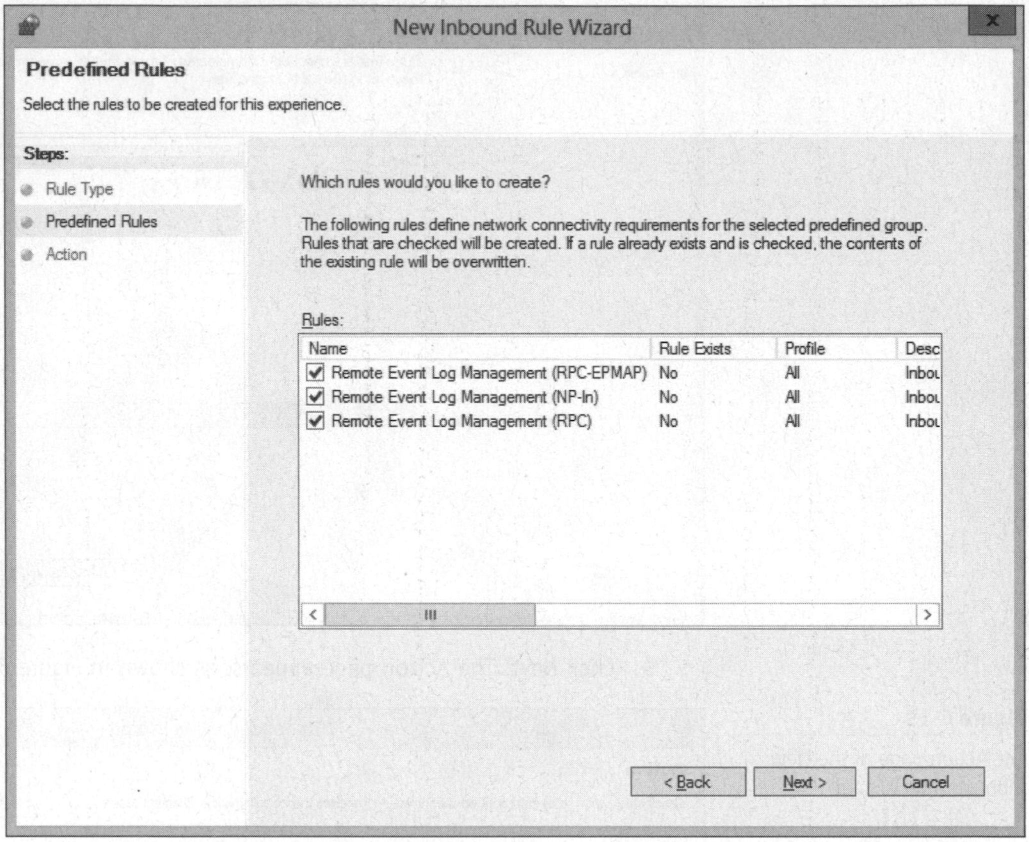

10. Leave the three rules selected and click Next. The page appears.

11. Leave the *Allow the connection* option selected and click Finish. The three rules appear in the Group Policy Management Editor console.

12. Close the Group Policy Management Editor.

13. In the Group Policy Management console, link the Server Firewall Configuration GPO you just created to your domain.

CLOSE the Group Policy Management console.

> **TAKE NOTE***
>
> To deploy the GPO to a subset of the servers on your network, you can use security filtering to limit the scope of the GPO to the servers you added to a particular group.

The settings in the GPO you created deploy to your remote servers the next time they recycle or restart, and you can use MMC snap-ins, such as Computer Management and Disk Management, on them.

Managing Down-Level Servers

The Windows Firewall rules to enable for remote servers running Windows Server 2012 are also disabled by default on computers running earlier versions of Windows Server, so you need to enable them there as well.

CERTIFICATION READY
Configure down-level
server management.
Objective 2.3

Unlike Windows Server 2012, however, earlier versions of the operating system also lack the WinRM support needed for them to be managed using the new Server Manager.

By default, after you add servers running Windows Server 2008 or Windows Server 2008 R2 to the Windows Server 2012 Server Manager, they appear with a manageability status that reads "Online – Verify WinRM 3.0 service is installed, running, and required firewall ports are open."

To add WinRM support to servers running Windows Server 2008 or Windows Server 2008 R2, you must download and install the following updates:

- .NET Framework 4.0
- Windows Management Framework 3.0

These updates are available from the Microsoft Download Center at Microsoft's website.

TAKE NOTE✱

In addition to the lack of WinRM support on Windows Server 2008 and Windows Server 2008 R2, a known issue also exists that prevents Server Manager from retrieving Performance Monitor data from the operating systems. Microsoft has published a Knowledge Base article on the problem and has released a hotfix. Both are available at Microsoft's Support website.

Figure 6-15

The Windows Remote
Management rules in the
Windows Firewall with
Advanced Security console

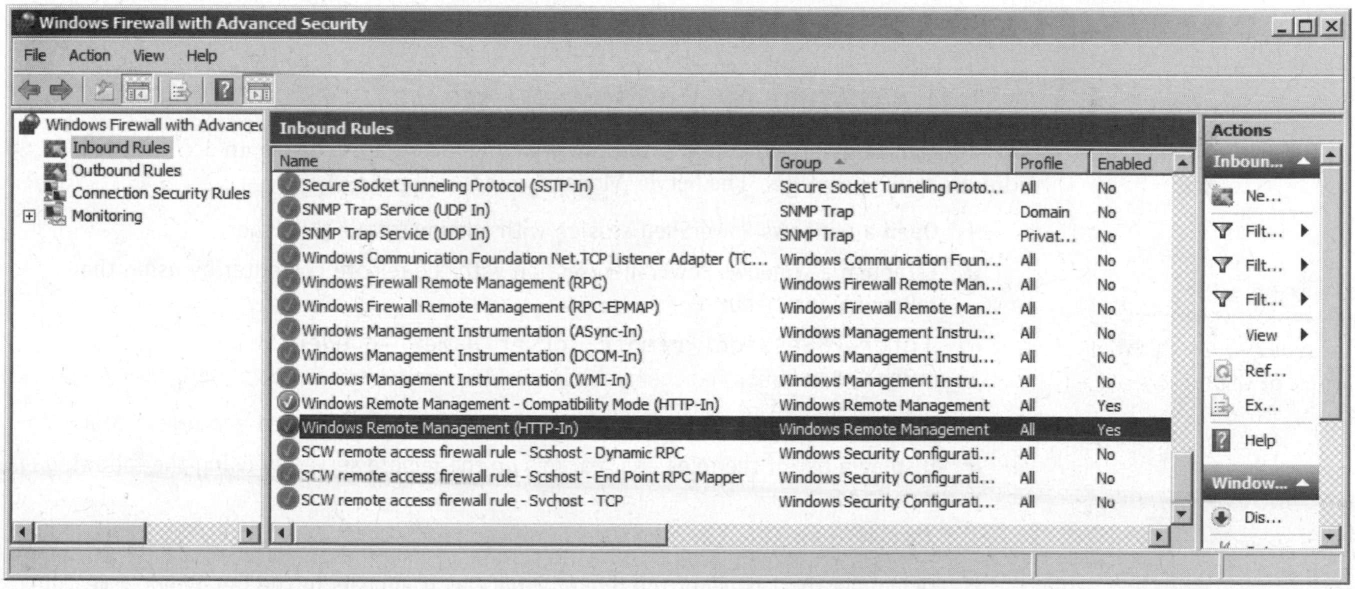

After you install the updates, the system automatically starts the Windows Remote Management service, but you must complete the following tasks on the remote server:

- Enable the Windows Remote Management (HTTP-In) rules in Windows Firewall, as shown in Figure 6-15.

- Create a WinRM listener by running the `winrm quickconfig` command at a command prompt with administrative privileges, as shown in Figure 6-16.

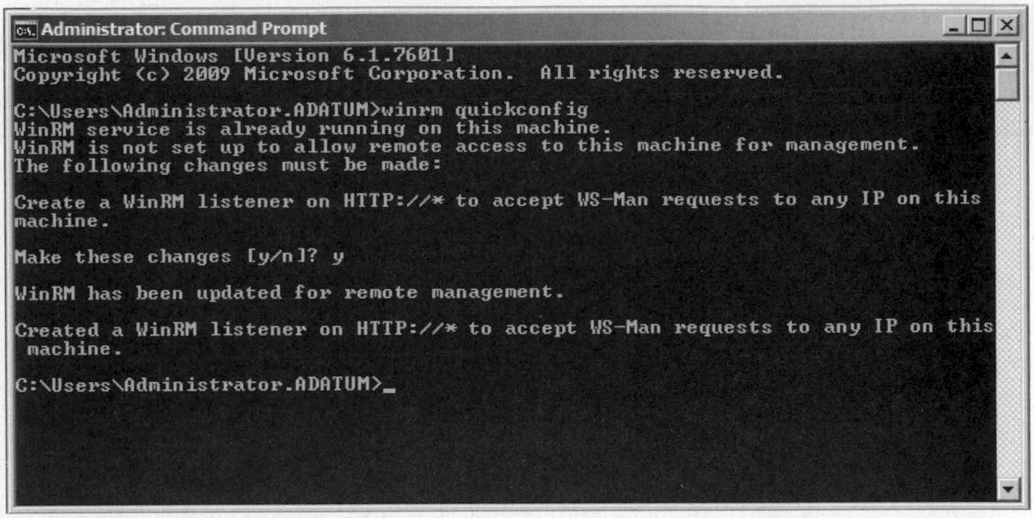

Figure 6-16

Creating a WinRM listener

```
Administrator: Command Prompt                                        _ □ ×
Microsoft Windows [Version 6.1.7601]
Copyright (c) 2009 Microsoft Corporation.  All rights reserved.

C:\Users\Administrator.ADATUM>winrm quickconfig
WinRM service is already running on this machine.
WinRM is not set up to allow remote access to this machine for management.
The following changes must be made:

Create a WinRM listener on HTTP://* to accept WS-Man requests to any IP on this
machine.

Make these changes [y/n]? y

WinRM has been updated for remote management.

Created a WinRM listener on HTTP://* to accept WS-Man requests to any IP on this
 machine.

C:\Users\Administrator.ADATUM>_
```

- Enable the COM+ Network Access and Remote Event Log Management rules in Windows Firewall, as described in the previous section.

After installing the previous updates, you still have limitations to the management tasks you can perform on down-level servers from a remote location. For example, you cannot use the Add Roles and Features Wizard in Server Manager to install roles and features on down-level servers. These servers do not appear in the server pool on the *Select destination server* page.

However, you can use Windows PowerShell to install roles and features on servers running Windows Server 2008 and Windows Server 2008 R2 remotely, as in the following procedure.

INSTALL A FEATURE ON A DOWN-LEVEL SERVER

GET READY. Log on to the server running Windows Server 2012 using an account with administrative privileges. The Server Manager window appears.

1. Open a Windows PowerShell session with administrative privileges.

2. Establish a Windows PowerShell session with the remote computer by using the following command:

   ```
   Enter-PSSession <remote server name> -credential
   <user name>
   ```

3. Type the password associated with the user name you specified and press Enter.

4. Display a list of the roles and features on the remote server by using the following command:

   ```
   Get-WindowsFeature
   ```

5. Using the short name of the role or service as it appears in the Get-WindowsFeature display, install the component using the following command:

   ```
   Add-WindowsFeature <feature name>
   ```

6. Close the session with the remote server by using the following command:

   ```
   Exit-PSSession
   ```

CLOSE the Windows PowerShell window.

TAKE NOTE *

When you install a role or feature on a remote server using Windows PowerShell, the installation does not include the role's management tools, as a wizard-based installation does. However, you can install the tools along with the role or feature if you include the `IncludeManagementTools` parameter in the `Install-WindowsFeature` command line. Be aware, however, that in the case of a Server Core installation, adding the `IncludeManagementTools` parameter does not install MMC snap-ins or other graphical tools.

Creating Server Groups

For enterprise network administrators, it might be necessary to add several servers to Server Manager. To avoid working with a long scrolling list of servers, you can create server groups, based on server locations, functions, or any other organizational paradigm.

After you create a server group, it appears as an icon in the navigation pane, and you can manage the servers in the group just as you would those in the All Servers group.

To create a server group, use the following procedure.

⊙ **CREATE A SERVER GROUP**

GET READY. Log on to the server running Windows Server 2012 using an account with administrative privileges. The Server Manager window appears.

1. In the navigation pane, click the All Servers icon. The All Servers homepage appears.
2. From the Manage menu, select Create Server Group. The Create Server Group dialog box appears, as shown in Figure 6-17.

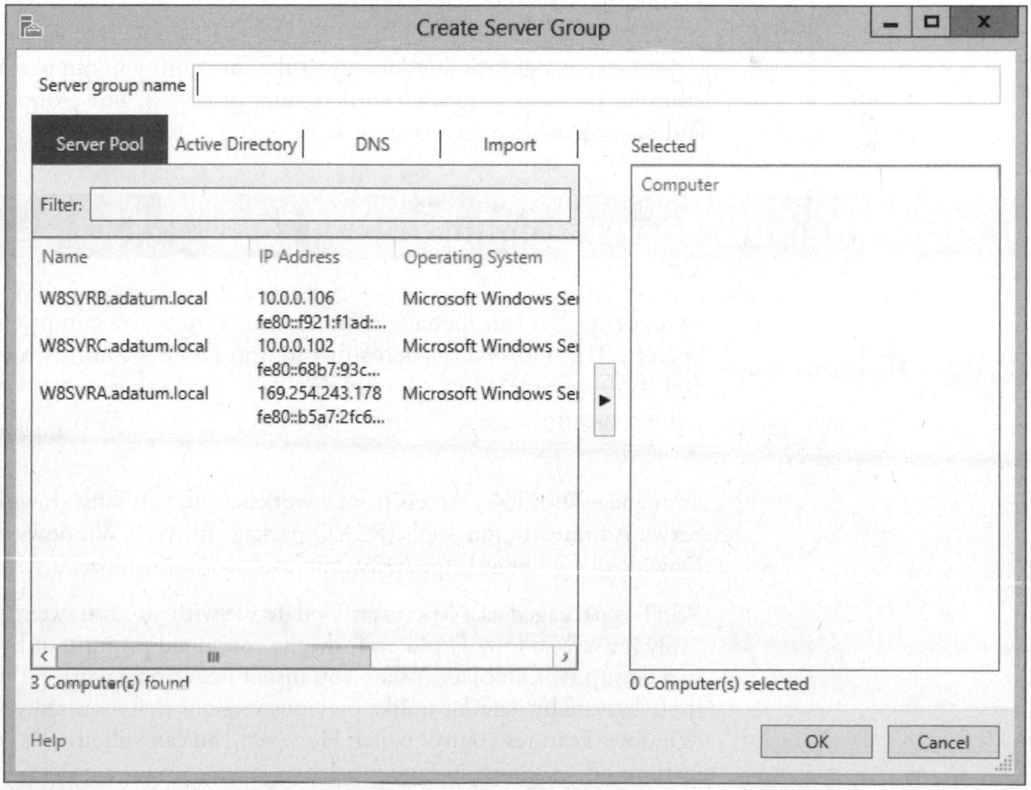

Figure 6-17

The Create Server Group dialog box in Server Manager

3. In the Server group name text box, type the name you want to assign to the server group.

4. Select one of the four tabs to choose a method for selecting servers.

5. Select the servers you want to add to the group and click the right arrow button to add them to the Selected box.

6. Click OK. A new server group icon with the name you specified appears in the navigational pane, as shown in Figure 6-18.

Figure 6-18

A server group in Server Manager

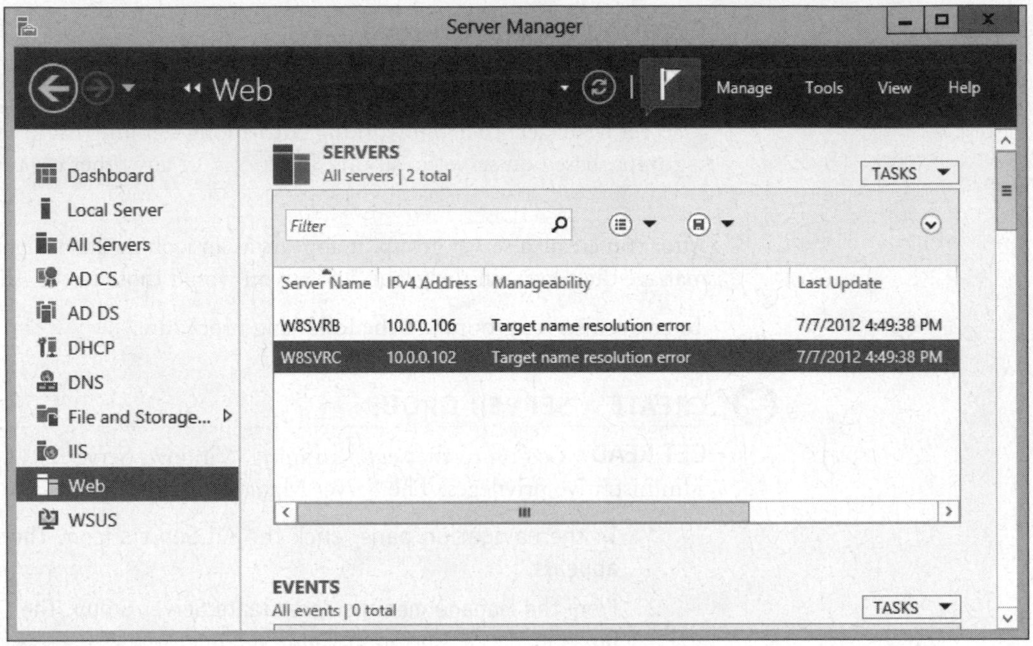

CLOSE the Server Manager console.

Creating server groups does not affect the functions you can perform on them. You cannot, for example, perform actions on entire groups of servers. The groupings enable you to organize and navigate several servers at once.

■ Using Remote Server Administration Tools

THE BOTTOM LINE

By default, you can manage remote servers from any computer running Windows Server 2012. However, Microsoft promotes a new administrative method that urges you to keep servers locked away and uses a workstation to manage servers from a remote location.

To manage Windows servers from a workstation, you must download and install the Remote Server Administration Tools (RSAT) package for your Windows version from the Microsoft Download Center at http://www.microsoft.com/download.

RSAT is packaged as a Microsoft Update file with an .msu extension, enabling you to deploy it easily from Windows Explorer, from the command prompt, or by using Software Distribution in a Group Policy object. When you install RSAT on a workstation running Windows 8, the tools activate by default, unlike previous versions that required you to turn them on using the Windows Features control panel. However, you can still use the control panel to turn selected features off, as shown in Figure 6-19.

Figure 6-19

RSAT in the Windows Features control panel

When you launch Server Manager on a Windows workstation, there is no local server, and there are no remote servers to manage, as shown in Figure 6-20, until you add some. You add servers by using the same process described previously in this lesson.

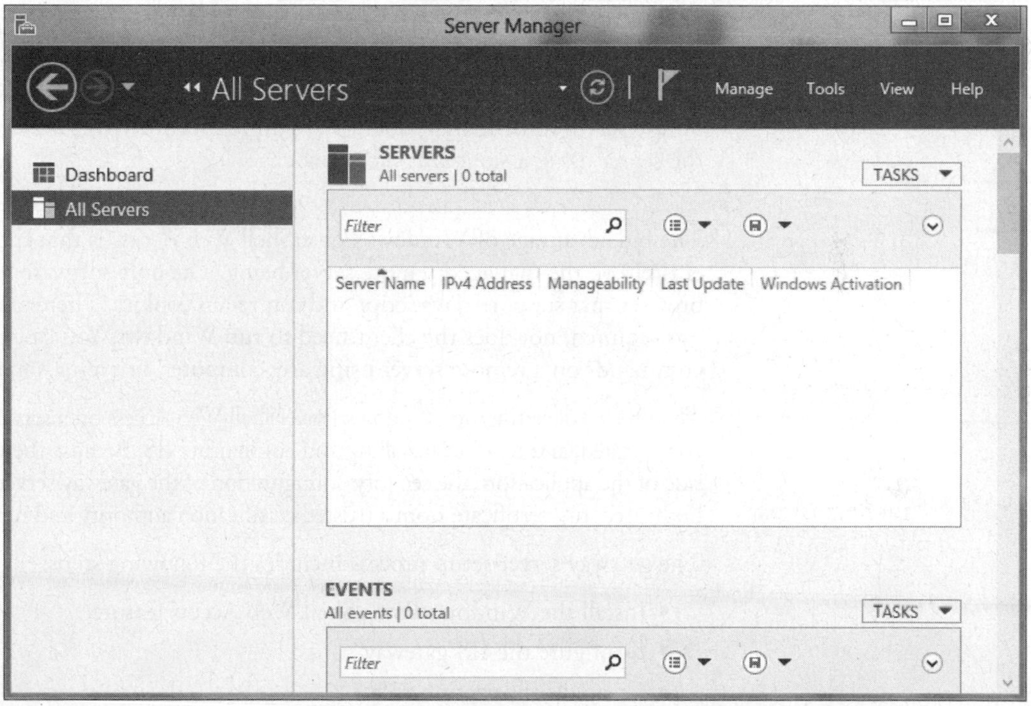

Figure 6-20

Server Manager on a Windows workstation

The access to the servers you add depends on the account you use to log on to the workstation. If an "Access denied" message appears, as shown in Figure 6-21, you can connect to the server using another account by right-clicking it and, from the context menu, selecting Manage As to display a standard Windows Security dialog box, in which you can supply alternative credentials.

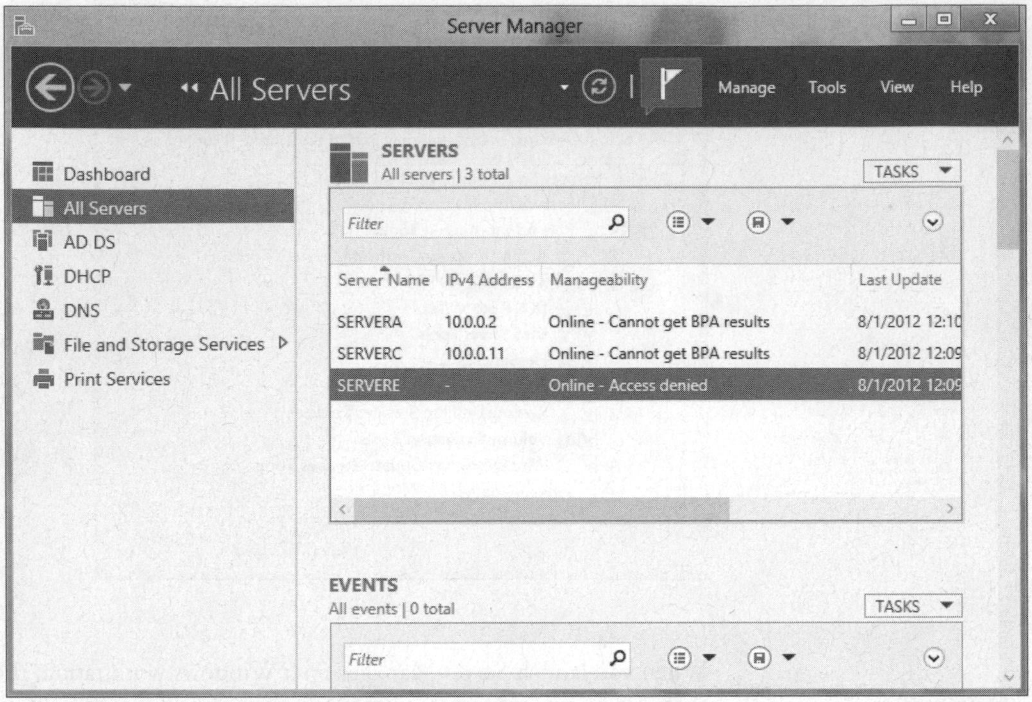

Figure 6-21

Failed remote server
authentication in Server
Manager

Using Windows PowerShell Web Access

THE BOTTOM LINE

Windows Server 2012 includes another new remote management tool called ***Windows PowerShell Web Access***. This web gateway, hosted by Internet Information Services (IIS) on the server to be managed, enables you to execute Windows PowerShell commands on the server using a standard web browser.

The bid advantage of Windows PowerShell Web Access is that the gateway is implemented entirely on the managed remote server being. The only software required on the client is a web browser that supports JavaScript and can retain cookies. There are no browser plug-ins or add-ons required, nor does the client need to run Windows. You can execute Windows PowerShell commands on a remote server using any computer, or even a smartphone or tablet.

The process of setting up Windows PowerShell Web Access on a server to create gateway is fairly complicated, and requires installing and configuring IIS. Because there is no security on the client side of the application, the security configuration of the gateway server is crucial, and should include both a security certificate from a trusted certification authority and user-specific authorization rules.

The gateway server setup process includes the following steps:

- Install the Windows PowerShell Web Access feature.
- Configure the IIS gateway.
- Create Authorization rules.

These steps are described in the following sections.

Installing Windows PowerShell Web Access

The default Windows Server 2012 configuration includes the Windows PowerShell 3.0 feature, as shown in Figure 6-22, but not the Windows PowerShell Web Access feature.

Figure 6-22

The Windows PowerShell Web Access feature in the Add Roles and Features Wizard

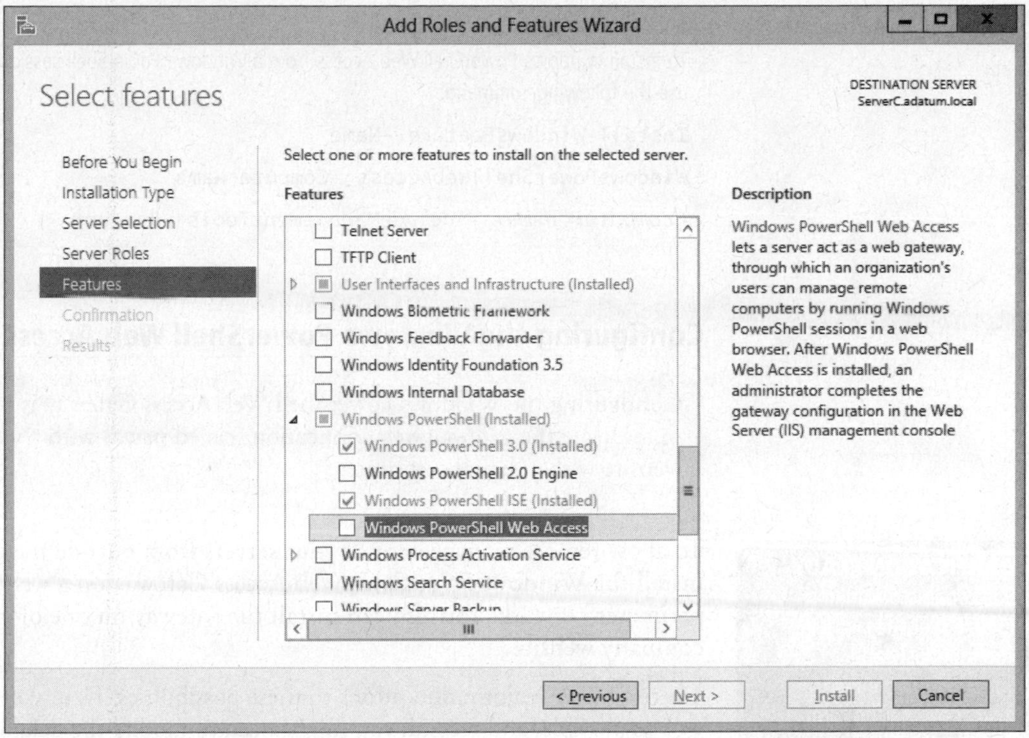

You must use the Add Roles and Features Wizard to install Windows PowerShell Web Access. Selecting this feature requires you to install .NET Framework 4.5 and the Web Server (IIS) role, as shown in Figure 6-23.

Figure 6-23

The Add Features that are required for Windows PowerShell Web Access dialog box

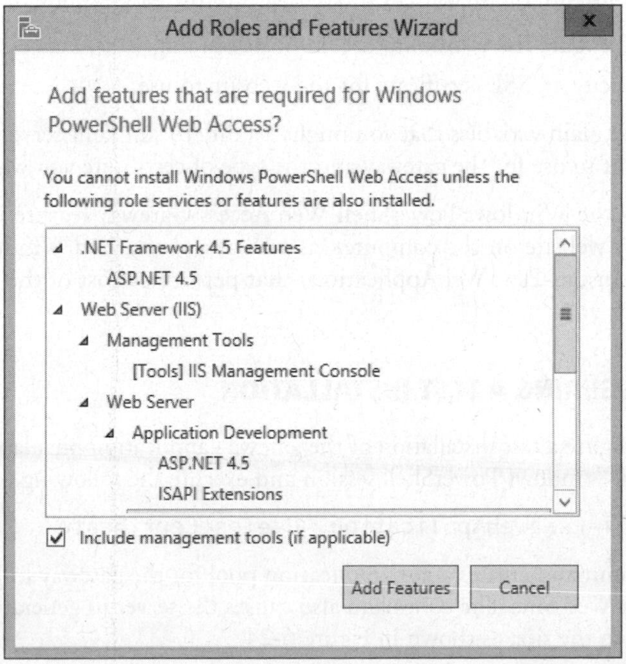

This installation configures the computer to function as a web server and provides the Windows PowerShell gateway function. However, before clients can use the gateway, you must configure it, as described in the next section.

To install Windows PowerShell Web Access from a Windows PowerShell session, as on a Server Core installation, use the following command:

```
Install-WindowsFeature -Name
WindowsPowerShellWebAccess -ComputerName
<computer name> -IncludeManagementTools -Restart
```

Configuring the Windows PowerShell Web Access Gateway

Configuring the Windows PowerShell Web Access Gateway is a matter of configuring IIS to associate the gateway web application (called **pswa**) with a website, and secure the website with a digital certificate.

CERTIFICATION READY
IIS is capable of running multiple websites simultaneously and supports multiple web applications, in the form of application pools. Exam 70-410 does not specifically cover IIS or website configuration, so this section does not explore all possible ways of deploying the Windows PowerShell Web Gateway on an existing IIS installation. Exam candidates should know that the gateway exists and be familiar with the deployment procedure and with the gateway's capabilities.

To allow remote management of your servers from outside the enterprise, you should install the Windows PowerShell Web Access Gateway on a web server located on a perimeter network. You also can install the gateway on one of your servers hosting your company websites.

There are two major ramifications to these possibilities. First, you must secure the server as well as possible, and second, you might need to modify the default gateway configuration to accommodate other websites running on the same server.

The gateway configuration process consists of the following IIS tasks:

1. Create an application pool for the pswa web application.
2. Associate the application pool with a website.
3. Configure the website to use the path to the gateway site files.
4. Configure the website to use an https binding.
5. Specify an SSL certificate for the website to use.

The two main variables that you might modify to suit your server installation are the website you want to use for the gateway and the type of certificate you want to use.

Adding the Windows PowerShell Web Access Gateway feature installs the code for the gateway website on the computer, as well as a specialized Windows PowerShell cmdlet (called Install-PswaWebApplication) that performs most of the basic gateway configuration tasks for you.

CONFIGURING A TEST INSTALLATION

To configure a test installation of the gateway application on a lab server, you can open an elevated Windows PowerShell session and execute the following command:

```
Install-PswaWebApplication -UseTestCertificate
```

This command creates a new application pool for the gateway in IIS and associates it with the Default Web Site. The command also causes the server to generate a self-signed certificate and bind it to the site, as shown in Figure 6-24.

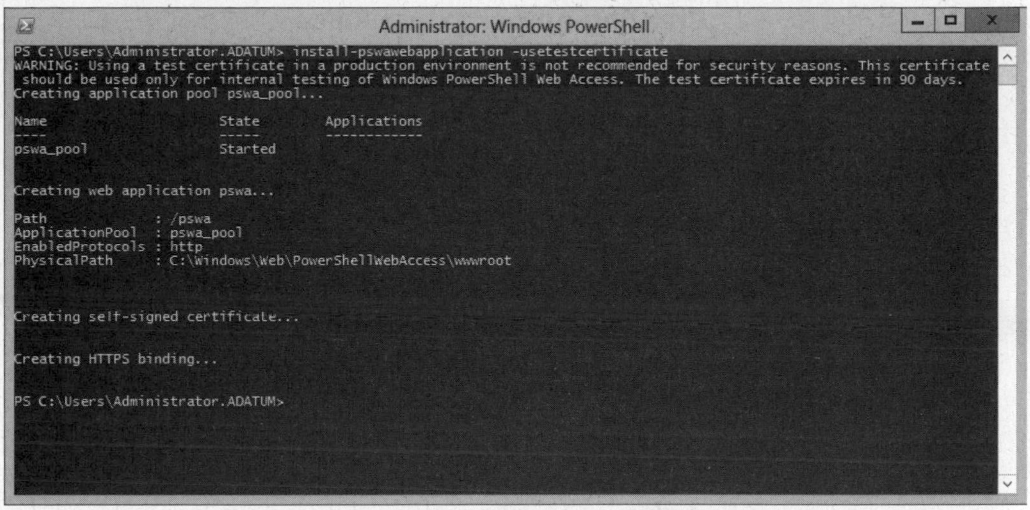

Figure 6-24

Configuring the Windows
PowerShell Web Gateway with
the default settings

Now, the gateway site is ready to accept client connections, using the default URL:
https://<server name>/pswa. You can change this default URL and other configuration settings
by altering the cmdlet parameters.

CUSTOMIZING A GATEWAY INSTALLATION

The Install-PswaWebApplication supports command-line parameters that enable you to
modify the default installation in several ways. The syntax of the cmdlet, with its main
parameters, is as follows:

```
Install-PswaWebApplication [-WebApplicationName
<app name>] [-WebSiteName <site name>]
[-UseTestCertificate]
```

The functions of the parameters are as follows:

- **-WebApplicationName** enables you to specify an alternative to the default application
  name, which is pswa. This is an important modification because it changes the URL that
  clients use to access the gateway. For example, adding the **-WebApplicationName
  pshell** parameter to the command line changes the URL of the gateway site to
  https://<server name>/ pshell.

- **-WebSiteName** enables you to specify an alternative to the default site in which the
  cmdlet installs the gateway application. By default, the cmdlet installs the gateway in the
  Default Web Site site. Adding the **-WebSiteName mgmt** parameter installs the gateway
  to an existing IIS site called mgmt.

- **-UseTestCertificate** causes the server to create a self-signed certificate and bind it
  to the website. This weakens the overall security of the site and is suitable only for a test
  installation in a lab environment. The certificate associated with the site enables clients
  to confirm that the server is operated by the supposed owner. This is only true, however,
  when the certificate is issued by an authority that the client trusts. Any server can issue
  its own self-signed certificate, so this is not a trustworthy arrangement. Instead, you
  should obtain a certificate from a third-party organization that is trusted by the server
  administrators and by the clients.

Rather than modifying the parameters of the Install-PswaWebApplication cmdlet, you can also
customize the gateway by manually configuring IIS by using the IIS Manager console. To do
this, you must create an application pool manually and associate it with a website that points
to the location of the gateway code, which is /Windows/Web/PowerShell/WebAccess/
wwwroot. Then, you must create a binding for the site and supply a certificate to secure it.

Creating Authorization Rules

The `Install-PswaWebApplication` cmdlet configures IIS to provide the website and the application pool needed to implement the Windows PowerShell Web Gateway. After running it, clients can connect to the site, but they cannot log on until you create authorization rules for them.

When the gateway is properly configured, there are four layers of security that users must go through before they can execute commands on a server. These four layers are as follows:

- IIS certificate authentication
- Windows PowerShell Web Access Gateway authentication
- Windows PowerShell Web authorization rules
- Target server authentication and authorization

Authorization rules form one of the layers, which enable you to associate specific users with specific servers and specific session configurations. A ***session configuration*** is a collection of settings that create the environment in which remote users work after they connect to the computer. The settings specify who can connect to the computer from a remote client and what Windows PowerShell commands they can run.

To create and manage authorization rules, you use the following Windows PowerShell cmdlets:

- Get-PswaAuthorizationRule
- Test-PswaAuthorizationRule
- Add-PswaAuthorizationRule
- Remove-PswaAuthorizationRule

TAKE NOTE★

There is no GUI-based method for creating authorization rules. You must use the Windows PowerShell cmdlets.

To create an authorization rule, you use the `Add-PswaAuthorizationRule` cmdlet, with the following syntax:

```
Add-PswaAuthorizationRule -UserName
<domain\user name> -ComputerName <computer name>
-ConfigurationName <session configuration name>
```

The following command is an example of creating an authorization rule:

```
Add-PswaAuthorizationRule -UserName
    adatum.com\Administrator -ComputerName
    ServerA.adatum.com -ConfigurationName
    microsoft.powershell
```

TAKE NOTE★

The `microsoft.powershell` session configuration cited in the example is one of the default session configurations included with Windows Server 2012. You can use these supplied configurations, but to create more specific security environments, you can also create your own.

After you create authorization rules on your gateway server, the users you specify in the rules can log on to the gateway and connect to the servers, displaying an interface like the one shown in Figure 6-25.

Figure 6-25

An active Windows PowerShell
Web Gateway session

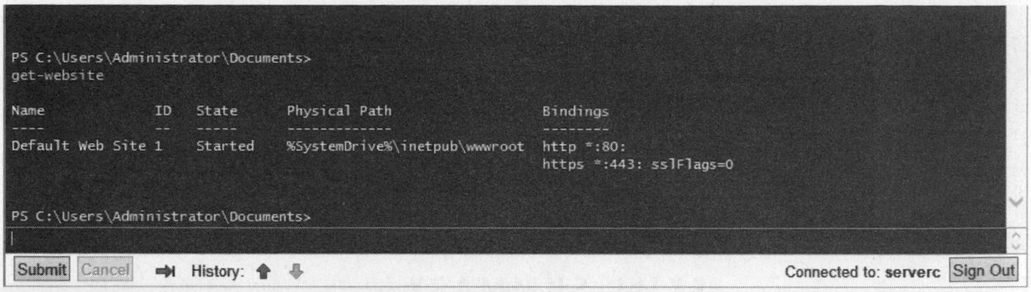

Working with Remote Servers

↓
THE BOTTOM LINE   After you add remote servers to Server Manager, you can access them using various remote administration tools.

CERTIFICATION READY
Configure servers for
day-to-day management
tasks.
Objective 2.3

Server Manager provides three basic methods for addressing remote servers, as follows:

- **Contextual tasks:** When you right-click a server in a Servers tile, anywhere in Server Manager, you see a context menu that provides access to tools and commands pointed at the selected server, as shown in Figure 6-26. Some are commands that Server Manager executes on the remote server, such Restart Server and Windows PowerShell. Others launch tools on the local system and direct them at the remote server, such as Microsoft Management Console snap-ins and the Install Roles and Features Wizard. Still others modify Server Manager itself, by removing servers from the interface. Other contextual tasks sometimes appear in the Tasks menus for specific panes.

Figure 6-26

Contextual tasks in Server
Manager

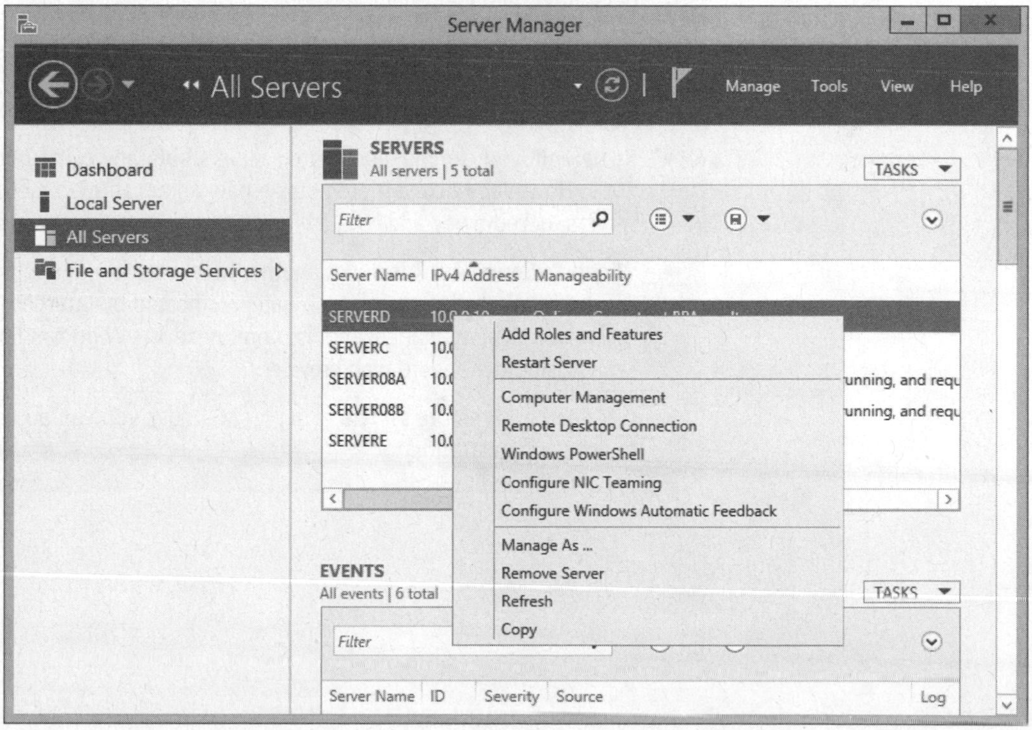

- **Non-contextual tasks:** The menu bar at the top of the Server Manager console provides access to internal tasks, such as launching the Add Server and Install Roles and Features Wizards, as well as the Server Manager Properties dialog box, in which you can specify the console's refresh interval.

- **Non-contextual tools:** The console's Tools menu provides access to external programs, such as MMC snap-ins and the Windows PowerShell interface, that are directed at the local system.

SKILL SUMMARY

IN THIS LESSON, YOU LEARNED:

- Windows Server 2012 facilitates remote server management, so that you do not need to work at the server console. This capability conserves server resources that can be devoted to applications.

- The primary difference between the Windows Server 2012 Server Manager and previous versions is the capability to add and manage multiple servers at once.

- Server Manager has been tested with nearly 100 servers added to the interface. However, the tool's performance is based on a number of factors, including the hardware resources of the computer running Server Manager and the amount of data the remote servers are transmitting to Server Manager over the network.

- After you add servers running Windows Server 2012 to Server Manager, you can immediately use the Add Roles and Features Wizard to install roles and features on any server you add.

- The Windows Firewall rules to enable for remote servers running Windows Server 2012 are also disabled by default on computers running earlier versions of Windows Server, so you need to enable them there as well.

- For enterprise networks administrators, it might be necessary to add several servers to Server Manager. To avoid working with a long scrolling list of servers, you can create server groups, based on server locations, functions, or any other organizational paradigm.

- By default, you can manage remote servers from any computer running Windows Server 2012. However, Microsoft promotes a new administrative method that urges you to keep servers locked away and uses a workstation to manage servers from a remote location.

- Windows Server 2012 includes another new remote management tool called Windows PowerShell Web Access. This web gateway, hosted by Internet Information Services (IIS) on the server to be managed, enables you to execute Windows PowerShell commands on the server using a standard web browser.

- After you add remote servers to Server Manager, you can access them using various remote administration tools.

■ Knowledge Assessment

Multiple Choice

Select one or more correct answers for each of the following questions.

1. Which of the following tasks must you perform before you can manage a remote server running Windows Server 2012 using the Computer Management snap-in?
   a. Enable WinRM on the remote server.
   b. Enable the COM+ Network Access rule on the remote server.
   c. Enable the Remote Event Log Management rules on the remote server.
   d. Install Remote Server Administration Tools on the remote server.

2. Which of the following PowerShell cmdlets can you use to list the existing Windows Firewall rules on a computer running Windows Server 2012?
   a. Get-NetFirewallRule
   b. Set-NetFirewallRule
   c. Show-NetFirewallRule
   d. New-NetFirewallRule

3. Which of the following updates must you install on a server running Windows Server 2008 before you can connect to it using Windows Server 2012 Server Manager?
   a. .NET Framework 3.5
   b. .NET Framework 4.0
   c. Windows Management Framework 3.0
   d. Windows Server 2008 R2

4. When you run Server Manager from a Windows 8 workstation using Remote Server Administration Tools, which of the following elements do not appear in the default display?
   a. The Dashboard
   b. The Local Server home page
   c. The All Servers home page
   d. The Welcome tile

5. Windows Firewall is enabled by default in Windows Server 2012. How are remote management tools affected?
   a. Both MMC and WinRM are blocked. You must alter inbound Windows Firewall rules on the remote server.
   b. MMC is blocked. You must alter inbound Windows Firewall rules on the remote server.
   c. WinRM is blocked. You must alter inbound Windows Firewall rules on the remote server.
   d. Neither MMC nor WinRM is blocked.

6. How can you remotely configure the firewall on several servers at once?
   a. Using the PowerShell command Set-NetFirewallRule -name -enabled All
   b. Applying the configuration change to the applicable server grouping in Server Manager
   c. Creating a configuration file for junior administrators to configure servers in parallel
   d. Applying a Group Policy related to Windows Firewall to the servers

7. The Server Manager interface accommodates several servers, tested at nearly 100. What did the lesson highlight as an element that can easily degrade Server Manager performance, and how to resolve it?
   a. The Event tile generates a large number of records. It is resolved by configuring the types, ages, and sources of events.

    b. The hardware resources of the Server Manager computer can degrade Server Manager. It is resolved by adding additional server memory.

    c. The server's screen resolution is set too high. It is resolved by choosing a lower resolution.

    d. The amount of data the server sends to all remote servers can degrade Server Manager. It is resolved by NIC teaming.

8. By default, Server Manager does not connect with down-level servers (for example, Windows Server 2008). What must be done to properly connect?

    a. Remotely manage the down-level server by MMC.

    b. Disable the Windows Firewall on the down-level server.

    c. Add WinRM 3.0 support by installing the necessary updates and hotfix.

    d. Perform in-place upgrades to Windows Server 2012 to all Windows Server 2008 R2 or lower-level servers.

9. Server Manager is properly connecting and managing your down-level servers (for example, Windows Server 2008). What tool do you use to add roles and features to the down-level server?

    a. Using the Add Roles and Features Wizard in Server Manager to install the role.

    b. Using Windows PowerShell to install the role.

    c. Using MMC and the applicable snap-in.

    d. You cannot add a role remotely to a down-level server.

10. PowerShell Web Access Gateway allows _____.

    a. users to remotely connect to their desktops.

    b. administrators to remotely manage IIS servers.

    c. users a command-line alternative to standard websites.

    d. administrators remote management of servers using commands.

Best Answer

Choose the letter that corresponds to the best answer. More than one answer choice may achieve the goal. Select the BEST answer.

1. What happens if you attempt to add workgroup servers to Server Manager?

    a. Server Manager allows only servers that are members of an Active Directory Domain Services (AD DS) domain to be managed.

    b. Server Manager adds and allows management of any computer, whether a member of an AD DS domain or workgroup.

    c. Server Manager will not permit workgroup servers to be added and managed.

    d. Server Manager usually allows you to add workgroup servers, but attempts to access the remote server fail with a "Credentials not valid" error.

2. Once a server is added to Server Manager, what actions are taken to permit remote server management?

    a. No further action is needed. For example, you may immediately use the Add Roles and Features Wizard.

    b. No further action is needed, because Windows Remote Management (WinRM) is enabled on the source Windows Server 2012.

    c. No further action is needed because WS-Management Protocol is already running.

    d. No further action is needed thanks to Windows Management Instrumentation (WMI) and Windows PowerShell.

3. What is the primary difference between the Windows Server 2012 Server Manager and previous versions?

    a. Windows Server 2012 Server Manager allows management of multiple remote servers at once.

    b. Windows Server 2012 Server Manager allows management of remote servers, categorized in role groups.

    c. Windows Server 2012 Server Manager allows remote management of other servers, including down-level Windows servers.

    d. Windows Server 2012 Server Manager has been tested with nearly 100 servers added to the interface.

4. What functional benefit is derived from creating server groups?

    a. Server groups allow administrators to add roles to several servers at once.

    b. Server groups allow administrators to navigate and organize several servers at once.

    c. Server groups allow administrators to navigate several servers at once.

    d. Server groups allow administrators to organize several servers at once.

5. The security configuration of the Windows PowerShell Web Access Gateway server is crucial, employing a security certificate from a trusted certification authority and user-specific authorization rules. Why are these security measures so crucial?

    a. There is often both client and server side security, but only server end measures are controlled.

    b. There is no mandatory security on the client side of the application, relying more on server side security.

    c. There is no security on the client side of the application, instead relying on robust server side security.

    d. There is often both client and server side security, but only client end measures are controlled.

Build a List

1. Order the steps to add servers to Server Manager. Not all steps will be used.

    a. Select the servers you want to add and click the right arrow button to add them to the Selected list.

    b. Log on to Windows Server 2012 with administrative privileges.

    c. From the Manage menu, select Add Servers. The Add Servers dialog box appears. Select one of the following tabs: Active Directory, DNS, or Import (all varying ways to search for the server to add).

    d. Have a second administrator authenticate the server addition.

    e. In the Server Manager navigation pane, click the All Servers icon.

2. Order the steps to set up a Windows PowerShell Web Access Gateway server.

    a. Create Authorization rules.

    b. Install the Windows PowerShell Web Access feature.

    c. Configure the IIS gateway.

    d. Install .NET Framework 4.5 and the Web Server (IIS) role.

3. Order the steps to install a feature on a down-level server. Not all steps will be used.

    a. Display a list of the roles and features on the remote server by using the following command:

        Get-WindowsFeature

    b. Open a PowerShell session with administrative privileges.

    c. Log on to Windows Server 2012 with administrative privileges.

    d. Establish a Windows PowerShell session with the remote computer by using the following command:

        `Enter-PSSession <remote server name> -credential <user name>`

    e. By using the short name of the role or service as it appears in the Get-WindowsFeature display, install the component using the following command:

        `Add-WindowsFeature <feature name>`

■ Business Case Scenarios

Scenario 6-1: Using Group Policy to Deploy Server Settings

Ralph is responsible for the 24 servers running a particular application, which are scattered all over his company's enterprise network. Ralph wants to use Server Manager on his Windows 8 workstation to manage those servers and monitor the events that occur on them. To do this, he must enable the incoming COM+ Network Access and Remote Event Log Management rules in Windows Firewall on the servers.

Because he can't travel to the locations of all the servers, and many of the sites do not have trustworthy IT personnel, Ralph has decided to use Group Policy to configure Windows Firewall on all of the servers. The company's Active Directory Domain Services tree is organized geographically, which means that Ralph's servers are located in many different OUs, all under one domain.

How can Ralph use Group Policy to deploy the required Windows Firewall rule settings to his 24 servers, and only those servers?

Scenario 6-2: Installing Windows PowerShell Web Access

You need a method to remotely manage a few servers from any client within the enterprise. You want to avoid any method that requires additional client software except a web browser. What will you use? Give an outline of tasks.

Creating and Configuring Virtual Machine Settings

70-410 EXAM OBJECTIVE

Objective 3.1 – Create and configure virtual machine settings. This objective may include but is not limited to: Configure dynamic memory; configure smart paging; configure Resource Metering; configure guest integration services.

LESSON HEADING	EXAM OBJECTIVE
Virtualizing Servers	
Virtualization Architectures	
Hyper-V Implementations	
Installing Hyper-V	
Using Hyper-V Manager	
Creating a Virtual Machine	
Installing an Operating System	
Configuring Guest Integration Services	Configure guest integration services
Allocating Memory	Configure dynamic memory Configure smart paging
Configuring Resource Metering	Configure Resource Metering

KEY TERMS

dynamic memory

guest integration services

hypervisor

Hyper-V

smart paging

virtual machines (VMs)

virtual machine monitor (VMM)

■ Virtualizing Servers

THE BOTTOM LINE

The concept of virtualizing servers has, in the past several years, grown from a novel experiment to a convenient lab and testing tool, as well as to a legitimate deployment strategy for production servers. Windows Server 2012 includes the **Hyper-V** role, which enables you to create virtual machines, each of which runs in its own isolated environment. **Virtual machine (VMs)** are self-contained units that you can easily move from one physical computer to another, greatly simplifying the process of deploying network applications and services.

Server virtualization in Windows Server 2012 is based on a module called a **hypervisor**. Sometimes called a **virtual machine monitor (VMM)**, the hypervisor is responsible for abstracting the computer's physical hardware and creating multiple virtualized hardware environments, called virtual machines (VMs). Each VM has its own (virtual) hardware configuration and can run a separate copy of an operating system. Therefore, with sufficient physical hardware and the correct licensing, a single computer running Windows Server 2012 with the Hyper-V role installed can support multiple VMs, which you can manage as though they were standalone computers.

Virtualization Architectures

Virtualization products can use several different architectures to share a computer's hardware resources among several virtual machines.

The earlier types of virtualization products, including Microsoft Windows Virtual PC and Microsoft Virtual Server, require a standard operating system installed on a computer. This becomes the "host" operating system. Then you install the virtualization product, which adds the hypervisor component. The hypervisor essentially runs as an application on the host operating system, as shown in Figure 7-1, and enables you to create as many virtual machines as the computer has hardware to support.

Figure 7-1

A hybrid VMM sharing hardware access with a host operating system

Host Operating System	Guest Operating System	Guest Operating System	Guest Operating System
	Virtual Machine	Virtual Machine	Virtual Machine
	Hypervisor		
Hardware			

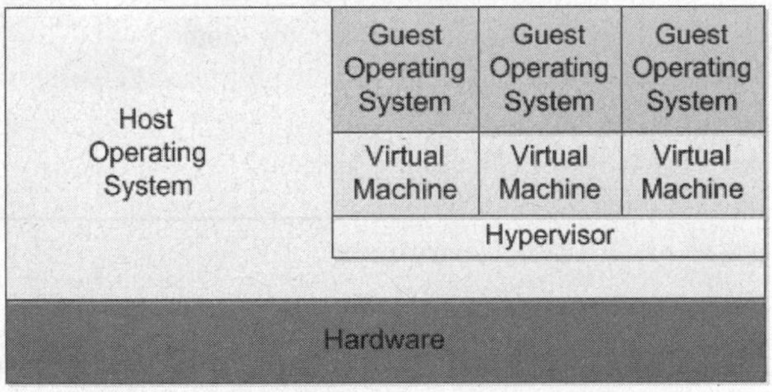

This arrangement, in which the hypervisor runs on top of a host operating system, is called a *Type II virtualization*. By using the Type II hypervisor, you create a virtual hardware environment for each virtual machine. You can specify how much memory to allocate to each VM, create virtual disk drives by using space on the computer's physical drives, and provide access to peripheral devices. You then install a "guest" operating system on each virtual machine as though you were deploying a new computer. The host operating system then shares access to the computer's processor with the hypervisor, with each taking the clock cycles it needs and passing control of the processor back to the other.

Type II virtualization can provide adequate virtual machine performance, particularly in classroom and laboratory environments, but it does not provide performance equivalent to separate physical computers. Therefore, it is not recommended for high-traffic servers in production environments.

The virtualization capability built into Windows Server 2012, called Hyper-V, uses a different type of architecture. Hyper-V uses *Type I virtualization*, in which the hypervisor is an abstraction layer that interacts directly with the computer's physical hardware—that is, without an intervening host operating system. The term *hypervisor* is intended to represent the next level beyond the term *supervisor*, concerning responsibility for allocating a computer's processor clock cycles.

The hypervisor creates individual environments called *partitions*, each of which has its own operating system installed and accesses the computer's hardware via the hypervisor. Unlike Type II virtualization, no host operating system shares processor time with the hypervisor. Instead, the hypervisor designates the first partition it creates as the parent partition and all subsequent partitions as child partitions, as shown in Figure 7-2.

Figure 7-2

A Type 1 VMM, with the hypervisor providing all hardware access

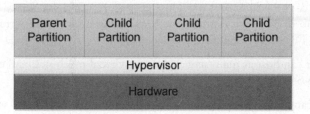

The parent partition accesses the system hardware through the hypervisor, just as the child partitions do. The only difference is that the parent runs the virtualization stack, which creates and manages the child partitions. The parent partition is also responsible for the subsystems that directly affect the performance of the computer's physical hardware, such as Plug and Play, power management, and error handling. These subsystems run in the operating systems on the child partitions as well, but they address only virtual hardware, whereas the parent, or root, partition handles the real thing.

TAKE NOTE * It might not seem as though the Hyper-V role in Windows Server 2012 provides Type I virtualization, because it requires the Windows Server operating system to be installed and running. However, adding the Hyper-V role actually converts the installed instance of Windows Server 2012 into the parent partition and causes the system to load the hypervisor before the operating system.

Hyper-V Implementations

Windows Server 2012 includes the Hyper-V role only in the Standard and Datacenter editions.

The Hyper-V role is required for the operating system to function as a computer's primary partition, enabling it to host other virtual machines. No special software is required for an operating system to function as a guest OS in a virtual machine. Therefore, although the Windows Server 2012 Essentials product does not include the Hyper-V role, it can function as a guest OS. Other guest OSes supported by Hyper-V include the current Windows workstation operating systems and many other non-Microsoft server and workstation products.

HYPER-V LICENSING

As far as Hyper-V is concerned, the primary difference between the Standard and Datacenter editions of Windows Server 2012 is the number of virtual machines they support. When you install a Windows Server 2012 instance on a virtual machine, you must have a license for it, just as when you install it on a physical machine. Purchasing the Datacenter edition licenses you to create an unlimited number of virtual machines running Windows Server 2012 on that one physical machine. The Standard license provides only two virtual instances of Windows Server 2012.

TAKE NOTE*

The licensing restrictions of the Windows Server 2012 Standard and Datacenter editions do not govern how many virtual machines you can create. They govern only what operating system you are permitted to install on the virtual machines. For example, you can use a Standard edition license to create only two virtual instances of Windows Server 2012, but you can also create any number of virtual machines running a free Linux distribution.

HYPER-V HARDWARE LIMITATIONS

The Windows Server 2012 version of Hyper-V contains massive improvements in the scalability of the system over previous versions. A Windows Server 2012 Hyper-V host system can have up to 320 logical processors, supporting up to 2,048 virtual CPUs and up to 4 terabytes (TB) of physical memory.

One server can host as many as 1,024 active virtual machines, and each virtual machine can have up to 64 virtual CPUs and up to 1 TB of memory.

Hyper-V can also support clusters with up to 64 nodes and 8,000 virtual machines.

HYPER-V SERVER

In addition to the Hyper-V implementation in Windows Server 2012, Microsoft also provides a dedicated Hyper-V Server product, which is a subset of Windows Server 2012. Hyper-V Server includes the Hyper-V role, which it installs by default during the operating system installation. With the exception of some limited File and Storage Services and Remote Desktop capabilities, the operating system includes no other roles, as shown in Figure 7-3.

TAKE NOTE*

Another major improvement in the Windows Server 2012 version of Hyper-V is the inclusion of a Hyper-V module for Windows PowerShell, which includes more than 160 new cmdlets dedicated to the creation and management of the Hyper-V service and its virtual machines.

Figure 7-3

Roles available in Hyper-V Server

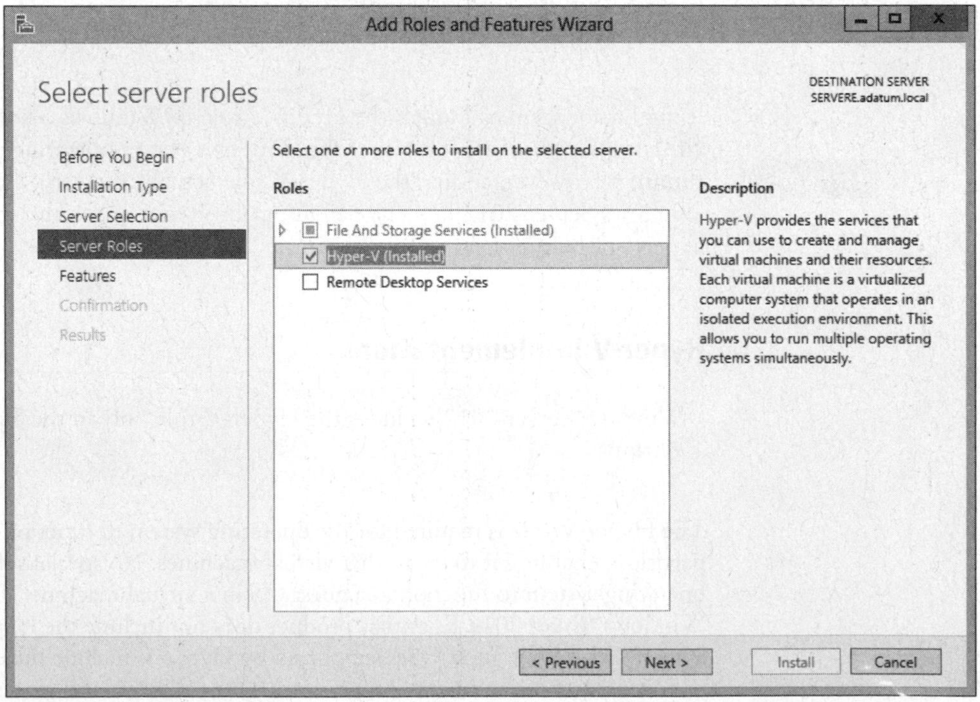

The Hyper-V Server product is also limited to the Server Core interface, although it also includes a simple, script-based configuration interface, as shown in Figure 7-4. You can also manage Hyper-V Server remotely, using Server Manager and Hyper-V Manager, just as you would with any other Server Core installation.

Figure 7-4

The Server Core interface in Hyper-V Server

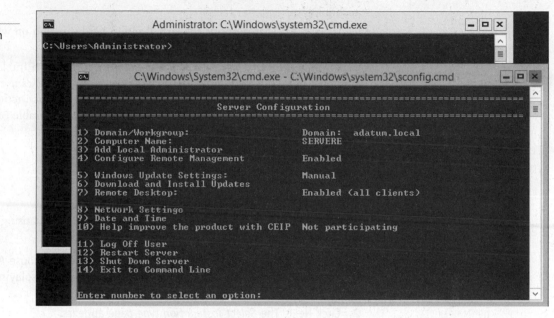

Unlike Windows Server 2012, Hyper-V Server is a free product, available for download from Microsoft's website. However, Hyper-V Server does not include any licenses for virtual instances. You must obtain and license all the operating systems you install on the virtual machines you create.

■ Installing Hyper-V

↓
THE BOTTOM LINE

As soon as you have the appropriate hardware and the required licenses, you can add the Hyper-V role to Windows Server 2012 via Server Manager, just as you would any other role.

Adding the Hyper-V role installs the hypervisor software, and, in the case of a full GUI installation, the management tools. The primary tool for creating and managing virtual machines and their components on Hyper-V servers is the Hyper-V Manager console. Hyper-V Manager provides you with a list of all the virtual machines on Windows Server 2012 systems and enables you to configure both the server environments and those of the individual VMs. Windows PowerShell also includes a set of Hyper-V cmdlets that enable you to exercise complete control over VMs using that interface.

Microsoft recommends that you do not install other roles with Hyper-V. Any other roles that you need the physical computer to perform are better off implemented within one of the virtual machines you create with Hyper-V. You also might want to consider installing Hyper-V on a computer using the Server Core installation option to minimize the overhead expended on the partition. As with other roles, installing Hyper-V on Server Core excludes the management tools, which you must install separately as a feature.

Before you can install the Hyper-V role on a server running Windows Server 2012, you must have appropriate hardware, as follows:

- A *64-bit processor* that includes hardware-assisted virtualization. This type of virtualization is available in processors that include a virtualization option, such of Intel Virtualization Technology (Intel VT) or AMD Virtualization (AMD-V) technology.

- A *system BIOS* that supports the virtualization hardware and on which the virtualization feature has been enabled.

- Hardware-enforced *Data Execution Prevention (DEP)*, which Intel describes as eXecuted Disable (XD) and AMD describes as No eXecute (NS). CPUs use this technology to segregate areas of memory for either storage of processor instructions or for storage of data. Specifically, you must enable Intel XD bit (execute disable bit) or AMD NX bit (no execute bit).

To install the Hyper-V role, use the following procedure.

INSTALL THE HYPER-V ROLE

GET READY. Log on to the server running Windows Server 2012 using an account with administrative privileges.

1. From the Manage menu of the *Server Manager* window, choose Add Roles and Features. The *Add Roles and Features Wizard* launches, displaying the *Before you begin* page.

2. Click Next. The *Select installation type* page appears.

3. Leave the *Role-based or feature-based installation* radio button selected and click Next. The *Select destination server* page appears.

4. Select the server on which you want to install Hyper-V and click Next. The *Select server roles* page appears, as shown in Figure 7-5.

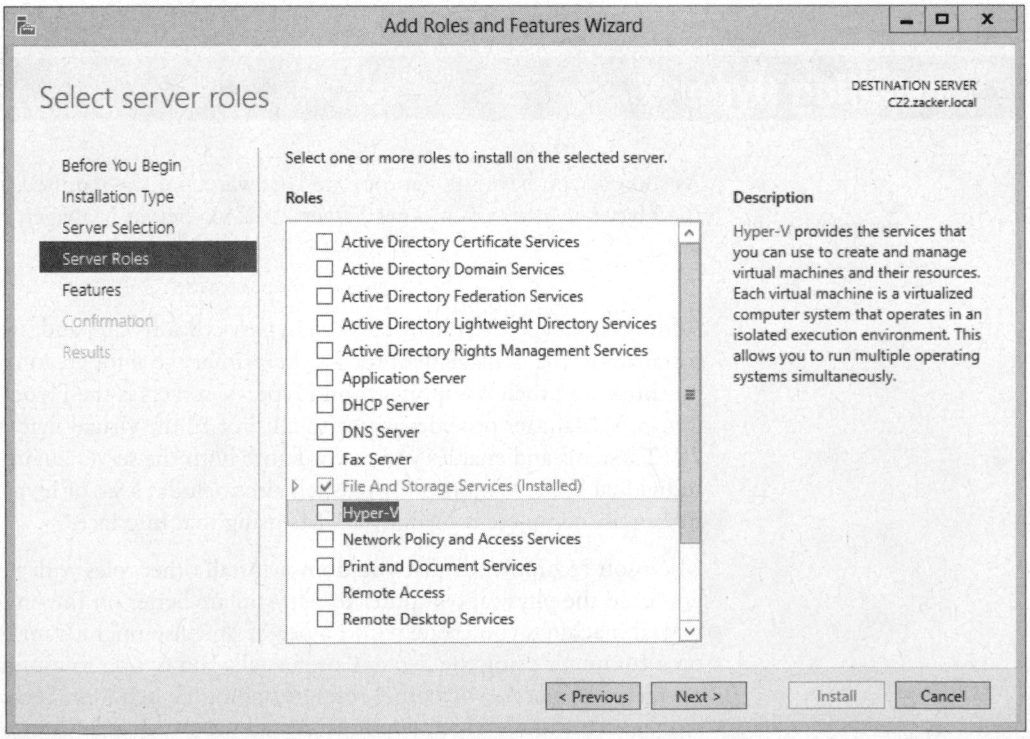

Figure 7-5

The *Select server roles* page of the Add Roles and Features Wizard

5. Select the Hyper-V role. The *Add features that are required for Hyper-V?* dialog box appears, as shown in Figure 7-6.

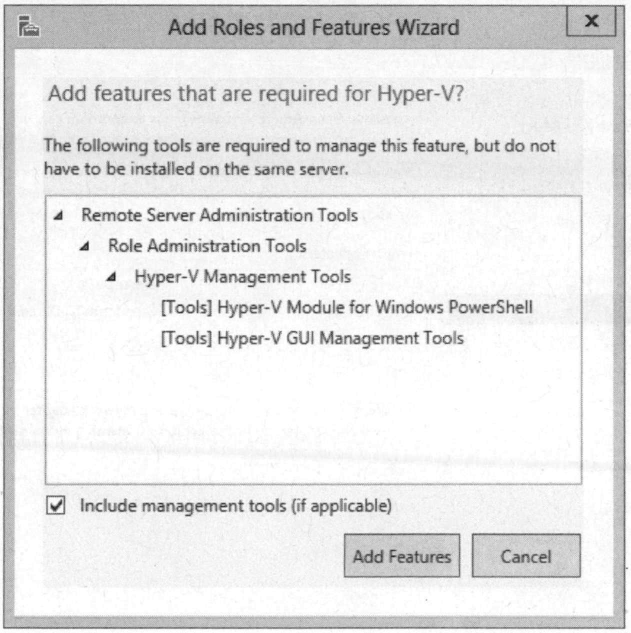

Figure 7-6

The *Add features that are required for Hyper-V?* dialog box in the Add Roles and Features Wizard

6. Click Add Features to accept the dependencies, and then click Next. The *Select features* page appears.
7. Click Next. The *Hyper-V* page appears, as shown in Figure 7-7.

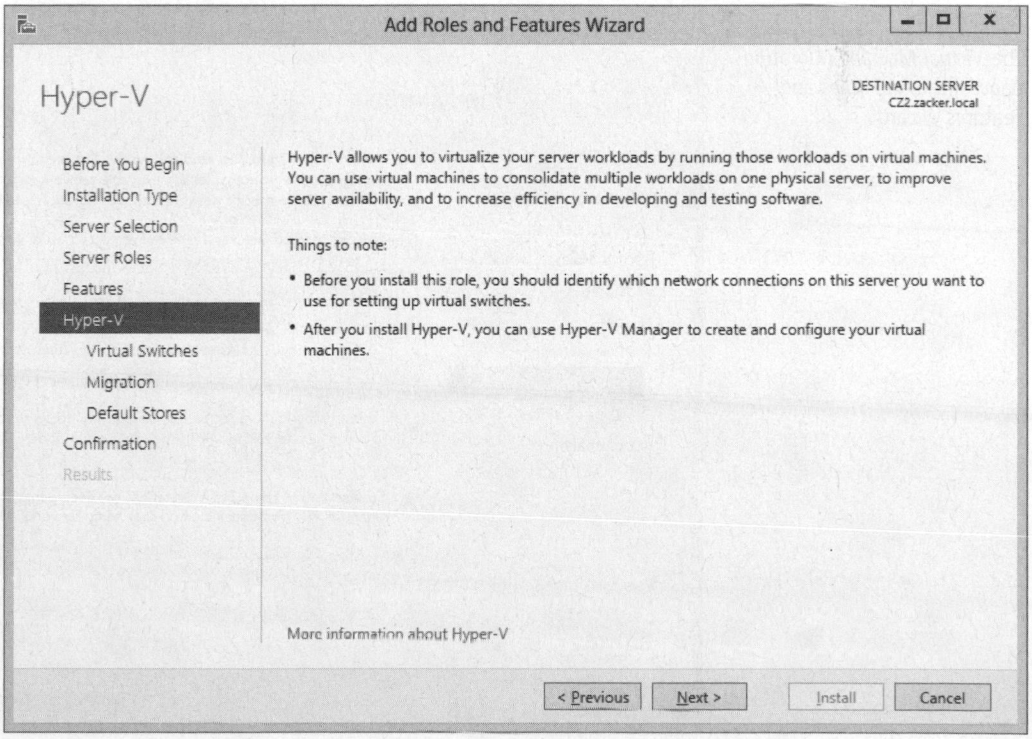

Figure 7-7

The Hyper-V page of the Add Roles and Features Wizard

8. Click Next. The *Create Virtual Switches* page appears, as shown in Figure 7-8.

Figure 7-8

The *Create Virtual Switches* page of the Add Roles and Features Wizard

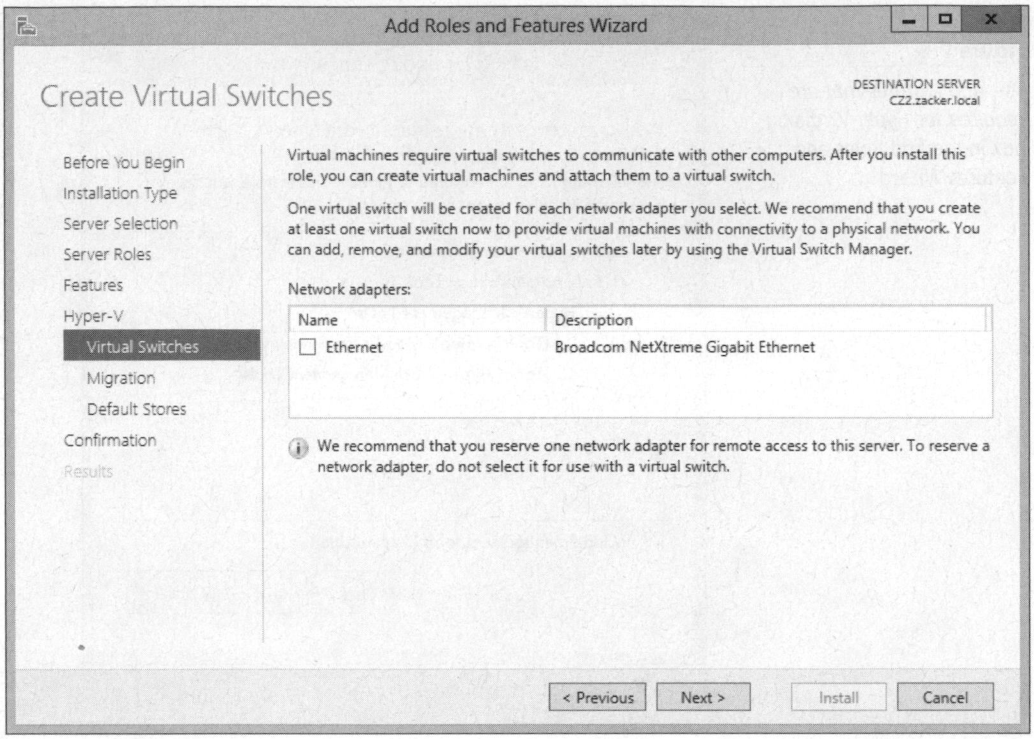

9. Select the check box for a network adapter and click Next. The *Virtual Machine Migration* page appears, as shown in Figure 7-9.

Figure 7-9

The *Virtual Machine Migration* page of the Add Roles and Features Wizard

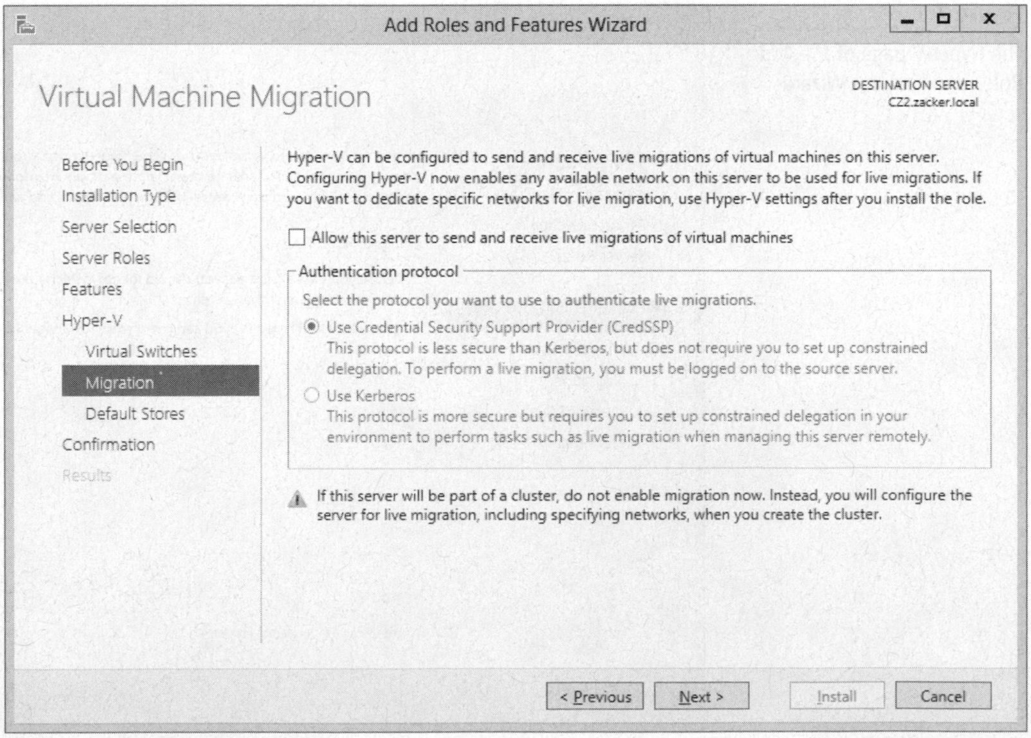

10. Click Next. The *Default Stores* page appears, as shown in Figure 7-10.

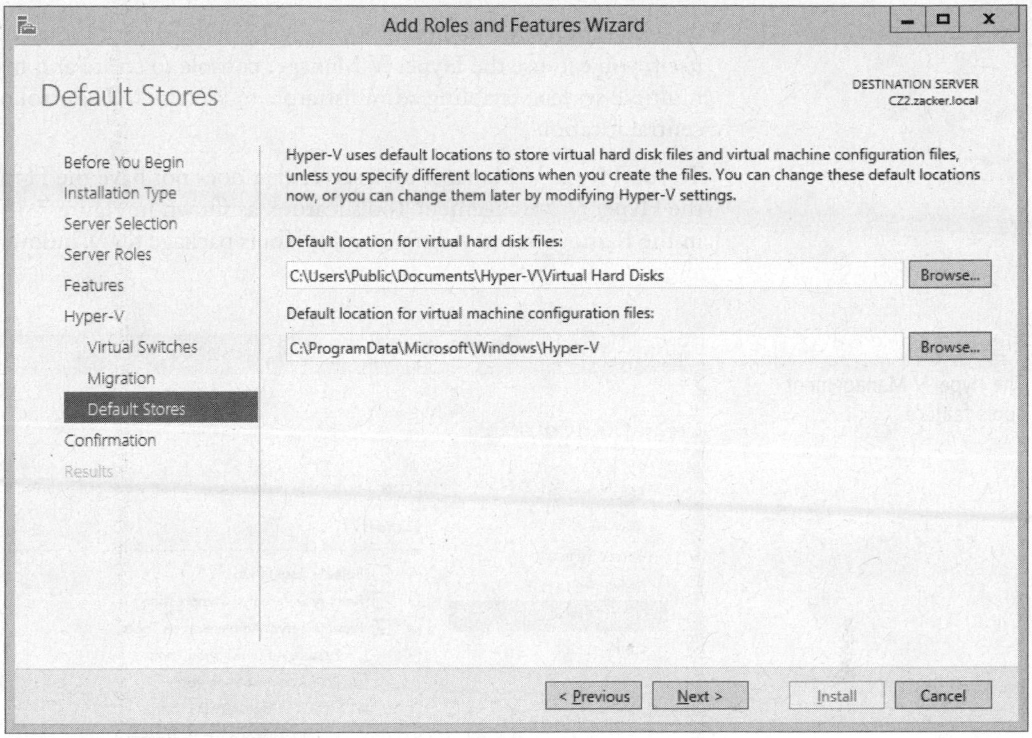

Figure 7-10

The *Default Stores* page of the
Add Roles and Features Wizard

11. Specify alternatives to the default locations for virtual hard disk and virtual machine configuration files, if desired, and click Next. The *Confirm Installation Selection* page appears.

12. Click Install. The *Installation Progress* page appears as the wizard installs the role.

13. Click Close to close the wizard.

RESTART the server.

Installing the role modifies the Windows Server 2012 startup procedure, so that the newly installed hypervisor can address the system hardware directly and then load the operating system as the primary partition on top of that.

USING WINDOWS POWERSHELL

You can also install the Hyper-V role with the Install-WindowsFeature cmdlet, using the following syntax:

```
Install–WindowsFeature –Name Hyper–V –ComputerName <name>
–IncludeManagementTools –Re start
```

■ Using Hyper-V Manager

↓
THE BOTTOM LINE   After you install the Hyper-V role and restart the computer, you can begin to create virtual machines and deploy operating systems on them.

The primary graphical tool for creating and managing virtual machines is the Hyper-V Manager console, which you can access from the *Tools* menu in Server Manager, just as you can any of the other server and Active Directory management tools.

As with most of the Windows Server 2012 management tools, including Server Manager itself, you can use the Hyper-V Manager console to create and manage virtual machines on multiple servers, enabling administrators to exercise full control over their servers from a central location.

To run Hyper-V Manager on a server that does not have the Hyper-V role, you must install the Hyper-V Management Tools feature, as shown in Figure 7-11. You also can find these tools in the Remote Server Administration Tools package for Windows 8.

Figure 7-11

The Hyper-V Management Tools feature

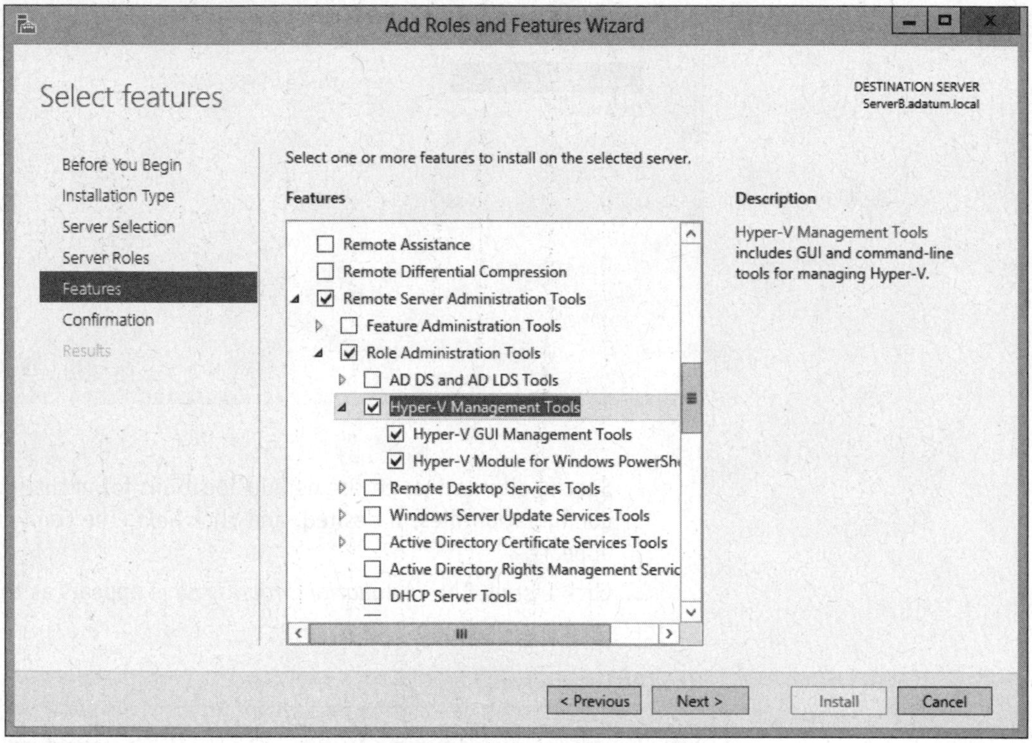

After you install and launch the Hyper-V Manager console, you can add servers to the display by right-clicking the *Hyper-V Manager* node in the left pane and selecting *Connect to Server* from the shortcut menu. In the *Select Computer* dialog box that appears, you can type or browse to the name of a Hyper-V server (see Figure 7-12).

Figure 7-12

The Select Computer dialog box

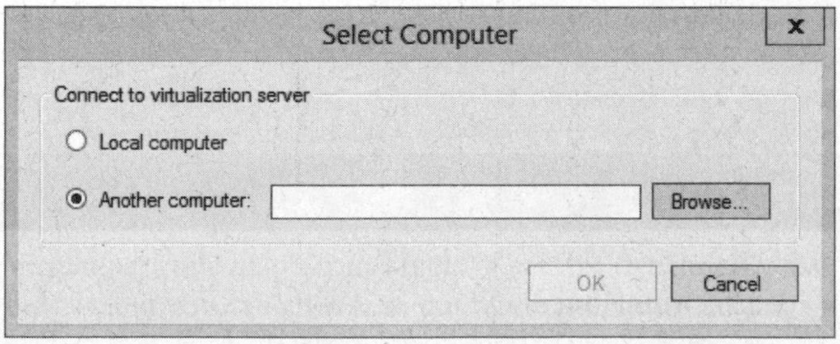

The Hyper-V Manager console lists all the virtual machines on the selected server, along with status information about each one (see Figure 7-13).

Figure 7-13

The Hyper-V Manager console

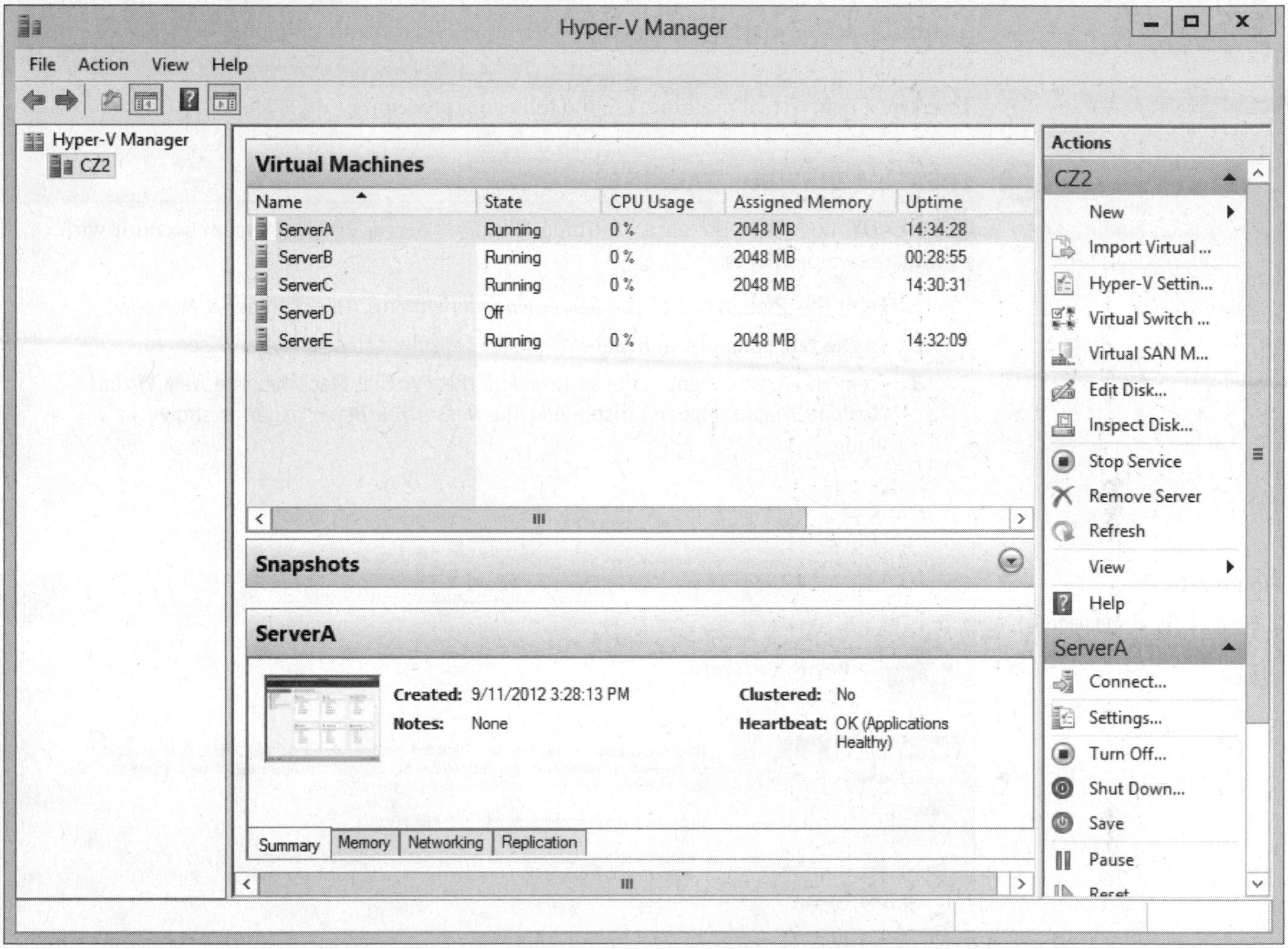

Creating a Virtual Machine

After installing Hyper-V and configuring Hyper-V Manager, you are ready to create virtual machines and install the operating system on each virtual machine that you create.

By using Hyper-V Manager, you can create new virtual machines and define the hardware resources that the system should allocate to them. In the settings for a particular virtual machine, depending on the physical hardware available in the computer and the limitations of the guest operating system, you can specify the number of processors and the amount of memory a virtual machine should use, install virtual network adapters, and create virtual disks using various technologies, including storage area networks (SANs).

By default, Hyper-V stores the files that make up virtual machines in the folders you specified on the *Default Stores* page during installation. Each virtual machine uses the following files:

- A virtual machine configuration (.vmc) file in XML format that contains the virtual machine configuration information, including all settings for the virtual machine
- One or more virtual hard disk (.vhd or .vhdx) files to store the guest operating system, applications, and data for the virtual machine

A virtual machine may also use a saved-state (.vsv) file, if the machine has been placed into a saved state.

To create a new virtual machine, use the following procedure.

CREATE A VIRTUAL MACHINE

GET READY. Log on to the server running Windows Server 2012, using an account with administrative privileges.

1. From the Tools menu of the *Server Manager* window, select Hyper-V Manager.
2. In the left pane of the *Hyper-V Manager* console, select a Hyper-V server.
3. From the Action menu, choose New and then Virtual Machine. The *New Virtual Machine Wizard* appears, displaying the *Before You Begin* page, as shown in Figure 7-14.

Figure 7-14

The *Before You Begin* page of the New Virtual Machine Wizard

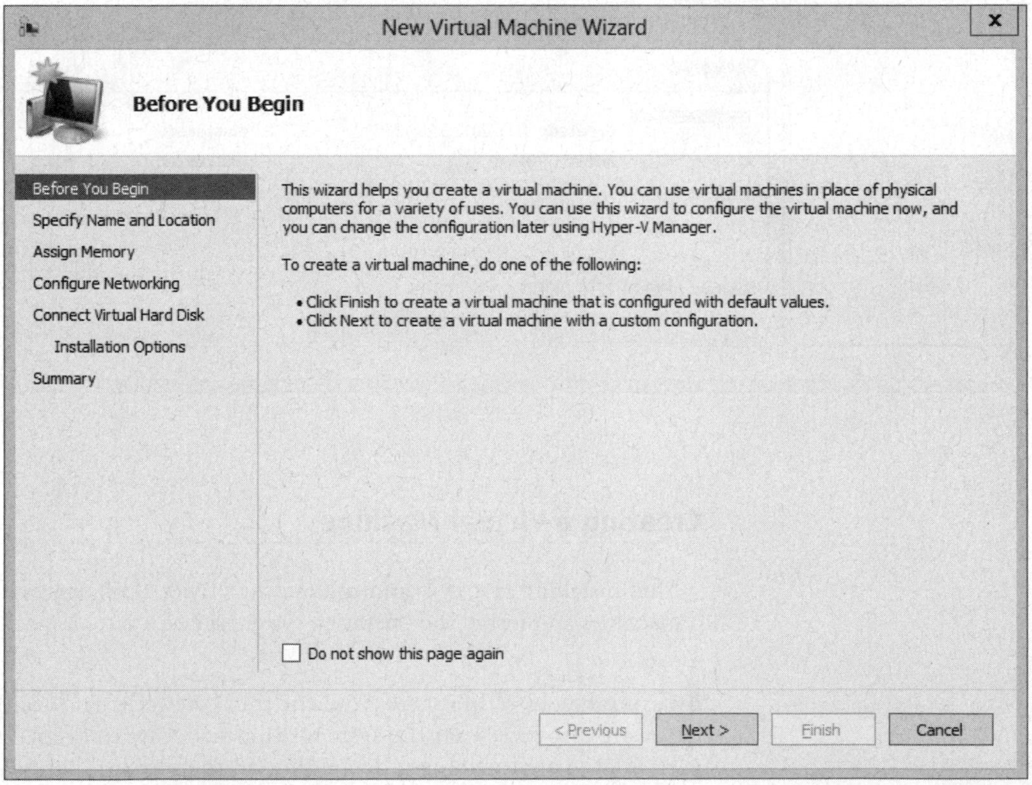

4. Click Next. The *Specify Name and Location* page appears, as shown in Figure 7-15.

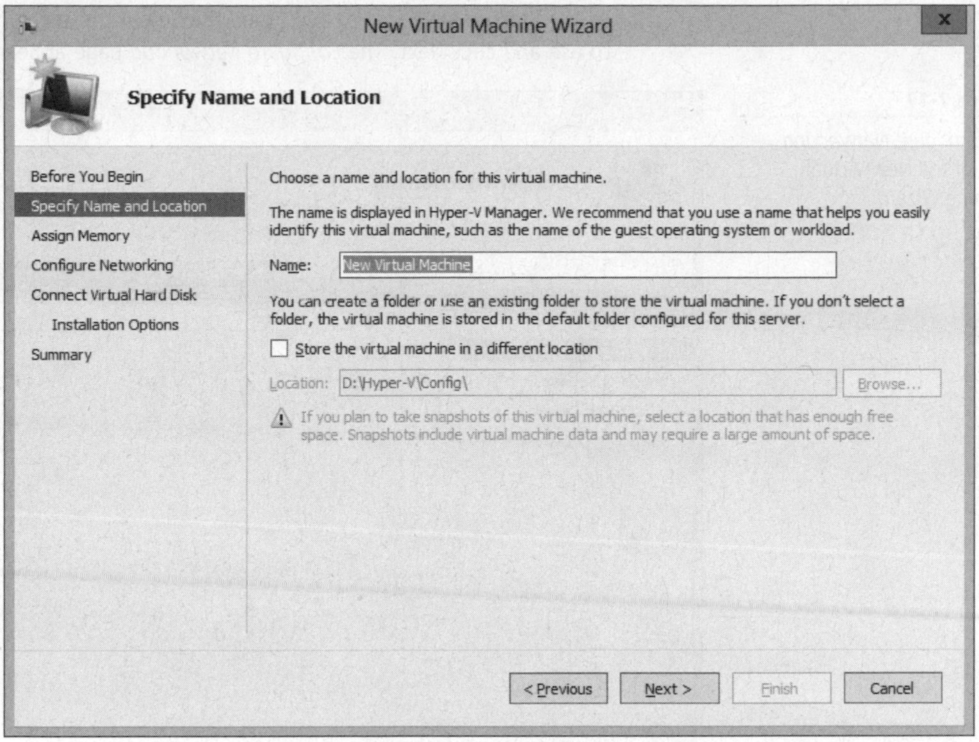

Figure 7-15

The *Specify Name and Location* page of the New Virtual Machine Wizard

5. In the Name text box, type a name for the virtual machine, keeping in mind that the system also uses this name to create the VM files and folders. To create the virtual machine files in a location other than the default, select the Store the virtual machine in a different location check box and type an alternate path in the Location text box. Then click Next. The *Assign Memory* page appears, as shown in Figure 7-16.

➕ MORE INFORMATION

For more information on how Hyper-V uses memory, see "Allocating Memory," later in this lesson.

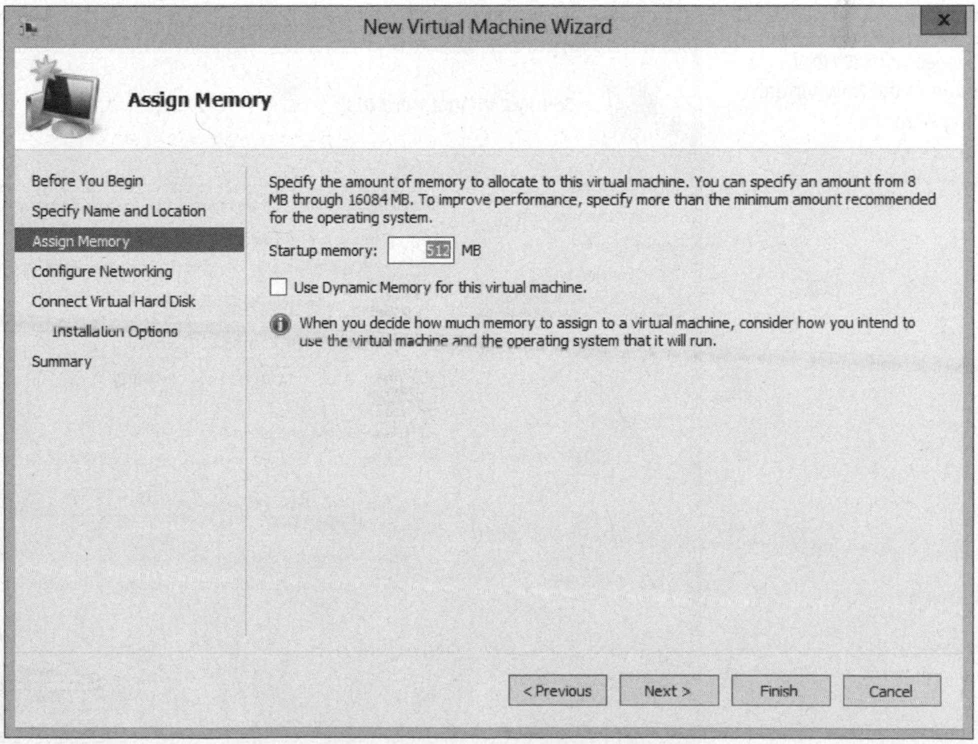

Figure 7-16

The *Assign Memory* page of the New Virtual Machine Wizard

6. In the Startup memory text box, type the amount of memory you want the virtual machine to use and click Next. The *Configure Networking* page appears, as shown in Figure 7-17.

Figure 7-17

The *Configure Networking* page of the New Virtual Machine Wizard

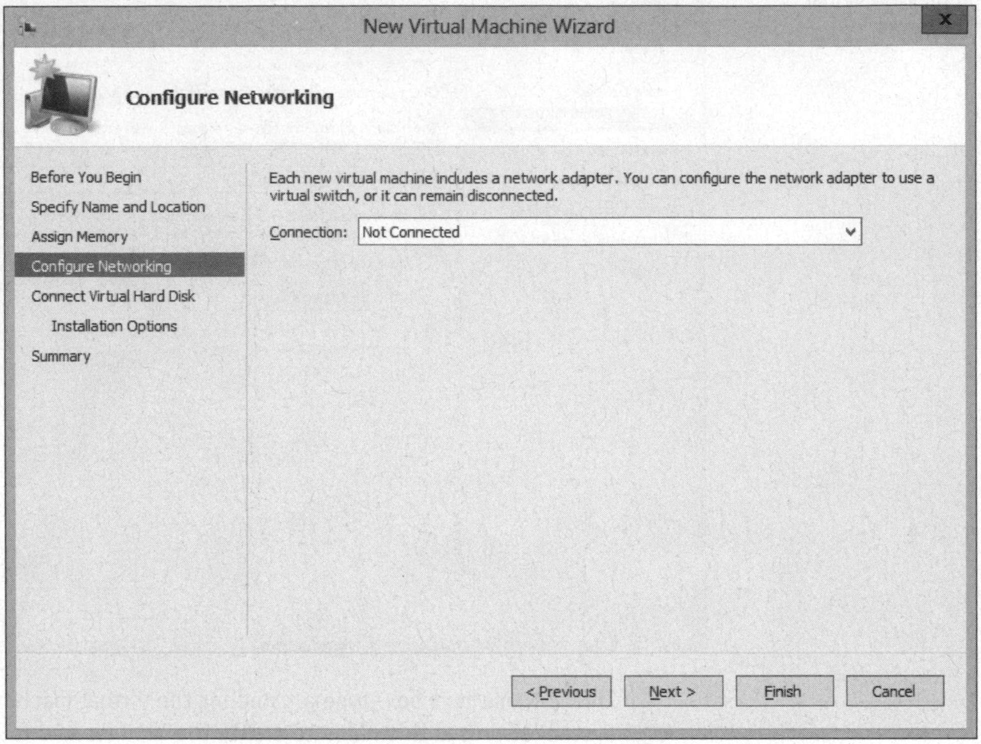

7. From the Connection drop-down list, select a virtual switch and click Next. The *Connect Virtual Hard Disk* page appears, as shown in Figure 7-18.

➕ **MORE INFORMATION**

For more information on virtual switches and networking virtual machines, see Lesson 9, "Creating and Configuring Virtual Networks."

Figure 7-18

The *Connect Virtual Hard Disk* page of the New Virtual Machine Wizard

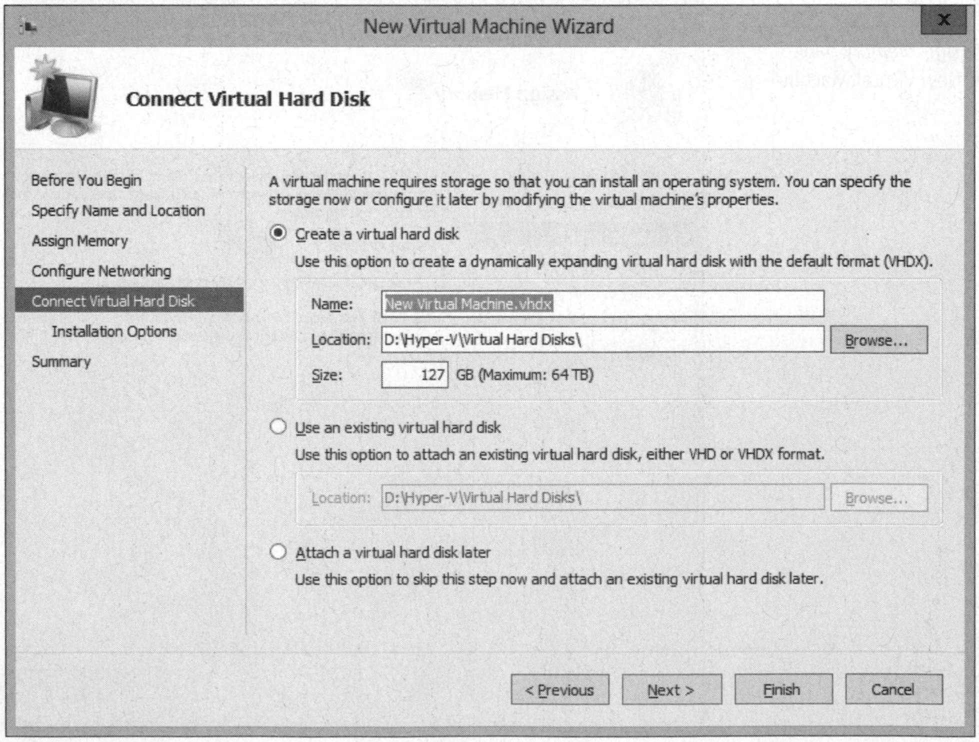

8. Leave the *Create a virtual hard disk* option selected and type values for the following fields:
   - Name specifies the filename for the virtual hard disk, using the .vhdx format new to Windows Server 2012.
   - Location specifies a location for the virtual hard disk other than the default you specified in the *Default Stores* page.
   - Size specifies the maximum size of the virtual hard disk.

> **＋ MORE INFORMATION**
>
> By default, the wizard creates a virtual hard disk file that starts small and dynamically expands up to the maximum size you specify. For more information on Hyper-V storage, see Lesson 8, "Creating and Configuring Virtual Machine Storage."

9. Click Next. The *Installation Options* page appears, as shown in Figure 7-19.

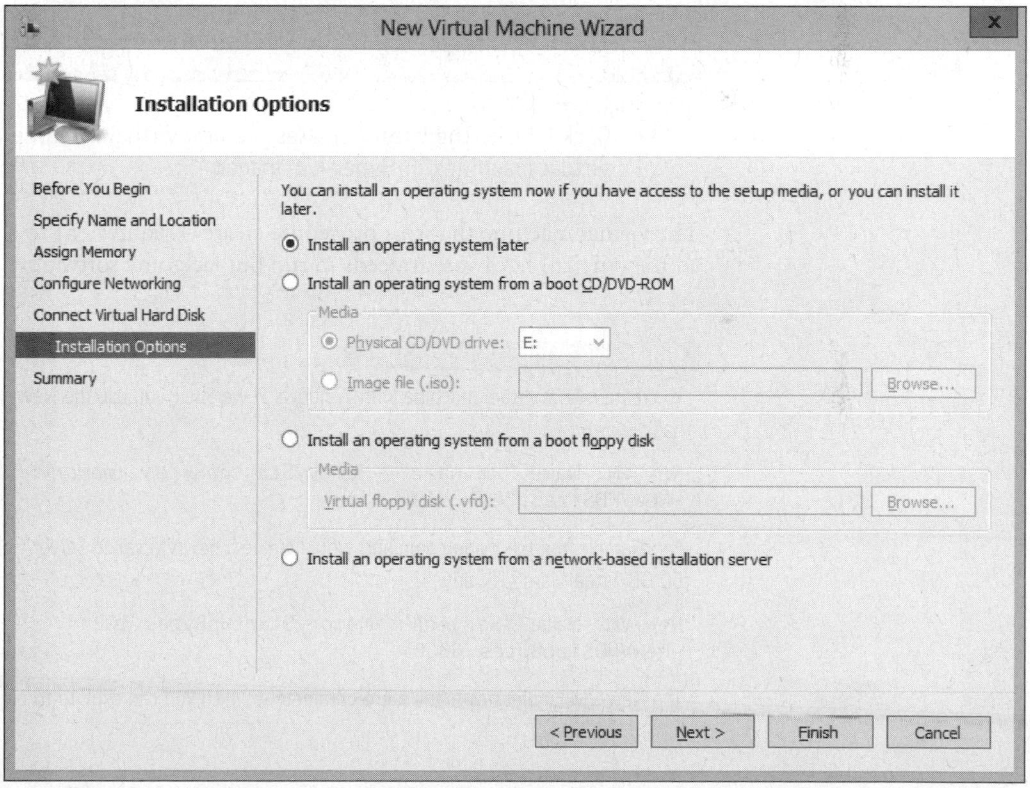

Figure 7-19

The *Installation Options* page of the New Virtual Machine Wizard

10. Leave the *Install an operating system later* option selected and click Next. The *Completing the New Virtual Machine Wizard* page appears, as shown in Figure 7-20.

Figure 7-20

The *Completing the New Virtual Machine Wizard* page of the New Virtual Machine Wizard

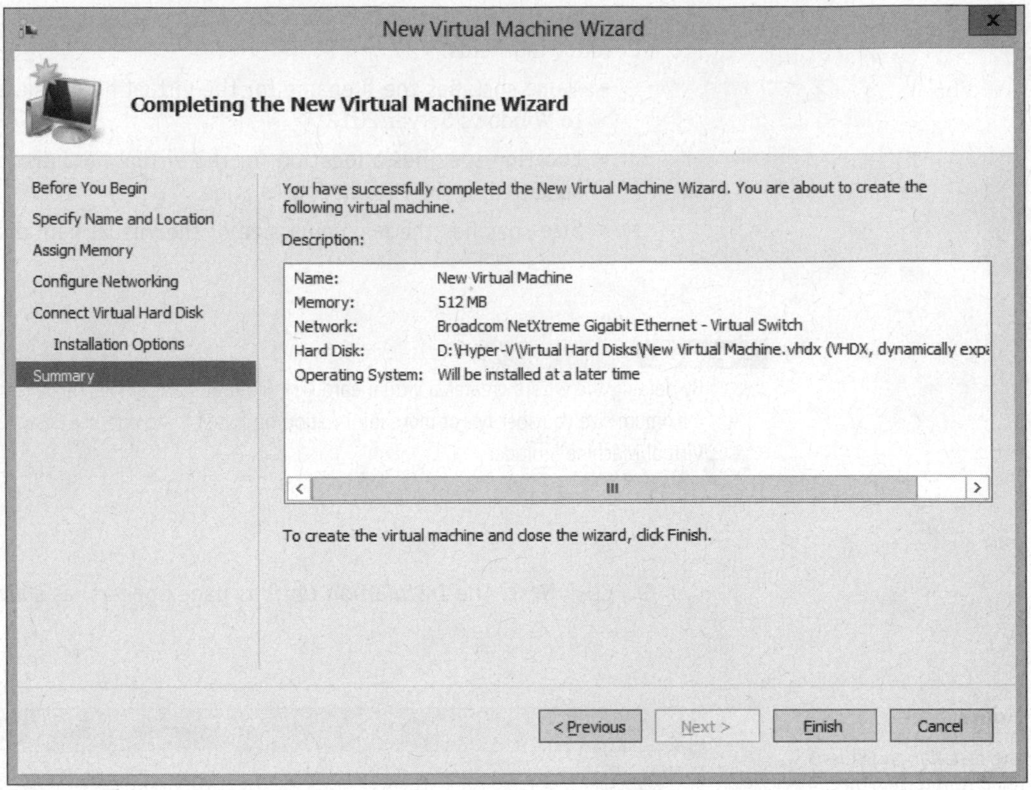

11. Click Finish. The wizard creates the new virtual machine and adds it to the list of virtual machines in Hyper-V Manager.

The virtual machine that this procedure creates is equivalent to a bare metal computer. It has all the (virtual) hardware it needs to run but lacks any software.

USING WINDOWS POWERSHELL

To create a new virtual machine with Windows PowerShell, you use the New-VM cmdlet with the following basic syntax:

```
New-VM -Name "VM name" -MemoryStartupBytes <memory>
-NewVHDSizeBytes <disk size>
```

For example, the following command would create a new VM called ServerA with 1 GB of memory and a new 60 GB virtual hard disk drive:

```
New-VM -Name "ServerA" -MemoryStartupBytes 1GB
-NewVHDSizeBytes 60GB
```

The New-VM cmdlet has many more parameters, which you can explore through the Get-Help cmdlet.

Each virtual machine on a Hyper-V server consists of a collection of settings that specify the hardware resources in the machine and the configuration settings that control those resources. You can manage and modify those settings by using the *Settings* dialog box for the particular virtual machine.

Selecting a virtual machine from the list in Hyper-V Manager displays a series of icons in the *Actions* pane. Clicking the *Settings* icon opens the *Settings* dialog box (see Figure 7-21), which is the primary configuration interface for that VM. Here, you can modify any settings that the New Virtual Machine Wizard configured for you.

Figure 7-21

The Settings dialog box for a virtual machine

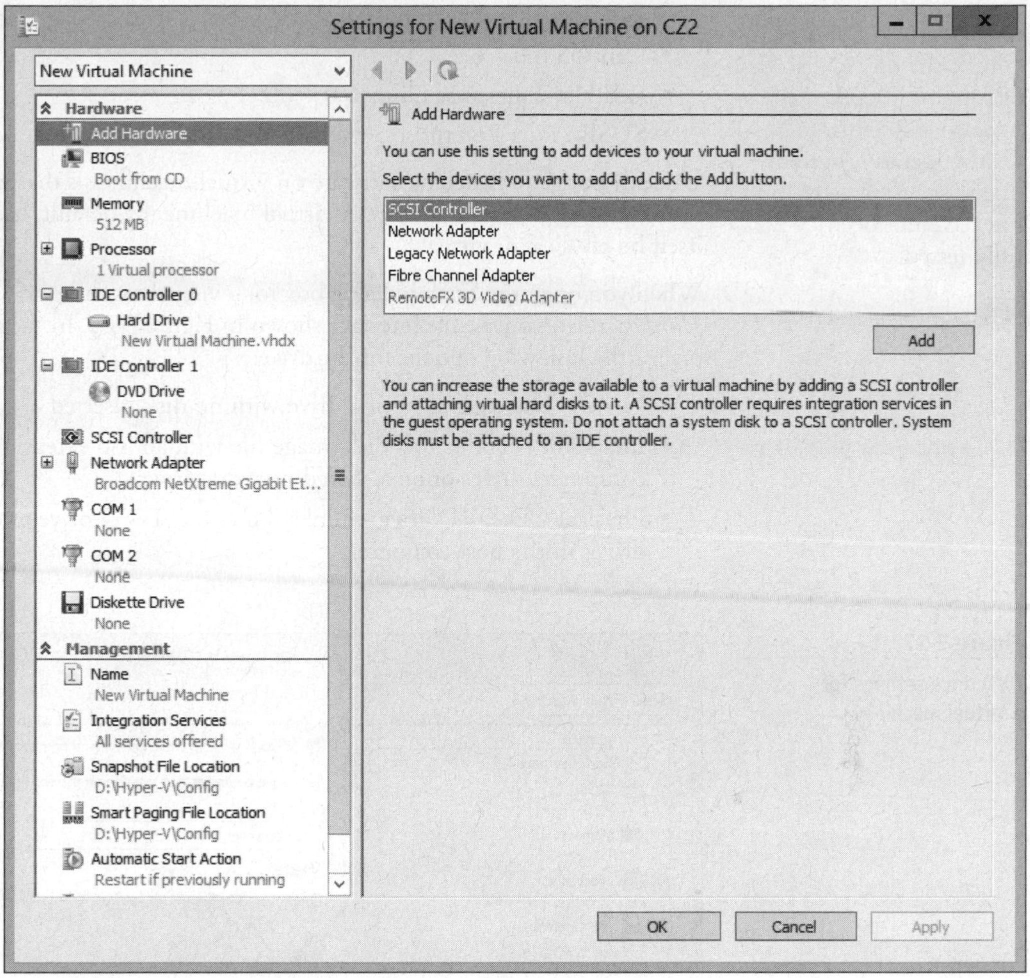

Installing an Operating System

After you create a virtual machine, you can install an operating system on it, just as you would on a new, bare metal computer.

Hyper-V in Windows Server 2012 supports all the following as operating systems you can install in virtual machines:

- Windows Server 2012
- Windows Server 2008 R2
- Windows Server 2008
- Windows Home Server 2011
- Windows Small Business Server 2011
- Windows Server 2003 R2
- Windows Server 2003 SP2
- Windows 8
- Windows 7 Enterprise and Ultimate
- Windows Vista Business, Enterprise, and Ultimate SP2
- Windows XP Professional SP3

TAKE NOTE*

This is the official list of supported guest operating systems. Other operating systems might function as well but have not been fully tested.

- Windows XP x64 Professional SP2
- CentOS 6.0 – 6.2
- Red Hat Enterprise Linux 6.0 – 6.2
- SUSE Linux Enterprise Server 11 SP2

One advantage to installing software on virtual machines is that you can access the installation files in several ways. A virtual machine, by default, has a DVD drive, which can itself be physical or virtual.

When you open the *Settings* dialog box for a virtual machine and select the DVD drive in the *Hardware* list, you see the interface shown in Figure 7-22. In the Media box, you can select one of the following options for the drive:

- None – The equivalent of a drive with no disk inserted
- Image file – Points to a disk image file with an .iso extension stored on one of the host computers drives or on a shared network drive.
- Physical CD/DVD drive – Links the virtual DVD drive to one of the physical DVD drives in the host computer.

Figure 7-22

DVD drive settings for a virtual machine

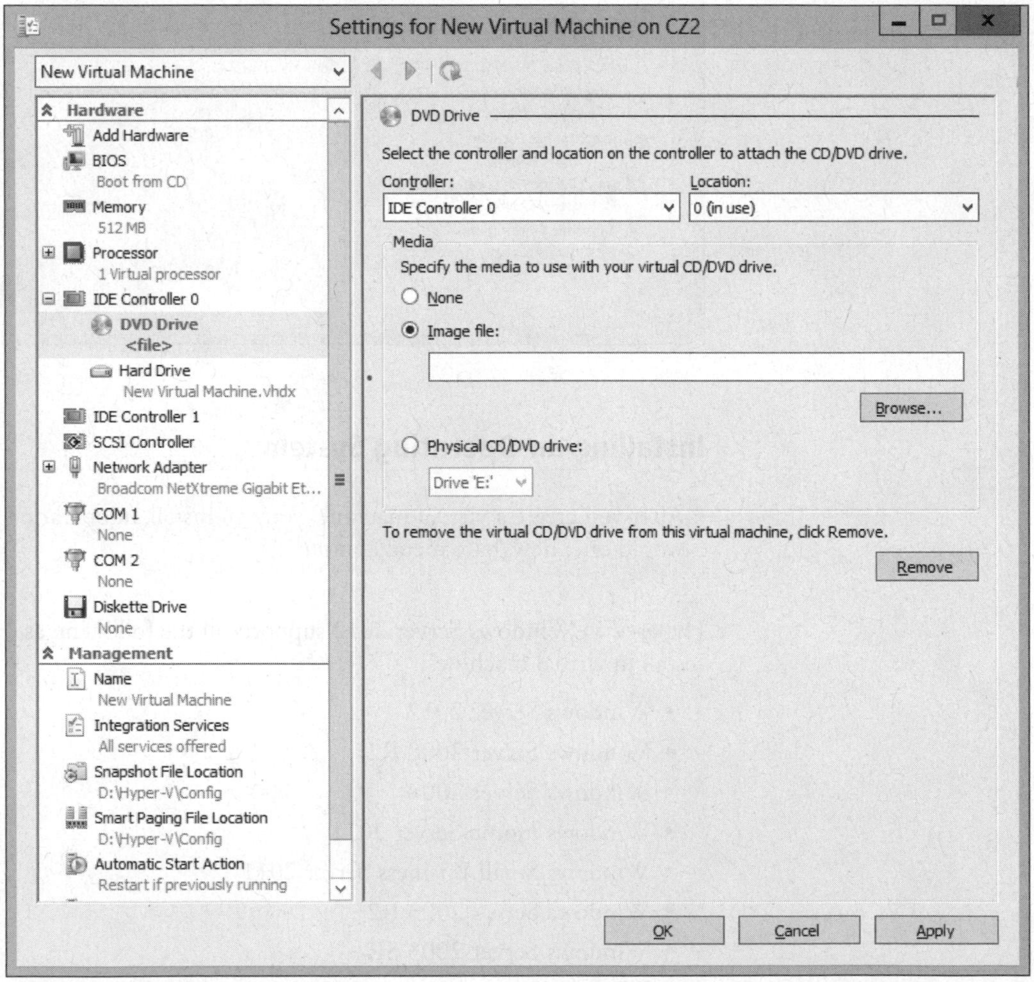

The ability to mount an image file to a virtual DVD drive is a particularly useful benefit for administrators who download operating system files as disk images. After you mount an installation disk, either physically or virtually, click *Start* in the *Actions* pane, which is the equivalent of turning on the virtual machine.

Starting a VM causes the thumbnail in the Hyper-V Manager to go live, displaying the contents of the computer's screen. To display the VM's activity at full size, click *Connect* in the *Actions* pane to open a new window for the virtual machine. You can then interact with the VM through that window as though you were sitting at a physical computer's console.

When the virtual machine boots from the disk you mounted, the operating system installation proceeds as though you were using a physical computer. During the installation process, you can work with the virtual hard disk drive just as you would a physical one, creating partitions of various sizes and selecting one for the operating system. When the installation is complete, the virtual machine restarts, and you can then log on and use it as you would normally.

Configuring Guest Integration Services

In some cases, certain Hyper-V guest operating system features do not function properly using the OS's own device drivers. Hyper-V, therefore, includes a software package called *guest integration services*, which you can install on your virtual machines for compatibility purposes.

Some functions provided by the guest integration services package are as follows:

- **Operating system shutdown** enables the Hyper-V Manager console to remotely shut down a guest operating system in a controlled manner, eliminating the need for you to log on and manually shut the system down.
- **Time synchronization** enables Hyper-V to synchronize the operating system clocks in parent and child partitions.
- **Data Exchange** enables the operating systems on parent and child partitions to exchange information, such as OS version information and fully qualified domain names.
- **Heartbeat** implements a service in which the parent partition sends regular heartbeat signals to the child partitions, which are expected to respond in kind. A failure of a child partition to respond indicates that the guest OS has frozen or malfunctioned.
- **Backup** allows backup of Windows virtual machines using Volume Shadow Copy Services.

The Windows Server 2012 and Windows 8 operating systems have the latest guest integration services software built in, so you do not need to install the package on VMs running those operating systems as guests. Earlier versions of Windows, however, have previous versions of the guest integration services package that need to be upgraded, and some Windows versions do not include the package at all.

To upgrade the guest integration services on a Windows guest OS, use the following procedure.

CERTIFICATION READY
Configure guest integration services.
Objective 3.1

TAKE NOTE*
For Linux guest operating systems, you must download and install Linux Integration Services Version 3.2 for Hyper-V from the Microsoft Download Center.

INSTALL GUEST INTEGRATION SERVICES

GET READY. Log on to the server running Windows Server 2012 using an account with administrative privileges.

1. From the Tools menu of the *Server Manager* window, choose Hyper-V Manager. The *Hyper-V Manager* console appears.
2. In the left pane, select a Hyper-V server.
3. In the Actions pane, start the virtual machine on which you want to install the guest integration services and click Connect. A *Virtual Machine Connection* window appears.
4. From the Action menu of the Virtual Machine Connection window, choose Insert Integration Services Setup Disk. Hyper-V mounts an image of the guest integration services disk to a virtual disk drive and displays an *Autoplay* window, as shown in Figure 7-23.

Figure 7-23

Launching Hyper-V
Integration Services

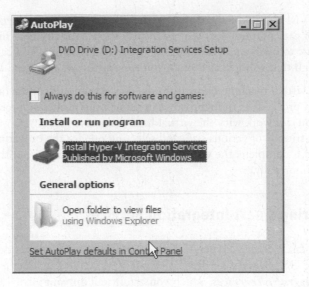

5. Click Install Hyper-V Integration Services. A message box appears, asking you to upgrade the existing installation.

6. Click OK. The system installs the package and prompts you to restart the computer.

7. Click Yes to restart the computer.

After you install or upgrade the guest integration services, you can enable or disable each individual function by opening the *Settings* dialog box for the virtual machine and selecting the *Integration Services* page, as shown in Figure 7-24.

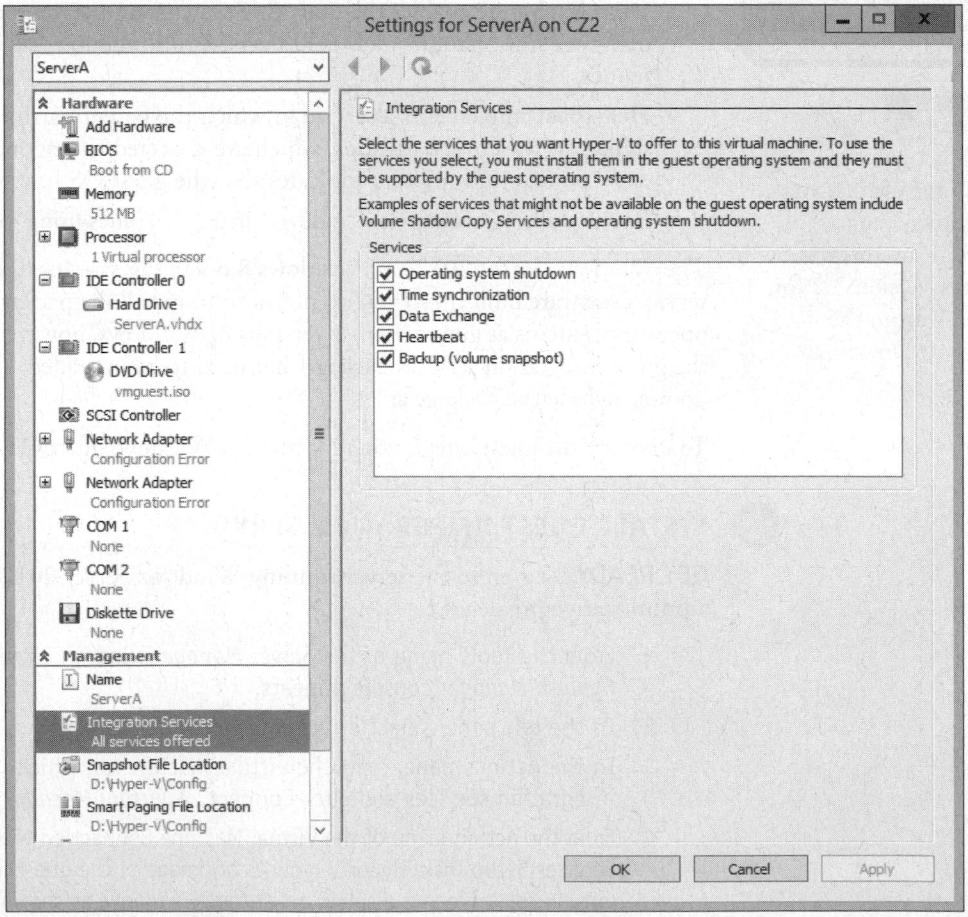

Figure 7-24

Integration Services settings
for a virtual machine

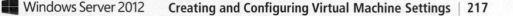

Now, you are ready to configure and manage the virtual machine as though you were working on a physical server. You can modify the network configuration, enable remote desktop, load the appropriate roles and features, and install applications.

Allocating Memory

Dynamic memory enables Hyper-V to adjust the amount of RAM allocated to virtual machines, depending on their ongoing requirements.

Some computer components can be virtualized. You can take some disk space and create a virtual hard drive out of it, and you can take an image file and create a virtual DVD drive. You can also create virtual network interface adapters and other components, which appear like the real thing in a VM. System memory is different, however; it has no substitute, so all Hyper-V can do is take the physical memory installed in the computer and allocate it among the various virtual machines.

When you create a virtual machine with the *New Virtual Machine Wizard*, you specify how much memory the VM should use on the *Assign Memory* page. Obviously, the amount of memory available for use is based on the physical memory installed in the computer.

After you create the virtual machine, you can modify the amount of memory allocated to it by shutting down the VM, opening its *Settings* dialog box, and changing the *Startup RAM* setting on the *Memory* page, as shown in Figure 7-25. This enables you to experiment with various amounts of memory and dial in the optimum performance level for the system.

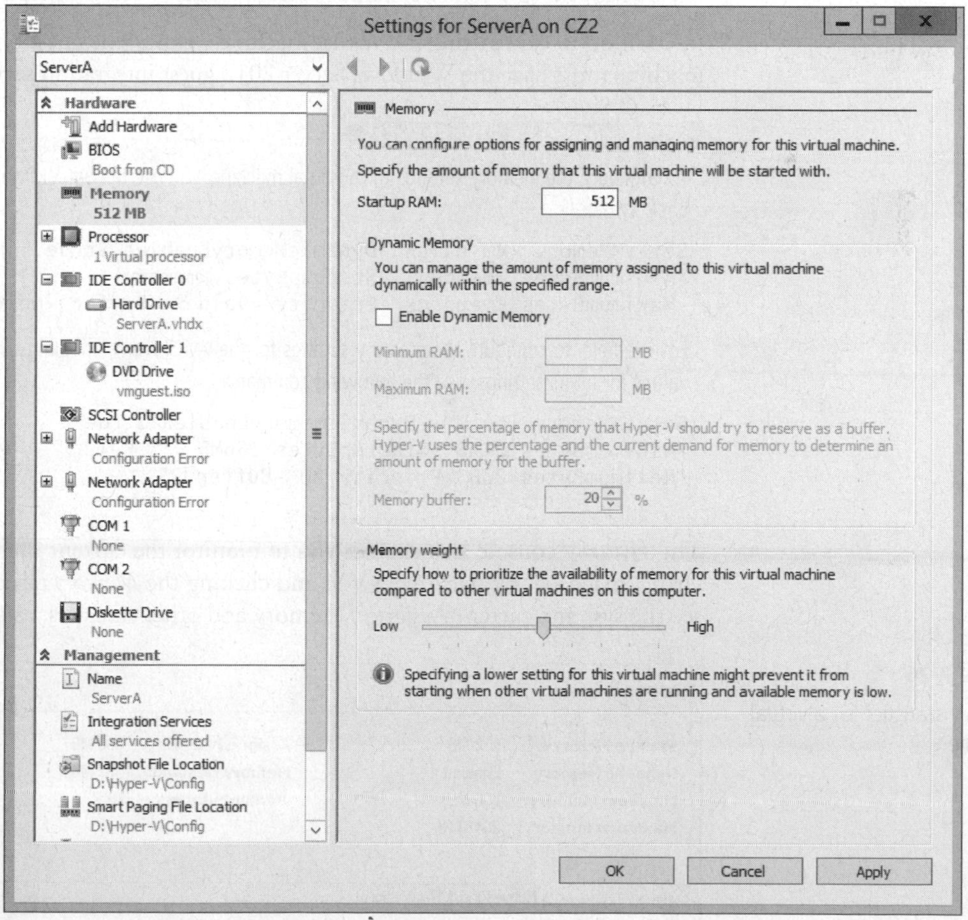

Figure 7-25

Memory settings for a virtual machine

USING DYNAMIC MEMORY

CERTIFICATION READY
Configure dynamic memory.
Objective 3.1

In the first versions of Hyper-V, shutting down the virtual machine was the only way to modify its memory allocation. In the Windows Server 2012 version, however, you can use a feature called dynamic memory to reallocate memory automatically to the VM from a shared memory pool as its demands change. If a virtualized server starts to experience larger amounts of client traffic, for example, Hyper-V can increase the memory allocated to the system, and then reduce it when the traffic subsides.

To use dynamic memory, you must enable it by selecting the *Enable Dynamic Memory* check box on the VM's *Memory* page of the *Settings* dialog box, and then configure the following settings:

- **Startup RAM** specifies the amount of memory that you want to allocate to the VM when it starts. When you are using dynamic memory, this value can be the minimum amount of memory needed to boot the system.

- **Minimum RAM** specifies the smallest amount of memory the VM can use at any time. Operating systems can conceivably require more memory to start up than they do to run, so this value can be smaller than the *Startup RAM* value.

- **Maximum RAM** specifies the largest amount of memory that the VM can use at any time. The value can range from a low equal to the *Startup RAM* value to a high of 64 GB.

TAKE NOTE *

You can change the Minimum RAM, Maximum RAM, Memory buffer, and Memory weight values at any time, but to enable or disable dynamic memory, you must shut down the virtual machine.

- **Memory buffer** contains a percentage that Hyper-V uses to calculate how much memory to allocate to the VM, compared to its actual utilization, as measured by performance counters. For example, with the *Memory buffer* value set to 20%, a VM with applications and operating system that consume 1 GB of memory receives a dynamic allocation of 1.2 GB.

- **Memory weight** contains a relative value that specifies the priority of this VM, compared to the other VMs on the same computer. When the physical memory in the computer is insufficient to allocate the full buffered amount specified for each VM, the VMs with the highest memory weight settings receive priority.

In addition to configuring the virtual machine settings, the guest operating system on the virtual machine must have the Windows Server 2012 guest integration services to use dynamic memory.

USING WINDOWS POWERSHELL

To configure the memory settings for a virtual machine, you use the Set-VMMemory cmdlet, using the following basic syntax

```
Set-VMMemory <VM name> -DynamicMemoryEnabled $true
-MinimumBytes <memory> -StartupBytes <memory>
-MaximumBytes <memory> -Priority <value> -Buffer <percentage>
```

For example, to configure the memory settings for the VM ServerA, enabling dynamic memory and configuring values for all its settings, use the following command:

```
Set-VMMemory TestVM -DynamicMemoryEnabled $true
-MinimumBytes 64MB -StartupBytes 256MB
-MaximumBytes 2GB -Priority 80 -Buffer 25
```

The *Hyper-V* console also enables you to monitor the current memory allocation for each virtual machine. By selecting a VM and clicking the *Memory* tab on the bottom pane, you can see the system's current Assigned Memory and other statistics, as shown in Figure 7-26.

Figure 7-26

Memory statistics for a virtual machine

ServerA			
Startup Memory:	512 MB	**Assigned Memory:**	580 MB
Dynamic Memory:	Enabled	**Memory Demand:**	487 MB
Minimum Memory:	256 MB	**Memory Status:**	OK
Maximum Memory:	2048 MB		

Summary | Memory | Networking | Replication

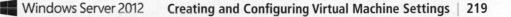

CONFIGURING SMART PAGING

CERTIFICATION READY
Configure smart paging.
Objective 3.1

Windows Server 2008 R2 Hyper-V introduced dynamic memory, but Windows Server 2012 improves on the concept by adding the *Minimum RAM* setting. This enables Hyper-V to reduce the memory used by a virtual machine to a level lower than that needed to start the system, reclaiming that memory for other uses.

The problem with having minimum RAM values that are lower than the startup RAM values is that the supply of physical memory can become depleted with too many VMs running simultaneously at their minimum RAM values. If this occurs, a VM that has to restart might be unable to do so because not enough free memory is available to increase its memory allocation from its minimum RAM value to its startup RAM value.

To address this possibility, Hyper-V includes a feature called ***smart paging***. If a VM has to restart and not enough memory is available to allocate its startup RAM value, the system uses hard disk space to make up the difference and begins paging memory contents to disk.

Disk-access rates are far slower than memory-access rates, of course, so smart paging incurs a severe performance penalty, but the paging occurs only for as long as it takes to restart the VM and return it to its minimum RAM allocation.

Hyper-V uses smart paging only in highly specific conditions, such as when a VM must be restarted, no free memory is available, and the memory needed cannot be freed up by other means.

You can use the *Smart Paging File Location* page in a VM's *Settings* dialog box to specify a location for the paging file, as shown in Figure 7-27. Selecting the fastest possible hard drive is recommended.

Figure 7-27

The *Smart Paging File Location* page in a VM's Settings dialog box

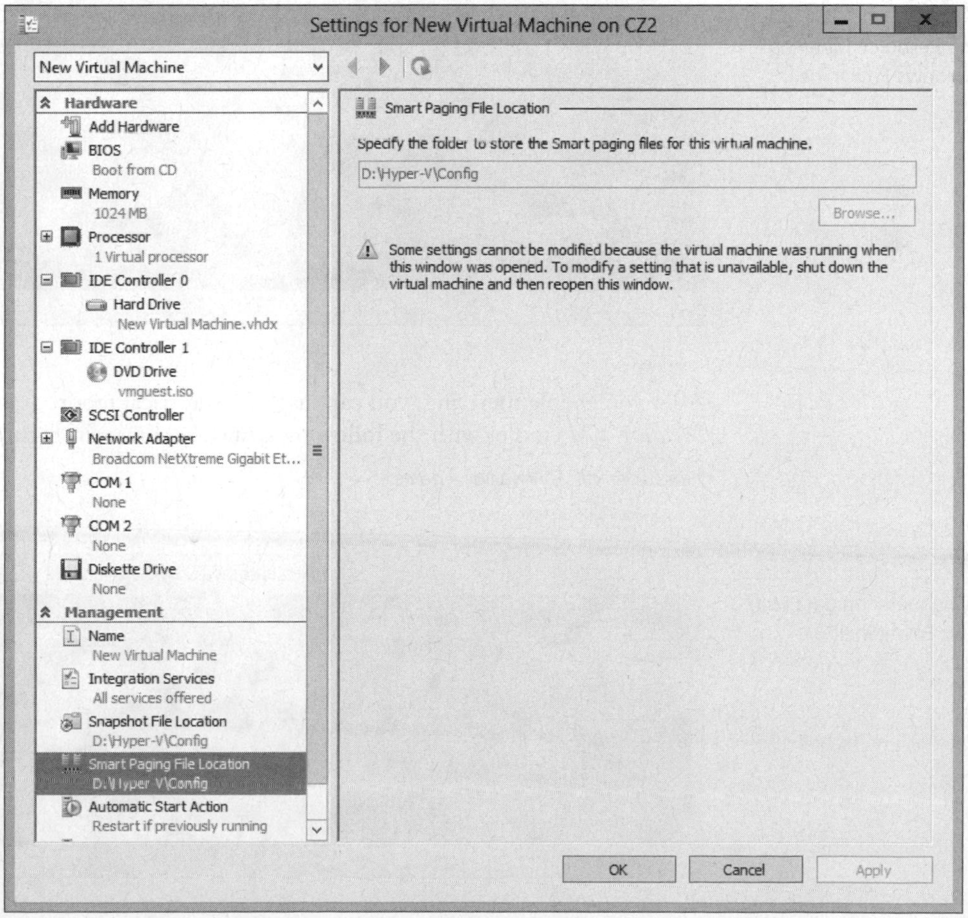

■ Configuring Resource Metering

THE BOTTOM LINE

Resource metering is a new Windows PowerShell-based feature in Windows Server 2012 Hyper-V that enables you to document virtual machine usage via a variety of criteria.

Organizations might want to track the use of virtual machines for various reasons. For large corporations, it might be a matter of internal accounting and controlling ongoing expenses, such as wide area network (WAN) bandwidth. For service providers, it might be necessary to bill customers based on the VM resources they use.

Resource metering uses Windows PowerShell cmdlets to track various performance metrics for individual VMs, including the following:

- CPU utilization
- Minimum/maximum/average memory utilization
- Disk space utilization
- Incoming/outgoing network traffic

Resource metering statistics remain consistent, even when you transfer VMs between host systems using live migration or move virtual hard disk files between VMs.

To use resource metering, you must first enable it for the specific VM that you want to monitor, using the *Enable-VMResourceMetering* cmdlet with the following syntax, as shown in Figure 7-28:

```
Enable-VMResourceMetering –VMName <name>
```

Figure 7-28

Enabling Resource Metering with Windows PowerShell

After you enable metering, you can display a statistical report at any time by using the *Measure-VM* cmdlet with the following syntax, as shown in Figure 7-29:

```
Measure-VM –VMName <name>
```

Figure 7-29

Displaying metering data with Windows PowerShell

In addition to metering resources for entire virtual machines, you can also create resource pools that help you monitor specific VM components, such as processors, memory, network adapters, or virtual hard disks. You create a resource pool using the *New-VMResourcePool* cmdlet and then enable metering for the pool using *Enable-VMResourceMetering*.

By using techniques such as pipelining, you can use the resource metering cmdlets to gather data on virtual machine performance and export it to applications or data files.

SKILL SUMMARY

IN THIS LESSON, YOU LEARNED:

- Virtualization is a process that adds a layer of abstraction between actual, physical hardware and the system making use of it. Rather than have the server access the computer's hardware directly, an intervening component called a *hypervisor* creates a virtual machine environment, and the server operating system runs in that environment.

- Virtualization is the process of deploying and maintaining multiple instances of an operating system, called *virtual machines (VMs)*, on a single computer.

- Microsoft Hyper-V is a hypervisor-based virtualization system for x64 computers starting with Windows Server 2008. The hypervisor—the main component that manages the virtual computers—is installed between the hardware and the operating system.

- For licensing purposes, Microsoft refers to each virtual machine that you create on a Hyper-V server as a *virtual instance*. Each Windows Server 2012 version includes a set number of virtual instances; you must purchase licenses to create additional ones.

- To keep a small footprint and minimal overhead, Hyper-V Server contains only the Windows Hypervisor, Windows Server driver model, and virtualization components.

■ Knowledge Assessment

Multiple Choice

Select one or more correct answers for each of the following questions.

1. Which of the following statements about Type I and Type II virtualization are true? (Choose all that apply)
   a. In Type I virtualization, the hypervisor runs on top of a host OS.
   b. In Type I virtualization, the hypervisor runs directly on the computer hardware.
   c. In Type II virtualization, the hypervisor runs on top of a host OS.
   d. In Type II virtualization, the hypervisor runs directly on the computer hardware.

2. Which of the following types of server virtualization provides the best performance for high-traffic servers in production environments?
   a. Type I virtualization
   b. Type II virtualization
   c. Presentation virtualization
   d. RemoteApp

3. Which of the following Microsoft operating systems includes a license that enables you to create an unlimited number of virtual instances?
   a. Hyper-V Server
   b. Windows Server 2012 Datacenter
   c. Windows Server 2012 Standard
   d. Windows Server 2012 Foundation

4. Which of the following Hyper-V features make it possible for a VM to function with a minimum RAM value that is lower than the startup RAM value?
   a. Smart Paging
   b. Dynamic Memory
   c. Memory Weight
   d. Guest Integration Services

5. When you install the Hyper-V role on a server running Windows Server 2012, the instance of the OS on which you installed the role is converted to what system element?
   a. The hypervisor
   b. The Virtual Machine Monitor
   c. The parent partition
   d. A child partition

6. If an administrator wants to install additional roles along with Hyper-V, what does Microsoft recommend the administrator do?
   a. Microsoft recommends that you install other roles on one of the VMs you create with Hyper-V.
   b. Microsoft recommends you install only roles related to Hyper-V.
   c. Microsoft recommends you install only roles on the parent partition.
   d. There are no recommendations against roles installed with Hyper-V.

7. What are the two files used for every VM?
   a. A saved-state file and a virtual machine configuration (.vmc) file in INF format
   b. A virtual machine configuration (.vmc) file in INF format and virtual hard disk (.vhd or .vhdx) files for the guest OS and data
   c. A saved-state file and virtual hard disk (.vhd or .vhdx) files for the guest OS, applications, and data
   d. A virtual machine configuration (.vmc) file in XML format and virtual hard disk (.vhd or .vhdx) files for the guest OS and data

8. When using the Create a Virtual Machine Wizard, how is the virtual hard disk created by default?
   a. You set the maximum size and it starts at that size.
   b. It starts at 40 GB and warns the administrator when nearly full.
   c. It starts small and dynamically expands up to the maximum size you specify.
   d. It starts small and continually expands to fill the available storage.

9. What operating systems can an administrator install on a VM?
   a. Windows Server 2008 and newer
   b. Windows Server 2003 and newer
   c. Any Microsoft Windows edition
   d. Several Microsoft products as well as Red Hat and SuSE Linux

10. In some cases, certain Hyper-V guest OS features do not function properly using the OS's own device drivers. What can an administrator do?
    a. Install and configure Guest Integration Services.
    b. Install Hyper-V Manager.
    c. Reinstall Hyper-V.
    d. Try a different operating system.

Best Answer

Choose the letter that corresponds to the best answer. More than one answer choice may achieve the goal. Select the BEST answer.

1. Hyper-V in Windows Server 2012 is a Type I virtualization architecture. What is the fundamental difference between Hyper-V and older, Type II virtualization architectures?

    a. Hyper-V creates environments called partitions, each with its own operating system installed.

    b. Its hypervisor designates the first partition as the parent partition and all subsequent partitions as child partitions.

    c. Its hypervisor is an abstraction layer and interacts directly with computer hardware, rather than as a host OS application.

    d. Computer subsystems such as Plug and Play and power management are managed by Hyper-V's parent partition.

2. Windows Server 2012 includes Hyper-V in which edition(s)?

    a. All editions

    b. The Datacenter edition

    c. The Standard and Datacenter editions

    d. The Essentials, Standard, and Datacenter editions

3. After installing the Hyper-V role, what is the startup procedure for Windows Server 2012?

    a. The newly installed hypervisor starts first, and then loads the operating system as the primary or parent partition.

    b. The actual startup procedure is not altered.

    c. The newly installed hypervisor starts first, and then loads the operating system as a child partition.

    d. The newly installed hypervisor starts second, after the operating system loads as a partition.

4. What is the primary purpose of the software package offered by Hyper-V called guest integration services?

    a. Guest integration services improves communications between the parent partition and child partitions.

    b. Guest integration services resolves compatibility issues of certain guest operating systems experiencing non-functioning features.

    c. Guest integration services improves data exchange between the parent partition and child partitions.

    d. Guest integration services improves time synchronization between the parent partition and child partitions.

5. What is Resource Monitoring in Windows Server 2012?

    a. Resource Monitoring is a PowerShell-based feature that enables you to document virtual machine usage.

    b. Resource Monitoring is a Server Manager feature that enables you to monitor virtual machine resources.

    c. Resource Monitoring is a PowerShell-based feature that enables you to redistribute virtual machine resources.

    d. Resource Monitoring is a Server Manager feature that enables you to document virtual machine communications.

Build a List

1. Order the steps to install the Hyper-V role.
   a. Choose Role-based or feature-based installation from the Select installation type page.
   b. Select network adapter on the Create Virtual Switches page.
   c. Select the server on which to add the Hyper-V role. Add applicable dependencies.
   d. From Server Manager's Manage menu, choose Add Roles and Features.
   e. Log on to Windows Server 2012 with administrative privileges.
   f. Specify virtual hard disk and virtual machine configuration file locations.

2. Order the steps to create a virtual machine.
   a. From Server Manager's Tools menu, select Hyper-V Manager.
   b. Specify the Name and Location of the virtual machine files.
   c. Log on to the server with administrative privileges.
   d. Select a Hyper-V server and, from the Action menu, choose New Virtual Machine.
   e. Specify the Startup memory and Network Connections.
   f. Decide whether to install the new OS now or later.

3. Order the steps to install a guest integration services.
   a. From Server Manager's Tools menu, choose Hyper-V Manager.
   b. From the Action menu of the Virtual Machine Connection window, choose Insert Integration Services Setup Disk.
   c. In the Actions pane, start the virtual machine on which you want to install the guest integration services, and then click Connect.
   d. Select a Hyper-V server.
   e. Log on to the server with administrative privileges.
   f. Click Install Hyper-V Integration Services.

■ Business Case Scenarios

Scenario 7-1: Isolating Server Applications

You have two network accounting applications, neither of which is processor hungry. Both of these applications must be kept totally isolated from each other and from all other applications. Both applications will access a centralized database server. What server configuration solution do you recommend?

Scenario 7-2: Configuring Virtual Machine Memory

Alice has a computer running Windows Server 2012 with 8 GB of memory installed, which she has configured as a Hyper-V server. After creating eight VMs with the New Virtual Machine Wizard, each with a startup RAM value of 1,024 MB, Alice is having trouble getting all eight VMs to boot. What settings can she modify to resolve the problem without changing the startup RAM value?

Creating and Configuring Virtual Machine Storage

70-410 EXAM OBJECTIVE

Objective 3.2 – Create and configure virtual machine storage. This objective may include but is not limited to: Create VHDs and VHDX; configure differencing drives; modify VHDs; configure pass-through disks; manage snapshots; implement a virtual Fibre Channel adapter.

LESSON HEADING	EXAM OBJECTIVE
Working with Virtual Disks	
Understanding Virtual Disk Formats	
Creating Virtual Disks	Create VHDs and VHDX Configure differencing drives
Configuring Pass-Through Disks	Configure pass-through disks
Modifying Virtual Disks	Modify VHDs
Creating Snapshots	Manage snapshots
Connecting to a SAN	
Understanding SAN Technologies	
Using Fibre Channel	
Connecting Virtual Machines to a SAN	Implement a virtual Fibre Channel adapter

KEY TERMS

dynamic hard disk

differencing hard disk

Fibre Channel

JBOD (Just a Bunch of Disks)

pass-through disk

snapshot

storage area network (SAN)

VHDX

virtual hard disk (VHD)

■ Working with Virtual Disks

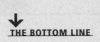

THE BOTTOM LINE

When you create a virtual machine (VM) in Windows Server 2012 Hyper-V, you emulate all the standard components that you typically find in a physical computer. When you virtualize memory, as discussed in Lesson 7, "Creating and Configuring Virtual Machine Settings," you take a portion of the physical memory in the computer and dedicate it to a VM. The same is true with hard disk space. Hyper-V uses a specialized *virtual hard disk (VHD)* format to package part of the space on a physical disk and make it appear to the virtual machine as though it is physical hard disk drive.

When you create a new virtual machine in Hyper-V by using the New Virtual Machine Wizard, the wizard creates a virtual storage subsystem that consists of two IDE (Integrated Drive Electronics) controllers and one SCSI (Small Computer Systems Interface) controller, as shown in Figure 8-1. The IDE controllers host the virtual machine's system drive and its DVD drive. As with their physical equivalents, each IDE controller can host two devices, so you can create two additional virtual drives and add them to the system.

Figure 8-1

The default VM drive controller configuration

```
┌──────────────────────────────────────────────────────────────────────────┐
│ 🖳                    Settings for ServerC on CZ2              [ _ ] [ □ ] [ X ]│
├──────────────────────────────────────────────────────────────────────────┤
│ ServerC                          ▼    ◀ ▶ | ↻                               │
│ ┌────────────────────────────────┐  ┌──────────────────────────────────┐   │
│ │ ☆ Hardware                  ^  │  │ 🖳  Add Hardware ───────────────── │   │
│ │  ➕🖳 Add Hardware             │  │                                   │   │
│ │  🖳 BIOS                        │  │ You can use this setting to add devices to your virtual machine. │
│ │     Boot from CD               │  │ Select the devices you want to add and click the Add button.     │
│ │  🖭 Memory                      │  │ ┌────────────────────────────────┐│   │
│ │     512 MB                     │  │ │ SCSI Controller                ││   │
│ │  ➕ ▢ Processor                 │  │ │ Network Adapter                ││   │
│ │     1 Virtual processor        │  │ │ Legacy Network Adapter         ││   │
│ │  ▭ 🖴 IDE Controller 0          │  │ │ Fibre Channel Adapter          ││   │
│ │    🗀 Hard Drive                │  │ │ RemoteFX 3D Video Adapter      ││   │
│ │       ServerC.vhdx             │  │ └────────────────────────────────┘│   │
│ │  ▭ 🖴 IDE Controller 1          │  │                          [  Add  ] │   │
│ │    💿 DVD Drive                 │  │                                   │   │
│ │       vmguest.iso              │  │ You can increase the storage available to a virtual machine by adding a SCSI controller │
│ │  ▣ SCSI Controller             │  │ and attaching virtual hard disks to it. A SCSI controller requires integration services in │
│ │  ➕ 🗔 Network Adapter          │  │ the guest operating system. Do not attach a system disk to a SCSI controller. System │
│ │     Private Virtual Switch ≡   │  │ disks must be attached to an IDE controller. │
│ │  📺 COM 1                       │  │                                   │   │
│ │     None                       │  │                                   │   │
│ │  📺 COM 2                       │  │                                   │   │
│ │     None                       │  │                                   │   │
│ │  🖬 Diskette Drive              │  │                                   │   │
│ │     None                       │  │                                   │   │
│ │ ☆ Management                   │  │                                   │   │
│ │  [I] Name                      │  │                                   │   │
│ │     ServerC                    │  │                                   │   │
│ │  📄 Integration Services       │  │                                   │   │
│ │     All services offered       │  │                                   │   │
│ │  📄 Snapshot File Location     │  │                                   │   │
│ │     D:\Hyper-V\Config          │  │                                   │   │
│ │  📄 Smart Paging File Location │  │                                   │   │
│ │     D:\Hyper-V\Config          │  │                                   │   │
│ │  ⏻ Automatic Start Action      │  │                                   │   │
│ │     Restart if previously running ▼│                                   │   │
│ └────────────────────────────────┘  └──────────────────────────────────┘   │
│                                   [  OK  ] [ Cancel ] [  Apply  ]           │
└──────────────────────────────────────────────────────────────────────────┘
```

The SCSI controller, in the default VM configuration, is unpopulated, and you can create additional drives and add them to that controller to provide the VM with additional storage. You can also create additional SCSI controllers and add drives to them. By creating multiple drives and controllers, Hyper-V makes it possible to construct virtual storage subsystems that emulate almost any physical storage solution you might devise.

Understanding Virtual Disk Formats

> Windows Server 2012 Hyper-V supports the original VHD disk image file and the new VHDX format.

The original VHD format was created by a company called *Connectix* for its Virtual PC product. Microsoft later acquired the product and used the VHD format for all its subsequent virtualization products, including Hyper-V. There are three types of VHD files, as follows:

- **Fixed hard disk image:** This image file is a specified size in which all the disk space required to create the image is allocated during its creation. Fixed disk images can be considered wasteful in terms of storage, because they can contain large amounts of empty space, but they are also efficient from a processing standpoint, because there is no overhead due to dynamic expansion.

- *Dynamic hard disk* **image:** This image file has a specified maximum size, which starts out small and expands as needed to accommodate the data the system writes to it.

- *Differencing hard disk* **image:** This child image file is associated with a specific parent image. The system writes all changes made to the data on the parent image file to the child image, to facilitate a rollback at a later time.

VHD images are limited to maximum size of 2 terabytes (TB) and are compatible with all versions of Hyper-V, as well as Microsoft's Type 2 hypervisor products, such as Virtual Server and Virtual PC. Windows Server 2012 introduced an updated version of the format, which uses a VHDX filename extension.

VHDX image files can be as large as 64 TB, and they also support 4 KB logical sector sizes, to provide compatibility with new 4 KB native drives. VHDX files can also use larger block sizes (up to 256 MB), which enable you to fine-tune the performance level of a virtual storage subsystem to accommodate specific applications and data file types. However, VHDX files are not backwards compatible and can be read only by Windows Server 2012 Hyper-V servers. If migrating your virtual machines from Windows Server 2012 to an older version of Hyper-V is a remote possibility, you should continue using the VHD file format.

Creating Virtual Disks

> Windows Server 2012 Hyper-V provides several ways to create virtual disk files. You can create them as part of a virtual machine, or create them later and add them to a VM.

CERTIFICATION READY
Create VHDs and VHDX.
Objective 3.2

The graphical interface in Hyper-V Manager provides access to most of the VHD parameters, but the new Windows PowerShell cmdlets included in Windows Server 2012 provide the most granular control over the disk image format.

CREATING A VIRTUAL DISK WITH A VM

The New Virtual Machine Wizard includes a Connect Virtual Hard Disk page, with which you can add a single disk to your new VM. The options for this disk are limited and consist of the following:

- **Create a virtual hard disk** enables you to specify the name, location, and size of a new virtual hard disk, but you can create only a dynamically expanding disk using the VHDX format.

- **Use an existing virtual hard disk** enables you to specify the location of an existing VHD or VHDX disk, which the VM presumably uses as its system disk.

- **Attach a virtual hard disk later** prevents the wizard from adding virtual disks to the VM configuration. The assumption is that you will manually add a disk later, before you start the virtual machine.

The object of this wizard page is to create the disk on which you will install the VM's operating system, or select an existing disk on which an OS is already installed. The disk the wizard creates is always a dynamically expanding one connected to IDE Controller 0.

It is a common practice for Microsoft to release evaluation copies of its products as preinstalled VHD files, as an alternative to the traditional installable disk images. After downloading one of these files, you can create a VM on a Hyper-V server and select the *Use an existing virtual hard disk* option to mount the VHD as its system drive.

CREATING A NEW VIRTUAL DISK

You can create a virtual hard disk file at any time, without adding it to a virtual machine, by using the *New Virtual Hard Disk Wizard in Hyper-V Manager.*

To create a new virtual disk, use the following procedure.

⊕ CREATE A NEW VIRTUAL DISK

GET READY. Log on to the server running Windows Server 2012 using an account with administrative privileges.

1. From the Tools menu in the *Server Manager* window, select Hyper-V Manager. The *Hyper-V Manager* console appears.
2. In the left pane, select a Hyper-V server.
3. From the Action menu, select New > Hard Disk. The *New Virtual Hard Disk Wizard* appears, displaying the *Before You Begin* page, as shown in Figure 8-2.

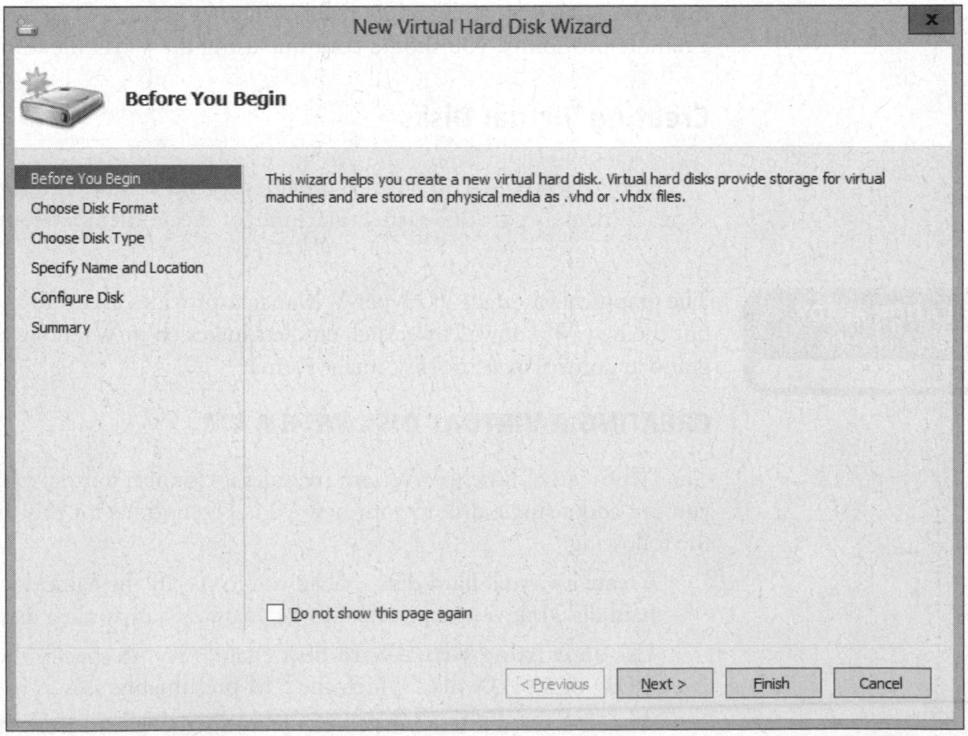

Figure 8-2

The *Before You Begin* page of the New Virtual Hard Disk Wizard

4. Click Next. The *Choose Disk Format* page appears, as shown in Figure 8-3.

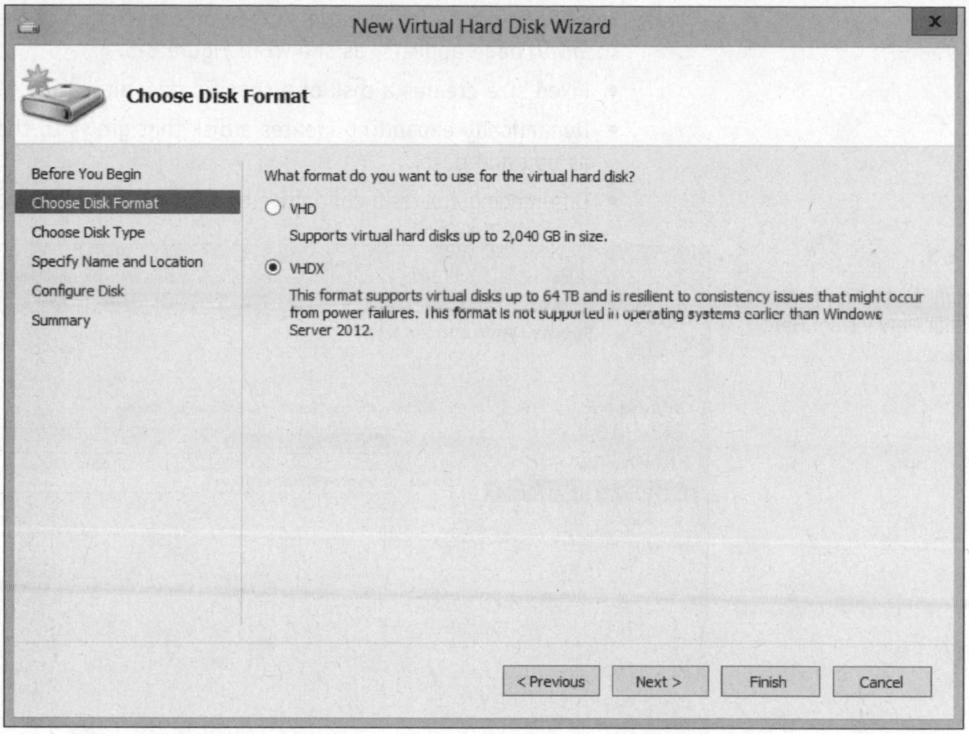

Figure 8-3

The *Choose Disk Format* page of the New Virtual Hard Disk Wizard

New Virtual Hard Disk Wizard

Choose Disk Format

Before You Begin
Choose Disk Format
Choose Disk Type
Specify Name and Location
Configure Disk
Summary

What format do you want to use for the virtual hard disk?

○ VHD

Supports virtual hard disks up to 2,040 GB in size.

◉ VHDX

This format supports virtual disks up to 64 TB and is resilient to consistency issues that might occur from power failures. This format is not supported in operating systems earlier than Windows Server 2012.

< Previous   Next >   Finish   Cancel

5. Select one of the following disk format options and click Next. The *Choose Disk Type* page appears, as shown in Figure 8-4.

- VHD creates an image no larger than 2 TB, using the highly compatible VHD format.

- VHDX creates an image up to 64 TB in size, using the new VHDX format.

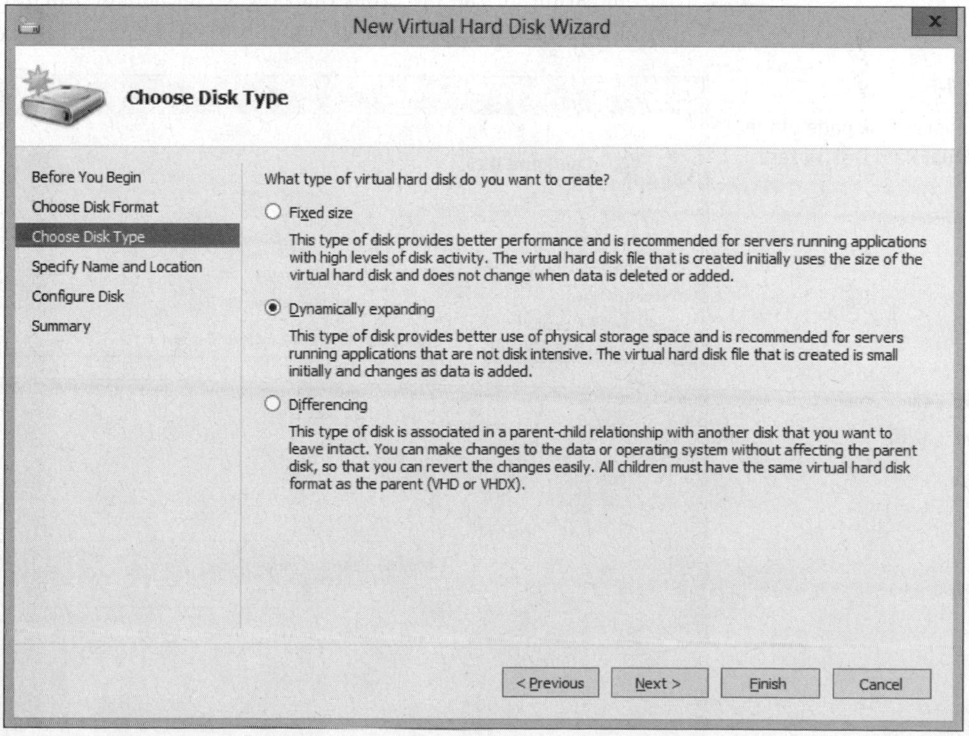

Figure 8-4

The *Choose Disk Type* page of the New Virtual Hard Disk Wizard

New Virtual Hard Disk Wizard

Choose Disk Type

Before You Begin
Choose Disk Format
Choose Disk Type
Specify Name and Location
Configure Disk
Summary

What type of virtual hard disk do you want to create?

○ Fixed size

This type of disk provides better performance and is recommended for servers running applications with high levels of disk activity. The virtual hard disk file that is created initially uses the size of the virtual hard disk and does not change when data is deleted or added.

◉ Dynamically expanding

This type of disk provides better use of physical storage space and is recommended for servers running applications that are not disk intensive. The virtual hard disk file that is created is small initially and changes as data is added.

○ Differencing

This type of disk is associated in a parent-child relationship with another disk that you want to leave intact. You can make changes to the data or operating system without affecting the parent disk, so that you can revert the changes easily. All children must have the same virtual hard disk format as the parent (VHD or VHDX).

< Previous   Next >   Finish   Cancel

6. Select one of the following disk type options and click Next. The *Specify Name and Location* page appears, as shown in Figure 8-5.

   • Fixed size creates a disk of a specific size, allocating all the space at once.

   • Dynamically expanding creates a disk that grows to the maximum size you specify as you add data.

   • Differencing creates a child drive that contains changes made to a specified parent drive.

Figure 8-5

The *Specify Name and Location* page of the New Virtual Hard Disk Wizard

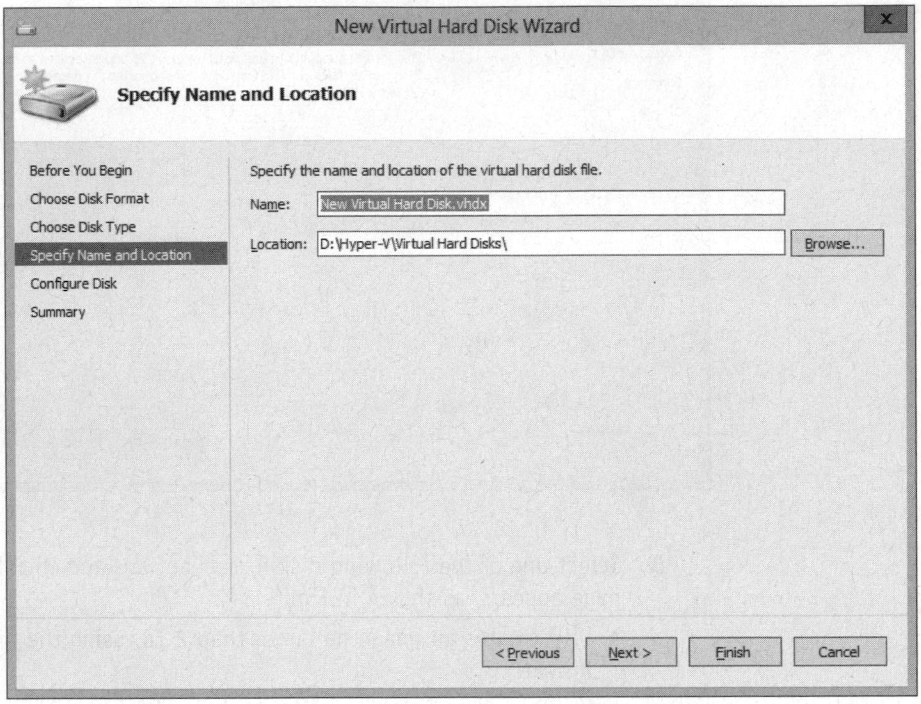

7. Specify a filename for the disk image in the Name text box and, if desired, specify a location for the file other than the server default. Then, click Next. The *Configure Disk* page appears, as shown in Figure 8-6.

Figure 8-6

The *Configure Disk* page of the New Virtual Hard Disk Wizard

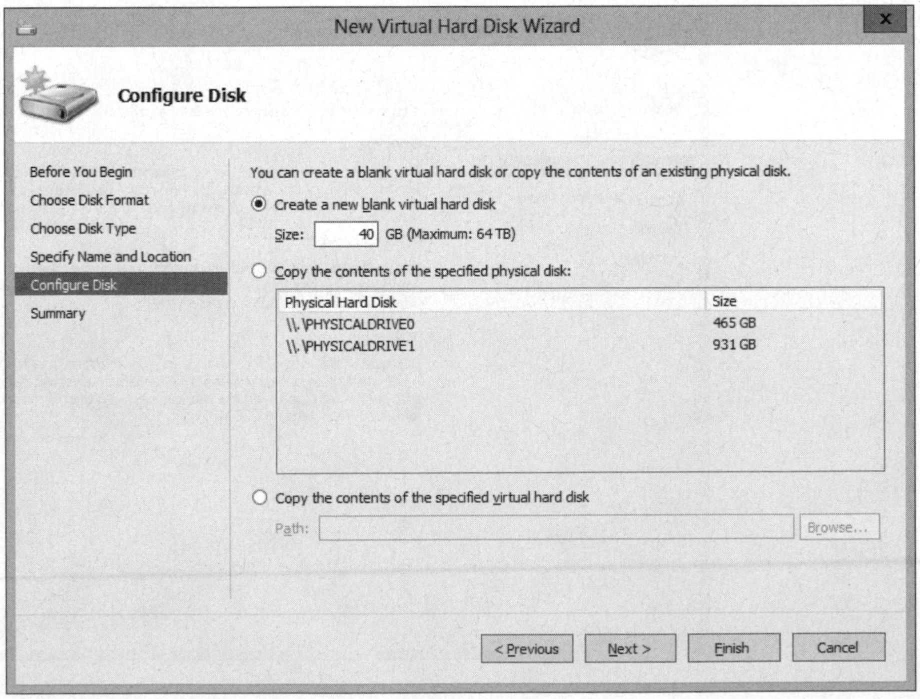

8. Select and configure one of the following options and click Next. The *Completing the New Virtual Hard Disk Wizard* page appears, as shown in Figure 8-7.

   • Create a new blank virtual hard disk specifies the size (or the maximum size) of the disk image file to create.

   • Copy the contents of the specified physical disk enables you to select one of the physical hard disks in the computer and copy its contents to the new disk image.

   • Copy the contents of the specified virtual hard disk enables you to select an existing virtual disk file and copy its contents to the new disk image.

Figure 8-7

The *Completing the New Virtual Hard Disk Wizard* page of the New Virtual Hard Disk Wizard

9. Click Finish.

The wizard creates the new image disk and saves it to the specified location.

USING WINDOWS POWERSHELL

You can create new virtual hard disk files using Windows PowerShell, with more control than is available through the graphical interface. To create a new disk image, you use the New-VHD cmdlet with the following basic syntax:

```
New-VHD -Path c:\filename.vhd|c:\filename.vhdx
-Fixed|-Dynamic|-Differencing -SizeBytes <size>
[-BlockSizeBytes <block size>]
[-LogicalSectorSizeBytes 512|4096] [-ParentPath <pathname>]
```

When using the cmdlet to create a disk image, the extension you specify for the filename determines the format (VHD or VHDX), and you can specify the block size and the logical sector size for the image, which you cannot do in the GUI. For example, the following command creates a 400 GB fixed VHDX image file with a logical sector size of 4 KB:

```
New-VHD -Path c:\diskfile.vhdx -Fixed
-SizeBytes 400GB -LogicalSectorSizeBytes 4096
```

ADDING VIRTUAL DISKS TO VIRTUAL MACHINES

Creating virtual disk image files as a separate process enables you to exercise more control over their capabilities. After creating the VHD or VHDX files, you must add them to a virtual machine for them to be useful.

To add a hard disk drive to a physical computer, you must connect it to a controller, and the same is true with a virtual machine in Hyper-V. When you open the *Settings* dialog box for a virtual machine in its default configuration, you see three controllers, labeled *IDE Controller 0*, *IDE Controller 1*, and *SCSI Controller*. These correspond to the controllers you might find in a typical physical server computer.

Each of the IDE controllers can support two devices, and the default virtual machine configuration uses one channel on IDE Controller 0 for the system hard disk and one channel on IDE Controller 1 for the system's DVD drive. If you did not create a virtual disk as part of the new Virtual Machine Wizard (that is, if you chose the *Attach a virtual hard disk later* option), then you must add a hard disk image to IDE Controller 0 to use as a system drive. The virtual machine cannot boot from the SCSI controller.

To add an existing virtual system drive to a virtual machine, use the following procedure.

→ ADD A VIRTUAL DISK TO A VIRTUAL MACHINE

GET READY. Log on to the server running Windows Server 2012 using an account with administrative privileges.

1. From the Tools menu in the *Server Manager* window, select Hyper-V Manager. The *Hyper-V Manager* console appears.
2. In the left pane, select a Hyper-V server.
3. Select a virtual machine and, in the Actions pane, select Settings. The *Settings* dialog box for the virtual machine appears.
4. Select IDE Controller 0, as shown in Figure 8-8.
5. In the IDE Controller box, select Hard Drive and click Add. The *Hard Drive* page appears, as shown in Figure 8-9.
6. In the Controller and Location drop-down lists, select the IDE controller and the channel you want to use for the hard disk.
7. With the Virtual hard disk option selected, click Browse and select the disk image file you want to add.
8. Click OK to close the *Settings* dialog box.

Although you cannot use a SCSI drive as the system disk in a virtual machine, you can add virtual data disks to the SCSI controller. Unlike the IDE connectors, which support only two devices each, a SCSI connector in Hyper-V can support up to 64 drives. You can also add SCSI controllers to a virtual machine, providing almost unlimited scalability for your virtual storage subsystem.

CREATING DIFFERENCING DISKS

A differencing disk enables you to preserve an existing virtual disk image file in its original state, while mounting it in an OS and even modifying its contents. For example, when building a laboratory setup, you can create a baseline system by installing a clean copy of an OS on a new virtual disk and configure the environment to your needs. Then, you can create a new child-differencing disk, using your baseline image as the parent. All subsequent changes you make to the system are written to the differencing disk, whereas the parent remains untouched. You can experiment on the test system, knowing that you can revert back to your baseline configuration by creating a new differencing disk.

CERTIFICATION READY
Configure differencing drives.
Objective 3.2

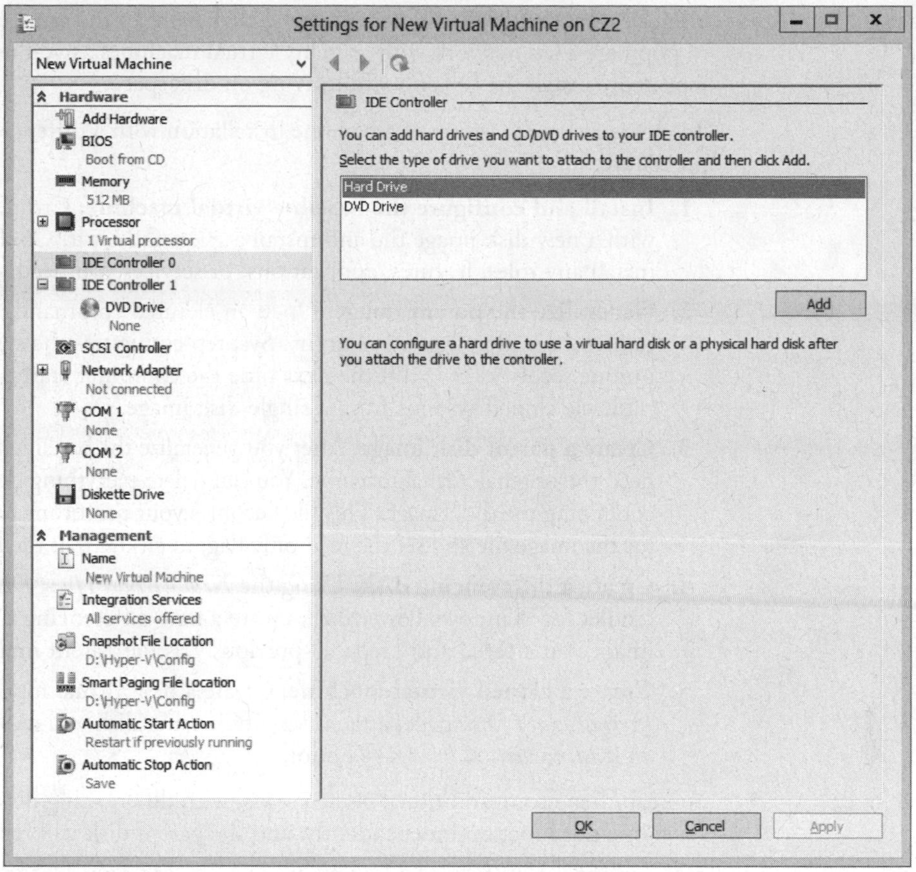

Figure 8-8

The IDE Controller interface in the Settings dialog box

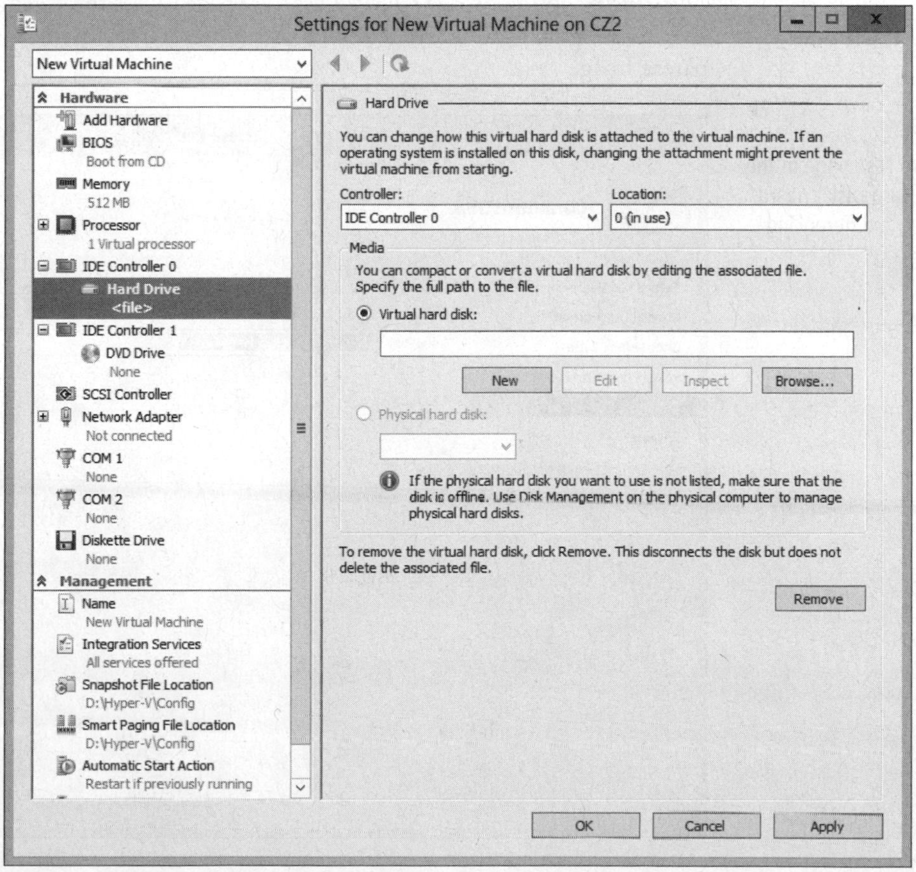

Figure 8-9

The Hard Drive interface in the Settings dialog box

You can create multiple differencing disks that point to the same parent image, enabling you to populate a lab network with as many virtual machines as you need, without having to repeatedly install the OS and while saving on disk space.

To create a cloned version of a baseline installation with a differencing disk, use the following procedure.

1. **Install and configure the baseline virtual machine:** Create a new virtual machine with a new disk image file and install a guest OS on it. Configure the OS as needed and install any roles, features, applications, or services you need.

2. **Generalize the parent image:** Open an elevated command prompt on the baseline system and run the *Sysprep.exe* utility. Sysprep configures the system to assign itself a new, unique security ID (SID) the next time the computer starts. This enables you to create multiple cloned systems from a single disk image.

3. **Create a parent disk image:** After you generalize the baseline installation, you no longer need the original virtual machine. You can delete everything except the VHD or VHDX file containing the disk image. This file becomes your parent image. Open the Properties sheet for the image file and set the read-only flag, to ensure that the baseline does not change.

4. **Create a differencing disk:** Using the *New Virtual Hard Disk Wizard* or the *New-VHD* cmdlet for Windows PowerShell, create a new differencing disk, pointing to the baseline image you created and prepared previously as the parent image.

5. **Create a cloned virtual machine:** Create a new virtual machine and, on the *Connect Virtual Hard Disk* page, attach the differencing disk you created to it, by using the *Use an existing virtual hard disk* option.

You can then create additional cloned VMs, with differencing disks that use the same parent. Each one can function independently, and the parent disk will remain unchanged.

When you create a differencing drive by using the *New Virtual Hard Disk Wizard*, selecting the *Differencing* option on the *Choose Disk Type* page causes the *Configure Disk* page to appear as shown in Figure 8-10. In the *Location* text box, you specify the name of the file to use as the parent image.

Figure 8-10

The *Configure Disk* page in the New Virtual Hard Disk Wizard, when creating a differencing disk

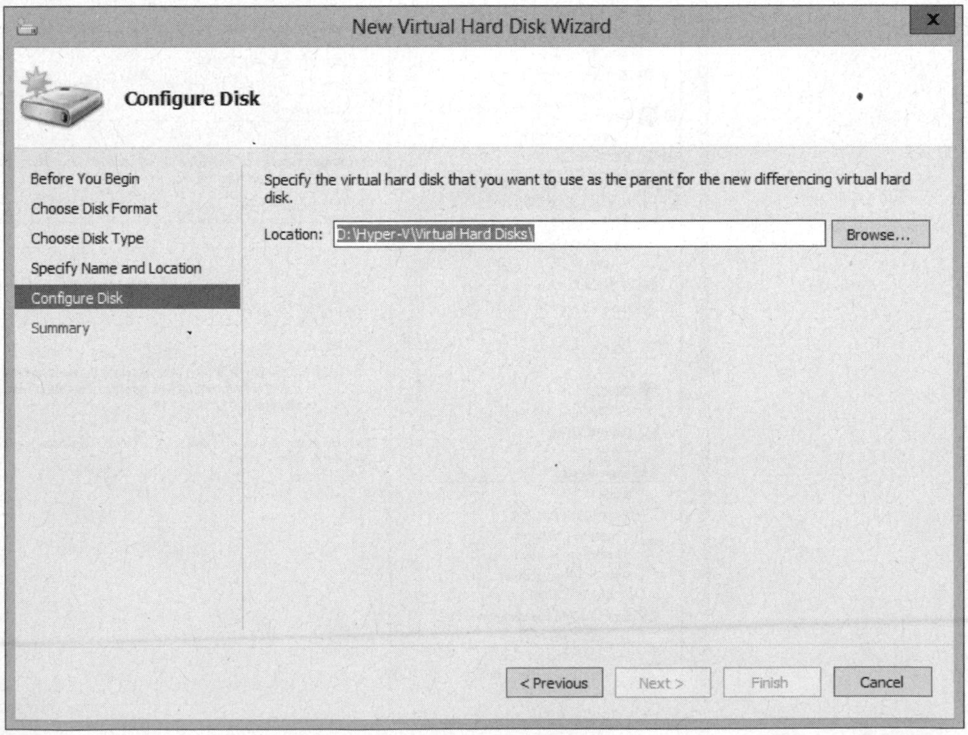

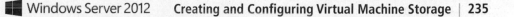

In the same way, if you create the differencing disk by using Windows PowerShell, you must run the New-VHD cmdlet with the `-Differencing` parameter and the `-ParentPath` parameter, specifying the location of the parent disk.

Configuring Pass-Through Disks

So far, this lesson focusses primarily on virtual hard disks—that is, areas of space on a physical disk drive allocated for use by virtual machines. However, it is also possible for VMs to access physical disks directly.

CERTIFICATION READY
Configure pass-through disks.
Objective 3.2

A ***pass-through disk*** is a type of virtual disk that points not to an area of space on a physical disk, but to a physical disk drive itself, installed on the host computer. When you add a hard drive to any of the controllers in a virtual machine, you can select a physical hard disk, as opposed to virtual one.

To add a physical hard disk to a virtual machine, however, the VM must have exclusive access to it. That is, you must first take the disk offline in the parent OS, by using the *Disk Management* snap-in, as shown in Figure 8-11, or the *Diskpart.exe* utility. After the disk is offline, it is available for selection in the *Physical hard disk* drop-down list.

Computer Management
File Action View Help
Computer Management (Local
System Tools
Task Scheduler
Event Viewer
Shared Folders
Performance
Device Manager
Storage
Windows Server Backup
Disk Management
Services and Applications
Volume | Layout | Type | File System | Status
(C:) Simple Basic NTFS Healthy (Boot, Page File, Crash Dump, P
System Reserved Simple Basic NTFS Healthy (System, Active, Primary Partitic
VMGUEST (D:) Simple Basic CDFS Healthy (Primary Partition)
Actions
Disk Manage...
More Actions
Disk 0
Basic
127.00 GB
Online
System Reserved
350 MB NTFS
Healthy (System, Ac
(C:)
126.66 GB NTFS
Healthy (Boot, Page File, Crash Dump, Prir
Disk 1
Basic
40.00 GB
Offline
Help
40.00 GB
Unallocated
Primary partition

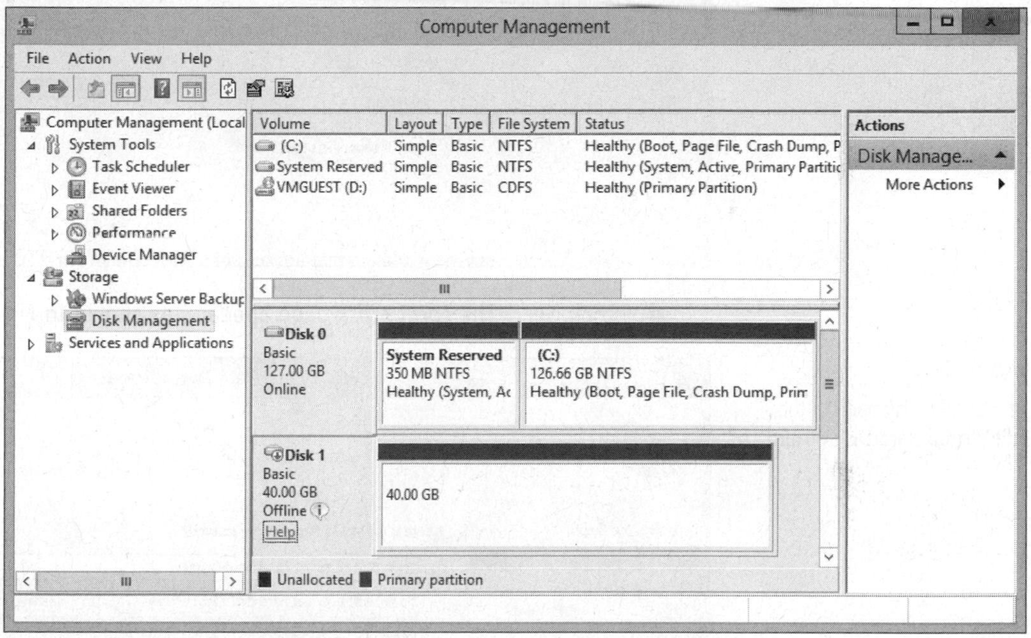

Figure 8-11
An offline disk in the Disk Management snap-in

Modifying Virtual Disks

Windows Server 2012 and Hyper-V provide several ways for you to manage and manipulate virtual hard disk images without mounting them in a virtual machine.

CERTIFICATION READY
Modify VHDs.
Objective 3.2

After you create a virtual hard disk, whether you attach it to a virtual machine or not, you can manage it by using the *Edit Virtual Hard Disk Wizard* in *Hyper-V Manager*. To edit an existing VHD or VHDX file, use the following procedure.

EDIT A VIRTUAL DISK

GET READY. Log on to the server running Windows Server 2012 using an account with administrative privileges.

1. From the Tools menu in the *Server Manager* window, select Hyper-V Manager. The *Hyper-V Manager* console appears.

2. In the left pane, select a Hyper-V server.

3. In the Actions pane, select Edit Disk. The *Edit Virtual Hard Disk Wizard* appears, displaying the *Before You Begin* page, as shown in Figure 8-12.

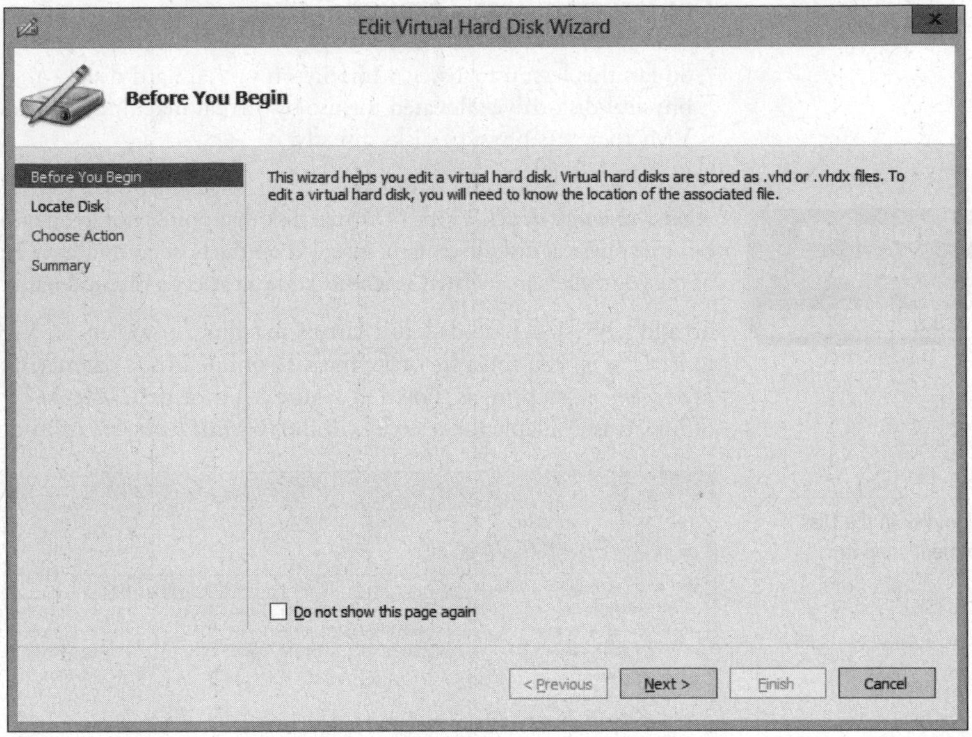

Figure 8-12

The *Before You Begin* page in the Edit Virtual Hard Disk Wizard

4. Click Next. The *Locate Disk* page appears, as shown in Figure 8-13.

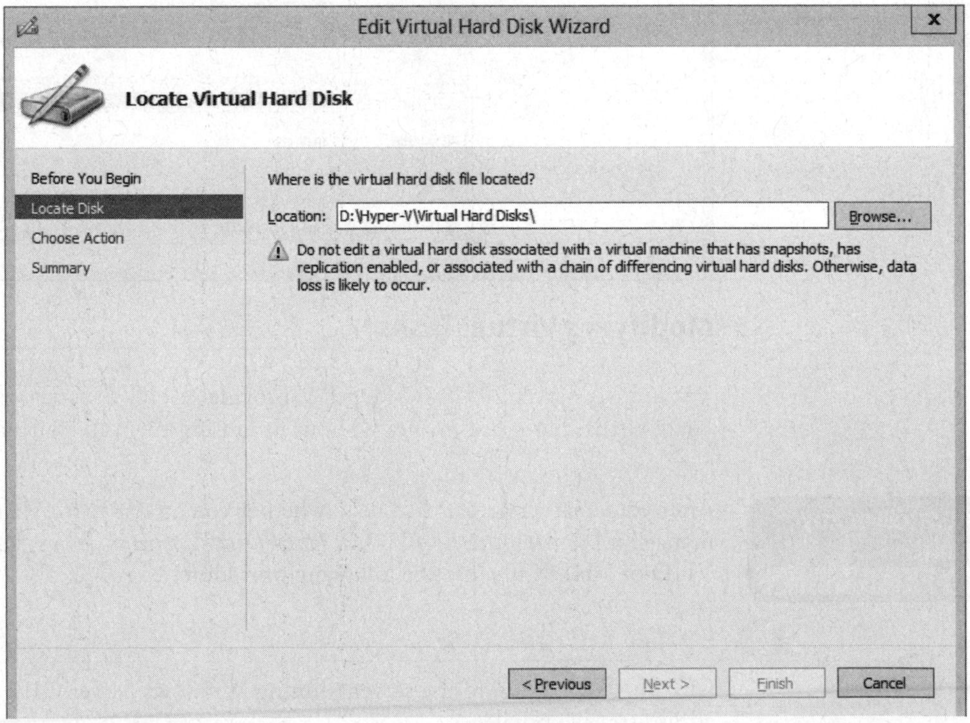

Figure 8-13

The *Locate Disk* page in the Edit Virtual Hard Disk Wizard

5. Type or browse to the name of the VHD or VHDX file you want to open and click Next. The *Choose Action* page appears, as shown in Figure 8-14.

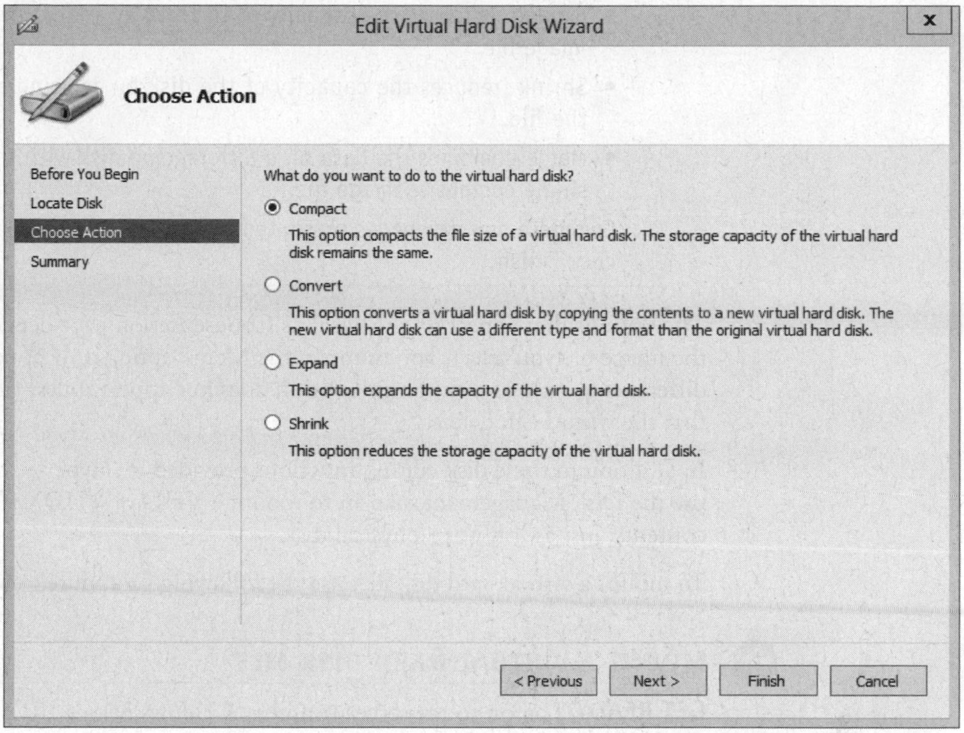

Figure 8-14

The *Choose Action* page in the Edit Virtual Hard Disk Wizard

6. Select one of the following functions and click Next. The *Completing the Edit Virtual Hard Disk Wizard* page appears, as shown in Figure 8-15.

   • Compact reduces the size of a dynamically expanding or differencing disk by deleting empty space, while leaving the disk's capacity unchanged.

   • Convert changes the type of format of a disk by copying the data to a new disk image file.

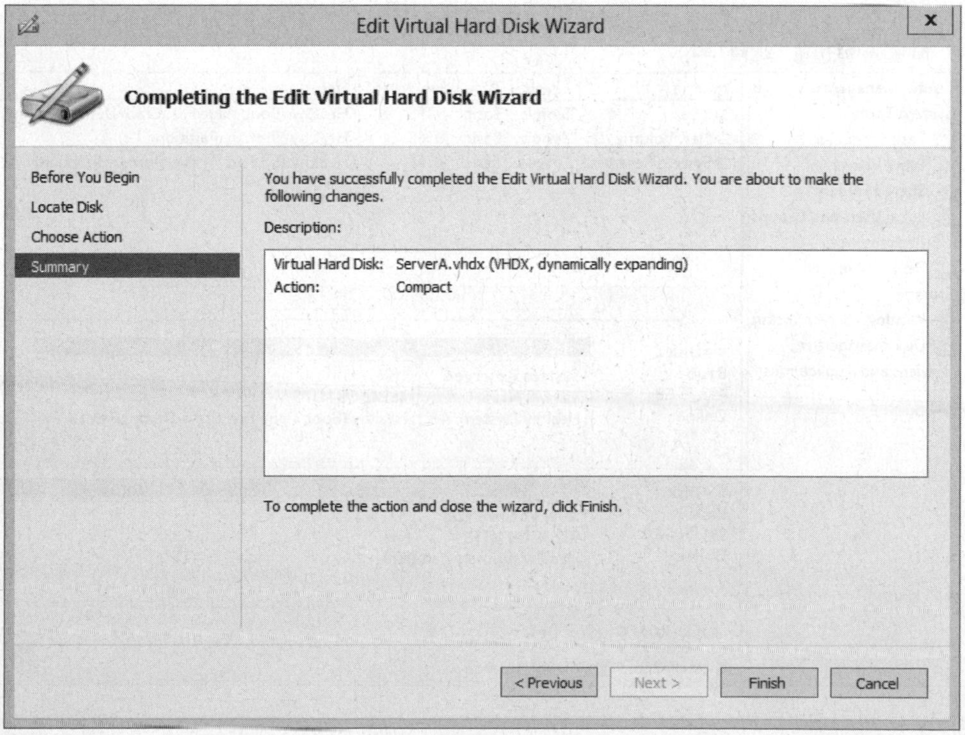

Figure 8-15

The *Completing the Edit Virtual Hard Disk Wizard* page in the Edit Virtual Hard Disk Wizard

- Expand increases the capacity of the disk by adding empty storage space to the image file.
- Shrink reduces the capacity of the disk by deleting empty storage space from the file.
- Merge combines the data on a differencing disk with the parent disk to form a single composite image file.

7. Complete any new pages presented by the wizard as a result of your selection and click Finish.

The options that appear on the wizard's Choose Action page depend on the current status of the image file you select. For example, the Merge option only appears if you choose a differencing disk, and the Shrink option does not appear unless there is free space in the file that the wizard can delete.

In addition to these disk editing functions provided by Hyper-V Manager, it is also possible to use the Disk Management snap-in to mount a VHD or VHDX file as a drive and access its contents, just as if it was a physical disk.

To mount a virtual hard disk file, use the following procedure.

MOUNT A VIRTUAL HARD DISK FILE

GET READY. Log on to the server running Windows Server 2012 using an account with administrative privileges.

1. From the Tools menu in the *Server Manager* window, select Computer Management. The *Computer Management* console appears.

2. In the left pane, select Disk Management. The *Disk Management* snap-in appears, as shown in Figure 8-16.

Figure 8-16

The Disk Management snap-in

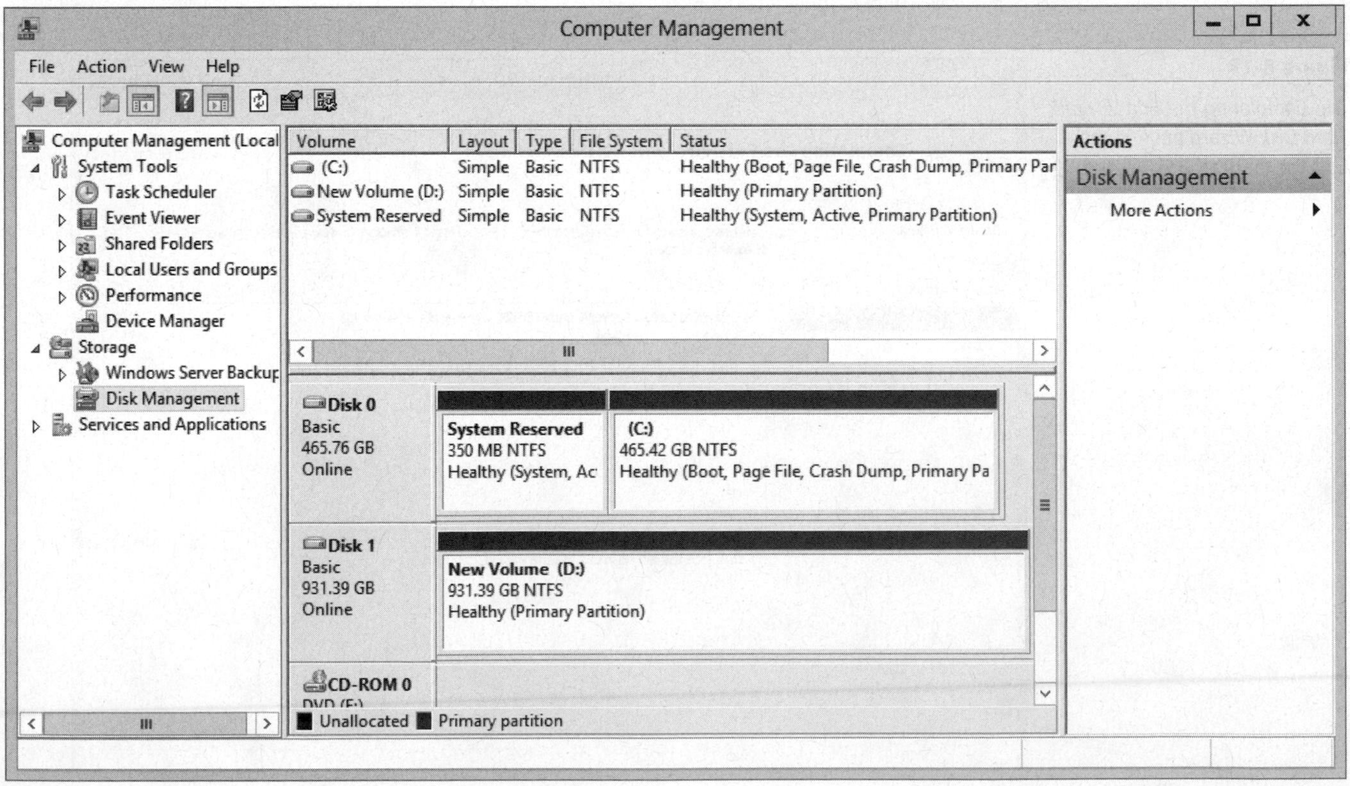

3. From the Action menu, select Attach VHD. The *Attach Virtual Hard Disk* dialog box appears, as shown in Figure 8-17.

Figure 8-17

The Attach Virtual Hard Disk dialog box

4. In the Location text box, type or browse to the image disk file you want to attach and click OK. The disk appears in the *Disk Management* interface.

CLOSE the *Computer Management* console.

At this point, you can work with the virtual disk and its contents using any standard tools, just as you would a physical hard disk drive.

USING WINDOWS POWERSHELL

You can execute some of the functions discussed in this section by using cmdlets included with Windows PowerShell 3.0, including the following:

- *Merge-VHD* merges a differencing disk into its parent disk.
- *Mount-VHD* mounts a virtual hard disk file into the local file system.
- *Dismount-VHD* dismounts a virtual hard disk file from the local file system.
- *Convert-VHD* converts the format, type, or block size of a virtual hard disk file.
- *ResizeVHD* expands or shrinks virtual hard disks.
- *OptimizeVHD* compacts dynamic or differencing disks.

Creating Snapshots

In Hyper-V, a ***snapshot*** is a captured image of the state, data, and hardware configuration of a virtual machine at a particular moment in time.

CERTIFICATION READY
Manage snapshots.
Objective 3.2

Creating snapshots is a convenient way for you to revert a virtual machine to a previous state at will. For example, if you create a snapshot just before applying a system update, and the update is somehow problematic, you can apply the snapshot and return the VM to the state it was in before you applied the update.

Creating a snapshot is as simple as selecting a running virtual machine in Hyper-V Manager and selecting Snapshot from the Actions pane. The system creates a snapshot file, with an AVHD or AVHDX extension, in the same folder as the virtual hard disk file, and adds the snapshot to Hyper-V Manager display, as shown in Figure 8-18.

Snapshots is a useful tool for you implementing a test environment in Hyper-V, but this tool is not recommended for heavy use in production environments. Apart from consuming disk space, the presence of snapshots can reduce the overall performance of a virtual machine's disk subsystem.

Figure 8-18

A snapshot in Hyper-V
Manager

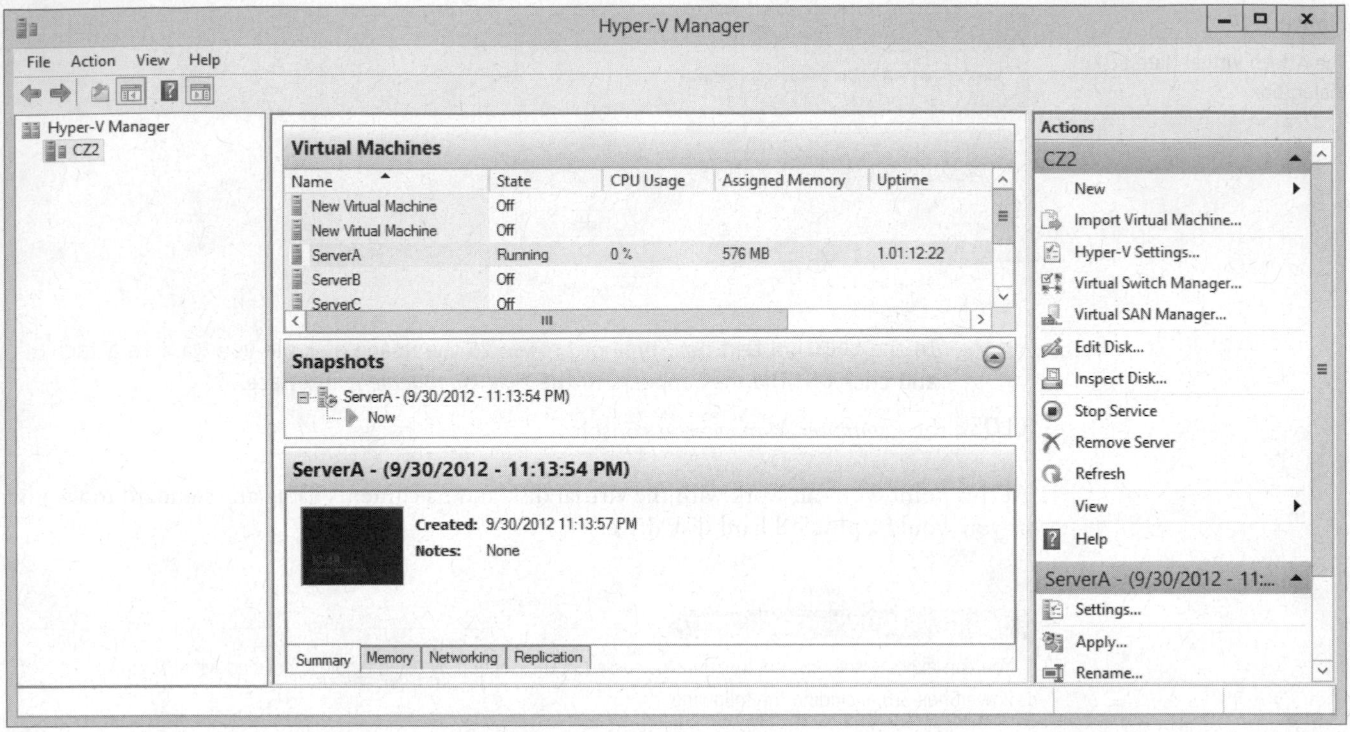

Connecting to a SAN

↓
THE BOTTOM LINE

At its most basic level, a *storage area network (SAN)* is a network dedicated to high-speed connections between servers and storage devices.

Rather than installing disk drives into servers, or connecting them by using an external SCSI bus, a SAN consists of one or more drive arrays equipped with network interface adapters, which you connect to your servers by using standard twisted pair or fiber optic network cables. A SAN-connected server, therefore, has a minimum of two network adapters, one for the standard LAN connection and one for the SAN, as shown in Figure 8-19.

The advantages of SANs are many. By connecting the storage devices to a network rather than to the servers themselves, you avoid the limitations imposed by the maximum number of devices you can connect directly to a computer. SANs also provide added flexibility in their communications capabilities. Because any device on a SAN can communicate with any other device on the same SAN, high-speed data transfers can occur in any of the following ways:

- **Server to storage:** Servers can access storage devices over the SAN just as if they were connected directly to the computer.

- **Server to server:** Servers can use the SAN to communicate directly with each other at high speeds, to avoid flooding the LAN with traffic.

- **Storage to storage:** Storage devices can communicate among themselves without server intervention, such as to perform backups from one medium to another or to mirror drives on different arrays.

Figure 8-19

A server connected to a SAN

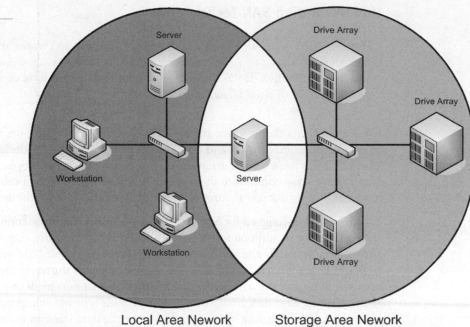

Although a SAN is not a high availability technology, you can make it into one by connecting redundant servers to the same network, as shown in Figure 8-20, enabling them to access the same data storage devices. If one server fails, another can assume its roles by accessing the same data, which is called *server clustering*.

Figure 8-20

Multiple servers connected to a SAN

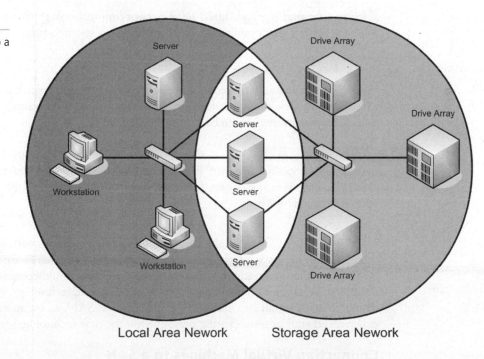

Because they use standard networking technologies, SANs can also greatly extend the distances between servers and storage devices. You can design a SAN that spans different rooms, different floors, or even different buildings, just as you would with a standard computer network.

Understanding SAN Technologies

External hard drives are now commonplace, on servers and workstations alike. The simplest devices consist of a single drive in a housing that includes a power supply and a Universal Serial Bus (USB) interface. These are suitable for local computer use, but not for the storage of shared data, as on a server.

Hard drive arrays that connect directly to a server are somewhat more complex, usually consisting of multiple drives and a SCSI interface. Some arrays include a RAID controller, whereas others use a simpler arrangement amusingly called *JBOD (Just a Bunch of Disks)*. This type of array connects to the server by using an external SCSI cable. The server must also have a SCSI host adapter that provides the other connection for the array.

The drive arrays designed for SANs are more complex than those connecting directly to servers, because in addition to the RAID and SCSI functionality, they also include support for networking protocols and intelligent agents that provide advanced functions, such as serverless backups. In a serverless backup, a server is responsible for initiating the backup job, but after the backup begins, the data travels directly from one storage medium on the SAN to another, such as from a hard disk array to a tape library. This type of backup not only eliminates the potential LAN bottleneck by using the SAN for the data transfer, it also eliminates the backup server itself as a possible bottleneck.

Servers and storage devices cannot exchange SCSI commands over a SAN connection the way they do when the devices are directly connected using a SCSI cable. To communicate over a SAN, servers and storage devices map their SCSI communications onto another protocol, such as Fibre Channel.

Using Fibre Channel

Fibre Channel is a high-speed serial networking technology that was originally designed for use with supercomputers, but which is now associated primarily with storage area networking.

Fibre Channel is a versatile technology, supporting various network media, transmission speeds, topologies, and upper-level protocols. Its primary disadvantage is that it requires specialized hardware that can be extremely expensive.

> **+ MORE INFORMATION**
>
> The non-standard spelling of the word "fibre" in Fibre Channel is deliberate, to distinguish the term from "fiber optic." Fibre Channel can run on either twisted pair copper or optical cables, whereas the spelling "fiber" always refers to an optical medium.

Installing a Fibre Channel SAN means building a new network with its own special medium, switches, and network interface adapters. In addition to the hardware costs, which can easily be 10 times that of a traditional Ethernet network, you should consider installation and maintenance expenses. Fibre Channel is a rather esoteric technology, with relatively few experts in the field. To install and maintain a Fibre Channel SAN, an organization must either hire experienced staff or train existing personnel on the new technology.

Connecting Virtual Machines to a SAN

In the past, the specialized networking technologies used to build Fibre Channel SANs made it difficult to use them with virtualized servers. However, Windows Server 2012 Hyper-V now supports the creation of virtual Fibre channel adapters.

CERTIFICATION READY
Implement a virtual Fibre Channel adapter.
Objective 3.2

A Hyper-V Fibre Channel adapter is essentially a pass-through device that enables a virtual machine to access a physical Fibre Channel adapter installed in the computer, and through that, the external resources connected to the SAN. With this capability, applications running on virtual machines can access data files stored on SAN devices, and you can use VMs to create server clusters with shared storage subsystems.

To support virtual Fibre Channel connectivity, the physical Fibre Channel host bus adapter(s) in the host computer must have drivers that explicitly support virtual Fibre Channel. At the time of Windows Server 2012's release, this support is relatively rare, but more manufacturers are expected to update their drivers to provide the necessary support. Your SAN must also be able to address its connected resources using logical unit numbers (LUNs).

Assuming you have the appropriate hardware and software installed on the host commuter, you implement the Fibre Channel capabilities in Hyper-V by first creating a virtual SAN. You do this by using the *Virtual SAN Manager*, accessible from *Hyper-V Manager*. When you create the virtual SAN, the World Wide Node Names (WWNNs) and World Wide Port Names (WWPNs) of your host bus adapter appear, as shown in Figure 8-21.

Figure 8-21
WWNNs and WWPNs in a virtual SAN

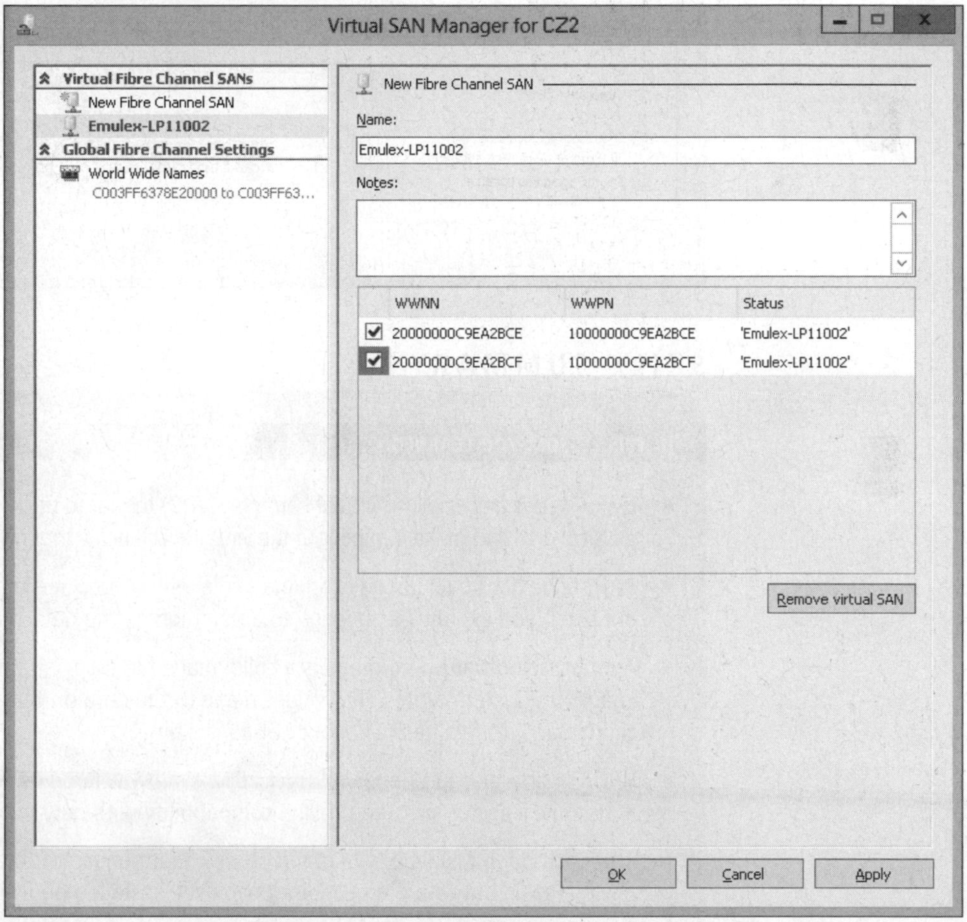

The next step is to add a Fibre Channel adapter to a virtual machine from the *Add Hardware* page in the *Settings* dialog box. Then, the virtual SAN you created previously is available in the *Fibre Channel Adapter* page, as shown in Figure 8-22. Hyper-V virtualizes the SAN and makes the WWNNs and WWPNs available to the VM.

Figure 8-22

A Fibre Channel adapter in a VM

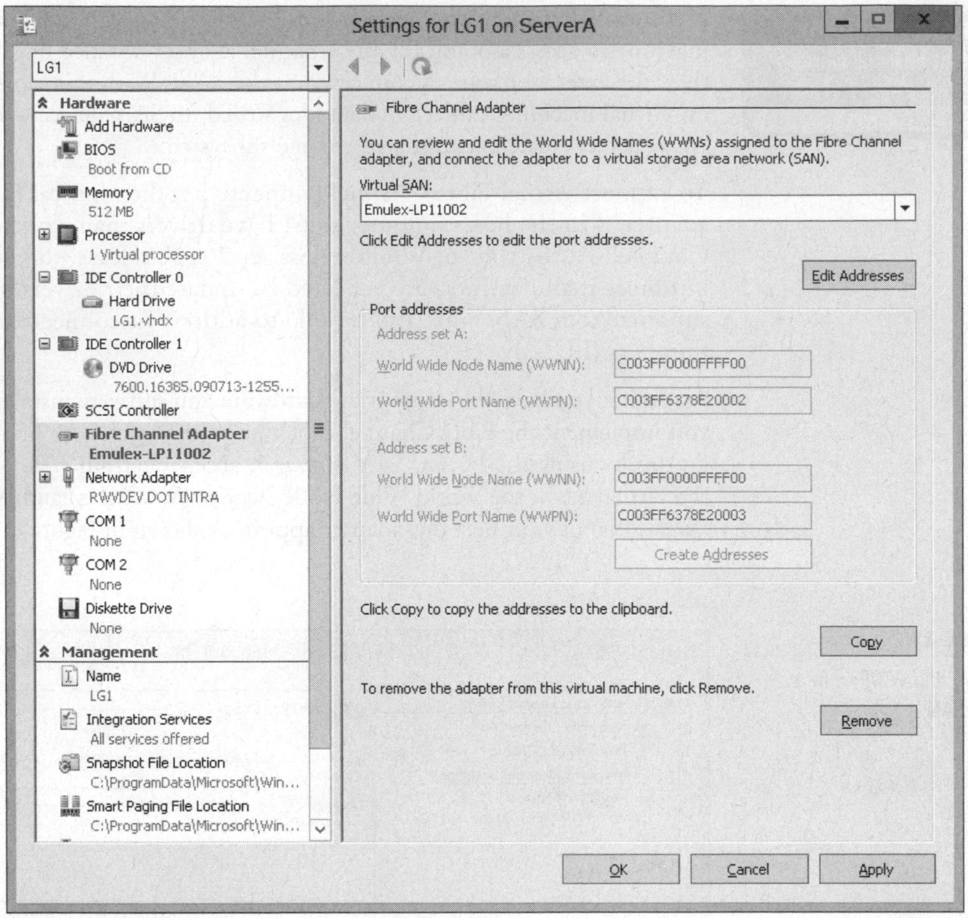

SKILL SUMMARY

IN THIS LESSON, YOU LEARNED:

- Hyper-V uses a specialized virtual hard disk (VHD) format to package part of the space on a physical disk and make it appear to the virtual machine as though it is physical hard disk drive.

- A dynamic hard disk image is an image file with a specified maximum size, which starts out small and expands as needed to accommodate the data the system writes to it.

- A differencing hard disk image is a child image file associated with a specific parent image. The system writes all changes made to the data on the parent image file to the child image, to facilitate a rollback at a later time.

- VHDX image files in Windows Server 2012 can be as large as 64 TB, and they also support 4 KB logical sector sizes, to provide compatibility with new 4 KB native drives.

- A pass-through disk is a type of virtual disk that points not to an area of space on a physical disk, but to a physical disk drive itself, installed on the host computer.

- In Hyper-V, a snapshot is a captured image of the state, data, and hardware configuration of a virtual machine at a particular moment in time.

- In the past, the specialized networking technologies used to build Fibre Channel SANs made it difficult to use them with virtualized servers. However, Windows Server 2012 Hyper-V now supports the creation of virtual Fibre channel adapters.

■ Knowledge Assessment

Multiple Choice

Select one or more correct answers for each of the following questions.

1. Which of the following statements about VHDX files is not true?
   a. VHDX files can be as large as 64 TB.
   b. VHDX files can only be opened by computers running Windows Server 2012.
   c. VHDX files support larger block sizes than VHD files.
   d. VHDX files support 4 KB logical sectors.

2. Which of the following must be true about a pass-through disk?
   a. A pass-through disk must be offline in the guest OS that will access it.
   b. A pass-through disk must be offline in the parent partition of the Hyper-V server.
   c. A pass-through disk can only be connected to a SCSI controller.
   d. A pass-through disk must be added to a VM with the Disk Management snap-in.

3. The Merge function only appears in the Edit Virtual Hard Disk Wizard under which of the following conditions?
   a. When you select a VHDX file for editing
   b. When you select two or more disks for editing
   c. When you select a disk with free space available in it
   d. When you select a differencing disk for editing

4. Which of the following are valid reasons not to take snapshots of VMs? (Choose all that apply.)
   a. Snapshots can consume a large amount of disk space.
   b. Each snapshot requires a separate copy of the VM's memory allocation.
   c. Each snapshot can take several hours to create.
   d. The existence of snapshots slows down VM performance.

5. Which of the following is not required to add a Fibre Channel adapter to a Hyper–V VM?
   a. You must create a Fibre Channel virtual SAN.
   b. You must have a physical Fibre Channel adapter installed in the host computer.
   c. You must have a Fibre Channel adapter driver that supports virtual networking.
   d. You must have a SCSI cable connecting the Fibre Channel adapter to the storage devices.

6. What Server Manager tool allows you to create a new virtual hard disk (VHD)?
   a. Hyper-V server
   b. Active Directory Domain Services (AD DS) manageability
   c. Hyper-V Manager
   d. File and storage services

7. When creating a new VHD, what feature does Windows PowerShell offer that the graphical interface does not?
   a. You can specify the block size and the logical sector sizes.
   b. You can decide between VHD and VHDX disk types.
   c. You can choose among Fixed, Dynamic, or Differencing.
   d. You can specify the path.

8. Can you modify an existing VHD file?
   a. No, once created, a VHD file is fixed.
   b. Yes, but you can modify it only through Windows PowerShell.
   c. No, but you change it into a VHDX file.
   d. Yes, you can even modify it without mounting it to a VM.

9. Do VMs ever directly access a physical hard disk?
   a. No, VMs access only VHDs, areas of space on the physical hard disk.
   b. Yes, VMs access a physical hard disk by way of a "pass-through disk," a special virtual disk that directly accesses the physical disk if it is made exclusively available to the VM.
   c. No, VMs access physical hardware only through the hypervisor.
   d. Yes, VHDs correlate one to one with physical hard disks.

10. Creating a virtual SAN allows you to _____.
    a. eliminate the physical disks
    b. have VHDs communicate with physical hard disks
    c. make distant storage accessible to VMs
    d. utilize the Fibre Channel adapters

Best Answer

Choose the letter that corresponds to the best answer. More than one answer choice may achieve the goal. Select the BEST answer.

1. Deciding between two virtual disk formats (VHD and VHDX), you need one to accommodate image sizes up to 2 TB (terabytes) and be compatible with both Windows Server 2012's Hyper-V and Microsoft's older product, Virtual PC. Which format do you choose and why?
   a. VHD, because it supports up to 2 TB image files.
   b. VHDX, because it supports file sizes far beyond 2 TB—up to 64 TB.
   c. VHD, because it supports both new and old hypervisor products.
   d. VHDX, because it supports larger block sizes for tuning storage performance.

2. You need to connect a virtual hard disk with a virtual machine (VM). What disk format do you choose and why?
   a. VHDX, because it's the only one available when creating a new disk.
   b. VHD or VHDX if using an existing virtual hard disk.
   c. VHD with an existing hard disk and a Type II hypervisor product.
   d. Either one is possible and applicable.

3. You intend to create a new virtual hard disk, specifying a 700 GB VHDX image file with a logical sector size of 4 KB. How do you proceed?
   a. With Server Manager, using Hyper-V Manager's New Disk feature.
   b. With the utilities included in Hyper-V's guest integration services.
   c. Those exact specifications are not possible in Hyper-V Manager.
   d. With PowerShell, using the New-VHD cmdlet with appropriate parameters.

4. Is it possible for a VM to access a hard disk directly?
   a. No. VMs access virtual hard disks, areas of space on the physical hard disk.
   b. Yes. VMs can have "pass-through disks," a special virtual disk that directly accesses the physical disk if made exclusively available to the VM.
   c. No. VMs can never access physical hardware, but only through the hypervisor.
   d. Yes. VMs use virtual hard disks, which are essentially the physical hard disks.

5. What is a key benefit of using differencing disks?
   a. They enable you to use baseline images.
   b. They enable you to keep a fixed image in its original state.
   c. They allow you to experiment without repercussions.
   d. They let you create parent and child-differencing disks.

Build a List

1. Order the steps to create a new virtual hard disk.
   a. Select one of the available hard disk formats.
   b. Choose the disk type, either VHD or VHDX.
   c. From the Action menu, select New > Hard Disk.
   d. Specify the Name and Location of the disk.
   e. From Server Manager's Tools menu, select Hyper-V Manager, and then select a Hyper-V server.
   f. Select to either create a blank virtual hard disk or to copy contents from an existing virtual or physical hard disk.

2. Order the steps to add a virtual disk to a VM.
   a. From Server Manager's Tools menu, select Hyper-V Manager, and then select a Hyper-V server.
   b. In the IDE Controller box, select Hard Drive, and click Add.
   c. In the Controller and Location drop-down lists, specify the IDE controller and the channel you want for the virtual hard disk.
   d. From the Action menu, select Settings.
   e. Select the IDE controller (for example, IDE Controller 0).
   f. With the Virtual hard disk option selected, click Browse and select the disk image file you want to add.

3. Order the steps to create a cloned installation with a differencing disk (in generalized steps).
   a. Create a parent disk image.
   b. Create a differencing disk.
   c. Install and configure the baseline VM and install the guest OS.
   d. Generalize the parent image.
   e. Create a cloned VM.

4. Order the steps to modify a virtual disk. Not all steps will be used.
   a. Browse to the name of the VHD or VHDX file to open.
   b. From Server Manager's Tools menu, select Hyper-V Manager, and then select a Hyper-V server.
   c. In the Actions pane, select Edit Disk to bring up the Edit Virtual Hard Disk Wizard.
   d. Open Disk Management snap-in to mount the VHD or VHDX file.
   e. Select one of the following edit options: Compact, Convert, Expand, Shrink, or Merge.

5. Order the steps to have a VM utilize a Fibre Channel Storage Area Network (SAN).
   a. Use World Wide Node Names and World Wide Port Names to add a Fibre Channel adapter to a VM.
   b. Open the Virtual SAN Manager to create a virtual SAN.
   c. From Server Manager's Tools menu, select Hyper-V Manager.
   d. Hyper-V makes the Virtual SAN available to the VM.

■ Business Case Scenarios

Scenario 8-1: Creating Differencing Disks

To conduct multiple tests, you require several VMs with the same baseline installation. You decide to employ differencing disks to create your VMs. Walk through the steps.

Scenario 8-2: Modifying Virtual Disks

You need to modify an existing VHD file. How do you proceed?

9 LESSON

Creating and Configuring Virtual Networks

70-410 EXAM OBJECTIVE

Objective 3.3 – Create and configure virtual networks. This objective may include but is not limited to: Implement Hyper-V Network Virtualization; configure Hyper-V virtual switches; optimize network performance; configure MAC addresses; configure network isolation; configure synthetic and legacy virtual network adapters.

Lesson Heading	Exam Objective
Using Virtual Networking	Implement Hyper-V Network Virtualization
Creating Virtual Switches	Configure Hyper-V virtual switches Configure MAC addresses
Creating Virtual Network Adapters	Configure synthetic and legacy virtual network adapters Optimize network performance Configure MAC addresses
Creating Virtual Network Configurations	Configure network isolation

KEY TERMS

emulated adapter

external network switch

internal network switch

legacy adapter

private network switch

synthetic adapter

virtual switch

Virtualization Service Client (VSC)

Virtualization Service Provider (VSP)

VMBus

■ Using Virtual Networking

Networking is a critical part of creating a virtual machine (VM) infrastructure. Depending on your network plan, the virtual machines you create on a Windows Server 2012 Hyper-V server can require communication with other virtual machines, with the computers on your physical network, and/or with the Internet.

When you build a network out of physical computers, you install a network interface adapter in each one and connect it to a hardware switch. The same principle is true in a Hyper-V environment, except that you use virtual components rather than physical ones. Each virtual machine you create has at least one virtual network adapter, and you can connect that adapter to a virtual switch. This enables you to connect the virtual machines on your Hyper-V server in various network configurations that either include or exclude the systems on your physical network.

Therefore, Hyper-V creates a pool of 256 MAC addresses during the installation. You can create multiple virtual switches on a Hyper-V server and multiple network adapters in each virtual machine. Multiple virtual switches and network adapters enable you to create a flexible networking environment, which is suitable for anything from a laboratory or classroom network to a production environment. In addition, Windows Server 2012 can create extensions for virtual switches, so that software developers can enhance their capabilities.

Creating Virtual Switches

A *virtual switch*, like its physical counterpart, is a device that functions at layer 2 of the Open Systems Interconnect (OSI) reference model. A switch has a series of ports, each of which is connected to a computer's network interface adapter. Any computer connected to the switch can transmit data to any other computer connected to the same switch.

Unlike physical switches, the virtual switches created by Hyper-V can have an unlimited number of ports, so you don't need to connect switches together or use uplinks and crossover circuits.

CREATING THE DEFAULT VIRTUAL SWITCH

The Windows Server 2012 Add Roles and Features Wizard provides the opportunity to create virtual switches when you install the Hyper-V role.

When you install Hyper-V on a server running Windows Server 2012, the Create Virtual Switches page, shown in Figure 9-1, provides you with the opportunity to create a virtual switch for each of the physical network adapters installed in the host computer. These switches enable virtual machines to participate on the networks to which the physical adapters are connected.

When you create a virtual switch in this manner, the networking configuration in the host operating system on the parent partition changes. The new virtual switch appears in the Network Connections window. If you examine its properties, notice that the switch is bound to the operating system's TCP/IP client, as shown in Figure 9-2.

Figure 9-1

The Create Virtual Switches page, displayed during a Hyper-V role installation

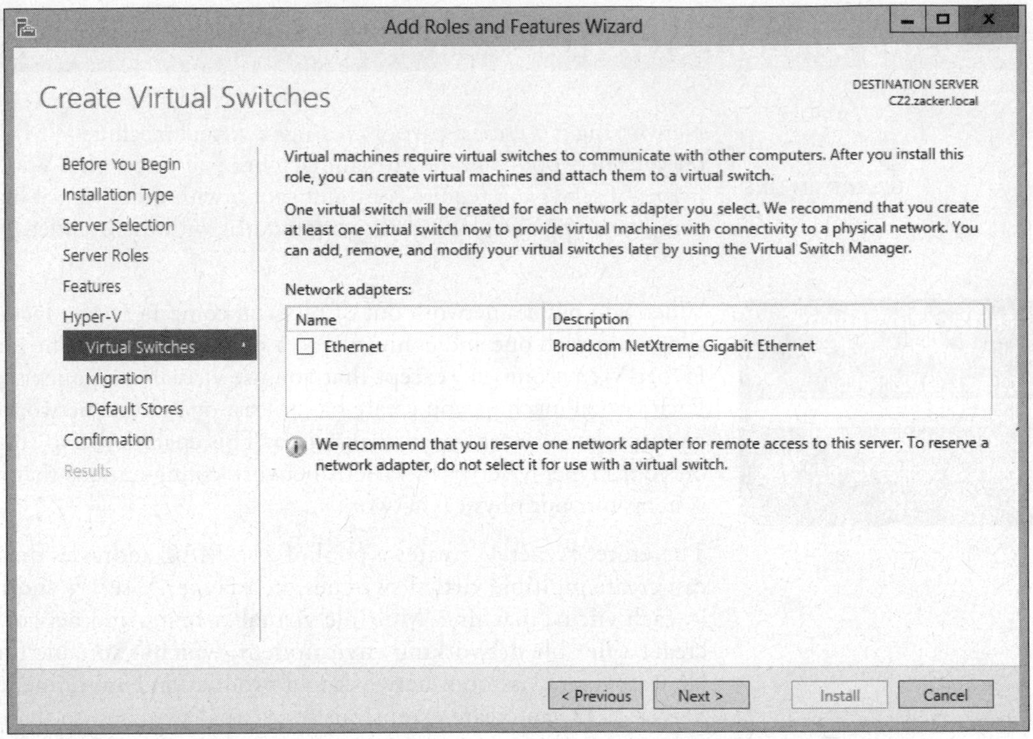

Figure 9-2

A virtual switch and its properties, displayed in the host operating system

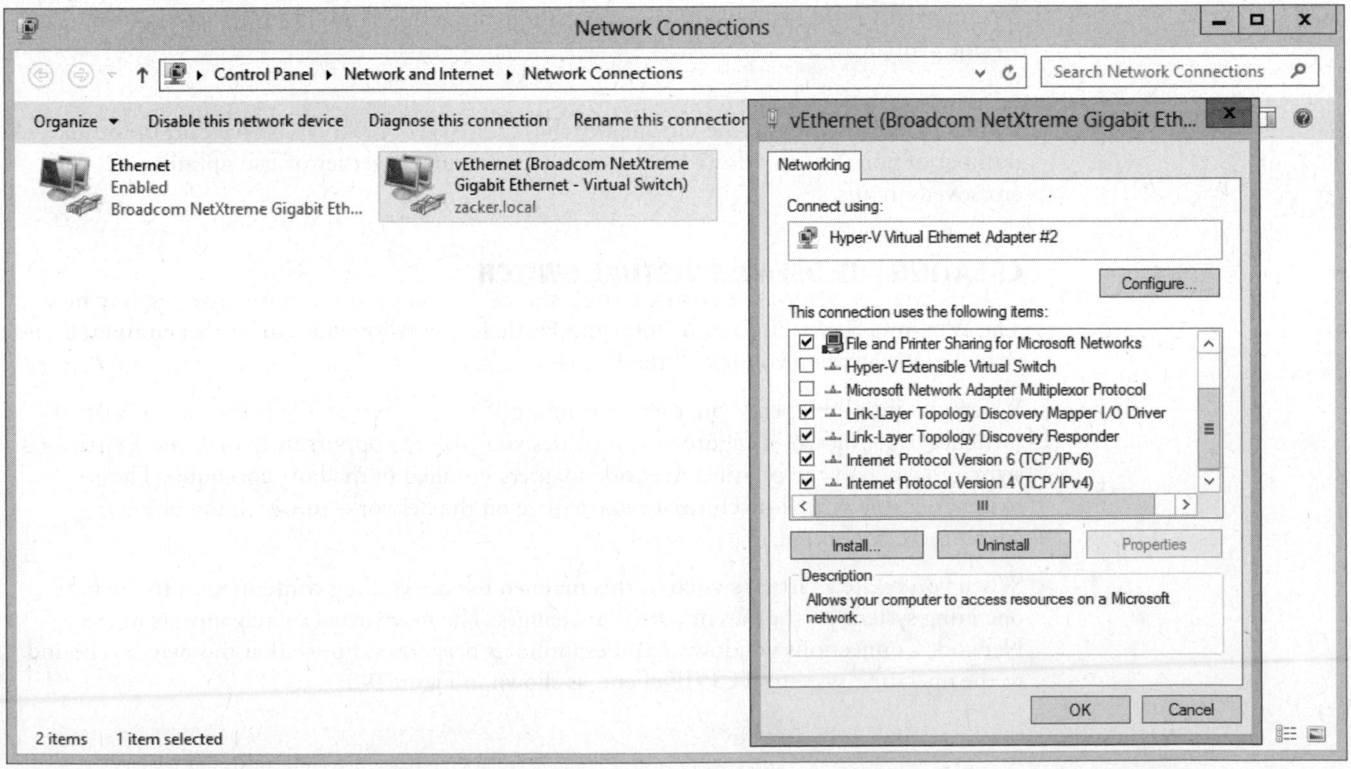

Figure 9-3

A network interface adapter in the host operating system, bound to a virtual switch

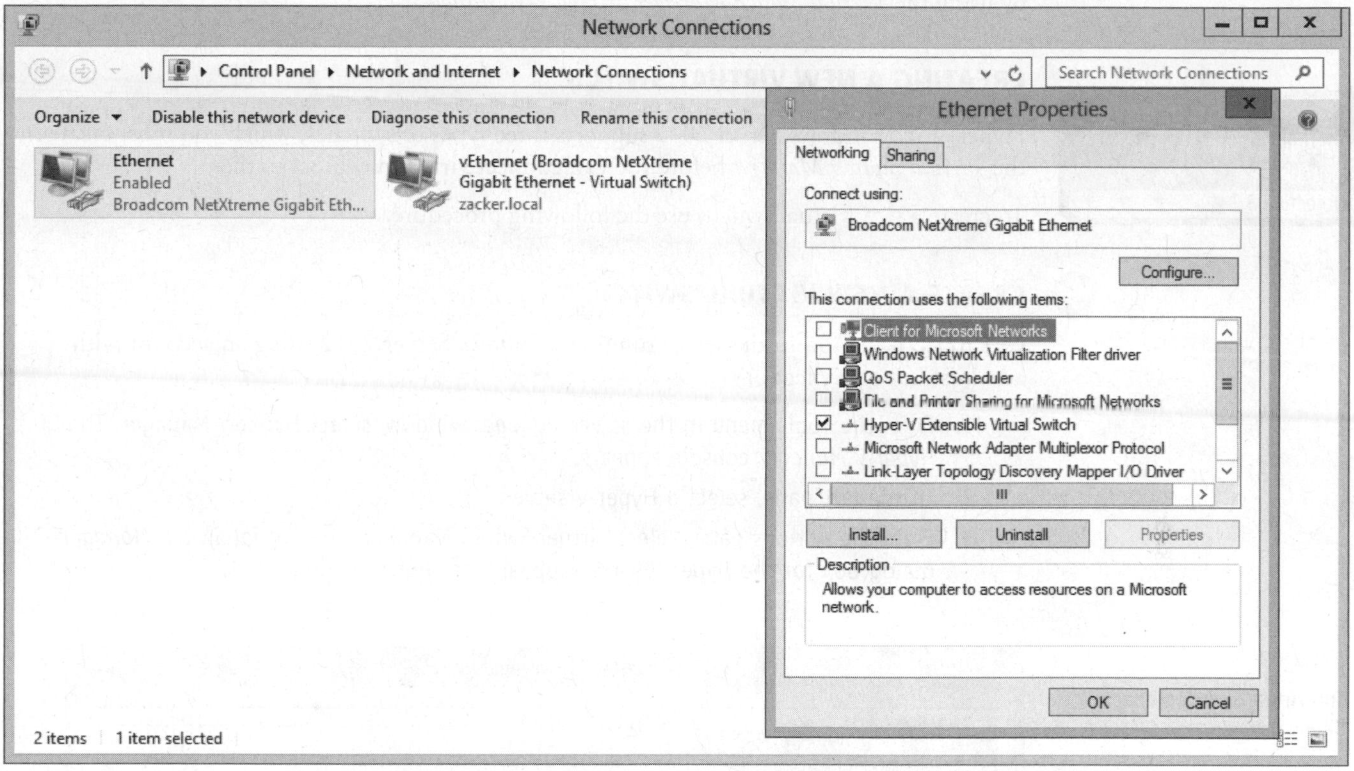

Meanwhile, Hyper-V also changes the properties of original network connection representing the physical network interface adapter in the computer. The physical network adapter is now bound only to the virtual switch, as shown in Figure 9-3.

The result is that the computer's physical network configuration, in which its network adapter is connected to an external physical switch, is overlaid by the virtual network configuration created by Hyper-V. In this virtual configuration, the virtual switch is connected to the physical switch and the network adapter in the host operating system is connected to the virtual switch. The internal virtual network and the external physical network are joined into a single local area network (LAN), just as if you connected two physical switches together.

After Hyper-V creates the virtual switch and makes the configuration changes, any new virtual machines that you connect to the virtual switch become part of this conjoined network, as do any physical computers connected to the physical network through an external switch.

This type of virtual switch is, in Hyper-V terminology, an *external network switch*, because it provides connections external to the Hyper-V environment. This is typically the preferred arrangement for a production network in which Hyper-V virtual machines provide and consume services for the entire network.

For example, a virtual machine connected to this switch automatically obtains an IP address from a DHCP server on the physical network, if one exists, or you can configure a virtual machine as a DHCP server and let it provide addresses to all the system on the network, virtual or physical.

Perhaps more importantly, this arrangement can also enable your virtual machines to access the Internet by using the router and DNS servers on the external network. The virtual machines can then download operating system updates from the Windows Update servers on the Internet, just as external machines often do.

This type of virtual switch is not appropriate in all situations. If you create a laboratory network for product testing or a classroom network, you might not want it to be accessible to or from the external network. In these cases, you must create a different type of virtual switch, by using the *Virtual Switch Manager* in *Hyper-V Manager*.

CREATING A NEW VIRTUAL SWITCH

CERTIFICATION READY
Configure Hyper-V virtual switches.
Objective 3.3

Hyper-V in Windows Server 2012 supports three types of switches, which you must create in the *Virtual Switch Manager* before you can connect virtual machines to them.

To create a new virtual switch, use the following procedure.

CREATE A NEW VIRTUAL SWITCH

GET READY. Log on to the server running Windows Server 2012 using an account with administrative privileges.

1. From the Tools menu in the *Server Manager* window, select Hyper-V Manager. The *Hyper-V Manager* console appears.

2. In the left pane, select a Hyper-V server.

3. From the Actions pane, select Virtual Switch Manager. The *Virtual Switch Manager* dialog box for the Hyper-V server appears, as shown in Figure 9-4.

Figure 9-4

The Virtual Switch Manager dialog box

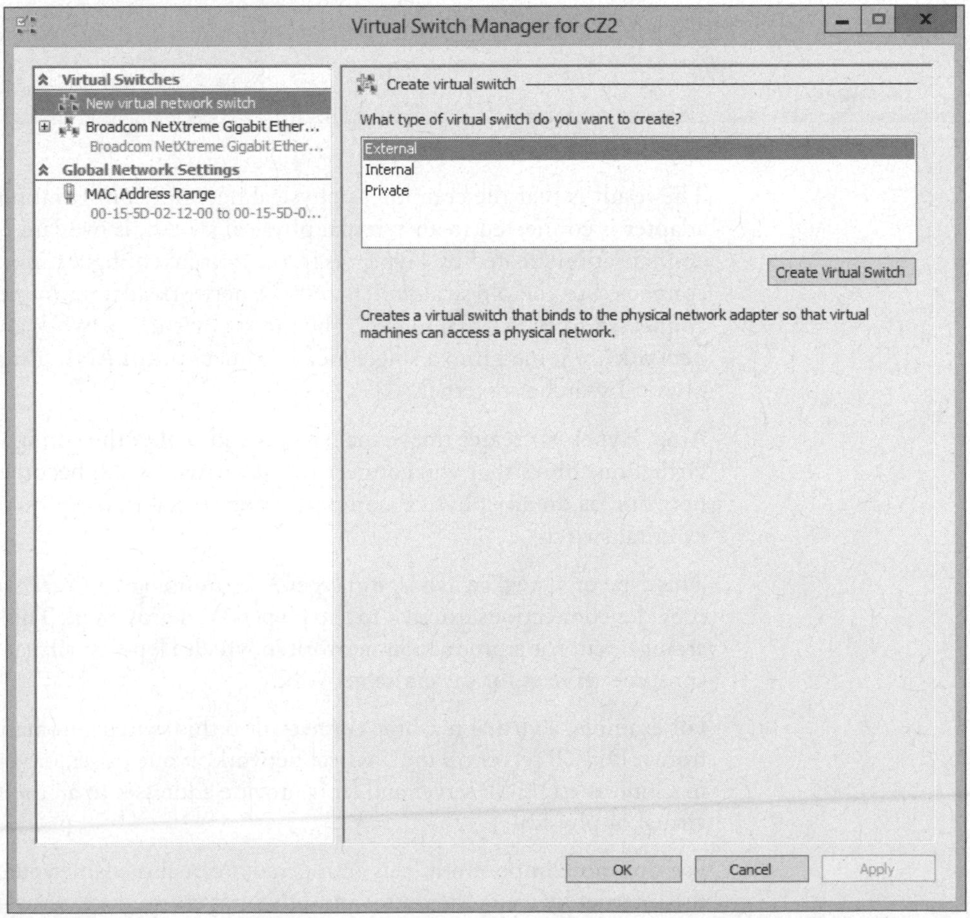

4. In the Create virtual switch box, select one of the following switch types and click Create Virtual Switch. The *Virtual Switch Properties* page appears, as shown in Figure 9-5.

- External: The virtual switch is bound to networking protocol stack in the host operating system and connected to a physical network interface adapter in the Hyper-V server. Virtual machines running on the server's parent and child partitions can access the physical network to which the physical adapter is connected.

- Internal: An ***internal network switch*** is bound to a separate instance of the networking protocol stack in the host operating system, independent from the physical network interface adapter and its connected network. Virtual machines running on the server's parent and child partitions can access the virtual network implemented by the virtual switch, and the host operating system on the parent partition can access the physical network through the physical network interface adapter, but the virtual machines on the child partitions cannot access the physical network through the physical adapter.

- Private: A ***private network switch*** exists only in the Hyper-V server and is accessible only to the virtual machines running on the child partitions. The host operating system on the parent partition can still access the physical network through the physical network interface adapter, but it cannot access the virtual network created by the virtual switch.

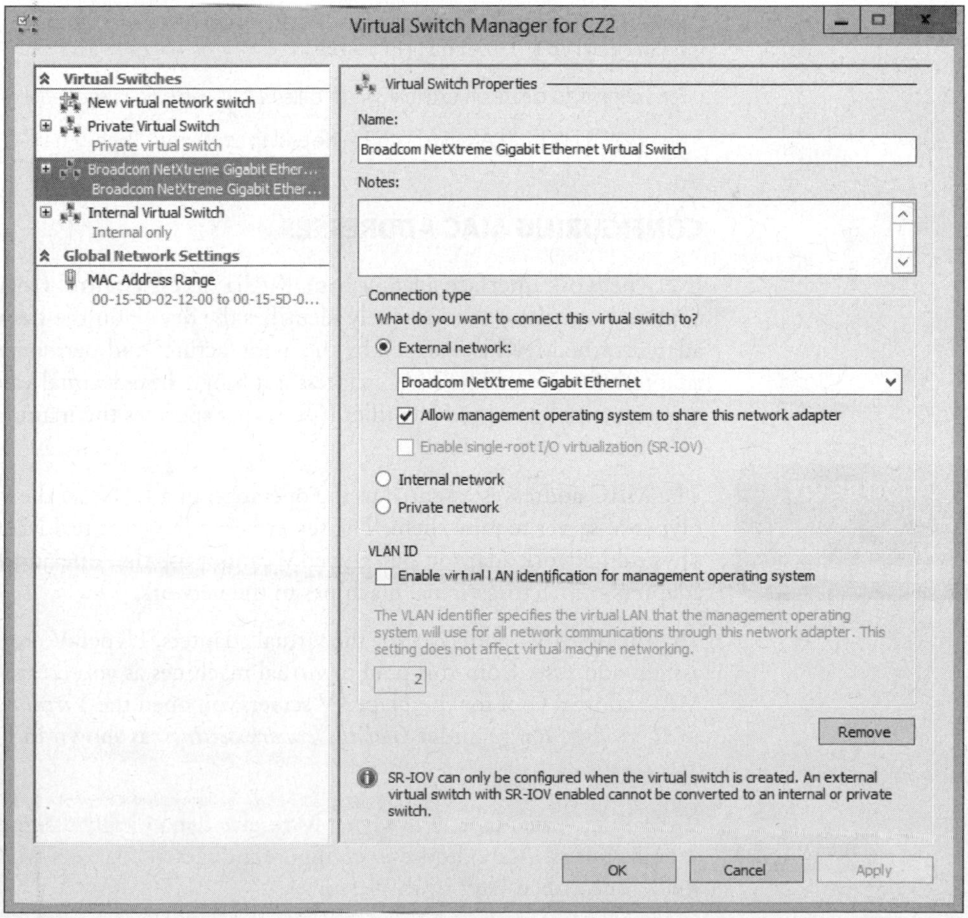

Figure 9-5

The *Virtual Switch Properties* page, with the private network switch selected

5. Configure the following options, if desired:

- Allow management operating system to share this network adapter: Selected by default when you create an external virtual switch, clearing this check box excludes the host operating system from the physical network, while allowing access to the child virtual machines.

- Enable single root I/O virtualization (SR-IOV): This option enables you to create an external virtual switch that is associated with a physical network adapter capable of supporting SR-IOV. This option is only available when creating a new virtual switch; you cannot modify an existing switch to use this option.

- Enable virtual LAN identification for management operating system: If your host computer is connected to a physical switching infrastructure that uses virtual LANs (VLANs) to create separate subnets, you can select the check box and enter a VLAN identifier to associate the virtual switch with a particular VLAN on your physical network.

6. Click OK. The new virtual switch appears in the left pane, in the list of virtual switches.

You can proceed to create additional virtual switches as needed. You can create only one switch for each physical network adapter in the computer, but you can create multiple internal or private switches, to create as many virtual networks as you need.

USING WINDOWS POWERSHELL

To create a new virtual switch with Windows PowerShell, you use the New-VMSwitch cmdlet with the following basic syntax:

```
New-VMSwitch <switch name> -NetAdapterName <adapter name>
[-SwitchType Internal|Private]
```

For example, to create an external switch called *LAN Switch*, you use the following command:

```
New-VMSwitch "LAN Switch" -NetAdapterName "Ethernet"
```

CONFIGURING MAC ADDRESSES

Every network interface adapter has a Media Access Control (MAC) address (sometimes called a *hardware address*) that uniquely identifies the device on the network. On physical network adapters, the MAC is assigned by the manufacturer and permanently entered in the adapter's firmware. The MAC address is a 6-byte hexadecimal value—the first 3 bytes is an organizationally unique identifier (OUI) that specifies the manufacturer, and the last 3 bytes identifies the adapter itself.

CERTIFICATION READY
Configure MAC addresses.
Objective 3.3

The MAC address is essential to the operation of a LAN, so the virtual network adapters on a Hyper-V server require them. The server has at least one real MAC address, provided in its physical network adaptor, but Hyper-V cannot use that one address for all of the virtual adapters connecting virtual machines to the network.

To provide MAC addresses for the virtual adapters, Hyper-V creates a pool of addresses and assigns addresses from this pool to virtual machines as you create them. To view or modify the MAC address pool for the Hyper-V server, you open the *Virtual Switch Manager* and select *MAC Address Range* under *Global Network Settings*, as shown in Figure 9-6.

TAKE NOTE*

Virtual network adapters in Hyper-V receive dynamically assigned MAC addresses by default, but you can choose to configure individual adapters with static MAC addresses as well, as described later in this lesson.

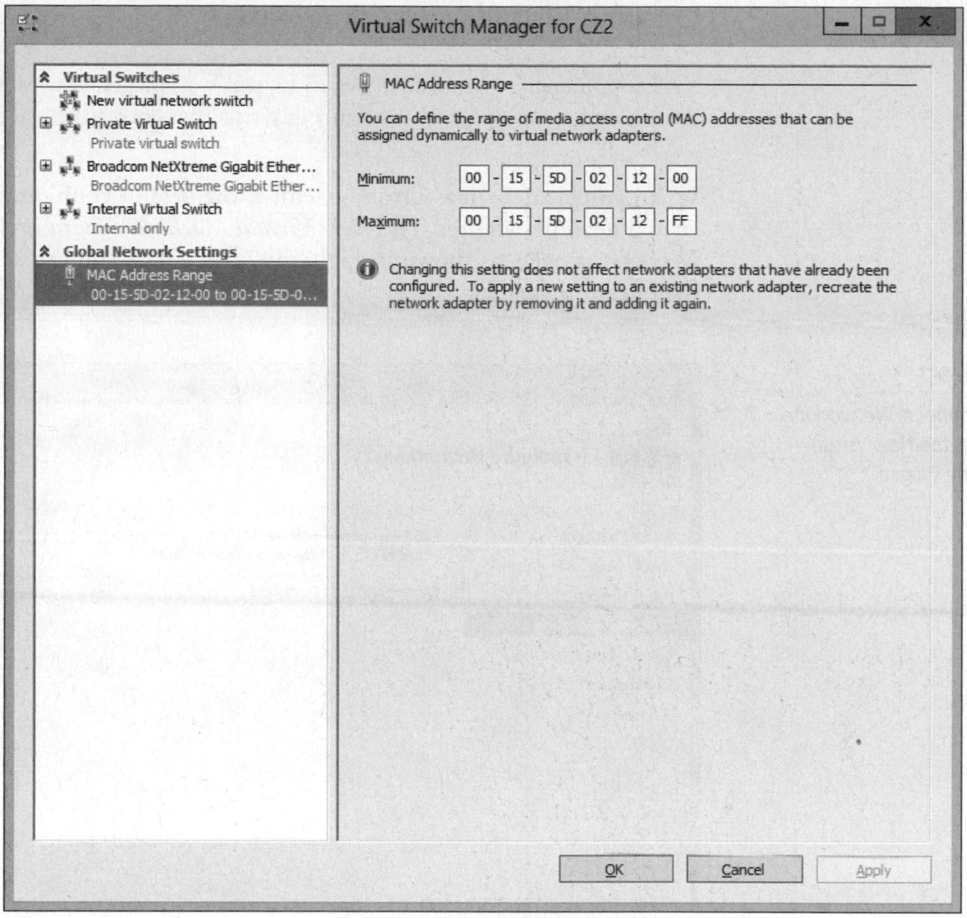

Figure 9-6

The *MAC Address Range* in the
Virtual Switch Manager

The first 3 bytes of MAC address range are always 00-15-5D, which is an OUI registered by Microsoft. The fourth and fifth bytes of the MAC address are the last 2 bytes of the IP address assigned to the server's physical network adapter, converted to hexadecimals. The sixth and last byte of the MAC address contains the range of values from 00 to FF, which provides 256 possible addresses.

The Hyper-V server assigns the MAC addresses to the network adapters in virtual machines as you create the adapters. The adapters retain their MAC addresses permanently, or until the adapter is removed from the virtual machine. The server reclaims any unused addresses and reuses them.

The default pool of 256 addresses is expected to be sufficient for most Hyper-V virtual machine configurations, but if it is not, you can modify the *Minimum* and *Maximum* values to enlarge the pool. To prevent address duplication, you should change the second to last byte only, by making it into a range of addresses like the last byte.

For example, if the range illustrated in Figure 9-6 provides 256 addresses with the following values:

```
00-15-1D-02-12-00 to 00-15-1D-02-12-FF
```

modifying only the least significant digit, as in the following values, increases the pool from 256 to 4,096.

```
00-15-1D-02-10-00 to 00-15-1D-02-1F-FF
```

WARNING When you modify the MAC address pool, and you have other Hyper-V servers on your network, you must be careful not to create the chance for duplicate MAC addresses, or networking problems can occur.

Creating Virtual Network Adapters

> After you create virtual switches in Hyper-V Manager, you can connect virtual machines to them by creating and configuring virtual network adapters.

When you create a new virtual machine, the default configuration includes one virtual network adapter. The *New Virtual Machine Wizard* includes a *Configure Networking* page, as shown in Figure 9-7, on which you can select one of the virtual switches you created.

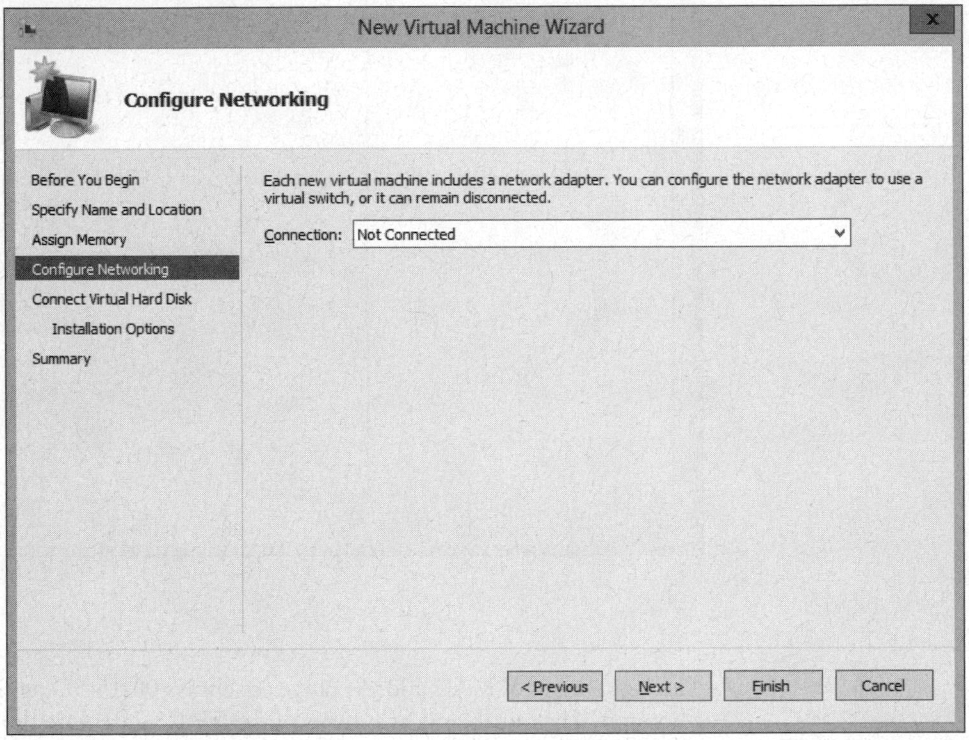

Figure 9-7

The *Configure Networking* page in the New Virtual Machine Wizard

If you create only the default external virtual switch when installing Hyper-V, then connecting a virtual machine to the switch joins the system to the physical network. To create additional network adapters in your virtual machines, you must use the following procedure.

CREATE A VIRTUAL NETWORK ADAPTER

GET READY. Log on to the server running Windows Server 2012 using an account with administrative privileges.

1. From the Tools menu in the *Server Manager* window, select Hyper-V Manager. The *Hyper-V Manager* console appears.
2. In the left pane, select a Hyper-V server.
3. In the Virtual Machines list, select a virtual machine and, in the Actions pane, click Settings. The *Settings* dialog box for the virtual machine appears, as shown in Figure 9-8.
4. In the Add Hardware list, select Network Adapter and click Add. A new adapter appears in the *Hardware* list, as shown in Figure 9-9.

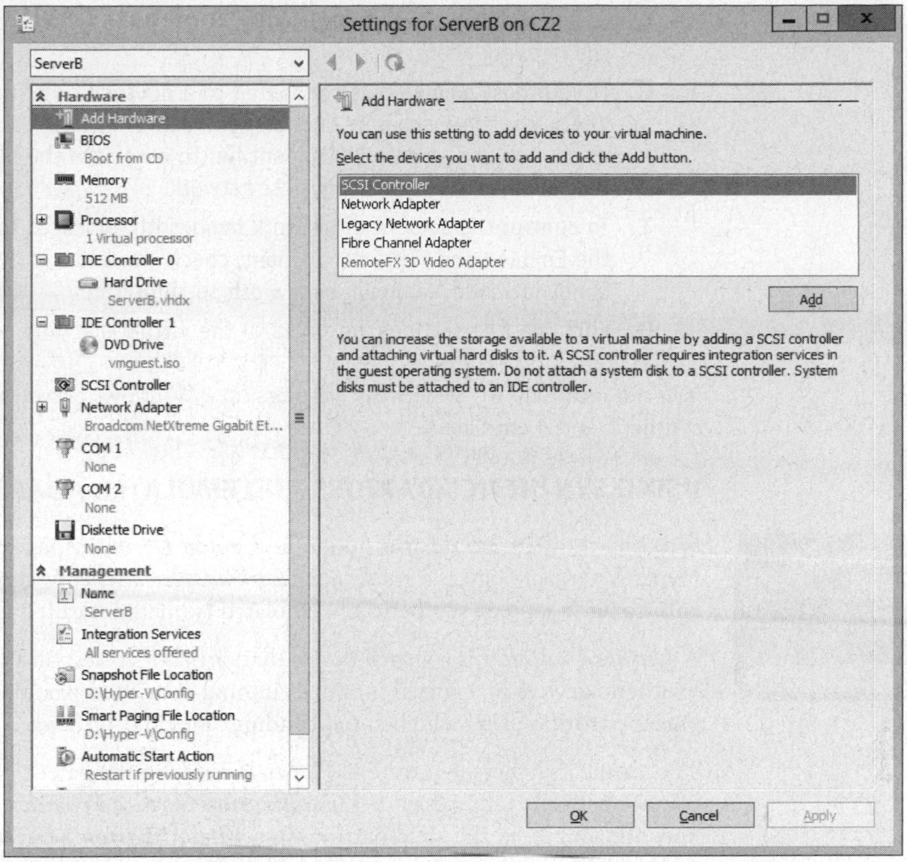

Figure 9-8

A virtual machine's Settings dialog box

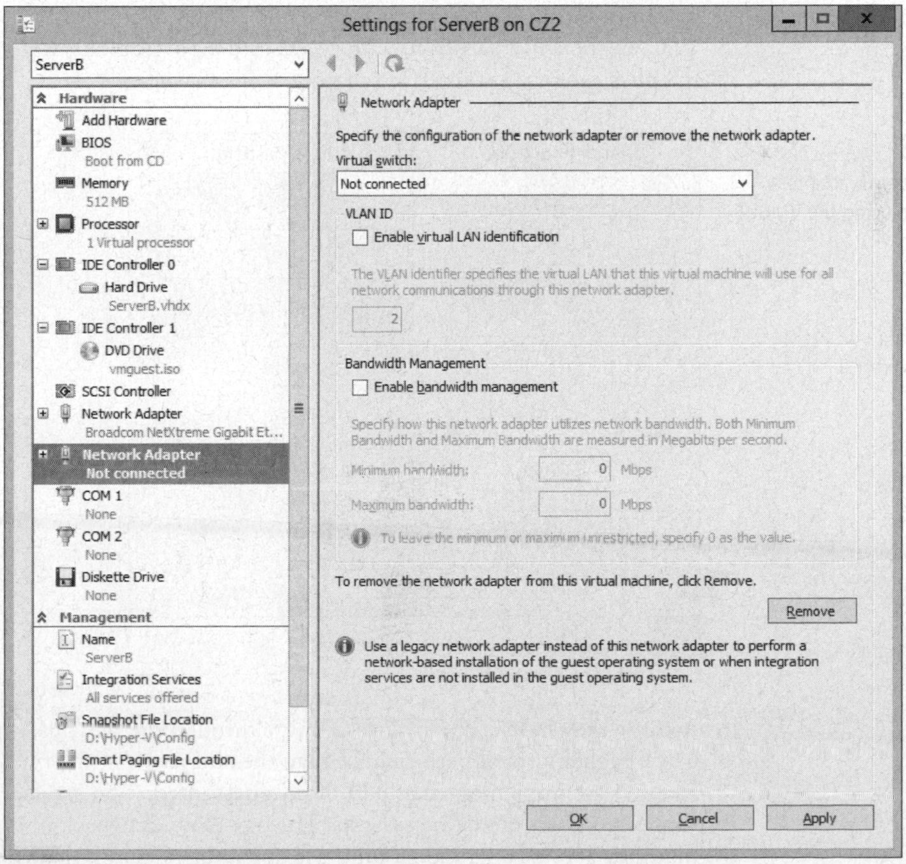

Figure 9-9

A new network adapter in the Settings dialog box

5. In the Virtual Switch drop-down list, select the switch to which you want to connect the network adapter.

6. If your host computer is connected to a physical switching infrastructure that uses VLANs to create separate subnets, you can select the Enable virtual LAN identification check box and enter a VLAN identifier to associate the network adapter with a particular VLAN on your physical network.

7. To control the amount of network bandwidth allocated to the network adapter, select the Enable bandwidth management check box and supply values for the Minimum bandwidth and Maximum bandwidth settings.

8. Click OK. The settings are saved to the virtual machine configuration.

You can create up to 12 network adapters on a Windows Server 2012 Hyper-V server—8 synthetic and 4 emulated.

USING SYNTHETIC ADAPTORS AND EMULATED ADAPTERS

Selecting the *Network Adapter* option in the *Add Hardware* page creates what is known in Hyper-V terminology as a *synthetic network adapter*. Hyper-V supports two types of network and storage adapters: synthetic and emulated (sometimes called *legacy*).

A ***synthetic adapter*** is a virtual device that does not correspond to a real-world product. Synthetic devices in a virtual machine running on a child partition communicate with the parent partition using a high-speed conduit called the ***VMBus***.

The virtual switches you create in Hyper-V reside in the parent partition and are part of a component called the network ***Virtualization Service Provider (VSP)***. The synthetic network adapter in the child partition is a ***Virtualization Service Client (VSC)***. The VSP and the VSC are both connected to the VMBus, which provides interpartition communications, as shown in Figure 9-10. The VSP, in the parent partition, provides the VSC, in the child partition, with access to the physical hardware in the host computer, that is, the physical network interface adaptor.

Figure 9-10

Synthetic network adapters communicate using the VMBUS

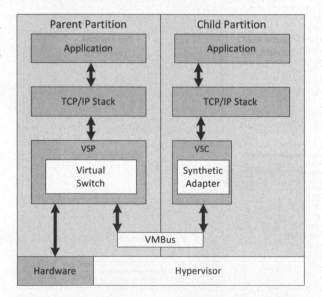

Because they have access to the hardware through the VMBus, synthetic adapters provide a much higher level of performance than the alternative—an emulated adapter. Synthetic adapters are implemented as part of the guest integration services package that run on supported guest operating systems. The one main drawback of synthetic network adapters is that they are not operational until the operating system is loaded on the virtual machine.

CERTIFICATION READY
Optimize network
performance.
Objective 3.3

An *emulated adapter* (sometimes called a *legacy adapter*) is a standard network adapter driver that communicates with the parent partition by making calls directly to the hypervisor, which is external to the partitions, as shown in Figure 9-11. This communication method is substantially slower than the VMBus used by the synthetic network adapters, and is therefore less desirable.

Figure 9-11

Emulated network adapters communicate using the hypervisor

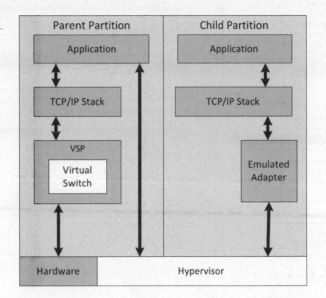

To install an emulated adapter, you use the same procedure described previously, except that you select *Legacy Network Adapter* in the *Add Hardware* list. Unlike synthetic adapters, emulated adapters load their drivers before the operating system, so you can boot the virtual machine using the Preboot eXecution Environment (PXE) and deploy an operating system over the network.

This is one of the only scenarios in which an emulated adapter is preferable to a synthetic adapter. The other is when you install an operating system on your virtual machines that does not have a guest integration services package available for it.

CONFIGURING HARDWARE ACCELERATION SETTINGS

CERTIFICATION READY
Optimize network
performance.
Objective 3.3

Some physical network interface adapters have features that are designed to improve performance by offloading certain functions from the system processor to components built into the adapter itself. Hyper-V includes support for some of these features, as long as the hardware in the physical network adapter supports them properly.

To configure these features, use the following procedure.

CONFIGURE NETWORK PERFORMANCE SETTINGS

GET READY. Log on to a server running Windows Server 2012 using an account with administrative privileges.

1. From the Tools menu in the *Server Manager* window, select Hyper-V Manager. The *Hyper-V Manager* console appears.
2. In the left pane, select a Hyper-V server.
3. In the Virtual Machines list, select a virtual machine and, in the Actions pane, click Settings. The *Settings* dialog box for the virtual machine appears.
4. Expand one of the network adapters installed in the virtual machine and select Hardware Acceleration. The *Hardware Acceleration* page appears, as shown in Figure 9-12.

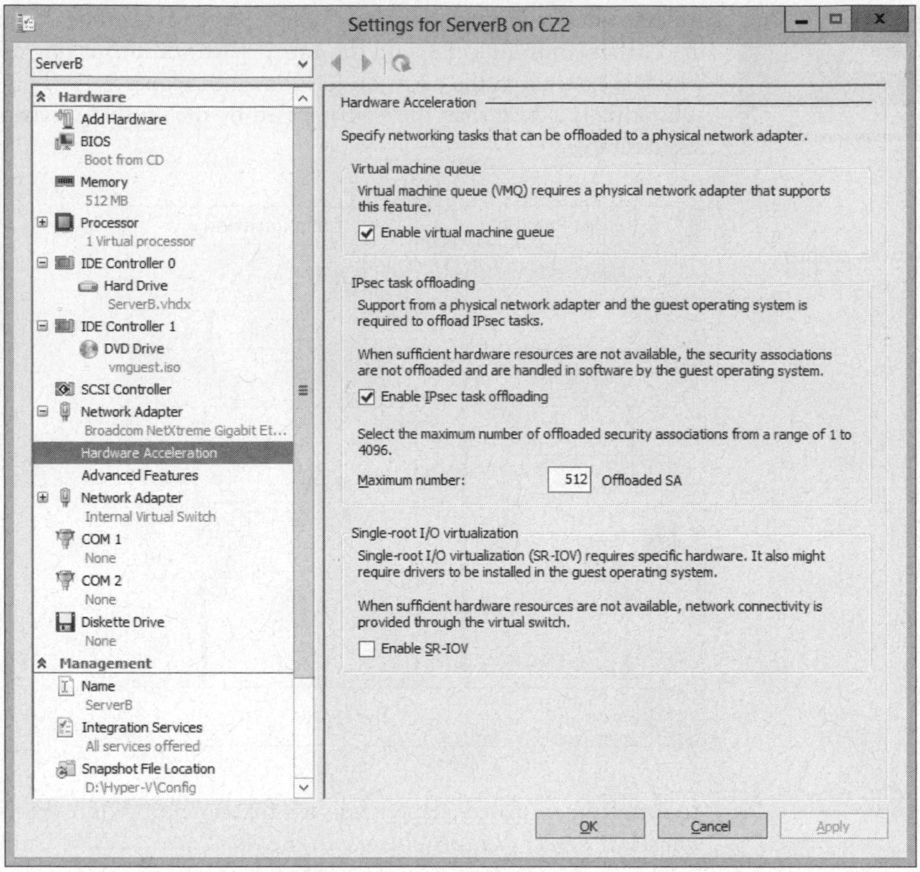

Figure 9-12

The Network Adapter *Hardware Acceleration* page in the Settings dialog box

5. Configure any or all of the following hardware acceleration settings:

   - Enable virtual machine queue: Virtual machine queue (VMQ) is a technique that stores incoming packets intended for virtual machines in separate queues on the physical network adapter and delivers them directly to the VMs, bypassing the processing normally performed by the virtual switch on the parent partition.

   - Enable IPsec task offloading: This setting uses the components on the network adapter to perform some of the cryptographic functions required by IPsec. You can also specify maximum number of security associations you want the adapter to be able to calculate.

   - Single-root I/O virtualization: This setting enables the virtual adapter to use the SR-IOV capabilities of the physical adapter.

6. Click OK to close the Settings dialog box.

CLOSE the Hyper-V Manager console.

CONFIGURING ADVANCED NETWORK ADAPTER FEATURES

To configure advanced network adapter features, use the following procedure.

CONFIGURE ADVANCED NETWORK ADAPTER FEATURES

GET READY. Log on to a server running Windows Server 2012 using an account with administrative privileges.

1. From the Tools menu in the *Server Manager* window, select Hyper-V Manager. The *Hyper-V Manager* console appears.

2. In the left pane, select a Hyper-V server.

3. In the Virtual Machines list, select a virtual machine and, in the Actions pane, click Settings. The *Settings* dialog box for the virtual machine appears.
4. Expand one of the network adapters installed in the virtual machine and select Advanced Features. The *Advanced Features* page appears, as shown in Figure 9-13.

Figure 9-13

The Network Adapter *Advanced Features* page in the Settings dialog box

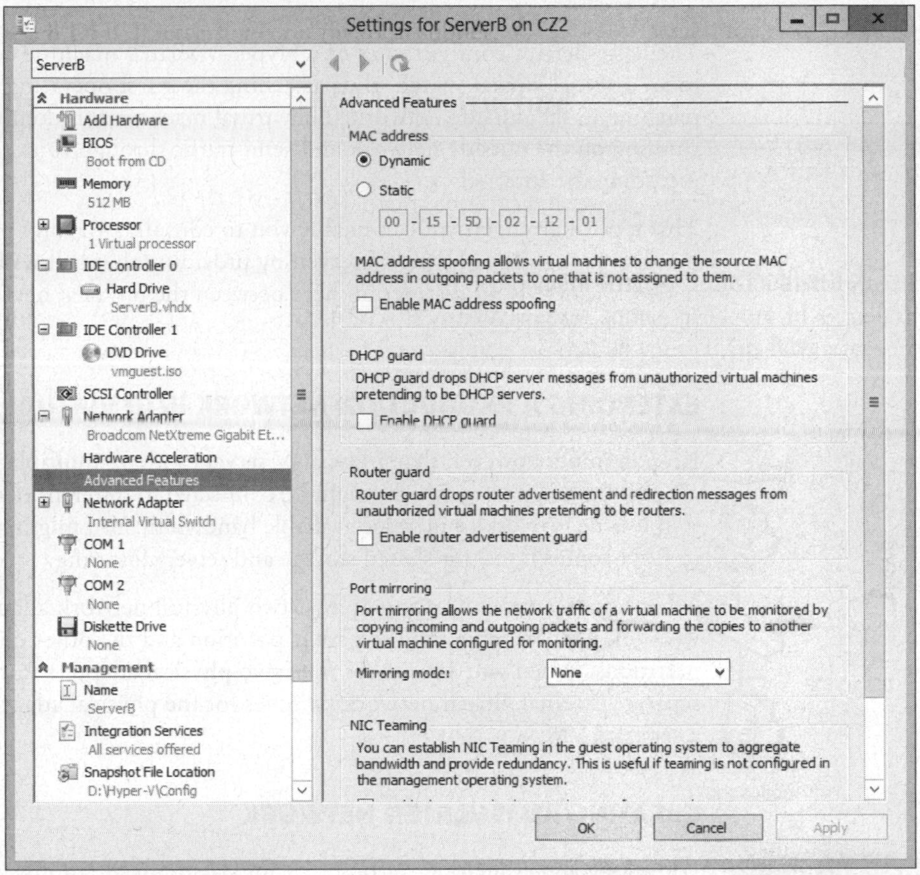

CERTIFICATION READY
Configure MAC addresses.
Objective 3.3

5. Configure any or all of the following advanced features:
   - Static MAC address: By default, virtual network adapters receive a dynamically assigned MAC address from the Hyper-V server. However, you can also opt to create a static MAC address, by using this option. The only requirement is that no other adapter, virtual or physical, on the same network uses the same address.
   - Enable MAC address spoofing: When enabled, the port in the virtual switch to which the virtual network adapter is connected can send and receive packets that contain any MAC address. The virtual switch port can also learn of new MAC addresses and add them in its forwarding table.
   - Enable DHCP guard: This option prevents the adapter from processing messages sent by rogue DHCP servers.
   - Port mirroring mode: This option enables the adapter to forward all the packets it receives over the network to another virtual adapter for analysis using an application such as Network Monitor.
   - NIC teaming: This option enables the adapter to add its bandwidth to other adapters in the same guest operating system in a NIC teaming arrangement.
6. Click OK to close the Settings dialog box.

CLOSE the Hyper-V Manager console.

Creating Virtual Network Configurations

Hyper-V makes it possible to extend virtually any existing physical network configuration into its virtual space, or create a completely separated and isolated network within the Hyper-V environment.

The basic default configuration of a Hyper-V virtual machine connects its network adapter to an external virtual switch, thus attaching the guest operating system on the virtual machine to the outside network. The virtual machine can then take advantage of services running on the outside network and send traffic through routers to other networks, including the Internet.

This type of arrangement can enable you to consolidate many physical servers into virtual machines on a single Hyper-V server, by providing them all with access to the entire network. There is no distinction here between the physical network and the virtual one in the Hyper-V space.

EXTENDING A PRODUCTION NETWORK INTO VIRTUAL SPACE

Keep in mind, however, that a Hyper-V server can have multiple physical network interface adapters installed in it, which might be connected to different networks to separate traffic, or to the same network to increase available bandwidth. You might also have adapters dedicated to SAN connections, for shared storage and server clustering.

Microsoft recommends using at least two physical network adapters in a Hyper-V server, with one adapter servicing the parent partition and the other connected to the child partitions. When you have more than two physical adapters in the server, you can create separate external virtual network switches for the physical adapters, and connect each one to a separate VM.

CREATING AN ISOLATED NETWORK

For testing and evaluation purposes, or for classroom situations, you might create isolated network environments. By creating internal or private virtual switches, you can create a network that exists only within the Hyper-V space, with or without the parent partition included.

An isolated network such as this suffers from the weaknesses of its strengths. If you want to install the guest operating systems using Windows Deployment Services or configure the virtual machines using DHCP, you must install and configure these services on your private network. The guest operating systems also do not have access to the Internet, which prevents them from downloading operating system updates. Again, you must deploy appropriate substitutes on the private network.

To provide your systems with updates, install two network adapters on each of your virtual machines, by connecting one to a private switch and one to an external switch. This procedure enables the virtual machines to access the Internet and the private network.

Another method for creating an isolated network is to use virtual LANs (VLANs). This is particularly helpful if you have virtual machines on different Hyper-V servers that you want to add to the isolated network. By connecting the network adapters to an external switch and configuring them with the same VLAN identifier, you can create a network within a network, which isolates the VLAN from other computers. You can, for example, deploy a DHCP server on your VLAN without it interfering with the other DHCP servers in your production environment.

SKILL SUMMARY

IN THIS LESSON, YOU LEARNED:

- Networking is a critical part of creating a virtual machine infrastructure. Depending on your network plan, the virtual machines you create on a Windows Server 2012 Hyper-V server can require communication with other virtual machines, with the computers on your physical network, and with the Internet.

- A virtual switch, like its physical counterpart, is a device that functions at layer 2 of the Open Systems Interconnect (OSI) reference model. A switch has a series of ports, each of which is connected to a computer's network interface adapter. Any computer connected to the switch can transmit data to any other computer connected to the same switch.

- Hyper-V in Windows Server 2012 supports three types of switches: external, internal, and private, which you must create in the virtual Switch Manager before you can connect virtual machines to them.

- Every network interface adapter has a Media Access Control (MAC) address (sometimes called a *hardware address*) that uniquely identifies the device on the network.

- After you have created virtual switches in Hyper-V Manager, you can connect virtual machines to them by creating and configuring virtual network adapters.

- Selecting the *Network Adapter* option in the *Add Hardware* page creates what is known in Hyper-V terminology as a *synthetic network adapter*. Hyper-V supports two types of network and storage adapters: synthetic and emulated (sometimes called *legacy*).

■ Knowledge Assessment

Multiple Choice

Select one or more correct answers for each of the following questions.

1. Which of the following are valid reasons for using an emulated network adapter rather than a synthetic one? (Choose all that apply.)
   a. You want to install the guest OS using a Windows Deployment Services server.
   b. There is no Guest Integration Services package available for the guest OS you plan to use.
   c. The manufacturer of your physical network adapter has not yet provided a synthetic network adapter driver.
   d. The emulated network adapter provides better performance.

2. Which of the following statements is not true about synthetic network adapters?
   a. Synthetic adapters communicate with the parent partition using the VMBus.
   b. Synthetic adapters require the Guest Integration Services package to be installed on the guest OS.
   c. Synthetic adapters provide faster performance than emulated adapters
   d. Synthetic adapters can start the child VM using a PXE network boot.

3. What is the maximum number of ports supported by a Hyper-V virtual switch?
   a. 8
   b. 256
   c. 4,096
   d. Unlimited

4. Which of the following virtual switch types does not enable guest OSs to communicate with the parent partition?
   a. External
   b. Internal
   c. Private
   d. Isolated

5. How many dynamically assigned MAC addresses can a Hyper-V server provide by default?
   a. 8
   b. 256
   c. 4,096
   d. Unlimited

6. You can create virtual switches after what role is installed?
   a. Hyper-V
   b. Application Server
   c. Remote Access
   d. Network Policy and Access Services

7. Creating the default virtual switch places it between _____ and _____.
   a. the physical switch; the network adapter in the host operating system
   b. the virtual adapter; the network adapter in the host operating system
   c. the network adapter; the virtual adapter in the host operating system
   d. the physical switch; the next upstream physical switch

8. How do you create a virtual switch for the purpose of isolating virtual machines (VMs) from the external network and the host operating system?
   a. You create an external virtual switch.
   b. You create an internal virtual switch.
   c. You create a private virtual switch.
   d. You cannot isolate VMs from the external network.

9. Which is faster, synthetic adapters or emulated adapters?
   a. Synthetic, because it does not correspond to a real-world device
   b. Emulated, because it is legacy and more compatible
   c. Synthetic, because it uses the VMBus
   d. Emulated, because it uses the VMBus

Best Answer

Choose the letter that corresponds to the best answer. More than one answer choice may achieve the goal. Select the BEST answer

1. What network interface configuration does Microsoft recommend in a Hyper-V server?
   a. Two physical adapters providing multiple virtual adapters
   b. One physical adapter per Hyper-V server, providing for several network and SAN connections
   c. One physical adapter per partition, providing for multiple network connections per partition
   d. At least two physical network adapters: one adapter servicing the parent partition and the other to the child partitions

2. What is the key benefit for creating a virtual switch?
   a. Virtual switches enable virtual machines (VMs) to participate on the networks to which the physical adapters are connected.
   b. Virtual switches require no physical space in the rack.
   c. Virtual switches enable the Hyper-V server to participate on the networks to which the physical adapters are connected.
   d. Virtual switches have unlimited ports, freeing network administrators from connecting physical switches by uplinks or crossover circuits.

3. What is the MAC address range in the Virtual Switch Manager?
   a. The MAC of the Hyper-V server is associated with the physical adapter's MAC address.
   b. First 3 bytes are fixed. Fourth and fifth associate to the adapter's IP address. Sixth provides 256 options.
   c. First 1 byte is fixed. Next 3 bytes associate to the adapter's IP address. Last 2 bytes provide 256 options.
   d. First 3 bytes are fixed. Fourth associates to the adapter's IP address. Fifth and sixth provides 256 options.

4. Where can an administrator make configuration changes to optimize network performance?
   a. In Server Manager, Advanced Network Features
   b. In the Settings dialog box of any VM
   c. In the Hardware Acceleration page under VM settings
   d. In any virtual network adapter, Advanced settings

5. What network communication occurs after creating a private virtual switch?
   a. The VM on the parent partition can communicate with the physical network.
   b. VMs on both the parent and child partitions can communicate with each other.
   c. VMs on the child partitions can communicate with each other only.
   d. VMs on child partitions and parent partition cannot communicate with each other.

Build a List

1. Order the steps to create a virtual switch.
   a. If applicable, configure the virtualization or management options.
   b. From the Actions pane, select Virtual Switch Manager.
   c. In the Server Manager Tools menu, select Hyper-V Manager, and then select a Hyper-V server.
   d. Click Create Virtual Switch after selecting a switch type option (External, Internal, or Private).

2. Order the steps to create a virtual network adapter.
   a. In the Virtual Machines list, select a virtual machine and, in the Actions pane, click Settings.
   b. In the Server Manager Tools menu, select Hyper-V Manager, and then select a Hyper-V server.
   c. In the Virtual Switch drop-down list, select the switch to which you want to connect the network adapter.
   d. In the Add Hardware list, select Network Adapter and click Add.
   e. If applicable, select the Enable virtual LAN identification check box.

3. You want to create a lab network disconnected to the company network. All lab servers are VMs on child partitions on a Hyper-V server. Order the steps to provide lab network connectivity.

   a. Test connectivity between child partition VMs. Test for no connectivity between the VMs and host OS or external network.

   b. Create a private virtual switch.

   c. Ensure you have either a DHCP virtual machine or the servers on child partitions have fixed network configurations.

   d. Create virtual network adapters for each desired VM.

■ Business Case Scenarios

Scenario 9-1: Creating a New Virtual Switch

You need all VMs networked to each other, plus to the host operating system. Only the host operating system will be connected to the external network. What do you do?

Scenario 9-2: Configuring Advanced Network Adapter Features

You are concerned about your VMs receiving rogue DHCP servers. How can you prevent this from happening?

Configuring IPv4 and IPv6 Addressing

LESSON 10

70-410 EXAM OBJECTIVE

Objective 4.1 – Configure IPv4 and IPv6 addressing. This objective may include but is not limited to: Configure IP address options; configure subnetting; configure supernetting; configure interoperability between IPv4 and IPv6; configure ISATAP; configure Teredo.

LESSON HEADING	EXAM OBJECTIVE
Understanding IPv4 Addressing	
IPv4 Classful Addressing	
Classless Inter-Domain Routing	
Public and Private IPv4 Addressing	
Using Network Address Translation	
Using a Proxy Server	
IPv4 Subnetting	Configure subnetting
Supernetting	Configure supernetting
Assigning IPv4 Addresses	Configure IP address options
Understanding IPv6 Addressing	
Introducing IPv6	
IPv6 Address Types	
Assigning IPv6 Addresses	
Planning an IP Transition	Configure interoperability between IPv4 and IPv6
Using a Dual IP Stack	
Tunneling	Configure ISATAP Configure Teredo

Understanding IPv4 Addressing

THE BOTTOM LINE

Many enterprise administrators are so comfortable working with IPv4 addresses that they are hesitant to change. Network Address Translation (NAT) and Classless Inter-Domain Routing (CIDR) have been excellent stopgaps to the depletion of the 32-bit IP address space for years, and many would like to see them continue as such. However, the IPv6 transition, long a specter on the distant horizon, is now suddenly approaching at frightening speed, and it is time for administrators not familiar with the new technologies to catch up—or be left behind.

The IPv4 address space consists of 32-bit addresses, notated as four 8-bit decimal values from 0 to 255, separated by periods, as in the example 192.168.43.100. This is known as dotted decimal notation, and the individual 8-bit decimal values are called *octets* or *bytes*.

Each address consists of *network bits*, which identify a network, and *host bits*, which identify a particular device on that network. To differentiate the network bits from the host bits, each address must have a subnet mask.

A **subnet mask** is another 32-bit value consisting of binary 1 bits and 0 bits. When compared to an IP address, the bits corresponding to the 1's in the mask are the network bits, whereas the bits corresponding to the 0's are the host bits. Thus, if the 192.168.43.100 address mentioned earlier has a subnet mask of 255.255.255.0 (which in binary form is 11111111.11 111111.11111111.00000000), the first three octets (192.168.43) identify the network and the last octet (100) identifies the host.

IPv4 Classful Addressing

Because the subnet mask associated with IP addresses can vary, so can the number of bits used to identify the network and the host.

The original Internet Protocol (IP) standard defines three classes of IP addresses, which provide support for networks of different sizes, as shown in Figure 10-1.

Figure 10-1

The three IPv4 address classes

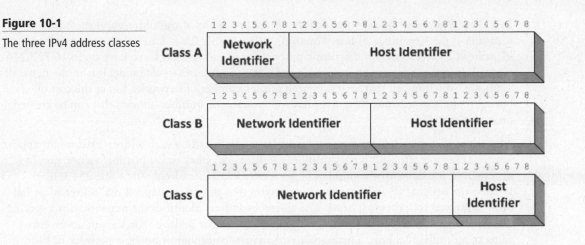

Table 10-1 lists the number of networks and hosts supported by each address class.

Table 10-1

IPv4 Address Classes

IP ADDRESS CLASS	CLASS A	CLASS B	CLASS C
First bit values (binary)	0	10	110
First byte value (decimal)	0–127	128–191	192–223
Number of network identifier bits	8	16	24
Number of host identifier bits	24	16	8
Number of possible networks	126	16,384	2,097,152
Number of possible hosts	16,777,214	65,534	254

TAKE NOTE *

In addition to classes A, B, and C, the IP standard also defines two additional address classes: D and E. Class D addresses begin with the bit values 1110, and Class E addresses begin with the values 11110. The Internet Assigned Numbers Authority (IANA) has allocated Class D addresses for use as multicast identifiers. A *multicast address* identifies a group of computers on a network, all of which possess a similar trait. Multicast addresses enable TCP/IP applications to send traffic to computers that perform specific functions (such as all the routers on the network), even if they are located on different subnets. Class E addresses are defined as experimental and are as of yet unused.

The *First bit values (binary)* row in Table 10-1 specifies the values that the first 1, 2, or 3 bits of an address in each class must have. Early TCP/IP implementations used these bit values instead of a subnet mask to determine the class of an address. The binary values of the first bits of each address class limit the possible decimal values for the first byte of the address. For example, because the first bit of Class A addresses must be 0, the possible binary values of the first byte in a Class A address range from 00000000 to 01111111, which in decimal form are values ranging from 1 to 127. Thus, when you see an IP address in which the first byte is a number from 1 to 127, you know that this is a Class A address.

In a Class A address, the network identifier is the first 8 bits of the address and the host identifier is the remaining 24 bits. Thus, only 126 possible Class A networks exist (network identifier 127 is reserved for diagnostic purposes), but each network can have up to 16,777,214 network interface adapters on it. Class B and Class C addresses devote more bits to the network identifier, which means that they support a greater number of networks, but at the cost of having fewer host identifier bits. This tradeoff reduces the number of hosts that can be created on each network.

The values in Table 10-1 for the number of hosts supported by each address class might appear low. For example, an 8-bit binary number can have 256 (that is, 2^8) possible values, not 254, as shown in the table for the number of hosts on a Class C address. The value 254 is used because the original IP addressing standard states that you cannot assign the "all zeros" or "all ones" addresses to individual hosts. The all-zeroes address identifies the network, not a specific host, and the all-ones identifier always signifies a broadcast address. You cannot assign either value to an individual host. Therefore, to calculate the number of possible network or host addresses you can create with a given number of bits, you use the formula $2^x - 2$, in which x is the number of bits.

SUBNETTING EXAMPLE 1

You can subnet a Class B network address by using the third byte, originally intended to be part of the host identifier, as a subnet identifier instead.

In the original address class, the first 16 bits identify the network and the last 16 bits identify the host, as represented by the letters N and H in the following diagram.

NNNNNNNN NNNNNNNN HHHHHHHH HHHHHHHH

By changing the subnet mask from 255.255.0.0 to 255.255.255.0, you divide the Class B address into 254 subnets of 254 hosts each. The third byte changes from host bits to subnet identifier bits, as represented by the letter S in the following diagram.

NNNNNNNN NNNNNNNN SSSSSSSS HHHHHHHH

To create addresses, you assign each of the physical segments on the network a different value for the third byte and number the individual systems using only the fourth byte. The result is that the routers on your network can use the value of the third byte to direct traffic to the appropriate segments.

TAKE NOTE*

The subnet identifier is purely a theoretical construction. To routers and other network systems, an IP address consists only of network and host identifiers, with the subnet bits incorporated into the network identifier.

Classless Inter-Domain Routing

When IP was developed, no one imagined that the 32-bit address space would ever be exhausted. In the early 1980s, no networks had 65,536 computers, never mind 16 million, and no one worried about the wastefulness of assigning IP addresses based on these classes.

Because of that wastefulness, classful addressing was gradually obsolesced by a series of subnetting methods, including variable-length subnet masking (VLSM) and eventually *Classless Inter-Domain Routing (CIDR)*. CIDR is a subnetting method that enables you to place the division between the network bits and the host bits anywhere in the address, not just between octets. This makes it possible to create networks of almost any size.

CIDR also introduces a new notation for network addresses. A standard dotted-decimal address representing the network is followed by a forward slash and a numeral specifying the size of the network-identifying prefix. For example, 192.168.43.0/24 represents a single Class C address that uses a 24-bit network identifier, leaving the other 8 bits for up to 254 host identifiers. Each of those hosts would receive an address from 192.168.43.1 to 192.168.43.254, using the subnet mask 255.255.255.0.

However, by using CIDR, you can subnet this address further by allocating some of the host bits to create subnets. To create subnets for four offices, for example, you can take two of the host identifier bits, changing the network address in CIDR notation to 192.168.43.0/26. Because the network identifier is now 26 bits, the subnet mask for all four networks is now 11111111.11111111.11111111.11000000 in binary form, or 255.255.255.192 in standard decimal form. Each of the four networks will have up to 62 hosts, using the IP address ranges shown in Table 10-2.

Table 10-2

Sample CIDR 192.168.43.0/26 Networks

NETWORK ADDRESS	STARTING IP ADDRESS	ENDING IP ADDRESS	SUBNET MASK
192.168.43.0	192.168.43.1	192.168.43.62	255.255.255.192
192.168.43.64	192.168.43.65	192.168.43.126	255.255.255.192
192.168.43.128	192.168.43.129	192.168.43.190	255.255.255.192
192.168.43.192	192.168.43.193	192.168.43.254	255.255.255.192

If you need more than four subnets, changing the address to 192.168.43.0/28 adds two more bits to the network address, for a maximum of 16 subnets, each of which can support up to 14 hosts. The subnet mask for these networks would therefore be 255.255.255.240.

SUBNETTING EXAMPLE 2

The previous example demonstrates the most basic type of subnetting, in which the boundaries of the subnet identifier fall between the bytes. However, with CIDR, you can use any number of host bits for the subnet identifier and adjust the subnet mask and IP address accordingly.

If, for example, you have an address with a /16 suffix, formerly known as a Class B address, and you decide to use 4 host bits for the subnet identifier, you would change the suffix to /20 and represent the arrangement using the following diagram:

NNNNNNNN NNNNNNNN SSSSHHHH HHHHHHHH

The subnet mask for this network would therefore have the following binary value.

11111111 11111111 11110000 00000000

The first 4 bits of the third byte are changed from 0s to 1s, to indicate that these bits are now part of the network identifier. The decimal equivalent of this number is 255.255.240.0, which is the value you would use for the subnet mask in the system's TCP/IP configuration. By borrowing 4 bits in this way, you can create up to 14 subnets, consisting of 4,094 hosts each, as determined by the formula $2^{12}-2$.

To determine the IP addresses you assign to particular systems, you increment the 4 bits of the subnet identifier separately from the 12 bits of the host identifier and convert the results into decimal form. Thus, assuming a network address of 172.16.0.0 with a subnet mask of 255.255.240.0, the first IP address of the first subnet will have the following binary address:

10101100 00010000 00010000 00000001

The first 2 bytes are the binary equivalents of 172 and 16. The third byte consists of the 4-bit subnet identifier, with the value 0001, and the first 4 bits of the 12-bit host

TAKE NOTE *

You can use the Windows Calculator program to convert between binary and decimal numbers by switching it into Programmer mode from the View menu. Once in Programmer mode, click either the Dec or Bin radio button, enter the number you want to convert, then click the other radio button to perform the conversion.

identifier. Because this is the first address on this subnet, the value for the host identifier is 000000000001.

Although these 12 bits are incremented as a single unit, when converting the binary values to decimals, you treat each byte separately. Therefore, the value of the third byte (00010000) in decimal form is 16, and the value of the fourth byte (00000001) in decimal form is 1, yielding an IP address of 172.16.16.1.

The last address in this subnet will have the following binary value:

`10101100 00010000 00011111 11111110`

which yields an IP address of 172.16.31.254.

For the next subnet, you increment the subnet identifier bits to 0010 and start again with 000000000001 as the first host in the new subnet. Thus, the first address in the second subnet is

`10101100 00010000 00100000 00000001`

or 172.16.32.1.

Proceeding in this way, you can create all 14 subnets, using the following address ranges:

```
172.16.16.1  -  172.16.31.25
172.16.32.1  -  172.16.47.25
172.16.48.1  -  172.16.63.25
172.16.64.1  -  172.16.79.25
172.16.80.1  -  172.16.95.25
172.16.96.1  -  172.16.111.25
172.16.112.1 -  172.16.127.25
172.16.128.1 -  172.16.143.25
172.16.144.1 -  172.16.159.25
172.16.160.1 -  172.16.175.25
172.16.176.1 -  172.16.191.25
172.16.192.1 -  172.16.207.25
172.16.208.1 -  172.16.223.25
172.16.224.1 -  172.16.239.25
```

Public and Private IPv4 Addressing

For a computer to be accessible from the Internet, it must have an IP address that is both registered and unique. All web servers on the Internet have registered addresses, as do all other types of Internet servers.

The IANA is the ultimate source for all registered addresses; managed by the Internet Corporation for Assigned Names and Numbers (ICANN), IANA allocates blocks of addresses to regional Internet registries (RIR), which in turn allocate smaller blocks to Internet service providers (ISPs). An organization that wants to host a server on the Internet typically obtains a registered address from an ISP.

Registered IP addresses are not necessary for workstations that merely access resources on the Internet. If organizations used registered addresses for all their workstations, the IPv4 address space would have been depleted long ago. Instead, organizations typically use private IP addresses for their workstations. Private IP addresses are blocks of addresses allocated specifically for private network use. Anyone can use these addresses without registering them, but they cannot make computers using private addresses directly accessible from the Internet.

The three blocks of addresses allocated for private use are as follows:

- 10.0.0.0/8
- 172.16.0.0/1212
- 192.168.0.0/16

Most enterprise networks use addresses from these blocks for their workstations. It does not matter if other organizations use the same addresses also, because the workstations are never directly connected to the same network.

Using Network Address Translation

The question still remains, however, of how workstations with unregistered private addresses communicate with registered servers on the Internet. An unregistered workstation can conceivably send messages to an Internet web server, but how can the web server respond when the workstation is using an address that is not visible from the Internet, and also might be shared by dozens of other computers?

The answer is by using a technology called network address translation or a slightly different mechanism called a proxy server.

Network address translation (NAT) is a Network-layer routing technology that enables a group of workstations to share a single registered address. A NAT router is a device with two network interfaces: one connected to a private network and one to the Internet. When a workstation on the private network wants to access an Internet resource, it sends a request to the NAT router.

Normally, a router passes traffic from one network to another without modifying the data. However, in this case, the NAT router substitutes its own registered IP address for the workstation's private address, and sends the request on to the Internet server. The server responds to the NAT router, thinking that the router generated the original request. The router then performs the same substitution in reverse and forwards the response back to the original unregistered workstation. The router, in essence, functions as an intermediary between the client and the server.

A single NAT router can perform this same service for hundreds of private workstations by maintaining a table of the address substitutions it has performed. In addition to conserving the IPv4 address space, NAT also provides a certain amount of protection to the network workstations. Because the workstations are functionally invisible to the Internet, attackers cannot readily probe them for open ports and other common exploits.

Using a Proxy Server

Because NAT routers function at the Network layer of the protocol stack, they can handle any kind of traffic, regardless of the application that generated it. A ***proxy server*** is another type of intermediary—functioning at the Application layer—which is designed to forward specific types of traffic to destinations on the Internet. In most cases, the primary function of a proxy server is to provide workstations with web access through a browser, such as Internet Explorer.

Like a NAT router, a proxy server receives requests from clients on a private network and forwards those requests to the destination on the Internet, using its own registered address to identify itself. The primary difference between a proxy server and a NAT router is that the proxy server interposes additional functions into the forwarding process. These functions can include the following:

- **Filtering:** Administrators can configure proxy servers to limit user access to the Internet by filtering out requests sent to undesirable sites.
- **Logging:** A proxy server can maintain logs of user Internet activity, for later evaluation and reporting.
- **Caching:** A proxy server can store frequently accessed Internet data in a local cache, which it can then use to satisfy subsequent requests for the same data at higher speeds.
- **Scanning:** A proxy server can scan incoming data from the Internet for various types of malware and outgoing data for confidential company information.

Unlike a NAT router, which is invisible to the workstation, applications must be configured to use a proxy server, a process that can be manual or automatic.

IPv4 Subnetting

In most cases, enterprise administrators use addresses in one of the private IP address ranges to create the subnets they need. If you are building a new enterprise network from scratch, you can choose any private address block and make things easy on yourself by subnetting along the octet boundaries.

CERTIFICATION READY
Configure subnetting.
Objective 4.1

For example, you can take the 10.0.0.0/8 private IP address range and use the entire second octet as a subnet ID. This enables you to create up to 256 subnets with as many as 65,536 hosts on each one. The subnet masks for all the addresses on the subnets will be 255.255.0.0, and the network addresses will proceed as follows:

- 10.0.0.0/16
- 10.1.0.0/16
- 10.2.0.0/16
- 10.3.0.0/16
- . . .
- 10.255.0.0/16

Of course, when you are working on an existing network, the subnetting process will likely be more difficult. You might, for example, be given a relatively small range of addresses and be asked to create a certain number of subnets out of them. To do this, use the following procedure.

⊘ CALCULATE IPV4 SUBNETS

1. Determine how many subnet identifier bits you need to create the required number of subnets.
2. Subtract the subnet bits you need from the host bits and add them to the network bits.
3. Calculate the subnet mask by adding the network and subnet bits in binary form and converting the binary value to decimal.
4. Take the least significant subnet bit and the host bits, in binary form, and convert them to a decimal value.
5. Increment the network identifier (including the subnet bits) by the decimal value you calculated to determine the network addresses of your new subnets.

By using the same example from earlier in this lesson, if you take the 192.168.43.0/24 address and allocate two extra bits for the subnet ID, you end up with a binary subnet mask value of 11111111.11111111.11111111.11000000 (255.255.255.192 in decimal form, as noted earlier).

The least significant subnet bit plus the host bits gives you a binary value of 1000000, which converts to a decimal value of 64. Therefore, if we know that the network address of your first subnet is 192.168.43.0, the second subnet must be 192.168.43.64, the third 192.168.43.128, and the fourth 192.168.43.192, as shown earlier in Table 10-2.

Supernetting

In addition to simplifying network notation, CIDR also makes possible a technique called *IP address aggregation* or *supernetting*, which can help reduce the size of Internet routing tables. A **supernet** combines contiguous networks that all contain a common CIDR prefix. When an organization possesses multiple contiguous networks that can be expressed as a supernet, listing those networks in a routing table using only one entry, instead of many, becomes possible.

For example, if an organization has the following five subnets, standard practice would be to create a separate routing table entry for each one:

- 172.16.43.0/24
- 172.16.44.0/24
- 172.16.45.0/24
- 172.16.46.0/24
- 172.16.47.0/24

To create a supernet encompassing all five of these networks, you must isolate the bits they have in common. When you convert the network addresses from decimal to binary, you get the following values:

- 172.16.43.0 **10101100.00010000.00101**011.00000000
- 172.16.44.0 **10101100.00010000.00101**100.00000000
- 172.16.45.0 **10101100.00010000.00101**101.00000000
- 172.16.46.0 **10101100.00010000.00101**110.00000000
- 172.16.47.0 **10101100.00010000.00101**111.00000000

In binary form, you can see that all five addresses have the same first 21 bits. Those 21 bits become the network identifier of the supernet address, as follows:

10101100.00010000.00101

After zeroing out the host bits to form the network address and converting the binary number back to decimal form, as follows, the resulting supernet address is 172.16.40.0/21.

10101100.00010000.00101000.00000000 172.16.40.0/21

This one network address can replace the original five in routing tables duplicated throughout the Internet. Obviously, this is just an example of a technique that you can use to combine dozens or even hundreds of subnets into single routing table entries.

Assigning IPv4 Addresses

In addition to understanding how IP addressing works, you must be familiar with the methods for deploying IP addresses to the computers on a network.

You have three alternatives for assigning IPv4 addresses:

- Manual configuration
- Dynamic Host Configuration Protocol (DHCP)
- Automatic Private IP Addressing (APIPA)

The following sections cover the advantages and disadvantages of these methods.

CERTIFICATION READY
Configure IP address options.
Objective 4.1

MANUAL IPV4 ADDRESS CONFIGURATION

Configuring a TCP/IP client manually is not terribly difficult, nor is it very time-consuming. Most operating systems provide a graphical interface that enables you to enter an IPv4 address, a subnet mask, and various other TCP/IP configuration parameters. To configure IP address settings in Windows Server 2012, use the following procedure.

CONFIGURE IP ADDRESS SETTINGS

GET READY. Log on to Windows Server 2012 using an account with Administrative privileges.

1. In the left pane of the *Server Manager* window, click the Local Server icon. The Properties tile for the server appears.

2. In the *Properties* tile, click the Ethernet hyperlink. The *Network Connections* window appears.

3. Right-click the Ethernet icon and, from the context menu, select Properties. The *Ethernet Properties* sheet appears.

4. Select the Internet Protocol Version 4 (TCP/IPv4) component and click Properties. The *Internet Protocol Version 4 (TCP/IPv4) Properties* sheet appears, as shown in Figure 10-2.

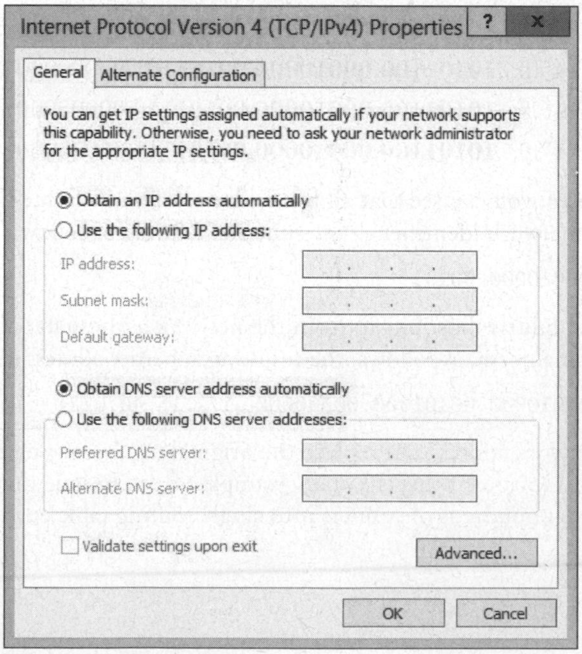

Figure 10-2

The *Internet Protocol Version 4 (TCP/IPv4) Properties* sheet

5. Select the Use the following IP address radio button and configure the following parameters with appropriate values:

   • IP address specifies the IP address on the local subnet that identifies the network interface in the computer.

   • Subnet mask specifies the mask associated with the local subnet.

   • Default gateway specifies the IP address of a router on the local subnet, which the system uses to access destinations on other networks.

6. Select the Use the following DNS server addresses radio button and configure the following parameter with appropriate values:

   • Preferred DNS server specifies the IP address of the DNS server that the system uses to resolve host names into IP addresses.

   • Alternate DNS server specifies the IP address of the DNS server that the system uses to resolve host names into IP addresses when the preferred DNS server is not available.

7. Click OK twice to close the *Internet Protocol Version 4 (TCP/IPv4)* and *Ethernet* Properties sheets.

   CLOSE the *Network Connections* window.

You also can configure the IP address settings on a Windows system from the command line, using the Netsh.exe program. However, the big problem with manual configuration is that a task requiring two minutes for one workstation requires several hours for 100 workstations and several days for 1,000. Manually configuring all but the smallest networks is highly impractical, and not just for reasons of time. You also need to track the IPv4 addresses you assign and make sure each system has a unique address. This can end up being a logistical nightmare, which is why few network administrators choose this option.

USING WINDOWS POWERSHELL

Prior to Windows Server 2012, configuring IP addresses and other network interface settings with Windows PowerShell was a complicated affair involving scripts and Windows Management Instrumentation (WMI) classes. Windows PowerShell 3.0, however, adds a NetTCPIP module that includes cmdlets that simplify these tasks.

To configure the basic settings for a network interface, including the IP address, the subnet mask, and the default gateway address, you use the **New-NetIPAddress** cmdlet with the following syntax:

```
New-NetIPAddress –InterfaceIndex <number>
-Ipaddress <address> -PreefixLength <number>
-DefaultGateway <address>
```

To determine the index number of the network interface you want to configure, you run the **Get-NetIPInterface** cmdlet, to generate a table like that shown in Figure 10-3.

Once you have the index number, you can configure the interface, as in the following example:

```
New-NetIPAddress –InterfaceIndex 12 -IPaddress 192.168.4.55
-PrefixLength 24 -DefaultGateway 192.168.4.1
```

The one essential parameter that the **New-NetIPAddress** cmdlet cannot configure is the DNS server address the system will use. To configure this, you must use the **Set-DNSClientServerAddress** cmdlet, with the following syntax:

```
Set-DNSClientServerAddress –InterfaceIndex <number> -ServerAddresses
("10.0.0.1","10.0.0.7")
```

Figure 10-3

Output from the Get-
NetIPInteface cmdlet for
Windows PowerShell

```
PS C:\Users\Administrator> get-netipinterface

ifIndex InterfaceAlias                    AddressFamily NlMtu(Bytes) InterfaceMetric Dhcp     ConnectionState PolicyStore
------- --------------                    ------------- ------------ --------------- ----     --------------- -----------
15      Ethernet 2                        IPv6                  1500               5 Enabled  Connected       ActiveStore
12      Ethernet                          IPv6                  1500               5 Enabled  Connected       ActiveStore
16      isatap.{739ECA29-9639-42C8-A...   IPv6                  1280              50 Disabled Disconnected    ActiveStore
13      isatap.zacker.local               IPv6                  1280              50 Disabled Disconnected    ActiveStore
1       Loopback Pseudo-Interface 1       IPv6            4294967295              50 Disabled Connected       ActiveStore
15      Ethernet 2                        IPv4                  1500               5 Disabled Connected       ActiveStore
12      Ethernet                          IPv4                  1500               5 Enabled  Connected       ActiveStore
1       Loopback Pseudo-Interface 1       IPv4            4294967295              50 Disabled Connected       ActiveStore


PS C:\Users\Administrator> _
```

DYNAMIC HOST CONFIGURATION PROTOCOL

The *Dynamic Host Configuration Protocol (DHCP)* is a client/server application as well as an Application-layer protocol that enables you to allocate IP addresses dynamically from a pool. Computers equipped with DHCP clients automatically contact a DHCP server when they start, and the server assigns them unique addresses and all the other configuration parameters the TCP/IP client requires.

The DHCP server leases addresses to clients, and after a predetermined interval, each client either renews its address or releases it back to the server for reallocation. DHCP not only automates the address assignment process, but it also keeps track of the addresses it assigns, preventing any address duplication on the network.

➕ **MORE INFORMATION**

For more information about DHCP, see Objective 4.2, "Deploy and Configure DHCP Service."

AUTOMATIC PRIVATE IP ADDRESSING (APIPA)

Automatic Private IP Addressing (APIPA) is the name assigned by Microsoft to a DHCP failover mechanism used by all current Microsoft Windows operating systems. On Windows computers, the DHCP client is enabled by default. If, after several attempts, a system fails to locate a DHCP server on the network, APIPA takes over and automatically assigns an address on the 169.254.0.0/16 network to the computer. The system then uses the Address Resolution Protocol (ARP) to ensure that no other computer on the local network is using the same address.

For a small network that consists of only a single LAN, APIPA is a simple and effective alternative to installing a DHCP server. However, for installations consisting of multiple LANs, with routers connecting them, you must take more positive control over the IP address assignment process. This usually means deploying one or more DHCP servers in some form.

■ Understanding IPv6 Addressing

↓ **THE BOTTOM LINE**

As most administrators know, IPv6 is designed to increase the size of the IP address space, thus providing addresses for many more devices than IPv4. The 128-bit address size of IPv6 allows for 2^{128} possible addresses, an enormous number that works out to over 54 million addresses for each square meter of the Earth's surface.

TAKE NOTE*

IPv6 was designed to provide a permanent solution for the IP address space depletion problem. Of course, when IP was conceived in the late 1970s, no one involved in the project imagined that the 32-bit IPv4 address space would ever be exhausted either. These people had no idea at the time that every home, every car, and nearly every pocket or purse in America would have at least one computer in it. You can only wonder what the world will look like if ever the IPv6 address space approaches depletion.

In addition to providing more addresses, IPv6 also reduces the size of the routing tables in the routers scattered around the Internet. This is because the size of the addresses provides for more than the two levels of subnetting currently possible with IPv4.

Introducing IPv6

IPv6 addresses are different from IPv4 addresses in many ways other than length.

Instead of the four 8-bit decimal numbers separated by periods that IPv4 uses, IPv6 addresses use a notation called *colon-hexadecimal format*, which consists of eight 16-bit hexadecimal numbers, separated by colons, as follows:

XX:XX:XX:XX:XX:XX:XX:XX

TAKE NOTE*

Hexadecimal notation is another name for Base 16, which means that each digit can have 16 possible values. To express hexadecimal numbers, you use the numerals 0 to 9 and the letters A to F to represent those 16 values. In binary (Base 2) notation, an 8-bit (1-byte) number can have 256 possible values, but to express those 256 possible values in hexadecimal form, two characters are required. This is why some of the 2-byte XX values in the sample IPv6 address require four digits in hexadecimal notation.

Each X represents 8 bits (or 1 byte), which in hexadecimal notation is represented by two characters, as in the following example:

21cd:0053:0000:0000:e8bb:04f2:003c:c394

CONTRACTING IPV6 ADDRESSES

When an IPv6 address has two or more consecutive 8-bit blocks of zeroes, you can replace them with a double colon, as follows (but you can use only one double colon in any IPv6 address):

21cd:0053::e8bb:04f2:003c:c394

You can also remove the leading zeros in any block where they appear:

21cd:53::e8bb:4f2:3c:c394

EXPRESSING IPV6 NETWORK ADDRESSES

IPv6 has no subnet masks. Network addresses use the same slash notation as CIDR to identify the network bits. In the example specified here, the network address is notated as follows:

21cd:53::/64

This is the contracted form for the following network address:

21cd:0053:0000:0000/64

IPv6 Address Types

IPv6 has no broadcast transmissions, and therefore no broadcast addresses, unlike IPv4.

IPv6 supports three address types:

- **Unicast:** provides one-to-one transmission service to individual interfaces, including server farms sharing a single address. IPv6 supports several types of unicast addresses, including global, link-local, and unique local, terms that identify the scope of the

TAKE NOTE✱

In IPv6, an address's *scope* refers to the size of its functional area. For example, the scope of a global unicast is unlimited—the entire Internet. The scope of a link-local unicast is the immediate link—that is, the local network. The scope of a unique local unicast consists of all the subnets within an organization.

address. Each type of unicast has a different *format prefix (FP)*, a sequence of bits that identifies the type, just as an IPv4 address uses a sequence of bits to identify its class.

- **Multicast:** provides one-to-many transmission service to groups of interfaces identified by a single multicast address.

- **Anycast:** provides one-to-one-of-many transmission service to groups of interfaces, only the nearest of which (measured by the number of intermediate routers) receives the transmission.

GLOBAL UNICAST ADDRESSES

A *global unicast address* is the equivalent of a registered IPv4 address, routable worldwide and unique on the Internet. The original format of the address, as shown in Figure 10-4, consists of the following elements:

- **Format prefix (FP):** An FP value of 001 identifies the address as a global unicast

- **Top Level Aggregator (TLA):** A 13-bit globally unique identifier allocated to regional internet registries by the IANA

- **Reserved:** A currently unused 8-bit field

- **Next Level Aggregator (NLA):** A 24-bit field that the TLA organization uses to create a multilevel hierarchy for allocating address blocks to its customers

- **Site Level Aggregator (SLA):** A 16-bit field that organizations can use to create an internal hierarchy of sites or subnets

- **Extended Unique Identifier (EUI-64) (64 bits):** A 64-bit field, derived from the network interface adapter's MAC address, identifying a specific interface on the network

Figure 10-4

The original IPv6 global unicast address format

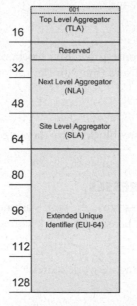

These original field definitions still appear in many IPv6 descriptions, but the standard was actually modified in 2003 to eliminate the separate TLA and NLA fields and rename the SLA field. The current official format for global unicast addresses, as shown in Figure 10-5, consists of the following elements:

- **Global routing prefix:** A 48-bit field beginning with the 001 FP value, the hierarchical structure of which is left up to the regional Internet registry (RIR)

- **Subnet ID:** Formerly known as the SLA, a 16-bit field that organizations can use to create an internal hierarchy of sites or subnets

- **Interface ID:** A 64-bit field identifying a specific interface on the network

Figure 10-5

The current IPv6 global unicast address format

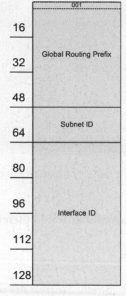

Theoretically, the global routing prefix and subnet ID fields can be any size. They are represented in the IPv6 standard by the letters *n* and *m*, with the size of the interface ID specified as *128-n-m*. In practice, however, organizations obtaining an address from an RIR or ISP are usually supplied with a 48-bit prefix, known colloquially as a */48*.

> **TAKE NOTE***
>
> As with IPv4 addresses, three hierarchical levels are involved in IPv6 global unicast address registration. At the top of the hierarchy is ICANN, which manages assignments for the IANA. At the second level are RIRs, which receive blocks of addresses from ICANN and allocate them in smaller blocks to ISPs.

Subnet IDs

The organization then has the 16-bit subnet ID with which to create an internal subnet hierarchy, if desired. Some possible subnetting options are as follows:

- **One-level subnet:** By setting all subnet ID bits to 0, all the computers in the organization are part of a single subnet. This option is suitable only for smaller organizations.
- **Two-level subnet:** By creating a series of 16-bit values, you can split the network into as many as 65,536 subnets. This is the functional equivalent of IPv4 subnetting, but with a much larger subnet address space.
- **Multi-level subnet:** By allocating specific numbers of subnet ID bits, you can create multiple levels of subnets, sub-subnets, and sub-sub-subnets, suitable for an enterprise of almost any size.

In one example, designed to support a large international enterprise, you could split the subnet ID as follows:

- **Country (4 bits):** Creates up to 16 subnets representing countries in which the organization has offices
- **State (6 bits):** Creates up to 64 sub-subnets within each country, representing states, provinces, or other geographical divisions
- **Office (2 bits):** Creates up to four sub-sub-subnets within each state or province, representing offices located in various cities
- **Department (4 bits):** Creates up to 16 sub-sub-sub-subnets within each office, representing the various departments or divisions.

To create a subnet ID for a particular office, you need to assign values for each field. To use the value 1 for the United States, the Country bits would be as follows:

```
0001------------
```

To create a subnet for an office in Alaska, you can use a value of 49 in the State field, which in binary form would appear as follows:

```
----110001------
```

For the second office in Alaska, use the value 2 for Office bits, as follows:

```
----------10----
```

For the Sales department in the office, use the value 9 for the Department bits, as follows:

```
------------1001
```

The resulting value for the subnet ID, in binary form, would therefore be as follows:

```
0001110001101001
```

In hexadecimal form, that would be 1c69.

Because the organization that owns the prefix wholly controls the subnet ID, enterprise administrators can adjust the number of levels in the hierarchy and the number of bits dedicated to each level as needed.

Interface IDs

Finally, the last field, the interface ID, contains a unique identifier for a specific interface on the network. The Institute for Electrical and Electronic Engineers (IEEE) defines the format for the 48-bit MAC address assigned to each network adapter by the manufacturer, as well as the EUI-64 identifier format derived from it.

A MAC address consists of two 24-bit values, which are usually already expressed in hexadecimal notation. The first 24 bits, an organizationally unique identifier (OUI), identifies the company that made the adapter. The second 24 bits is a unique value for each individual device.

To derive the 64-bit interface ID for an interface, an IPv6 implementation takes the two 24-bit values and adds a 16-bit value between them: *11111111 11111110* in binary or *fffe* in hexadecimal. Then, it changes the seventh bit in the OUI, called the universal/local bit, from a 0 to a 1. This changes the hexadecimal value of the first byte in the address from 00 to 02.

Therefore, as shown in Figure 10-6, a computer with a network adapter that has a MAC address of *00-1a-6b-3c-ba-1f* would have an IPv6 global unicast address with the following interface ID:

```
021a:6bff:fe3c:ba1f
```

Figure 10-6

Converting a MAC address to an IPv6 interface ID

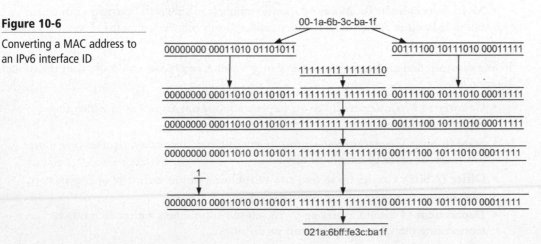

One perceived problem with this method of deriving interface IDs from the computer's hardware is that a mobile computer's location can be tracked based on its IPv6 address. This raises privacy concerns. Rather than use MAC addresses, Windows operating systems generate random interface IDs by default. Figure 10-7 demonstrates this, by showing a system with a randomly generated IPv6 address that does not match the Physical Address value.

Figure 10-7

A randomly generated
IPv6 address

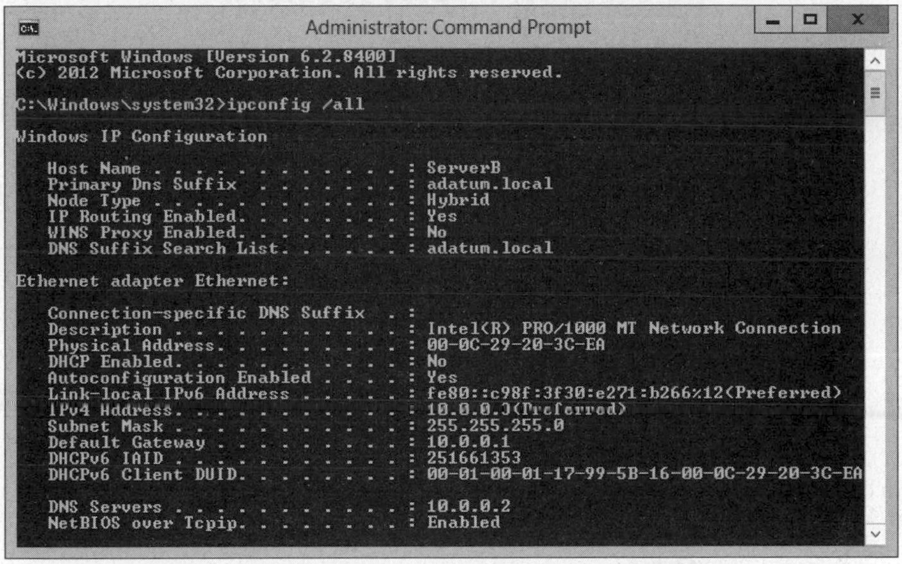

To modify this default behavior, you can type the following at an elevated command prompt:

```
netsh interface ipv6 set global randomizeidentifiers=disabled
```

With this feature disabled, the system reverts to the standard practice of creating an interface ID from the MAC address, as shown in Figure 10-8.

Figure 10-8

An IPv6 address generated
from the MAC address

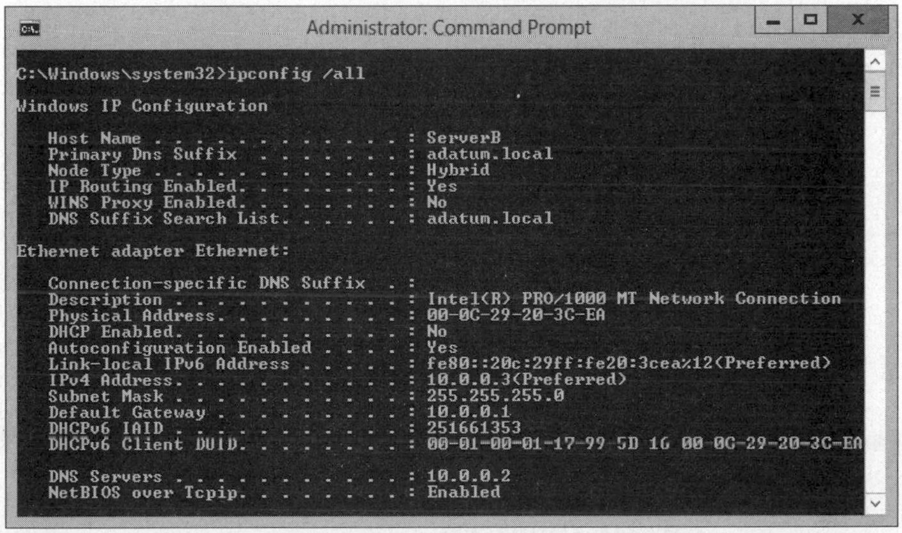

TAKE NOTE＊

In IPv6, the term *link* refers to the local network segment, which in IPv4 is called the *broadcast domain*. However, because IPv6 has no broadcasts, that latter term does not apply.

LINK-LOCAL UNICAST ADDRESSES

In IPv6, systems that assign themselves an address automatically create a ***link-local unicast address***, which is essentially the equivalent of an APIPA address in IPv4. All link-local addresses have the same network identifier: a 10-bit FP of 11111110 010 followed by 54 zeroes, resulting in the following network address:

```
fe80:0000:0000:0000/64
```

In its more compact form, the link-local network address is as follows:

`fe80::/64`

Because all link-local addresses are on the same network, they are not routable, and systems possessing them can communicate only with other systems on the same link.

UNIQUE LOCAL UNICAST ADDRESSES

Unique local unicast addresses are the IPv6 equivalent of the 10.0.0.0/8, 172.16.0.0/12, and 192.168.0.0/16 private network addresses in IPv4. Like the IPv4 private addresses, unique local addresses are routable within an organization. You can also subnet them as needed to support an organization of any size.

The format of a unique local unicast address, as shown in Figure 10-9, is as follows:

- **Global ID:** A 48-bit field beginning with an 8-bit FP of 11111101 in binary, or fd00::/8 in hexadecimal. The remaining 40 bits of the global ID are randomly generated.
- **Subnet ID:** A 16-bit field that organizations can use to create an internal hierarchy of sites or subnets
- **Interface ID:** A 64-bit field identifying a specific interface on the network

Figure 10-9

The IPv6 unique local unicast address format

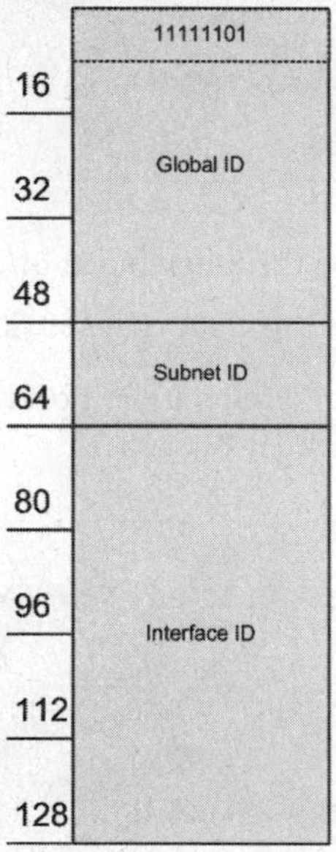

Because unique local addresses are not routable outside the organization, the global ID does not have to be unique in most cases. In fact, because part of the global ID value is randomly generated, two organizations might possibly end up using the same value. However, the IPv6 standards make every attempt short of creating a central registrar to keep these identifiers unique. This is so that addressing conflicts will not likely occur when organizations merge, when virtual private network (VPN) address spaces overlap, or when mobile computers connect to different enterprise networks.

SPECIAL ADDRESSES

Two other IPv6 unicast addresses with special purposes correspond to equivalents in IPv4. The loopback address returns back any messages sent to it to the sending system. In IPv6, the loopback address is 0:0:0:0:0:0:0:1, more commonly notated as follows:

`::1`

The other special address is 0:0:0:0:0:0:0:0, also known as the unspecified address. A system uses this address while requesting an address assignment from a DHCP server.

MULTICAST ADDRESSES

Multicast addresses always begin with an FP value of 11111111, in binary, or ff in hexadecimal. The entire multicast address format, as shown in Figure 10-10, is as follows:

- **FP:** An 8-bit field that identifies the message as a multicast
- **Flags (4 bits):** A 4-bit field that specifies whether the multicast address contains the address of a rendezvous point (0111), is based on a network prefix (0010), and is permanent (0000) or transient (0001)
- **Scope:** A 4-bit field that specifies how widely routers can forward the address. Values include interface-local (0001), link-local (0010), site-local (0101), organization-local (1000), and global (1110).
- **Group ID:** A 112-bit field uniquely identifying a multicast group

> **TAKE NOTE***
>
> Many sources of IPv6 information continue to list *site-local unicast addresses* as a valid type of unicast, with a function similar to that of the private IPv4 network addresses. Site-local addresses have an FP of 11111110 11 in binary, or fec0::/10 in hexadecimal. For various reasons, site-local unicast addresses have been deprecated, and although their use is not forbidden, their functionality has been replaced by unique local unicast addresses.

Figure 10-10

The IPv6 multicast address format

> **TAKE NOTE***
>
> IPv6 can simulate the functionality of a broadcast transmission with a transmission to the *all hosts* multicast group, when necessary. However, the elimination of the broadcast traffic generated by the Address Resolution Protocol (ARP) is one of the advantages of IPv6.
>
> ARP resolves IPv4 addresses into the media access control (MAC) address coded into network adapters by transmitting broadcasts containing addresses and waiting for the computers with those addresses to reply. However, every computer on the local network must process all broadcast messages, which increases the burden on the computers, as well as the network traffic levels. IPv6 replaces ARP with a protocol called Neighbor Discovery (ND), which performs the same function without using broadcast messages.

ANYCAST ADDRESSES

The function of an anycast address is to identify the routers within a given address scope and send traffic to the nearest router, as determined by the local routing protocols. Organizations can use anycast addresses to identify a particular set of routers in the enterprise, such as those that provide access to the Internet. To use anycast, the routers must be configured to recognize the anycast addresses as such.

Anycast addresses do not have a special network identifier format; they are derived from any of the standard unicast formats and consist of the entire subnet identifier and an interface identifier set to all 0s. Thus, the scope of an anycast address is the same as that of the unicast address from which it is derived.

As an example, the anycast address for the sample network used earlier in this lesson would be as follows, with the first 64 bits serving as the subnet ID:

`21cd:0053:0000:0000:0000:0000:0000:0000`

Assigning IPv6 Addresses

> The processes by which you assign IPv6 addresses to network computers are similar to those in IPv4.

As with IPv4, a Windows computer can obtain an IPv6 address by three possible methods:

- **Manual allocation:** A user or administrator manually supplies an address and other information for each network interface.
- **Self-allocation:** The computer creates its own address using a process called stateless address autoconfiguration.
- **Dynamic allocation:** The computer solicits and receives an address from a Dynamic Host Configuration Protocol (DHCPv6) server on the network.

MANUAL IPV6 ADDRESS ALLOCATION

For the enterprise administrator, manual allocation of IPv6 addresses is even more impractical than in IPv4, because of the length of the addresses involved. However, it is possible, and the procedure for doing so in Windows Server 2012 is the same as that for IPv4, except that you open the *Internet Protocol Version 6 (TCP/IPv6) Properties* sheet, as shown in Figure 10-11.

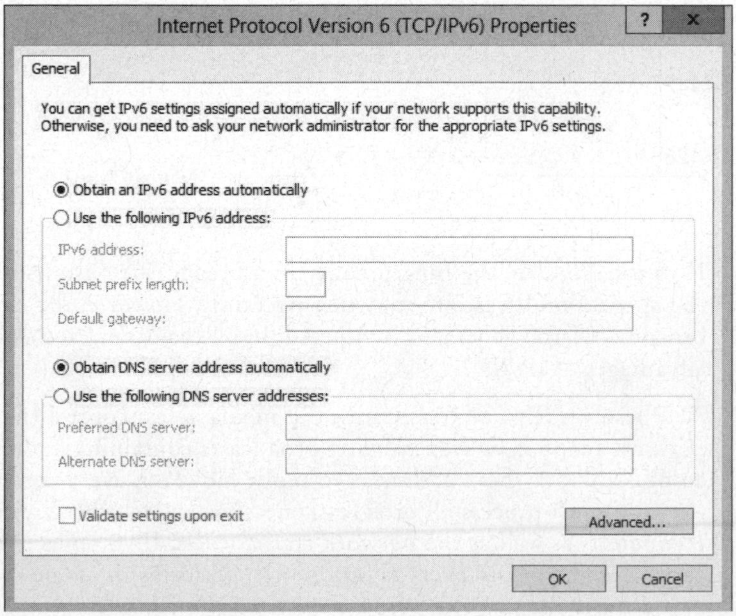

Figure 10-11

The *Internet Protocol Version 6 (TCP/IPv6) Properties* sheet

Because of the difficulties working with IPv6 addresses manually, the following two options are far more prevalent.

STATELESS IPV6 ADDRESS AUTOCONFIGURATION

When a Windows computer starts, it initiates the *stateless address autoconfiguration* process, during which it assigns each interface a link-local unicast address. This assignment always occurs, even when the interface is to receive a global unicast address later. The link-local address enables the system to communicate with the router on the link, which provides additional instructions.

The steps of the stateless address autoconfiguration process are as follows.

PERFORM A STATELESS ADDRESS AUTOCONFIGURATION

1. **Link-local address creation:** The IPv6 implementation on the system creates a link-local address for each interface by using the fe80::/64 network address and generating an interface ID, either using the interface's MAC address or a pseudorandom generator.

2. **Duplicate address detection:** By using the IPv6 Neighbor Discovery (ND) protocol, the system transmits a Neighbor Solicitation message to determine if any other computer on the link is using the same address and listens for a Neighbor Advertisement message sent in reply. If no reply occurs, the system considers the address to be unique on the link. If a reply does occur, the system must generate a new address and repeat the procedure.

3. **Link-local address assignment:** When the system determines that the link-local address is unique, it configures the interface to use that address. On a small network consisting of a single segment or link, this may be the interface's permanent address assignment. On a network with multiple subnets, the primary function of the link-local address assignment is to enable the system to communicate with a router on the link.

4. **Router advertisement solicitation:** The system uses the ND protocol to transmit Router Solicitation messages to the *all routers* multicast address. These messages compel routers to transmit the Router Advertisement messages more frequently.

5. **Router advertisement:** The router on the link uses the ND protocol to transmit Router Advertisement messages to the system, which contain information on how the autoconfiguration process should proceed. The Router Advertisement messages typically supply a network prefix, which the system uses with its existing interface ID to create a global or unique local unicast address. The messages might also instruct the system to initiate a stateful autoconfiguration process by contacting a specific DHCPv6 server. If the link has no other router, as determined by the system's failure to receive Router Advertisement messages, the system must attempt to initiate a stateful autoconfiguration process.

6. **Global or unique local address configuration:** By using the information it receives from the router, the system generates a suitable address—one that is routable, either globally or within the enterprise—and configures the interface to use it. If so instructed, the system might also initiate a stateful autoconfiguration process by contacting the DHCPv6 server specified by the router and obtaining a global or unique local address from that server, along with other configuration settings.

DYNAMIC HOST CONFIGURATION PROTOCOL V6

If you deal with a multi-segment network, you need to use unique local or global addresses for internetwork communication, so you need either routers that advertise the appropriate network prefixes or DHCPv6 servers that can supply addresses with the correct prefixes.

The Remote Access role in Windows Server 2012 supports IPv6 routing and advertising, and the DHCP Server role supports IPv6 address allocation.

■ Planning an IP Transition

Many enterprise administrators are so comfortable working with IPv4 addresses that they are hesitant to change. Network Address Translation (NAT) and Classless Inter-Domain Routing (CIDR) have been excellent stopgaps to the depletion of the 32-bit IP address space for years, and many would like to see them continue as such. However, the IPv6 transition, long a specter on the distant horizon, is now suddenly approaching at frightening speed, and it is time for administrators not familiar with the new technologies to catch up—or be left behind.

The exhaustion of the IANA unallocated address pool occurred on January 31, 2011. One of the regional Internet registries (RIRs), the Asia Pacific Network Information Center (APNIC), was depleted on April 15, 2011, and the other RIRs are expected to follow suit before long.

The networking industry, and particularly the Internet, has made huge investments in IPv4 technologies, and replacing them with IPv6 has had to be a gradual process. In fact, this gradual process was supposed to have begun in earnest in 1998. However, many people treat their IPv4 equipment like household appliances; unless they stop working, replacing them is not necessary. Unfortunately, the day in which that equipment stops working is approaching rapidly. So, while it might not yet be time to embrace IPv6 exclusively, you should have the transition in mind as you design your networks and make your purchasing decisions.

Enterprise administrators can do as they want within the enterprise itself. If all network devices in the organization support IPv6, they can begin to use IPv6 addresses at any time. However, the Internet is still firmly based on IPv4 and will continue to be so for several years. There, an IPv4-to-IPv6 transition must be a gradual project that includes some period of support for both IP versions.

Now and for the immediate future, you must work under the assumption that the rest of the world is using IPv4, and that you must implement a mechanism for transmitting your IPv6 traffic over an IPv4 connection. Eventually, the situation will be reversed. Most of the world will be running IPv6, and the remaining IPv4 technologies will have to transmit their older traffic over new links.

Using a Dual IP Stack

The simplest and most obvious method for transitioning from IPv4 to IPv6 is to run both, and this is what all current versions of Windows do, going back as far as Windows Server 2008 and Windows Vista.

By default, these operating systems install both IP versions and use them simultaneously. In fact, even if you have never heard of IPv6 until today, your computers are likely already using it and have IPv6 link-local addresses that you can see by running the ipconfig/all command.

The Network-layer implementations in Windows are separate, so you configure them separately. For both IPv4 and IPv6, you can choose to configure the address and other settings manually, or use autoconfiguration.

Because Windows supports both IP versions, the computers can communicate with TCP/IP resources running either IPv4 or IPv6. However, an enterprise network includes other devices also, most particularly routers, that might not yet support IPv6. The Internet also is nearly all still based on IPv4.

Beginning immediately, you should ensure that any Network-layer equipment you purchase includes support for IPv6. Failure to do so will almost certainly cost you later.

Tunneling

Right now, many network services are IPv4 only, and comparatively few require IPv6. Those IPv6 services are coming, however.

The DirectAccess remote networking feature in Windows Server 2012 and Windows 8 is an example of an IPv6-only technology, and much of its complexity is due to the need to establish IPv6 connections over the IPv4 Internet.

Tunneling is the primary method for transmitting IPv6 traffic over an IPv4 network. *Tunneling*, in this case, is the process by which a system encapsulates an IPv6 datagram within an IPv4 packet, as shown in Figure 10-12. The system then transmits the IPv4 packet to its destination, with none of the intermediate systems aware of the packet's contents.

Figure 10-12

IPv6 traffic encapsulated inside an IPv4 datagram

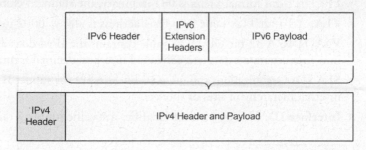

Tunneling can work in various configurations, depending on the network infrastructure, including router-to-router, host-to-host, router-to-host, and host-to-router. However, the most common configuration is router-to-router, as in the case of an IPv4-only connection between an IPv6 branch office and an IPv6 home office, as shown in Figure 10-13.

Figure 10-13

Two IPv6 networks connected by an IPv4 tunnel

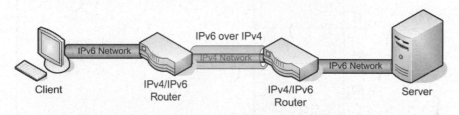

The two routers support both IPv4 and IPv6, and the local networks at each site use IPv6. However, the link connecting the two sites is IPv4 only. By creating a tunnel between the routers in the two offices, using their IPv4 interfaces, they can exchange IPv6 traffic as needed. Computers at either site can send IPv6 traffic to the other site, and the routers are responsible for encapsulating the IPv6 data in IPv4 packets for the trip through the tunnel.

Windows supports several different tunneling methods, both manual and automatic, as described in the following sections.

CONFIGURING TUNNELS MANUALLY

You can manually create semi-permanent tunnels that carry IPv6 traffic through an IPv4-only network. When a computer running Windows Server 2012 or Windows 8 is functioning as one end of the tunnel, you can use the following command:

```
netsh interface ipv6 add v6v4tunnel "interface" localaddress remoteaddress
```

In this command, *interface* is a friendly name you want to assign to the tunnel you are creating; *localaddress* and *remoteaddress* are the IPv4 addresses forming the two ends of the tunnel. An example of an actual command would be as follows:

```
netsh interface ipv6 add v6v4tunnel "tunnel"
206.73.118.19 157.54.206.43
```

CONFIGURING TUNNELS AUTOMATICALLY

A number of mechanisms automatically create tunnels over IPv4 connections. These are technologies designed to be temporary solutions during the transition from IPv4 to IPv6. All of them include a mechanism for expressing an IPv4 address in the IPv6 format. The following sections describe IPv4-to-IPv6 transition technologies that Windows supports.

6to4

The *6to4* mechanism essentially incorporates the IPv4 connections in a network into the IPv6 infrastructure by defining a method for expressing IPv4 addresses in IPv6 format and encapsulating IPv6 traffic into IPv4 packets.

To enable IPv4 links to function as part of the IPv6 infrastructure, 6to4 translates public IPv4 addresses into IPv6 using the following format, as shown in Figure 10-14:

- **FP:** The 3-bit format prefix is 001 in binary, the standard global unicast value.
- **TLA:** A 13-bit TLA value for a 6to4 address is always 0002 in hexadecimal.
- **V4ADDR:** A 32-bit V4ADDR value contains the IPv4 dotted decimal address, split into four separate octets and converted into hexadecimal form.
- **SLA ID:** Organizations can use a 16-bit SLA ID (or subnet ID) field to create an internal hierarchy of sites or subnets.
- **Interface ID:** This 64-bit field identifies a specific interface on the network.

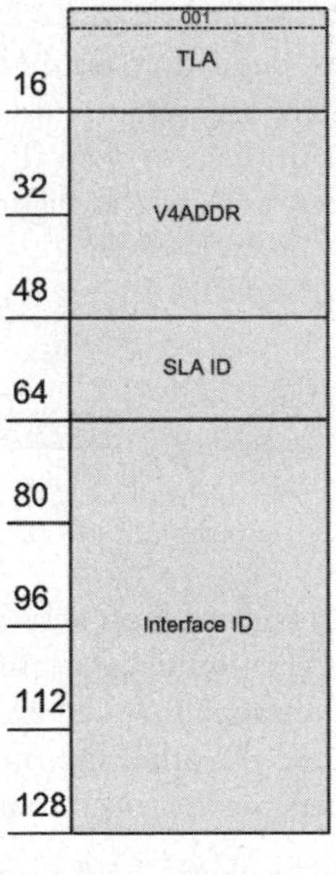

Figure 10-14

The 6to4 address format

For example, to convert the IPv4 address 157.54.176.7 into a 6to4 IPv6 address, you begin with 2002 for the FP and TLA fields, and then convert the four decimal values from the IPv4 address into hexadecimal, as follows:

- 157 = 9d
- 54 = 36
- 176 = b0
- 7 = 07

Therefore, you end up with the following IPv6 address:

`2002:9d36:b007:subnetID:interfaceID`

The subnet and interface identifiers use the same values as any other IPv6 link on the network. The encapsulation method is the same as that for a manually created tunnel, with a standard

IPv4 header and containing the IPv6 data as the payload. A 6to4 router examines incoming packets and, if it detects the 2002 value in the first block, knows to transmit the packet over the IPv4 interface, using the 32 bits following the 2002 block as the IPv4 address.

ISATAP

CERTIFICATION READY
Configure ISATAP.
Objective 4.1

Intra-Site Automatic Tunnel Addressing Protocol (ISATAP) is an automatic tunneling protocol used by the Windows workstation operating systems that emulates an IPv6 link using an IPv4 network.

ISATAP also converts IPv4 addresses into an IPv6 Link-layer address format, but it uses a different method than 6to4. An ISATAP address uses the following format, as shown in Figure 10-15:

- The first 64 bits consist of the standard link-local network identifier, the value fe80 following by 48 bits of 0s.
- The first 16-bit block of the interface identifier consists of all 0s, except for the seventh bit, which is set to 1 when the IPv4 address is globally unique, and the eighth bit, which is set to 1 when the IPv4 address identifies a multicast group. In most cases, this block consists of all 0s.
- The second 16-bit block of the interface ID consists of the value 5efe, which represents the concatenated OUI for ISATAP (5e) and the standardized value fe.
- The final 32 bits of the interface identifier consist of the IPv4 address in hexadecimal form.

Figure 10-15
The ISATAP address format

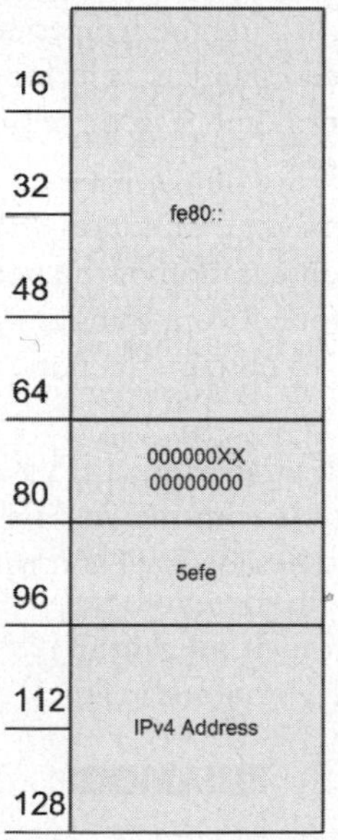

Therefore, the IPv4 address 157.54.176.7 would have the following as its ISATAP address:

```
fe80:0000:0000:0000:0000:5efe:9d36:b007
```

In compressed form, the address appears as follows:

```
fe80::5efe:9d36:b007
```

ISATAP does not support multicasting, so it cannot locate routers in the usual manner, using the Neighbor Discovery protocol. Instead, the system compiles a potential routers list (PRL) using DNS queries and sends Router Discovery messages to them regularly, using Internet Control Message Protocol version 6 (ICMPv6).

Teredo

To use 6to4 tunneling, both endpoints of the tunnel must have registered IPv4 addresses. However, on many networks, the system that would function as the endpoint is located behind a NAT router, and therefore has an unregistered address. In such a case, the only registered address available is assigned to the NAT router itself, and unless the router supports 6to4 (which many do not), establishing the tunnel is impossible.

Teredo is a mechanism that addresses this shortcoming by enabling devices behind non-IPv6 NAT routers to function as tunnel endpoints. To do this, Teredo encapsulates IPv6 packets within Transport-layer User Datagram Protocol (UDP) datagrams, rather than Network-layer IPv4 datagrams, as 6to4 does.

For a Teredo client to function as a tunnel endpoint, it must have access to a Teredo server, with which it exchanges Router Solicitation and Router Advertisement messages to determine whether the client is located behind a NAT router.

Teredo clients have the most complicated form of IPv6 address yet, which uses the following format, as shown in Figure 10-16:

- **Prefix:** A 32-bit field that identifies the system as a Teredo client. Windows clients use the prefix value 2001:0000, or 2001::/32.
- **Server IPv4:** A 32-bit field containing the IPv4 address of the Teredo server the client uses.
- **Flags:** A 16-bit field, the first bit of which is the Cone flag, set to 1 when the NAT device providing access to the Internet is a cone NAT, which stores the mappings between internal and external addresses and port numbers. The second bit is reserved for future use. The seventh and eighth bits are the Universal/Local and Individual/Group flags, which are both set to 0. The Teredo standard calls for the remaining 12 bits to be set to 0, but Windows assigns a random number to these bits to prevent attackers from attempting to discover the Teredo address.
- **Port:** A 16-bit field that specifies the external UDP port that the client uses for all Teredo traffic, in obscured form. The obscuration of the port number (and the following IPv4 address) helps prevent the NAT router from translating the port as it normally would as part of its packet processing. To obscure the port, the system runs an exclusive OR (XOR) with the value ffff.
- **Client IPv4:** A 32-bit field that specifies the external IPv4 address that the client uses for all Teredo traffic, in obscured form. As with the Port field, the obscuration is the result of converting the IPv4 address to hexadecimal and running an XOR with the value ffffffff.

Figure 10-16

The Teredo address format

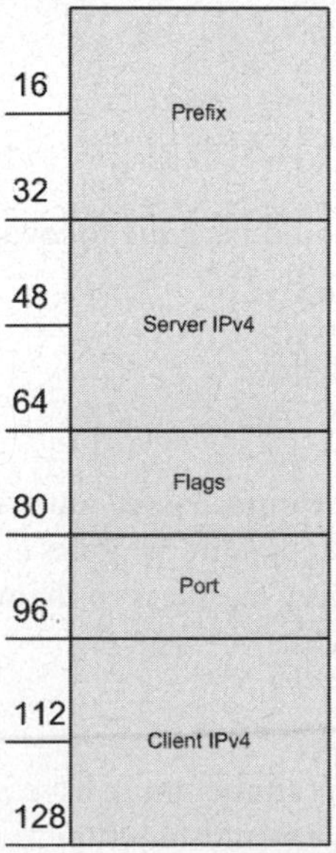

If, for example, the IPv4 address and port of the Teredo client are both 192.168.31.243:32000, the Teredo server uses the address 157.54.176.7, and the client is behind a cone NAT router, the Teredo address, in standard format, would consist of the elements listed in Table 10-3.

Table 10-3

Standard Teredo Address Format

ELEMENT	DESCRIPTION
2001:0000	Standard Teredo prefix
9d36:b007	Server IPv4 address (157.54.176.7) converted to hexadecimal
8000	Flags field with first bit set to 1 and all others 0
82ff	Client UDP port number (32000), converted to hexadecimal (7d00) and XORed with ffff
3f57:e00c	Client IPv4 address (192.168.31.243), converted to hexadecimal (C0a8:1ff3) and XORed with ffffffff

Thus, the final Teredo address is as follows:

`2001:0000:9d36:b007:8000:82ff:3f57:e00c`

To initiate communications, a Teredo client exchanges null packets called *bubbles* with the desired destination, using the Teredo servers at each end as intermediaries. The function of the bubble messages is to create mappings for both computers in each other's NAT routers.

SKILL SUMMARY

IN THIS LESSON, YOU LEARNED:

- The IPv4 address space consists of 32-bit addresses, notated as four 8-bit decimal values from 0 to 255, separated by periods, as in the example 192.168.43.100. This is known as *dotted decimal notation*, and the individual 8-bit decimal values are called *octets* or *bytes*.

- Because the subnet masks associated with IP addresses can vary, so can the number of bits used to identify the network and the host. The original Internet Protocol (IP) standard defines three address classes for assignment to networks, which support different numbers of networks and hosts.

- Because of its wastefulness, classful addressing was gradually made obsolete by a series of subnetting methods, including variable-length subnet masking (VLSM) and eventually Classless Inter-Domain Routing (CIDR). CIDR is a subnetting method that enables you to place the division between the network bits and the host bits anywhere in the address, not just between octets.

- When a Windows computer starts, it initiates the IPv6 stateless address autoconfiguration process, during which it assigns each interface a link-local unicast address.

- The simplest and most obvious method for transitioning from IPv4 to IPv6 is to run both, and this is what all current versions of Windows do.

- The primary method for transmitting IPv6 traffic over an IPv4 network is called tunneling, the process by which a system encapsulates an IPv6 datagram within an IPv4 packet.

Knowledge Assessment

Multiple Choice

Select one or more correct answers for each of the following questions.

1. Which of the following is the primary method for transmitting IPv6 traffic over an IPv4 network?
   a. Subnetting
   b. Tunneling
   c. Supernetting
   d. Contracting

2. Which of the following is the IPv6 equivalent to a private IPv4 address?
   a. Link-local unicast address
   b. Global unique unicast address
   c. Unique local unicast address
   d. Anycast address

3. Which of the following is an automatic tunneling protocol used by Windows operating systems that are located behind NAT routers?
   a. Teredo
   b. 6to4
   c. ISATAP
   d. APIPA

4. What subnet mask would you use when configuring a TCP/IP client with an IPv4 address on the 172.16.32.0/19 network?
   a. 255.224.0.0
   b. 255.240.0.0
   c. 255.255.224.0
   d. 255.255.240.0
   e. 255.255.255.240

5. What are the classes of IPv4 addresses used to provide support for networks?
   a. Class A
   b. Classes A and B
   c. Classes A, B, and C
   d. Classes A, B, C, and D

6. How does Classless Inter-Domain Routing (CIDR) help reduce waste of IP addresses?
   a. Uses a subnetting method also called variable length subnet masking
   b. Uses a subnetting method that divides between network bits and host bits anywhere, not just between octets
   c. Uses network address translation
   d. Converts between IPv4 and IPv6

7. There are three alternatives to assigning an IPv4 address. Two are manual configuration and DHCP. What is the third?
   a. Automatic Private IP Addressing (APIPA)
   b. Network address translation (NAT)
   c. Automatic Public Addressing (APA)
   d. Group Policy

8. Instead of the four 8-bit decimal numbers separated by periods that IPv4 uses, IPv6 addresses use a notation called _____.
   a. hexadecimal fold
   b. double-colon format
   c. bi-octet
   d. colon-hexadecimal format

9. What does a double-colon in an IPv6 address signify?
   a. Two or more 8-bit blocks of ones
   b. Abbreviated form, leaving out company ID
   c. Two consecutive 8-bit blocks of zeros
   d. The division between subnet mask and host ID

10. What is the stateless address autoconfiguration process, during a Windows computer start?
    a. The computer assigns itself an anycast address.
    b. The computer pings for an DHCP address.
    c. The computer assigns itself 192.168.0.1.
    d. The computer assigns itself a link-local unicast address.

Best Answer

Choose the letter that corresponds to the best answer. More than one answer choice may achieve the goal. Select the BEST answer.

1. What is the primary reason IPv6 has not completely replaced IPv4?
   a. Administrators are hesitant and reluctant to change.
   b. Stopgap technologies such as Network Address Translation (NAT) and Classless Inter-Domain Routing (CIDR) alleviate the lack of registered IPv4 addresses.
   c. IPv4 addresses have only been depleted since early 2011.
   d. IPv6 has already replaced IPv4 on the Internet.

2. What is the primary difference between a NAT server and a proxy server?
   a. There is no difference; they are functionally the same.
   b. There is little difference because NAT servers and proxy servers; both act as an intermediary between networks.
   c. Proxy servers offer additional functions such as they can scan, cache, and filter certain types of data.
   d. NAT servers translate at the Network layer of the protocol stack, whereas proxy servers function at the Application layer.

3. Your company environment includes Windows Server versions 2003, 2008, and 2012. Desktops range from Windows XP and Vista. To transition to IPv6, what versions have IPv6 support running by default?
   a. Windows Server 2008, Windows Server 2012, and Vista have IPv6 running by default.
   b. All versions have IPv6 running by default, except the Windows 2003 servers.
   c. Windows Server 2003 and Windows XP both include support for IPv6, but they do not install it by default.
   d. Only Windows Server 2012 has IPv6 running by default.

4. What Windows Server 2012 services and applications offer IPv6 support?
   a. Nearly all server roles provide IPv6 support.
   b. Few offer IPv6 support, but they are expected soon.
   c. All offer IPv6 support in Windows Server 2012.
   d. Remote Access supports IPv6 routing and advertising, and the DHCP Server role can allocate IPv6 addresses.

5. What is Intra-Site Automatic Tunnel Addressing Protocol (ISATAP)?
   a. ISATAP converts IPv4 address for an IPv6 network just as 6to4 offers.
   b. ISATAP emulates an IPv6 link for use on an IPv4 network.
   c. ISATAP is a method of multicasting for IPv6 networks.
   d. ISATAP translates between IPv4 and IPv6 networks without client configuration.

Build a List

1. Order the steps to calculate an IPv4 subnet mask.
   a. Calculate the subnet mask by adding the network and subnet bits in binary form and converting the binary value to decimal.
   b. Take the least significant subnet bit and the host bits, in binary form, and convert them to a decimal value.
   c. Determine how many subnet identifier bits you need to create the required number of subnets.
   d. Subtract the subnet bits you need from the host bits and add them to the network bits.
   e. Increment the network identifier (including the subnet bits) by the decimal value you calculated to determine the network addresses of your new subnets.

2. Order the steps to configure IP address settings.
   a. Select the Internet Protocol Version 4 (TCP/IPv4) component and click Properties. The Internet Protocol Version 4 (TCP/IPv4) Properties sheet appears.
   b. In the Properties tile, click the Ethernet hyperlink. The Network Connections window appears.
   c. Right-click the Ethernet icon and, from the context menu, select Properties. The Ethernet Properties sheet appears.
   d. In the left pane of the Server Manager window, click the Local Server icon.
   e. Specify the preferred and alternate DNS server address.
   f. Set the IP address, subnet mask, and default gateway.

3. Order the steps to configure IP address settings using Windows PowerShell.
   a. Run the New-NetIPAddress cmdlet with the following syntax:
   ```
   New-NetIPAddress –InterfaceIndex <number>
   -Ipaddress <address> –PrefixLength <number>
   -DefaultGateway <address>
   ```
   b. Run the Get-NetIPInterface cmdlet to get the network interface Index number.
   c. Test connectivity of the network adapter.
   d. Run the Set-DNSClientServerAddress cmdlet, with the following syntax:
   ```
   Set-DNSClientServerAddress–InterfaceIndex <number> -ServerAddresses
   ("10.0.0.1","10.0.0.7"]
   ```

■ Business Case Scenarios

Scenario 10-1: Calculating IPv4 Subnets

The enterprise administrator has assigned Arthur the network address 172.16.85.0/25 for the branch office network that he is constructing. Arthur calculates that this gives him 126 (27) IP addresses, which is enough for his network, but he has determined that he needs six subnets with at least 10 hosts on each one. How can Arthur subnet the address he has been given to satisfy his needs? What IP addresses and subnet masks will the computers on his branch office network use?

Scenario 10-2: Calculating IPv6 Interface IDs

Ed has three servers running Windows Server 2012, for which he has to configure IPv6 global unicast addresses manually. The MAC addresses for the network interfaces in the three machines are as follows:

- 60-EB-69- 93-5E-E5

- 00-15-5D-02-12-05

- D4-AE-52-BF-C3-2D

What are the EUI-64 interface IDs that Ed will use for these three MAC addresses?

LESSON

Deploying and Configuring the DHCP Service

70-410 EXAM OBJECTIVE

Objective 4.2 – Deploy and configure Dynamic Host Configuration Protocol (DHCP) service. This objective may include but is not limited to: Create and configure scopes; configure a DHCP reservation; configure DHCP options; configure client and server for PXE boot; configure DHCP relay agent; authorize DHCP server.

LESSON HEADING	EXAM OBJECTIVE
Understanding DHCP	
DHCP Packets	
DHCP Options	
DHCP Communications	
Designing a DHCP Infrastructure	
Using a Distributed DHCP Infrastructure	
Using a Centralized DHCP Infrastructure	
Using a Hybrid DHCP Infrastructure	
Regulating DHCP Network Traffic	
Deploying a DHCP Server	Authorize DHCP server
Creating a Scope	Create and configure scopes Configure DHCP options
Configuring DHCP Options	Configure DHCP options
Creating a Reservation	Configure a DHCP reservation
Using PXE	Configure client and server for PXE boot
Deploying a DHCP Relay Agent	Configure DHCP relay agent

KEY TERMS

automatic allocation

centralized DHCP infrastructure

DHCP relay agent

distributed DHCP infrastructure

dynamic allocation

Dynamic Host Configuration Protocol (DHCP)

manual allocation

Pre-boot Execution Environment (PXE)

■ Understanding DHCP

THE BOTTOM LINE
The ***Dynamic Host Configuration Protocol (DHCP)*** service automatically configures the Internet Protocol (IP) address and other TCP/IP settings on network computers by assigning addresses from a pool (called a *scope*) and reclaiming them when they are no longer in use.

Aside from being a time-consuming chore, manually configuring TCP/IP clients can result in typographical errors that cause addressing conflicts, which interrupt network communications. DHCP prevents these errors and provides many other advantages, including automatic assignment of new addresses when computers are moved from one subnet to another, and automatic reclamation of addresses that are no longer in use.

DHCP consists of three components:

- A *DHCP server application* responds to client requests for TCP/IP configuration settings.
- A *DHCP client* issues requests to servers and applies the TCP/IP configuration settings it receives to the local computer
- A *DHCP communications protocol* defines the formats and sequences of the messages exchanged by DHCP clients and servers

All Microsoft Windows operating systems include DHCP client capabilities, and all the server operating systems (including Windows Server 2012) include Microsoft DHCP Server. Microsoft's DHCP implementation is based on public domain standards published by the Internet Engineering Task Force (IETF) as RFC 2131, "Dynamic Host Configuration Protocol," and RFC 2132, "DHCP Options and BOOTP Vendor Extensions," and is interoperable with other DHCP implementations.

➕ MORE INFORMATION

The standards on which TCP/IP communication is based are published in public domain documents called Requests for Comments (RFCs) by the Internet Engineering Task Force. These documents are freely available on the Internet at *http://www.ietf.org* and many other sites. Unlike many other networking standards, which are highly technical and directed at engineers, students and beginning networkers can comprehend many RFCs, making them well worth examining.

The overall objectives Microsoft used when designing DHCP are as follows:

- The DHCP server should be able to provide a workstation with all the settings needed to configure the TCP/IP client so that no manual configuration is needed.
- The DHCP server should be able to function as a repository for the TCP/IP configuration parameters for all network clients.
- The DHCP server should assign IP addresses in such a way as to prevent the duplication of addresses on the network.
- The DHCP server should be able to configure clients on other subnets through relay agents.
- DHCP servers should support the assignment of specific IP addresses to specific client systems.
- DHCP clients should be able to retain their TCP/IP configuration parameters despite a reboot of either the client or the server system.

The DHCP standards define three different IP address allocation methods:

- *Dynamic allocation:* The DHCP server assigns an IP address to a client computer from a scope for a specified length of time. DHCP servers using dynamic allocation only lease addresses to clients. Each client must periodically renew the lease to continue using the address. If the client allows the lease to expire, the address is returned to the scope for reassignment to another client.

- *Automatic allocation:* The DHCP server permanently assigns an IP address to a client computer from a scope. After the DHCP server assigns the address to the client, the only way to change it is to reconfigure the computer manually. Automatic allocation is suitable for networks where you do not often move computers to different subnets. It reduces network traffic by eliminating the periodic lease renewal messages needed for dynamic allocation. In the Windows Server 2012 DHCP server, automatic allocation is essentially dynamic allocation with an indefinite lease.

- *Manual allocation:* The DHCP server permanently assigns a specific IP address to a specific computer on the network. In the Windows Server 2012 DHCP server, manually allocated addresses are called *reservations*. You use manually allocated addresses for computers that must have the same IP address at all times, such as Internet web servers that have specific IP addresses associated with their host names in the DNS namespace. Although you can just as easily configure such computers manually, DHCP reservations prevent the accidental duplication of permanently assigned IP addresses.

> **+ MORE INFORMATION**
>
> DHCP is an extension of the Bootstrap Protocol (BOOTP), designed to enable diskless workstations to retrieve an IP address and other TCP/IP configuration settings from a network server. BOOTP's primary limitation is that an administrator must manually enter the configuration parameters for each workstation on the server. DHCP improves on this concept by dynamically assigning IP addresses to clients from a range of addresses specified by an administrator.

In addition to IP addresses, DHCP also can provide clients with values for the other parameters needed to configure a TCP/IP client, including a subnet mask, default gateway, and DNS server addresses. The object is to eliminate the need for any manual TCP/IP configuration on a client system. For example, the Microsoft DHCP server includes more than 50 configuration parameters, which it can deliver along with the IP address, even though Windows clients can use only a subset of those parameters.

The RFC 2132 document, "DHCP Options and BOOTP Vendor Extensions," defines an extensive list of parameters that compliant servers should support, and most major DHCP server packages adhere closely to this list. Many of these parameters are designed for use by specific system configurations and are submitted by vendors for inclusion in the standard document.

DHCP Packets

> DHCP communications use eight different types of messages, all of which use the same basic packet format. Standard UDP/IP datagrams carry DHCP traffic, using port 67 at the server and port 68 at the client.

Figure 11-1 shows the packet format, which contains the fields listed in Table 11-1.

Figure 11-1

The DHCP packet format

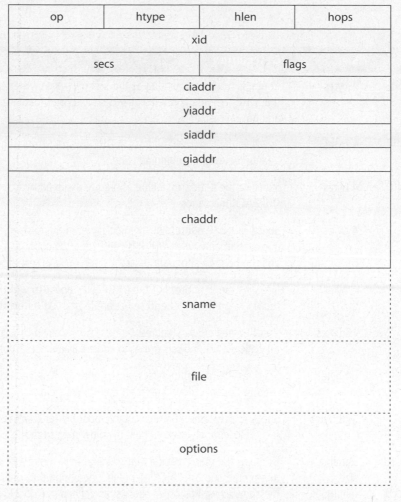

Table 11-1

DHCP Packet Fields

Field	Size	Description
op (Op Code)	1 byte	Specifies whether the message is a request or a reply.
htype (Hardware Type)	1 byte	Specifies the type of hardware address used in the chaddr field.
hlen (Hardware Address Length)	1 byte	Specifies the length (in bytes) of the hardware address in the chaddr field.
hops	1 byte	Specifies the number of network segments between the client and the server. The client sets the value to 0, and each DHCP relay system increments it by 1 during the journey to the server.
xid (Transaction ID)	4 bytes	Contains a transaction identifier used to associate the request and response messages of a single DHCP transaction.
secs (Seconds)	2 bytes	Specifies the number of seconds elapsed since the IP address was assigned or the lease last renewed.

(continued)

Table 11-1

(continued)

Field	Size	Description
flags	2 bytes	Contains the broadcast flag as the first bit, which, when set to a value of 1, specifies that DHCP servers and relay agents should use broadcasts to transmit to the client and not unicasts.
ciaddr (Client IP Address)	4 bytes	Specifies the client's IP address in DHCPREQUEST messages transmitted while in the bound, renewal, or rebinding state.
yiaddr (Your IP Address)	4 bytes	Specifies the IP address being offered or assigned by a server in DHCPOFFER or DHCPACK messages.
siaddr (Server IP Address)	4 bytes	Specifies the IP address of the next server in a bootstrap sequence. Servers include this information only when DHCP is configured to supply an executable boot file to clients, and the boot files for various client platforms are stored on different servers.
giaddr (Gateway IP Address)	4 bytes	Specifies the IP address of the DHCP relay agent to which a server should send its replies when the client and server are located on different subnets.
chaddr (Client Hardware Address)	16 bytes	Specifies the hardware address of the client system in DHCPDISCOVER and DHCPREQUEST messages, which the server uses to address its unicast responses to the client.
sname (Server Host Name)	64 bytes	Specifies the (optional) host name of the DHCP server. This field is more commonly used to hold overflow data from the options field.
file (Boot File Name)	128 bytes	Specifies the name of an executable boot file for diskless client workstations. This field is more commonly used to hold overflow data from the options field.
options	Variable size, minimum 312 bytes	Contains the magic cookie that specifies how the rest of the field should be interpreted and the DHCP Message Type option that defines the function of the message, as well as other options, as defined in RFC 2132.

DHCP Options

The DHCP options field is a catchall area designed to carry the various parameters (other than the IP address) used to configure the client system's TCP/IP stack.

Because you can configure a DHCP server to deliver many options to clients, defining separate fields for each one would be impractical.

THE MAGIC COOKIE

The options field always begins with the so-called *magic cookie*, which informs the server about what is contained in the rest of the field. The magic cookie is a 4-byte subfield containing the dotted decimal value 99.130.83.99.

THE OPTION FORMAT

The individual options in the options field contain various types and amounts of data, but most of them use the same basic structure, which consists of three subfields, as shown in Figure 11-2. Table 11-2 lists the functions of the subfields.

Figure 11-2

The DHCP option format

```
1 2 3 4 5 6 7 8 1 2 3 4 5 6 7 8 1 2 3 4 5 6 7 8 1 2 3 4 5 6 7 8
┌─────────────────┬─────────────────┬───────────────────────────────────┐
│      code       │     length      │               data                │
└─────────────────┴─────────────────┴───────────────────────────────────┘
```

Table 11-2

Subfield Functions

Subfield	Size	Description
code	1 byte	Contains a code specifying the function of the option, as defined in RFC 2132
length	1 byte	Specifies the length of the data field associated with the option
data	Variable	Contains information used by the client in various ways, depending on the code value and the message type

THE DHCP MESSAGE TYPE OPTION

All DHCP packets require the DHCP Message Type option, which identifies the overall function of the DHCP message. The code subfield for the option is 53 and the length is 1.

The DHCP communication protocol defines eight different message types:

- **DHCPDISCOVER:** Used by clients to request configuration parameters from a DHCP server
- **DHCPOFFER:** Used by servers to offer IP addresses to requesting clients
- **DHCPREQUEST:** Used by clients to accept or renew an IP address assignment
- **DHCPDECLINE:** Used by clients to reject an offered IP address
- **DHCPACK:** Used by servers to acknowledge a client's acceptance of an offered IP address
- **DHCPNAK:** Used by servers to reject a client's acceptance of an offered IP address
- **DHCPRELEASE:** Used by clients to terminate an IP address lease
- **DHCPINFORM:** Used by clients to obtain additional TCP/IP configuration parameters from a server

THE PAD OPTION

The Pad option is not really an option at all, but instead is a filler used to pad out fields so their boundaries fall between 8-byte words. Unlike most other options, the Pad option has no length or data field and consists only of a 1-byte code field with a value of 0.

THE OPTION OVERLOAD OPTION

Because User Datagram Protocol (UDP) datagrams carry DHCP messages, the packets are limited to a maximum size of 576 bytes, and the inclusion of a large number of options can test this limit. Because the DHCP message's sname and file fields are rarely used today, the DHCP standard allows these fields to be used to contain options that do not fit in the standard options field.

To include options in the sname and/or file fields, the packet's option field must contain the Option Overload option. This option has a value of 52 in the code subfield and a length of 1. The data subfield specifies which of the two auxiliary fields will carry additional options.

THE VENDOR-SPECIFIC INFORMATION OPTION

An option is defined in the standard as code 43, which is specifically intended for use by vendors to supply information required for the operation of their products. This Vendor-Specific Information option can itself contain multiple options for use by a vendor's products. To identify the vendor of the products for which the information in the Vendor-Specific Information option is intended, a message uses the Vendor Class Identifier option, which has a code value of 60 and a variable length with a minimum of 1 byte.

THE END OPTION

The End option signifies the end of the option field. Any bytes in the option field coming after the End option must contain nothing but 0 (Pad option) bytes. Like the Pad option, the End option consists only of a 1-byte code, with no length or data fields. The code has a value of 255.

OTHER CONFIGURATION OPTIONS

The DHCP options defined in RFC 2132 fall into several functional categories, as discussed in the following sections. Each category includes a list containing some of the available options, as well as their code field values.

BOOTP Vendor Information Extensions

These options are included in the DHCP standard exactly as defined in RFC 1497 for use with BOOTP and include many of the basic TCP/IP configuration parameters used by most client systems, such as those listed in Table 11-3.

Table 11-3

BOOTP Vendor Information Extensions

PARAMETER	CODE	DESCRIPTION
Subnet Mask	Code 1	Specifies which bits of the IP address identify the host system and which bits identify the network where the host system resides
Router	Code 3	Specifies the IP address of the router (or default gateway) on the local network segment the client should use to transmit to systems on other network segments
Domain Name Server	Code 6	Specifies the IP addresses of the servers the client will use for DNS name resolution
Host Name	Code 12	Specifies the DNS host name the client system will use
Domain name	Code 15	Specifies the name of the DNS domain on which the system will reside

IP Layer Parameters

These options affect the functionality of the IP protocol on the client system (see Table 11-4).

Table 11-4

IP Layer Parameters

PARAMETER	CODE	DESCRIPTION
IP Forwarding Enable/Disable	code 19	Specifies whether IP forwarding (that is, routing) should be enabled on the client system
Default IP Time-to-Live	code 23	Specifies the Time to Live (TTL) value the client should use in its outgoing IP datagrams
Interface MTU	code 26	Specifies the maximum transfer unit to be used by the Internet Protocol on this network interface only

DHCP Extensions

Table 11-5

DHCP Extensions

These options provide parameters that govern the DHCP lease negotiation and renewal processes (see Table 11-5).

PARAMETER	CODE	DESCRIPTION
Requested IP Address	Code 50	Used by the client to request a particular IP address from the server
IP Address Lease Time	Code 51	Specifies the duration of a dynamically allocated IP address lease
Server Identifier	Code 54	Specifies the IP address of the server involved in a DHCP transaction; used by the client to address unicasts to the server
Parameter Request List	Code 55	Used by the client to send a list of requested configuration options (identified by their code numbers) to the server
Message	Code 56	Carries an error message from the server to the client in a DHCPNAK message
Renewal (T1) time value	Code 58	Specifies the amount of time that must elapse before an IP address lease enters the renewing state
Rebinding (T2) time value	Code 59	Specifies the amount of time that must elapse before an IP address lease enters the rebinding state

DHCP Communications

To design a DHCP strategy for an enterprise network and deploy it properly requires an understanding of the communications that occur between DHCP clients and servers.

In Windows computers, the DHCP client is enabled by default, although it is not mentioned by name in the interface. The *Obtain an IP address automatically* option in the *Internet Protocol Version 4 (TCP/IPv4) Properties* sheet (see Figure 11-3) and the *Internet Protocol Version 6 (TCP/IPv6) Properties* sheet controls the activation of the client for IPv4 and IPv6 respectively.

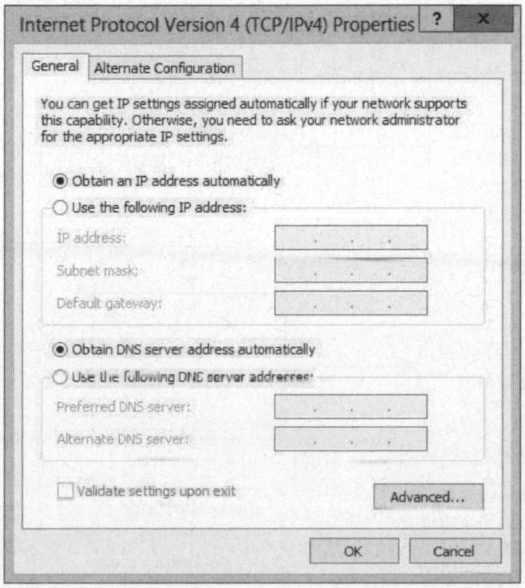

Figure 11-3

The *Internet Protocol Version 4 (TCP/IPv4) Properties* sheet

DHCP LEASE NEGOTIATION

The client always initiates DHCP communication, as shown in Figure 11-4, and proceeds as follows:

1. When a computer boots for the first time with the DHCP client active, the client generates a series of DHCPDISCOVER messages to solicit an IP address assignment from a DHCP server and broadcasts them on the local network. At this point, the client has no IP address and is said to be in the *init* state.

Figure 11-4

The DHCP IP address assignment process

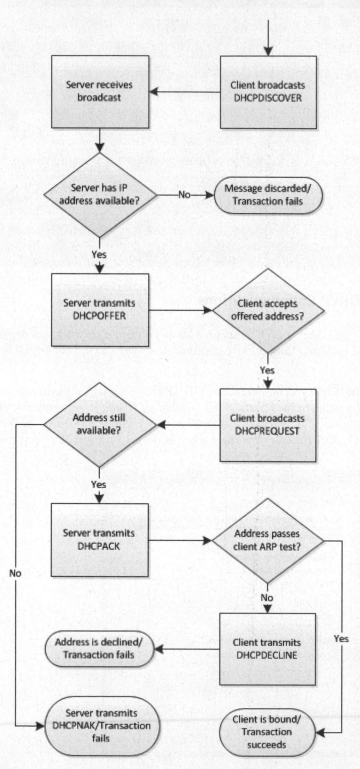

2. All DHCP servers receiving the DHCPDISCOVER broadcast messages generate DHCPOFFER messages containing an IP address and whatever other TCP/IP configuration parameters the server is configured to supply, and then transmit them to the client. Because the client broadcasts its DHCPDISCOVER messages, it may receive DHCPOFFER responses from multiple servers.

3. After a specified time, the client stops broadcasting and signals its acceptance of one of the offered addresses by generating a DHCPREQUEST message, containing the address of the server from which it is accepting the offer along with the offered IP address, and then broadcasting it on the local network. This broadcast notifies the selected server that the client is accepting the offered address. It also notifies any other servers on the network that the client is rejecting their offers.

4. When the server offering the accepted IP address receives the DHCPREQUEST message, it adds the offered IP address and other settings to its database using a combination of the client's hardware address and the offered IP address as a unique identifier for the assignment. This is known as the *lease identification cookie.*

5. The server transmits a DHCPACK message to the client, acknowledging completion of the process. If the server cannot complete the assignment for any reason (for example, because it has already assigned the offered IP address to another system), it transmits a DHCPNAK message to the client, and the whole process begins again.

6. As a final test, the client transmits the offered IP address in a broadcast using the Address Resolution Protocol (ARP) to ensure that no other system on the network is using the same address. If the client receives no response to the ARP broadcast, the DHCP transaction is complete and the client enters what is known as the *bound* state. If another system does respond to the ARP message, the client discards the IP address and transmits a DHCPDECLINE message to the server, nullifying the transaction. The client then restarts the entire process with a new series of DHCPDISCOVER messages.

DHCP LEASE RENEWAL

By default, the DHCP Server service in Windows Server 2012 uses dynamic allocation, leasing IP addresses to clients for eight-day periods. At periodic intervals during the course of the lease, the client attempts to contact the server to renew the lease, as shown in Figure 11-5, by using the following procedure:

1. When the DHCP client reaches the 50 percent point of the lease's duration (called the *renewal time value* or *T1 value*), the client enters the *renewing* state and begins generating DHCPREQUEST messages and transmitting them as unicasts to the DHCP server holding the lease. DHCP clients also renew their leases each time they restart.

2. If the server does not respond by the time the client reaches the 87.5 percent point of the lease's duration (called the *rebinding time value* or *T2 value*), the client enters the rebinding state and begins transmitting its DHCPREQUEST messages as broadcasts, in an attempt to solicit an IP address assignment from any DHCP server on the network.

3. If the server receives the DHCPREQUEST message from the client, it can respond with either a DHCPACK message, approving the lease renewal request, or a DHCPNAK message, which terminates the lease. If the client receives no responses to its DHCPREQUEST messages by the time the lease expires, or if it receives a DHCPNAK message, the client releases its IP address and returns to the *init* state. All TCP/IP communication then ceases, except for the transmission of DHCPDISCOVER broadcasts.

Figure 11-5

The DHCP IP address renewal
process

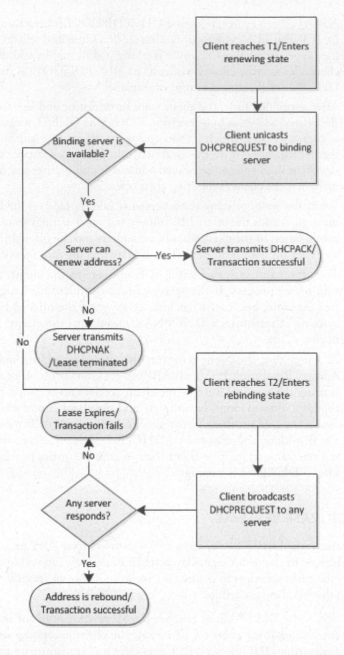

TAKE NOTE*

The DHCP message formats and communication processes are not Microsoft-specific. Defined in the RFC 2131 document, they are interoperable with the DHCP server and client implementations in all earlier versions of Microsoft Windows, as well as with those in other implementations based on the same standards.

■ Designing a DHCP Infrastructure

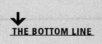

THE BOTTOM LINE

The Windows Server 2012 DHCP Server service theoretically can support many thousands of clients. However, for several reasons, virtually all enterprise networks require more than one DHCP server.

The primary reason for distributing the DHCP Server service is its reliance on broadcast messaging. When a DHCP client starts for the first time, it has no IP address of its own and no way of knowing the addresses of the DHCP servers on the network. Therefore, it can send its DHCPDISCOVER messages only as broadcast transmissions. By definition, broadcast transmissions are limited to the local subnet on which they are transmitted; routers do not propagate them to other networks. As a result, a client's DHCPDISCOVER messages can reach DHCP servers only on the local subnet.

Using a Distributed DHCP Infrastructure

Because of DHCP's reliance on broadcast messaging, it might seem at first that you must have a DHCP server on each of your enterprise network's subnets.

On some networks, this is a viable DHCP deployment strategy, called a distributed DHCP infrastructure. In a *distributed DHCP infrastructure*, shown in Figure 11-6, you install at least one DHCP server on each of your subnets, so that all your clients have access to a local DHCP server.

Figure 11-6

A distributed DHCP infrastructure

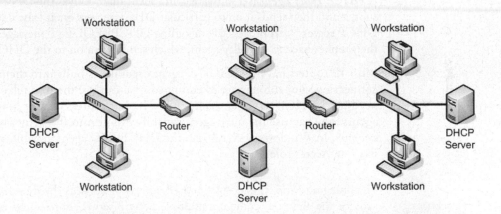

A distributed DHCP infrastructure has distinct advantages:

- Your clients have ready access to their DHCP servers.
- You do not have to worry about DHCP traffic adding to the burden of your routers, because all the client/server traffic is local.

The potential disadvantage of this arrangement is the need to install and configure a large number of DHCP servers. This is especially true if you plan to have multiple servers on each subnet for fault tolerance.

A distributed DHCP infrastructure does not necessarily mean that you must have a separate server dedicated to DHCP on every subnet, however. The DHCP Server role in Windows Server 2012 co-exists well with other roles. Because each DHCP server has to support only the local subnet, the impact of the role on each server's disk subsystem and network traffic burden is significant, but relatively light. If your network design already calls for at least one server on every subnet, adding the DHCP Server role to each subnet can be an acceptable solution.

Using a Centralized DHCP Infrastructure

Despite the limitation of DHCP broadcast traffic, you can design a DHCP infrastructure that does not have a separate DHCP server on every subnet.

In a ***centralized DHCP infrastructure***, DHCP servers are all placed in a single location, such as a server closet or data center. To enable the broadcast traffic on each subnet to reach the DHCP servers, you must install a DHCP relay agent on each subnet, as shown in Figure 11-7.

Figure 11-7

A centralized DHCP infrastructure

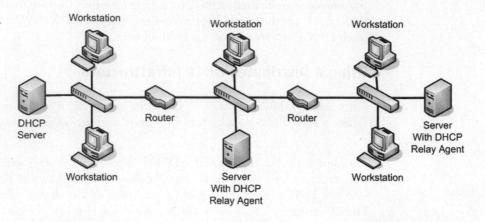

A ***DHCP relay agent*** is a software component that receives the DHCP broadcast traffic on a subnet and then sends it on to particular DHCP servers on at least one other subnet. The DHCP servers then process the incoming DHCPREQUEST messages as usual and transmit their replies back to the relay agent, which sends them on to the DHCP client.

Most IP routers have DHCP relay agent capabilities built into them. If the routers connecting your subnets are so equipped, you can use them as relay agents, eliminating the need for a DHCP server on each subnet. If your routers cannot function as DHCP relay agents, you can use the relay agent capability built into the Windows server operating systems. In Windows Server 2012, the DHCP relay agent capability is built into the Remote Access role.

TAKE NOTE*

To conform to the RFC 1542 standard, a relay agent must be disabled by default and must provide the ability to configure multiple DHCP server addresses on other subnets. Therefore, you must always activate and configure your relay agents, whether they are router-based or Windows-based.

The advantages of a centralized DHCP infrastructure include a reduced administrative burden, because you have fewer DHCP servers to install, configure, manage, and monitor. DHCP relay agents incur virtually no additional burden on your servers or routers, so you do not need to scale up your hardware to accommodate them.

A centralized DHCP infrastructure has some disadvantages, though. The DHCP Server services impose a burden both on the servers running it and on the subnet to which they are connected. When you consolidate your DHCP Server deployment to a relatively small number of servers, all located on the same subnet, the burden on those servers and on that subnet increases accordingly.

On a large enterprise network, a centralized DHCP infrastructure can result in a large convergence of network traffic on the single subnet hosting the DHCP servers. Depending on your organization's work schedule, DHCP traffic can be particularly heavy at the beginning of the day, when a large number of users are turning on their workstations at nearly the same time. This burden can negatively affect the performance of other servers on the same subnet, as well as on the routers connecting that subnet to the rest of the network.

For example, if you have your high-volume DHCP servers in a data center on the same subnet as your file or application servers, your users might have trouble accessing the tools they need during periods of peak DHCP usage. This traffic congestion can be particularly burdensome if you have

DHCP clients on remote subnets accessing DHCP over wide area network (WAN) links. WAN connections are, in most cases, relatively slow and relatively expensive, and burdening them with DHCP traffic can be a big problem in terms of performance and expense.

Using a Hybrid DHCP Infrastructure

The distributed and centralized DHCP infrastructures represent the extremes at opposite ends of the design spectrum. In practice, as with most things, the ideal solution often resides somewhere between those two extremes. A hybrid DHCP infrastructure is one that uses multiple DHCP servers on different subnets but does not necessarily require a DHCP server on every subnet.

By scattering the DHCP servers on subnets throughout the enterprise, you can avoid the traffic congestion common to a centralized design. By substituting DHCP relay agents for DHCP servers on some of your subnets, you also can reduce the administrative burden of your design.

Take as an example an enterprise network that consists of a home office and a large number of branch offices in remote cities connected by WAN links. A centralized infrastructure with all DHCP servers located in the home office would result in massive amounts of traffic on the WAN links connecting the branch offices to the home office.

A distributed infrastructure would eliminate the WAN traffic congestion, but having a separate DHCP server for each subnet at each branch office could be prohibitively expensive in terms of hardware, and generate a huge administrative burden for the IT staff working remotely from the home office.

A compromise between the two infrastructure designs, with one DHCP server and several relay agents at each branch office, would seem to be an ideal solution in this case. All users would have access to a local DHCP server, the WAN links would be free of DHCP traffic, and administrators would have to set up and manage only one DHCP server at each remote location.

Thus, by designing an infrastructure that uses DHCP servers on some subnets and relay agents on others, you can exercise control over the amount of internetwork traffic DHCP generates, without incurring too much additional hardware expense and creating an administrative bottleneck.

Regulating DHCP Network Traffic

As explained earlier, the number of DHCP servers on a network and their locations can affect the amount of network traffic passing through potential bottlenecks, such as routers and WAN links. Distributing your DHCP servers on different subnets is one way to prevent large amounts of traffic from converging on a single location.

Another way of reducing DHCP traffic levels is to adjust the length of your IP address leases. The default lease interval for a Windows Server 2012 DHCP server is eight days, which means that clients enter the renewing state and start transmitting renewal messages every four days. The handful of messages generated by one client might not seem like a lot, but when you multiply that by many thousands of clients, DHCP can generate a significant amount of traffic. By increasing the length of your DHCP leases, you increase the amount of time between lease renewals and, therefore, reduce the amount of renewal traffic.

When you consider how long to make your DHCP leases, you might begin to wonder whether using dynamic allocation is needed at all. When you set the lease duration for a scope to Unlimited, you are effectively switching that scope to automatic allocation. Whether this is a viable solution for your network depends on factors such as the following:

- The number of IP addresses you have available on each subnet
- The number of computers you have on each subnet
- How often you move computers from one subnet to another

The main reason for leasing IP addresses, rather than assigning them permanently, is that you can reclaim them for assignment to other computers. If nearly all available IP addresses in each of your subnets are allocated, you are better off keeping your lease intervals relatively short because you might have need for the unallocated addresses at any time. However, if you have a large number of unused addresses on each subnet, you can safely increase the lease intervals because you are unlikely to experience a shortage of addresses.

One advantage of DHCP is that as you move a computer from one subnet to another, it automatically retrieves an appropriate IP address on the new subnet. When the old address lease expires, it returns to the old subnet's scope. You should consider the frequency of computer relocations on your network when configuring your lease durations. If your network consists largely of mobile computers that move frequently from one subnet to another, as on a university network supporting student laptops, keeping the lease intervals short is better. For networks with computers that rarely change locations, long leases are appropriate.

Deploying a DHCP Server

↓ THE BOTTOM LINE DHCP servers operate independently, so you must install the service and configure scopes on every computer that will function as a DHCP server.

The DHCP Server service is packaged as a role in Windows Server 2012, which you can install by using the *Add Roles and Features Wizard*, accessible from the Server Manager console. To install the DHCP Server service on a Windows Server 2012 computer with Server Manager, use the following procedure.

TAKE NOTE★ A DHCP server should not also be an active DHCP client. Before you install the DHCP Server role, be sure to configure the target server with a static IP address.

➡ DEPLOY A DHCP SERVER

GET READY. Log on to Windows Server 2012 using an account with Administrative privileges.

1. In the *Server Manager* window, click **Manage** and then click **Add Roles and Features**. The *Add Roles and Features Wizard* appears, displaying the *Before you begin* page.
2. Click **Next**. The *Select Installation Type* page appears.
3. Leave the *Role-based or feature-based installation* radio button selected and click **Next**. The *Select Destination Server* page appears.
4. Select the server on which you want to install the roles and/or features and click **Next**. The *Select Server Roles* page appears.
5. Select the **DHCP Server** check box. An *Add features that are required for DHCP Server* dialog box appears.
6. Click **Add Features**, and then click **Next**. The *Select features* page appears.
7. Click **Next**. The *DHCP Server* page appears.
8. Click **Next**. The *Confirm installation selections* page appears.

TAKE NOTE★

If your computer does not have a static IP address, a message box appears, recommending that you reconfigure the TCP/IP client with a static address before you install the DHCP Server role.

9. Click Install. The *Installation progress* page appears as the wizard installs the role.

10. Click Close. The wizard closes.

CLOSE Server Manager.

USING WINDOWS POWERSHELL

To install the DHCP Server role using Windows PowerShell, use the following syntax:

```
Install-WindowsFeature DHCP [-ComputerName <computer_name>]
```

CERTIFICATION READY
Authorize DHCP server.
Objective 4.2

When you install the DHCP Server role on a computer that is a member of an AD DS domain, the DHCP Server is automatically authorized to allocate IP address to clients that are also members of the same domain. If the server is not a domain member when you install the role, and you join it to a domain later, you must manually authorize the DHCP server in the domain. To do this, right-click the server node in the DHCP console and, from the context menu, select *Authorize*.

After installing the DHCP Server role, you must configure the service by creating a scope before it can serve clients.

Creating a Scope

A *scope* is a range of IP addresses on a particular subnet that a DHCP server has selected for allocation.

CERTIFICATION READY
Create and configure scopes.
Objective 4.2

In Windows Server versions prior to 2012, you can create a scope as you install the DHCP Server role. However, in Windows Server 2012, the procedures are separate. To create a scope using the DHCP snap-in for Microsoft Management Console (MMC), use the following procedure.

➔ CREATE A DHCP SCOPE

GET READY. Log on to Windows Server 2012, using an account with Administrative privileges.

1. In the *Server Manager* window, click Tools and then click DHCP. The *DHCP* console appears, as shown in Figure 11-8.

Figure 11-8

The DHCP console

2. Expand the server and IPv4 nodes.

3. Right-click the IPv4 node and, from the context menu, select New Scope. The *New Scope Wizard* appears, displaying the *Welcome* page.

4. Click Next. The *Scope Name* page appears, as shown in Figure 11-9.

Figure 11-9

The *Scope Name* page in the New Scope Wizard

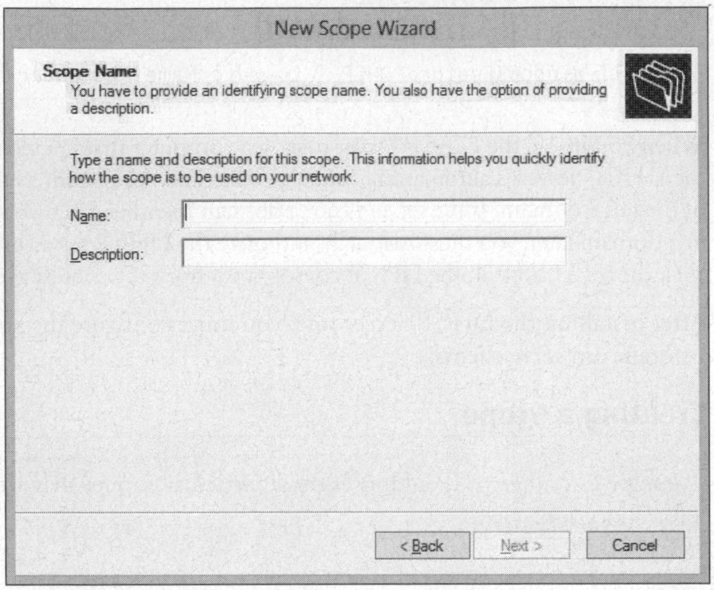

5. Type a name for the scope into the Name text box and click Next. The *IP Address Range* page appears, as shown in Figure 11-10.

Figure 11-10

The *IP Address Range* page in the New Scope Wizard

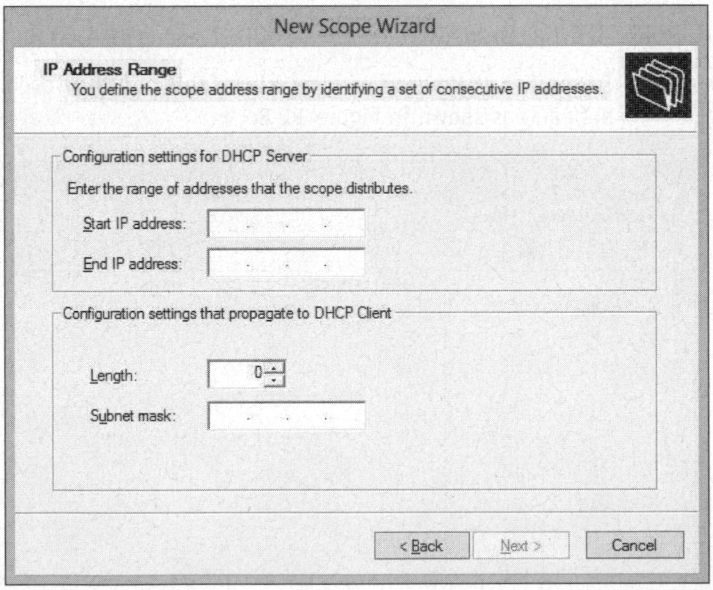

6. In the Start IP address text box, type the first in the range of addresses you want to assign. In the End IP address text box, type the last address in the range.

7. In the Subnet Mask text box, type the mask value for the subnet on which the scope will operate and click Next. The *Add Exclusions and Delay* page appears, as shown in Figure 11-11.

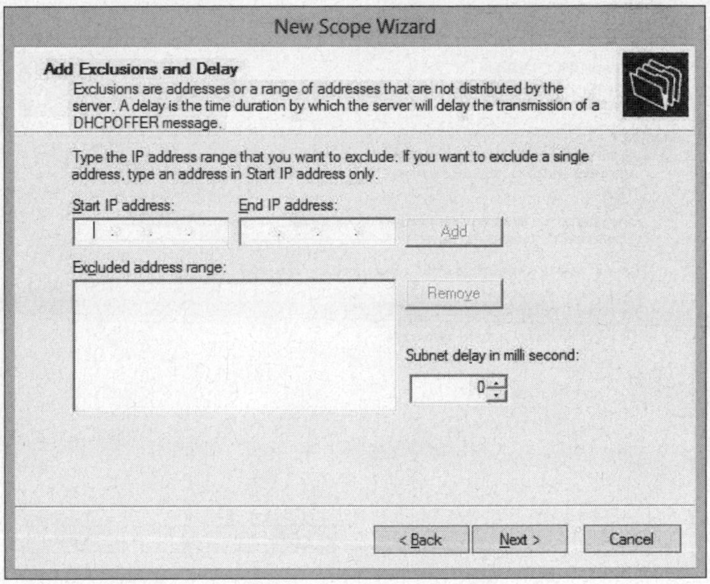

Figure 11-11

The *Add Exclusions and Delay* page in the New Scope Wizard

8. In the Start IP address and End IP address text boxes, specify a range of addresses you want to exclude from the scope. You can also specify a delay interval between the server's receipt of DHCPDISCOVER messages and its transmission of DHCPOFFER messages. Then click Next. The *Lease Duration* page appears, as shown in Figure 11-12.

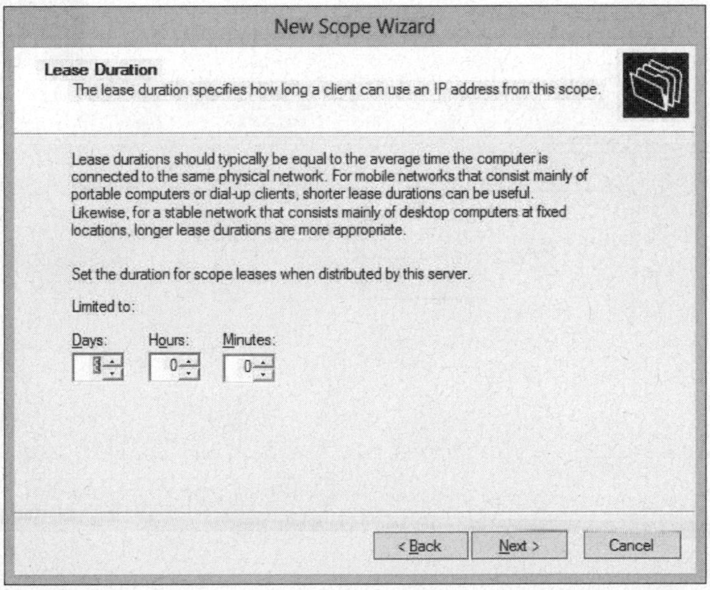

Figure 11-12

The *Lease Duration* page in the New Scope Wizard

CERTIFICATION READY
Configure DHCP options.
Objective 4.2

9. Specify the length of the leases for the addresses in the scope and click Next. The *Configure DHCP Options* page appears, as shown in Figure 11-13.

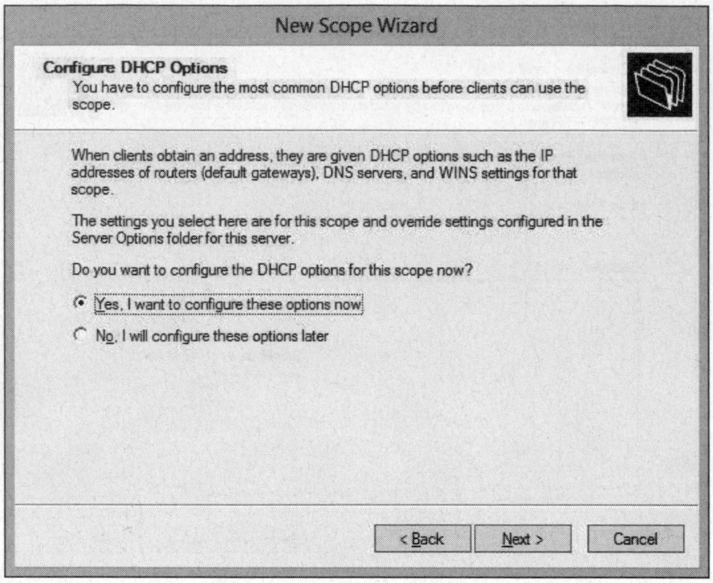

Figure 11-13

The *Configure DHCP Options* page in the New Scope Wizard

10. Select Yes, I want to configure these options now and click Next. The *Router (Default Gateway)* page appears, as shown in Figure 11-14.

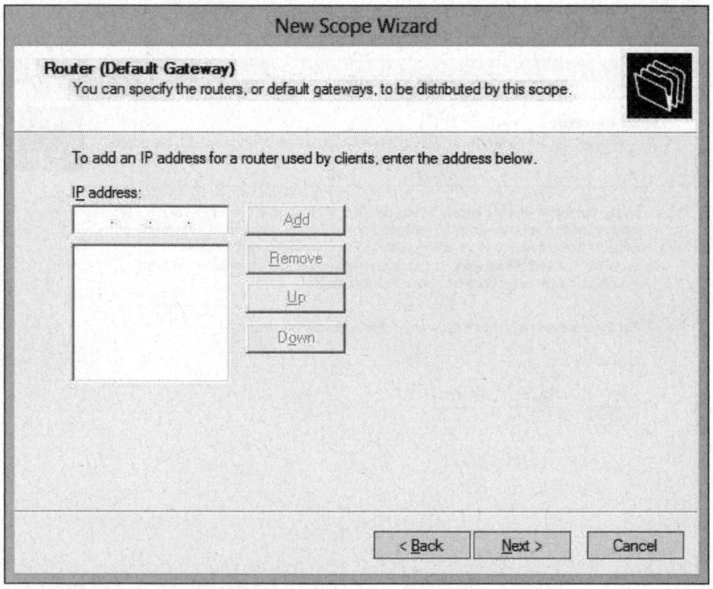

Figure 11-14

The *Router (Default Gateway)* page in the New Scope Wizard

11. In the IP address text box, specify the address of a router on the subnet served by the scope and click Add. Then click Next. The *Domain Name and DNS Servers* page appears, as shown in Figure 11-15.

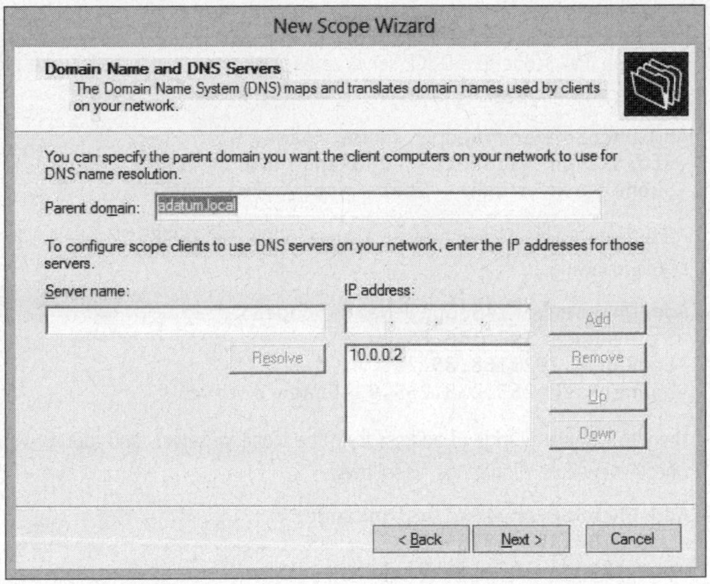

Figure 11-15

The *Domain Name and DNS Servers* page in the New Scope Wizard

12. In the Server name text box, type the name of a DNS server on the network and click Resolve, or type the address of a DNS server in the IP address text box and click Add. Then click Next. The *WINS Servers* page appears.

13. Click Next. The *Activate Scope* page appears, as shown in Figure 11-16.

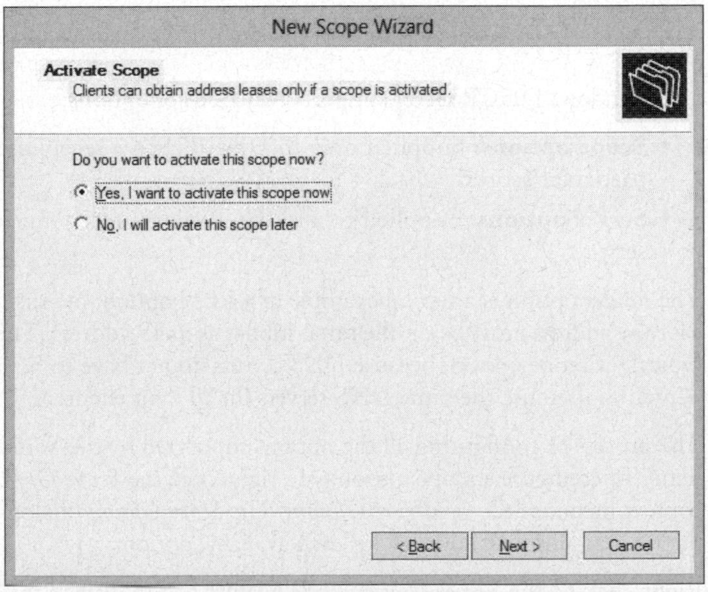

Figure 11-16

The *Activate Scope* page in the New Scope Wizard

14. Select Yes, I want to activate this scope now and click Next. The *Completing the New Scope Wizard* page appears.

15. Click Finish. The wizard closes.

CLOSE the DHCP console.

After the role installation is complete, all DHCP clients on the subnet identified in the scope you created can obtain their IP addresses and other TCP/IP configuration settings via DHCP. You can also use the DHCP console to create additional scopes for other subnets.

To add an IPv4 scope to a DHCP server using Windows PowerShell, you use the Add-DhcpServerv4Scope cmdlet with the following basic syntax.

```
Add-DhcpServerv4Scope -Name <name>
-StartRange <address> -EndRange <address>
-SubnetMask <mask> -State Active|Inactive
```

For example, to create and activate a scope for the 192.168.85.0/24 network, you would use a command such as the following:

```
Add-DhcpServerv4Scope -Name Scope85
-StartRange 192.168.85.1
-EndRange 192.168.85.255
-SubnetMask 255.255.255.0 -State Active
```

Then, to exclude a range of address from the scope for servers and routers, you must use the Add-DhcpServerv4ExclusionRange, as follows:

```
Add-DhcpServerv4ExclusionRange
-ScopeID 192.168.85.0
-StartRange 192.168.85.1
-EndRange 192.168.85.10
```

Configuring DHCP Options

The *New Scope Wizard* enables you to configure a few of the most commonly used DHCP options as you create a new scope, but you can always configure the many other options at a later time.

CERTIFICATION READY
Configure DHCP options.
Objective 4.2

The Windows DHCP server supports two kinds of options:

- **Scope options:** Supplied only to DHCP clients receiving addresses from a particular scope.
- **Server options:** Supplied to all DHCP clients receiving addresses from the server.

The *Router* option is a typical example of a scope option, because a DHCP client's default gateway address must be on the same subnet as its IP address. The *DNS Servers* option is typically a scope option, because DNS servers do not have to be on the same subnet, and networks often use the same DNS servers for all their clients.

The process of configuring all the options supported by the Windows DHCP server is the same. To configure a scope option, you right-click the *Scope Options* node and, from the context menu, select *Configure Options*. The *Scope Options* dialog box (see Figure 11-17) provides appropriate controls for each available option.

Right-clicking the *Server Options* node enables you to display the *Server Options* dialog box, which behaves in exactly the same way as the *Scope Options* dialog box.

To configure DHCP options using Windows PowerShell, you use the Set-DhcpServerv4OptionValue cmdlet, with the following basic syntax:

```
Set-DhcpServerv4OptionValue -ScopeID <address>
-DnsServer <address> -DnsDomain <name>
-Router <address> -WinsServer <address>
```

Figure 11-17

The Scope Options dialog box

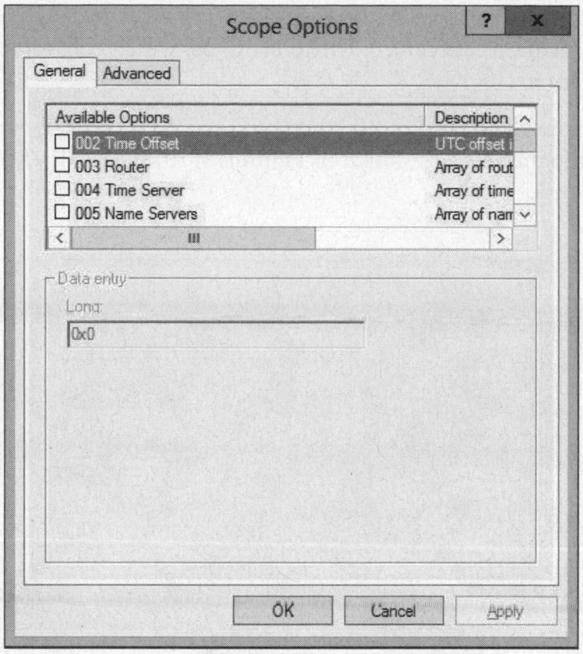

Creating a Reservation

> While DHCP is an excellent TCP/IP configuration solution for most computers on a network, it is not such a good solution for a few components. Domain controllers, Internet web servers, and DHCP servers themselves need static IP addresses.

CERTIFICATION READY
Configure a DHCP reservation.
Objective 4.2

Because the DHCP dynamic allocation method allows for the possibility that a computer's IP address could change, it is not appropriate for these particular roles. However, it is still possible to assign addresses to these computers with DHCP by using manual, instead of dynamic, allocation.

In a Windows DHCP server, a manually allocated address is called a *reservation*. You create a reservation by expanding the scope node, right-clicking the *Reservations* node, and, from the context menu, selecting *New Reservation*. The *New Reservation* dialog box appears, as shown in Figure 11-18.

Figure 11-18

A DHCP server's New Reservation dialog box

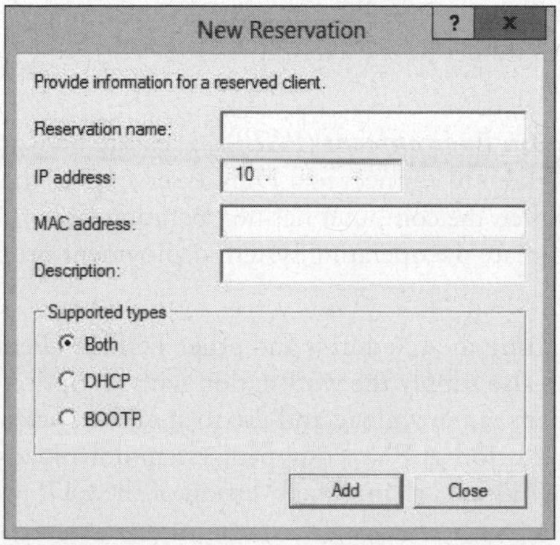

In this dialog box, you specify the IP address you want to assign and associate it with the client computer's media access control (MAC) address, which is hard-coded into its network interface adapter.

To discover the MAC address of a network interface adapter, run the Ipconfig.exe program with the /all parameter, as shown in Figure 11-19, where the MAC address appears as *Physical Address*.

Figure 11-19

A MAC address in the Ipconfig display

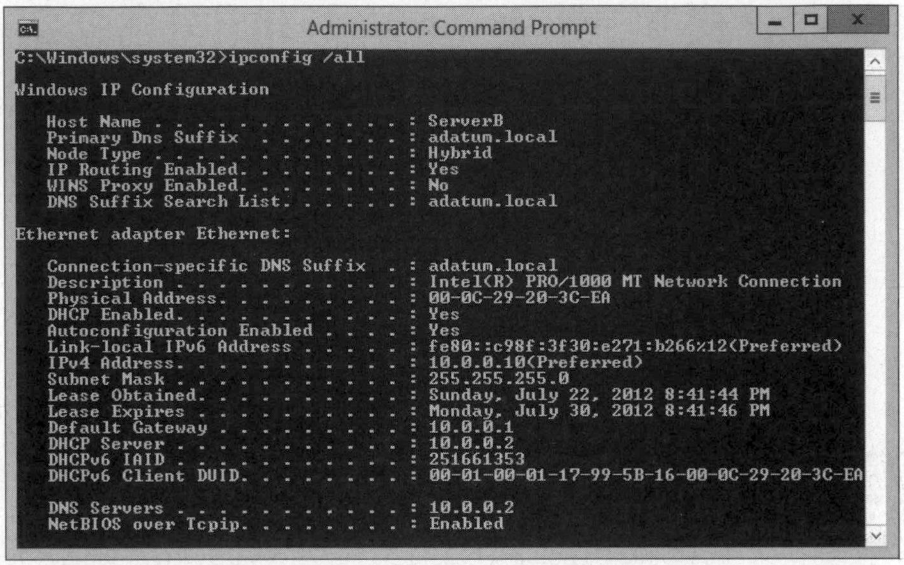

Of course, you also can manually configure the computer's TCP/IP client, but creating a DHCP reservation ensures that your DHCP servers manage all your IP addresses. In a large enterprise, where various administrators might be dealing with DHCP and TCP/IP configuration issues, the IP address that one technician manually assigns to a computer might be included in a DHCP scope by another technician, resulting in potential addressing conflicts. Reservations create a permanent record of the IP address assignment on the DHCP server.

Using PXE

The Windows operating systems include a DHCP client that can configure the IP address and other TCP/IP settings of computers with an operating system already installed. However, it is also possible for a bare metal computer—that is, a computer with no operating system—to use DHCP.

CERTIFICATION READY
Configure client and server for PXE boot.
Objective 4.2

The *Pre-boot Execution Environment (PXE)* is a feature built into many network interface adapters that enables them to connect to a DHCP server over the network and obtain TCP/IP client settings, even when the computer has no operating system. Administrators typically use this capability to automate the operating system deployment process on large fleets of workstations.

In addition to configuring the IP address and other TCP/IP client settings on the computer, the DHCP server can also supply the workstation with an option specifying the location of a boot file that the system can download and use to start the computer and initiate a Windows operating system installation. A PXE-equipped system downloads boot files using the Trivial File Transfer Protocol (TFTP), a simplified version of the FTP protocol that requires no authentication.

USING PXE WITH WDS

Windows Server 2012 includes a role called Windows Deployment Services (WDS), which enables you to manage image files that remote workstations can use to start up and install Windows. For a PXE adapter to access WDS images, the DHCP server on the network must have a custom PXEClient option (option 60) configured with the location of the WDS server on the network.

The PXE client on the workstation typically needs no configuration, except possibly to change the boot device order, so that the computer attempts a network boot before using the local devices.

In a properly configured WDS installation of Windows 8, the client operating system deployment process proceeds as follows:

1. The client computer starts and, finding no local boot device, attempts to perform a network boot.
2. The client computer connects to a DHCP server on the network from which it obtains a DHCPOFFER message containing an IP address and other TCP/IP configuration parameters, plus the 060 PXEClient option containing the name of a WDS server.
3. The client connects to the WDS server and is supplied with a boot image file, which it downloads using the Trivial File Transfer Protocol (TFTP).
4. The client loads Windows PE and the Windows Deployment Services client from the boot image file onto a RAM disk (a virtual disk created out of system memory) and displays a boot menu containing a list of the install images available from the WDS server.
5. The user on the client computer selects an install image from the boot menu, and the operating system installation process begins.
6. From this point, the setup process proceeds just like a manual installation.

> **➕ MORE INFORMATION**
>
> For more information on using Windows Deployment Services (WDS), see Objective 1.1, "Deploy and Manage Server Images," in Exam 70-411, "Administering Windows Server 2012."

CONFIGURING A CUSTOM DHCP OPTION

The WDS server configuration procedure discussed earlier in this lesson assumes that you have installed DHCP on the same computer as Windows Deployment Services. In many instances, this is not the case, however.

When you are using an external DHCP server, you must also configure it manually to include the custom option that provides WDS clients with the name of the WDS server. To configure this option on a Windows Server 2008 DHCP server, use the following procedure.

➡ CONFIGURE A CUSTOM DHCP OPTION

GET READY. Log on to Windows Server 2012, using an account with Administrative privileges.

1. In the *Server Manager* window, click Tools and then click DHCP. The *DHCP* console appears.
2. Expand the server and IPv4 nodes.

3. Right-click the IPv4 node and, from the context menu, select Set Predefined Options. The *Predefined Options and Values* dialog box appears, as shown in Figure 11-20.

Figure 11-20

The *Predefined Options and Values* dialog box

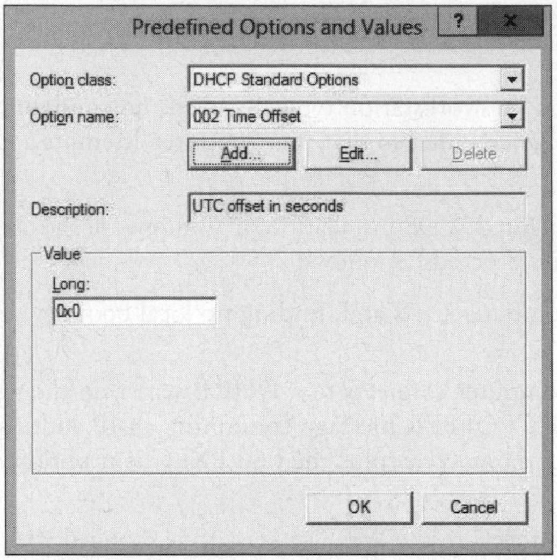

4. Click Add. The *Option Type* dialog box appears, as shown in Figure 11-21.

Figure 11-21

The Option Type dialog box

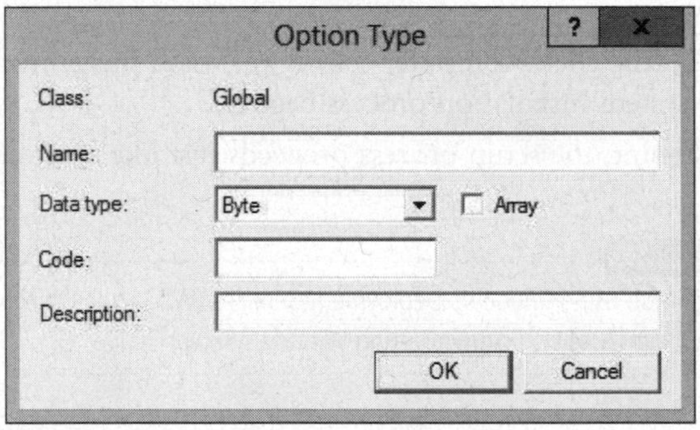

5. In the Name text box, type PXEClient.

6. From the Data type drop-down list, select String.

7. In the Code text box, type 060.

8. Click OK twice to close the *Option Type* and *Predefined Options and Values* dialog boxes.

9. In the scope pane, right-click the Server Options node and, from the context menu, select Configure Options. The *Server Options* dialog box appears.

10. In the Available Options list box, scroll down and select the 060 PXEClient option you just created, as shown in Figure 11-22.

Figure 11-22

The Server Options dialog box

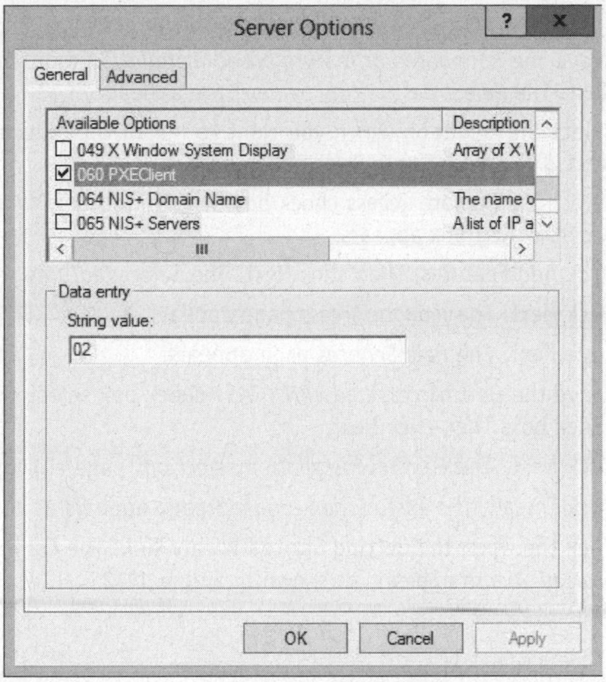

11. In the String value text box, type the name or IP address of your WDS server. Then, click OK.

CLOSE the DHCP console.

This procedure adds the 060 custom option value you defined to all the DHCPOFFER packets the DHCP server sends out to clients. When a client computer boots from a local device, such as a hard drive or CD-ROM, the 060 option has no effect. However, when a client performs a network boot after receiving and accepting an offered IP address from the DHCP server, it connects to the WDS server specified in the 060 PXEClient option and uses it to obtain the boot image file it needs to start.

■ Deploying a DHCP Relay Agent

↓
THE BOTTOM LINE   If you opt to create a centralized or hybrid DHCP infrastructure, you need a DHCP relay agent on every subnet that does not have a DHCP server on it.

CERTIFICATION READY
Configure DHCP relay agent.
Objective 4.2

Many routers can function as DHCP relay agents, but in situations where they cannot, you can configure a Windows Server 2012 computer to function as a relay agent by using the following procedure.

⊙ **DEPLOY A DHCP RELAY AGENT**

GET READY. Log on to Windows Server 2012, using an account with Administrative privileges.

1. In the *Server Manager* window, click Manage and then click Add Roles and Features. The *Add Roles and Features Wizard* appears, displaying the *Before you begin* page.

2. Click Next. The *Select Installation Type* page appears.

3. Leave the *Role-based or feature-based installation* radio button selected and click Next. The *Select Destination Server* page appears.

4. Select the server on which you want to install the roles and/or features and click Next. The *Select Server Roles* page appears.

5. Select the **Remote access** check box. An *Add features that are required for Remote Access* dialog box appears.

6. Click **Add Features**. Then click **Next**. The *Select features* page appears.

7. Click **Next**. The *Remote Access* page appears.

8. Click **Next**. The *Role Services* page appears.

9. Leave the *DirectAccess and VPN (RAS)* check box selected and select the Routing check box. Then click **Next**.

10. Click **Next**. The *Confirm installation selections* page appears.

11. Click **Install**. The *Installation progress* page appears as the wizard installs the role.

12. Click the **Open the Getting Started Wizard** link. The *Configure Remote Access – Getting Started Wizard* appears, as shown in Figure 11-23.

Figure 11-23

The Configure Remote Access – Getting Started Wizard

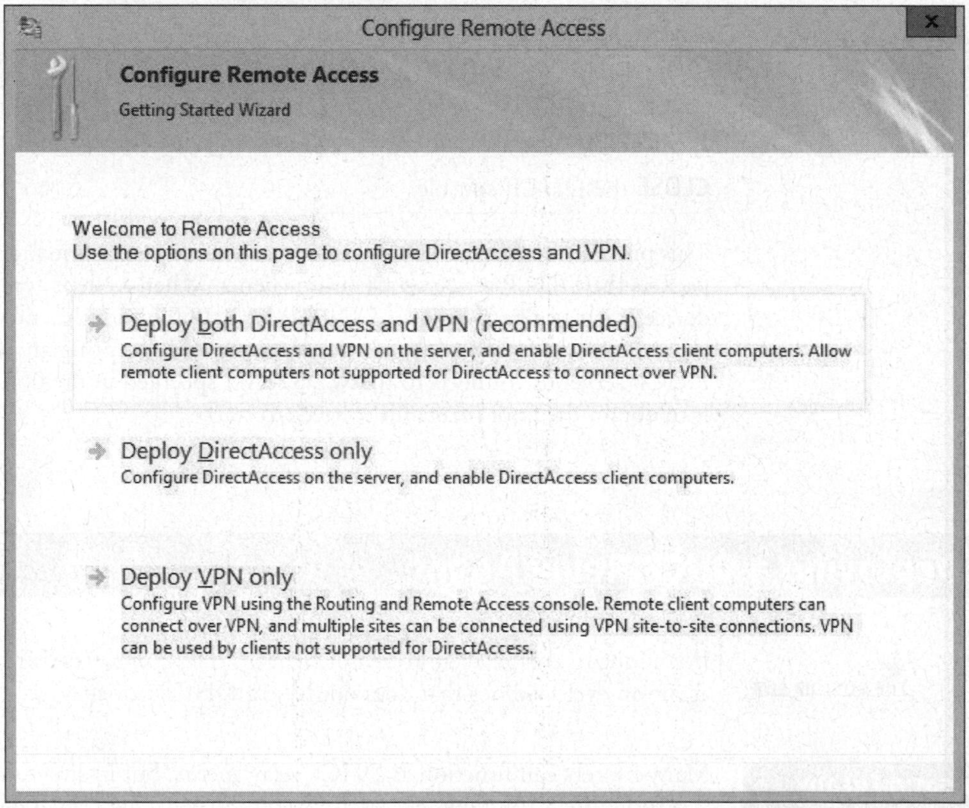

13. Click **Deploy VPN only**. The *Routing and Remote Access* console appears, as shown in Figure 11-24.

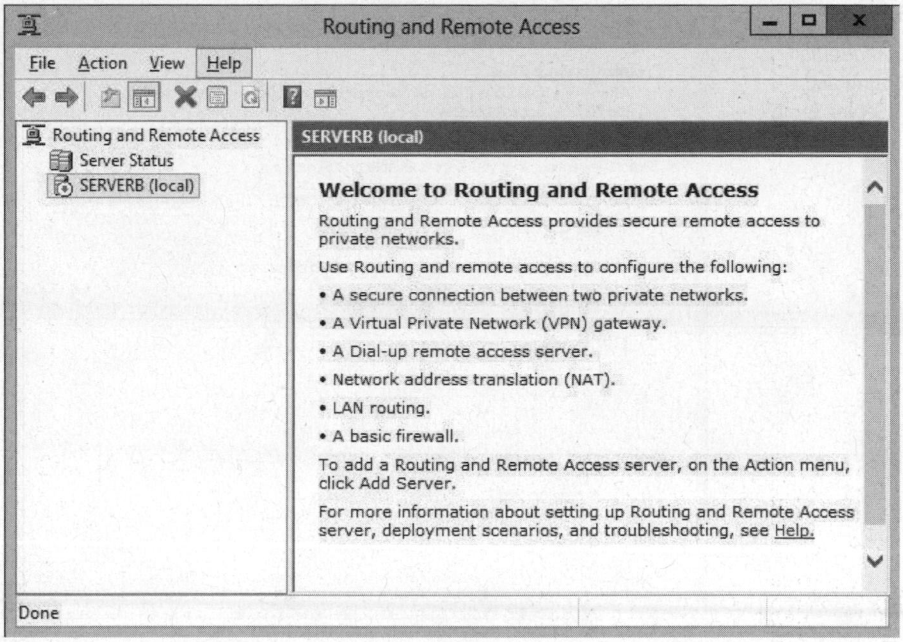

Figure 11-24

The *Routing and Remote Access* console

14. Right-click the server node and, on the context menu, select Configure and Enable Routing and Remote Access. The *Routing and Remote Access Server Setup Wizard* launches.

15. Click Next to bypass the *Welcome* page. The *Configuration* page appears, as shown in Figure 11-25.

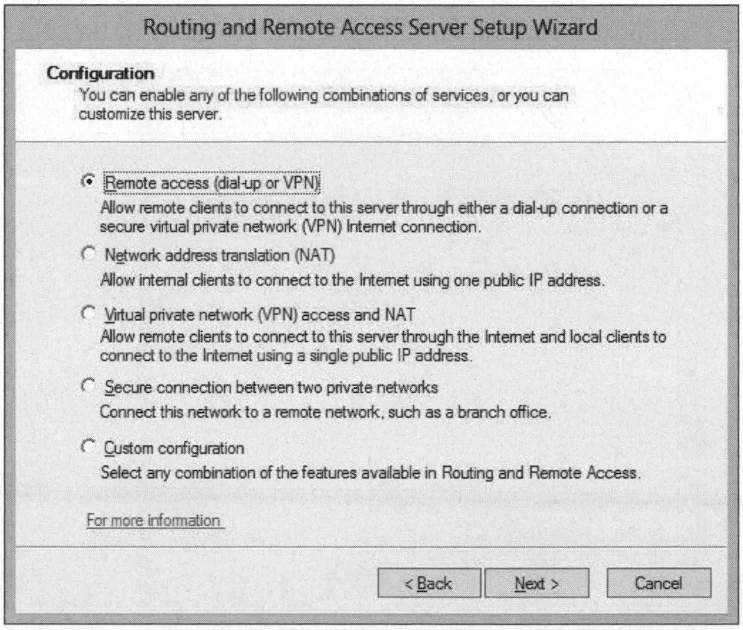

Figure 11-25

The *Configuration* page of the Routing and Remote Access Server Setup Wizard

16. Select Custom configuration and click Next. The *Custom Configuration* page appears, as shown in Figure 11-26.

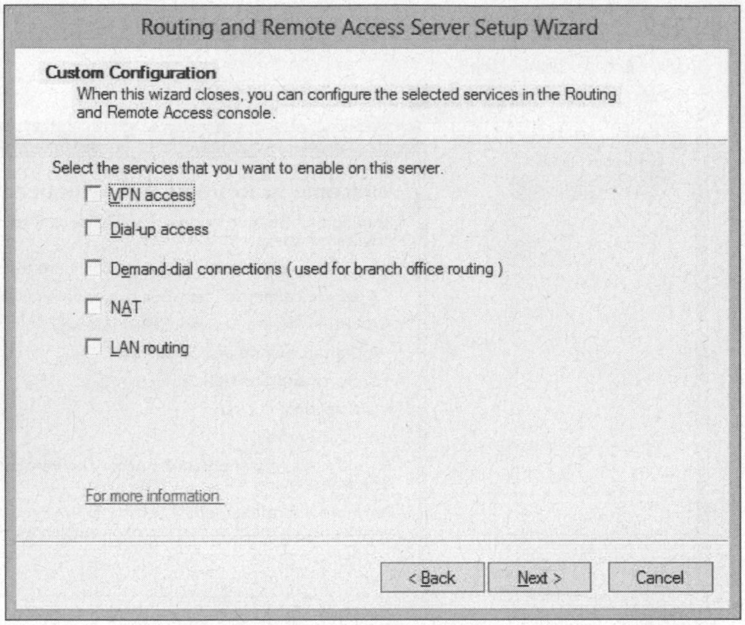

Figure 11-26

The *Custom Configuration* page of the Routing and Remote Access Server Setup Wizard

Routing and Remote Access Server Setup Wizard

Custom Configuration
When this wizard closes, you can configure the selected services in the Routing and Remote Access console.

Select the services that you want to enable on this server.

☐ VPN access

☐ Dial-up access

☐ Demand-dial connections (used for branch office routing)

☐ NAT

☐ LAN routing

For more information

[< Back] [Next >] [Cancel]

17. Select the LAN routing check box and click Next. The *Completing the Routing and Remote Access Server Setup Wizard* page appears.

18. Click Finish. A *Routing and Remote Access* message box appears, prompting you to start the service.

19. Click Start Service.

20. Expand the IPv4 node. Then, right-click the General node and, in the context menu, select New Routing Protocol. The *New Routing Protocol* dialog box appears, as shown in Figure 11-27.

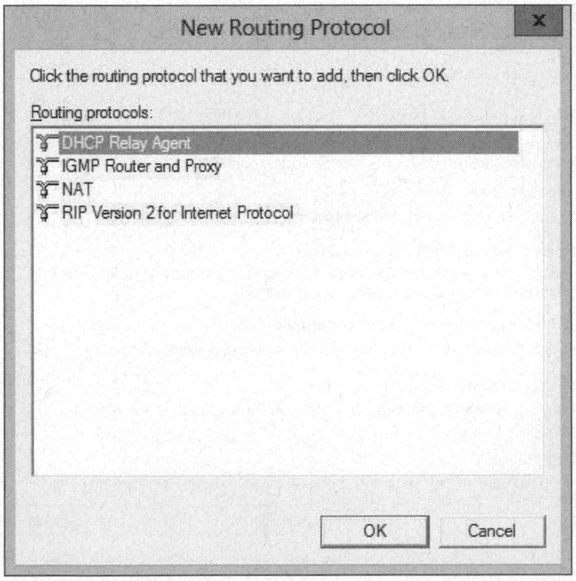

Figure 11-27

The New Routing Protocol dialog box

New Routing Protocol [x]

Click the routing protocol that you want to add, then click OK.

Routing protocols:

- DHCP Relay Agent
- IGMP Router and Proxy
- NAT
- RIP Version 2 for Internet Protocol

[OK] [Cancel]

21. Select DHCP Relay Agent and click OK. A *DHCP Relay Agent* node appears, subordinate to the IPv4 node.

22. Right-click the DHCP Relay Agent node and, on the context menu, select New Interface. The *New Interface for DHCP Relay Agent* dialog box appears, as shown in Figure 11-28.

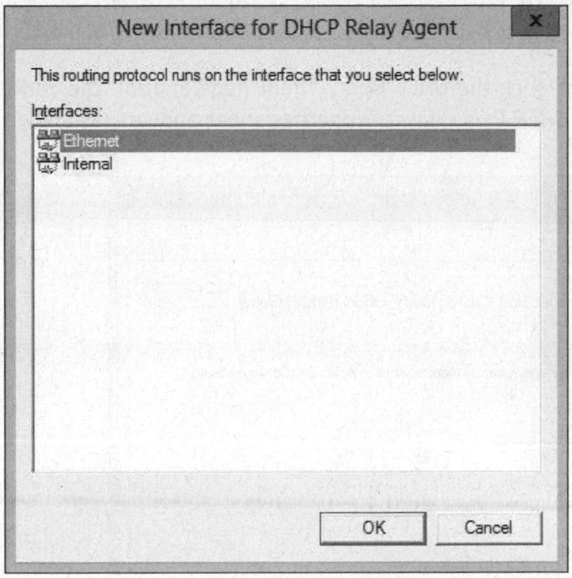

Figure 11-28

The *New Interface for DHCP Relay Agent* dialog box

23. Select the interface to the subnet on which you want to install the relay agent and click OK. The *DHCP Relay Properties* sheet for the interface appears, as shown in Figure 11-29.

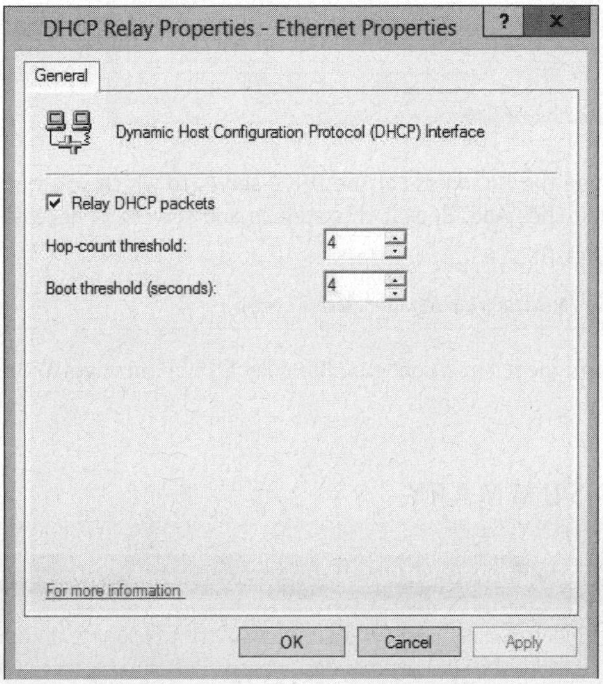

Figure 11-29

The *DHCP Relay Properties* sheet for a selected interface

24. Leave the *Relay DHCP packets* check box selected and configure the following settings, if needed:

- Hop-count threshold specifies the maximum number of relay agents that DHCP messages can pass through before being discarded. The default value is 4 and the maximum value is 16. This setting prevents DHCP messages from being relayed endlessly around the network.

- Boot threshold specifies the time interval (in seconds) that the relay agent should wait before forwarding each DHCP message it receives. The default value is 4 seconds. This setting enables you to control which DHCP server processes the clients for a particular subnet.

25. Click OK.

26. Right-click the DHCP Relay Agent node and, on the context menu, select Properties. The *DHCP Relay Agent Properties* sheet appears, as shown in Figure 11-30.

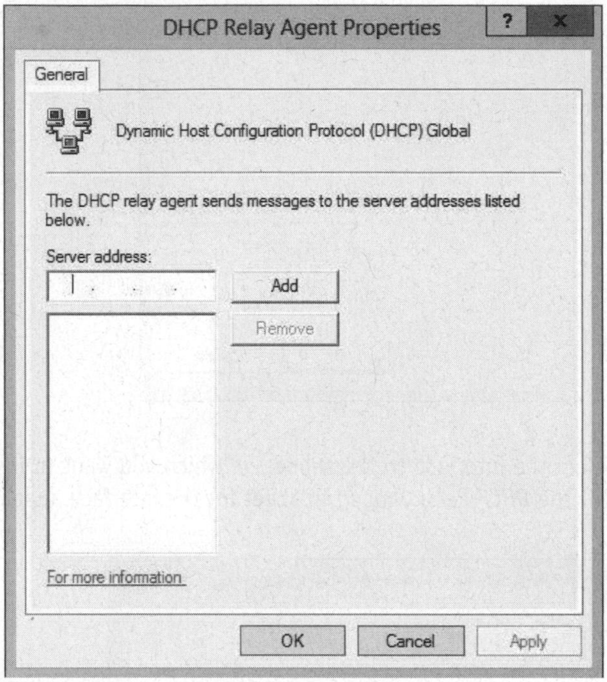

Figure 11-30

The *DHCP Relay Agent Properties* sheet

> **DHCP Relay Agent Properties** ? X
>
> General
>
> Dynamic Host Configuration Protocol (DHCP) Global
>
> The DHCP relay agent sends messages to the server addresses listed below.
>
> Server address:
>
> [.............] [Add]
>
> [Remove]
>
> For more information
>
> [OK] [Cancel] [Apply]

27. Type the IP address of the DHCP server to which you want the agent to relay messages and click Add. Repeat this step to add servers, if necessary.

28. Click OK.

CLOSE the *Routing and Remote Access* console.

At this point, the server is configured to relay DHCP messages to the server addresses you specified.

SKILL SUMMARY

IN THIS LESSON, YOU LEARNED:

- The Dynamic Host Configuration Protocol (DHCP) service automatically configures the Internet Protocol (IP) address and other TCP/IP settings on network computers by assigning addresses from a pool (called a *scope*) and reclaiming them when they are no longer in use.

- DHCP consists of three components: a *DHCP server application*, which responds to client requests for TCP/IP configuration settings; a *DHCP client*, which issues requests to server and applies the TCP/IP configuration settings it receives to the local computer; and a *DHCP communications protocol*, which defines the formats and sequences of the messages exchanged by DHCP clients and servers.

- The DHCP standards define three different IP address allocation methods: *dynamic allocation*, in which a DHCP server assigns an IP address to a client computer from a scope for a specified length of time; *automatic allocation*, in which the DHCP server permanently assigns an IP address to a client computer from a scope; and *manual allocation*, in which a DHCP server permanently assigns a specific IP address to a specific computer on the network.

- In a distributed DHCP infrastructure, you install at least one DHCP server on each of your subnets, so that all your clients have access to a local DHCP server. In a centralized DHCP infrastructure, all DHCP servers are placed in a single location, such as a server closet or data center. To enable the broadcast traffic on each subnet to reach the DHCP servers, you must install a DHCP relay agent on each subnet.

■ Knowledge Assessment

Multiple Choice

Select one or more correct answers for each of the following questions.

1. Which of the following message types is not used during a successful DHCP address assignment?
   - **a.** DHCPDISCOVER
   - **b.** DHCPREQUEST
   - **c.** DHCPACK
   - **d.** DHCPINFORM

2. Which of the following is not one of the techniques you can use to provide fault tolerance for DHCP servers?
   - **a.** splitting scopes
   - **b.** using stand-by servers
   - **c.** DHCP servers using identical scopes
   - **d.** failover clustering

3. Which of the following DHCP infrastructure designs requires the largest number of DHCP server implementations?
   - **a.** hybrid
   - **b.** centralized
   - **c.** dynamic
   - **d.** distributed

4. Which of the following types of DHCP address allocation is the equivalent of a reservation in Windows Server 2012?
   - **a.** dynamic allocation
   - **b.** automatic allocation
   - **c.** manual allocation
   - **d.** hybrid allocation

5. Which of the following DHCP message types is sent first in process of obtaining an address lease?
   - **a.** DHCPOFFER
   - **b.** DHCPACK
   - **c.** DHCPDISCOVER
   - **d.** DHCPREQUEST

6. At which layer of the OSI model does DHCP operate?
   a. Session layer
   b. Network layer
   c. Application layer
   d. Presentation layer

7. A DHCP client first attempts to reacquire its lease at half the lease time, which is known as:
   a. DHCP reservation
   b. T1
   c. T2
   d. DHCP lease

8. The following is an administrative grouping of scopes that is used to support multiple logical subnets on a single network segment:
   a. host
   b. scope
   c. superscope
   d. multinet

9. The following is a hexadecimal address that is uniquely associated with a specific Network Interface Card (NIC):
   a. MAC
   b. JET
   c. BOOTP
   d. IETF

10. Which of the following network components are typically capable of functioning as DHCP relay agents?
    a. Windows 8 computers
    b. routers
    c. switches
    d. Windows Server 2012 computers

Best Answer

Choose the letter that corresponds to the best answer. More than one answer choice may achieve the goal. Select the BEST answer.

1. One method a Dynamic Host Configuration Protocol (DHCP) server allocates IP addresses is called manual allocation. This process involves manually assigning an IP address to a particular server. What is the key benefit of DHCP manual allocation over manually configuring the address directly on the server?
   a. The DHCP server then contains a centralized list of permanently assigned addresses.
   b. The DHCP server might pass on more information than just an IP address.
   c. This process prevents accidental duplication of permanently assigned IP addresses.
   d. This manually assigned address is officially known as a reservation.

2. Your DHCP servers are burdened with heavy traffic, most related to IP address renewals. Unfortunately, virtually all the IP addresses in each of your subnets are allocated. Which of the following options is the best way to lower the renewal traffic?
   a. Increase the lease time.
   b. Deploy additional DHCP servers on the most burdened subnets.
   c. Shorten the lease time.
   d. Switch to manual allocation.

3. You are preparing to deploy Windows 8 to a large number of new workstations. Which of the following options would be best?
   a. Install Windows 8 using Pre-boot Execution Environment (PXE) and Windows Deployment Services (WDS).
   b. Delegate the work to a team of local administrators to divide up.
   c. Manually install the operating system yourself.
   d. Manually configure each workstation's IP address.

4. To make use of Pre-boot Execution Environment (PXE) and Windows Deployment Services (WDS), what special configuration do you require on the server and client?
   a. The client must have a special PXE-enabled network adapter.
   b. Both client and server are capable by default.
   c. The client and server both require some preparatory configuration.
   d. The DHCP server on the network must have a custom PXEClient option (option 60) configured with the location of the WDS server on the network.

5. What servers should not be DHCP clients?
   a. Web servers, DHCP servers, and domain controllers
   b. Workstations
   c. End user laptops
   d. Computers, which might have IP addresses in the exclusion range

Build a List

1. List the order in which DHCP messages are exchanged by the client and the server during a successful IP address assignment.
   a. DHCPOFFER
   b. DHCPACK
   c. DHCPREQUEST
   d. DHCPDISCOVER

2. Order the steps to demonstrate the DHCP IP address assignment process.
   a. The computer broadcasts an Address Resolution Protocol (ARP) message to ensure that no other system uses an identical IP address.
   b. When a computer boots up and has no IP address assigned, it begins broadcasting DHCPDISCOVER messages.
   c. The selected DHCP server records the computers information and responds with a DHCPACK message.
   d. All DHCP servers receiving DHCPDISCOVER messages reply with DHCPOFFER messages with an IP address and other TCP/IP configuration information.
   e. The computer selects an offer, broadcasting with a DHCPREQUEST message. The broadcast signals its acceptance to one DHCP server as well as its rejection to the other offering DHCP servers.

3. Order the steps to deploy a DHCP server.
   a. In the Server Manager window, click Manage and then click Add Roles and Features.
   b. Select the DHCP Server check box. An Add features that are required for DHCP Server dialog box appears.
   c. Leave the Role-based or feature-based installation radio button selected and click Next.
   d. Select the server on which you want to install the roles and/or features and click Next.
   e. Click Next through to Confirm.

4. Order the steps to create a DHCP scope.
   a. Expand the server and IPv4 nodes. Right-click the IPv4 node and, from the context menu, select New Scope. The New Scope Wizard appears.
   b. Configure IP address range, from starting to ending IP address. Configure the subnet mask.
   c. In the Server Manager window, click Tools and then click DHCP. The DHCP console appears.
   d. Type a name for the scope into the Name text box and click Next.
   e. Configure the IP exclusion range, from starting to ending IP address. You can also specify a delay interval between the server's receipt of DHCPDISCOVER messages and its transmission of DHCPOFFER messages.
   f. Specify the default gateway, DNS, and activate the scope.
   g. Specify the length of leases for the scope's addresses.

Business Case Scenarios

Scenario 11-1: Configuring DHCP Servers

After deploying a large number of wireless laptop computers on the network, Taylor, the IT director at Contoso, Ltd. decides to use DHCP to enable the laptop users to move from one subnet to another without having to manually reconfigure their IP addresses. Soon after the DHCP deployment, however, Taylor notices that some of the IP address scopes are being depleted, resulting in some computers being unable to connect to a new subnet. What can Taylor do to resolve this problem without altering the network's subnetting?

Scenario 11-2: Maximizing Lease Availability

You are configuring DHCP scope options for Contoso, Ltd. The company has a limited number of IP addresses available for clients, and it wants to configure DHCP to maximize IP address availability. Choose all of the following actions that will accomplish this objective:

   a. Set long lease durations for IP addresses.
   b. Set short lease durations for IP addresses.
   c. Configure a DHCP option to automatically release an IP address when the computer shuts down.
   d. Create DHCP reservations for all portable computers.

Deploying and Configuring the DNS Service

70-410 EXAM OBJECTIVE

Objective 4.3 – Deploy and configure DNS service. This objective may include but is not limited to: Configure Active Directory integration of primary zones; configure forwarders; configure Root Hints; manage DNS cache; create A and PTR resource records.

LESSON HEADING	EXAM OBJECTIVE
Understanding the DNS Architecture	
Creating a DNS Standard	
Understanding DNS Naming	
Understanding the DNS Domain Hierarchy	
Using DNS Messaging	
Understanding DNS Communications	
Comprehending DNS Server Caching	Manage DNS cache
Understanding DNS Referrals and Queries	
Using DNS Forwarders	Configure forwarders
Understanding Reverse Name Resolution	
Designing a DNS Deployment	
Resolving Internet Names	
Hosting Internet Domains	
Hosting Active Directory Domains	
Integrating DHCP and DNS	
Separating DNS Services	
Creating Internet Domains	
Creating Internal Domains	
Creating Subdomains	
Combining Internal and External Domains	
Creating Host Names	

Deploying a DNS Server	
Creating Zones	Configure Active Directory integration of primary zones
Creating Resource Records	Create A and PTR resource records
Configuring DNS Server Settings	Configure Root Hints

KEY TERMS

caching-only server

country-code top level
    domain (ccTLD)

domain

forwarder

fully qualified domain
    name (FQDN)

generic top-level domain (gTLD)

global domain

host

host table

iterative query

name resolution

negative caching

recursive query

referral

resolver

resource record

reverse name
    resolution

root name server

zone

zone transfer

■ Understanding the DNS Architecture

THE BOTTOM LINE

The Domain Name System (DNS) is a crucial element of both Internet and Active Directory communications.

All TCP/IP communication is based on IP addresses. Each computer on a network has at least one network interface, which is called a *host*, in TCP/IP parlance, and each host has an IP address that is unique on that network. Every datagram transmitted by a TCP/IP system contains the sending computer's IP address and the intended recipient's IP address. However, when users access a shared folder on the network or a website on the Internet, they do so by specifying or selecting a host name, not an IP address. This is because names are easier to remember and use than IP addresses.

For TCP/IP systems to use these friendly host names, they must have some way to discover the IP address associated with a specific name. In the early days of TCP/IP networking, each computer had a list of names and their equivalent IP addresses, called a *host table*. At that time, there were few enough computers on the fledgling Internet for the maintenance and distribution of a single host table to be practical.

Today, millions of computers are on the Internet, and the idea of maintaining and distributing a single file containing names for all of them is absurd. Rather than a host table stored on every computer, TCP/IP networks today use DNS servers to convert host names into IP addresses. This conversion process is referred to as *name resolution*.

Creating a DNS Standard

When the developers of what became the Internet recognized the increasing impracticality of the host table, they set about devising a solution that would not only solve their immediate maintenance and distribution problems, but would also remain a viable solution for decades to come.

The objectives of what became the DNS were as follows:

- To create a means for administrators to assign host names to their computers without duplicating the names of other systems.
- To store the host names in a database that would be accessible by any system, anywhere on the network.
- To distribute the host name database among servers all over the network, to avoid creating traffic bottlenecks and a single point of failure.
- To create a standardized system for host naming accessing electronic mailboxes.

The resulting solution was the Domain Name System (DNS), as defined and published by the Internet Engineering Task Force (IETF) in 1983 in two documents called RFC 882, "Domain Names: Concepts and Facilities," and RFC 883, "Domain Names: Implementation Specification." These documents were updated in 1987, published as RFC 1034 and RFC 1035, respectively, and ratified as an IETF standard. Since that time, the IETF has published numerous other RFCs that update the information in the standard to address current networking issues.

At its core, the DNS is still a list of names and their equivalent IP addresses, but the method for creating, storing, and retrieving the names is different from those in a host table. The DNS consists of three elements, as follows:

- **The DNS name space:** The DNS standards define a tree-structured name space in which each branch of the tree identifies a *domain*. Each domain contains a collection of *resource records* that contain host names, IP addresses, and other information. Query operations are attempts to retrieve specific resource records from a particular domain.
- **Name servers:** A DNS server is an application running on a server computer that maintains information about the domain tree structure and (usually) contains authoritative information about one or more specific domains in that structure. The application is capable of responding to queries for information about the domains for which it is the authority, and also of forwarding queries about other domains to other name servers. This enables any DNS server to access information about any domain in the tree.
- **Resolvers:** A *resolver* is a client program that generates DNS queries and sends them to a DNS server for fulfillment. A resolver has direct access to at least one DNS server and can also process referrals to direct its queries to other servers when necessary.

In its most basic form, the DNS name resolution process consists of a resolver submitting a name resolution request to its designated DNS server. When the server does not possess information about the requested name, it forwards the request to another DNS server on the network. The second server generates a response containing the IP address of the requested name and returns it to the first server, which relays the information in turn to the resolver, as shown in Figure 12-1. In practice, however, the DNS name resolution process can be considerably more complex, as you learn in the following sections.

TAKE NOTE*

The term *domain*, in the context of DNS, has a different meaning than it does when used in the Microsoft Windows directory services. A Windows Server 2012 domain is a grouping of Windows computers and devices that are administered as a unit. In DNS, a domain is a group of hosts and possibly subdomains that represent a part of the DNS namespace.

Figure 12-1

DNS servers relay requests and replies to other DNS servers

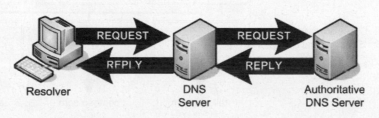

Understanding DNS Naming

To facilitate the continued growth of the namespace, the developers of the DNS created a two-tiered system, consisting of domain names and host names. The basic principle is that the administrators of individual networks obtain domain names from a centralized authority, and then assign the host names within that domain themselves. This process enables administrators to assign host names without worrying about duplication, as long as each host name is unique within its domain.

In the days of host tables, if two administrators each named one of their computers Server01, a conflict occurred, resulting in misdirected data packets. Today, the two administrators can both use the host name *Server01*, as long as the two hosts are in different domains. Each computer is uniquely identified by the combination of its host name and its domain name.

One of the most common examples of this principle is found in the Internet websites you see every day. It is common for the administrators of websites to assign the host name *www* to their web servers. Therefore, millions of web servers on the Internet have identical host names. However, when you type a Uniform Resource Locator (URL) such as *http://www.contoso.com* in your browser, it is the domain name (contoso.com) that distinguishes that particular www server from millions of others.

➕ MORE INFORMATION

When you study the structure of a DNS name, notice the similarity between DNS names and IP addresses, which also consist of two parts: a network identifier and a host identifier. This two-part hierarchy is a recurring theme in the architecture of TCP/IP networks, because it enables administrative responsibilities to be distributed throughout the network. In the same way that you receive the network identifiers for their IP addresses and are responsible for assigning the host identifiers on that network, you also receive DNS domain names and are responsible for assigning host names within that domain.

The domain name part of a DNS name is hierarchical and consists of two or more words, separated by periods. The DNS namespace takes the form of a tree that, much like a file system, has its root at the top. Just beneath the root is a series of top-level domains, and beneath each top-level domain is a series of second-level domains, as shown in Figure 12-2. At minimum, the complete DNS name for a computer on the Internet consists of a host name, a second-level domain name, and a top-level domain name, written in this order and separated by periods. The complete DNS name for a particular computer is called its ***fully qualified domain name (FQDN)***.

Figure 12-2

The DNS domain hierarchy

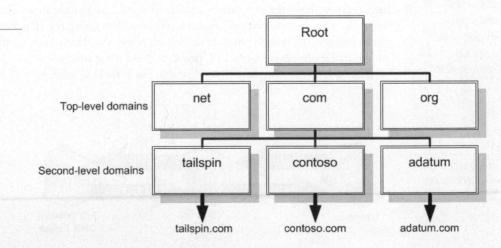

Unlike an IP address, which places the network identifier first and follows it with the host, the notation for an FQDN places the host name first, followed by the domain name, with the top-level domain name last. In the example cited previously, the FQDN *www.contoso.com* consists of a host (or computer) called *www* in the *contoso.com* domain. In the contoso.com domain name, *com* is the top-level domain and *contoso* is the second-level domain. Technically, every FQDN should end with a period, representing the root of the DNS tree, as follows:

`www.contoso.com.`

However, the period is rarely included in FQDNs today.

Understanding the DNS Domain Hierarchy

The hierarchical nature of the DNS namespace is designed to make it possible for any DNS server on the Internet to locate the authoritative source for any domain name, by using a minimum number of queries. This efficiency results from the domains at each level of the hierarchy are responsible for maintaining information about the domains at the next lower level.

The authoritative source for any domain is the DNS server (or servers) responsible for maintaining that domain's resource records. Each level of the DNS domain hierarchy has name servers responsible for the individual domains at that level.

At the top of the DNS hierarchy are the root name servers. The ***root name servers*** are the highest-level DNS servers in the entire namespace, and they maintain information about the top-level domains. All DNS server implementations are preconfigured with the IP addresses of the root name servers, because these servers are the ultimate source for all DNS information. When a computer attempts to resolve a DNS name, it begins at the top of the namespace hierarchy with the root name servers and works down the levels until it reaches the authoritative server for the domain in which the name is located.

TOP-LEVEL DOMAINS

Just beneath the root name servers are the top-level domains (TLDs). The original DNS name space called for six ***generic top-level domains (gTLDs),*** dedicated to specific purposes, as follows:

- *com:* Commercial organizations
- *edu:* Four-year, degree-granting educational institutions in North America
- *gov:* United States government institutions
- *mil:* United States military applications
- *net:* Networking organizations
- *org:* Noncommercial organizations

The *edu*, *gov*, and *mil* domains are reserved for use by certified organizations, but the *com*, *org*, and *net* domains are called ***global domains***, because organizations anywhere in the world can register second-level domains within them.

Originally, these top-level domains were managed by a company called *Network Solutions, Inc.* (NSI, formerly known as InterNIC, the Internet Network Information Center) as a result of a cooperative agreement with the United States government.

In 1998, however, the agreement with the U.S. government was changed to permit other organizations to compete with NSI in providing domain registrations. An organization called the *Internet Corporation for Assigned Names and Numbers (ICANN)* is responsible for the accreditation of domain name registrars. Under this new policy, the procedures and fees for registering names in the *com*, *net*, and *org* domains might vary, but there is no difference in the functionality of the domain names, nor are duplicate names permitted. The complete list of registrars that are accredited by ICANN is available at its website.

ICANN is also responsible for the ratification of new top-level domains. Numerous proposals for the establishment of various new top-level domains have been submitted; the proposals selected for negotiation of agreements in November 2000 are *aero*, *biz*, *coop*, *info*, *museum*, *name*, and *pro*. After discussion, the TLDs have become active, along with a number of sponsored TLDs, including *asia*, *cat*, *jobs*, *mobi*, *tel*, and *travel*.

The top two levels of the DNS hierarchy, the root and the top-level domains, are represented by servers that exist primarily to respond to queries for information about other domains. No hosts exist in the root or top-level domains, except for the name servers themselves. For example, you do not see a DNS name consisting of only a host and a top-level domain, such as *www.com*. The root name servers do nothing but respond to millions of requests by sending out the addresses of the authoritative servers for the top-level domains, and the top-level domain servers do the same for the second-level domains.

Country-Code Domains

In addition to the generic TLDs, hundreds of two-letter **country-code top level domains (ccTLDs)** exist, named for specific countries in their own languages, such as *fr* for France and *de* for Deutschland (Germany). The two letter codes for countries, territories, and other geographical entities are taken from the ISO 3166 standard, published by International Organization for Standardization. Not all the countries listed in the standard exist in the DNS database, and for the countries that are listed, some do not have domains registered to them.

The Internet Assigned Numbers Authority (IANA) has on record an authoritative trustee for each abbreviation, typically a government organization or official, or someone affiliated with a university. Each domain is permitted to establish its own prices and requirements for registration of subdomains. Some ccTLDs allow open registration to anyone, whereas others maintain citizenship or residence requirements.

➕ MORE INFORMATION

For a list of the top-level domains, as maintained by the IANA, see the IANA website.

Some countries that permit open registration of ccTLDs have been more aggressive than others in marketing their services for the registration of company domains, which has resulted in the fairly common appearance in URLs of top-level domains from obscure island countries, such as *nu* (Niue), *to* (Tonga), and *cc* (Cocos-Keeling Islands).

A top-level domain, called *us*, is a viable alternative for organizations unable to obtain a satisfactory name in the *com* domain. The *us* domain is administered by the Information Sciences Institute of the University of Southern California, which registers second-level domains to businesses and individuals, as well as to government agencies, educational institutions, and other organizations. The only restriction is that all *us* domains must conform to a naming hierarchy that uses two-letter state abbreviations at the third level and local city or county names at the fourth level. Thus, an example of a valid domain name is *adatum.chicago.il.us*.

Infrastructure Domains

Another top-level domain category is the infrastructure domain, which has only one. The IANA manages the *arpa* domain for the use of the IETF, most notably as the host for the reverse name resolution domains, as discussed in "Understanding Reverse Name Resolution," later in this lesson.

SECOND-LEVEL DOMAINS

Each top-level domain has its own collection of second-level domains. Individuals and organizations can purchase these domains for their own use. For example, the second-level domain *contoso.com* belongs to a company that purchased the name from one of the many Internet registrars now in the business of selling domain names to consumers. For the payment of an annual fee, you can purchase the rights to a second-level domain.

To use the domain name, you must supply the registrar with the IP addresses of two DNS servers that you want to be the authoritative sources for information about the domain. A DNS server is a software program that runs on a computer. DNS server products are available for all the major network operating systems. The DNS servers do not need to be located on the registrant's network; many companies outsource their Internet server hosting chores and use their service provider's DNS servers.

The administrators of the top-level domain servers create resource records pointing to these authoritative servers, so that any *com* server receiving a request to resolve a name in the *contoso.com* domain can reply with the addresses of the *contoso.com* servers.

Thus, in its simplest form, the Domain Name System refers requests for the address of a particular host name to a top-level domain server, which passes the request to the authoritative server for the second-level domain and responds with the requested information. Therefore, the DNS is described as a *distributed database*. The information about the hosts in specific domains is stored on their authoritative servers, which can be located anywhere. There is no single list of all the host names on the entire Internet. This is a good thing because at the time that the DNS was developed, no one imagined that the Internet would grow as large as it has.

This distributed nature of the DNS database eliminates the traffic-congestion problem caused by the use of a host table maintained on a single computer. The top-level domain servers handle millions of requests a day, but they are requests only for the DNS servers associated with second-level domains. If the top-level domains had to maintain records for every host in every second-level domain they registered, the resulting traffic would bring the entire system to a standstill.

Distributing the database in this way also splits the chores of administering the database among thousands of network administrators around the world. Domain name registrants are responsible for their own area of the name space, and can maintain it as they want with complete autonomy.

> **TAKE NOTE** *
>
> To create authoritative sources for your Internet domain, you can deploy your own DNS servers, using Windows Server 2012 or another operating system, or you can pay to use your ISP's DNS servers. Remember, however, that if you host an Internet domain on your own DNS servers, these servers must be accessible from the Internet and have registered IP addresses.

SUBDOMAINS

After you purchase the rights to a second-level domain, you can create as many hosts as you want in that domain, by creating new resource records on the authoritative servers. You can also create as many additional domain levels as you want. For example, once you own the *contoso.com* domain, you can create the subdomains *sales.contoso.com* and *marketing.contoso.com*, and then populate these subdomains with hosts, such as *www.sales.contoso.com* and *ftp.marketing.contoso.com*. The only limitations to the subdomains and hosts you can create in your second-level domain are as follows:

- Each individual domain name can be no more than 63 characters long.
- The total FQDN (including the trailing period) can be no more than 255 characters long.

For the convenience of users and administrators, most domain names do not approach these limitations.

In some cases, large organizations use subdomains to subdivide their networks according to geographical or organizational boundaries. A large corporation might create a third-level domain for each city or country in which it has an office, such as *paris.contoso.com* and *newyork.contoso.com*, or for each of several departments, such as the *sales.contoso.com* and *marketing.contoso.com* domains noted previously. The organizational paradigm for the subdomains and hosts within a second-level domain is left completely up to its administrators.

The use of subdomains can make it easier to identify hosts on a large network, but many organizations also use them to delegate domain maintenance chores. The DNS servers for a top-level domain contain the addresses for each second-level domain's authoritative servers. In the same way, a second-level domain's servers can refer to authoritative servers for third-level administrators at each site to maintain their own DNS servers.

Using DNS Messaging

DNS name resolution transactions use User Datagram Protocol (UDP) datagrams on port 53 for servers and an ephemeral port number for clients. Communication between two servers uses port 53 on both machines.

The DNS uses a single message format for all its communications that consists of the following five sections:

- **Header:** contains information about the nature of the message.
- **Question:** contains the information requested from the destination server.
- **Answer:** contains resource records supplying the information requested in the Question section.
- **Authority:** contains resource records pointing to an authority for the information requested in the Question section.
- **Additional:** contains resource records with additional information in response to the Question section.

Every DNS message has a Header section, and the other four sections are included only if they contain data. For example, a query message contains the DNS name to be resolved in the Question section, but the Answer, Authority, and Additional sections aren't needed. When the server receiving the query constructs its reply, it makes some changes to the Header section, leaves the Question section intact, and adds entries to one or more of the remaining three sections. Each section can have multiple entries, so that a server can send more than one resource record in a single message.

If the data to be transmitted does not fit in a single UDP datagram, as in the case of zone transfers, the two systems establish a standard TCP connection, also using port 53 on both machines, and transmit the data using as many segments as needed.

Understanding DNS Communications

Although all Internet applications use DNS to resolve host names into IP addresses, this name resolution process is easiest to see when you use a web browser to access an Internet site.

When you type a URL containing a DNS name (such as *www.microsoft.com*) into the browser's *Address* box and press the *Enter* key, you might see a message that says, "Finding Site: www.microsoft.com." Then, a few seconds later, you might see a message that says, "Connecting to," followed by an IP address. It is during this interval that the DNS name resolution process occurs.

From the client's perspective, the procedure that occurs during these few seconds consists of the application sending a query message to its designated DNS server that contains the name to be resolved. The server replies with a message containing the IP address corresponding to that name. Using the supplied address, the application can transmit a message to the intended destination. When you examine the DNS server's role in the process, you see the procedure's complexity.

The following procedure diagrams the Internet name resolution process.

1. A user on a client system specifies the DNS name of an Internet server in an application such as a web browser. The application generates an API call to the resolver on the client system, and the resolver creates a DNS recursive query message containing the server name, which it transmits to the DNS server identified in computer's TCP/IP configuration, as shown in Figure 12-3.

Figure 12-3

DNS servers relay requests and replies to other DNS servers

2. The client's DNS server, after receiving the query, checks its resource records to see whether it is the authoritative source for the zone containing the requested server name. If it is not, which is typical, the DNS server generates an iterative query and submits it to one of the root name servers, as shown in Figure 12-4. The root name server examines the name requested by the client's DNS server and consults its resource records to identify the authoritative servers for the name's top-level domain. The root name server transmits a reply to the client's DNS server that contains a referral to the top-level domain server addresses.

Figure 12-4

DNS servers relay requests and replies to other DNS servers

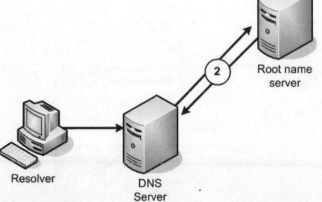

3. The client's DNS server, now in possession of the top-level domain server address for the requested name, generates a new iterative query and transmits it to the top-level domain server, as shown in Figure 12-5. The top-level domain server examines the second-level domain in the requested name and transmits a referral containing the addresses of authoritative servers for that second-level domain back to the client's DNS server.

Figure 12-5

DNS servers relay requests and replies to other DNS servers

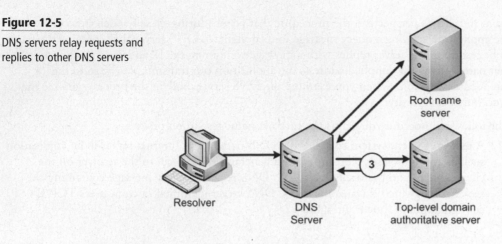

 In the DNS name resolution process, the process of resolving the top-level and second-level domain names are portrayed as separate steps, but this is often not the case. The most commonly used top-level domains, such as *com*, *net*, and *org*, are hosted by the root name servers, which eliminates one entire referral from the name resolution process.

4. The client's DNS server generates yet another iterative query and transmits it to the second-level domain server, as shown in Figure 12-6. If the second-level domain server is the authority for the zone containing the requested name, it consults its resource records to determine the IP address of the requested system and transmits it in a reply message back to the client's DNS server.

Figure 12-6

DNS servers relay requests and replies to other DNS servers

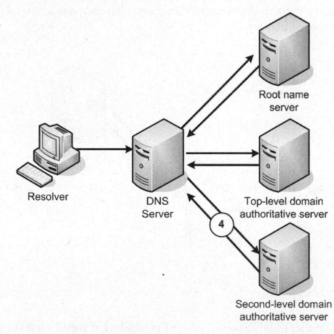

5. The client's DNS server receives the reply from the authoritative server and transmits the IP address back to the resolver on the client system, as shown in Figure 12-7. The resolver relays the address to the application, which can then initiate IP communications with the system specified by the user.

Figure 12-7

DNS servers relay requests and replies to other DNS servers

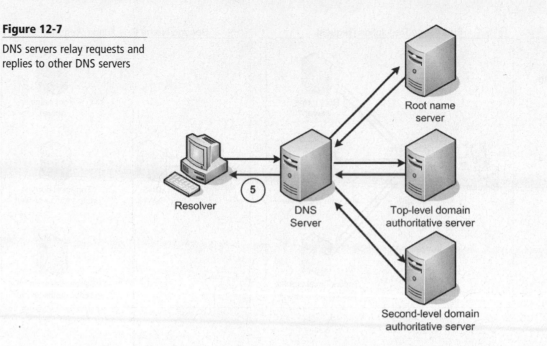

Depending on the name the client is trying to resolve, this process can be simpler or considerably more complex than the one shown here. If, for example, the client's DNS server is the authority for the domain in which the requested name is located, no other servers or iterative requests are necessary. On the other hand, if the requested name contains three or more levels of domains, additional iterative queries might be necessary.

This procedure also assumes a successful completion of the name resolution procedure. If any of the authoritative DNS servers queried returns an error message to the client's DNS server stating (for example, that one of the domains in the name does not exist), then this error message is relayed back to the client and the name resolution process fails.

Comprehending DNS Server Caching

The DNS name resolution process might seem long and complex, but in many cases, it isn't necessary for the client's DNS server to send queries to the servers for each domain specified in the requested DNS name. That is, DNS servers are capable of retaining the information they learn about the DNS name space in the course of their name resolution procedures and storing it in a cache on the local drive.

CERTIFICATION READY
Manage DNS cache.
Objective 4.3

A DNS server that receives requests from clients, for example, caches the addresses of the requested systems, as well as the addresses for authoritative servers of particular domains. The next time that a client requests the resolution of a previously resolved name, the server can respond immediately with the cached information, as shown in Figure 12-8. In addition, if a client requests another name in one of the same domains, the server can send a query directly to an authoritative server for that domain, and not to a root name server. Thus, the names in commonly accessed domains generally resolve more quickly because one of the servers along the line has information about the domain in its cache, whereas names in obscure domains take longer because the entire request/referral process is needed.

Figure 12-8

Name caching enables the second name resolution request for the same name to bypass the referral process.

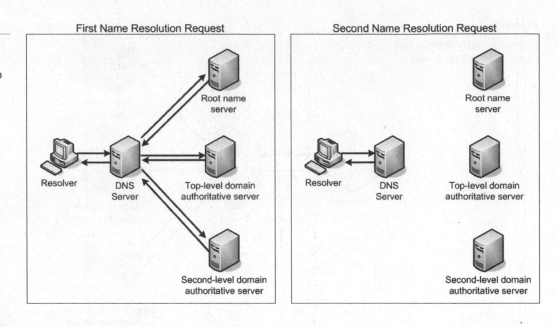

NEGATIVE CACHING

In addition to storing information that aids in the name resolution process, most modern DNS server implementations are also capable of negative caching. *Negative caching* occurs when a DNS server retains information about names that do not exist in a domain. If, for example, a client sends a query to its DNS server containing a name in which the second-level domain does not exist, the top-level domain server will return a reply containing an error message to that effect. The client's DNS server will then retain the error message information in its cache. The next time a client requests a name in that domain, the DNS server will be able to respond immediately with its own error message, without consulting the top-level domain.

CACHE DATA PERSISTENCE

Caching is a vital element of the DNS architecture, because it reduces the number of requests sent to the root name and top-level domain servers, which, being at the top of the DNS tree, are the most likely to act as a bottleneck for the whole system. However, caches must be purged eventually, and there is a fine line between effective and ineffective caching.

Because DNS servers retain resource records in their caches, it can take hours or even days for changes made in an authoritative server to be propagated around the Internet. During this period, users might receive incorrect information in response to a query. If information remains in server caches too long, then the changes that administrators make to the data in their DNS servers take too long to propagate around the Internet. If caches are purged too quickly, then the number of requests sent to the root name and top-level domain servers increases precipitously.

The amount of time that DNS data remains cached on a server is called its *Time To Live (TTL)*. Unlike most data caches, the TTL is not specified by the administrator of the server where the cache is stored. Instead, the administrators of each authoritative DNS server specify how long the data for the resource records in their domains or zones should be retained in the servers where it is cached. This enables administrators to specify a TTL value based on the volatility of their server data. On a network where changes in IP addresses or the addition of new resource records is frequent, a lower TTL value increases the likelihood that clients will receive current data. On a network that rarely changes, you can use a longer TTL value, and minimize the number of requests sent to the parent servers of your domain or zone.

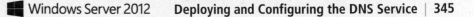

To modify the TTL value for a zone on a Windows Server 2012 DNS server, right-click the zone, open the Properties sheet, and click the *Start Of Authority (SOA)* tab, as shown in Figure 12-9. On this tab, you can modify the TTL for this record setting from its default value of one hour.

Figure 12-9

The Start of Authority (SOA) tab on a DNS server's Properties sheet

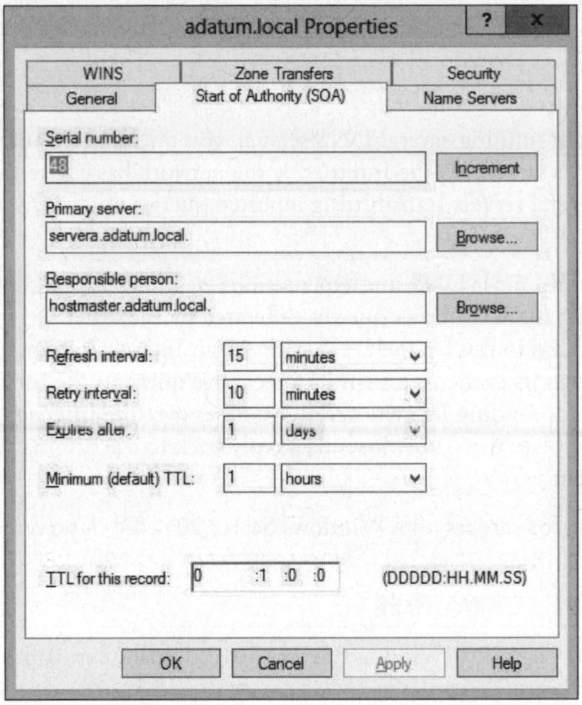

adatum.local Properties

WINS	Zone Transfers	Security
General	Start of Authority (SOA)	Name Servers

Serial number:

48   [Increment]

Primary server:

servera.adatum.local.   [Browse...]

Responsible person:

hostmaster.adatum.local.   [Browse...]

Refresh interval: 15 minutes

Retry interval: 10 minutes

Expires after: 1 Days

Minimum (default) TTL: 1 hours

TTL for this record: 0 :1 :0 :0   (DDDDD:HH.MM.SS)

[OK] [Cancel] [Apply] [Help]

Understanding DNS Referrals and Queries

The process by which one DNS server sends a name resolution request to another DNS server is called a *referral*. Referrals are essential to the DNS name resolution process.

As described previously, the DNS client is not involved in the name resolution process, except for sending one query and receiving one reply. The client's DNS server might need to send referrals to several servers before it reaches the one with the necessary information.

DNS servers recognize two types of name resolution requests, as follows:

- *Recursive query:* The DNS server receiving the name resolution request takes full responsibility for resolving the name. If the server possesses information about the requested name, it replies immediately to the requestor. If the server has no information about the name, it sends referrals to other DNS servers until it obtains the necessary information. TCP/IP client resolvers always send recursive queries to their designated DNS servers.

- *Iterative query:* The server that receives the name resolution request immediately responds with the best information it possesses at the time. This information can be cached or authoritative, and it can be a resource record containing a fully resolved name or a reference to another DNS server. DNS servers use iterative queries when communicating with each other. In most cases, it is improper to configure one DNS server to send a recursive query to another DNS server. For example, if DNS servers send iterative queries to the root name servers rather than recursive queries, the additional burden on the root name servers would be immense, and probably cause the entire Internet to grind to a halt. The only time a DNS server sends iterative queries to another server is in the case of a special type of server called a *forwarder*, which is specifically configured to interact with other servers in this way.

Using DNS Forwarders

> DNS servers send recursive queries to other servers when you configure a server to function as a forwarder.

On a network running several DNS servers, you might not want all the servers sending queries to other DNS servers on the Internet. If the network has a slow connection to the Internet, for example, several servers transmitting repeated queries might use too much of the available bandwidth.

CERTIFICATION READY
Configure forwarders.
Objective 4.3

To prevent this, most DNS implementations enable you to configure one server to function as the forwarder for all Internet queries generated by the other servers on the network. Any time that a server has to resolve the DNS name of an Internet system and fails to find the needed information in its cache, it transmits a recursive query to the forwarder, which is then responsible for sending its own iterative queries over the Internet connection. After the forwarder resolves the name, it sends a reply back to the original DNS server, which relays it to the client.

To configure forwarders on a Windows Server 2012 DNS server, use the following procedure.

 CONFIGURE FORWARDERS

GET READY. Log on to Windows Server 2012 domain controller by using an account with administrative privileges.

1. In the *Server Manager* window, click Tools > DNS. The *DNS Manager* console appears.
2. Right-click the server node and, from the context menu, select Properties. The server's Properties sheet appears.
3. Click the Forwarders tab, as shown in Figure 12-10.

Figure 12-10

The Forwarders tab on a DNS server's Properties sheet

| SERVERA Properties | ? | X |

| Debug Logging | Event Logging | Monitoring | Security |
| Interfaces | Forwarders | Advanced | Root Hints |

Forwarders are DNS servers that this server can use to resolve DNS queries for records that this server cannot resolve.

| IP Address | Server FQDN |

☑ Use root hints if no forwarders are available   Edit...

Note: If conditional forwarders are defined for a given domain, they will be used instead of server-level forwarders. To create or view conditional forwarders, navigate to the Conditional Forwarders node in the scope tree.

OK   Cancel   Apply   Help

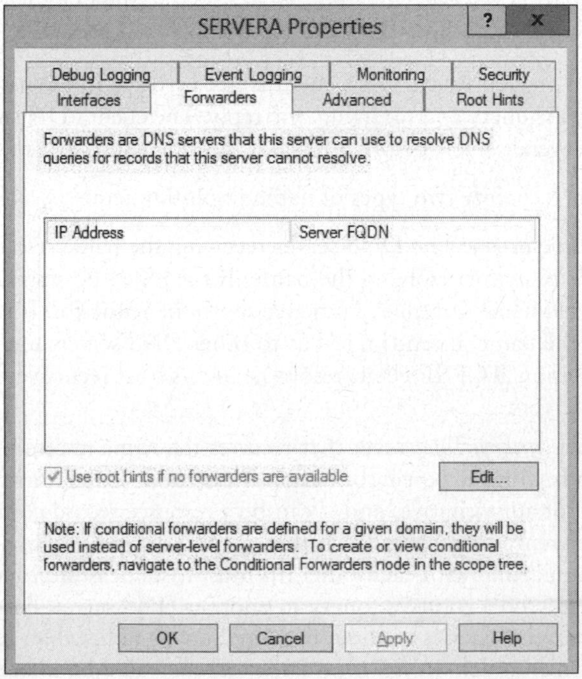

4. Click Edit. The Edit Forwarders dialog box appears, as shown in Figure 12-11.

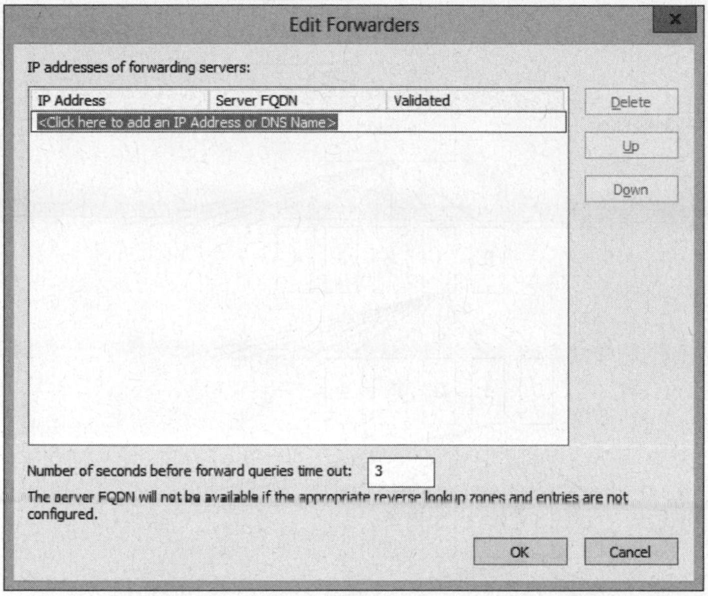

Figure 12-11

The Edit Forwarders dialog box

Figure 12-11

The Edit Forwarders dialog box

5. Type the name or address of the DNS server you want to function as a forwarder and press Enter. The system validates the name or address by connecting to the DNS server.

6. Click OK to close the Edit Forwarders dialog box and add the servers to the Forwarders tab.

7. Click OK to close the server's Properties sheet.

CLOSE the *DNS Manager* console.

Understanding Reverse Name Resolution

The name resolution process described previously converts DNS names into IP addresses. However, it might be necessary for a computer to convert an IP address into a DNS name, which is called a ***reverse name resolution***.

Because the domain hierarchy is broken down by domain names, there is no apparent way to resolve an IP address into a name by using iterative queries, except by forwarding the reverse name resolution request to every DNS server on the Internet in search of the requested address, which is obviously impractical.

To overcome this problem, the developers of the DNS created a special domain called *in-addr. arpa*, specifically designed for reverse name resolution. The in-addr.arpa second-level domain contains four additional levels of subdomains. Each of the four levels consists of subdomains that are named using the numerals 0 to 255. For example, 256 third-level domains, which have names ranging from 0.in-addr.arpa to 255.in-addr.arpa, are located beneath in-addr.arpa. Each of the 256 third-level domains has 256 fourth-level domains beneath it, also numbered from 0 to 255, and each fourth-level domain has 256 fifth-level domains, as shown in Figure 12-12. Each of the fifth-level domains can have up to 256 hosts, also numbered from 0 to 255.

Figure 12-12

The DNS reverse lookup domain

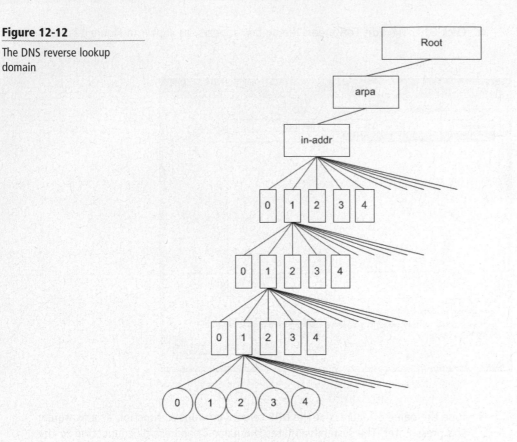

Using this hierarchy of subdomains, it is possible to express the first 3 bytes of an IP address as a DNS domain name, and to create a resource record named for the fourth byte in the appropriate fifth-level domain. For example, to resolve the IP address 192.168.89.34 into a name, a DNS server locates a domain called *89.168.192.in-addr.arpa* in the usual manner and reads the contents of a resource record named *34* in the domain.

TAKE NOTE*

In the in-addr.arpa domain, the IP address is reversed in the domain name because IP addresses have the least pertinent bit (that is, the host identifier) on the right and in DNS FQDNs, the host name is on the left.

■ Designing a DNS Deployment

↓
THE BOTTOM LINE

All the DNS information in the preceding sections might at first seem gratuitous, but understanding the structure of the DNS and how the clients and servers communicate is crucial to creating an effective DNS deployment plan.

Every computer on a TCP/IP network needs access to a DNS server, but this does not mean that you must deploy your own DNS servers on your network. Internet service providers (ISPs) nearly always include the use of their DNS servers into their rates, and in some cases, it might be better to use other DNS servers, rather than run your own.

When designing a DNS deployment, you should first determine what DNS services your network requires. Consider the information in the following sections as you create your design.

Resolving Internet Names

If you provide your network users with access to the Internet, as most organizations do, then every user must have at least one DNS server address specified in its TCP/IP configuration settings. If you use DHCP servers to assign IP addresses to the network computers, you can configure the servers to configure the clients' DNS server addresses as well.

For Internet name resolution purposes, the only functions required of the DNS server are the capability to process incoming queries from resolvers and send its own queries to other DNS servers on the Internet. A DNS server that performs only these functions is known as a *caching-only server*, because it is not the authoritative source for any domain and hosts no resource records of its own.

Installing your own caching-only DNS server is a simple matter, or you can use the DNS servers supplied by your ISP. The important factor to consider in this decision is the amount of traffic generated by the server's query process. In the DNS name resolution process, the client resolver and its DNS server exchange one query message and one reply. If the clients on your local network use the DNS servers on your ISP's network, then your Internet connection has to handle only these two messages, as shown in Figure 12-13.

Figure 12-13

Using an ISP's caching-only DNS server

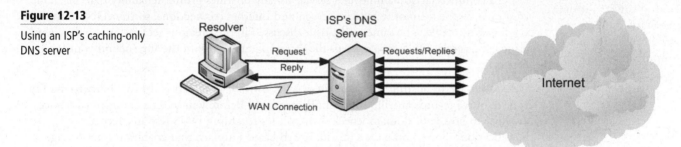

If, however, you install a DNS server on your local network, the recursive queries the server receives from clients cause it to send numerous iterative queries to various other DNS servers on the Internet. These multiple message exchanges must all pass over the Internet connection, as shown in Figure 12-14. When you have hundreds or thousands of clients using the DNS server, the amount of iterative query traffic the server generates can overburden your Internet connection or greatly increase its cost.

Figure 12-14

Using your own caching-only DNS server

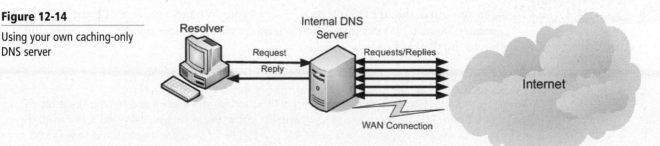

As a general rule, if your network requires no DNS services other than name resolution, you should consider using off-site DNS servers.

Hosting Internet Domains

> If you host a domain on the Internet, you must pay an annual fee to register a second-level domain name with a commercial registrar and supply it with the IP addresses of your DNS servers. These servers are the authoritative source for information about your domain. Therefore, they must have registered IP addresses and be accessible from the Internet at all times.

The two main reasons for registering an Internet domain name are to host web servers and to create e-mail addresses. The authoritative DNS servers for the domain must have resource records that can provide Internet users with the IP addresses of your web servers and e-mail servers. If the authoritative DNS servers are offline, Internet users might be unable to access your web servers, and e-mail messages destined for your domain could bounce back to their senders.

As with name resolution, the DNS servers you use to host your domain can be computers on your own network or servers supplied by a commercial entity. The DNS servers that host your domain do not need to be located in that domain, nor do they need to be supplied by the registrar from whom you obtained your domain name. You can usually pay an additional fee to your domain registrar and have them host the domain on their servers, or you can use you ISP's servers, also for an additional fee.

Using a commercial domain hosting service usually provides greater reliability than installing your own, in the form of redundant servers and Internet connections, so your DNS records are always available. The same traffic issue discussed in the previous section also applies here; using commercial DNS servers keeps the incoming queries from the Internet off your local network.

One advantage to hosting your domain on your own DNS servers is the capability to modify your resource records at will, using familiar controls. Before you select a commercial service provider to host your domain, check their policies regarding DNS resource record modifications. Some companies provide a web-based interface that enables you to manage your resource records, whereas others might require you to call them to make DNS changes, and might even charge you an additional fee for each modification.

Hosting Active Directory Domains

> If you run Active Directory Domain Services (AD DS) on your network, you must have at least one DNS server on the network that supports the Service Location (SRV) resource record, such as the DNS Server service in Windows Server 2012.

When you install the AD DS role on a server running Windows Server 2012, the Active Directory Domain Services Installation Wizard checks for an appropriate DNS server, and offers to install one if none is available.

> **+ MORE INFORMATION**
>
> The SRV resource record was not part of the original DNS standards; it is a recent development. As a result, you might encounter DNS server implementations that do not support this record type. Before you deploy an AD DS network, be sure your DNS servers support RFC 2052, "A DNS RR for Specifying the Location of Services (DNS SRV)," published by the IETF.

Computers on the network running Windows 2000 and later versions use DNS to locate AD DS domain controllers. To support AD DS clients, the DNS server does not need to have a registered IP address or an Internet domain name.

For AD DS domain hosting, it is preferable to deploy your own DNS servers on the network. It is pointless to force your AD DS clients on the local network to send queries to a DNS server on the Internet, so they can locate a domain controller on the same local network as themselves. This action introduces an unnecessary delay into the already complex communications process, and also adds to the traffic on your Internet connection for no good reason.

Integrating DHCP and DNS

To resolve a DNS name into an IP address, the DNS server must have a resource record for that name, which contains the equivalent address. The original DNS specifications call for you to manually create the DNS resource records. Using DHCP complicates this process, however.

When computers lease their IP addresses from DHCP servers, the possibility exists for a particular computer's address to change. For example, a computer that is offline for some time might come back online after its lease expires, and the DHCP server, having given the computer's address to another client, might assign it a different address. However, a manually created DNS resource record still contains the old IP address, leading to name resolution errors.

To address this problem, the DNS server included in Windows Server 2012 is compliant with the RFC 2136 document, called *Dynamic Updates in the Domain Name System (DNS UPDATE)*. The dynamic update standard enables a DNS server to modify resource records at the request of DHCP servers and clients. Therefore, when a DHCP server assigns an address to a client, it can also send the appropriate commands to the DNS server, enabling it to create or update the resource records for the client. The dynamic update standard also enables AD DS domain controllers to create their own SRV resource records.

This relationship between the DNS and DHCP server services is another compelling reason to run your own DNS servers on your network.

Separating DNS Services

As discussed in the previous sections, the name resolution and Internet domain hosting functions are often better served by DNS servers that are external to the enterprise network, whereas organizations that use AD DS and DHCP typically require internal DNS servers.

In many cases, a network requires some or all of the DNS functions, and you must decide which ones you want to implement yourself and which you want to delegate.

It is possible to use a single DNS server to host both Internet and Active Directory domains, as well as to provide clients with name resolution services and DHCP support. However, just because you need all four services does not mean that you must compromise by choosing to deploy only internal or external DNS servers.

Because the services are independent from each other, you might consider splitting up the functions by using several DNS servers. For example, you can use your ISP's DNS servers for client name resolution, to conserve your network's Internet bandwidth, even if you run your own DNS servers for other purposes. You can also use a commercial service provider to host your Internet domain, while keeping your Active Directory domain hosting and dynamic update services internal.

> **+ MORE INFORMATION**
>
> The client computers on the network can only send their queries to a single DNS server, so you must use the server's configuration capabilities to delegate the various DNS functions among multiple servers. For example, a **forwarder** is a DNS server that receives queries from other DNS servers that are explicitly configured to send them. With Windows Server 2008 DNS servers, the forwarder requires no special configuration. However, you must configure the other DNS servers to send queries to the forwarder. By using a forwarder, you can configure all the clients on your network to use the local domain controller as a DNS server, and then have the domain controller forward Internet domain name resolution requests as recursive queries to the ISP's DNS server.

However, when you deploy your own DNS servers for any reason, you should always run at least two instances, to provide fault tolerance.

■ Creating Internet Domains

↓ THE BOTTOM LINE
Designing a DNS namespace for your organization's Internet presence is usually the easiest part of deploying DNS. Most organizations register a single second-level domain and use it to host all their Internet servers.

In most cases, the selection of a second-level domain name depends on what is available. A large portion of the most popular top-level domain, *com*, is already depleted, and you might find that the name you want to use is already taken. In this case, you have three alternatives:

- Choose a different domain name.
- Register the name in a different top-level domain.
- Attempt to purchase the domain name from its current owner.

If you still want to use the second-level domain name you have chosen, such as when the name is a recognizable brand of your organization, you should register the name in another top-level domain. Although the *org* and *net* domains are available to anyone, these domains are traditionally associated with non-profit and network infrastructure organizations, respectively, and might not fit your business. As an alternative, a number of countries around the world with attractive top-level domain names register second-level domains commercially.

> **+ MORE INFORMATION**
>
> You can find an extensive list of the Internet domain name registrars that the ICANN has accredited on its website,

Some organizations maintain multiple sites on the Internet, for various reasons. Your organization might be involved in several separate businesses that warrant individual treatment, or your company might have independent divisions with different sites. You might also create different sites for retail customers, wholesale customers, and providers. Whatever the reason, the following two basic ways can help you implement multiple sites on the Internet:

- **Register a single second-level domain name and then create multiple subdomains beneath it:** For the price of a single domain registration, you can create as many third-level domains as you need, and you can also maintain a single brand across all your sites. For example, a company called *Contoso Pharmaceuticals* might register the contoso.com domain, and then create separate websites for doctors and patients, in domains called *doctors.contoso.com* and *patients.contoso.com*.

- **Register multiple second-level domains:** If your organization consists of multiple, completely unrelated brands or operations, this is often the best solution. You must pay a separate registration fee for each domain name, however, and you must maintain a separate DNS namespace for each domain. A problem might also arise when you try to integrate your Internet domains with your internal network. You can select one of your second-level domains to integrate with your internal namespace, or you can leave your internal and external namespaces completely separate, as discussed later in this lesson.

■ Creating Internal Domains

↓ **THE BOTTOM LINE**   Using DNS on an internal Windows Server 2012 network is similar to using DNS on the Internet in many ways. You can create domains and subdomains to support the organizational hierarchy of your network in any way you want.

When you design a DNS namespace for a network that uses AD DS, the DNS domain name hierarchy is directly related to the directory service hierarchy. For example, if your organization consists of a headquarters and a series of branch offices, you might choose to create a single AD DS tree and assign the name *contoso.com* to the root domain in the tree. Then, for the branch offices, you create subdomains beneath contoso.com with names such as *seattle.contoso. com* and *pittsburgh.contoso.com*. These names correspond directly to the domain hierarchy in your DNS namespace.

When selecting names for your internal domains, you should observe the following rules:

- **Keep domain names short:** Internal DNS namespaces tend to run to more levels than Internet ones, and using long names for individual domains can result in excessively long FQDNs.

- **Avoid an excessive number of domain levels:** To keep FQDNs a manageable length and to keep administration costs down, limit your DNS namespace to no more than five levels from the root.

- **Create a naming convention and stick to it:** When creating subdomains, establish a rule that enables users to deduce what the name of a domain should be. For example, you can create subdomains based on political divisions, such as department names, or geographical divisions, such as names of cities, but do not mix the two at the same domain level.

- **Avoid obscure abbreviations:** Don't use abbreviations for domain names unless they are immediately recognizable by users. Domains using abbreviations such as NY for New York or HR for Human Resources are acceptable, but avoid creating your own cryptic abbreviations just to keep names short.

- **Avoid names that are difficult to spell:** Even though you might have established a domain-naming rule that calls for city names, a domain called *albuquerque.contoso.com* is impossible for most people (outside of New Mexico) to spell correctly the first time.

When you are designing an internal DNS namespace for a network that connects to the Internet, consider the following rules:

- **Use registered domain names:** Although using a domain name on an internal network that you have not registered is technically not a violation of Internet protocol, this practice can interfere with the client name resolution process on your internal network.

- **Do not use top-level domain names or names of commonly known products or companies:** Naming your internal domains using names found on the Internet can interfere with the name resolution process on your client computers. For example, if you create an internal domain called *microsoft.com*, you cannot predict whether a query for a name in that domain will be directed to your DNS server or to the authoritative servers for microsoft.com on the Internet.

- **Use only characters that are compliant with the Internet standard:** The DNS server included with Microsoft Windows Server 2012 supports the Unicode characters in UTF-8 format, but the RFC 1123 standard, "Requirements For Internet Hosts— Applications and Support," limits DNS names to uppercase characters (A–Z), lowercase characters (a–z), numerals (0–9), and the hyphen (-). You can configure the Windows Server 2012 DNS server to disallow the use of UTF-8 characters.

Creating Subdomains

Owning a registered second-level domain gives you the right to create any number of subdomains beneath that domain.

The primary reason for creating subdomains is to delegate administrative authority for parts of the namespace. For example, if your organization has offices in different cities, you might maintain a single DNS namespace, but grant the administrators at each site autonomous control over the DNS records for their computers. The best way to do this is to create a separate subdomain for each site, locate it on a DNS server at that site, and delegate authority for the server to local network support personnel. This procedure also balances the DNS traffic load among servers at different locations, preventing a bottleneck that can affect name resolution performance.

Combining Internal and External Domains

When you are designing a DNS namespace that includes both internal and external (that is, Internet) domains, you can use three possible strategies.

These strategies are as follows:

- **Use the same domain name internally and externally:** Using the same domain name for your internal and external namespaces is a practice that Microsoft strongly discourages. When you create an internal domain and an external domain with the same name, you make it possible for a computer in the internal network to have the same DNS name as a computer on the external network. This duplication wreaks havoc with the name resolution process.

TAKE NOTE * It is possible to make this arrangement work by copying all the zone data from your external DNS servers to your internal DNS servers, but the extra administrative difficulties make this a less than ideal solution.

- **Create separate and unrelated internal and external domains:** When you use different domain names for your internal and external networks, you eliminate the potential name resolution conflicts that come with using the same domain name for both networks. However, using this solution requires you to register (and pay for) two domain names and to maintain two separate DNS namespaces. The different domain names can also confuse users who need to distinguish between internal and external resources.

• **Make the internal domain a subdomain of the external domain:** To combine internal and external networks, Microsoft recommends registering a single Internet domain name and using it for external resources, and then creating a subdomain beneath that domain name and using it for your internal network. For example, if you register the name *contoso.com*, you use that domain for your external servers and create a subdomain, such as *int.contoso.com* for your internal network. If you need to create additional subdomains, you can create fourth-level domains beneath it for the internal network, and additional third-level domains beneath contoso for the external network, as shown in Figure 12-15. The advantages of this solution are that it makes it impossible to create duplicate FQDNs, and it lets you delegate authority across the internal and external domains, which simplifies the DNS administration process. In addition, you only need to register and pay for one Internet domain name.

Figure 12-15

Internal and external domain names

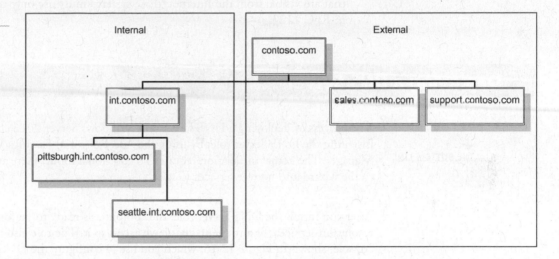

Creating Host Names

After you create the domain structure for your DNS namespace, you need to populate the domains with hosts. You should create hosts the same way you create domains, by devising a naming rule and then sticking to it. In many cases, host-naming rules are based on users, geographical locations, or the function of the computer.

For workstations, a common practice is to create host names from some variation on the user's name, such as a first initial followed by the user's surname. For example, the host name for Tony Madigan's computer might be *tmadigan*. Many organizations also use similar naming rules to create user account names and e-mail addresses. Following the same pattern for DNS host names enables users to keep track of only one name. For servers, the most common practice is to create host names describing the server's function or the department that uses it, such as *Mail1* or *Sales1*.

For whatever naming rules you use for your namespace, you should adhere to the following basic practices:

• **Create easily remembered names:** Users and administrators should be able to figure out the host name assigned to a particular computer using your naming rules alone.

• **Use unique names throughout the organization:** Although it is possible to create identical host names as long as they are located in different domains, this practice is strongly discouraged. You might need to move a computer and put it in a new domain that already has a host by that name, causing duplication that interferes with name resolution.

- **Do not use case to distinguish names:** Although you can use both uppercase and lowercase characters when creating a computer name on a computer running a Windows operating system, DNS itself is not case-sensitive. Therefore, you should not create host names that are identical except for the case of the letters, nor should you create host names that rely on case to be understandable.

- **Use only characters supported by all your DNS servers:** As with domain names, avoid using characters that are not compliant with the DNS standard, unless all the DNS servers processing the names support these characters. The NetBIOS namespace supports a larger character set than DNS does. When you are upgrading a Windows network that uses NetBIOS names to one that uses DNS names, you might use the Unicode (UTF-8) character support in the Windows Server 2012 DNS server to avoid having to rename all your computers. However, you must not do this on computers that are visible from the Internet; these systems must use only the character set specified in RFC 1123.

Deploying a DNS Server

THE BOTTOM LINE

The process of deploying a DNS server on a Windows Server 2012 computer is a matter of installing the DNS Server role, by using the Add Roles and Features Wizard in Server Manager. The actual installation requires no additional input; there are no additional pages in the wizard and no role services to select.

After you install the DNS Server role, the computer is ready to perform caching-only name resolution services for any clients that have access to it. The role also installs the DNS Manager console, shown in Figure 12-16, which you use to configure the DNS server's other capabilities. To configure the server to perform other services, consult the following sections.

Figure 12-16

The DNS Manager console

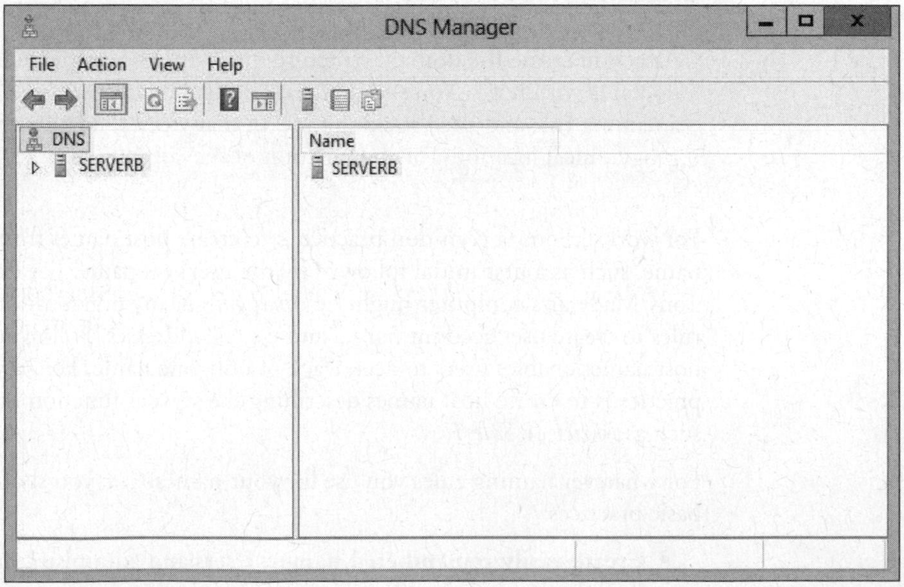

Creating Zones

A **zone** is an administrative entity you create on a DNS server to represent a discrete portion of the DNS namespace.

Administrators typically divide the DNS namespace into zones to store them on different servers and to delegate their administration to different people. Zones always consist of entire domains or subdomains. You can create a zone that contains multiple domains, as long as those domains are contiguous in the DNS namespace. For example, you can create a zone containing a parent domain and its child, because they are directly connected, but you cannot create a zone containing two child domains without their common parent, because the two children are not directly connected, as shown in Figure 12-17.

Figure 12-17

Valid zones must consist of contiguous domains

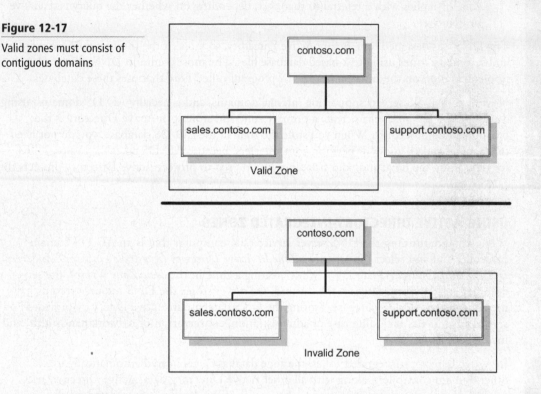

You can divide the DNS namespace into multiple zones and host them on a single DNS server, although there is usually no persuasive reason to do so. The DNS server in Windows Server 2012 can support as many as 200,000 zones on a single server, although it is hard to imagine a scenario that would require that many. In most cases, an administrator creates multiple zones on a server and then delegates most of them to other servers, which then become responsible for hosting them.

Every zone consists of a zone database, which contains the resource records for the domains in that zone. The DNS server in Windows Server 2012 supports three zone types, which specify where the server stores the zone database and what kind of information it contains. These zone types are as follows:

- **Primary zone:** creates a primary zone that contains the master copy of the zone database, where administrators make all changes to the zone's resource records. If the *Store The Zone In Active Directory (Available Only If DNS Server Is A Domain Controller)* check box is cleared, the server creates a primary master zone database file on the local drive. This is a simple text file that is compliant with most non-Windows DNS server implementations.

- **Secondary zone:** creates a duplicate of a primary zone on another server. The secondary zone contains a backup copy of the primary master zone database file, stored as an identical text file on the server's local drive. You cannot modify the resource records in a secondary zone manually; you can update them only by replicating the primary master zone database file, using a process called a *zone transfer*. You should always create at least one secondary zone for each file-based primary zone in your namespace, both to provide fault tolerance and to balance the DNS traffic load.

- **Stub zone:** creates a copy of a primary zone that contains the key resource records that identify the authoritative servers for the zone. The stub zone forwards or refers requests. When you create a stub zone, you configure it with the IP address of the server that hosts the zone from which you created the stub. When the server hosting the stub zone receives a query for a name in that zone, it either forwards the request to the host of the zone or replies with a referral to that host, depending on whether the query is recursive or iterative.

The DNS was designed long before Active Directory, so most of the Internet relies on primary and secondary zones using text-based database files. The most common DNS server implementation on the Internet is a UNIX program called *bind* that uses these databases.

However, for DNS servers supporting internal domains, and especially AD DS domains, using the Windows DNS server to create a primary zone and store it in Active Directory is the recommended procedure. When you store the zone in the AD DS database, you do not need to create secondary zones or perform zone transfers, because AD DS takes the responsibility for replicating the data, and your backup solution used to protect Active Directory protects the DNS data.

CERTIFICATION READY
Exam 70-410 covers only the process of creating a primary zone stored in Active Directory. The procedures for creating text-based primary and secondary zones and configuring zone transfers are covered in Exam 70-411, "Administering Windows Server 2012," on Objective 3.1, "Configure DNS zones."

USING ACTIVE DIRECTORY-INTEGRATED ZONES

When you are running the DNS server service on a computer that is an AD DS domain controller and you select the *Store The Zone In Active Directory (Available Only If DNS Server Is A Domain Controller)* check box while creating a zone in the *New Zone Wizard*, the server does not create a zone database file. Instead, the server stores the DNS resource records for the zone in the AD DS database. Storing the DNS database in Active Directory provides several advantages, including ease of administration, conservation of network bandwidth, and increased security.

CERTIFICATION READY
Configure Active Directory integration of primary zones.
Objective 4.3

In Active Directory-integrated zones, the zone database is replicated automatically to other domain controllers, along with all other Active Directory data. Active Directory uses a multiple master replication system so that copies of the database are updated on all domain controllers in the domain. You can modify the DNS resource records on any domain controller hosting a copy of the zone database, and Active Directory will update all of the other domain controllers automatically. You don't need to create secondary zones or manually configure zone transfers, because Active Directory performs all database replication activities.

By default, Windows Server 2012 replicates the database for a primary zone stored in Active Directory to all the other domain controllers running the DNS server in the AD DS domain where the primary is located. You can also modify the scope of zone database replication to keep copies on all domain controllers throughout the enterprise, or on all domain controllers in the AD DS domain, whether or not they are running the DNS server. You can also create a custom replication scope that copies the zone database to the domain controllers you specify.

Active Directory conserves network bandwidth by replicating only the DNS data that has changed since the last replication, and by compressing the data before transmitting it over the network. The zone replications also use the full security capabilities of Active Directory, which are considerably more robust than those of file-based zone transfers.

CREATING AN ACTIVE DIRECTORY ZONE

To create a new primary zone and store it in Active Directory, use the following procedure.

CREATE AN ACTIVE DIRECTORY ZONE

GET READY. Log on to Windows Server 2012 domain controller using an account with administrative privileges.

1. In the *Server Manager* window, click Tools > DNS. The *DNS Manager* console appears.

2. Expand the server node and select the Forward Lookup Zones folder.

3. Right-click the Forward Lookup Zones folder and, from the context menu, select New Zone. The *New Zone Wizard* appears.

4. Click Next to bypass the *Welcome* page. The *Zone Type* page appears, as shown in Figure 12-18.

Figure 12-18

The *Zone Type* page of the New Zone Wizard

> **New Zone Wizard**
>
> **Zone Type**
> The DNS server supports various types of zones and storage.
>
> Select the type of zone you want to create:
>
> ⦿ Primary zone
> Creates a copy of a zone that can be updated directly on this server.
>
> ◯ Secondary zone
> Creates a copy of a zone that exists on another server. This option helps balance the processing load of primary servers and provides fault tolerance.
>
> ◯ Stub zone
> Creates a copy of a zone containing only Name Server (NS), Start of Authority (SOA), and possibly glue Host (A) records. A server containing a stub zone is not authoritative for that zone.
>
> ☑ Store the zone in Active Directory (available only if DNS server is a writeable domain controller)
>
> [< Back] [Next >] [Cancel]

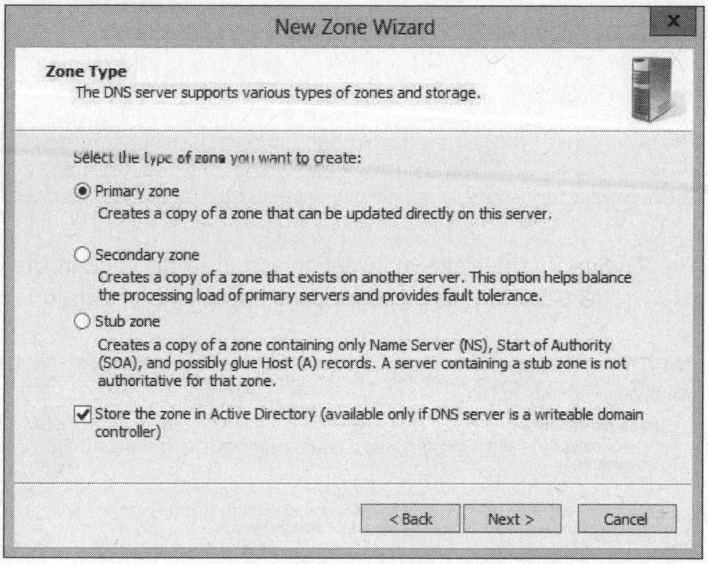

5. Leave the *Primary Zone* option and the *Store The Zone In Active Directory (Available Only If DNS Server Is A Domain Controller)* check box selected and click Next. The *Active Directory Zone Replication Scope* page appears, as shown in Figure 12-19.

Figure 12-19

The *Active Directory Zone Replication Scope* page of the New Zone Wizard

> **New Zone Wizard**
>
> **Active Directory Zone Replication Scope**
> You can select how you want DNS data replicated throughout your network.
>
> Select how you want zone data replicated:
>
> ◯ To all DNS servers running on domain controllers in this forest: adatum.local
>
> ⦿ To all DNS servers running on domain controllers in this domain: adatum.local
>
> ◯ To all domain controllers in this domain (for Windows 2000 compatibility): adatum.local
>
> ◯ To all domain controllers specified in the scope of this directory partition:
>
> [⌄]
>
> [< Back] [Next >] [Cancel]

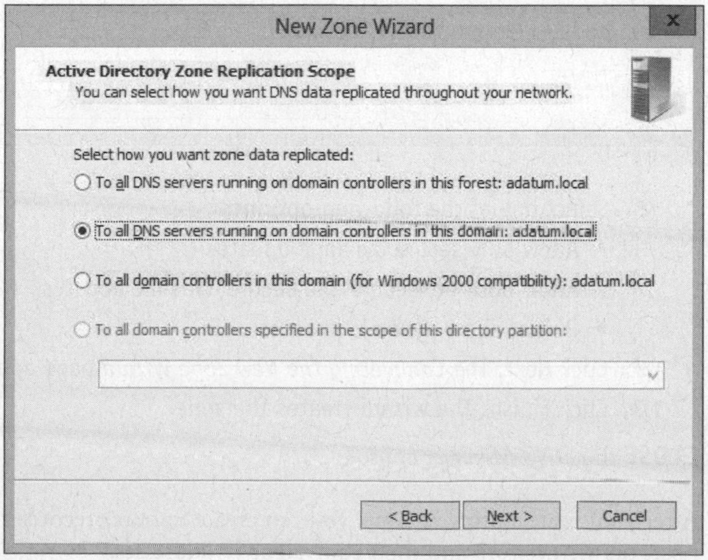

6. Click Next. The *Zone Name* page appears, as shown in Figure 12-20.

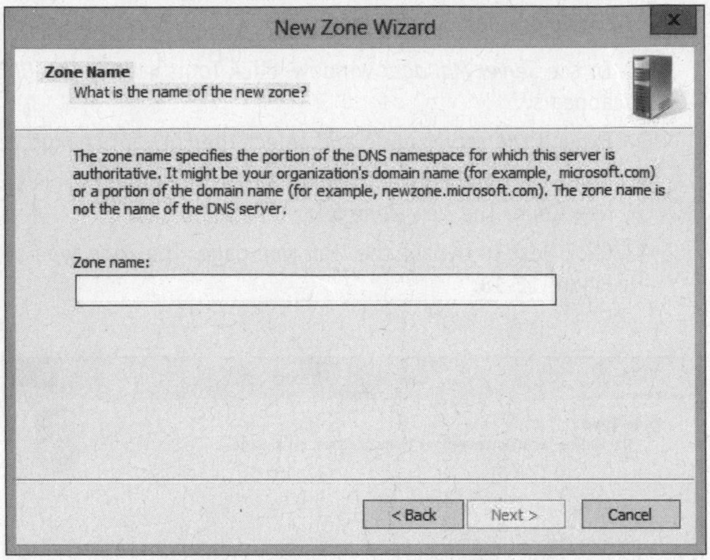

Figure 12-20

The *Zone Name* page of the New Zone Wizard

7. Specify the name you want to assign to the zone in the Zone Name text box and click Next. The *Dynamic Update* page appears, as shown in Figure 12-21.

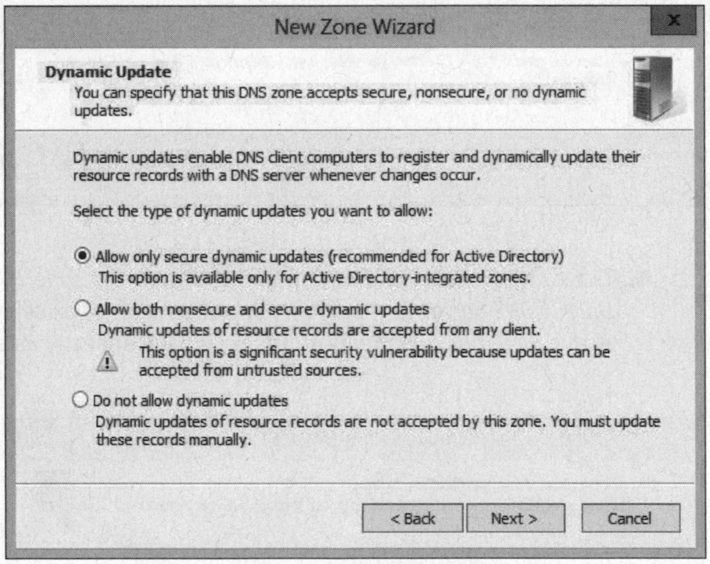

Figure 12-21

The *Dynamic Update* page of the New Zone Wizard

8. Select one of the following options:
  - Allow only secure dynamic updates
  - Allow both nonsecure and secure dynamic updates
  - Do not allow dynamic updates

9. Click Next. The *Completing the New Zone Wizard* page appears.

10. Click Finish. The wizard creates the zone.

CLOSE the *DNS Manager* console.

After you create a primary zone, you can create resource records that specify the names of the hosts on the network and their equivalent IP addresses.

Windows Server 2012 includes a new Windows PowerShell module that, for the first time, enables you to manage DNS servers from the command line without using elaborate Windows Management Information (WMI) scripts. After installing the DNS Server role using the `Install-WindowsFeatures` cmdlet, you can create a zone on the DNS server using the `Add-DnsServerPrimaryZone` cmdlet with the following basic syntax:

```
Add-DnsServerPrimaryZone -Name <name>
-ReplicationScope Forest|Domain|Legacy|Custom
[-DynamicUpdate None|Secure|NonSecureAndSecure]
```

For example, to create a zone called Paris in the adatum.com domain, you would use the following command:

```
Add-DnsServerPrimaryZone -Name Paris.adatum.com
-ReplicationScope Forest
```

Creating Resource Records

When you run your own DNS server, you create a resource record for each host name that you want to be accessible by the rest of the network.

There are several different types of resource records used by DNS servers, the most important of which are as follows:

- **SOA (Start of Authority):** indicates that the server is the best authoritative source for data concerning the zone. Each zone must have an SOA record, and only one SOA record can be in a zone.

- **NS (Name Server):** identifies a DNS server functioning as an authority for the zone. Each DNS server in the zone (whether primary master or secondary) must be represented by an NS record.

- **A (Address):** provides a name-to-address mapping that supplies an IPv4 address for a specific DNS name. This record type performs the primary function of the DNS, converting names to addresses.

- **AAAA (Address):** provides a name-to-address mapping that supplies an IPv6 address for a specific DNS name. This record type performs the primary function of the DNS, converting names to addresses.

- **PTR (Pointer):** provides an address-to-name mapping that supplies a DNS name for a specific address in the *in-addr.arpa* domain. This is the functional opposite of an A record, used for reverse lookups only.

- **CNAME (Canonical Name):** creates an alias that points to the *canonical* name (that is, the "real" name) of a host identified by an A record. Administrators use CNAME records to provide alternative names by which systems can be identified.

- **MX (Mail Exchanger):** identifies a system that directs e-mail traffic sent to an address in the domain to the individual recipient, a mail gateway, or another mail server.

To create a new Address resource record, use the following procedure.

→ CREATE AN ADDRESS RESOURCE RECORD

GET READY. Log on to Windows Server 2012 using an account with Administrative privileges.

1. In the *Server Manager* window, click Tools > DNS. The *DNS Manager* console appears.
2. Expand the server node and select the Forward Lookup Zones folder.
3. Right-click the zone in which you want to create the record and, from the context menu, select New Host (A or AAAA). The *New Host* dialog box appears, as shown in Figure 12-22.

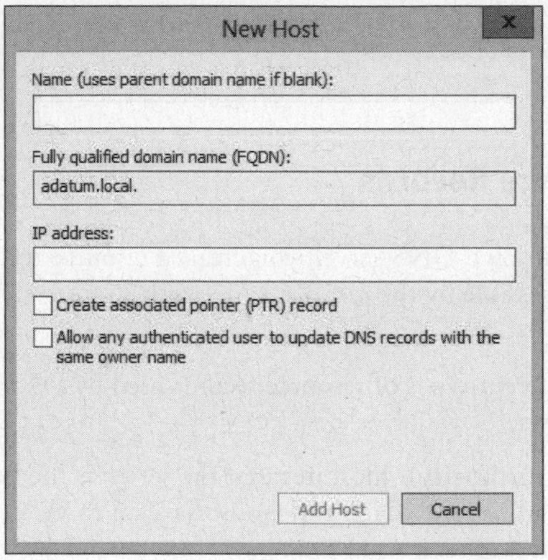

Figure 12-22

The New Host dialog box

4. In the Name text box, type the host name for the new record. The FQDN for the record appears.
5. In the IP address text box, type the IPv4 or IPv6 address associated with the host name.
6. Select the following check boxes, if necessary:
   - Create associated pointer (PTR) record creates a reverse name lookup record for the host in the in-addr.arpa domain
   - Allow any authenticated use to update DNS records with the same owner name enables users to modify their own resource records
7. Click Add Host. The new resource record is created in the zone you selected.

CLOSE the *DNS Manager* console.

USING WINDOWS POWERSHELL

To create an Address resource record with Windows PowerShell, you use the **Add-DnsServerResourceRecordA** cmdlet, using the following syntax:

```
Add-DnsServerResourceRecordA –Name <name>
–ZoneName <name> -IPv4Address <address>
```

For example, to create a resource record for a host called Client1, use the following command:

```
Add-DnsServerResourceRecordA –Name Client1
–ZoneName paris.adatum.com -IPv4Address 192.168.4.76
```

To create a PTR record for a new host, you can select the *Create associated pointer (PTR) record* check box in the *New Host* dialog box, but that will only be effective if a reverse lookup zone already exists on the server. To create the zone, you follow the same procedure described previously, but select the *Reverse Lookup Zones* folder. This causes the *New Zone Wizard* to add a *Reverse Lookup Zone Name* page like the one shown in Figure 12-23.

Figure 12-23

The *Reverse Lookup Zone Name* page in the New Zone Wizard

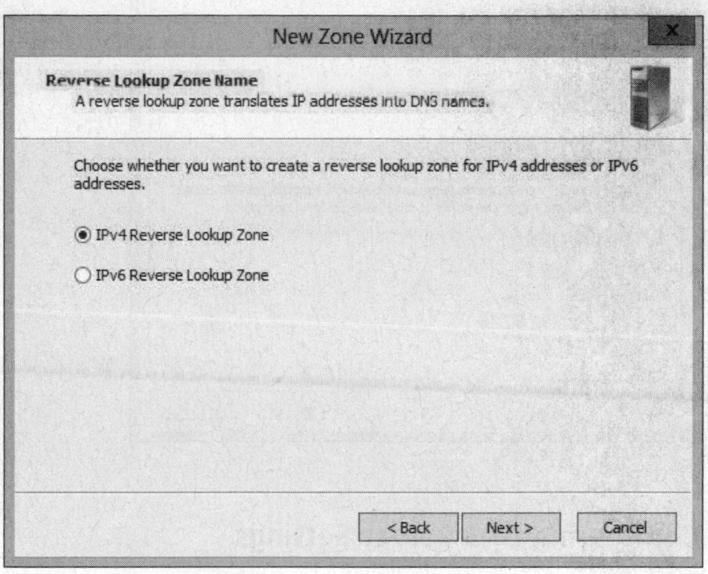

A second page then appears, as shown in Figure 12-24, in which you supply the Network ID that the wizard uses to create the zone.

Figure 12-24

The second *Reverse Lookup Zone Name* page in the New Zone Wizard

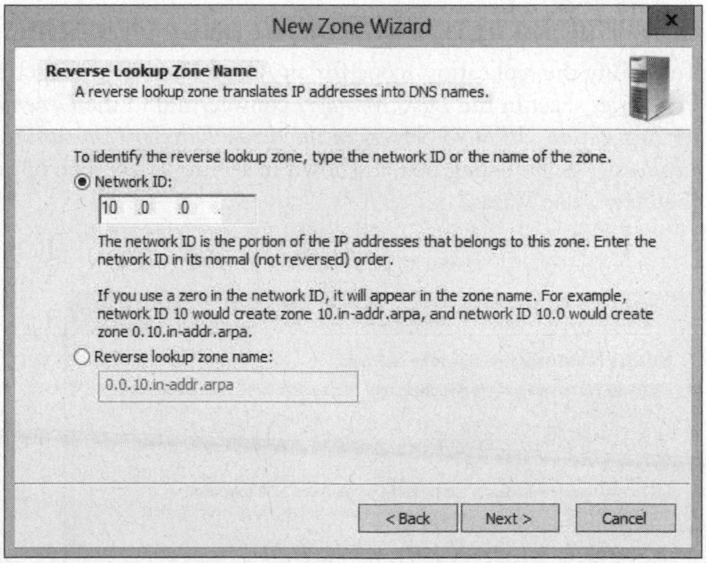

After the zone is created, you can either create PTR records along with A or AAAA records, or create a new PTR record by using the interface shown in Figure 12-25.

Figure 12-25

The New Resource Record
dialog box

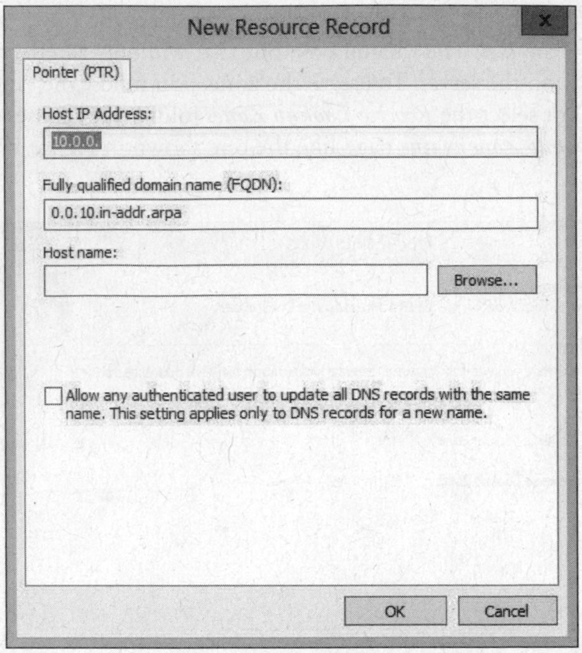

New Resource Record ✕

Pointer (PTR)

Host IP Address:

10.0.0.

Fully qualified domain name (FQDN):

0.0.10.in-addr.arpa

Host name:

Browse...

☐ Allow any authenticated user to update all DNS records with the same
name. This setting applies only to DNS records for a new name.

OK   Cancel

Configuring DNS Server Settings

> After you install a DNS server and create zones and resource records on it, you can alter
> settings to modify its behavior.

The following sections describe some of these settings.

CONFIGURING ACTIVE DIRECTORY DNS REPLICATION

To modify the replication scope for an Active Directory-integrated zone, open the zone's
Properties sheet in the *DNS Manager* console, and in the *General* tab, click the *Change button
for Replication: All DNS Servers In the Active Directory Domain* to display the *Change Zone
Replication Scope* dialog box, as shown in Figure 12-26. The options are the same as those in
the New Zone Wizard.

Figure 12-26

The *Change Zone Replication
Scope* dialog box

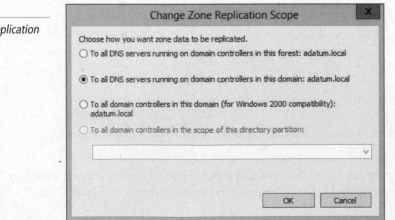

Change Zone Replication Scope ✕

Choose how you want zone data to be replicated.

○ To all DNS servers running on domain controllers in this forest: adatum.local

◉ To all DNS servers running on domain controllers in this domain: adatum.local

○ To all domain controllers in this domain (for Windows 2000 compatibility):
adatum.local

○ To all domain controllers in the scope of this directory partition:

⌄

OK   Cancel

CONFIGURING ROOT HINTS

Every DNS server must be able to contact the root name servers to initiate name resolution processes. Most server implementations, including Microsoft DNS Server, are preconfigured with the names and addresses of multiple root name servers. These are called *root hints.*

CERTIFICATION READY
Configure Root Hints.
Objective 4.3

The 13 root name server names are located in a domain called *root-servers.net*, and are named using letters of the alphabet. The servers are scattered around the world on different subnets, to provide fault tolerance.

To modify the root hints on a Windows Server 2012 DNS server, right-click the server node, open the Properties sheet, and click the *Root Hints* tab, as shown in Figure 12-27. On this tab, you can add, edit, or remove root hints from the list provided.

Figure 12-27

The Root Hints tab on a DNS server's Properties sheet

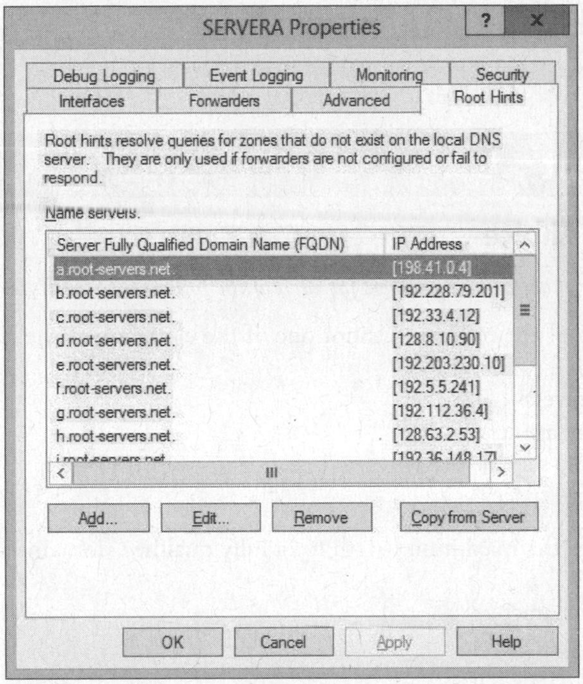

SKILL SUMMARY

In this lesson, you learned:

- TCP/IP networks today use DNS servers to convert host names into IP addresses. This conversion process is referred to as *name resolution*.
- The DNS consists of three elements: the DNS namespace, which takes the form of a tree structure and consists of domains, containing resource records that contain host names, IP addresses, and other information; name servers, which are applications running on server computers that maintains information about the domain tree structure; and resolvers, which are client programs that generate DNS queries and send them to DNS servers for fulfillment.
- The hierarchical nature of the DNS namespace makes it possible for any DNS server on the Internet to locate the authoritative source for any domain name, using a minimum number of queries. This efficiency results from the fact that the domains at each level of the hierarchy are responsible for maintaining information about the domains at the next lower level.

(continued)

- In a recursive query, the DNS server receiving the name resolution request takes full responsibility for resolving the name. In an iterative query, the server that receives the name resolution request immediately responds with the best information it possesses at the time.

- For Internet name resolution purposes, the only functions required of the DNS server are the capability to process incoming queries from resolvers and send its own queries to other DNS servers on the Internet. A DNS server that performs only these functions is known as a *caching-only server*, because it is not the authoritative source for any domain and hosts no resource records of its own.

Knowledge Assessment

Multiple Choice

Select one or more correct answers for each of the following questions.

1. Which of the following is not one of the elements of the Domain Name System (DNS)?
   a. resolvers
   b. relay agents
   c. name servers
   d. name space

2. What is the maximum length for a fully qualified domain name, including the trailing period?
   a. 50 characters
   b. 63 characters
   c. 255 characters
   d. 255 characters for each individual domain name

3. Which of the following would be the correct FQDN for a resource record in a reverse lookup zone if the computer's IP address is 10.75.143.88?
   a. 88.143.75.10.in-addr.arpa
   b. 10.75.143.88. in-addr.arpa
   c. in-addr.arpa.88.143.75.10
   d. arpa.in-addr. 10.75.143.88

4. Which of the following are types of zone transfers supported by the DNS server in Windows Server 2012?
   a. network zone transfers
   b. full zone transfers
   c. incremental zone transfers
   d. partial zone transfers

5. In the fully qualified domain name www.sales.contoso.com, which of the following is the second-level domain?
   a. www
   b. sales
   c. contoso
   d. com

6. This DNS configuration item will forward DNS queries to different servers based on the domain name of the query.
   a. Iterative forwarder
   b. Recursive forwarder
   c. Conditional forwarder
   d. IPv6 forwarder

7. The IPv6 DNS host record is referred to as a(n):
   a. A record
   b. AA record
   c. AAA record
   d. AAAA record

8. A DNS server that hosts a primary or secondary zone containing a particular record can issue the following response to a query for that record:
   a. Authoritative answer
   b. Non-authoritative answer
   c. Referral answer
   d. Non-referral answer

9. Data from a primary zone is transmitted to secondary zones using the following:
   a. Zone transfer
   b. Zone transmission
   c. DNS Zone
   d. Active Directory replication

10. The following feature is available only on Active Directory-integrated DNS zones:
    a. Dynamic updates
    b. Incremental zone transfers
    c. Reverse lookup zones
    d. Secure dynamic updates

Best Answer

Choose the letter that corresponds to the best answer. More than one answer choice may achieve the goal. Select the BEST answer.

1. What client applications utilize Domain Name System (DNS) to resolve host names into IP addresses?
   a. Client web browsers, or any application that uses HyperText Transfer Protocol (HTTP) use DNS to resolve host names into IP addresses.
   b. All Internet applications working with host names must use DNS to resolve host names into IP addresses.
   c. Any application on a system that has connectivity to the Internet use DNS to resolve host names into IP addresses.
   d. DNS does not resolve host names into IP addresses.

2. What is the primary purpose of name caching?
   a. Name caching saves extraordinary amount of time for the user.
   b. Name caching greatly reduces traffic on the company network.
   c. Name caching validates why you should deploy caching-only servers.
   d. Name caching enables the second name resolution request for the same name to bypass the referral process.

3. What are the dangerous consequences of a poorly chosen Time To Live (TTL)?
   a. Specifying a TTL that is too long can greatly increase traffic, especially to the root name and top-level domain servers.
   b. Specifying a TTL that is too long can delay referrals from being propagated.
   c. Specifying a TTL that is too short can overburden root name and top-level domain servers with requests.
   d. Specifying a TTL that is too short can cause incorrectly cached information to remain before changes get recorded.

4. What is the primary benefit of a DNS forwarder?
   a. Exchanging iterative queries for recursive queries across the network perimeter
   b. Reducing the traffic and making efficient use of available bandwidth across the network perimeter
   c. Making the most of iterative queries to other DNS servers
   d. Reducing the burden on the Internet's root name servers

5. What are some best practices when creating internal DNS namespaces.
   a. Avoid an excessive number of domain levels.
   b. Keep domain names full and descriptive; avoid concise subdomains.
   c. Place less importance on a convention compared to spelling.
   d. Never abbreviate.

Build a List

1. You type a web address in your web browser. Order the steps that describe the Internet name resolution process for the web address.
   a. Client's DNS server, with the top-level domain server address, generates a new iterative query and sends it to the top-level domain server. The top-level domain server responds with a referral to the second-level domain server.
   b. Client's DNS server checks its own records for the authoritative source for the zone containing the web address. Because it does not, the DNS server generates an iterative query and sends it to one of the root servers. Root server responds with a referral to the top-level domain server address.
   c. Client system sends a recursive query message with the web address to the DNS server as specified in the system's TCP/IP configuration.
   d. Client's DNS generates another iterative query and transmits it to the second-level domain server. Assuming the second-level server is the authoritative server for the zone containing the web address, it consults its records to determine the IP address of the requested system and messages it back to the client's DNS server.
   e. Client's DNS receives the reply from the authoritative server and transmits the IP address back to the client. The client's web browser now knows the IP address of the web server.

2. Order the steps to configure a DNS forwarder.
   a. In the Server Manager window, click Tools > DNS. The DNS Manager console appears.
   b. Click the Forwarders tab. Click Edit. The Edit Forwarders dialog box appears.
   c. Type the name or address of the DNS server you want to function as a forwarder and press Enter. The system validates the name or address by connecting to the DNS server.
   d. Right-click the server node and, from the context menu, select Properties. The server's Properties sheet appears.
   e. Click OK to close the Edit Forwarders dialog box and add the servers to the Forwarders tab. Click OK to close the server's Properties sheet. Close the DNS Manager console.

3. Order the steps to create an Active Directory zone.

    a. Specify the name you want to assign to the zone in the Zone Name text box and click Next. The Dynamic Update page appears.

    b. Expand the server node and select the Forward Lookup Zones folder.

    c. Right-click the Forward Lookup Zones folder and, from the context menu, select New Zone. The New Zone Wizard appears. Click Next to bypass the Welcome page. The Zone Type page appears.

    d. Leave the Primary Zone option and the Store The Zone In Active Directory (Available Only If DNS Server Is A Domain Controller) check box selected and click Next. The Active Directory Zone Replication Scope page appears. Click Next. The Zone Name page appears.

    e. In the Server Manager window, click Tools > DNS. The DNS Manager console appears.

    f. Select one of the following options: Allow only secure dynamic updates, Allow both nonsecure and secure dynamic updates, or Do not allow dynamic updates. Click Finish. Close the DNS Manager console.

■ Business Case Scenarios

Scenario 12-1: Deploying DNS Servers

Harold is a freelance networking consultant who has designed a network for a small company with a single location. The owner of the company wants to use an Active Directory domain, so Harold installs a Windows Server 2012 domain controller with the Active Directory Domain Services and DNS Server roles. Harold also uses DHCP to configure all of the workstations on the network to use the DNS services provided by the domain controller.

Soon after the installation, however, the owner of the company reports extremely slow Internet performance. After examining the traffic passing over the Internet connection, you determine that it is being flooded with DNS traffic. What can you do to reduce the amount of DNS traffic passing over the internet connection?

Scenario 12-2: Regulating DNS Traffic

Ralph is an enterprise administrator for Wingtip Toys, which has recently expanded its customer service division by adding 100 workstations. All of the workstations on the company network are configured to use a server on the perimeter network as their primary DNS server and a server on their ISP's network as a secondary. As a result of the expansion, Internet performance has slowed down perceptibly, and a Network Monitor trace indicates that there is a disproportionate amount of DNS traffic on the link between the perimeter network and the ISP's network. What are two ways that Ralph can reduce the amount of DNS traffic passing over the Internet connection?

Installing Domain Controllers

70-410 EXAM OBJECTIVE

Objective 5.1 – Install domain controllers. This objective may include but is not limited to: Add or remove a domain controller from a domain; upgrade a domain controller; install Active Directory Domain Services (AD DS) on a Server Core installation; install a domain controller from Install from Media (IFM); resolve DNS SRV record registration issues; configure a global catalog server.

LESSON HEADING	EXAM OBJECTIVE
Introducing Active Directory	
Understanding Active Directory Functions	
Understanding Active Directory Architecture	
Understanding Active Directory Communications	
Deploying Active Directory Domain Services	
Installing the Active Directory Domain Services Role	
Creating a New Forest	
Adding a Domain Controller to an Existing Domain	Add or remove a domain controller from a domain
Creating a New Child Domain in a Forest	
Installing AD DS on Server Core	Install Active Directory Domain Services (AD DS) on a Server Core installation
Using Install from Media (IFM)	Install a domain controller from Install from Media (IFM)
Upgrading Active Directory Domain Services	Upgrade a domain controller
Removing a Domain Controller	Add or remove a domain controller from a domain
Configuring the Global Catalog	Configure a global catalog server
Troubleshooting DNS SRV Registration Failure	Resolve DNS SRV record registration issues

KEY TERMS

Active Directory Domain Services (AD DS)

attributes

authentication

authorization

container object

Directory Access Protocol (DAP)

directory schema

domain

domain controller

domain tree

forest

forest root domain

global catalog

leaf object

Lightweight Directory Access Protocol (LDAP)

multiple-master replication

organizational unit (OU)

Read-Only Domain Controller (RODC)

single-master replication

site

■ Introducing Active Directory

THE BOTTOM LINE

A directory service is a repository of information about the resources—hardware, software, and human—connected to a network. Users, computers, and applications throughout the network can access the repository for various purposes, including user authentication, storage of configuration data, and even simple white pages–style information lookups. *Active Directory Domain Services (AD DS)* is the directory service that Microsoft first introduced in Windows 2000 Server and has upgraded in each successive server operating system release, including Windows Server 2012.

AD DS is a directory service that enables you to create organizational divisions called domains. A *domain* is a logical container of network components, hosted by at least one server designated as a *domain controller*. The domain controllers for each domain replicate their data among themselves for fault tolerance and load-balancing purposes.

Understanding Active Directory Functions

In addition to making services and resources available, the primary functions of Active Directory Domain Services are to provide authentication and authorization services for hardware and software resources on the network.

Simply put, *authentication* is the process of verifying a user's identity; *authorization* is the process of granting users access only to the resources they are permitted to use. Users joined to an AD DS domain can log on to the domain, as opposed to an individual computer or application, and can access any resources in that domain for which administrators have granted them the proper permissions. Without AD DS, users must have separate accounts on every computer they access, which results in problems creating and maintaining the accounts, synchronizing passwords, and performing multiple logons.

When a user logs on to an Active Directory domain, the client computer performs an elaborate authentication procedure that involves locating the nearest domain controller and exchanging a series of messages using Kerberos, a complex security protocol. In most cases, users authenticate themselves by supplying a password, but AD DS can also use smart cards and biometrics (such as fingerprint scans) to verify a user's identity.

After the authentication process is completed (and assuming it is successful), an Active Directory authorization process occurs whenever the user attempts to access a network resource. Network administrators grant users access to resources by assigning them permissions using their Active Directory user objects. No transactions between clients and protected resources involve a transaction using a domain controller as a third party. The design of an AD DS infrastructure, therefore, calls for the distribution of domain controllers around the network so that all clients have ready access to them.

Understanding Active Directory Architecture

Active Directory is a hierarchical directory service, based on the domain, that is scalable in both directions.

In AD DS, you can subdivide a domain into organizational units and populate it with objects. You can also create multiple domains and group them into sites, trees, and forests. As a result, AD DS provides a highly flexible architecture that can accommodate the smallest and the largest organizations, as well as provide various design options.

The following sections examine the components you can use to design and build an Active Directory structure.

UNDERSTANDING OBJECTS AND ATTRIBUTES

An AD DS domain is a hierarchical structure that takes the form of a tree, much like a file system. The domain consists of objects, each of which represents a logical or physical resource. Objects come in two basic classes: container objects and leaf objects. A *container object* can have other objects subordinate to it, whereas a *leaf object* cannot have subordinate objects. The container objects essentially form the branches of the tree, with the leaf objects growing on the branches.

The domain itself is a container object, as are the organizational unit objects within the domain. Leaf objects can represent users, computers, groups, applications, and other resources on the network.

Every object consists of *attributes*, which store information about the object. A container object has, as one of its attributes, a list of all the other objects it contains. Leaf objects have attributes that contain information about the specific resource the object represents. Some attributes are created automatically, such as the globally unique identifier (GUID) that the domain controller assigns to each object when it creates it, whereas you must supply information for other attributes manually.

For example, a user object can have attributes that specify the user's name, address, telephone number, and other identifying information. This enables AD DS to function as a directory in the purest sense of the word, much like a telephone book. When you open a user object in the Active Directory Users and Computers console, you can see many of its attributes in its Properties sheet, as shown in Figure 13-1.

Different object types have different sets of attributes, depending on their functions. The attributes each type of object can possess (both required and optional), the type of data that each attribute can store, and the object's place in the directory tree are all defined in the *directory schema*. The AD DS schema elements are extensible, enabling applications to add their own object types to the directory or add attributes to existing object types. For example, when you install Microsoft Exchange on an AD DS network, the application alters the directory schema to add its own attributes to the user object type. When you open a user's Properties sheet after the Exchange installation, you see additional tabs containing the Exchange attributes.

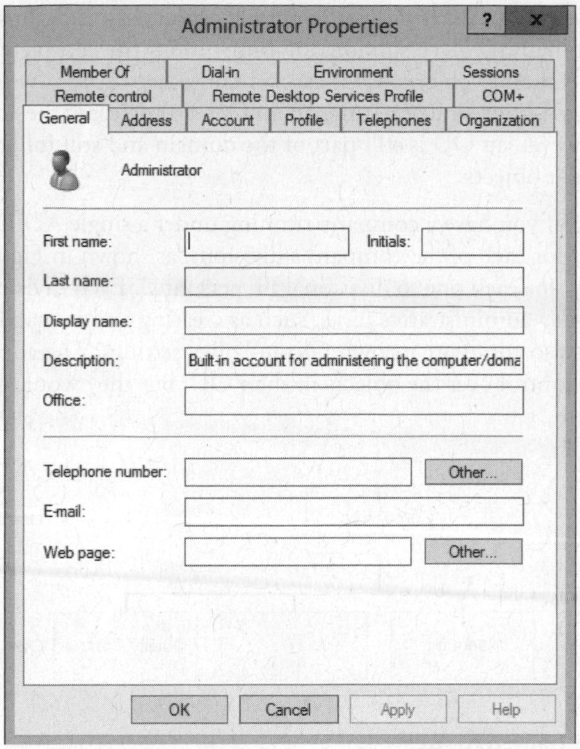

Figure 13-1

The attributes of a user object, as displayed in its Properties sheet

The hierarchical structure of container and leaf objects used in an AD DS domain, and the design and composition of the individual objects themselves, are based on a standard called X.500, which was developed by the International Telecommunications Union (ITU) in the late 1980s.

TAKE NOTE*

UNDERSTANDING DOMAINS

As mentioned earlier, the domain is the fundamental component of the Active Directory architecture. You can zoom into a domain and create a hierarchy within it, and you can zoom out and create a hierarchy out of multiple domains. In AD DS, domains function by default as the boundaries for virtually all directory functions, including administration, access control, database management, and replication. You begin the process of designing an Active Directory infrastructure by deciding what domains to create, and you begin deploying AD DS by creating your first domain.

Domains are not security boundaries, in the strict sense of the term. Although users in one domain cannot access the resources of another domain unless they receive explicit permissions to do so, domains are not completely isolated from one another. You can perform tasks in one domain that affect all other domains in the forest. To completely isolate one domain from another, you must create them in different forests. Therefore, the forest functions as the security boundary, not the domain.

TAKE NOTE*

ZOOMING IN: ORGANIZATIONAL UNITS

As mentioned earlier, the domain is still the fundamental division in the Active Directory service. However, the extreme scalability that AD DS provides can result in domains containing many thousands of objects. When domains grow this large, dividing the security and administrative responsibility for the domain among several divisions or departments can become necessary. To make this possible, you can create objects within a domain called organizational units.

An *organizational unit (OU)* is a container object that functions in a subordinate capacity to a domain, something like a subdomain, but without the complete separation of security policies. As container objects, OUs can contain other OUs, as well as leaf objects. You can apply separate Group Policy settings to an OU and delegate the administration of an OU as needed. However, an OU is still part of the domain and still inherits policies and permissions from its parent objects.

For example, if you have a company running under a single AD DS domain, you can create a separate OU for each of the company's divisions, as shown in Figure 13-2, and delegate the responsibility for each one to divisional IT personnel. Each division could then perform its own day-to-day administrative tasks, such as creating and managing user objects, and each division can also configure its own Group Policy settings. The administrators for each division would have control over the objects in their OU, but they would have limited access to the rest of the domain.

Figure 13-2

Organizational units subordinate to a domain

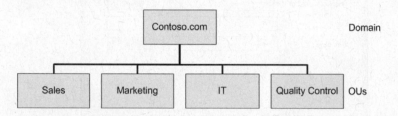

ZOOMING IN: GROUPS

Group objects are not containers, as OUs are, but they perform a similar function, with important differences. Groups are not full-fledged security divisions, as OUs are; you cannot apply Group Policy settings to a group object directly. However, group members—which can be leaf objects, such as users or computers, as well as other groups—inherit permissions assigned to that group.

> **+ MORE INFORMATION**
>
> Although you cannot link Group Policy Objects (GPOs) directly to a group, as you can to an OU, you can use a technique called *security filtering* to restrict the application of a GPO's settings to members of a specific group. For more information on using groups, see Objective 5.3, "Create and Manage Active Directory Groups and Organizational Units (OUs)," in Lesson 15.

One of the most important differences between groups and OUs is that group memberships are independent of the domain's tree structure. A group can have members located anywhere in the domain and, in some cases, can have members from other domains.

For example, you might design a domain with OUs representing the various divisions in your organization. Therefore, each division can have its own Group Policy settings and permissions propagated through the domain tree structure. However, you might want to assign certain special permissions to the director in charge of each division. You can do this by creating a group object and adding the directors' user objects as members of the group. This prevents you from having to assign permissions to each director individually.

ZOOMING OUT: DOMAIN TREES

When designing an AD DS infrastructure, you might, in some cases, want to create multiple domains. Active Directory scales upward from the domain, just as easily as it scales downward.

Active Directory uses the Domain Name System (DNS) naming conventions for its domains. You can create an Active Directory domain using the registered domain name you use on the Internet, or you can create an internal domain name, without registering it.

When you create your first domain on an Active Directory network, you are, in essence, creating the root of a ***domain tree***. You can populate the tree with additional domains as long as they are part of the same contiguous namespace (see Figure 13-3). For example, you might create a root domain called *contoso.com*, and then create additional subdomains for each of the organization's branch offices, with names such as *baltimore.contoso.com* and *dallas.contoso.com*. These subdomains are said to be part of the same tree as *contoso.com* because they use the same top- and second-level domain names.

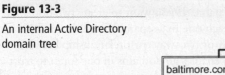

Figure 13-3

An internal Active Directory domain tree

If you are using a registered Internet domain name, you can use it as a parent and create a child, or subdomain, for internal use, such as *int.contoso.com*, and then create another level of child domains beneath that for the branch offices (see Figure 13-4).

Figure 13-4

An Active Directory domain tree using an Internet domain name

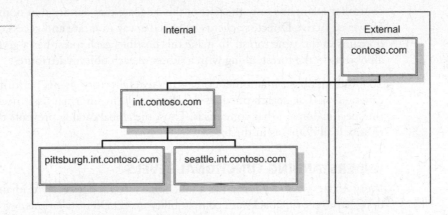

You can add as many domains to the tree as you need, using any number of levels, as long as you conform to the DNS naming limitations, which call for a maximum of 63 characters per domain name and 255 characters for the fully qualified domain name (FQDN).

Each domain in a tree is a separate security entity. Each has its own separate Group Policy settings, permissions, and user accounts. However, unlike OUs, subdomains in a tree do not inherit permissions and policies from their parent domains. Domains in the same tree do have bidirectional trust relationships between them, though, which Active Directory creates automatically when you create each subdomain. These trust relationships mean that an administrator of a particular domain can grant any user in the tree access to that domain's resources. As a result, you do not need to create duplicate user objects, just because an individual needs access to resources in a different domain.

ZOOMING OUT: FORESTS

An organization might want to use multiple domains that cannot be part of the same tree, because they are not contiguous. For example, a single corporation might run two operations out of the same facilities, each with its own Internet domain name, such as *contoso.com* and *adatum.com*. You can create two separate Active Directory domains using these two names, but they cannot be parts of the same tree, because one is not subordinate to the other. You can, however, create two separate domain trees and join them together in a parent structure called a ***forest***.

An Active Directory forest consists of one or more separate domain trees, which have the same two-way trust relationships between them as two domains in the same tree. When you create the first domain on an Active Directory network, you are in fact creating a new forest, and that first domain becomes the **forest root domain**. Therefore, if you create the *contoso.com* domain first, that domain becomes the root of the *contoso.com* forest. When you create the *adatum.com* domain in the same forest, it retains its status as a separate domain in a separate tree, but it is still considered part of the *contoso.com* forest.

It is important to understand that separate trees in the same forest still have trust relationships between them, even though they do not share a domain name. If you want to create two domains completely separate from one another, you must create each one in a separate forest. Even if this is the case, however, you can still manually create a one-way or two-way trust relationship between domains in different forests, or even a forest trust, which enables all domains in one forest to trust all domains in the other. In fact, trusts between domains in different forests must be explicitly created manually, unlike those between subdomains in the same tree. If, for example, two companies with separate Active Directory forests should merge, it is possible for administrators to establish a trust relationship between the two, rather than redesign the entire infrastructure.

INTRODUCING THE GLOBAL CATALOG

Domains also function as the hierarchical boundaries for the AD DS database. A domain controller maintains only the part of the database that defines that domain and its objects. However, Active Directory clients still need a way to locate and access the resources of other domains in the same forest. To make this possible, each forest has a **global catalog**, which lists all objects in the forest, along with a subset of each object's attributes.

To locate an object in another domain, Active Directory clients perform a search of the global catalog first. This search provides the client with the information it needs to find the object in the specific domain that contains it. Thus, the global catalog prevents the client from having to search all domains in the forest.

UNDERSTANDING FUNCTIONAL LEVELS

Every Active Directory forest has a functional level, as does every domain. Functional levels are designed to provide backward compatibility in AD DS installations, with domain controllers running various versions of the Windows Server operating system. Each successive version of Windows Server includes new Active Directory features that are not directly compatible with previous versions. By selecting the functional level representing the oldest Windows version running on your domain controllers, you disable these new features, so that the various domain controllers can interoperate properly. After you have all the domain controllers running the latest version of Windows, you can raise the functional levels to activate the latest features.

To raise the forest functional level or domain functional level, you can use Active Directory Administrative Center or the *Raise Domain* (or *Forest*) *Functional Level* dialog box, as shown in Figure 13-5, in the *Active Directory Domains and Trusts* console. As soon as you raise the functional level of a forest or a domain, you cannot lower it again.

Figure 13-5

Raising functional levels

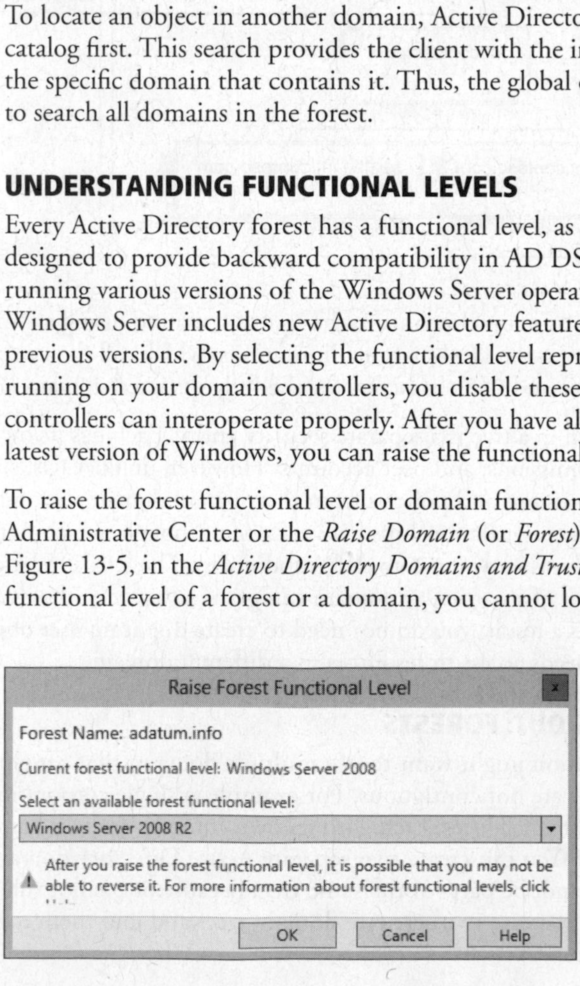

Raise Forest Functional Level

Forest Name: adatum.info

Current forest functional level: Windows Server 2008

Select an available forest functional level:

Windows Server 2008 R2

⚠ After you raise the forest functional level, it is possible that you may not be able to reverse it. For more information about forest functional levels, click Help.

OK   Cancel   Help

Understanding Active Directory Communications

> Active Directory services are implemented in the network's domain controllers. Each domain controller hosts one (and only one) domain, storing the domain's objects in a database. AD DS clients—that is, users and computers that are members of a domain—access the domain controller frequently as they log on to the domain and access domain resources.

Each domain on an AD DS network should have at least two domain controllers to ensure that clients have the Active Directory database available at all times, and to provide clients with ready access to a nearby domain controller. How many domain controllers you install for each of your domains, and where you locate them, is an important part of designing an Active Directory infrastructure. Also important is an understanding of how and why the domain controllers communicate—with each other and with clients.

If a domain has only one domain controller and it fails, you must restore the Active Directory database from a recent backup. When a single domain has two or more domain controllers, you can repair or replace a failed domain controller, and it automatically replicates the database from the other domain controller.

INTRODUCING LDAP

The original X.500 directory service standard calls for the use of *Directory Access Protocol (DAP)*, a highly complex communications protocol that includes many features, requires a great deal of work from the directory service client, and is based on the Open Systems Interconnection (OSI) protocol stack. Today, the OSI stack remains a purely theoretical construct, as the Internet and Windows networks are all based on TCP/IP (Transmission Control Protocol/Internet Protocol) instead.

To avoid the use of DAP and the OSI stack, a team at the University of Michigan worked throughout the 1990s to develop a more practical communications protocol for use with X.500 directory services. This team created a series of standards, published as Requests For Comments (RFCs) by the Internet Engineering Task Force (IETF), which defines the *Lightweight Directory Access Protocol (LDAP)*. RFC 2251, "Lightweight Directory Access Protocol (v3)," published in December 1997, has become the standard communications protocol for directory service products, including Active Directory.

LDAP defines the format of the queries that Active Directory clients send to domain controllers, as well as provides a compound naming structure for uniquely identifying objects in the directory.

UNDERSTANDING REPLICATION

When a domain has two or more domain controllers, each controller must have a database that is identical to those of the others. To stay synchronized, the domain controllers communicate by sending database information to each other, a process called *replication*. Replication comes in two basic types. In *single-master replication*, a single primary system replicates the contents of its database to one or more secondary systems on the network. In this model (see Figure 13-6), replication traffic moves in only one direction—from the primary to the secondaries—so it is possible to modify the database only on the primary system.

Figure 13-6

Single-master replication

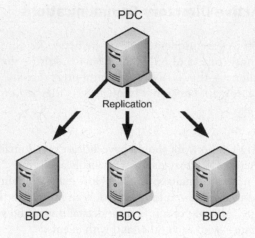

Single-master replication can make managing the database difficult, especially if administrators are located in remote offices and must work over a slow wide-area network (WAN) link. To avoid this problem, Active Directory uses ***multiple-master replication***, in which you can make changes to domain objects on any domain controller, which replicates those changes to all the other domain controllers, as shown in Figure 13-7.

Figure 13-7

Multiple-master replication

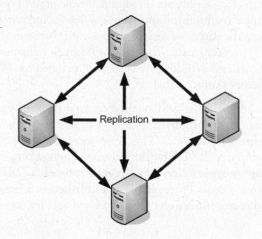

Multiple-master replication is much more complicated than single-master replication, because two administrators can be working on the same object at the same time, using the databases on two different domain controllers. The replication messages exchanged by the domain controllers include timestamps and other transaction identifiers that enable each computer to determine which version of an object is the latest and most relevant. This is why accurate timekeeping is essential on Active Directory networks.

USING READ-ONLY DOMAIN CONTROLLERS

One Active Directory feature introduced in Windows Server 2008 is the ability to create a ***Read-Only Domain Controller (RODC),*** a domain controller that supports only incoming replication traffic. As a result, you cannot create, modify, or delete Active Directory objects via the RODC.

RODCs are used in locations that require a domain controller but have less stringent physical security or have no administrators who need read/write access to the Active Directory database. To install an RODC, the domain must have at least one other domain controller running Windows Server 2008 or later.

EXPANDING OUTWARD: SITES

To facilitate the replication process, Active Directory includes another administrative division called the site. A *site* is defined as a collection of subnets that have good connectivity between them. Good connectivity is understood to be at least T-1 speed (1.544 megabits per second). Generally speaking, this means that a site consists of all the local area networks (LANs) at a specific location. A different site would be a network at a remote location, connected to the other site using a T-1 or a slower WAN technology.

Sites are one of the three AD DS objects (along with domains and OUs) that can have their own Group Policy settings assigned to them. However, site divisions are wholly independent of domain, tree, and forest divisions. You can have multiple sites as part of a single domain, or you can have separate domains, trees, or forests for each site.

The primary reason for creating different sites on an Active Directory network is to control the amount of traffic passing over the relatively slow and expensive WAN links between locations. If your entire network is located in one building or campus, with all subnets connected via high-speed, low-cost LAN technologies, you do not need to have more than one site.

If, however, your network spans multiple locations and uses WAN connections running at various speeds, you should create a site topology for your network. A site topology consists of three AD DS object types:

- **Sites:** A site object represents the group of subnets at a single location, with good connectivity.
- **Subnets:** A subnet object represents an IP network at a particular site.
- **Site links:** A site link object represents a WAN connection between two sites.

When you create a site topology, you create site objects, specify the subnets located at each site by creating subnet objects, and then specify the access schedules and relative costs of the WAN links between the sites (in terms of bandwidth and transmission speed, not monetary costs) by creating and configuring site link objects.

After the site topology is in place, AD DS uses it to provide two regulatory functions:

- **Domain controller location:** When an Active Directory client attempts to access a domain controller, it uses its IP address to determine what subnet it belongs to and which site contains that particular subnet. The client then accesses a domain controller at that same site or, if one is not available, at the remote site with the fastest site link connection. This prevents clients from using slow WAN connections to access a domain controller when a closer one is available.
- **Replication traffic control:** A component called the Knowledge Consistency Checker (KCC) automatically creates replication links between domain controllers in the same site and schedules their replication activities. When you connect multiple sites using site link objects, you specify the relative cost of each link and the hours during which it can be used for replication. The KCC then creates an intersite replication schedule for each pair of domain controllers, using the routes with coincident schedules and the lowest aggregate costs.

Unlike many other elements of an Active Directory deployment, the creation of a site topology is not automatic. You must manually create and configure the site, subnet, and site link objects.

■ Deploying Active Directory Domain Services

↓ THE BOTTOM LINE After you create an Active Directory design, you need to think about the actual deployment process. As with most major network technologies, installing AD DS on a test network first, before you put it into actual production, is a good idea.

Many variables can affect the performance of an Active Directory installation, including the hardware you select for your domain controllers, your network capabilities, and the types of WAN links connecting your remote sites. In many cases, an Active Directory design that looks good on paper will not function well in your environment, and you might want to modify the design before you proceed with the live deployment.

Active Directory is one of the more difficult technologies to test, because an isolated lab environment usually cannot emulate many of the factors that can affect the performance of a directory service. Most test labs cannot duplicate the network traffic patterns of the production environment, and few have the WAN links necessary to simulate an actual multisite network. Wherever possible, you should try to test your design under real-life conditions, using your network's actual LAN and WAN technologies but limiting the domain controllers and AD DS clients to laboratory computers.

To create a new forest or a new domain, or to add a domain controller to an existing domain, you must install the Active Directory Domain Services role on a Windows Server 2012 computer, and then run the *Active Directory Domain Services Configuration Wizard*.

To use a Windows Server 2012 computer as a domain controller, you must configure it to use static IP addresses, not addresses supplied by a Dynamic Host Configuration Protocol (DHCP) server. If you are creating a domain in an existing forest, or adding a domain controller to an existing domain, you also must configure the computer to use the DNS server that hosts the existing forest or domain, at least during the Active Directory installation.

Installing the Active Directory Domain Services Role

Although the Active Directory Domain Services role does not actually convert the computer into a domain controller, installing it prepares the computer for the conversion process.

To install the Active Directory Domain Services role, use the following procedure.

⊙ INSTALL THE ACTIVE DIRECTORY DOMAIN SERVICES ROLE

GET READY. Log on to the server running Windows Server 2012 using an account with administrative privileges.

1. From the *Server Manager*'s Manage menu, select Add Roles and Features. The *Add Roles and Features Wizard* appears, displaying the *Before you begin* page.
2. Click Next. The *Select Installation Type* page appears.
3. Leave the *Role-based or feature-based installation* radio button selected and click Next. The *Select Destination Server* page appears.
4. Select the server that you want to promote to a domain controller and click Next. The *Add Roles and Features Wizard* displays the *Select server roles* page, as shown in Figure 13-8.

Figure 13-8

The *Select server roles* page in the *Add Roles and Features Wizard*

Add Roles and Features Wizard

Select server roles

DESTINATION SERVER
LabSvrA

Before You Begin
Installation Type
Server Selection
Server Roles
Features
Confirmation
Results

Select one or more roles to install on the selected server.

Roles

- [ ] Active Directory Certificate Services
- [ ] Active Directory Domain Services
- [ ] Active Directory Federation Services
- [ ] Active Directory Lightweight Directory Services
- [ ] Active Directory Rights Management Services
- [ ] Application Server
- [ ] DHCP Server
- [ ] DNS Server
- [ ] Fax Server
- ▷ [■] File And Storage Services (Installed)
- [ ] Hyper-V
- [ ] Network Policy and Access Services
- [ ] Print and Document Services
- [ ] Remote Access
- [ ] Remote Desktop Services

Description

Active Directory Domain Services (AD DS) stores information about objects on the network and makes this information available to users and network administrators. AD DS uses domain controllers to give network users access to permitted resources anywhere on the network through a single logon process.

< Previous   Next >   Install   Cancel

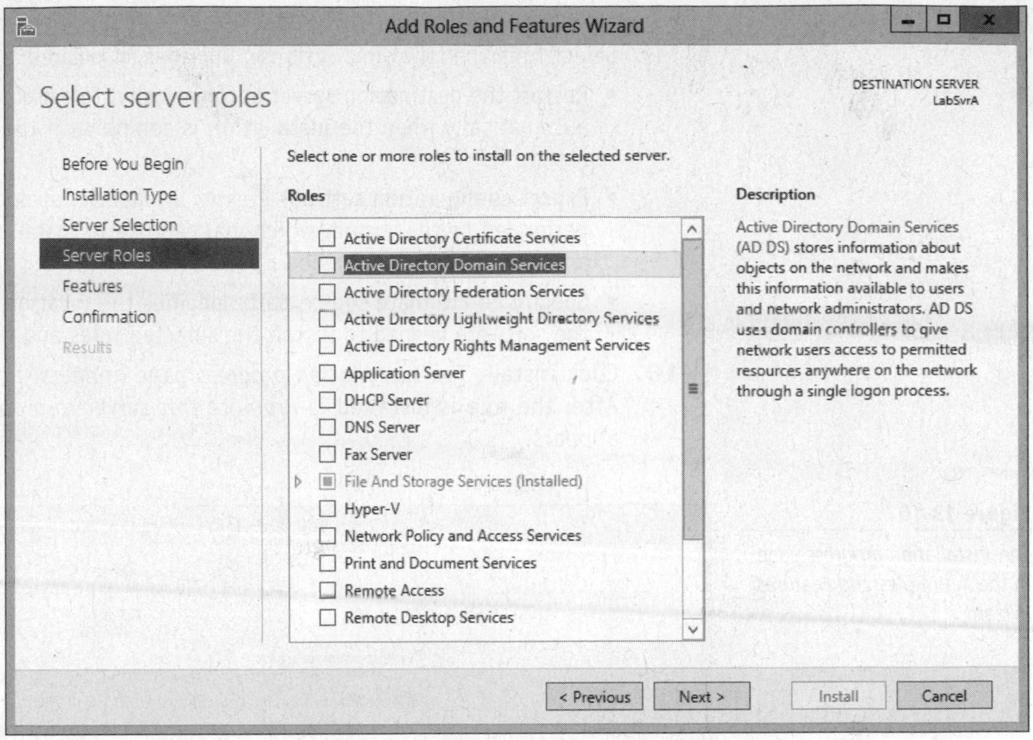

5. Select the Active Directory Domain Service role. The *Add features that are required for Active Directory Domain Services?* page appears, as shown in Figure 13-9.

Figure 13-9

The *Add features that are required for Active Directory Domain Services?* dialog box in the *Add Roles and Features Wizard*

Add Roles and Features Wizard

Add features that are required for Active Directory Domain Services?

You cannot install Active Directory Domain Services unless the following role services or features are also installed.

[Tools] Group Policy Management
▲ Remote Server Administration Tools
  ▲ Role Administration Tools
    ▲ AD DS and AD LDS Tools
        Active Directory module for Windows PowerShell
      ▲ AD DS Tools
          [Tools] Active Directory Administrative Center
          [Tools] AD DS Snap-Ins and Command-Line Tools

[✓] Include management tools (if applicable)

Add Features   Cancel

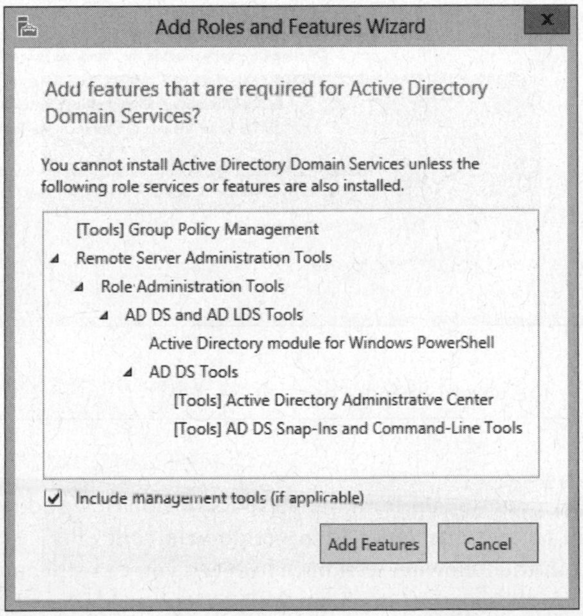

6. Click Add Features to accept the dependencies, and then click Next. The *Select features* page appears.

7. Click Next. The *Active Directory Domain Services* page appears, displaying information about the role.

8. Click Next. A *Confirm installation selections* page appears.

9. Select from the following optional functions, if desired:

   - Restart the destination server automatically if desired causes the server to restart automatically when the installation is complete, if the selected roles and features require it.

   - Export configuration settings creates an XML script documenting the procedures performed by the wizard, which you can use to install the same configuration on another server using Windows PowerShell.

   - Specify an alternate source path specifies the location of an image file containing the software needed to install the selected roles and features.

10. Click Install. The *Installation progress* page appears, as shown in Figure 13-10. After the role is installed, a *Promote this server to a domain controller* link appears.

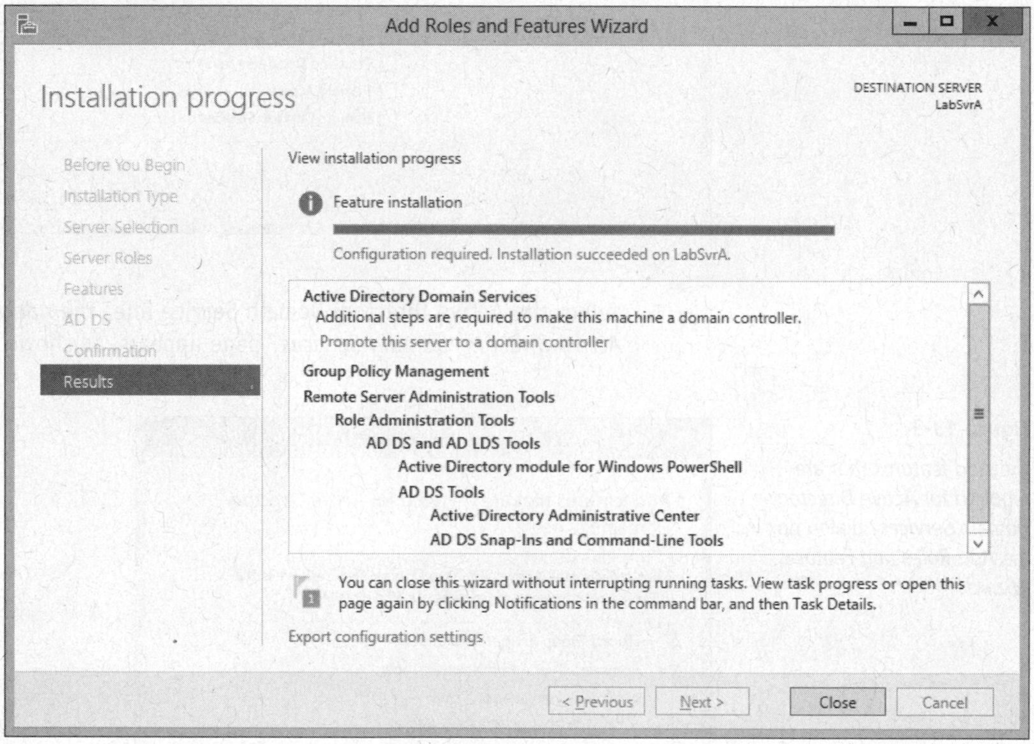

Figure 13-10

The *Installation progress* page in the *Add Roles and Features Wizard*

PAUSE. Leave the wizard open.

TAKE NOTE * The Dcpromo.exe program from the previous version of Windows Server has been deprecated in favor of the Server Manager domain controller installation process documented in the following sections. However, you can still automate AD DS installations by running Dcpromo.exe with an answer file.

After you install the role, you can proceed to run the *Active Directory Domain Services Installation Wizard*. The wizard procedure varies, depending on what function the new domain controller will serve. The following sections describe the procedures for the most common types of domain controller installations.

Creating a New Forest

> When beginning a new AD DS installation, you first need to create a new forest, which you do by creating the first domain in the forest, the forest root domain.

To create a new forest, use the following procedure.

➔ CREATE A NEW FOREST

GET READY. Log on to the server running Windows Server 2012 using an account with administrative privileges and install the Active Directory Domain Services role, as described earlier in this lesson.

1. On the *Installation progress* page that appears at the end of the Active Directory Domain Services role installation procedure, click the Promote this server to a domain controller hyperlink. The *Active Directory Domain Services Configuration Wizard* appears, displaying the *Deployment Configuration* page, as shown in Figure 13-11.

Figure 13-11

The *Deployment Configuration* page of the *Active Directory Domain Services Configuration Wizard*

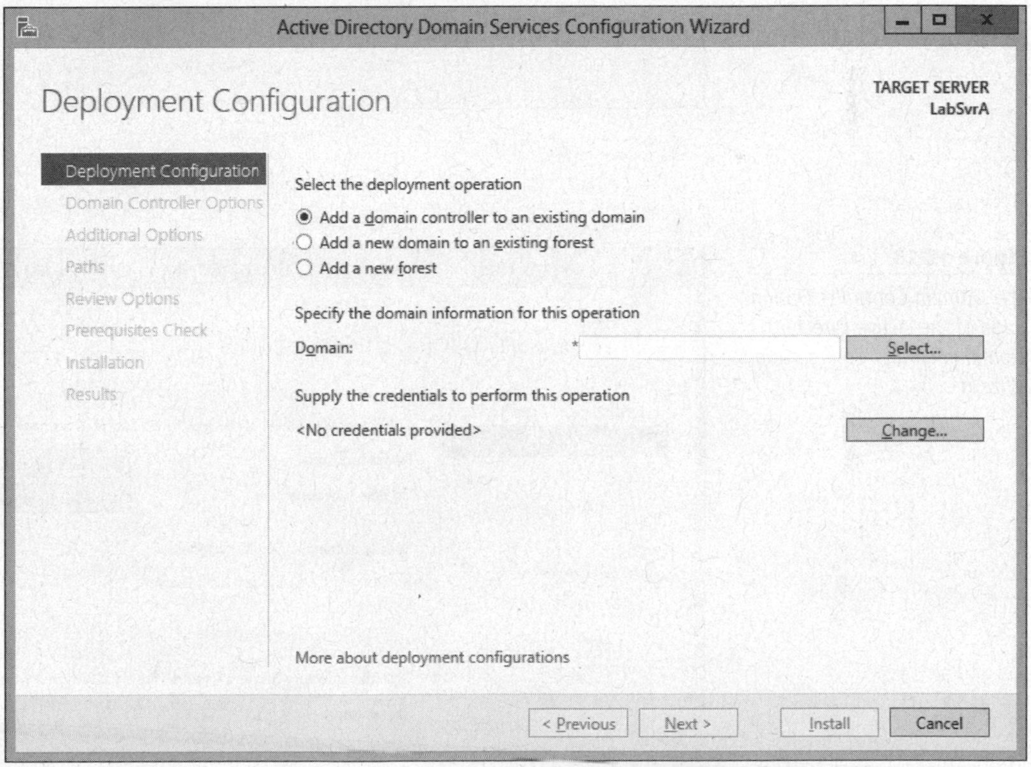

2. Select the Add a new forest option, as shown in Figure 13-12, and, in the Root domain name text box, type the name of the domain you want to create.

3. Click Next. The *Domain Controller Options* page appears, as shown in Figure 13-13.

Figure 13-12

The *Deployment Configuration* page of the *Active Directory Domain Services Configuration Wizard* for the *Add a new forest* option

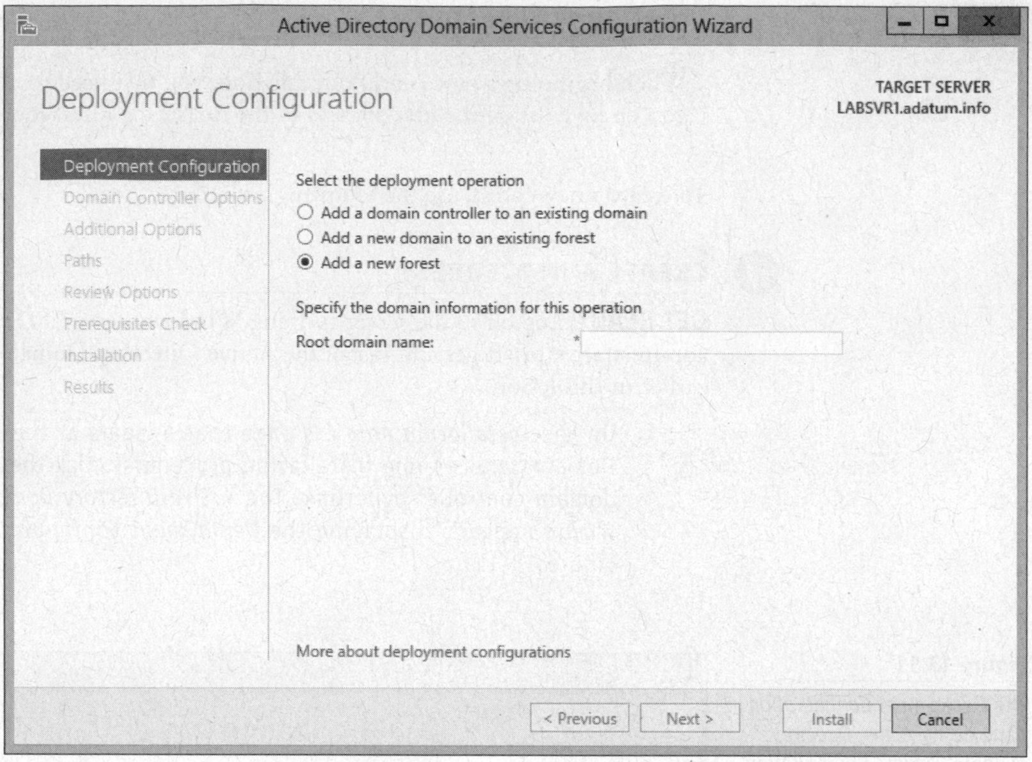

Active Directory Domain Services Configuration Wizard

Deployment Configuration

TARGET SERVER
LABSVR1.adatum.info

Deployment Configuration
Domain Controller Options
Additional Options
Paths
Review Options
Prerequisites Check
Installation
Results

Select the deployment operation
○ Add a domain controller to an existing domain
○ Add a new domain to an existing forest
◉ Add a new forest

Specify the domain information for this operation
Root domain name: *[   ]

More about deployment configurations

< Previous   Next >   Install   Cancel

Figure 13-13

The *Domain Controller Options* page of the *Active Directory Domain Services Configuration Wizard*

Active Directory Domain Services Configuration Wizard

Domain Controller Options

TARGET SERVER
ServerC

Deployment Configuration
Domain Controller Options
DNS Options
Additional Options
Paths
Review Options
Prerequisites Check
Installation
Results

Select functional level of the new forest and root domain
Forest functional level: [Windows Server 2012 ▼]
Domain functional level: [Windows Server 2012 ▼]

Specify domain controller capabilities
☑ Domain Name System (DNS) server
☑ Global Catalog (GC)
☐ Read only domain controller (RODC)

Type the Directory Services Restore Mode (DSRM) password
Password: *[   ]
Confirm password: *[   ]

More about domain controller options

< Previous   Next >   Install   Cancel

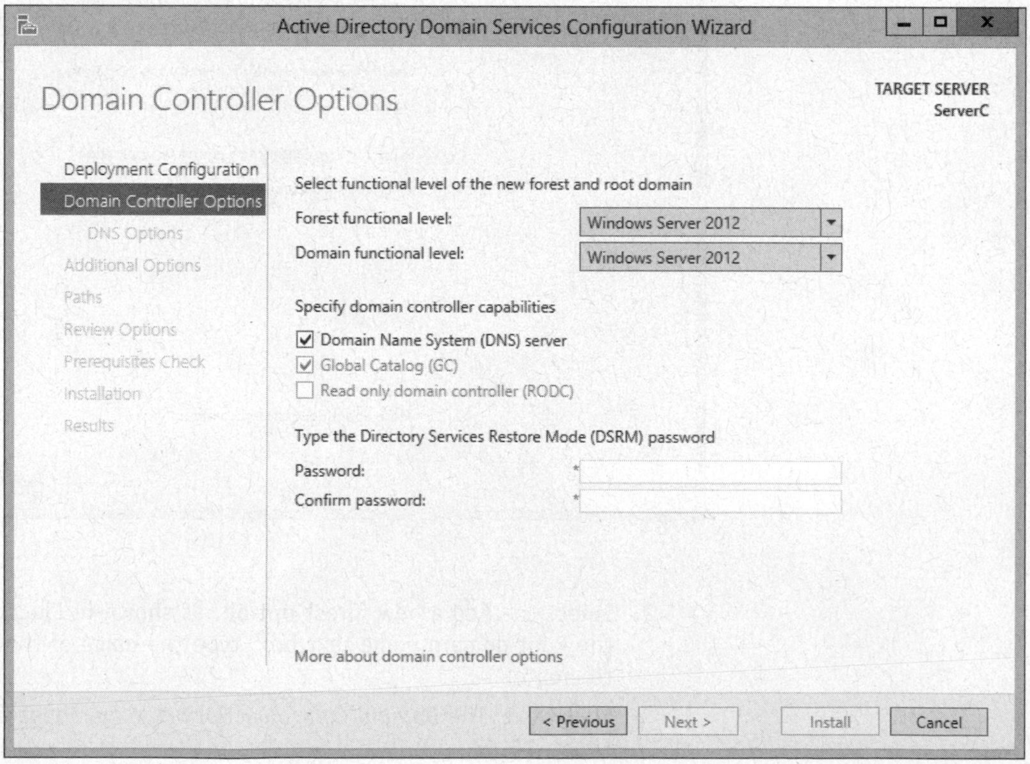

4. Make changes on the *Domain Controller Options* page, as needed:
   - If you plan to add domain controllers running earlier versions of Windows Server to this forest, select the earliest Windows version you plan to install from the Forest functional level drop-down list.
   - If you plan to add domain controllers running earlier versions of Windows Server to this domain, select the earliest Windows version you plan to install from the Domain functional level drop-down list.
   - If you do not already have a DNS server on your network, leave the Domain Name System (DNS) server check box selected. If you have a DNS server on the network and the domain controller is configured to use that server for DNS services, clear the check box.

> **TAKE NOTE** *
>
> The *Global Catalog (GC)* and *Read only domain controller (RODC)* options are grayed out because the first domain controller in a new forest must be a Global Catalog server; it cannot be a read-only domain controller.

5. In the Password and Confirm password text boxes, type the password you want to use for Directory Services Restore Mode (DSRM) and click Next. The *DNS options* page appears, with a warning that a delegation for the DNS server cannot be created, because the DNS Server service is not installed yet.

6. Click Next. The *Additional Options* page appears, as shown in Figure 13-14, displaying the NetBIOS equivalent of the domain name you specified.

Figure 13-14

The *Additional Options* page of the *Active Directory Domain Services Configuration Wizard*

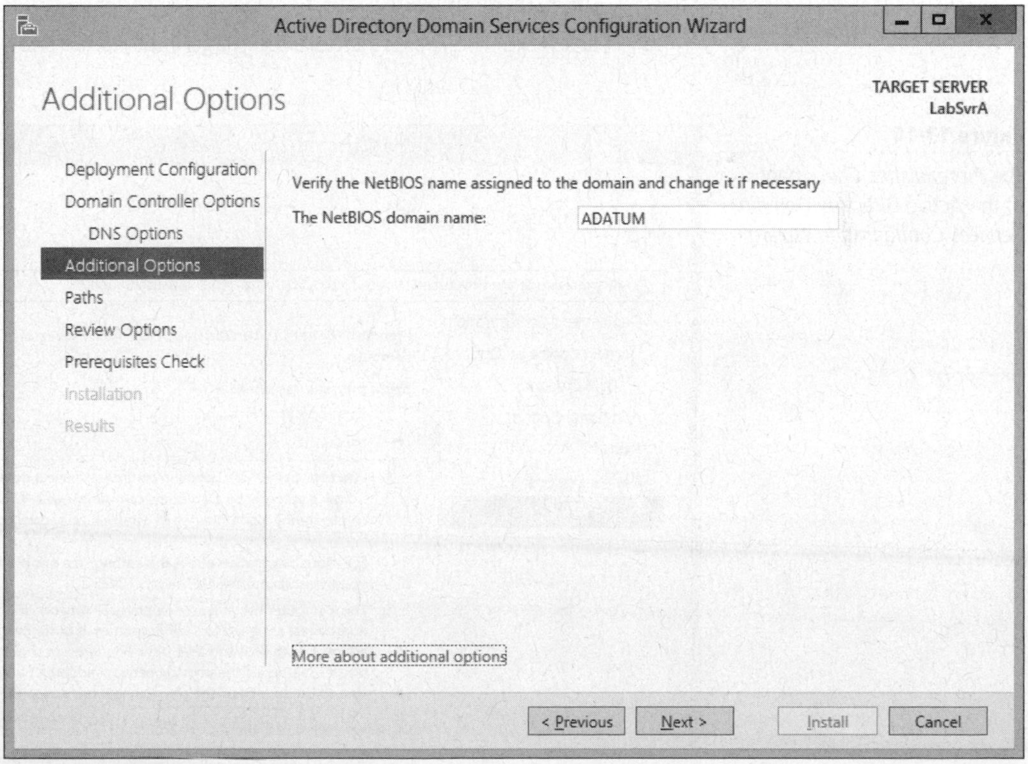

7. Modify the name, if desired, and click Next. The *Paths* page appears, as shown in Figure 13-15.

Figure 13-15

The *Paths* page of the *Active Directory Domain Services Configuration Wizard*

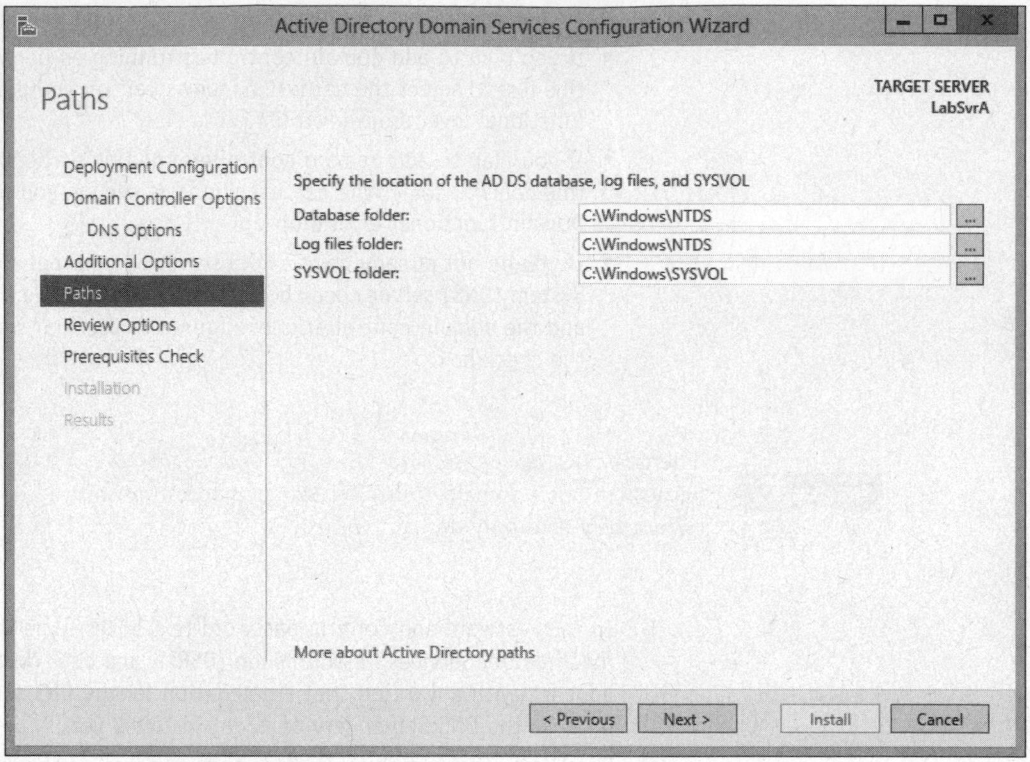

8. Modify the default locations for the AD DS files, if desired, and click Next. The *Review Options* page appears.

9. Click Next. The *Prerequisites Check* page appears, as shown in Figure 13-16.

Figure 13-16

The *Prerequisites Check* page of the *Active Directory Domain Services Configuration Wizard*

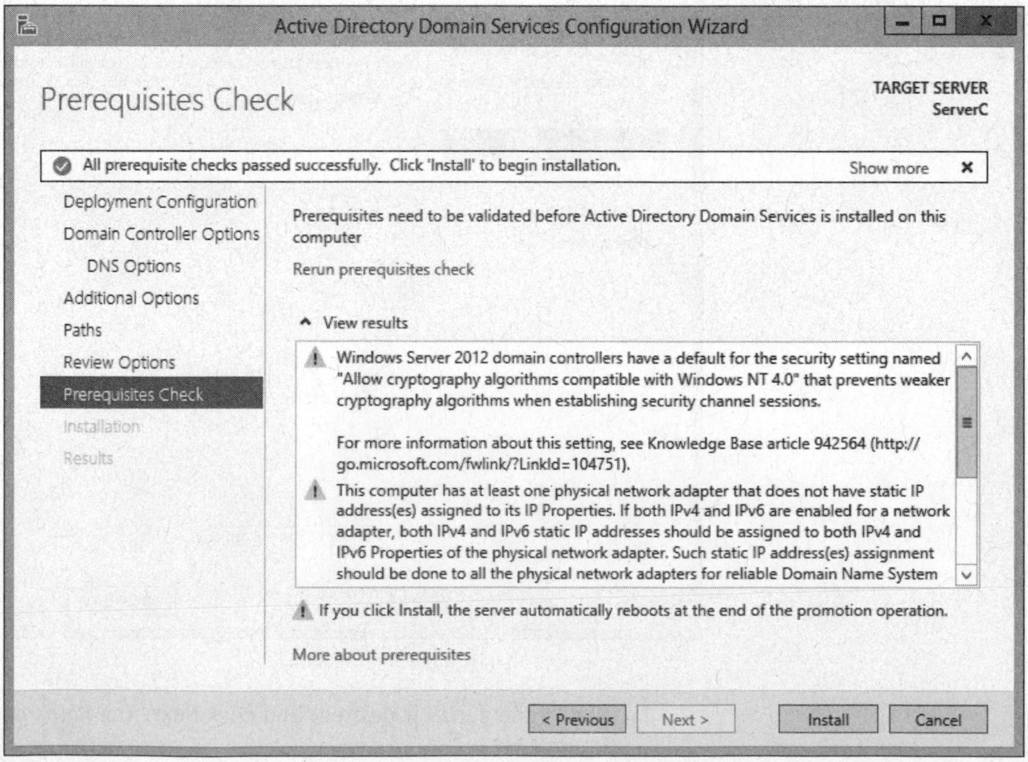

The wizard performs a number of environment tests to determine whether the system can function as a domain controller. The results can appear as cautions, which enable the procedure to continue, or warnings, which require you to perform certain actions before the server can be promoted.

10. After the system passes all the prerequisite checks, click Install. The wizard creates the new forest and configures the server to function as a domain controller.

RESTART the computer.

With the forest root domain in place, you can now proceed to create additional domain controllers in that domain, or add new domains to the forest.

Adding a Domain Controller to an Existing Domain

Every Active Directory domain should have a minimum of two domain controllers.

CERTIFICATION READY
Add or remove a domain controller from a domain.
Objective 5.1

To add a domain controller to an existing Windows Server 2012 domain, use the following procedure.

ADD A DOMAIN CONTROLLER TO AN EXISTING DOMAIN

GET READY. Log on to the server running Windows Server 2012 using an account with administrative privileges and install the Active Directory Domain Services role, as described earlier in this lesson.

1. On the *Installation progress* page that appears at the end of the Active Directory Domain Services role installation procedure, click the Promote this server to a domain controller hyperlink. The *Active Directory Domain Services Configuration Wizard* appears, displaying the *Deployment configuration* page.

2. Select the Add a domain controller to an existing domain option and then click Select.

3. If you are not logged on to an existing domain in the forest, a *Credentials for deployment operation* dialog box appears, in which you must supply administrative credentials for the domain to proceed. After you are authenticated, a *Select a domain from the forest* dialog box appears, as shown in Figure 13-17.

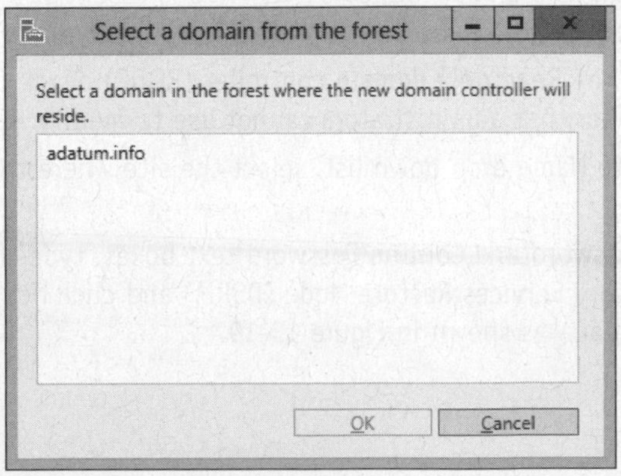

Figure 13-17

The *Select a domain from the forest* page of the *Active Directory Domain Services Configuration Wizard*

4. Select the domain to which you want to add a domain controller and click OK. The selected domain name appears in the *Domain* field.

5. Click Next. The *Domain Controller Options* page appears, as shown in Figure 13-18.

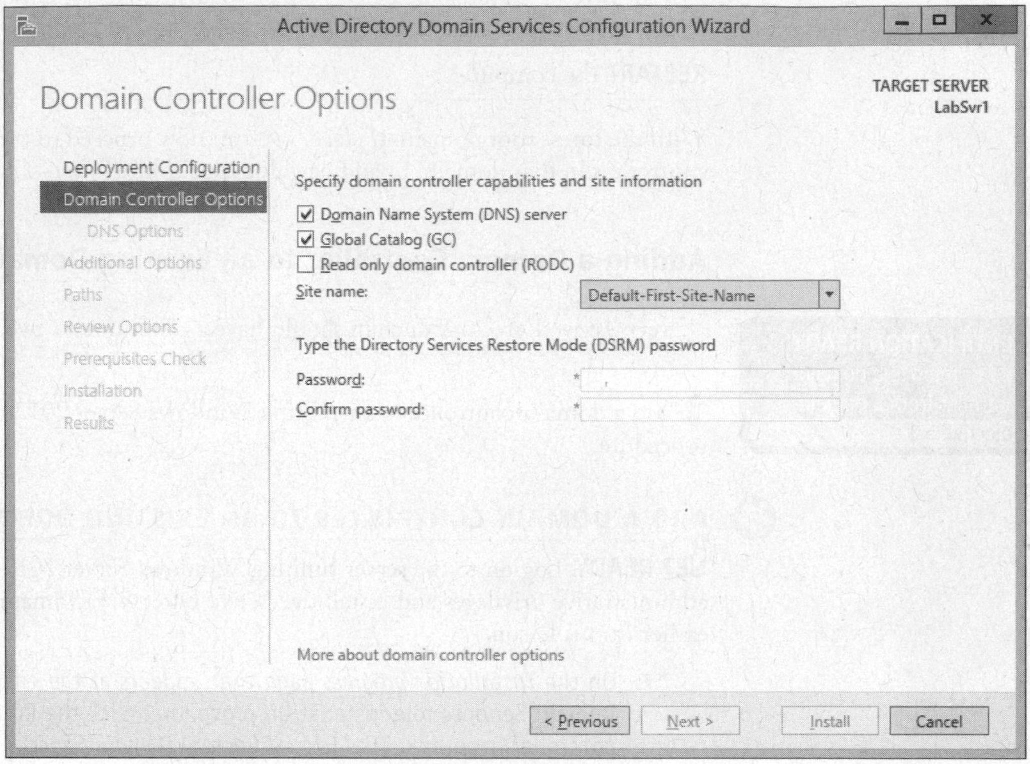

Figure 13-18

The *Domain Controller Options* page of the *Active Directory Domain Services Configuration Wizard*

6. Select or clear the check boxes on the *Domain Controller Options* page as needed:

   • If you want to install the DNS Server service on the computer, leave the Domain Name System (DNS) server check box selected. Otherwise, the DNS server the computer is configured to use will host the domain.

   • Leave the Global Catalog (GC) check box selected if you want the computer to function as a global catalog server. This is essential if you are deploying the new domain controller at a site that does not already have a GC server.

   • Select the Read only domain controller (RODC) check box to create a domain controller that administrators cannot use to modify AD DS objects.

7. In the Site Name drop-down list, select the site where the domain controller will be located.

8. In the Password and Confirm Password text boxes, type the password you want to use for Directory Services Restore Mode (DSRM) and click Next. The *Additional Options* page appears, as shown in Figure 13-19.

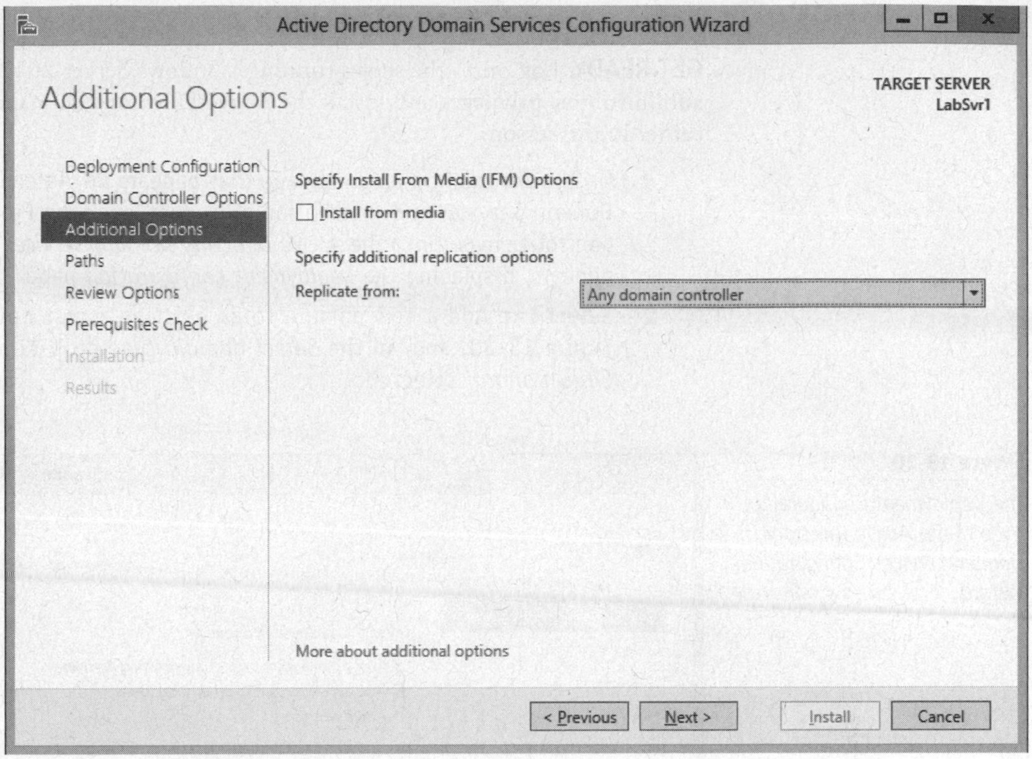

Figure 13-19

The *Additional Options* page of the *Active Directory Domain Services Configuration Wizard*

9. To use the Install From Media (IFM) option, select the Install from media check box.

+ MORE INFORMATION

For more information on deploying replicate domain controllers using Install From Media, see "Using Install From Media (IFM)," later in this lesson.

10. In the Replicate from drop-down list, select the existing domain controller that the server should use as a data source. Then click Next. The *Paths* page appears.
11. Modify the default locations for the AD DS files, if desired, and click Next. The *Review Options* page appears.
12. Click Next. The *Prerequisites Check* page appears.
13. After the system passes all the prerequisite checks, click Install. The wizard configures the server to function as a domain controller.

RESTART the computer.

The domain controller is now configured to service the existing domain. If the new domain controller is located in the same site as another, AD DS replication between the two begins automatically.

Creating a New Child Domain in a Forest

When you have a forest with at least one domain, you can add a child domain beneath any existing domain.

To create a child domain in an existing forest, use the following procedure.

CREATE A NEW CHILD DOMAIN IN A FOREST

GET READY. Log on to the server running Windows Server 2012 using an account with administrative privileges and install the Active Directory Domain Services role, as described earlier in this lesson.

1. On the *Installation progress* page that appears at the end of the Active Directory Domain Services role installation procedure, click the Promote this server to a domain controller hyperlink. The *Active Directory Domain Services Configuration Wizard* appears, displaying the *Deployment Configuration* page.

2. Select the Add a new domain to an existing forest option, as shown in Figure 13-20, and, in the *Select domain type* drop-down list, leave *Child Domain* selected.

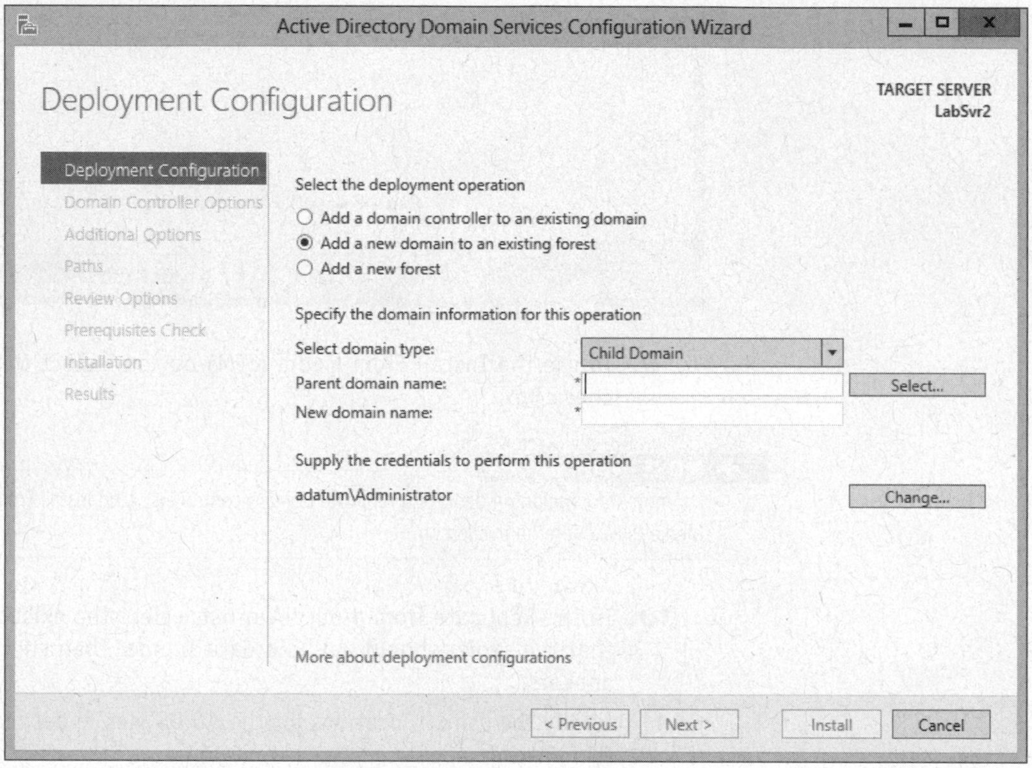

Figure 13-20

The *Deployment Configuration* page of the *Active Directory Domain Services Configuration Wizard*

> **TAKE NOTE**＊ The wizard also supplies the option to create a *tree domain*, a new domain that is not subordinate to an existing domain in the forest.

3. Click Select. If you are not logged on to an existing domain in the forest, a *Credentials for deployment operation* dialog box appears, in which you must supply administrative credentials for the domain to proceed. After you are authenticated, a *Select a domain from the forest* dialog box appears.

4. Select the domain beneath which you want to create a child domain and click OK. The selected domain name appears in the *Parent domain name* field of the *Deployment Configuration* page.

5. In the New domain name text box, type the name of the child domain you want to create and click Next. The *Domain Controller Options* page appears, as shown in Figure 13-21.

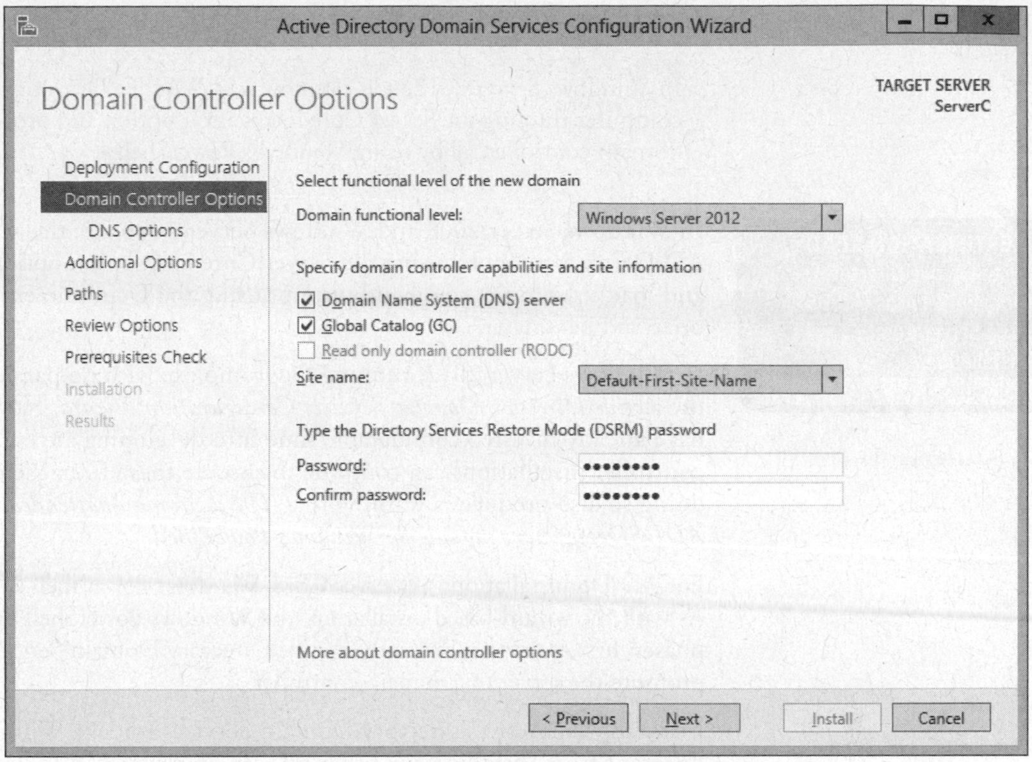

Figure 13-21

The *Domain Controller Options* page of the *Active Directory Domain Services Configuration Wizard*

6. If you plan to add domain controllers running earlier versions of Windows Server to this domain, select the earliest Windows version you plan to install from the Domain functional level drop-down list.

7. If you want to install the DNS Server service on the computer, leave the Domain Name System (DNS) server check box selected. Otherwise, the DNS server the computer is configured to use will host the domain.

8. Leave the Global Catalog (GC) check box selected if you want the computer to function as a global catalog server. This is essential if you are deploying the new domain controller at a site that does not already have a GC server.

9. In the Site Name drop-down list, select the site where the domain controller will be located.

10. In the Password and Confirm Password text boxes, type the password you want to use for Directory Services Restore Mode (DSRM) and click Next. The *DNS Options* page appears.

11. If you are using another server for DNS, leave the Create DNS delegation check box selected. If you are installing DNS on the new domain controller, you can clear the check box. Click Next. The *Additional Options* page appears, displaying the NetBIOS equivalent of the domain name you specified.

12. Modify the name, if desired, and click Next. The *Paths* page appears.

13. Modify the default locations for the AD DS files, if desired, and click Next. The *Review Options* page appears.

14. Click Next. The *Prerequisites Check* page appears.

15. After the system passes all the prerequisite checks, click Install. The wizard creates the new domain and configures the server to function as a domain controller.

RESTART the computer.

The new domain you have just created appears beneath the parent domain you specified.

TAKE NOTE *

The Read only domain controller (RODC) option is grayed out because the first domain controller in a new domain cannot be a read-only domain controller.

Installing AD DS on Server Core

In Windows Server 2012, you can now install Active Directory Domain Services on a computer running the Server Core installation option and promote the system to a domain controller, all by using Windows PowerShell.

In Windows Server 2008 and Windows Server 2008 R2, the accepted method for installing AD DS on a computer using the Server Core installation option is to create an answer file and load it from the command prompt using the Dcpromo.exe program with the / unattend parameter.

In Windows Server 2012, running Dcpromo.exe with no parameters no longer launches the *Active Directory Domain Services Configuration Wizard*. However, administrators who have already invested considerable time into developing answer files for unattended domain controller installations can continue to execute them from the command prompt, although doing so also produces a warning that *The dcpromo unattended operation is replaced by the ADDSDeployment module for Windows PowerShell*.

For AD DS installations on Server Core, Windows PowerShell is now the preferred method. As with the wizard-based installation, the Windows PowerShell procedure occurs in two phases: first, you must install the Active Directory Domain Services role; then, you must promote the server to a domain controller.

Installing the Active Directory Domain Services role via Windows PowerShell is no different from installing any other role. In an elevated Windows PowerShell session, use the following command:

```
Install-WindowsFeature -name AD-Domain-Services
-IncludeManagementTools
```

As with other Windows PowerShell role installations, the Install-WindowsFeature cmdlet does not install the management tools for the role, such as Active Directory Administrative Center and Active Directory Users and Computers, unless you include the -IncludeManagementTools parameter in the command.

After you install the role, promoting the server to a domain controller is somewhat more complicated. The ADDSDeployment Windows PowerShell module includes separate cmdlets for the three deployment configurations covered in the previous sections:

- Install-AddsForest
- Install-AddsDomainController
- Install-AddsDomain

Each of these cmdlets has a great many possible parameters to support the many configuration options you find in the Active Directory Domain Services Configuration Wizard. In its simplest form, the following command would install a domain controller for a new forest called *adatum.com*:

```
Install-AddsForest -DomainName "adatum.com"
```

The defaults for all the cmdlet's other parameters are the same as those in the *Active Directory Domain Services Configuration Wizard*. Running the cmdlet with no parameters steps through the options, prompting you for values. You can also display basic syntax information using the Get-Help command, as shown in Figure 13-22.

Figure 13-22

Syntax for the Install-
AddsForest cmdlet in Windows
PowerShell

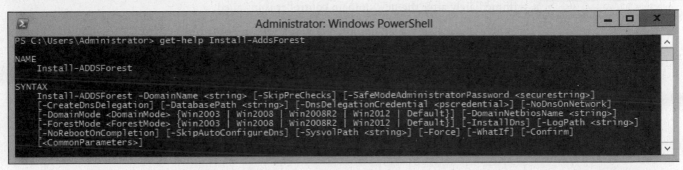

```
Administrator: Windows PowerShell

PS C:\Users\Administrator> get-help Install-AddsForest

NAME
    Install-ADDSForest

SYNTAX
    Install-ADDSForest -DomainName <string> [-SkipPreChecks] [-SafeModeAdministratorPassword <securestring>]
    [-CreateDnsDelegation] [-DatabasePath <string>] [-DnsDelegationCredential <pscredential>] [-NoDnsOnNetwork]
    [-DomainMode <DomainMode> {Win2003 | Win2008 | Win2008R2 | Win2012 | Default}] [-DomainNetbiosName <string>]
    [-ForestMode <ForestMode> {Win2003 | Win2008 | Win2008R2 | Win2012 | Default}] [-InstallDns] [-LogPath <string>]
    [-NoRebootOnCompletion] [-SkipAutoConfigureDns] [-SysvolPath <string>] [-Force] [-WhatIf] [-Confirm]
    [<CommonParameters>]
```

Another way to perform a complex installation using Windows PowerShell is to use a computer
running Windows Server 2012 with the full GUI option to generate a script. Begin by running
the *Active Directory Domain Services Configuration Wizard*, configuring all the options with your
desired settings. When you reach the *Review Option* page, click the *View Script* button to display
the Windows PowerShell code for the appropriate cmdlet, as shown in Figure 13-23.

Figure 13-23

An installation script generated
by the Active Directory Domain
Services Configuration Wizard

```
tmpD4C6.tmp - Notepad

File  Edit  Format  View  Help

#
# Windows PowerShell script for AD DS Deployment
#

Import-Module ADDSDeployment
Install-ADDSDomainController `
-NoGlobalCatalog:$true `
-Credential (Get-Credential) `
-CriticalReplicationOnly:$false `
-DatabasePath "C:\Windows\NTDS" `
-DomainName "adatum.info" `
-InstallDns:$false `
-LogPath "C:\Windows\NTDS" `
-NoRebootOnCompletion:$false `
-SiteName "Default-First-Site-Name" `
-SysvolPath "C:\Windows\SYSVOL" `
-Force:$true
```

This feature works as it does because Server Manager is actually based on Windows
PowerShell, so the script contains the cmdlets and parameters that are actually running
when the wizard performs an installation. You can also use this scripting capability with
the Install-AddsDomainController cmdlet to deploy multiple domain controllers for the
same domain.

Using Install from Media (IFM)

Earlier in this lesson, in the procedure for installing a replica domain controller, the
Additional Options page of the *Active Directory Domain Services Configuration Wizard*
included an *Install from media* check box. This option enables you to streamline the
process of deploying replica domain controllers to remote sites.

Normally, installing a domain controller on an existing domain creates the AD DS database structure, but it has no data until the server can receive replication traffic from the other domain controllers. When the domain controllers for a particular domain are well connected, such as by a local area network (LAN), replication occurs automatically and almost immediately after the new domain controller is installed.

When you install a domain controller at a remote location, however, the connection to the other domain controllers is most likely a wide area network (WAN) link, which is typically slower and more expensive than a LAN connection. In this case, the initial replication with the other domain controllers can be much more of a problem. The slow speed of the WAN link might cause the replication to take a long time and might flood the connection, delaying regular traffic. If the domain controllers are located in different AD DS sites, no replication occurs until an administrator creates and configures the required site links.

TAKE NOTE The first replication that occurs after the installation of a new domain controller is the only one that requires the servers to exchange a complete copy of the AD DS database. In subsequent replications, the domain controllers exchange information about only the objects and attributes that have changed since the last replication.

By using a command-line tool called Ndtsutil.exe, you can avoid these problems by creating domain-controller installation media that include a copy of the AD DS database. By using this media when installing a remote domain controller, the data is installed along with the database structure, and no initial replication is necessary.

To create Install From Media (IFM) media, you must run the Ntdsutil.exe program on a domain controller running the same version of Windows that you intend to deploy. The program is interactive, requiring you to enter a sequence of commands such as the following:

- `Ntdsutil` launches the program.
- `Activate instance ntds` focuses the program on the installed AD DS instance.
- `Ifm` switches the program into IFM mode.
- `Create Full|RODC <path name>` creates media for either a full read/write domain controller or a read-only domain controller and saves it to the folder specified by the path name variable.

TAKE NOTE The Ntdsutil.exe create command also supports parameters that include the contents of the SYSVOL volume with the AD DS data. The Windows Server 2012 version of the program adds a nodefrag parameter, which speeds up the media creation process by skipping the defragmentation.

When you execute these commands, the Ntdsutil.exe program creates a snapshot of the AD DS database, mounts it as a volume to defragment it, and then saves it to the specified folder, along with a copy of the Windows Registry (see Figure 13-24).

After you create the IFM media, you can transport it to the servers you intend to deploy as domain controllers by any convenient means. To use the media, you run the *Active Directory Domain Services Configuration Wizard* in the usual way, select the *Install from media* check box, and specify the path to the location of the folder.

Figure 13-24

An Ntdsutil.exe command sequence

```
C:\Windows\system32>ntdsutil
ntdsutil: activate instance ntds
Active instance set to "ntds".
ntdsutil: ifm
ifm: create full c:\ifm
Creating snapshot...
Snapshot set {807a3a63-c75e-4ae3-8e4d-d3fd2dd4bfc7} generated successfully.
Snapshot {b350adae-bca3-4ff7-a57a-389727c68c99} mounted as C:\$SNAP_201208171630
_VOLUMEC$\
Snapshot {b350adae-bca3-4ff7-a57a-389727c68c99} is already mounted.
Initiating DEFRAGMENTATION mode...
    Source Database: C:\$SNAP_201208171630_VOLUMEC$\Windows\NTDS\ntds.dit
    Target Database: c:\ifm\Active Directory\ntds.dit

             Defragmentation  Status  (% complete)

          0    10   20   30   40   50   60   70   80   90   100
          |----|----|----|----|----|----|----|----|----|----|
          ...................................................

Copying registry files...
Copying c:\ifm\registry\SYSTEM
Copying c:\ifm\registry\SECURITY
Snapshot {b350adae-bca3-4ff7-a57a-389727c68c99} unmounted.
IFM media created successfully in c:\ifm
ifm:
```

Upgrading Active Directory Domain Services

Introducing Windows Server 2012 onto an existing AD DS installation is easier than it has ever been in previous versions of the operating system.

CERTIFICATION READY
Upgrade a domain controller.
Objective 5.1

You can upgrade an AD DS infrastructure in two ways. You can upgrade the existing down-level domain controllers to Windows Server 2012, or you can add a new Windows Server 2012 domain controller to your existing installation.

As noted in Lesson 1, "Installing Servers," the upgrade paths to Windows Server 2012 are few. You can upgrade a Windows Server 2008 or Windows Server 2008 R2 domain controller to Windows Server 2012, but no earlier versions are upgradable.

In the past, if you wanted to add a new domain controller to an existing AD DS installation based on previous Windows versions, you had to run the Adprep.exe program to upgrade the domains and forest. Depending on the installation's complexity, this could involve logging on to various domain controllers with different credentials, locating different versions of Adprep. exe, and running the program several times using /domainprep parameter for each domain and the /forestprep parameter for the forest.

In Windows Server 2012, the Adprep.exe functionality has been fully incorporated into Server Manager in the *Active Directory Domain Services Configuration Wizard*. When you install a new Windows Server 2012 domain controller, you have to supply only appropriate credentials, and the wizard takes care of the rest.

TAKE NOTE*

To install the first Windows Server 2012 domain controller into a down-level AD DS installation, you must supply credentials for a user that is a member of the Enterprise Admins and Schema Admins groups, and a member of the Domain Admins group in the domain that hosts the schema master.

Adprep.exe, still included with the operating system, supports the old preparation method, if you prefer it, but you have no compelling reason to use it.

CERTIFICATION READY
Add or remove a domain controller from a domain.
Objective 5.1

Removing a Domain Controller

With the loss of Dcpromo.exe, the process of demoting a domain controller has changed, and it is not immediately intuitive.

To remove a domain controller from an AD DS installation, you must begin by running *the Remove Roles and Features Wizard*, as shown in the following procedure.

REMOVE A REPLICA DOMAIN CONTROLLER

GET READY. Log on to the server running Windows Server 2012 using an account with administrative privileges.

1. From the Server Manager's Manage menu, select Remove Roles and Features. The *Remove Roles and Features Wizard* appears, displaying the *Before you begin* page.
2. Click Next. The *Select Destination Server* page appears.
3. Select the server that you want to demote from a domain controller and click Next. The *Remove Server Roles* page appears.
4. Clear the Active Directory Domain Services check box. A *Remove features that require Active Directory Domain Services* dialog box appears.
5. Click Remove Features. A *Validation Results* dialog box appears, as shown in Figure 13-25.

Figure 13-25

The *Validation Results* dialog box of the *Remove Roles and Features Wizard*

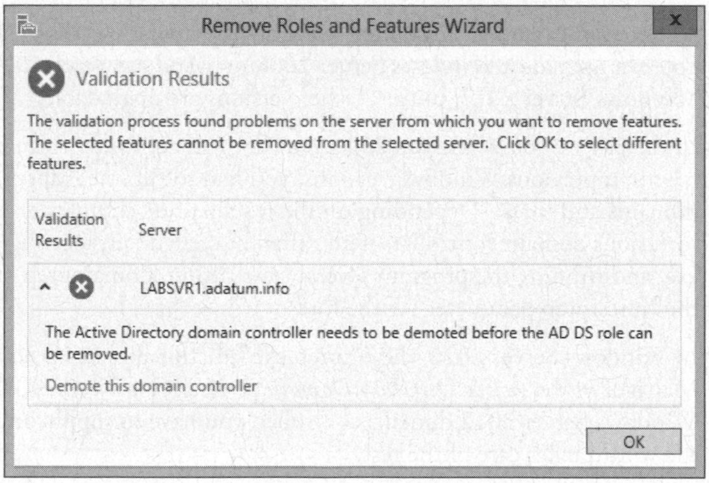

6. Click the Demote this domain controller hyperlink. The *Active Directory Domain Services Configuration Wizard* appears, displaying the *Credentials* page, as shown in Figure 13-26.

Figure 13-26

The *Credentials* page of the *Active Directory Domain Services Configuration Wizard*

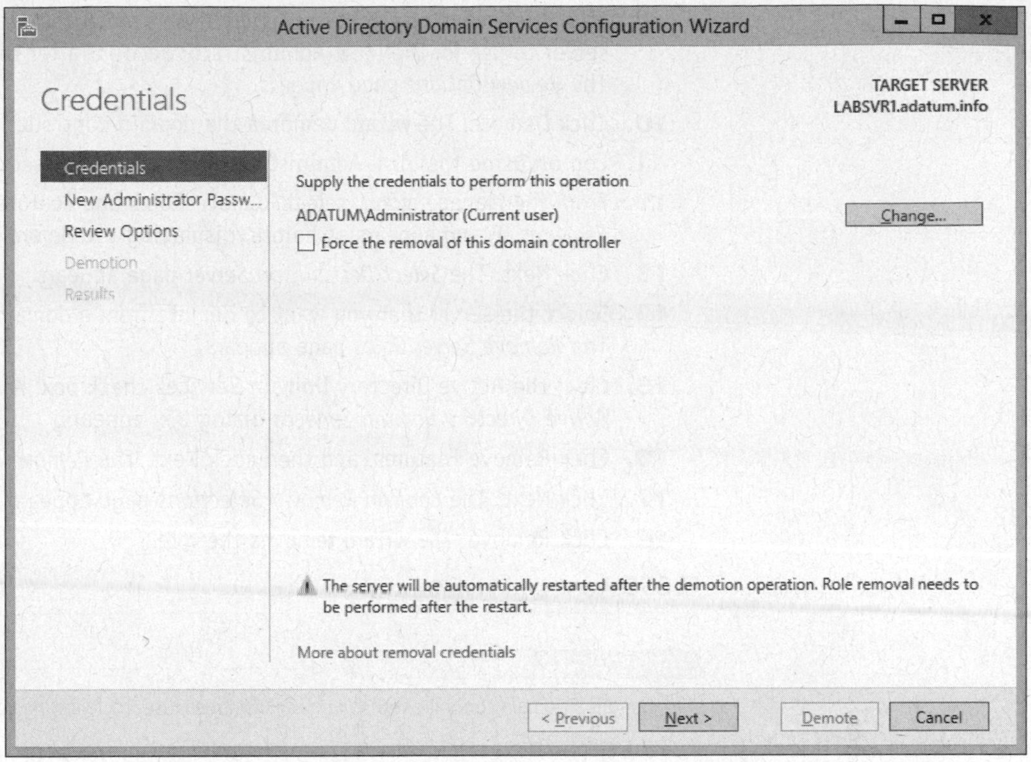

7. Click Change to supply alternative credentials for demoting the domain controller, if necessary.

8. Select the Force the removal of this domain controller check box and click Next. The *New Administrator Password* page appears, as shown in Figure 13-27.

Figure 13-27

The *Net Administrator Password* page of the *Active Directory Domain Services Configuration Wizard*

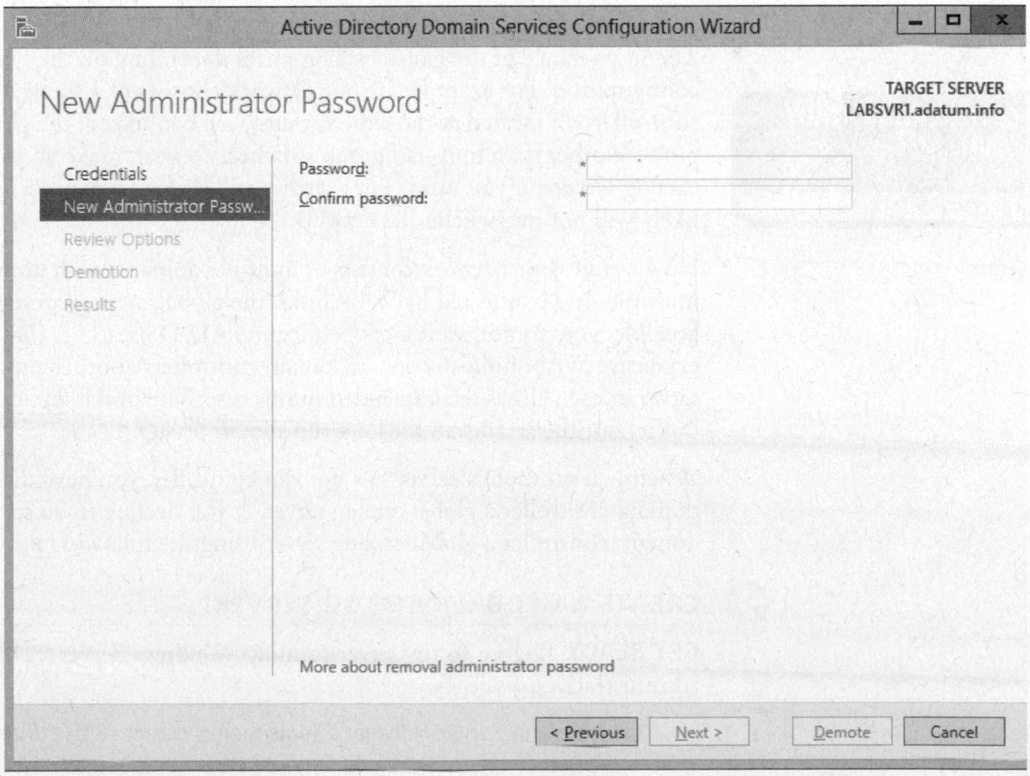

9. In the Password and Confirm Password text boxes, type the password you want the server to use for the local Administrator account after the demotion. Then click Next. The *Review Options* page appears.

10. Click Demote. The wizard demotes the domain controller and restarts the system.

11. Log on using the local Administrator password you specified earlier.

12. From the Manage menu, select Remove Roles and Features. The *Remove Roles and Features Wizard* appears as before, displaying the *Before you begin* page.

13. Click Next. The *Select Destination Server* page appears.

14. Select the server that you want to demote from a domain controller and click Next. The *Remove Server Roles* page appears.

15. Clear the Active Directory Domain Services check box. A *Remove features that require Active Directory Domain Services* dialog box appears.

16. Click Remove Features, and then click Next. The *Remove Features* page appears.

17. Click Next. The *Confirm Removal Selections* page appears.

18. Click Remove. The wizard removes the role.

CLOSE the wizard and restart the server.

USING WINDOWS POWERSHELL

To demote a domain controller with Windows PowerShell, use the following command:

```
Uninstall-ADDSDomainController -ForceRemoval
-LocalAdminisdtratorPassword <password> -Force
```

Configuring the Global Catalog

As noted earlier, the global catalog is an index of all AD DS objects in a forest that prevents systems from having to perform searches among multiple domain controllers.

CERTIFICATION READY
Configure a global catalog server.
Objective 5.1

The importance of the global catalog varies depending on the size of your network and its site configuration. For example, if your network consists of a single domain, with domain controllers all located at the same site and well connected, the global catalog serves little purpose other than universal group searches. You can make all your domain controllers global catalog servers, if you want. The searches will be load balanced, and the replication traffic likely will not overwhelm the network.

However, if your network consists of multiple domains with domain controllers located at multiple sites connected by WAN links, the global catalog configuration is critical. If at all possible, you do not want users performing AD DS searches that must reach across slow, expensive WAN links to contact domain controllers at other sites. Placing a global catalog server at each site is recommended in this case. The initial replication might generate a lot of traffic, but the savings in the long run should be significant.

When you promote a server to a domain controller, you have the option of making the domain controller a global catalog server. If you decline to do so, however, you can make any domain controller a global catalog server using the following procedure.

⊙ **CREATE A GLOBAL CATALOG SERVER**

GET READY. Log on to the server running Windows Server 2012 using an account with administrative privileges.

1. From the Server Manager's Tools menu, select Active Directory Sites and Services. The *Active Directory Sites and Services* console appears.

2. Expand the site where the domain controller you want to function as a global catalog server is located. Then expand the Servers folder and select the server you want to configure, as shown in Figure 13-28.

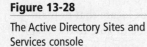

Figure 13-28

The Active Directory Sites and Services console

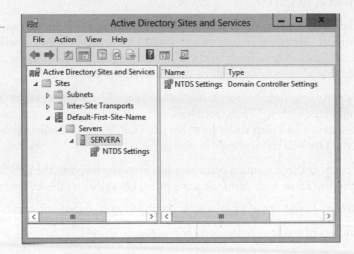

3. Right-click the NTDS Settings node for the server and, from the context menu, select Properties. The *NTDS Settings Properties* sheet appears, as shown in Figure 13-29.

Figure 13-29

The NTDS Settings Properties sheet

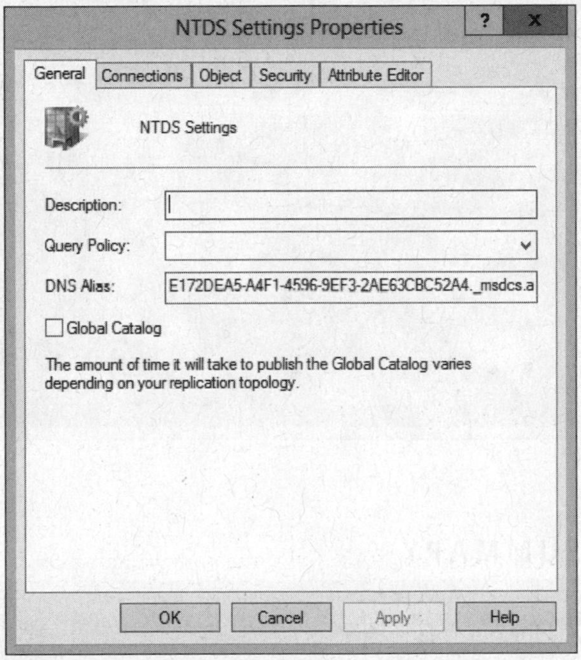

4. Select the Global Catalog check box and click OK.

CLOSE the *Active Directory Sites and Services* console.

Troubleshooting DNS SRV Registration Failure

The Domain Name System (DNS) is essential to the operating of Active Directory Domain Services. To accommodate directory services such as AD DS, a special DNS resource record was created that enables clients to locate domain controllers and other vital AD DS services.

CERTIFICATION READY
Resolve DNS SRV record registration issues.
Objective 5.1

When you create a new domain controller, one of the most important parts of the process is the registration of the server in the DNS. This automatic registration is the reason an AD DS network must have access to a DNS server that supports the Dynamic Updates standard defined in RFC 2136.

If the DNS registration process fails, computers on the network cannot locate that domain controller, the consequences of which can be serious. Computers will be unable to use that domain controller to join the domain; existing domain members will be unable to log on; and other domain controllers will be unable to replicate with it.

DNS problems are, in most cases, due to general networking faults or DNS client configuration error. When troubleshooting these problems, you should first try pinging the DNS server, and then make sure that the TCP/IP client configuration has the correct addresses for the DNS servers it should be using.

To confirm that a domain controller has been registered in the DNS, open a command-prompt window with administrative privileges and enter the following command:

```
dcdiag /test:registerindns /dnsdomain:<domain name> /v
```

A successful result appears, as shown in Figure 13-30.

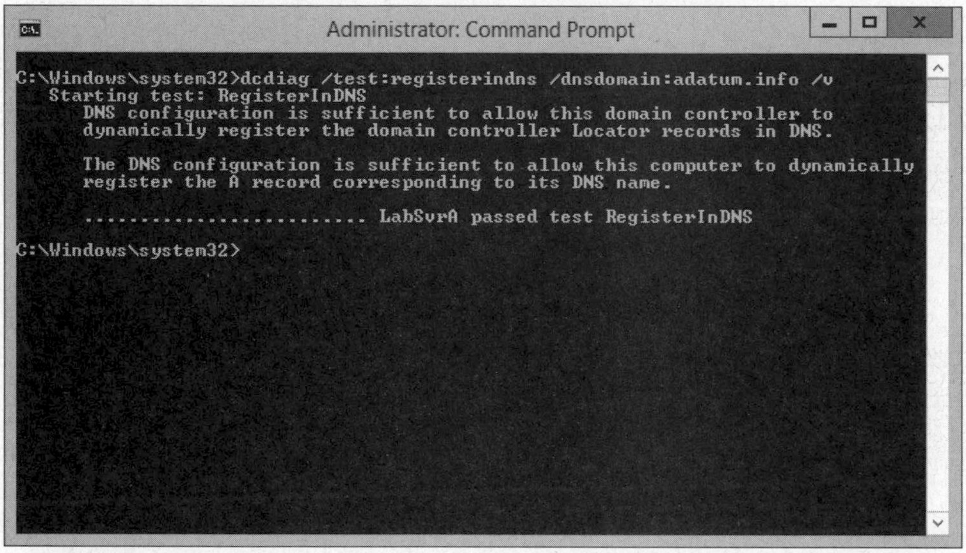

Figure 13-30

A successful dcdiag test

SKILL SUMMARY

IN THIS LESSON, YOU LEARNED:

- A directory service is a repository of information about the resources—hardware, software, and human—connected to a network. Microsoft first introduced the Active Directory service in Windows 2000 Server, and they have upgraded it in each successive server operating system release, including Windows Server 2012.

- When you create your first domain on an Active Directory network, you are, in essence, creating the root of a domain tree. You can populate the tree with additional domains, as long as they are part of the same contiguous name space.

- When beginning a new Active Directory Domain Services installation, the first step is to create a new forest, which you do by creating the first domain in the forest, the forest root domain.

- In Windows Server 2012, you can now install AD DS on a computer running the Server Core installation option, as well as promote the system to a domain controller, all using Windows PowerShell.

- Install from media (IFM) is an option that enables administrators to streamline the process of deploying replica domain controllers to remote sites.

- You can upgrade an AD DS infrastructure in two ways: upgrade the existing down-level domain controllers to Windows Server 2012, or add a new Windows Server 2012 domain controller to your existing installation.

- As noted earlier, the global catalog is an index of all the AD DS objects in a forest that prevents systems from having to perform searches among multiple domain controllers.

- The Domain Name System (DNS) is essential to the operating of Active Directory Domain Services. To accommodate directory services such as AD DS, a special DNS resource record was created that enables clients to locate domain controllers and other vital AD DS services.

■ Knowledge Assessment

Multiple Choice

Select one or more correct answers for each of the following questions.

1. Which of the following items is a valid leaf object in Active Directory?
   a. Domain
   b. User
   c. Application partition
   d. OU

2. What is required by DNS for Active Directory to function?
   a. Dynamic update support
   b. DHCP forwarding support
   c. SRV records support
   d. Active Directory integration

3. What is the first domain installed in a new Active Directory forest called?
   a. Forest root domain
   b. Parent root domain
   c. Domain tree root
   d. Domain root

4. Which of the following cannot contain multiple Active Directory domains?
   a. organizational units
   b. sites
   c. trees
   d. forests

5. What are the two basic classes of Active Directory objects?
   a. Resource
   b. Leaf
   c. Domain
   d. Container

6. Which of the following is not true about an object's attributes?
   a. Administrators must manually supply information for certain attributes.
   b. Every container object has, as an attribute, a list of all the other objects it contains.
   c. Leaf objects do not contain attributes.
   d. Active Directory automatically creates the globally unique identifier (GUID).

7. Which of the following is not a reason why you should try to create as few domains as possible when designing an Active Directory infrastructure?
   a. Creating additional domains increases the administrative burden of the installation.
   b. Each additional domain you create increases the hardware costs of the Active Directory deployment.
   c. Some applications might have problems working in a forest with multiple domains.
   d. You must purchase a license from Microsoft for each domain you create.

8. Which of the following does an Active Directory client use to locate objects in another domain?
   a. DNS
   b. Global Catalog
   c. DHCP
   d. Site Link

9. What is the default trust relationship between domains in one forest?
   a. Two-way trust relationship between domain trees
   b. By default, no trust relationship between domain trees
   c. One-way trust relationship between domain trees
   d. Each domain tree trusts the forest, but not between each other

10. What is an important difference between groups and organizational units (OUs)?
   a. An OU can represent the various divisions of your organization.
   b. Group membership can be a subset of an OU.
   c. OUs are a security entity.
   d. Group memberships are independent of the domain's tree structure.

Best Answer

Choose the letter that corresponds to the best answer. More than one answer choice may achieve the goal. Select the BEST answer.

1. What is the key difference between groups and Organizational Units (OUs)?
   a. Because groups are independent from domain structure, its members may be located anywhere in the domain or outside the domain.
   b. You cannot apply Group Policy settings directly to group objects.
   c. OUs are containers, whereas groups are not containers.
   d. There is essentially no difference between OUs and groups.

2. An Active Directory functional level must be low enough to ensure interoperability between domain controllers running different versions of Windows Server. How does the functional level affect the AD forest?
   a. Higher functional level means more efficient AD communication.
   b. Higher functional level means few Global Catalog errors.
   c. Lower functional level means fewer features available.
   d. Lower functional level means time to upgrade the lowest servers.

3. What is the primary reason for creating different sites on an Active Directory network?
   a. To create geographical divisions within the Active Directory
   b. To provide another boundary when applying Group Policy settings (along with domains and OUs)
   c. To provide a layer of access control between objects in differing sites
   d. To control the amount of traffic passing over the relatively slow and expensive WAN links between locations

4. What is the simplest way for administrators to upgrade their Active Directory Domain Services (AD DS) infrastructure to Windows Server 2012?
   a. Upgrade all existing down-level domain controllers (DCs) to Windows Server 2012.
   b. In Server Manager, use the Active Directory Domain Services Configuration Wizard to update a DC.
   c. Add a new Windows Server 2012 server to your existing Directory Services installation.
   d. Use Adprep.exe, included in the operating system.

5. Is it possible to add AD DS on a computer running Server Core?
   a. No, you require the full GUI installation of Windows Server 2012.
   b. Yes, you use Dcpromo.exe and accompanying answer files.
   c. No, unless all servers are already running Windows 2012.
   d. Yes, you use PowerShell, by first installing AD DS role, and then promoting the server to a DC.

Build a List

1. Order the steps to create a site topology. Not all steps will be used.
   a. Manually create the sites.
   b. Configure site link objects.
   c. Create and configure the subnets.
   d. There are no steps needed beyond site creation needed. Full site topology is done automatically in Active Directory.

2. Order the steps to install AD DS role.
   a. Confirm installation if not selecting from optional functions.
   b. Select the server that you want to promote to a DC and click Next. Select the Active Directory Domain Service role.
   c. Leave the Role-based or feature-based installation radio button selected and click Next.
   d. Click Add Features to accept the dependencies, and then click Next.
   e. From the Server Manager's Manage menu, select Add Roles and Features.

3. Order the steps to create a new forest.
   a. Select the Add a new forest option and in the Root domain name text box, type the name of the domain you want to create.
   b. Consider the earliest Windows versions you plan to install as DCs to specify the Forest and Domain functional levels.
   c. On the Installation progress page that appears at the end of the AD DS role installation procedure, click the Promote this server to a domain controller hyperlink. The Active Directory Domain Services Configuration Wizard appears.
   d. Specify the password for Directory Services Restore Mode (DSRM).
   e. Confirm the NetBIOS equivalent of the domain and paths for AD DS file where applicable.

4. Order the steps to add a DC to an existing domain.

   a. On the Installation progress page that appears at the end of the AD DS role installation procedure, click the Promote this server to a domain controller hyperlink. The Active Directory Domain Services Configuration Wizard appears.

   b. Select an existing DC to function as a Replication source.

   c. Select any options as needed: Install DNS, Leave a Global Catalog, or Select Read only domain controller.

   d. Select the Add a domain controller to an existing domain option and then click Select.

   e. Select a site where the DC will be located.

   f. Specify the password for Directory Services Restore Mode (DSRM).

   g. After authenticating if necessary, specify the domain from the forest to which the new server will be added.

5. Order the steps to install AD DS on a computer running the Server Core installation. Not all steps will be used.

   a. Promote the server to a DC using the appropriate cmdlet and parameters.

   b. Use Adprep.exe with necessary parameters.

   c. In an elevated Windows PowerShell session, use the following command:
   ```
   Install-WindowsFeature -name AD-Domain-Services
   -IncludeManagementTools
   ```

   d. Use Dcpromo.exe with necessary parameters.

■ Business Case Scenarios

Scenario 13-1: Creating AD DS Domains

Robert is designing a new Active Directory Domain Services infrastructure for a company called Litware, Inc., which has its headquarters in New York and two additional offices in London and Tokyo. The London office consists only of sales and marketing staff; it does not have its own IT department. The Tokyo office is larger, with representatives from all of the company departments, including a full IT staff. The Tokyo office is connected to the headquarters using a 64 Kbps demand-dial link, and the London office has a 512-Kbps frame relay connection. The company has registered the litware.com domain name, and Robert has created a subdomain called inside.litware.com for use by Active Directory.

Based on this information, design an Active Directory infrastructure for Litware, Inc. that is as economical as possible, specifying how many domains to create, what to name them, how many domain controllers to install, and where. Explain each of your decisions.

Scenario 13-2: Using Install from Media (IFM)

As you prepare some remote sites for domain controllers, you need the most efficient way to deploy replica DCs. You learn about Install from Media checkbox on the Additional Options page of the Active Directory Domain Services Configuration Wizard. Outline the steps taken in the interactive IFM wizard.

Creating and Managing Active Directory Users and Computers

70-410 EXAM OBJECTIVE

Objective 5.2 – Create and manage Active Directory users and computers. This objective may include but is not limited to: Automate the creation of Active Directory accounts; create, copy, configure, and delete users and computers; configure templates; perform bulk Active Directory operations; configure user rights; offline domain join; manage inactive and disabled accounts.

LESSON HEADING	EXAM OBJECTIVE
Creating User Objects	Create, copy, configure, and delete users and computers
Understanding User Creation Tools	
Creating Single Users	
Creating User Templates	Configure templates
Creating Multiple Users	Automate the creation of Active Directory accounts Perform bulk Active Directory operations
Creating Computer Objects	
Creating Computer Objects Using Active Directory Users and Computers	
Creating Computer Objects Using Active Directory Administrative Center	
Creating Computer Objects Using Dsadd.exe	
Managing Active Directory Objects	
Managing Multiple Users	
Joining Computers to a Domain	Configure user rights Offline domain join
Managing Disabled Accounts	Manage inactive and disabled accounts

■ Creating User Objects

THE BOTTOM LINE

The user account is the primary means by which people using an Active Directory Domain Services (AD DS) network access resources.

Resource access for individuals takes place through their individual user accounts. To gain access to the network, prospective network users must authenticate to a network with a specific user account. Authentication is the process of confirming a user's identity by using a known value such as a password, a smart card, or a fingerprint. When a user supplies a name and password, the authentication process validates the credentials supplied in the logon against information that is stored within the AD DS database. Do not confuse authentication with authorization, which is the process of confirming that an authenticated user has the correct permissions to access one or more network resources.

The following two types of user accounts run on Windows Server 2012 systems:

CERTIFICATION READY
Create, copy, configure, and delete users and computers.
Objective 5.2

- *Local users* can access only resources on the local computer and are stored in the local *Security Account Manager (SAM)* database on the computer where they reside. Local accounts are never replicated to other computers, nor do these accounts provide domain access. A local account configured on one server cannot be used to access resources on a second server; you need to configure a second local account in that case.

- *Domain users* can access AD DS or network-based resources, such as shared folders and printers. Account information for these users is stored in the AD DS database and replicated to all domain controllers within the same domain. A subset of the domain user account information is replicated to the global catalog, which is then replicated to other global catalog servers throughout the forest.

By default, two built-in user accounts are created on a computer running Windows Server 2012: the Administrator account and the Guest account. Built-in user accounts can be local accounts or domain accounts, depending on whether the server is a standalone server or a domain controller. In the case of a standalone server, the built-in accounts are local accounts on the server itself. On a domain controller, the built-in accounts are domain accounts that are replicated to each domain controller.

On a member server or standalone server, the built-in local Administrator account has full control of all files and complete management permissions for the local computer. On a domain controller, the built-in Administrator account created in Active Directory has full control of the domain in which it was created. By default, each domain has only one built-in administrator account. Neither the local Administrator account on a member server or standalone server nor a domain Administrator account can be deleted; however, they can be renamed.

The following list summarizes several security guidelines you should consider regarding the Administrator account:

- **Rename the Administrator account:** This guideline staves off attacks that are targeted specifically at the "administrator" username on a server or domain. This protects only against fairly unsophisticated attacks; therefore, you should not rely on this as the only means of protecting the accounts on your network.
- **Set a strong password:** Make sure that the password has at least seven characters and contains uppercase and lowercase letters, numbers, and alphanumeric characters.
- **Limit knowledge of administrator passwords to only a few individuals:** Limiting the distribution of administrator passwords decreases the risk of security breaches using this account.
- **Do not use the Administrator account for daily non-administrative tasks:** Microsoft recommends using a non-administrative user account for normal work and using the *Run As* command when administrative tasks need to be performed.

You use the built-in Guest account to provide temporary access to the network for a user such as a vendor representative or a temporary employee. Like the Administrator account, you cannot delete this account, but you should rename it. In addition, the Guest account is disabled by default and is not assigned a default password. In most environments, you should consider creating unique accounts for temporary user access rather than relying on the Guest account. In this way, you can be sure the account follows corporate security guidelines defined for temporary users. However, if you decide to use the Guest account, review the following guidelines:

- **Rename the Guest account after enabling it for use:** As we discuss with the Administrator account, this denies intruders a username, which is half of the information necessary to gain access to your domain.
- **Set a strong password:** By default, the Guest account is configured with a blank password. For security reasons, you should not allow a blank password. Make sure that the password is at least seven characters and contains uppercase and lowercase letters, numbers, and alphanumeric characters.

Understanding User Creation Tools

One of the most common tasks for administrators is the creation of Active Directory user objects. Windows Server 2012 includes several tools you can use to create objects. The specific tool you use depends on how many objects you need to create, the time frame available for the creation of these groups, and any special circumstances, such as importing users from an existing database.

When creating a single user, you can use Active Directory Administrative Center (ADAC) or the Active Directory Users and Computers console. However, when you need to create multiple users in a short time frame or you have an existing database from which to import these objects, you should choose a more efficient tool. Windows Server 2012 provides several tools you can choose according to what you want to accomplish. The following list describes the most commonly used methods for creating multiple users and groups. These tools are detailed in the upcoming sections.

- ***Dsadd.exe:*** The standard command line tool for creating AD DS leaf objects, which you can use with batch files to create AD DS objects in bulk.
- ***Windows PowerShell:*** The currently approved Windows maintenance tool, with which you can create object creation scripts of nearly unlimited complexity.
- ***Comma-Separated Value Directory Exchange (CSVDE.exe):*** A command-line utility that can create new AD DS objects by importing information from a comma-separated value (.csv) file.

- *LDAP Data Interchange Format Directory Exchange (LDIFDE.exe):* Like CSVDE, a utility that can import AD DS information and use it to add, delete, or modify objects, in addition to modifying the schema, if necessary.

These tools have their roles in network administration; it is up to you to select the best tool to suit your skill set and a particular situation. For example, you might have two tools that can accomplish a job, but your first choice might be the tool that you are most familiar with or the one that can accomplish the task in a shorter amount of time.

The following sections examine various scenarios for using these tools to create user objects.

Creating Single Users

For some administrators, creating individual user accounts is a daily task, and there are many ways to go about it.

Windows Server 2012 redesigned the Active Directory Administrative Center (ADAC) application, first introduced in Windows Server 2008 R2, to fully incorporate new features such as the Active Directory Recycle Bin and fine-grained password policies. You can also use the tool to create and manage AD DS user accounts.

To create a single user account with the Active Directory Administrative Center, use the following procedure.

CREATE A USER WITH ACTIVE DIRECTORY ADMINISTRATIVE CENTER

GET READY. Log on to the server running Windows Server 2012 using an account with administrative privileges.

Figure 14-1

The Active Directory Administrative Center console

1. From the Tools menu in the *Server Manager* window, select Active Directory Administrative Center. The *Active Directory Administrative Center* console appears, as shown in Figure 14-1.

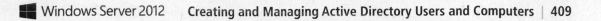

Figure 14-2

A container in the Active
Directory Administrative
Center console

2. In the left pane, find the domain in which you want to create the user object and select a container in that domain, as shown in Figure 14-2.

Active Directory Administrative Center

◄◄ adatum (local) ▸ Users   ▾ ↻ | Manage   Help

Active Directory... ‹   **Users (21)**   **Tasks**

▪ Overview

▸ adatum (local)

   Users

   Domain Controllers

▸ Dynamic Access Control

🔍 Global Search

Filter 🔍   ⊟ ▾ ⊞ ▾   ⌄

Name	Type	Description
Administrator	User	Built-in account for admini...
Allowed RODC Password...	Group	Members in this group ca...
Cert Publishers	Group	Members of this group ar...
Cloneable Domain Control...	Group	Members of this group th...
Denied RODC Password R...	Group	Members in this group ca...

Administrator   ⌄

User logon: Administrator   Expiration: <Never>
E-mail: Last log on: 8/16/2012 11:26 PM
Modified: 8/16/2012 11:38 PM
Description: Built-in account for administering the computer/domain

Summary

WINDOWS POWERSHELL HISTORY

Tasks panel:

Administrator ⌃
Reset password...
View resultant password settin...
Add to group...
Disable
Delete
Move...
Properties

Users ⌃
New ▸
Delete
Search under this node
Properties

☑ Show All

---

3. In the Tasks pane, under the container name, click New > User. The *Create User* window appears, as shown in Figure 14-3.

Figure 14-3

The *Create User window* in the
Active Directory Administrative
Center console

Create User: TASKS ▾   SECTIONS ▾

✳ Account   **Account**   ? ✱ ⌃
   Organization
   Member Of   First name: [   ]   Account expires: ● Never
   Password Settings Middle initials: [   ]   ○ End of [   ]
   Profile   Last name: [   ]
                      Full name: ✳ [   ]   Password options:
                      User UPN logon: [   ] @ [▾]   ● User must change password at next log on
                      User SamAccoun... adatum \✳ [   ] ○ Other password options
                                                        ☐ Smart card is required for interactive log...
                      Password: [   ]   ☐ Password never expires
                      Confirm password: [   ]   ☐ User cannot change password
                      Create in: CN=Users,DC=adatum,DC=info Change... Encryption options: ▾
                      ☐ Protect from accidental deletion   Other options: ▾
                         Log on hours...   Log on to...

Organization   ⊗ ⌃
   Display name: [   ]   Job title: [   ]
   Office: [   ]   Department: [   ]
   E-mail: [   ]   Company: [   ]
   Web page: [   ]   Manager: [   ] Edit... Clear
             Other web pages...   Direct reports:

⌃ More Information   OK   Cancel

TAKE NOTE＊

By default, the *User must change password at next logon* option will compel the user to supply his or her own new password later.

4. Type the user's name in the Full Name field and an account name in the User SamAccountName Logon field.

5. Type an initial password for the user in the Password and Confirm password fields.

6. Supply information for any of the optional fields on the page you want.

7. Click OK. The user object appears in the container.

CLOSE the *Active Directory Administrative Center* console.

Administrators who are comfortable with the familiar Active Directory Users and Computers console can still create user objects with this tool, by using the following procedure.

CREATE A USER WITH ACTIVE DIRECTORY USERS AND COMPUTERS

GET READY. Log on to the server running Windows Server 2012 using an account with administrative privileges.

1. From the Tools menu in the *Server Manager* window, select Active Directory Users and Computers. The *Active Directory Users and Computers* console appears, as shown in Figure 14-4.

Figure 14-4

The Active Directory Users and Computers console

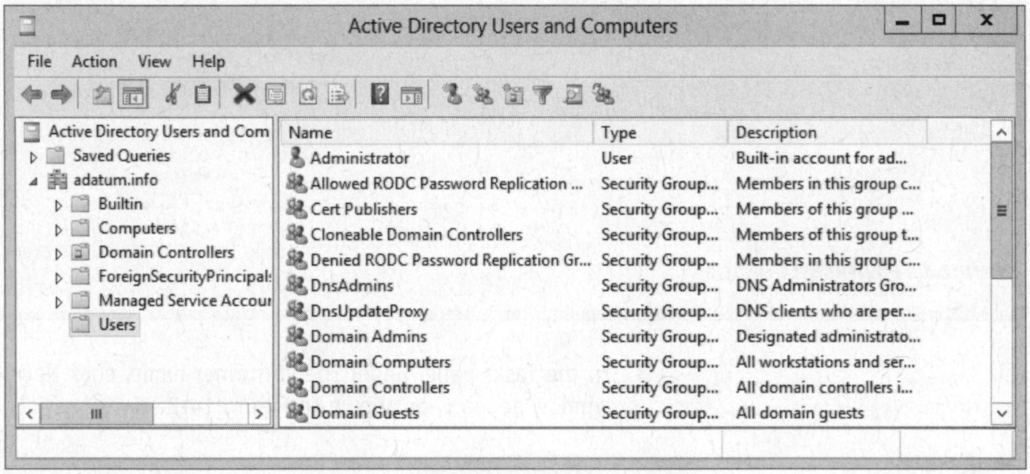

2. In the left pane, find the domain in which you want to create the user object and select a container in that domain.

3. From the Action menu, select New > User. *The New Object – User Wizard* appears, as shown in Figure 14-5.

Figure 14-5

The New Object - User Wizard

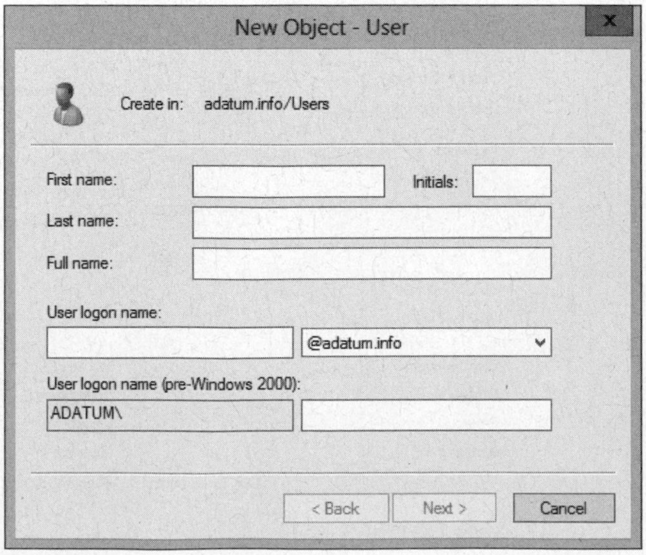

4. Type the user's name in the Full Name field and an account name in the User logon name field.

5. Click Next. The second page of the *New Object – User Wizard* appears, as shown in Figure 14-6.

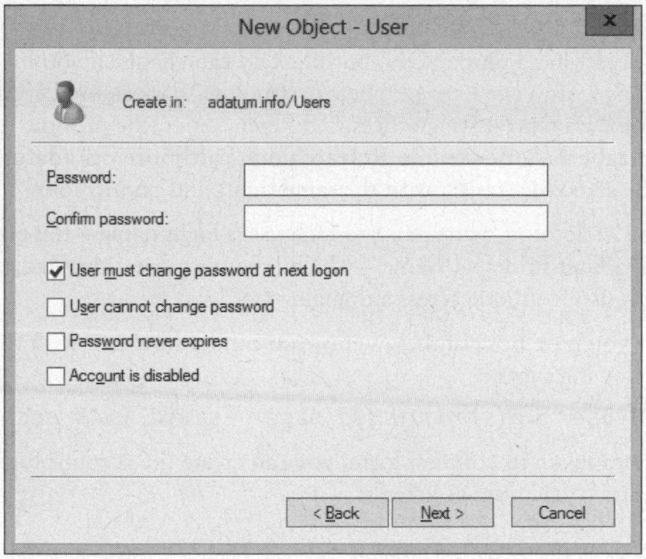

Figure 14-6

The second page of the New Object - User Wizard

6. Type an initial password for the user in the Password and Confirm password fields.

7. Click Next. A confirmation page listing the settings you configured appears.

8. Click Finish. The wizard creates the user object and closes.

CLOSE the *Active Directory Users and Computers* console.

For administrators working on Server Core installations, or for those who are just more comfortable with the command line, it is also possible to create user objects without a graphical interface.

USING DSADD.EXE

For administrators more comfortable with the traditional command prompt, the Dsadd.exe program can create new user objects by using the syntax shown in Figure 14-7.

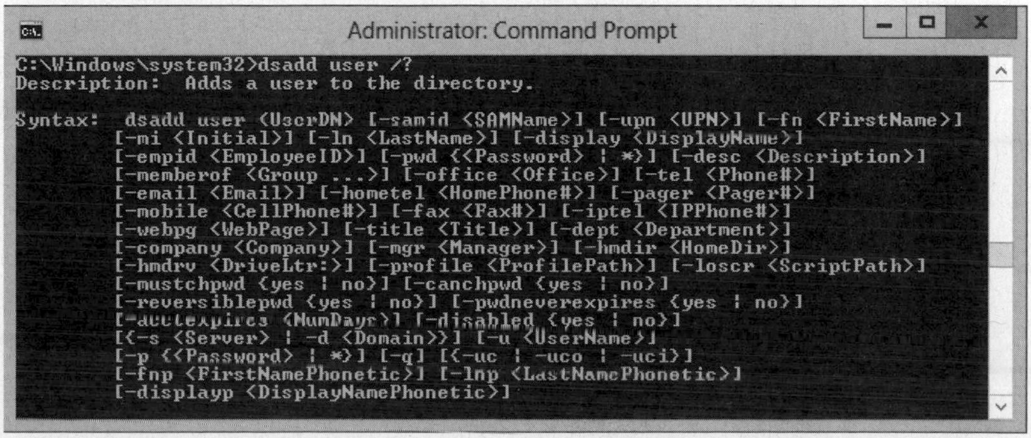

Figure 14-7

Syntax of the Dsadd.exe program

To create a user by using the Dsadd.exe utility, you must know the distinguished name (DN) for the user and the user's login ID, also known as the **SAM account name** attribute within AD DS. The distinguished name of an object signifies its relative location within the Active Directory structure. For example, in the distinguished name **cn=Elizabeth Andersen,ou=Research,dc=adatum,dc=com**, the "cn" refers to the common name for Elizabeth Andersen's user account, which resides in the Research OU, which resides in the adatum.com domain.

Each object has a unique DN, but this DN can change if you move the object to different locations within the Active Directory structure. For example, if you create an additional layer of OUs representing offices in different cities, the previous DN might change to **cn=Elizabeth Andersen,ou=Research,ou=Baltimore,dc=adatum,dc=com**, even though it is the same user object with the same rights and permissions.

The SAM account name refers to each user's login name—the portion to the left of the "@" within a User Principal Name—which is **eander** in **eander@adatum.com**. The SAM account name must be unique across a domain.

When you have both of these items, you can create a user with the Dsadd.exe utility by using the following syntax:

```
dsadd user <distinguished name> -samid <SAM account name>
```

For example, in its simplest form, you can create the account for Elizabeth Andersen referenced previously as follows:

```
dsadd user
cn="Elizabeth Andersen,ou=Research,dc=adatum,dc=com"
-samid eander
```

You can also add attribute values with the Dsadd.exe tool. The following command adds some of the most common attributes to the user object:

```
Dsadd.exe User
"CN=Elizabeth Andersen,OU=Research,DC=adatum,DC=local"
-samid "eander"
-fn "Elizabeth"
-ln "Andersen"
-disabled no
-mustchpwd yes
-pwd "Pa$$w0rd"
```

USING WINDOWS POWERSHELL

Microsoft is placing increased emphasis on Windows PowerShell as a server management tool and provides a cmdlet called *New-ADUser*, which you can use to create a user account and configure any or all the attributes associated with it. The New-ADUser cmdlet has many parameters, to enable access to all the user object's attributes, as shown in Figure 14-8.

For example, to create a new user object for Elizabeth Andersen in an organizational unit called *Research*, you can use the New-ADUser command with the following parameters:

```
new-ADUser
-Name "Elizabeth Andersen"
-SamAccountName "eander"
-GivenName "Elizabeth"
-SurName "Andersen"
-path 'OU=Research,DC=adatum,dc=local'
-Enabled $true
-AccountPassword "Pa$$w0rd"
-ChangePasswordAtLogon $true
```

The `-Name` and `-SamAccountName` parameters are required to identify the object. The `-path` parameter specifies the location of the object in the AD DS hierarchy. The `-Enabled` parameter ensures that the account is active.

Figure 14-8

Syntax of the New-ADUser
cmdlet

```
                        Administrator: Windows PowerShell                    _  □  X

NAME
    New-ADUser

SYNTAX
    New-ADUser [-Name] <string> [-WhatIf] [-Confirm] [-AccountExpirationDate <datetime>] [-AccountNotDelegated <bool>]
    [-AccountPassword <securestring>] [-AllowReversiblePasswordEncryption <bool>] [-AuthType <ADAuthType> {Negotiate |
    Basic}] [-CannotChangePassword <bool>] [-Certificates <X509Certificate[]>] [-ChangePasswordAtLogon <bool>] [-City
    <string>] [-Company <string>] [-CompoundIdentitySupported <bool>] [-Country <string>] [-Credential <pscredential>]
    [-Department <string>] [-Description <string>] [-DisplayName <string>] [-Division <string>] [-EmailAddress
    <string>] [-EmployeeID <string>] [-EmployeeNumber <string>] [-Enabled <bool>] [-Fax <string>] [-GivenName
    <string>] [-HomeDirectory <string>] [-HomeDrive <string>] [-HomePage <string>] [-HomePhone <string>] [-Initials
    <string>] [-Instance <ADUser>] [-KerberosEncryptionType <ADKerberosEncryptionType> {None | DES | RC4 | AES128 |
    AES256}] [-LogonWorkstations <string>] [-Manager <ADUser>] [-MobilePhone <string>] [-Office <string>]
    [-OfficePhone <string>] [-Organization <string>] [-OtherAttributes <hashtable>] [-OtherName <string>] [-PassThru]
    [-PasswordNeverExpires <bool>] [-PasswordNotRequired <bool>] [-Path <string>] [-POBox <string>] [-PostalCode
    <string>] [-PrincipalsAllowedToDelegateToAccount <ADPrincipal[]>] [-ProfilePath <string>] [-SamAccountName
    <string>] [-ScriptPath <string>] [-Server <string>] [-ServicePrincipalNames <string[]>] [-SmartcardLogonRequired
    <bool>] [-State <string>] [-StreetAddress <string>] [-Surname <string>] [-Title <string>] [-TrustedForDelegation
    <bool>] [-Type <string>] [-UserPrincipalName <string>] [<CommonParameters>]
```

Creating User Templates

In some cases, you need to create single users on a regular basis, but the user accounts contain so many attributes that creating them individually becomes time-consuming.

CERTIFICATION READY
Configure templates.
Objective 5.2

One way to speed up the process of creating complex user objects is to use the New-ADUser cmdlet or the Dsadd.exe program and retain your commands in a script or batch file. However, if you prefer a graphical interface, you can do roughly the same thing by creating a user template.

A user template is a standard user object containing boilerplate attribute settings. To create a new user with these settings, you copy the template to a new user object and change the name and any other attributes that are unique to the user.

To create a user template with the Active Directory Users and Computers console, use the following procedure.

➡ **CREATE A USER TEMPLATE**

GET READY. Log on to the server running Windows Server 2012 using an account with administrative privileges.

1. From the Tools menu in the *Server Manager* window, select Active Directory Users and Computers. The *Active Directory Users and Computers* console appears.

2. In the left pane, find the domain in which you want to create the user object and select a container in that domain.

3. From the Action menu, select New > User. The *New Object – User Wizard* appears.

4. Type Default Template, or a similarly descriptive name, in the Full Name field and an account name in the User logon name field.

5. Click Next. The second page of the *New Object – User Wizard* appears.

6. Type an initial password for the user in the Password and Confirm password fields.

7. Clear the *User must change password at next logon* check box.

8. Select the Account is disabled check box and click Next. A confirmation page listing the settings you configured appears.

9. Click Finish. The wizard creates the user object and closes.

10. Locate the user you just created in the console and double-click it to open its Properties sheet, as shown in Figure 14-9.

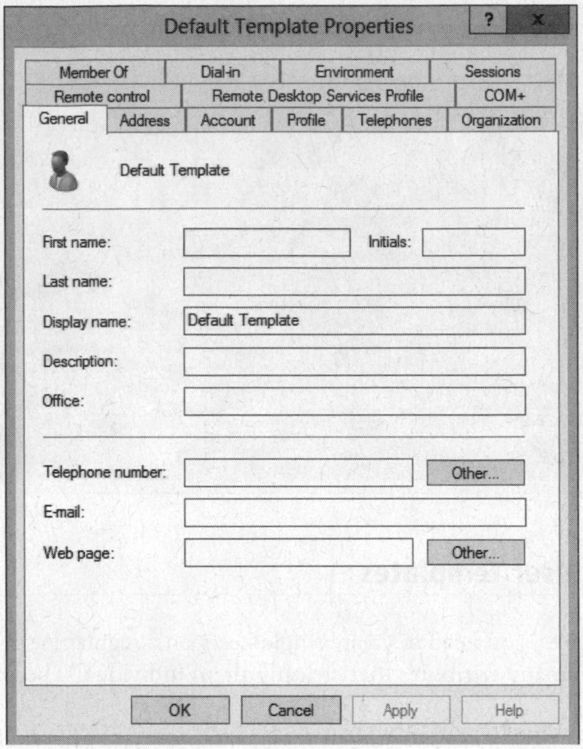

Figure 14-9

A user object's Properties sheet

11. Modify the attributes on the various tabs with values common to all the users you create.
12. Click OK.

CLOSE the *Active Directory Users and Computers* console.

To use the template, right-click the *Default Template* user object and, from the context menu, select *Copy*. The *Copy Object – User Wizard* appears, as shown in Figure 14-10.

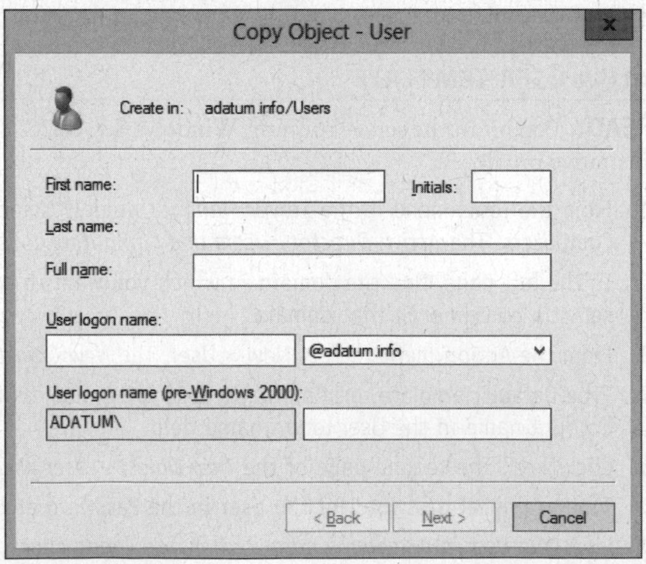

Figure 14-10

The Copy Object – User Wizard

Enter the required unique information for the user and clear the *Account is disabled* check box before clicking *OK*. The wizard creates a new user object with all the attributes you configured in the template.

Creating Multiple Users

> Administrators sometimes have to create hundreds or thousands of user objects, which makes the single object creation procedures impractical.

CERTIFICATION READY
Automate the creation
of Active Directory
accounts.
Objective 5.2

The previous sections in this lesson describe the procedures for creating single users and group objects by using the graphical user interface (GUI) and some of the available command-line tools in Windows Server 2012. The following sections examine some of the mechanisms for automating the creation of large numbers of Active Directory objects.

USING BATCH FILES

Batch files are commonly used files that can be written using any text editor. You can write a batch file to create objects in AD DS by following standard batch file rules and calling the Dsadd.exe program. You can also use Dsadd.exe to create, delete, view, and modify Active Directory objects, including users, groups, and OUs.

To create multiple objects (including users, groups, or any other object type) by using a batch file, open *Notepad* and use the Dsadd.exe syntax described previously, by placing a single command on each line. After you enter the commands you need, save the file and name it using a .cmd or .bat extension. Files with .cmd or .bat extensions are processed line by line when you execute the batch file at a command prompt or double-click on the file in Windows Explorer.

USING CSVDE.EXE

Some applications such as Microsoft Excel can generate a number of users, along with their accompanying information, to add to the AD DS database. In these cases, you can export information from the applications by saving it to a file in *Comma-Separated Values (CSV)* format. CSV format also can be used to import information into and export it from other third-party applications. For example, you might need to export user account information to a file for use in another third-party application, such as a UNIX database. CSVDE.exe provides this capability as well.

A CSV file is a plain text file that consists of records, each on a separate line that are divided into fields and separated by commas. The format saves database information in a universally understandable way.

CERTIFICATION READY
Perform bulk Active
Directory operations.
Objective 5.2

The CSVDE.exe command-line utility enables you to import or export Active Directory objects. It uses a CSV file that is based on a header record, which identifies the attribute contained in each comma-delimited field. The *header record* is the first line of the text file that uses proper attribute names. To import into AD DS, the attribute names in the CSV file must match the attributes allowed by the Active Directory schema. For example, to import a list of people and telephone numbers as users into the Active Directory database, you need to create a header record that accurately reflects the object names and attributes you want to create. Review the following attributes that are commonly used for creating user accounts.

- *dn* specifies the distinguished name of the object so that the object can be properly placed in Active Directory.
- *samAccountName* populates the SAM account field
- *objectClass* specifies the type of object to be created, such as user, group, or OU.
- *telephoneNumber* populates the Telephone Number field.
- *userPrincipalName* populates the User Principal Name field for the account.

As you create your CSV file, you must order the data to reflect the sequence of the attributes in the header record. If fields and data are out of order, you will either encounter an error when running the CSVDE.exe utility or you might not get accurate results in the created objects. The following header record example uses the previously listed attributes to create a user object.

```
dn,samAccountName,userPrincipalName,telephoneNumber,
objectClass
```

A data record conforming to this header record appears as follows:

```
"cn=Elizabeth
Andersen,ou=Research,dc=adatum,dc=com",eander,eander@
adatum.com,586-555-1234,user
```

After you add a record for each account you want to create, save the file using .csv as the extension. You then use the following command syntax to run the CSVDE.exe program and import the file.

```
csvde.exe -i -f <filename.csv>
```

The -i switch tells CSVDE.exe that this operation will import data. The -f switch specifies the .csv file containing the records to be imported.

USING LDIFDE.EXE

LDIFDE.exe is a utility that has the same basic functionality as CSVDE.exe and provides the capability to modify existing records in Active Directory. For this reason, LDIFDE.exe is a more flexible option. Consider an example where you need to import 200 new users into your AD DS structure. In this case, you can use CSVDE.exe or LDIFDE.exe to import the users. However, you can use LDIFDE.exe to modify or delete the objects later, whereas CSVDE.exe does not provide this option.

You can use any text editor to create the LDIFDE.exe input file, which is formatted according to the *LDAP Data Interchange Format (LDIF)* standard. The format for the data file containing the object records you want to create is significantly different from CSVDE.exe. The following example shows the syntax for a data file to create the same user account discussed in the CSVDE.exe example.

```
dn: "cn=Elizabeth
Andersen,ou=Research,dc=adatum,dc=com"

changetype: add
ObjectClass: user
SAMAccountName: eander
UserPrincipalName: eander@adatum.com
telephoneNumber: 586-555-1234
```

By using LDIFDE.exe, you can specify one of three actions to perform with the LDIF file:

- *Add* creates new objects using the LDIF records.
- *Modify* modifies existing object attributes using the LDIF records.
- *Delete* deletes existing objects using the LDIF records.

After creating the data file and saving it using the .LDF file extension, use the following syntax to execute the LDIFDE.exe program.

```
ldifde -i -f <filename.ldf>
```

The next example illustrates the LDIF syntax to modify the telephone number of an existing user object. Note that the hyphen in the last line is required for the file to function correctly.

```
dn: "cn=Elizabeth
Andersen,ou=Research,dc=adatum,dc=com

changetype: modify
replace: telephoneNumber
telephoneNumber: 586-555-1111
-
```

USING WINDOWS POWERSHELL

It also is possible to use CSV files to create user objects with Windows PowerShell, by using the Import-CSV cmdlet to read the data from the file and piping it to the New-ADUser cmdlet. To insert the data from the file into the correct user object attributes, you use the New-ADUser cmdlet parameters to reference the field names in the CSV file's header record.

An example of a bulk user creation command is as follows:

```
Import-CSV users Finance.csv | foreach
{New-ADUser -SamAccountName $_.SamAccountName
-Name $_.Name -Surname $_.Surname
-GivenName $_.GivenName -Path
"OU=Research,DC=adatum,DC=COM" -AccountPassword
Pa$$w0rd -Enabled $true}
```

■ Creating Computer Objects

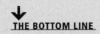

THE BOTTOM LINE

Because an AD DS network uses a centralized directory, you need a way to track the computers that are part of the domain. To do this, Active Directory uses computer accounts, which are realized in the form of computer objects in the Active Directory database. You might have a valid Active Directory user account and a password, but if your computer is not represented by a computer object, you cannot log on to the domain.

Computer objects are stored in the Active Directory hierarchy just as user objects are, and they possess many of the same capabilities, such as the following:

- Computer objects consist of properties that specify the computer's name, where it is located, and who is permitted to manage it.
- Computer objects inherit group policy settings from container objects such as domains, sites, and organizational units.
- Computer objects can be members of groups and inherit permissions from group objects.

When a user attempts to log on to an Active Directory domain, the client computer establishes a connection to a domain controller to authenticate the user's identity. However, before the user authentication occurs, the two computers perform a preliminary authentication using their respective computer objects, to ensure that both systems are part of the domain. The NetLogon service running on the client computer connects to the same service on the domain controller, and then each one verifies that the other system has a valid computer account. When this validation is completed, the two systems establish a secure communications channel between them, which they can then use to begin the user authentication process.

The computer account validation between the client and the domain controller is a genuine authentication process using account names and passwords, just as when a user authenticates to the domain. The difference is that the passwords used by the computer accounts generate automatically and keep hidden. You can reset a computer account, but you do not need to supply passwords for everyone.

What all this means for administrators is that, in addition to creating user accounts in the domain, they have to make sure that the network computers are part of the domain as well. Adding a computer to an AD DS domain consists of two steps:

- **Creating a computer account:** You create a computer account by creating a new computer object in Active Directory and assigning the name of an actual computer on the network.

- **Joining the computer to the domain:** When you join a computer to the domain, the system contacts a domain controller, establishes a trust relationship with the domain, locates (or creates) a computer object corresponding to the computer's name, alters its security identifier (SID) to match the computer object, and modifies its group memberships.

How these steps are performed, and who performs them, depends on the way in which you deploy computers on your network. You can create new computer objects in many ways, but how you elect to do this depends on several factors, including the number of objects you need to create, where you will be when creating the objects, and what tools you prefer to use.

Generally speaking, you create computer objects when you deploy new computers in the domain. After an object represents a computer and joins to the domain, any user in the domain can log on from that computer. For example, you do not need to create new computer objects or rejoin computers to the domain when employees leave the company and new hires start using their computers. However, if you reinstall the operating system on a computer, you must create a new computer object for it (or reset the existing one), because the newly installed computer will have a different SID.

The creation of a computer object must always occur before the corresponding computer can join the domain, although it sometimes does not appear that way. You can use the following two basic strategies for creating Active Directory computer objects:

- Create the computer objects in advance by using an Active Directory tool, so that the computers can locate the existing objects when they are in the domain.
- Begin the joining process first and let the computer create its own computer object.

In each case, the computer object exists before the joining takes place. In the second strategy, the joining process appears to begin first, but the computer creates the object before the joining process begins.

When you have a number of computers to deploy, particularly in different locations, you might prefer to create the computer objects in advance. For large numbers of computers, you can automate the computer object creation process by using command-line tools and batch files. The following sections examine the tools you can use for computer object creation.

Creating Computer Objects Using Active Directory Users and Computers

As with user objects, you can create computer objects with the *Active Directory Users and Computers* console.

To create computer objects in an Active Directory domain, using the Active Directory Users and Computers console or any tool, you must have the appropriate permissions for the container in which the objects will be located. By default, the Administrators group has permission to create objects anywhere in the domain and the Account Operators group has the special permissions needed to create computer objects in and delete them from the Computers container, as well as from any new organizational units you create. The Domain Admins and Enterprise Admins groups are members of the Administrators group, so members of these groups can create computer objects anywhere, as well. You also can explicitly delegate control of containers to particular users or groups, enabling them to create computer objects in these containers.

The process of creating a computer object in Active Directory Users and Computers is similar to creating a user object. You select the container in which you want to place the object and, from the *Action* menu, select *New > Computer*. The *New Object – Computer Wizard* appears, as shown in Figure 14-11.

Figure 14-11

The New Object – Computer
wizard

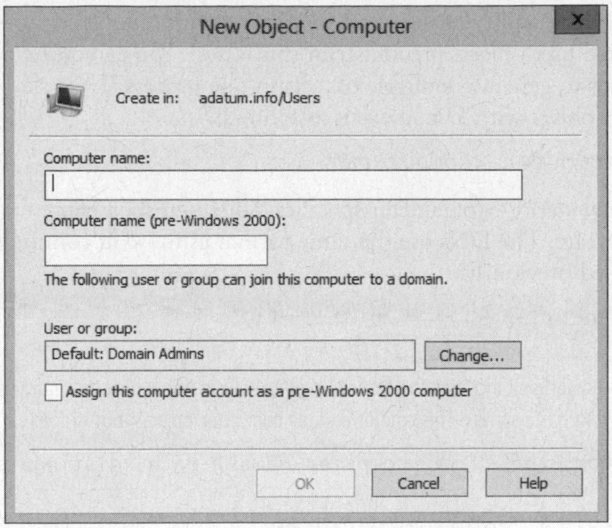

Computer objects have relatively few attributes, and in most cases, you will most likely just supply them with a name, which can be up to 64 characters long. This name must match the name of the computer joined with the object.

Creating Computer Objects Using Active Directory Administrative Center

As with users, you also can create computer objects in the ADAC.

To create a computer object, you choose a container and then select *New > Computer* from the *Tasks* list to display the *Create Computer* dialog box, as shown in Figure 14-12.

Figure 14-12

The Create Computer
dialog box

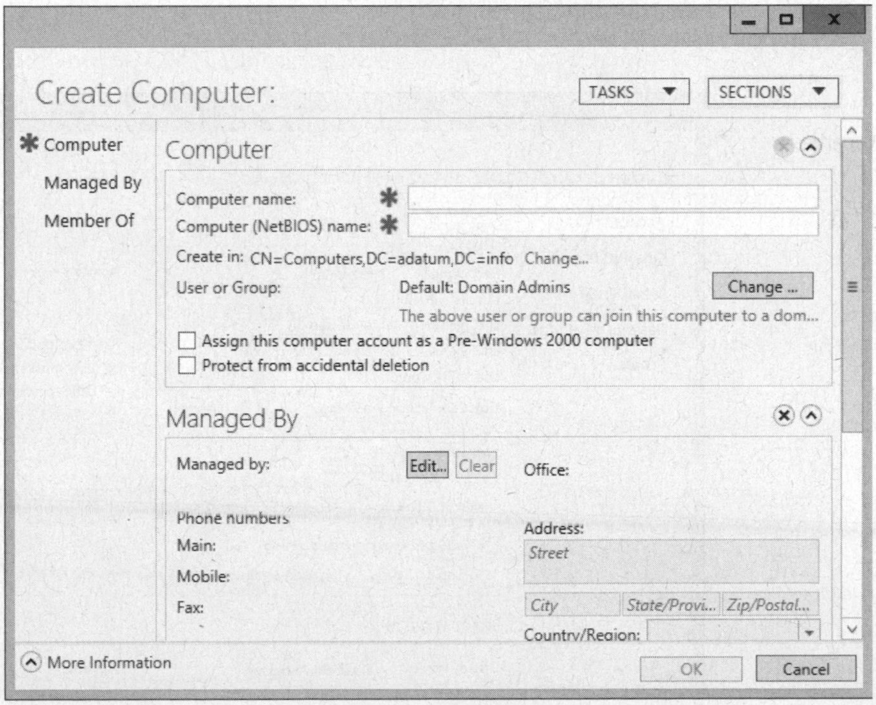

Creating Computer Objects Using Dsadd.exe

As with users, the graphical tools provided with Windows Server 2012 are good for creating and managing single objects, but many administrators turn to the command line when they need to create multiple objects.

The Dsadd.exe utility enables you to create computer objects from the command line, just as you created user objects previously in this lesson. You can create a batch file of Dsadd.exe commands to generate multiple objects in one process. The basic syntax for creating a computer object with Dsadd.exe is as follows:

```
dsadd computer <ComputerDN>
```

The *<ComputerDN>* parameter specifies a distinguished name for the new group object you want to create. The DNs use the same format as those in comma-separated value (CSV) files, as discussed previously.

USING WINDOWS POWERSHELL

Windows PowerShell includes the New-ADComputer cmdlet, which you can use to create computer objects with the following basic syntax. This cmdlet creates computer objects, but it does not join them to a domain.

```
new-ADComputer -Name <computer name> -path <distinguished name>
```

■ Managing Active Directory Objects

↓ THE BOTTOM LINE

After you create user and computer objects, you can manage them and modify them in many of the same ways that you created them.

Double-clicking any object in the ADAC (see Figure 14-13) or the Active Directory Users and Computers console (see Figure 14-14) opens the Properties sheet for that object. The windows appear different, but they contain the same information and provide the same capability to alter the object attributes.

Figure 14-13

A user object's Properties sheet in ADAC

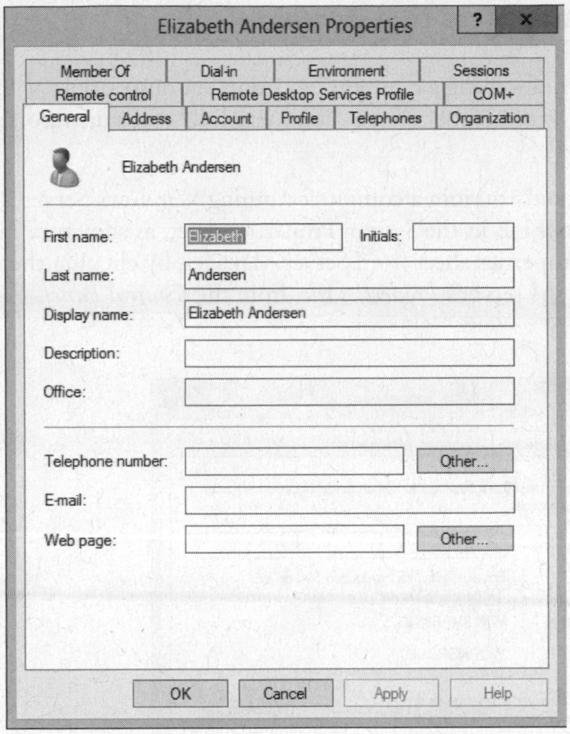

Figure 14-14

A user object's Properties sheet in Active Directory Users and Computers

Managing Multiple Users

When managing domain user accounts, you might need to make the same changes to multiple user objects, and modifying each one individually would be a tedious chore.

In these instances, you can modify the properties of multiple user accounts simultaneously, by using the *ADAC* or the *Active Directory Users and Computers* console. You simply select several user objects by holding down the *CTRL* key as you click each user, and then select Properties. A *Properties* sheet appears, containing the attributes you can manage for the selected objects simultaneously, as shown in Figure 14-15.

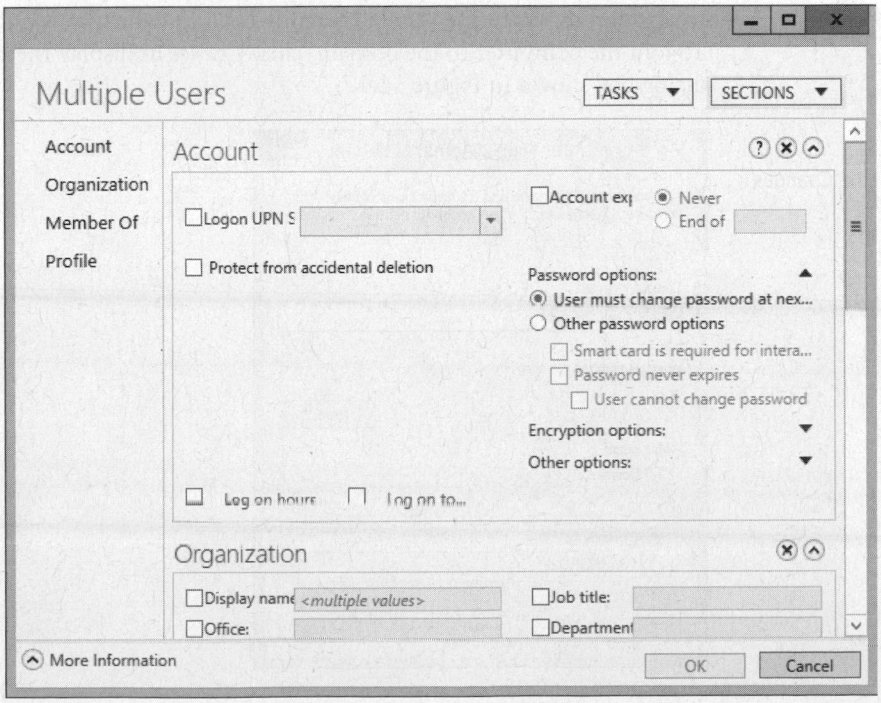

Figure 14-15

A Multiple Users Properties sheet in ADAC

TAKE NOTE*

When you select multiple objects to modify, the objects must be all the same class. For example, you can select multiple user objects, but you cannot select a user object and a computer object.

Joining Computers to a Domain

The process of joining a computer to a domain must occur at the computer itself and be performed by a member of the computer's local Administrators group.

After logging on, you join a computer running Windows Server 2012 to a domain from the *Computer Name* tab in the System Properties sheet, as shown in Figure 14-16. You can access the System Properties sheet from Server Manager, by clicking the *Computer name or domain* hyperlink on the server's *Properties tile*, from the *Control Panel.*

Figure 14-16

The Computer Name tab in the System Properties dialog box

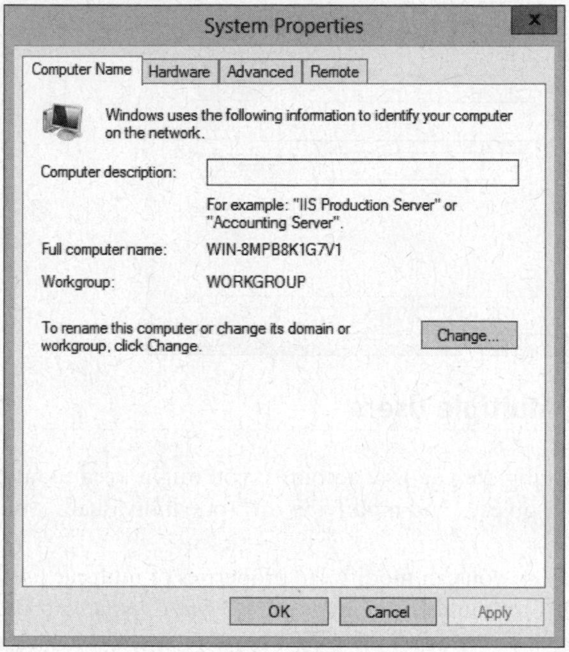

On a computer that is not joined to a domain, the Computer Name tab displays the name assigned to the computer during the operating system installation, and the name of the workgroup to which the system currently belongs (which is WORKGROUP, by default). To join the computer to the domain, click *Change* to display the *Computer Name Changes* dialog box shown in Figure 14-17.

Figure 14-17

The Computer Name Changes dialog box

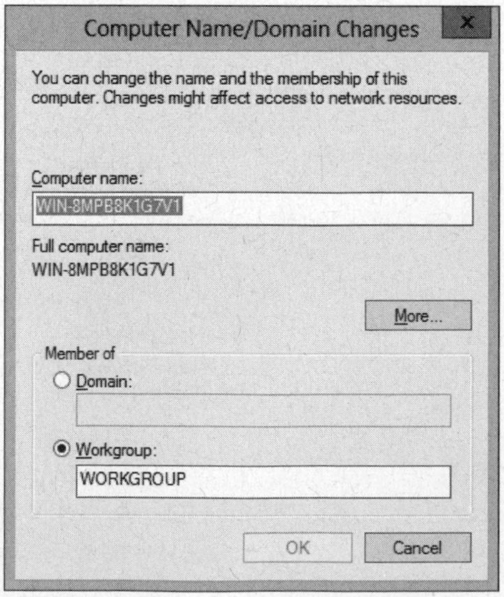

In this dialog box, the Computer name field enables you to change the name assigned to the computer during installation. Depending on whether you have already created a computer object, observe the following precautions:

- To join a domain in which you have already created a computer object for the system in AD DS, the name in this field must match the name of the object exactly.
- If you intend to create a computer object during the joining process, the name in this field must not already exist in the domain.

When you select the *Domain* option button and enter the name of the domain the computer will join, the computer establishes contact with a domain controller for the domain and a second *Computer Name Changes* dialog box appears, which prompts you for the name and password of a domain user account with permission to join the computer to the domain.

After you authenticate with the domain controller, the computer is welcomed to the domain and you are instructed to restart the computer.

JOINING A DOMAIN USING NETDOM.EXE

It is also possible to use the Netdom.exe command-line utility to join a computer to a domain.

The syntax for the command is as follows:

```
netdom join <computername> /Domain:<DomainName>
[/UserD:<User> /PasswordD:<UserPassword>] [/OU:OUDN]
```

The functions of the command-line parameters are as follows:

- *<computername>* specifies the name of the computer to be joined.
- /Domain:*<DomainName>* specifies the name of the domain the computer will join.
- /UserD:*<User>* specifies the name of the domain user account that the program should use to join the computer to the domain.
- /PasswordD:*<UserPassword>* specifies the password associated with the domain user account indicated by the /UserD parameter.
- /OU:*<OUDN>.>* specifies the DN of the organizational unit in which the program should create a computer object. When omitted, the program creates the object in the Computers container.

CREATING COMPUTER OBJECTS WHILE JOINING

You can join a computer to a domain whether or not you have already created a computer object for it. After the computer authenticates to the domain controller, the domain controller scans the Active Directory database for a computer object with the same name as the computer. If it does not find a matching object, the domain controller creates one in the Computers container, using the name supplied by the computer.

To create the computer object automatically in this manner, you might expect that the user account you specify when connecting to the domain controller must have object creation privileges for the Computers container, such as membership in the administrators group. However, this is not always the case.

Domain users also can create computer objects themselves through an interesting, indirect process. The Default Domain Controllers Policy GPO grants a user right called *Add Workstations To The Domain* to the Authenticated Users special identity, as shown in Figure 14-18. Any user who is successfully authenticated to Active Directory is permitted to join up to ten workstations to the domain, and create 10 associated computer objects, even if the user does not possess explicit object creation permissions.

With Add Workstations To The Domain user right, "workstations" is the operative word. Authenticated users can add up to 10 workstations to the domain, but not servers.

➕ MORE INFORMATION

Assigning User Rights

User rights are Group Policy settings that provide users with the capability to perform certain system-related tasks. For example, logging on locally to a domain controller requires that a user has the Log On Locally right assigned to his or her account or be a member of the Account Operators, Administrators, Backup Operators, Print Operators, or Server Operators group on the domain controller. Other similar settings included in this collection are related to user rights associated with system shutdown, taking ownership privileges of files or objects, restoring files and directories, and synchronizing directory service data. For more information on user rights assignment, refer to Objective 6.2, "Configure Security Policies," in Lesson 17.

JOINING A DOMAIN WHILE OFFLINE

It is typical for you to join computers to domains while the computers are connected to the network and have access to a domain controller. However, there are situations in which you might want to set up computers without access to a domain controller, such as a new branch office installation. In these cases, it is possible to perform an offline domain join, by using a command-line program called *Djoin.exe*.

The offline domain join procedure requires you to run the Djoin.exe program twice, once on a computer with access to a domain controller, and then again on the computer to be joined. When connected to the domain controller, the program gathers computer account metadata for the system to be joined and saves it to a file. The syntax for this phase of the process is as follows:

```
djoin /provision /domain <domain name>
/machine <computer name> /savefile <filename.txt>
```

You then transport the metadata file to the computer to be joined and run Djoin.exe again, specifying the name of the file. The program saves the metadata from the file to the computer, so that the next time it has access to a domain controller, the system is automatically joined to the domain. The syntax for the second phase of the process is as follows:

```
djoin /requestODJ /loadfile <filename.txt>
/windowspath %SystemRoot% /localos
```

Managing Disabled Accounts

> Disabling a user account prevents anyone from using it to log on to the domain until an administrator with the appropriate permissions enables it again.

You can disable user accounts manually, to prevent their use while preserving all their attributes, but it is also possible for a system to automatically disable them. For example, repeated violations of password policy settings can disable an account, to prevent intruders from making further attack attempts.

To disable or enable a user or computer account in ADAC or Active Directory Users and Computers, you simply right-click the object and select *Disable* or *Enable* from the context menu. You can also disable and enable multiple accounts by selecting multiple objects and right-clicking.

To disable or enable a user or computer account with Windows PowerShell, use the following cmdlet syntax:

```
Disable-ADAccount –Identity <account name>
Enable-ADAccount –Identity <account name>
```

SKILL SUMMARY

IN THIS LESSON, YOU LEARNED:

- The user account is the primary means by which people using an AD DS network access resources.

- One of the most common tasks for administrators is the creation of Active Directory user objects. Windows Server 2012 includes several tools you can use to create objects.

- Windows Server 2012 redesigned the ADAC application, first introduced in Windows Server 2008 R2, to fully incorporate new features such as the Active Directory Recycle Bin and fine-grained password policies. You can also use the tool to create and manage AD DS user accounts.

- Microsoft Excel and Microsoft Exchange are two common applications in which you can have a number of users, along with their accompanying information, to add to the AD DS database. In these cases, you can export information from the applications by saving it to a file in *Comma-Separated Values (CSV)* format.

- LDIFDE.exe is a utility that has the same basic functionality as CSVDE.exe and provides the capability to modify existing records in Active Directory.

- Because an AD DS network uses a centralized directory, you need a way to track the computers that are part of the domain. To do this, Active Directory uses computer accounts, which are realized in the form of computers objects in the Active Directory database.

(continued)

- The process of joining a computer to a domain must occur at the computer itself and be performed by a member of the computer's local Administrators group.

- It is typical for administrators to join computers to domains while the computers are connected to the network and have access to a domain controller. However, there are situations in which administrators might want to set up computers without access to a domain controller, such as a new branch office installation. In these cases, it is possible to perform an offline domain join, by using a command-line program called *Djoin.exe*.

■ Knowledge Assessment

Multiple Choice

Select one or more correct answers for each of the following questions.

1. What can be used to add, delete, or modify objects in Active Directory, in addition to modifying the schema if necessary?
   a. DCPROMO
   b. LDIFDE
   c. CSVDE
   d. NSLOOKUP

2. When using CSVDE, what is the first line of the text file that uses proper attribute names?
   a. header row
   b. header record
   c. name row
   d. name record

3. Which of the following utilities do you use to perform an offline domain join?
   a. net join
   b. join
   c. djoin
   d. dconnect

4. Which of the following is not a type of user account that can be configured in Windows Server 2012?
   a. local accounts
   b. domain accounts
   c. network accounts
   d. built-in accounts

5. Which of the following are the two built-in user accounts created automatically on a computer running Windows Server 2012?
   a. Network
   b. Interactive
   c. Administrator
   d. Guest

6. What is the PowerShell cmdlet syntax for creating a new user account?
   a. New-ADUser
   b. New-User

    c. `New-SamAccountName`

    d. There is no PowerShell cmdlet for user creation.

7. What is the PowerShell cmdlet syntax for creating a new computer object
    a. `New-Computer -Name <computer name> -path <distinguished name>`
    b. `New-ADComputer -Name <computer name> -path <distinguished name>`
    c. `New-ComputerName <computer name> -path <distinguished name>`
    d. There is no PowerShell cmdlet for creating computer objects.

8. When using Netdom.exe to join an account, you may add the parameter [/OU:OUDN]. If this parameter is left out, where is the object placed?
    a. In the same organizational unit (OU) as the administrator running Netdom.exe
    b. In the Users container
    c. In the Computers container
    d. Without the OU specified, the program will fail.

9. Who may join a computer to the domain?
    a. No one, the computer does this itself when authenticating.
    b. The computer joins the domain as part of the object creation process.
    c. Only the domain administrator may join the computer to the domain.
    d. Members of the computer's local Administrators group may join the computer to the domain.

Best Answer

Choose the letter that corresponds to the best answer. More than one answer choice may achieve the goal. Select the BEST answer.

1. What is the primary means by which people access resources on an Active Directory Domain Service (AD DS) network?
    a. By having a computer account
    b. Being within the proper site and domain
    c. By having elevated privileges
    d. By having a user account

2. What differences matter most in creating a single user versus multiple users?
    a. Single user creation is often done from the graphical user interface (GUI), whereas creating multiple users typically requires using command-line tools.
    b. Creating a single user is simple, but manual work.
    c. Time does not permit automating the creation of a single user.
    d. When creating multiple users, not as many parameters are involved.

3. What two graphical tools will help create either user or computer objects?
    a. Server Manager and PowerShell
    b. Active Directory Administrative Center and Active Directory Users and Computer
    c. Server Core and PowerShell
    d. LDIFDE.exe and CSVDE.exe

4. What is a key benefit to using ADAC or the Active Directory Users and Computers console?
    a. ADAC allows you to modify the properties of both multiple users and multiple computers at once.
    b. ADAC allows you to import multiple objects at once.
    c. ADAC allows you to modify the properties of multiple users or multiple computers at once.
    d. ADAC not only helps create user and computer objects, but it helps join them to a domain.

5. Are typical, authenticated users able to create computer objects in an Active Directory?
   a. No, it requires administrative rights to create a computer object.
   b. Yes, if they are specially granted the Add Workstations To The Domain right.
   c. No, users are not able to do so by default.
   d. Yes, by default, users who are successfully authenticated to Active Directory are permitted to join up to 10 workstations to the domain, thus creating up to 10 associated computer objects.

Build a List

1. Order the steps to create a user in Active Directory Users and Computers.
   a. From the Tools menu in the Server Manager window, select Active Directory Users and Computers.
   b. Type an initial password for the user in the Password and Confirm password fields.
   c. Confirm the settings you configured and click Finish.
   d. In the left pane, find the domain in which you want to create the user object and select a container in that domain. From the Action menu, select New > User.

2. Order the steps to create a user template.
   a. Specify an initial password. Clear the User must change password at next logon check box.
   b. Type "Default Template," or a similarly descriptive name, in the Full Name field and an account name in the User logon name field.
   c. In the left pane, find the domain in which you want to create the user object and select a container in that domain. From the Action menu, select New > User.
   d. From the Tools menu in the Server Manager window, select Active Directory Users and Computers.
   e. Select the Account is disabled check box and click Next.
   f. Finish new user creation and modify any attributes needed.
   g. To use the template, right-click the Default Template user object and, from the context menu, select Copy. The Copy Object – User Wizard appears.

3. Order the steps that occur for a user to authenticate.
   a. User attempts to log on to an AD domain. The client computer establishes a connection to a domain controller to authenticate the user's identity.
   b. The NetLogon service running on the client computer connects to the same service on the domain controller, and then each one verifies that the other system has a valid computer account.
   c. The two systems establish a secure communications channel over which the user authentication process begins.
   d. The two systems perform a preliminary authentication by using their respective computer objects, to ensure both systems are part of the domain.

■ Business Case Scenarios

Scenario 14-1: Creating User Objects

You are a network administrator who is in the process of building an Active Directory network for a company called Fabrikam, Inc., and you have to create user objects for the 75 users in the Inside Sales department. You have already created the fabrikam.com domain and an OU called Inside Sales for this purpose. The Human Resources department has provided you with a list of the users' names and has instructed you to create the account names by using the first initial and the last name. Each user object must also have the value

Inside Sales in the Department property and Fabrikam, Inc. in the Company property. Using the first name in the list, Oliver Cox, as an example, which of the following command-line formats would enable you to create the 75 user objects, with the required property values?

   a. dsadd "Oliver Cox" –company "Fabrikam, Inc." –dept "Inside Sales"
   b. dsadd user CN=Oliver Cox,CN=Inside Sales,DC=fabrikam,DC=com –company Fabrikam, Inc. –dept Inside Sales
   c. dsadd –company "Fabrikam, Inc." –dept "Inside Sales" "CN=Oliver Cox,CN=Inside Sales,DC=fabrikam,DC=com"
   d. dsadd user "CN=Oliver Cox,CN=Inside Sales,DC=fabrikam,DC=com" –company "Fabrikam, Inc." –dept "Inside Sales"

Scenario 14-2: Considering Security Guidelines

You are preparing a new branch office with new computers. You would like to join the computers to the domain. Unfortunately, the branch office network is available. How would you proceed?

15 LESSON

Creating and Managing Active Directory Groups and Organizational Units

70-410 EXAM OBJECTIVE

Objective 5.3 – Create and manage Active Directory groups and organizational units (OUs). This objective may include but is not limited to: Configure group nesting; convert groups including security, distribution, universal, domain local, and domain global; manage group membership using Group Policy; enumerate group membership; delegate the creation and management of Active Directory objects; manage default Active Directory containers; create, copy, configure, and delete groups and OUs.

LESSON HEADING	EXAM OBJECTIVE
Designing an Internal Domain Structure	
Understanding Inheritance	
Using Organizational Units	
Using Group Objects	
Working with Organizational Units	
Creating OUs	Create, copy, configure, and delete groups and OUs
Using OUs to Delegate Active Directory Management Tasks	Delegate the creation and management of Active Directory objects
Working with Groups	
Understanding Group Types	
Understanding Group Scopes	
Working with Default Groups	Manage default Active Directory containers
Nesting Groups	Configure group nesting
Using Special Identities	
Creating Groups	Create, copy, configure, and delete groups and OUs

Managing Group Memberships	Enumerate group membership Manage group membership using Group Policy
Converting Groups	Convert groups including security, distribution, universal, domain local, and domain global
Deleting a Group	

KEY TERMS

access token	domain local groups	security groups
Delegation of Control Wizard	global groups	universal groups
distribution groups	group nesting	

Designing an Internal Domain Structure

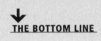 **THE BOTTOM LINE**
After you create a design for your Active Directory domains and the trees and forests superior to them, you can zoom in on each domain and consider the hierarchy you want to create inside it.

Within a domain, the primary hierarchical building block is the organizational unit (OU). As a general rule, it is easier to build an Active Directory hierarchy using OUs than it is using domains. Unlike domains, it is a simple matter to create new OUs, rename existing ones, and move them around. You can even move OUs between domains, as needed. By contrast, creating a new domain means deploying additional domain controllers. Although it is possible to rename a domain, it is not a simple process.

Understanding Inheritance

One of the critical differences between a domain tree hierarchy and the OU hierarchy within a domain is inheritance.

When you assign Group Policy settings to a domain, the settings apply to all the leaf objects in that domain, but not to the subdomains that are subordinate to it. However, when you assign Group Policy settings to an OU, the settings apply to all the leaf objects in the OU and are inherited by any subordinate OUs it contains.

The result of this inheritance is that when you have multiple levels of OUs within a domain, individual leaf objects in the lower levels of the hierarchy can conceivably receive settings from each of their parent containers, tracing a path through each level of OUs up to the parent domain, as shown in Figure 15-1.

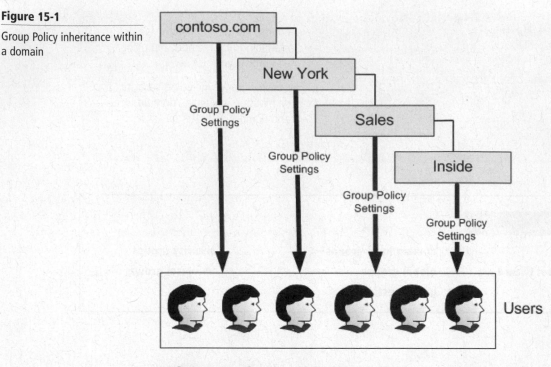

Using Organizational Units

Adding organizational units to your Active Directory hierarchy is not as difficult as adding domains; you don't need additional hardware, and you can easily move or delete an OU at will.

However, you should create an OU for only the following reasons:

- **Duplicating organizational divisions:** The structure of OUs within your domains should be an extension of the model you used to design the Active Directory domain structure. If, for example, you created domains based on a geographical model, you might want to create OUs that correspond to the departments in each domain. Conversely, if you used a political model to create your domains, you might want to create OUs based on the geographical distribution of your objects.

- **Assigning Group Policy settings:** Another reason for creating an OU is to assign different Group Policy settings to a particular collection of objects. When you assign Group Policy settings to an OU, every object contained by that OU receives those settings, including other OUs.

- **Delegating administration:** One of the primary reasons for creating an OU is to grant certain individuals administrative responsibility for a portion of the Active Directory hierarchy, without giving them full access to the entire domain. After you give someone administrative access to an OU, he or she can create, modify, and delete any type of object beneath that OU. Every OU should have at least two administrators (in case one gets locked out).

TAKE NOTE*

The administrators of OUs, despite their limited access, must still be responsible individuals who can be trusted not to abuse their powers. It is still possible for an administrator with access to one OU to corrupt an entire domain tree with improper actions.

When designing an internal domain structure, you can create as many organizational unit levels as you need. The name of an OU does not become part of the fully qualified domain name (FQDN) for the objects it contains, as the domain name does, so there are no naming limitations that restrict the number of OU layers you can create. Microsoft recommends that you create no more than 10 layers of OUs, however.

Using Group Objects

When you want to grant a collection of users permission to access a network resource, such as a file system share or a printer, you cannot assign permissions to an organizational unit; you must use a security group instead. Although they are container objects, groups are not part of the Active Directory hierarchy in the same way as domains and OUs.

You can create a group object in just about any location and add members from anywhere in the domain, and in most cases, from other domains as well. The group members inherit any permissions that you assign to the group, but they do not inherit the Group Policy settings from the group's parent OUs and domain.

The standard strategy when creating groups is to assign the permissions needed to access a network resource to one group and add the users who require the permissions to another group. Then, you make the user group a member of the resource group. This enables you to exercise precise control over the access permissions without having to repeatedly add users to multiple groups.

This strategy, in its original form, called for the use of a domain local group for the resource permissions and a global group for the users. This was due to the group nesting limitations when using Windows NT domain controllers. In Windows Server 2012, you can use all global groups or all universal groups, depending on the network's site topology.

The primary difference between global and universal groups is that universal groups add more data to the global catalog, thereby increasing the amount of replication traffic between sites. If your network consists of a single site, then you can use universal groups across the board. For a multisite network, you might want to consider using global groups instead, to reduce the replication traffic.

■ Working with Organizational Units

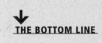

THE BOTTOM LINE

OUs can be nested to create a design that enables you to take advantage of the inheritance described previously. You should limit the number of nested OUs, because too many levels can slow the response time to resource requests and complicate the application of Group Policy settings.

When you install Active Directory Domain Services (AD DS), only one OU is in the domain, by default: the Domain Controllers OU. The domain administrator must create all other OUs.

TAKE NOTE*

OUs are not considered security principals. Therefore, you cannot assign access permissions to a resource based on membership to an OU. Herein lies the difference between OUs and global, domain local, and universal groups. Groups are used for assigning access permissions, whereas OUs are used for organizing resources and delegating permissions.

You can find another type of container object in a domain, called a *container*. For example, a newly created domain has several container objects, including one called *Users*, which contains the domain's predefined users and groups, and another called *Computers*, which contains the computer objects for all the systems joined to the domain.

Unlike organizational units, you cannot assign Group Policy settings to computer objects, nor can you delegate their administration. You also cannot create new container objects by using the standard Active Directory administration tools, such as the Active Directory Users and Computers console. You can create container objects by using scripts, but there is no compelling reason to do so. Organizational units are the preferred method of subdividing a domain.

Creating OUs

CERTIFICATION READY
Create, copy, configure, and delete groups and OUs.
Objective 5.3

The OU is the easiest object type to create in the AD DS hierarchy. You need to supply only a name for the object and define its location in the Active Directory tree.

To create an organizational unit object by using the Active Directory Administrative Center, use the following procedure.

CREATE AN OU WITH ACTIVE DIRECTORY ADMINISTRATIVE CENTER

GET READY. Log on to the server running Windows Server 2012 using an account with administrative privileges.

1. From the Tools menu in the *Server Manager* window, select Active Directory Administrative Center. The *Active Directory Administrative Center* console appears.
2. In the left pane, right-click the object beneath which you want to create the new OU and, from the context menu, select New > Organizational Unit. The *Create Organizational Unit* window appears, as shown in Figure 15-2.

Figure 15-2

The *Create Organizational Unit* window in the Active Directory Administrative Center console

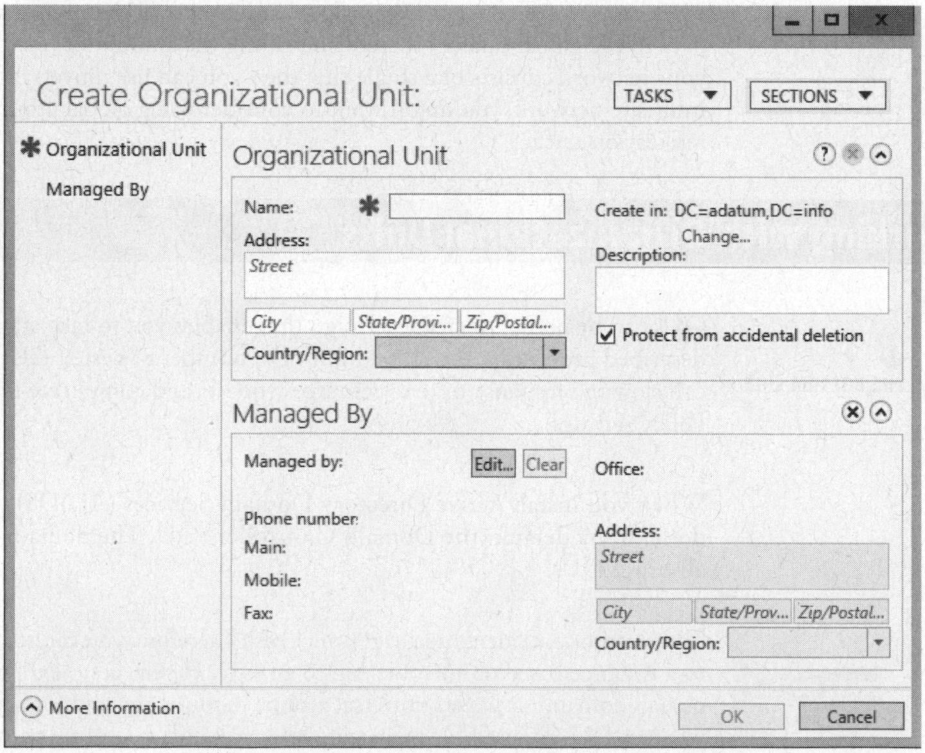

3. In the Name field, type a name for the OU and add any optional information you want.
4. Click OK. The organizational unit object appears in the container.

CLOSE the *Active Directory Administrative Center* console.

Creating an OU in the Active Directory Users and Computers console works in a similar way, although the *New Object – Organizational Unit* dialog box is different in appearance, as shown in Figure 15-3.

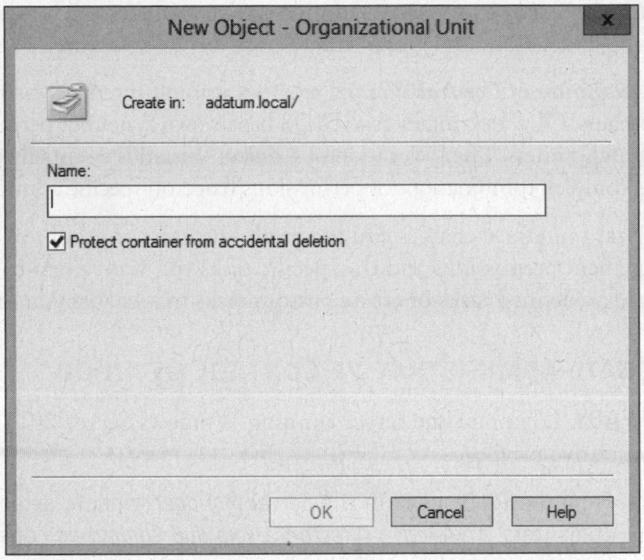

Figure 15-3

The *New Object – Organizational Unit* dialog box in the Active Directory Users and Computers console

After you create an OU, you can double-click it to open its Properties sheet, in which you can modify its attributes, or right-click it and select *Move*, to open the *Move* dialog box, as shown in Figure 15-4.

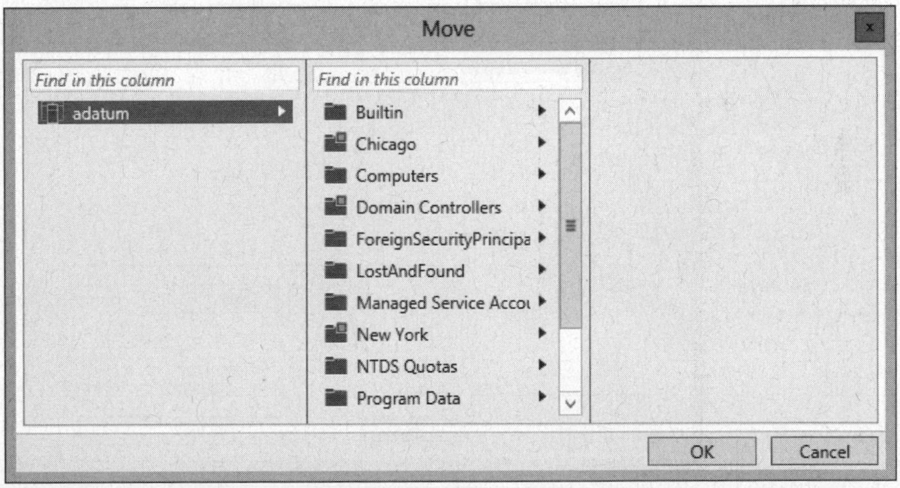

Figure 15-4

The *Move* dialog box in the Active Directory Administrative Center console

Using OUs to Delegate Active Directory Management Tasks

Creating OUs enables you to implement a decentralized administration model, in which others manage portions of the AD DS hierarchy, without affecting the rest of the structure.

Delegating authority at a site level affects all domains and users within the site. Delegating authority at the domain level affects the entire domain. However, delegating authority at the

OU level affects only that OU and its subordinate objects. By granting administrative authority over an OU structure, as opposed to an entire domain or site, you gain the following advantages:

- **Minimal number of administrators with global privileges:** By creating a hierarchy of administrative levels, you limit the number of people who require global access.
- **Limited scope of errors:** Administrative mistakes, such as a container deletion or group object deletion, affect only the respective OU structure.

The *Delegation of Control Wizard* provides a simple interface you can use to delegate permissions for domains, OUs, or containers. AD DS has its own system of permissions, much like those of NTFS and printers. The Delegation of Control Wizard is essentially a front-end interface that creates complex combinations of permissions based on specific administrative tasks.

The wizard interface enables you to specify the users or groups to which you want to delegate management permissions and the specific tasks you want them to be able to perform. You can delegate predefined tasks or create custom tasks that enable you to be more specific.

CERTIFICATION READY
Delegate the creation and management of Active Directory objects.
Objective 5.3

DELEGATE ADMINISTRATIVE CONTROL OF AN OU

GET READY. Log on to the server running Windows Server 2012 using an account with administrative privileges.

1. From the Tools menu in the *Server Manager* window, select Active Directory Users and Computers. The *Active Directory Users and Computers* console appears.
2. Right-click the object over which you want to delegate control, and click Delegate Control. The *Delegation of Control Wizard* appears, displaying the *Welcome* page.
3. Click Next. The *Users or Groups* page appears, as shown in Figure 15-5.

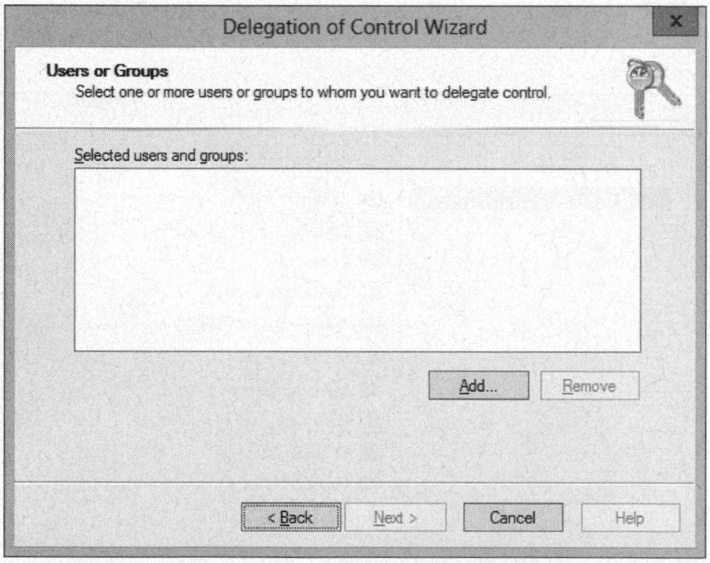

Figure 15-5

The *Users or Groups* page of the Delegation of Control Wizard

4. Click Add. The *Select Users, Computers, or Groups* dialog box appears.///
5. Type the name of the user or group to which you want to delegate control of the object, and click OK. The user or group appears in the *Selected users and groups* list.
6. Click Next. The *Tasks to Delegate* page appears, as shown in Figure 15-6, with the following options:
   - **Delegate the following common tasks:** This option enables you to choose from a list of predefined tasks.
   - **Create a custom task to delegate:** This option enables you to be more specific about the task delegation.

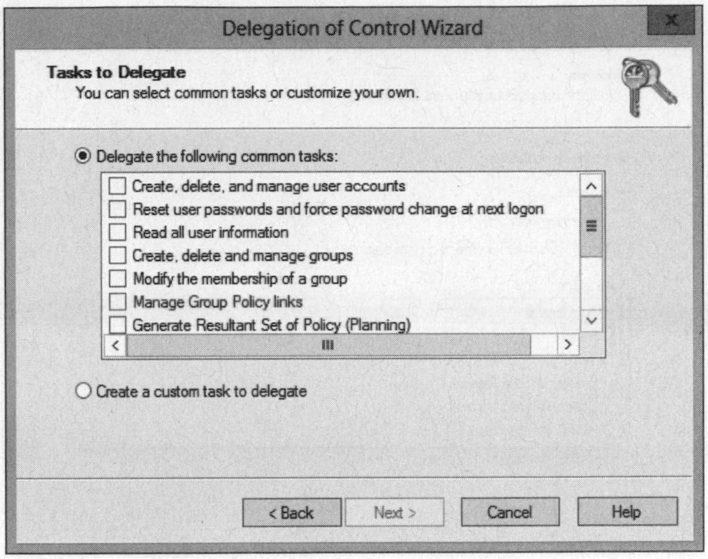

Figure 15-6

The *Tasks to Delegate* page of the Delegation of Control Wizard

7. Select Create a custom task to delegate and click Next. The *Active Directory Object Type* page appears, displaying the following options, as shown in Figure 15-7.

   • **This folder, existing objects in this folder, and creation of new objects in this folder:** This option delegates control of the container, including all its current and future objects.

   • **Only the following objects in the folder:** This option enables you to select specific objects to be controlled. You can select *Create selected objects in this folder* to allow selected object types to be created, or select *Delete selected objects in this folder* to allow selected object types to be deleted.

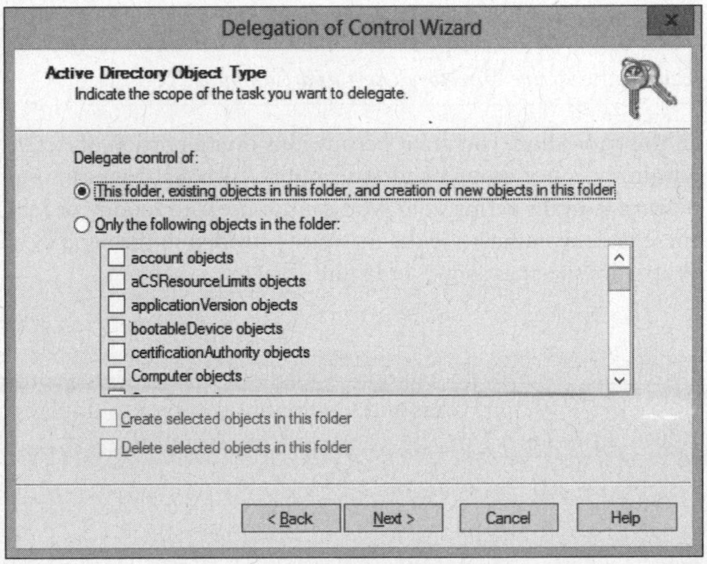

Figure 15-7

The *Active Directory Object Type* page of the Delegation of Control Wizard

8. Select This folder, existing objects in this folder, and creation of new objects in this folder and click Next. The *Permissions* page appears, as shown in Figure 15-8.

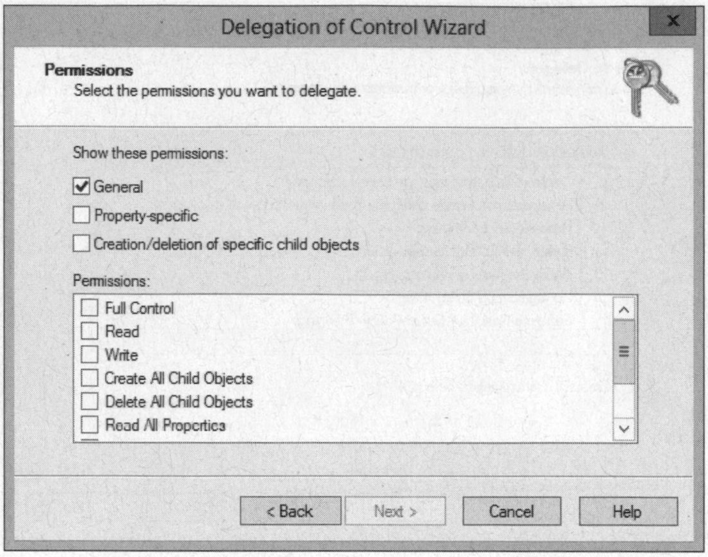

Figure 15-8

The Permissions page of the
Delegation of Control Wizard

Delegation of Control Wizard

Permissions
Select the permissions you want to delegate.

Show these permissions:
- ☑ General
- ☐ Property-specific
- ☐ Creation/deletion of specific child objects

Permissions:
- ☐ Full Control
- ☐ Read
- ☐ Write
- ☐ Create All Child Objects
- ☐ Delete All Child Objects
- ☐ Read All Properties

[< Back] [Next >] [Cancel] [Help]

9. Set the delegated permissions according to your needs for the user or group to which you delegate control. You can combine permissions from all three of the following options:
   - **General:** displays general permissions, which are equal to those displayed on the *Security* tab in an object's properties. For example, selecting Full Control for general permissions is inclusive of all property rights as well.
   - **Property-specific:** displays permissions that apply to specific attributes or properties of an object. If you select the Read permission using the General option, all read-specific properties are selected.
   - **Creation/deletion of specific child objects:** displays permissions that apply to creation and deletion permissions for specified object types.
10. Click Next. The *Completing the Delegation of Control Wizard* page appears.
11. Click Finish.

CLOSE the *Active Directory Users and Computers* console.

In this procedure, you grant permissions over a portion of Active Directory to a specified administrator or group of administrators. Although you can use the *Delegation of Control Wizard* to grant permissions, you cannot use it to modify or remove permissions. To perform these tasks, you must use the interface provided in the *Security* tab in the AD DS object's Properties sheet, as shown in Figure 15-9.

TAKE NOTE*

By default, the Security tab does not appear in an organizational unit's Properties sheet in the Active Directory Users and Computers console. To display the tab, you must select Advanced Features from the console's View menu.

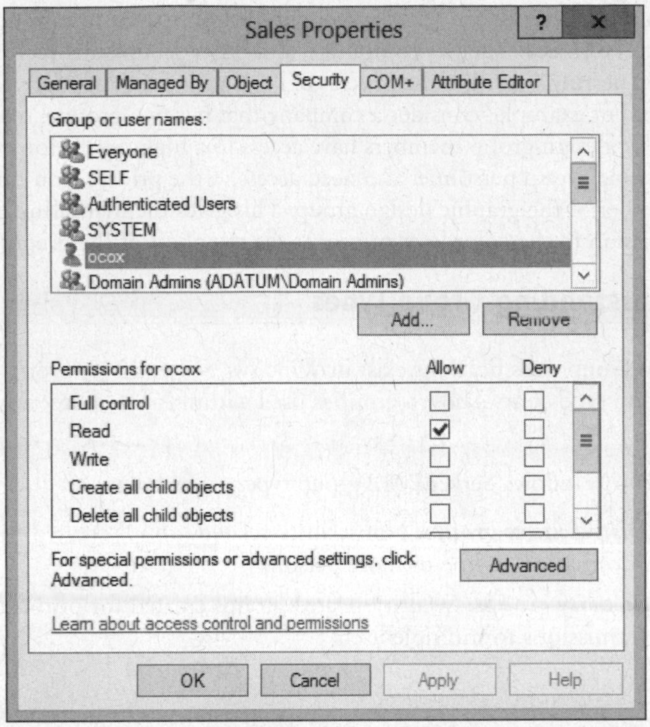

Figure 15-9

The Security tab of an organizational unit's Properties sheet

■ Working with Groups

THE BOTTOM LINE

Since the early days of the Microsoft server operating system, administrators have used *groups* to manage network permissions. Groups enable you to assign permissions to multiple users simultaneously. A group can be defined as a collection of user or computer accounts that functions as a security principal, in much the same way that a user does.

In Windows Server 2012, when a user logs on to Active Directory, an *access token* is created that identifies the user and all the user's group memberships. Domain controllers use this access token to verify a user's permissions when the user attempts to access a local or network resource. By using groups, you can grant multiple users the same permission level for resources on the network. If, for example, you have 25 users in the graphics department who need access to a color printer, you can either assign each user the appropriate permissions for the printer, or you can create a group containing the 25 users and assign the appropriate permissions to the group. By using a group object to access a resource, you accomplish the following:

- When users need access to the printer, you can add them to the group. Once added, the user receives all permissions assigned to this group. Similarly, you can remove users from the group when you want to revoke their access to the printer.
- You need to make only one change to modify the level of access to the printer for all the users. Changing the group's permissions changes the permission level for all group members. Without the group, you need to modify all 25 user accounts individually.

TAKE NOTE*

A user's access token is generated only after the user first logs on to the network from the workstation. If you add a user to a group, he or she will need to log off and log back on again for the change to take effect.

Users can be members of more than one group. In addition, groups can contain other Active Directory objects, such as computers, and other groups in a technique called *group nesting*. Group nesting describes the process of configuring one or more groups as members of another group. For example, consider a company that has two groups: marketing and graphic design. Graphic design group members have access to a high-resolution color laser printer. If the marketing group personnel also need access to the printer, you can add the marketing group as a member of the graphic design group. This gives the marketing group members the same permission to the color laser printer as the members of the graphic design group.

Understanding Group Types

Two group classifications exist in Windows Server 2012: group type and group scope. Group type defines how a group is used within Active Directory.

The two Windows Server 2012 group types are as follows:

- *Distribution groups:* Nonsecurity-related groups created for the distribution of information to one or more persons
- *Security groups:* Security-related groups created for purposes of granting resource access permissions to multiple users

TAKE NOTE * You can use a security group to grant permissions to resources and to enable e-mail access. A distribution group, however, can be used only for e-mail purposes; it cannot be used to secure resources on your network.

Active Directory–aware applications can use distribution groups for nonsecurity-related functions. For example, Microsoft Exchange uses distribution groups to send messages to multiple users. Only applications that are designed to work with Active Directory can use distribution groups in this manner.

Groups that you use to assign permissions to resources are referred to as *security groups*. You make multiple users that need access to the same resource members of a security group. They then grant the security group permission to access the resource. After you create a group, you can convert it from a security group to a distribution group, or vice versa, at any time.

Understanding Group Scopes

In addition to security and distribution group types, several group scopes are available within Active Directory.

The group scope controls which objects the group can contain, limiting the objects to the same domain or permitting objects from remote domains as well, and also controls the location in the domain or forest where the group can be used. Group scopes available in an Active Directory domain include domain local groups, global groups, and universal groups.

DOMAIN LOCAL GROUPS

Domain local groups can have any of the following as members:

- User accounts
- Computer accounts
- Global groups from any domain in the forest
- Universal groups
- Domain local groups from the same domain

You use domain local groups to assign permissions to resources in the same domain as the domain local group. Domain local groups can make permission assignment and maintenance easier to manage.

For example, if you have 10 users that need access to a shared folder, you can create a domain local group that has the appropriate permissions to the shared folder. Next, you create a global or universal group and add the 10 user accounts as members of this group. Finally, you add the global group to the domain local group. The 10 users have access to the shared folder via their membership in the global group. If any additional users need access to the shared folder, you can simply add them to the global group, and they will automatically receive the necessary permissions.

GLOBAL GROUPS

Global groups can have the following as members:

- User accounts
- Computer accounts
- Other global groups from the same domain

You can use global groups to grant or deny permissions to any resource located in any domain in the forest. You accomplish this by adding the global group as a member of a domain local group that has the desired permissions. Global group memberships are replicated only to domain controllers within the same domain. Users with common resource needs should be members of a global group, to facilitate the assignment of permissions to resources. You can change the membership of the global group as frequently as necessary to provide users with the necessary resource permissions.

UNIVERSAL GROUPS

Universal groups can contain the following members:

- User accounts
- Computer accounts
- Global groups from any domain in the forest
- Other universal groups

If a cross-forest trust exists, universal groups can contain similar accounts from a trusted forest. Universal groups, like global groups, can organize users according to their resource access needs. You can use them to provide access to resources located in any domain in the forest through the use of domain local groups.

You can also use universal groups to consolidate groups and accounts that either span multiple domains or span the entire forest. A key point in the application and utilization of universal groups is that group memberships in universal groups should not change frequently, because universal groups are stored in the global catalog. Changes to universal group membership lists are replicated to all global catalog servers throughout the forest. If these changes occur frequently, the replication process can consume a significant amount of bandwidth, especially on relatively slow and expensive wide area network (WAN) links.

Working with Default Groups

Although there are many situations in which you might create groups to organize users or computers and then assign permissions, there are several built-in security groups that the system creates when you install AD DS on Windows Server 2012. Many of the built-in groups have predefined user rights that enable their members to perform certain system-related tasks, such as backup and restore. You can add accounts to the default groups, to grant users the same rights, in addition to any resource access permissions the groups possess.

CERTIFICATION READY
Manage default Active
Directory containers.
Objective 5.3

The default groups are located in the Built-in and Users container objects in AD DS. The list of predefined groups in these containers varies depending on the installed services. For example, installing the Dynamic Host Configuration Protocol (DHCP) server role creates two new groups in the Users container, called *DHCP Administrators* and *DHCP Users*.

All the default groups are security groups. Active Directory does not include any default distribution groups. Table 15-1 lists the default groups found in the Built-in container, which are domain local groups.

Table 15-1

Default Groups Created in the Built-In Container

Group Name	Default Members	Purpose
Account Operators	None	Members can administer domain user and group accounts. Members do not have permission to modify the Administrators, Domain Admins, and Enterprise Admins groups.
Administrators	Administrator, Domain Admins, and Enterprise Admins	Members have complete and unrestricted access to the computer or domain controller locally, including the right to change their own permissions.
Backup Operators	None	Members can back up and restore all files on a computer, regardless of the permissions that protect the files. Members can log on to the computer and shut it down.
Certificate Service DCOM Access	None	Members are allowed to connect to Certification Authorities across the Active Directory forest.
Cryptographic Operators	None	Members are allowed to perform cryptographic operations.
Distributed COM Users	None	Members are permitted to use Distributed COM objects on all domain controllers.
Event Log Readers	None	Members are permitted to read event logs from all domain controllers.
Guests	Domain Guests, Guests	Members have the same privileges as members of the Users group. The Guest account is disabled by default.
IIS_IUSRS	IUSR special identity	Built-in group used by IIS.
Incoming Forest Trust Builders	None	Members can create incoming, one-way trusts to this forest.
Network Configuration Operators	None	Members have the same default rights as members of the Users group.
Performance Log Users	None	Members have remote access to schedule logging of performance counters on this computer.
Performance Monitor Users	Network Service from the NT Authority folder.	Members have remote access to monitor this computer.
Pre–Windows 2000 Compatible Access	Authenticated Users from the NT Authority folder	Members have read access on all users and groups in the domain.

Table 15-1

(continued)

Group Name	Default Members	Purpose
Print Operators	None	Members can manage printers and document queues.
Remote Desktop Users	None	Members can log on to a computer from a remote location.
Replicator	None	This group supports directory replication functions and is used by the file replication service on domain controllers. The only member should be a domain user account that is used to log on to the replicator services of the domain controller.
Server Operators	None	Members can do the following: log on to a server interactively, create and delete network shares, start and stop some services, back up and restore files, format the hard disk, shut down the computer, and modify the system date and time.
Terminal Server License Servers	None	Members of this group can update Active Directory user accounts with information about licensing usage.
Users	Domain Users, Authenticated Users and Interactive	Members can run applications, use printers, shut down and start the computer, and use network shares for which they are assigned permissions.
Windows Authorization Access Group	Enterprise Domain Controllers	Members of this group can view the attribute on User objects to determine their rights to a given resource.

Table 15-2

Default Groups Created in the Users Container

Table 15-2 lists the default groups found in the Users container, which have various scopes.

Group Name	Group Scope	Default Members	Purpose
Allowed RODC Password Replication Group	Domain local	None	Members of this group are eligible to have their passwords stored on any RODC in the domain.
Cert Publishers	Domain local	None	Members of this group are permitted to publish certificates to Active Directory.
Denied RODC Password Replication Group	Domain local	Cert Publishers, Domain Admins, Domain Controllers, Enterprise Admins, Group Policy Creator Owners, krbtgt, Read-only Domain Controllers, Schema Admins	Members of this group are *not* eligible to have their passwords stored on any RODC in the domain.

(continued)

Table 15-2

(continued)

Group Name	Group Scope	Default Members	Purpose
DnsAdmins (installed with DNS)	Domain local	None	Members of this group are permitted administrative access to the DNS server service.
DnsUpdate-Proxy (installed with DNS)	Global	None	Members of this group are DNS clients permitted to perform dynamic updates on behalf of some other clients such as DHCP servers.
Domain Admins	Global	Administrator	Members can perform administrative tasks on any computer in the domain.
Domain Computers	Global	All workstations and servers joined to the domain, and any computer accounts manually created	Any computer account created in a domain is automatically added to this group.
Domain Controllers	Global	All domain controllers in the domain	All member servers promoted to domain controllers are automatically added to this group.
Domain Guests	Global	Guest account	Members of this group can only access the system from across the network and have very limited privileges.
Domain Users	Global	All domain user accounts	Members can assign permissions to all users in the domain.
Enterprise Admins (appears only on forest root domain controllers)	Universal	Administrator user account for the forest root domain	This group is added to the Administrators group on all domain controllers in the forest.
Enterprise Read-only Domain Controllers	Universal	None	This group contains all read-only domain controllers within an entire forest.
Group Policy Creator Owners	Global	Administrator user account for the domain	Members can modify group policy for the domain.
RAS and IAS Servers	Domain local	None	Servers in this group are permitted access to the users' remote access properties.
Read-only Domain Controllers	Global	None	This group contains the computer accounts for all read-only domain controllers within a single domain.
Schema Admins (appears only on forest root domain controllers)	Universal	Administrator from the forest root domain	Members can manage and modify the Active Directory schema.

You can view the groups described in Tables 15-1 and 15-2 and manage their memberships by using the *Active Directory Administrative Center* or *Active Directory Users and Computers*. The only difference between these groups and the ones you create yourself is that you cannot delete the default groups.

Nesting Groups

> As discussed previously, *group nesting* is the term used when groups are added as members of other groups. For example, when you make a global group a member of a universal group, it is nested within the universal group.

Group nesting reduces the number of times you need to assign permissions to users in different domains in a multidomain forest. For example, if you have multiple child domains in your AD DS hierarchy, and the users in each domain need access to an enterprise database application located in the parent domain, the simplest way to set up access to this application is as follows:

1. Create global groups in each domain that contain all users needing access to the enterprise database.
2. Create a universal group in the parent domain. Include each location's global group as a member.
3. Add the universal group to the required domain local group to assign the necessary permission to access and use the enterprise database.

This traditional approach to group nesting in AD DS is often referred to using the mnemonic *AGUDLP*: you add **A**ccounts to **G**lobal groups, add those global groups to **U**niversal groups, add universal groups to **D**omain **L**ocal groups, and, finally, assign **P**ermissions to the domain local groups.

CERTIFICATION READY
Configure group nesting.
Objective 5.3

This same policy can apply to your administrative model. For the Built-in container, the default domain local groups are based on administrative tasks.

For example, the Backup Operators group enables members to perform backups on the computers in the domain, because the Backup Operators group receives the *Backup files and directories* user right through the Default Domain Controllers Policy and Local Security Policy GPOs.

You can use the same method to create your own domain local groups, which you delegate administrative tasks and user rights for particular OUs. Then, after creating global groups (or universal groups, for forest-wide assignments) and adding them to the domain local groups, the structure is in place.

For example, if you run a single-domain enterprise and want to grant the manager of your Boston office the ability to back up the computers at that site, you could use a procedure like the following:

1. Create an OU for the branch office called *Boston*.
2. Create a domain local group called *Boston Backup*.
3. Create a GPO called *Boston OU Backup* and grant the Boston Backup group the *Backup files and directories* user right.
4. Link the GPO to the Boston OU.
5. Create a global group called *Boston Office Managers*.
6. Add the Boston Office Managers group to the Boston Backup group as a member.

All that remains is to add the user account for the Boston branch manager to the Boston Office Managers global group. If the manager goes on vacation or leaves the company, the administrator at the central office just has to add another user from the Boston office to the Boston Office Managers group in order to grant someone else the rights to perform backups.

This procedure grants one user the rights needed to perform one task at one site. Obviously, it is not efficient to delegate every task individually this way. A more efficient method is for enterprise administrators to organize their lists of tasks into groups, which they or others will assign to IT staffers. Microsoft refers to these groups as management roles and has published lists of recommended roles for service management and data management tasks, as shown in Table 15-3.

Table 15-3

Active Directory Management Roles

SERVICE MANAGEMENT ROLES	DATA MANAGEMENT ROLES
Forest Configuration Operators	Business Unit Administrators
Domain Configuration Operators	Account Administrators
Security Policy Administrators	Workstation Administrators
Service Administration Managers	Server Operators
Domain Controller Administrators	Resource Administrators
Backup Operators	Security Group Administrators
Schema Administrators	Help Desk Operators
Replication Management Administrators	Application-Specific Administrators
Replication Monitoring Operators	
DNS Administrators	

TAKE NOTE*

The use of domain local groups for resource permissions and global groups for user accounts is a holdover from Windows NT and early Windows Server versions that that did not enable global groups to have other global groups as members. Beginning with the Windows 2000 Native functional level and including the Windows Server 2003 functional level (the earliest supported by Windows Server 2012), you can nest global groups within other global groups. There is, therefore, no reason why you cannot use a global group for resource permissions and another global group for users, and then make the user group a member of the resource group.

Using Special Identities

Special identities exist on all computers running Windows Server 2012. These are not groups because you cannot create them, delete them, or directly modify their memberships. Special identities do not appear as manageable objects in the AD DS utilities, but you can use them like groups, by adding them to the access control lists ACLs of system and network resources, as shown in Figure 15-10.

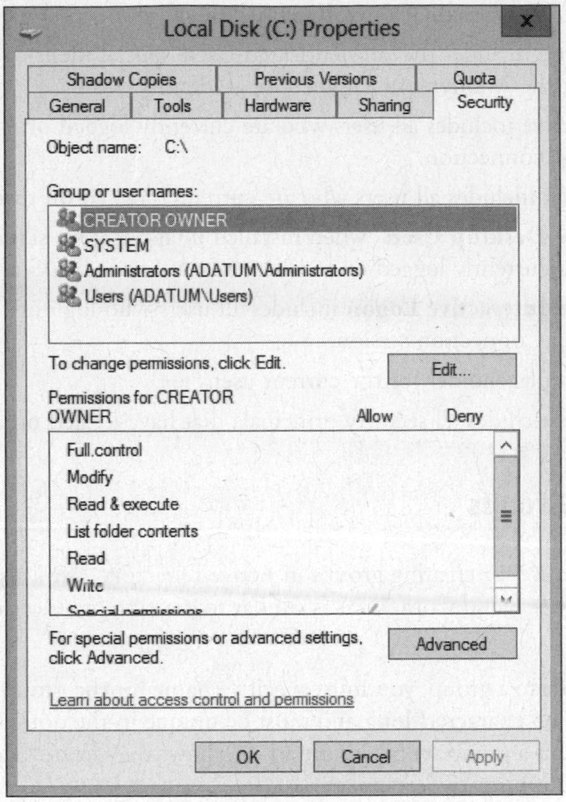

Figure 15-10

The Creator Owner special
identity on a Security tab

Special identities are placeholders for one or more users. When you add a special identity to an ACL, the system substitutes the users that conform to the identity at the moment the ACL is processed. Special identities represent different users at different times, depending on how users access a computer or resource. For example, the Authenticated Users special identity includes all users that are currently logged on, which have successfully been authenticated by a computer or domain controller. At any given moment, the list of users represented by the Authenticated Users special identity can change, as users log on and log off. The exact list of users substituted for the Authenticated Users placeholder is determined at the time a resource is accessed and its ACL processed, not at the time the special identity is added to the ACL.

The special identities included in Windows Server 2012 are as follows:

- **Anonymous Logon** includes all users who connected to the computer without authenticating.
- **Authenticated Users** includes all users with a valid local or domain user account whose identities have been authenticated. The Authenticated Users special identity does not include the Guest user even if the Guest account has a password.
- **Batch** includes all users who are currently logged on through a batch facility such as a task scheduler job.
- **Creator Group** includes the primary group of the users who created or took ownership of the resource.
- **Creator Owner** includes the account for the user who created or took ownership of a resource.
- **Dialup** includes all users who are currently logged on through a dial-up connection.
- **Digest Authentication** includes all users who have authenticated using digest authentication.

- **Enterprise Domain Controllers** includes all domain controllers in the forest.
- **Everyone** includes the Authenticated Users special identity plus the Guest user account, but not the Anonymous Logon special identity.
- **Interactive** includes all users who are currently logged on locally or through a Remote Desktop connection.
- **Network** includes all users who are currently logged on through a network connection.
- **Remote Desktop Users**, when installed in application serving mode, includes any users who are currently logged on to the system using an RDS terminal server.
- **Remote Interactive Logon** includes all users who log onto a computer using a Remote Desktop Connection session.
- **Self** is a placeholder for the current user.
- **Service** includes all security principals that have logged on as a service.

Creating Groups

The procedure for creating groups in Active Directory Administrative Center or Active Directory Users and Computers is similar to creating organizational units.

CERTIFICATION READY
Create, copy, configure, and delete groups and OUs.
Objective 5.3

When you create a group, you must specify a name for the group object. The name you select can be up to 64 characters long and must be unique in the domain. You must also choose a group type and a group scope. Figure 15-11 shows the Create Group window in Active Directory Administrative Center.

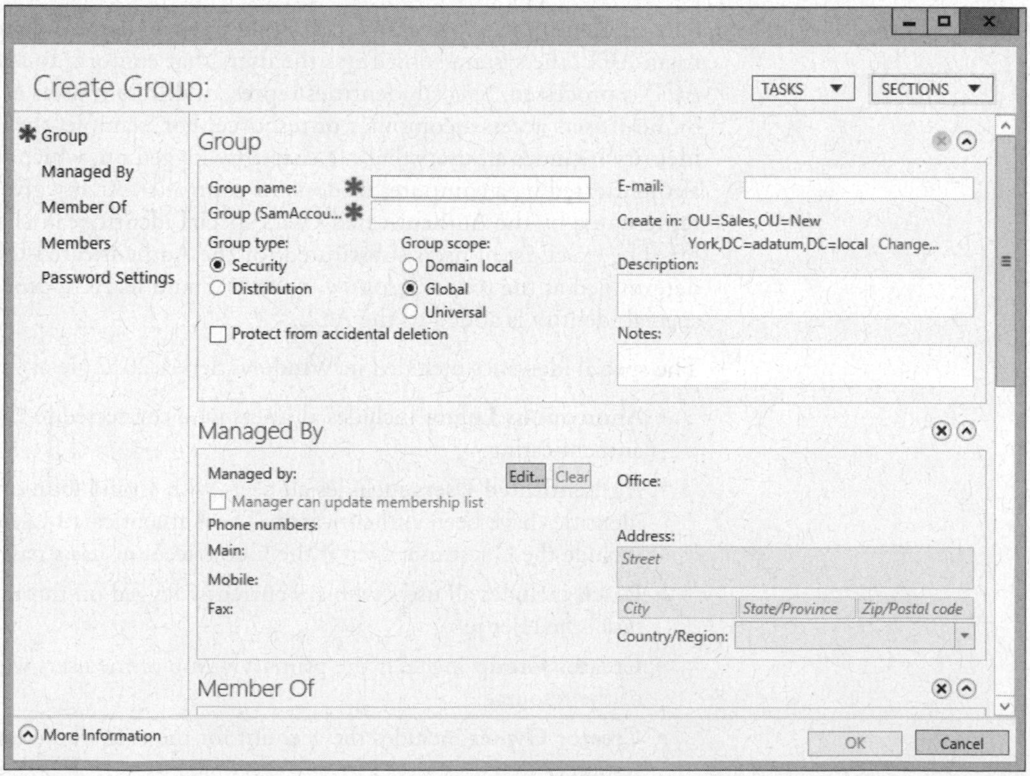

Figure 15-11

Creating a group in Active Directory Administrative Center

The New Object – Group dialog box in Active Directory Users and Computers is slightly different in appearance, but contains the same basic controls, as shown in Figure 15-12.

Figure 15-12

Creating a group in Active
Directory Users and Computers

New Object - Group

Create in: adatum.local/New York/Sales

Group name:

Group name (pre-Windows 2000):

Group scope
- ○ Domain local
- ◉ Global
- ○ Universal

Group type
- ◉ Security
- ○ Distribution

OK   Cancel

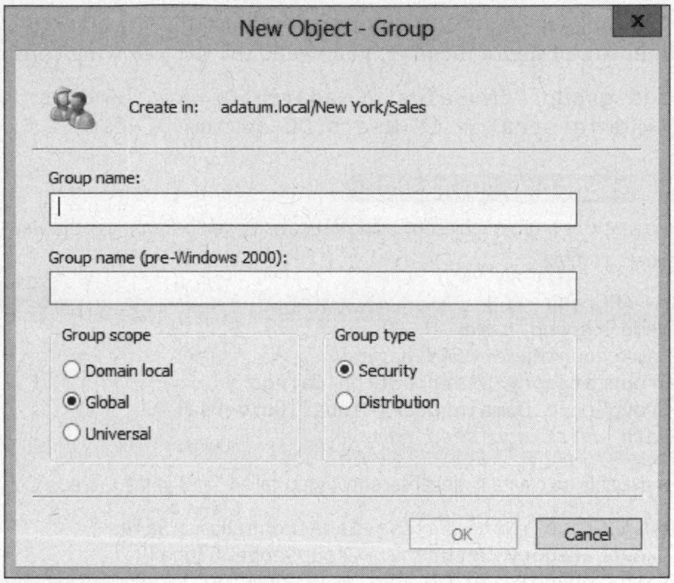

Although the graphical AD DS utilities are a convenient tool for creating and managing groups individually, they are not the most efficient method for creating large numbers of security principals. The command-line tools included with Windows Server 2012 enable you to create and manage groups in large numbers by using batch files or other types of scripts, as discussed in Lesson 14, "Creating and Managing Active Directory Users and Computers." Some of these tools are discussed in the following sections.

 TAKE NOTE* To create nested groups, you must create the groups first and then add one to the membership list of the other. You cannot create a new group directly within the membership list of another group.

CREATING GROUPS FROM THE COMMAND LINE

Just as you used the Dsadd.exe tool in Lesson 14 to create new user objects, you can use the same program to create group objects. The basic syntax for creating group objects with Dsadd.exe is as follows:

```
dsadd group <GroupDN> [parameters]
```

The *<GroupDN>* parameter is a distinguished name (DN) for the new group object you want to create. The DNs use the same format as those in CSV files.

By default, Dsadd.exe creates global security groups, but you can use command-line parameters to create groups with other types and scopes, as well as to specify members and memberships for the groups and other group object properties. The most commonly used command-line parameters are as follows:

- -secgrp yes|no specifies whether the program should create a security group (yes) or a distribution group (no). The default value is yes.
- -scope l|g|u specifies whether the program should create a domain local (l), global (g), or universal (u) group. The default value is g.
- -samid *<SAMName>* specifies the SAM name for the group object.
- -desc *<description>* specifies a description for the group object.
- -memberof *<GroupDN>* specifies the DNs of one or more groups of which the new group should be made a member.
- -member *<GroupDN>* specifies the DNs of one or more objects that should be made members of the new group.

For example, to create a new group called *Sales* in the Users container and make the Administrator user a member, you would use the following command:

```
dsadd group "CN=Sales,DC=adatum,DC=com" -member
"CN=Administrator,CN=Users,DC=adatum,DC=com"
```

USING WINDOWS POWERSHELL

To create a new group object by using Windows PowerShell, you use the New-ADGroup cmdlet, with the following syntax:

```
New-ADGroup
-Name <group name>
-SamAccountName <SAM name>
-GroupCategory Distribution|Category
-GroupScope DomainLocal|Global|Universal
-Path <distinguished name>
```

For example, to create a global security group called *Sales in the Chicago OU*, you use the following command:

```
New-ADGroup -Name Sales -SamAccountName Sales
-GroupCategory Security -GroupScope Global
-Path "OU=Chicago,DC=Adatum,DC=Com"
```

Managing Group Memberships

Unlike the Active Directory Administrative Center, which enables you to specify a group's members as you create the group, in Active Directory Users and Computers, you must create the group object first, and then add members to it.

CERTIFICATION READY
Enumerate group membership.
Objective 5.3

To add members to a group, you select it in the console and, from the *Action* menu, select *Properties* to open the group's Properties sheet, and then select the *Members* tab, as shown in Figure 15-13.

Figure 15-13

The Members tab of a group object's Properties sheet

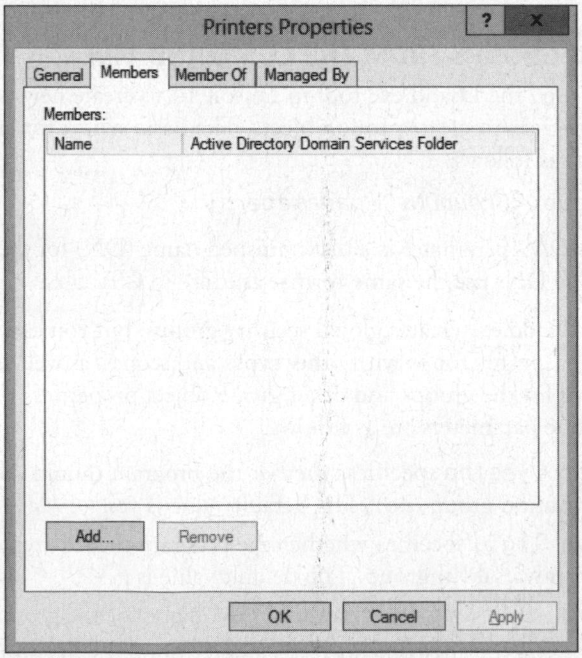

By using the *Members* tab, you can add objects to the group's membership list. On the *Member Of* tab, you can add the group to the membership list of another group. For both of these tasks, you use the standard *Select Users, Contacts, Computers, Service Accounts, or Groups* dialog box, as shown in Figure 15-14, to choose objects.

Figure 15-14

The *Select Users, Contacts, Computers, Service Accounts, or Groups* dialog box

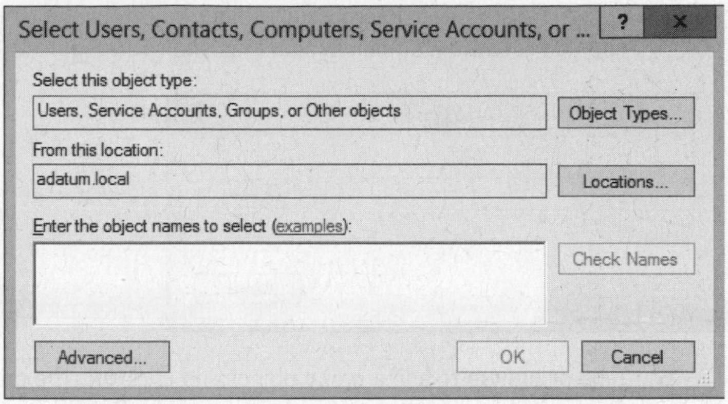

Select Users, Contacts, Computers, Service Accounts, or ...   ?   X

Select this object type:

| Users, Service Accounts, Groups, or Other objects | Object Types... |

From this location:

| adatum.local | Locations... |

Enter the object names to select (examples):

| | Check Names |

Advanced...   OK   Cancel

After you enter or find the objects you want to add, click *OK* to close the Properties sheet and add the objects to the group's membership list.

MANAGING GROUP MEMBERSHIP USING GROUP POLICY

It is also possible to control group memberships by using Group Policy. When you create Restricted Groups policies, you can specify the membership for a group and enforce it, so that no one can add or remove members.

To create Restricted Groups policies, use the following procedure.

CERTIFICATION READY
Manage group membership using Group Policy.
Objective 5.3

 CREATE A RESTRICTED GROUPS POLICY

GET READY. Log on to the server running Windows Server 2012 using an account with administrative privileges.

1. From the Tools menu in the *Server Manager* window, select Group Policy Management. The *Group Policy Management* console appears.

2. Create a new Group Policy object (GPO) and link it to your domain.

3. Open the GPO in the *Group Policy Management Editor* and browse to the Computer Configuration\Policies\Windows Settings\Security Settings\Restricted Groups folder, as shown in Figure 15-15.

Figure 15-15

The Restricted Groups folder in the Group Policy object

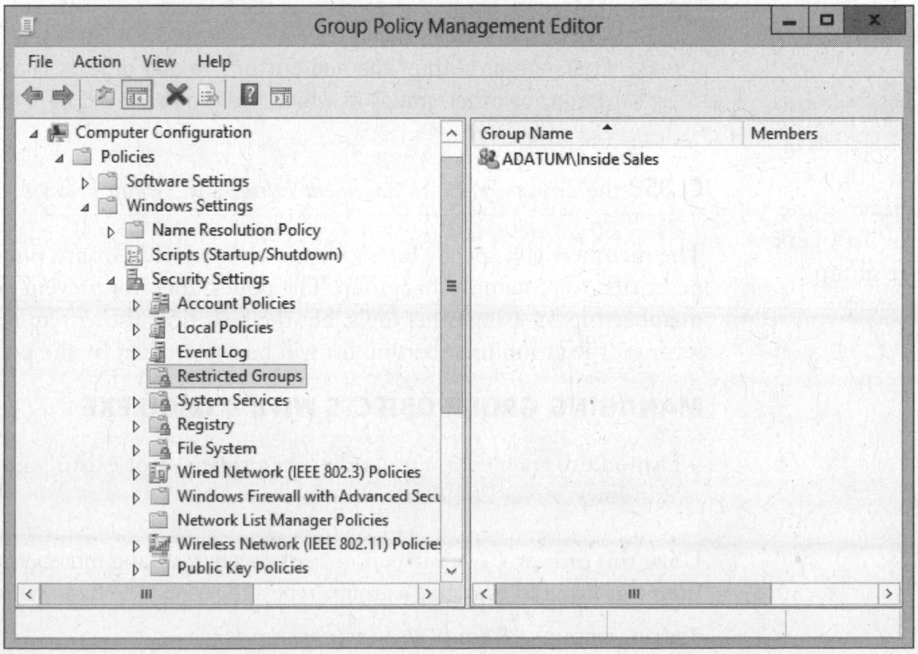

Group Policy Management Editor   _ □ x

File   Action   View   Help

Computer Configuration
  Policies
    Software Settings
    Windows Settings
      Name Resolution Policy
      Scripts (Startup/Shutdown)
      Security Settings
        Account Policies
        Local Policies
        Event Log
        Restricted Groups
        System Services
        Registry
        File System
        Wired Network (IEEE 802.3) Policies
        Windows Firewall with Advanced Secu
        Network List Manager Policies
        Wireless Network (IEEE 802.11) Policies
        Public Key Policies

| Group Name ▲ | Members |
| ADATUM\Inside Sales | |

4. Right-click the Restricted Groups folder and from the context menu, select Add Group. The *Add Group* dialog box appears, as shown in Figure 15-16.

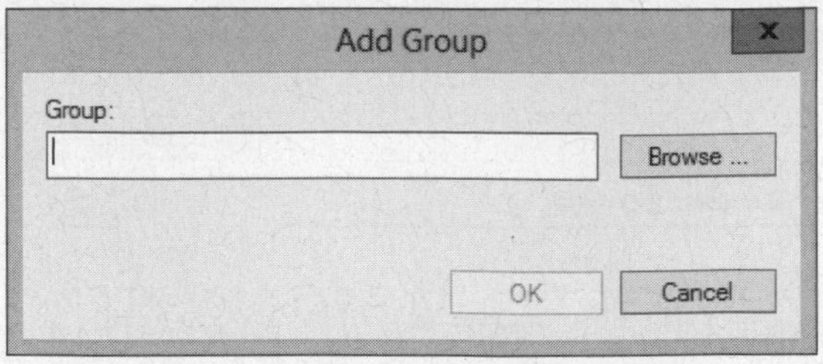

Figure 15-16

The Add Group dialog box

5. Type or browse to add a group object and click OK. The group appears in the *Restricted Groups* folder and a Properties sheet for the policy appears, as shown in Figure 15-17.

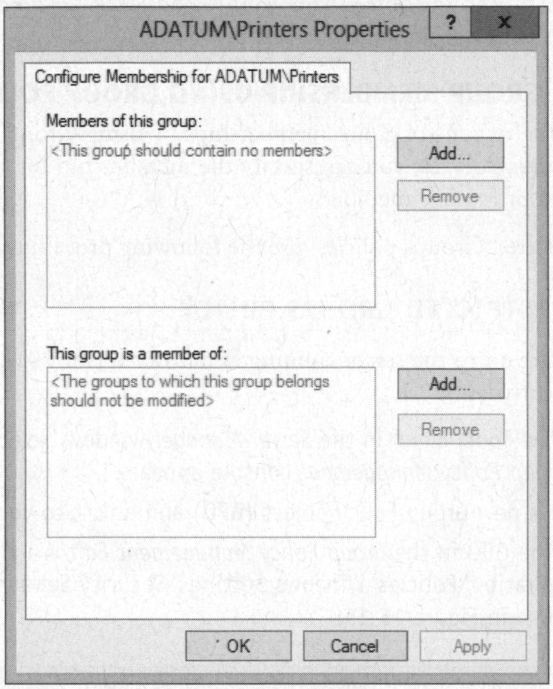

Figure 15-17

The Properties sheet for a Restricted Groups policy

6. Click one or both of the Add buttons to add objects that should be members of the group, or other groups of which the group should be a member.

7. Click OK.

CLOSE the *Group Policy Management Editor* and *Group Policy Management* consoles.

TAKE NOTE*

Creating a Restricted Groups policy for a group and leaving the membership list blank prevents the group from having any members at all.

The members you specify for a group in a Restricted Groups policy are the only members permitted to remain in that group. The policy does not prevent you from modifying the group membership by using other tools, but the next time the system refreshes its group policy settings, the group membership list will be overwritten by the policy.

MANAGING GROUP OBJECTS WITH DSMOD.EXE

Dsmod.exe enables you to modify the properties of existing group objects from the Windows Server 2012 command prompt.

Using this program, you can perform tasks such as adding members to a group, removing them from a group, and changing a group's type and scope. The basic syntax for Dsmod.exe is as follows:

```
dsmod group <GroupDN> [parameters]
```

The most commonly used command-line parameters for Dsmod.exe are as follows:

- `-secgrp yes|no` sets the group type to security group (yes) or distribution group (no).
- `-scope l|g|u` sets the group scope to domain local (l), global (g), or universal (u).
- `-addmbr <members>` adds members to the group. Replace members with the DNs of one or more objects.
- `-rmmbr <members>` removes members from the group. Replace members with the DNs of one or more objects.
- `-chmbr <members>` replaces the complete list of group members. Replace members with the DNs of one or more objects.

For example, to add the Administrator user to the Guests group, you use the following command:

```
dsmod group "CN=Guests,CN=Builtin,DC=adatum,DC=com"-
addmbr "CN=Administrator,CN=Users,DC=adatum,DC=com"
```

Converting Groups

> As group functions change, you might need to change a group object from one type to another.

CERTIFICATION READY
Convert groups including security, distribution, universal, domain local, and domain global.
Objective 5.3

For example, you might have created a distribution group that contains 100 members from multiple departments working on the same project for the purpose of sending e-mail messages. As the project progresses, members might need to access a common database. By converting the distribution group to a security group and assigning permissions to the group, you can provide the project members with access to the common database without having to create a new group and add 100 members to it again.

To change the type of a group, open the group's Properties sheet in the *Active Directory Administrative Center* or the *Active Directory Users and Computers* console, as shown in Figure 15-18. On the *General* tab, you can modify the *Group Type* option and click *OK*.

Figure 15-18

The General tab in a group object's Properties sheet

The process for changing the group's scope is the same, except that you select one of the *Group Scope* options on the *General* tab. The AD DS utilities enable you to perform only permissible scope changes. In Figure 15-18, for example, the Global option is disabled because you cannot change a domain local group to a global group. Table 15-4 lists the scope changes that are permitted.

Table 15-4

Active Directory Group Scope
Conversion Restrictions

	To Domain Local	To Global	To Universal
From Domain Local	Not applicable	Not permitted	Permitted only when the domain local group does not have other domain local groups as members
From Global	Not permitted	Not applicable	Permitted only when the global group is not a member of another global group
From Universal	No restrictions	Permitted only when the universal group does not have other universal groups as members	Not applicable

Deleting a Group

As with user objects, each group object that you create in AD DS has a unique, nonreusable security identifier (SID). Windows Server 2012 uses the SID to identify the group and the permissions assigned to it.

When you delete a group, Windows Server 2012 does not use the same SID for that group again, even if you create a new group with the same name as the one you deleted. Therefore, you cannot restore the access permissions you assigned to resources by re-creating a deleted group object. You must add the newly recreated group as a security principal in the resource's ACL again.

When you delete a group, you delete only the group object and the permissions and rights specifying that group as the security principal. Deleting a group does not delete the objects that are members of the group.

SKILL SUMMARY

IN THIS LESSON, YOU LEARNED:

- After you create a design for your Active Directory domains and the trees and forests superior to them, you can zoom in on each domain and consider the hierarchy you want to create inside it.

- Adding organizational units to your Active Directory hierarchy is not as difficult as adding domains; you don't need additional hardware, and you can easily move or delete an OU at will.

- When you want to grant a collection of users permission to access a network resource, such as a file system share or a printer, you cannot assign permissions to an organizational unit; you must use a security group instead. Although they are container objects, groups are not part of the Active Directory hierarchy in the same way as domains and OUs.

- The OU is the easiest object type to create in the AD DS hierarchy. You need to supply only a name for the object and define its location in the Active Directory tree.

- Creating OUs enables you to implement a decentralized administration model, in which others manage portions of the AD DS hierarchy, without affecting the rest of the structure.

- Groups enable you to assign permissions to multiple users simultaneously. A group can be defined as a collection of user or computer accounts that functions as a security principal, in much the same way that a user does.

- Active Directory contains two types of groups: security and distribution, and three group scopes: domain local, global, and universal.

- *Group nesting* is the term used when groups are added as members of other groups.

- It is possible to control group memberships by using Group Policy. When you create Restricted Groups policies, you can specify the membership for a group and enforce it, so that no one can add or remove members.

Knowledge Assessment

Multiple Choice

Select one or more correct answers for each of the following questions.

1. You are planning an Active Directory implementation for a company that currently has sales, accounting, and marketing departments. All department heads want to manage their own users and resources in Active Directory. What feature will permit you to set up Active Directory to allow each manager to manage his or her own container but not any other containers?
   a. Delegation of control
   b. Read-only domain controller
   c. Multimaster replication
   d. SRV records

2. If the user named Amy is located in the sales OU of the central.cohowinery.com domain, what is the correct syntax for referencing this user in a command line utility?
   a. amy.cohowinery.com
   b. cn=amy.ou=sales.dc=cohowinery.com
   c. cn=amy,ou=sales,dc=central,dc=cohowinery,dc=com
   d. dc=com,dn=cohowinery,ou=sales,cn=amy

3. Which of the following is a container object within Active Directory?
   a. Folder
   b. Group
   c. User
   d. OU

4. Which of the following groups do you use to consolidate groups and accounts that either span multiple domains or the entire forest?
   a. Global
   b. Domain local
   c. Built-in
   d. Universal

5. Which of the following is not a correct reason for creating an OU?
   a. To create a permanent container that cannot be moved or renamed
   b. To duplicate the divisions in your organization
   c. To delegate administration tasks
   d. To assign different Group Policy settings to a specific group of users or computers

6. Which of the following group scope modifications are not permitted? (Choose all answers that are correct.)
   a. Global to universal
   b. Global to domain local
   c. Universal to global
   d. Domain local to universal

7. In a domain running at the Windows Server 2012 domain functional level, which of the following security principals can be members of a global group? (Choose all answers that are correct.)
   a. Users
   b. Computers
   c. Universal groups
   d. Global groups

8. You are attempting to delete a global security group in the Active Directory Users and Computers console, and the console will not let you complete the task. Which of the following could possibly be causes for the failure? (Choose all answers that are correct.)
   a. There are still members in the group.
   b. One of the group's members has the group set as its primary group.
   c. You do not have the proper permissions for the container in which the group is located.
   d. You cannot delete global groups from the Active Directory Users and Computers console.

Best Answer

Choose the letter that corresponds to the best answer. More than one answer choice may achieve the goal. Select the BEST answer.

1. Select the best reasons for using organizational units (OUs)?
   a. Organizing by geography, assigning Group Policy settings, and applying security boundaries
   b. Applying security boundaries, assigning Group Policy settings, and organizing by geography
   c. Duplicating organizational divisions, assigning Group Policy settings, and delegating administration
   d. Assigning Group Policy settings, administering delegation, and delegating administration

2. What is the primary difference between universal groups and global groups in Windows Server 2012?
   a. Global groups use less data in the global catalog. So, in considering replication traffic, universal groups should be within a site.
   b. Universal groups use less data in the global catalog. So, in considering replication traffic, global groups should be within a site.
   c. Universal groups use more data in the global catalog. However, global groups are best in general, both within a site and across sites.
   d. Global groups use less data than universal groups, but not significantly.

3. Generally, how do groups differ from OUs?
   a. Groups are security principals, meaning you assign access permissions to a resource based on membership to a group. OUs are for organization and for assigning Group Policy settings.
   b. Groups are created by the Server Manager, but you create OUs by scripts.
   c. OUs are security principals, meaning you assign access permissions to a resource based on membership to an organizational unit. Groups are for organization and for delegating permissions.
   d. Organizational units are container objects made from the Active Directory Users and Computers console.

4. What are the different kinds of groups?
   a. There are two types: security and distribution.
   b. There are two types: security and distribution, and three group scopes: domain local, global, and universal.
   c. There are three group scopes: domain local, global, and universal.
   d. There are three group types: domain local, global, and universal.

5. What command-line utility allows administrators to modify groups' type and scope as well as add or remove members?
   a. PowerShell and the applicable cmdlet
   b. Active Directory Users and Computers console
   c. Active Directory Administrative Center
   d. Dsmod.exe

Build a List

1. Order the steps to create an OU with Active Directory Administrative Center.
   a. Click OK. The organizational unit object appears in the container.
   b. In the left pane, right-click the object beneath which you want to create the new OU and, from the context menu, select New > Organizational Unit.
   c. From Server Manager's Tools menu, select Active Directory Administrative Center.
   d. In the Name field, type a name for the OU and add any optional information you want.

2. Order the steps to delegate Administrative Control of an OU.
   a. In the Users or Groups page, click Add.
   b. Right-click the object over which you want to delegate control, and click Delegate Control.
   c. In the Select Users, Computers, or Groups dialog box, type the name of the user or group to which you want to delegate control of the object, and click OK. The user or group appears in the Selected users and groups list.
   d. Select the Tasks to delegate, whether common tasks or custom tasks.
   e. From the Tools menu in the Server Manager window, select Active Directory Users and Computers.
   f. Set the delegated permissions for the user or group to which you delegate control.

3. Order the steps to create a restricted groups policy.
   a. Open the GPO in the Group Policy Management Editor and browse to the Computer Configuration\Policies\Windows Settings\Security Settings\Restricted Groups folder.
   b. Right-click the Restricted Groups folder and from the context menu, select Add Group. The Add Group dialog box appears.
   c. From the Tools menu in the Server Manager window, select Group Policy Management. The Group Policy Management console appears.

    d. Create a new Group Policy object (GPO) and link it to your domain.

    e. Type or browse to add a group object and click OK. The group appears in the Restricted Groups folder and a Properties sheet for the policy appears.

    f. Click one or both of the Add buttons to add objects that should be members of the group, or other groups of which the group should be a member.

■ Business Case Scenarios

Scenario 15-1: Administering Groups for Humongous Insurance

You are a network administrator for Humongous Insurance. Humongous Insurance has a multidomain forest. The forest root is humongousinsurance.com. There are also two child domains named west.humongousinsurance.com and east.humongousinsurance.com. The company has approximately 7,000 users, 7,000 client workstations, and 100 servers.

All domains are Windows Server 2013 domains. The forest root domain has 10 domain controllers. Five of those domain controllers are configured as DNS servers and two are configured as global catalog servers. The West domain has three domain controllers. Two of those domain controllers are configured as DNS servers. One of those domain controllers is configured as a global catalog server. The East domain has two Windows Server 2012 domain controllers and three Windows 2008 domain controllers.

The forest root domain is located in College Station, Texas. The East domain is located in Gainesville, Florida. The West domain is located in San Diego, California. An Active Directory site is configured for each of these locations. The site for College Station is named Main_Site. The Gainesville site is named East_Site. The San Diego site is named West_Site.

You are one of several network administrators assigned to handle the forest root domain and College Station site. Your manager, Jean Trenary, has called a meeting of all network and desktop administrators. She wants to address several issues.

1. Jean says four internal auditors are in the forest root domain. Two internal auditors are in each of the child domains. Each set of internal auditors has been placed in a global group within each domain. These groups are named IA_Main, IA_East, and IA_West after their respective locations. Jean wants all of the members of these groups to be able to access a common set of resources in the Main domain, while still segregating the audi-tors' ability to access other resources in domains other than their own. What is the rec-ommended way to configure the groups to allow the desired functionality?

2. The network administrators from the West domain want to know why everyone always recommends placing global groups into universal groups, instead of placing the users directly into the universal groups. What should you tell them?

3. Jean approves a plan to hire assistants for each domain to create and manage user accounts. How can you give the assistants the immediate ability to help in this way, without making them domain administrators?

4. Two employees have been hired to back up data and manage printers for the Main_Site. Which built-in groups will give these users the permissions they require to manage the domain controllers? How should you set up their accounts and group memberships?

Scenario 15-2: Planning GPOs for Tailspin Toys

Tailspin Toys is running a single Windows Server 2012 Active Directory domain with mul-tiple OUs configured for each of its 12 locations. An administrator at each location is respon-sible for managing GPOs and user accounts. You are the enterprise administrator responsible for planning the infrastructure. For each of the following challenges, document your options and be prepared to share them with other students.

1. Administrators located at each location should be able to create new GPOs and edit any that they have created. They should not be able to change or delete GPOs that they have not created. What are your options for providing this functionality?

2. All users in each location are currently in one OU. Certain group policies should only apply to users in some departments and not others. What options should you consider that will allow group policies to be applied to only the necessary users?

3. Although you have created a domain-wide policy that enforces restrictions on administrative tools, you do not want those settings to apply to users for which you have delegated administrative permissions on each location's OU. What are your options to solve this?

Creating Group Policy Objects

70-410 EXAM OBJECTIVE

Objective 6.1 – Create Group Policy objects (GPOs). This objective may include but is not limited to: Configure a Central Store; manage starter GPOs; configure GPO links; configure multiple local group policies; configure security filtering.

LESSON HEADING	EXAM OBJECTIVE
Introducing Group Policy	
Understanding Group Policy Objects	
Viewing the Group Policy Container	
Viewing Group Policy Templates	
Configuring a Central Store	Configure a Central Store
Using the Group Policy Management Console	
Creating and Linking Nonlocal GPOs	Configure GPO links
Using Security Filtering	Configure security filtering
Understanding Group Policy Processing	
Managing Starter GPOs	Manage starter GPOs
Configuring Group Policy Settings	
Creating Multiple Local GPOs	Configure multiple local group policies

KEY TERMS

ADMX

asynchronous processing

Block Policy Inheritance

Central Store

domain GPO

Enforce

folder redirection

GPO inheritance

Group Policy

Group Policy container (GPC)

Group Policy Management console

Group Policy Management Editor

Group Policy Object (GPO)

Group Policy template (GPT)

linking

local GPO

Loopback Processing

LSDOU

multiple local GPO

security filtering

starter GPO

synchronous processing

SYSVOL bloat

■ Introducing Group Policy

> **Group Policy** is a mechanism for controlling and deploying operating system settings to computers all over your network. Group Policy consists of user and computer settings for the various Microsoft Windows operating systems, which the systems implement during computer startup and shutdown and user logon and logoff. You can configure one or more Group Policy objects (GPOs) and then use a process called **linking** to associate them with specific Active Directory Domain System (AD DS) objects. When you link a GPO to a container object, all the objects in that container receive the settings you configured in the GPO. You can link multiple GPOs to a single AD DS container or link one GPO to multiple containers throughout the AD DS hierarchy.

↓
THE BOTTOM LINE

You can use Group Policy objects to manage any or all of the following types of settings:

- Registry-based policies, such as user desktop settings and environment variables, provide a consistent, secure, manageable working environment that addresses the users' needs and the organization's administrative goals. As the name implies, these settings modify the Windows Registry.

- Software installation policies ensure that users always have the latest versions of applications. If application files are inadvertently deleted, the policies can make repairs without user intervention.

- *Folder redirection* enables users to store local files on a network drive for backup, making them accessible from anywhere on the network.

- Offline file storage works with folder redirection to provide local file caching. This enables users to access their files even when the network is inaccessible.

- Scripts, including logon, logoff, startup, and shutdown commands, can assist in configuring the user environment.

- Windows Deployment Services (WDS) assists in rebuilding or deploying workstations quickly and efficiently in an enterprise environment.

- Microsoft Internet Explorer settings provide quick links and bookmarks for user accessibility, in addition to browser options, such as proxy use, acceptance of cookies, and caching options.

- Security settings protect resources on computers in the enterprise.

Depending on the organization's needs, you can choose which features and settings to implement. For example, you can create a policy for a public access computer in a library that configures the desktop environment with a proprietary library-access system. In addition, you can disable the capability to write to the computer's hard drive. As you determine the needs of different users and address the needs within corporate security and computing policies, you can plan the best methods to implement Group Policy.

Although the name *Group Policy Object* implies that policies are linked directly to groups, this is not the case. Group Policies can be linked to sites, domains, or organizational units (OUs) to apply the settings to all users and computers within the Active Directory containers. However, an advanced technique, called *security filtering*, enables you to apply GPO settings to only one or more users or groups within a container by selectively granting the "Apply Group Policy" permission to one or more users or security groups.

Users might initially view Group Policies as a heavy-handed management tactic to keep them from using certain computer functions. However, if presented appropriately, users will understand that they can also benefit from Group Policies. The following are just some of the benefits of Group Policy implementation to users:

- Users can access their files, even when network connectivity is intermittent. This is accomplished by using folder redirection and offline files.
- Users can work with a consistent computing environment, regardless of which workstation or location they use to log on.
- User files redirected to a server location can be backed up regularly, saving users from data loss due to workstation failure.
- Applications that become damaged or need to be updated can be reinstalled or maintained automatically.

Group Policies have the largest impact on network efficiency due to the administrative benefits. Administrators find that Group Policy implementation helps them to achieve centralized management. The following list identifies administrative benefits to Group Policy implementation:

- You have control over centralized configuration of user settings, application installation, and desktop configuration.
- Problems due to missing application files and other minor application errors often can be alleviated by the automation of application repairs.
- Centralized administration of user files eliminates the need and cost of trying to recover files from a damaged drive. (Note, however, that this does not eliminate the need to establish a regular backup schedule for server data.)
- The need to manually make security changes is reduced by the rapid deployment of new settings through Group Policy.

Understanding Group Policy Objects

Group Policy objects (GPOs) contain the Group Policy settings to deploy to user and computer objects within a site, domain, or organizational unit. To deploy a GPO, you must associate it with the container to which it is deployed. This association links the GPO to the desired Active Directory Domain Services object. Administrative tasks for Group Policy include creating GPOs, specifying where they are stored, and managing the AD DS links.

There are three types of GPOs: *local GPOs*, *domain GPOs,* and *starter GPOs*.

LOCAL GPOS

All Windows operating systems have support for local Group Policy objects, sometimes known as LGPOs. Windows versions since Windows Server 2008 R2 and Windows Vista can support *multiple local GPOs*. This enables you to specify a different local GPO for administrators or to create specific GPO settings for one or more local users configured on a workstation. This capability is particularly valuable for computers in public locations such as libraries and kiosks, which are not part of an Active Directory infrastructure.

Older Windows releases (prior to Windows Vista) can support only one local GPO, and the settings in that local GPO can apply only to the computer, not to individual users or groups.

Local GPO settings are stored on the local computer in the %systemroot%/System32/GroupPolicy folder.

A local GPO has the following characteristics:

- Local GPOs contain fewer options than domain GPOs. They do not support folder redirection or Group Policy software installation. Fewer security settings are available.
- When a local and a nonlocal (Active Directory-based) GPO have conflicting settings, the local GPO settings are overwritten by those of the nonlocal GPO.

DOMAIN GPOS

Nonlocal GPOs are created in Active Directory and are linked to sites, domains, or OUs. After linked to a container, the settings in the GPO are applied to all users and computers within the container by default. The content of each nonlocal GPO is stored in the following two locations:

- *Group Policy container (GPC)* is an Active Directory object that stores the properties of the GPO.
- *Group Policy template (GPT)* is located in the Policies subfolder of the SYSVOL share; the GPT is a folder that stores policy settings, such as security settings and script files.

STARTER GPOS

Starter GPOs is a feature introduced in Windows Server 2008. A starter GPO is a template for the creation of domain GPOs based on a standard collection of settings. When you create a new GPO from a starter GPO, all the policies in the starter are automatically copied to the new GPO as its default settings.

Viewing the Group Policy Container

> The Group Policy container (GPC) directory object includes subcontainers that hold GPO policy information.

By default, when you install Active Directory Domain Services on Windows Server 2012, the wizard creates two GPOCs, corresponding to the two default GPOs: Default Domain Policy and Default Domain Controller Policy. The two GPCs are named using globally unique identifiers (GUIDs) assigned to the GPOs during their creation. For each additional GPO you create later, the system creates a new GPC.

Each GPC contains two subcontainers—one for machine (that is, computer) configuration information and another for user configuration information. The more specific information included in each GPC is as follows:

- Status information that indicates whether the GPO is enabled or disabled
- Version information to ensure that the GPC is synchronized and up-to-date with the current information
- A list of components that have settings in the GPO
- Information for Software Installation and Folder Redirection policies

⊙ VIEW THE GROUP POLICY CONTAINER

GET READY. Log on to a server running Windows Server 2012, using an account with domain Administrator privileges. The Server Manager console appears.

1. From the Tools menu, select Active Directory Administrative Center. The Active Directory Administrative Center console appears.
2. In the left pane, select the Tree View icon, as shown in Figure 16-1.
3. Expand the domain node and the System node, and select the Policies node. This opens the folder, displaying the default policies, named using GUIDs, as shown in Figure 16-2.

Figure 16-1

Tree view in Active Directory
Administrative Center

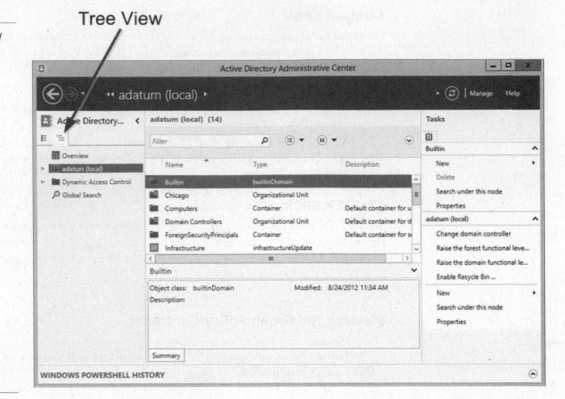

Figure 16-2

Contents of the Policies folder
in Active Directory
Administrative Center

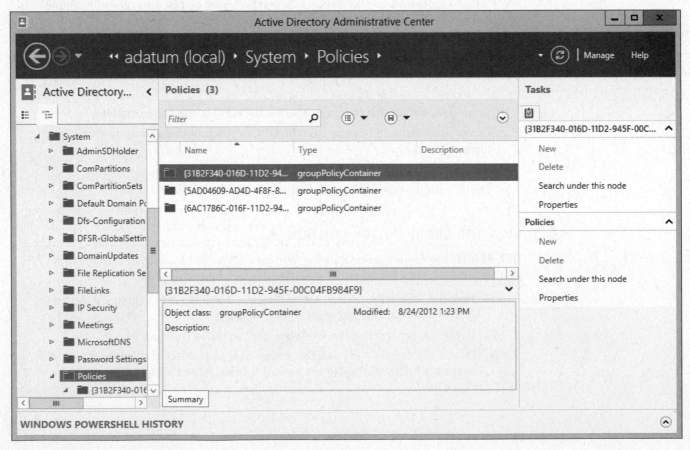

CLOSE the Active Directory Administrative Center console.

It is also possible to view the Group Policy Containers by using the Active Directory Users and Computers console, as shown in Figure 16-3.

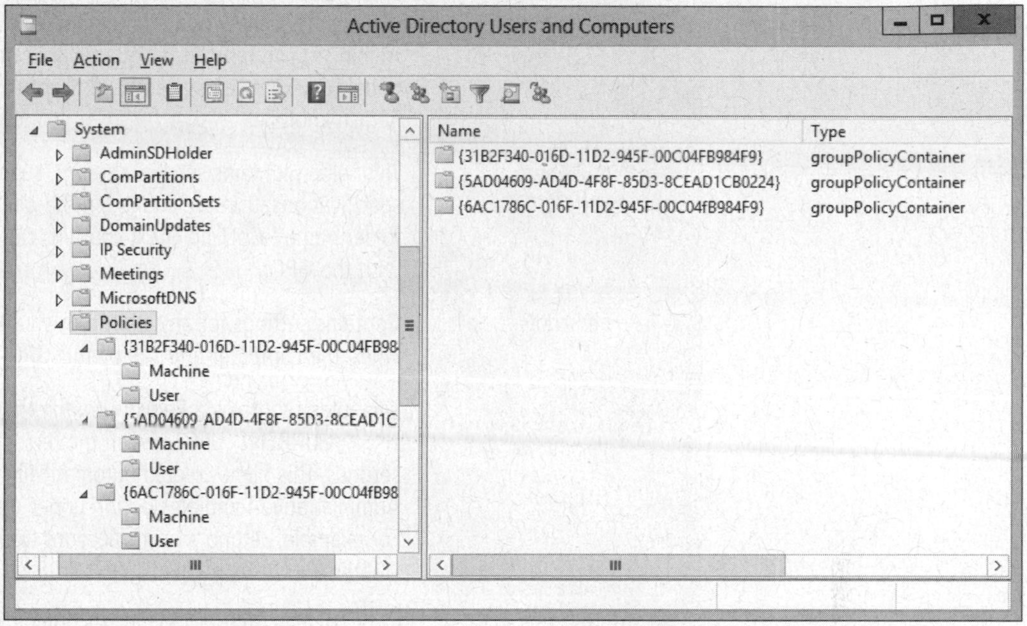

Figure 16-3

Group Policy Containers in Active Directory Users and Computers

> **TAKE NOTE** *
>
> Before you can see the System folder beneath a domain in the Active Directory Users and Computers console, you must select Advanced Features from the View menu to toggle the console's Advanced view.

Computers access the GPC to locate Group Policy templates via a link or connection reference to the Group Policy template. Domain controllers access the GPC to get version information. If the version information for a GPO is not current, replication occurs to update the GPO with the latest version.

Viewing Group Policy Templates

> The Group Policy templates (GPT) folder structure is located in the shared SYSVOL folder on a domain controller.

By default, there are two folders corresponding to the default domain policies, named using the same GUIDs as those for the GPCs. After you create an additional GPO, a corresponding GPT folder structure is created that contains all the policy's settings and information. As with the GPC, computers connect to the GPT folder structure to read the settings.

The path to the default GPT structure for a domain is %systemroot%\SYSVOL\sysvol\<*domain name*>\Policies. For example, in a standard Windows installation for a domain called adatum.com, the path would be C:\WINDOWS\SYSVOL\sysvol\adatum.com\Policies. In Universal Naming convention (UNC) notation, the folder would be \\<*domain name*>\SYSVOL\<*domain name*>\Policies.

Each GUID that refers to a policy in the GPT structure has several subfolders and a gpt.ini file. This file contains the version and status information regarding the specific GPO. The subfolders contain more specific settings that are defined within the policy. Table 16-1 identifies several of the subfolders that are part of the GPT structure and describes their contents. (This table is not all-inclusive; some folders and their contents are created when policy settings are defined.)

Table 16-1

GPT Subfolders

FOLDER	CONTENTS
\Machine	This folder contains a Registry.pol file that makes changes to the HKEY_LOCAL_MACHINE hive in the registry based on machine-specific settings. This file is created automatically when a policy has used the Administrative Templates option within the Computer Configuration node. For example, enabling Disk Quotas for a machine creates a Registry.pol file.
\Machine\Microsoft \WindowsNT\SecEdit	This folder contains security settings, such as account lockout specifications, that are defined in the policy. A file is created in this folder named GptTmpl.inf. It contains the specific settings to be applied with the GPO.
\Machine\Scripts	Contains settings for any startup or shutdown scripts that are in effect when the computer affected by this GPO starts or shuts down.
\User	This folder contains a Registry.pol file that makes changes to the HKEY_CURRENT_USER hive in the registry based on user-specific settings. This file is created automatically when a policy has used the Administrative Templates option under the User Configuration node. For example, setting a user's account to autoenroll for a certificate creates a Registry.pol file.
\User\Applications	Contains files that include instructions for assigned or published application packages. This folder does not exist until package files used to deploy software applications are assigned to the User Configuration node of the GPO.
\User\Scripts	Contains settings for logon and logoff scripts that are applied when a user affected by this GPO logs on or off the network.

As discussed previously, the two default GPOs represented by the GPCs and the GPT folders are called Default Domain Policy and Default Domain Controllers Policy, respectively. The Default Domain Policy GPO is linked to the domain object, so its settings are propagated to all the users and computers throughout the domain. The Default Domain Controllers Policy GPO is linked to the Domain Controllers OU, into which AD DS places all the computer objects representing domain controllers. Therefore, all the domain controllers for the domain receive the settings in the GPO.

These two policies are critically important, because their settings can affect security and your administrative capabilities throughout the domain. It is generally recommended that you do not modify these two GPOs by adding new settings or changing the existing ones. You can instead create new GPOs and use them to augment or override the existing settings.

Configuring a Central Store

In Windows Server 2008 and Windows Vista, Microsoft replaced the token-based administrative template (ADM) files used with previous versions of Group Policy with an XML-based file format (*ADMX*). Administrative templates are the files defining the registry-based settings that appear in Group Policy objects.

CERTIFICATION READY
Configure a Central Store.
Objective 6.1

Earlier Windows versions created a copy of the ADM files for each GPO you created and placed it in the SYSVOL volume of a domain controller. A large Active Directory installation could easily have dozens of GPOs, and each copy of the ADM files required 4 megabytes of storage. The result was a condition called **SYSVOL bloat**, in which hundreds of megabytes of redundant information was stored on SYSVOL volumes, which had to be replicated to all the domain controllers for the domain.

To address this problem, Group Policy tools can now access the ADMX files from a **Central Store**, a single copy of the ADMX files stored on domain controllers. To use a Central Store, however, you must create the appropriate folder in the SYSVOL volume on a domain controller.

By default, tools such as the Group Policy Management console save the ADMX files to the \%systemroot%\PolicyDefinitions folder, which on most computers is C:\Windows\PolicyDefinitions. To create a Central Store, you must copy the entire PolicyDefinitions folder to the same location as the Group Policy templates, that is, %systemroot%\SYSVOL\sysvol\<domain name>\Policies, or, in UNC notation, \\<domain name>\SYSVOL\<domain name>\Policies.

TAKE NOTE*

Using a Central Store presents a potential problem. Windows 7 and Windows Server 2008 R2 added two new registry types: REG_MULTI_SZ and REG_QWORD, to the ADMX format. To use these registry types, your Central Store must contain the ADMX files generated by a computer running Windows 7 or Windows Server 2008 R2. When you have the latest ADMX files in your Central Store, however, using Group Policy tools on computers running Windows Vista or Windows Server 2008 can result in parsing errors. The only solutions to this problem are to make sure that you manage your GPOs on computers running Windows 7 or Windows Server 2008 R2 or higher, or to eliminate the Central Store by deleting the PolicyDefinitions folder from the SYSVOL volume.

Using the Group Policy Management Console

THE BOTTOM LINE

The **Group Policy Management console** is the Microsoft Management Console (MMC) snap-in that you use to create Group Policy objects and manage their deployment to Active Directory Domain Services objects. The **Group Policy Management Editor** is a separate snap-in that opens GPOs and enables you to modify their settings.

There are several different ways of working with these two tools, depending on what you want to accomplish. You can create a GPO and then link it to a domain, site, or OU, or create and link a GPO in a single step. Windows Server 2012 implements the tools as the Group Policy Management feature, as shown in Figure 16-4, and installs them automatically with the Active Directory Domain Services role. You can install the feature manually on a member server by using the Add Roles and Features Wizard in Server Manager, and it is also included in the Remote Server Administration Tools package for Windows workstations.

Figure 16-4

The Group Policy Management feature in the Add Roles and Features Wizard

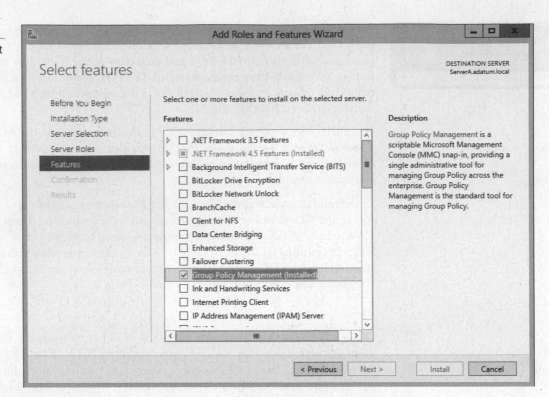

Creating and Linking Nonlocal GPOs

If, as recommended previously, you leave the default GPOs unaltered, the first steps in deploying your own customized Group Policy settings are to create one or more new Group Policy objects and link them to appropriate AD DS objects.

To use the Group Policy Management console to create a new GPO and link it to an organizational unit object in AD DS, perform the following procedure.

⊙ CREATE AND LINK A GPO TO AN OU

GET READY. Log on to a domain controller running Windows Server 2012, using an account with domain Administrator privileges. The Server Manager console appears.

1. Open the Active Directory Administrative Center and create an OU called "Sales" in your domain.
2. From the Tools menu, select Group Policy Management. The Group Policy Management console appears, as shown in Figure 16-5.

TAKE NOTE*

You can also launch the Group Policy Management console from a member server on which you have previously installed the Group Policy Management feature, or from a workstation running the Remote Server Administration Tools package.

3. Expand the forest container and browse to your domain. Then expand the domain container and select the Group Policy Objects folder. The GPOs that currently exist in the domain appear in the *Contents* tab, as shown in Figure 16-6.

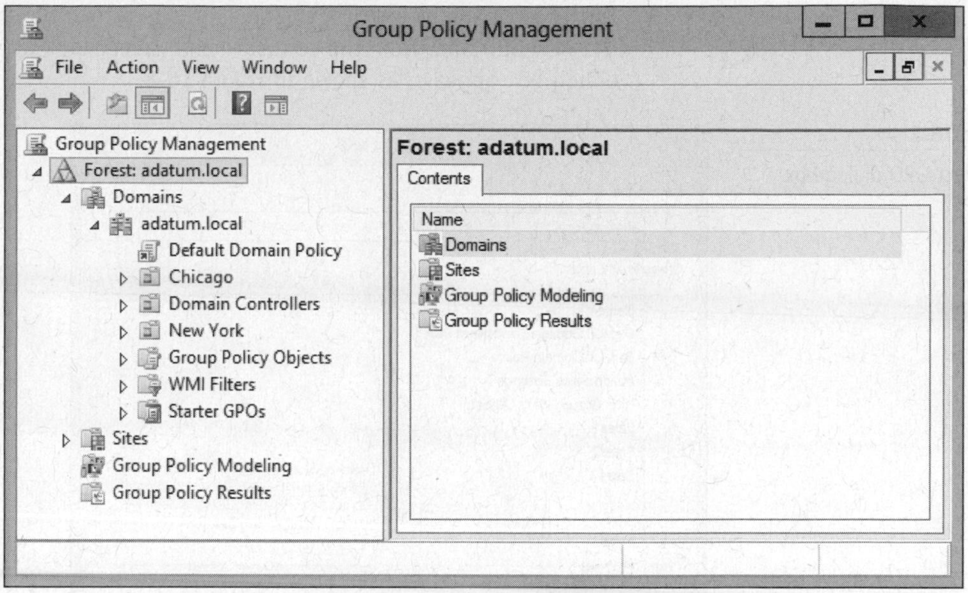

Figure 16-5

The Group Policy Management console

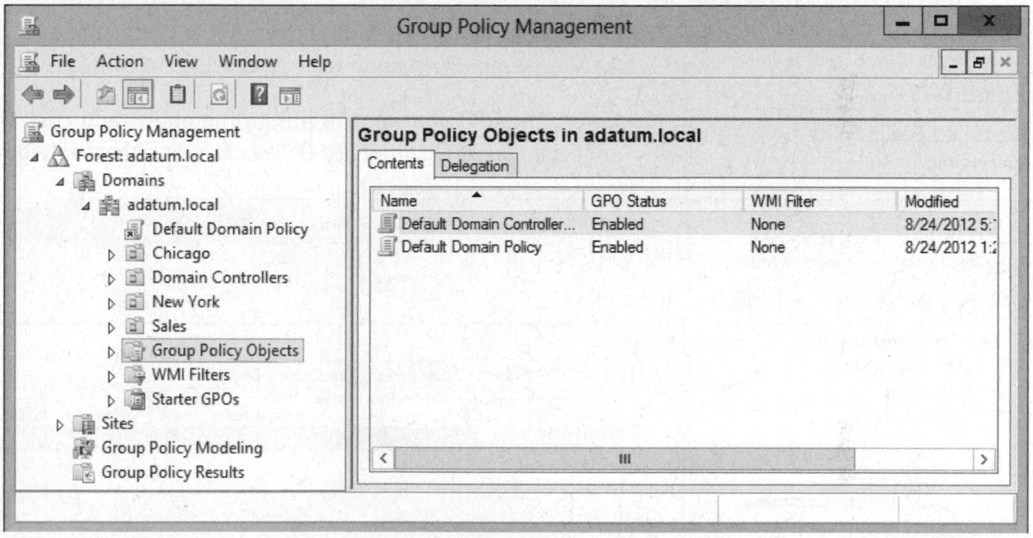

Figure 16-6

Contents of the Group Policy Objects folder

4. Right-click the Group Policy Objects folder and, from the context menu, select New. The *New GPO* dialog box appears, as shown in Figure 16-7.

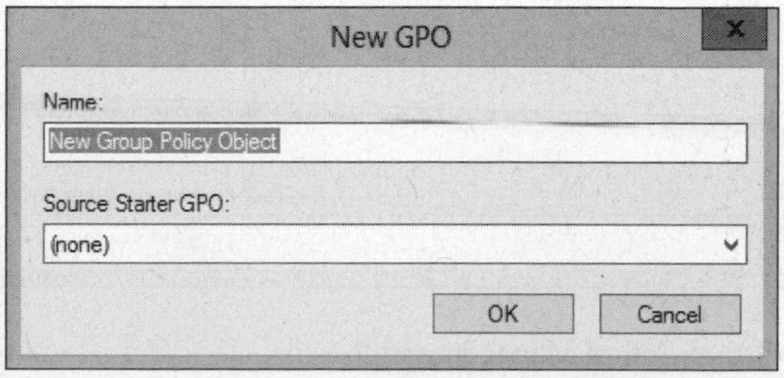

Figure 16-7

The New GPO dialog box

TAKE NOTE*

At any time, you can right-click the GPO you created, select Edit from the context menu to open it in the Group Policy Management Editor, and modify the settings it contains.

5. In the Name text box, type a name for the new GPO and, if desired, select a *Source Starter GPO* from the drop-down list and click OK. The new GPO appears in the Contents list.

6. In the left pane, right-click the domain, site, or OU object to which you want to link the new GPO and, from the context menu, select Link an existing GPO. The *Select GPO* dialog box appears, as shown in Figure 16-8.

Figure 16-8

The Select GPO dialog box

Figure 16-9

The Linked Group Policy Objects tab

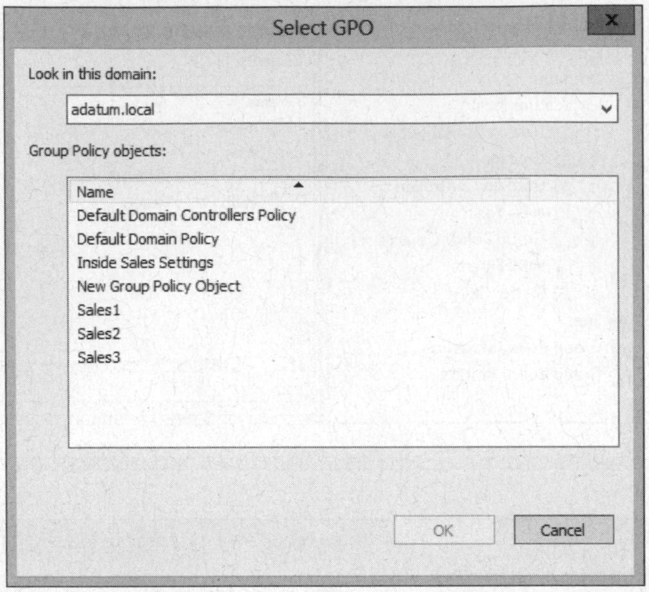

7. Select the GPO you want to link to the object and click OK. The GPO appears on the object's *Linked Group Policy Objects* tab, as shown in Figure 16-9.

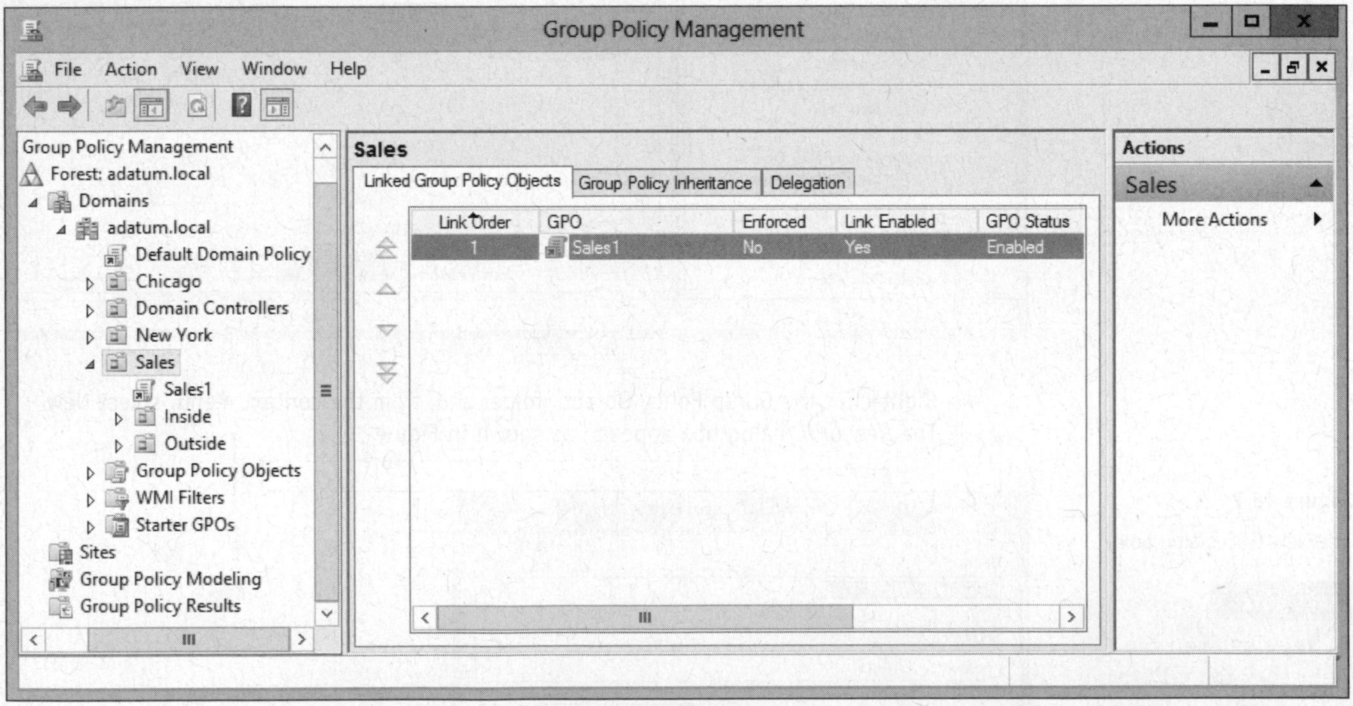

CLOSE the Group Policy Management console.

You can also create and link a GPO to an AD container in a single step, by right-clicking an object and selecting Create a GPO in this Domain and Link it here from the context menu.

If you link a GPO to a domain object, it applies to all users and computers in the domain. On a larger scale, if you link a GPO to a site that contains multiple domains, the Group Policy settings are applied to all the domains and the child objects beneath them. This process is referred to as *GPO inheritance*.

USING WINDOWS POWERSHELL

The Group Policy module in Windows PowerShell provides cmdlets that enable you to create and manage Group Policy objects. To create a new GPO, you use the New-GPO cmdlet with the following syntax:

```
New-GPO –Name <name> –Domain <name> –StarterGpoName <name>
```

When you run the New-GPO cmdlet, the cmdlet returns the name of the newly created GPO. You can therefore pipe that name to the New-GPLink cmdlet, which links the GPO to the domain, site, or OU object you specify, using the following syntax:

```
New-GPLink –Name <link name> –Target <LDAP path>
```

For example, to create a new GPO called Test1 and link it to the adatum.com domain, you would use the following command:

```
New-GPO –Name Test1 | New-GPLink –Target "dc=adatum,dc=com"
```

Using Security Filtering

> By default, linking a GPO to a container causes all the users and computers in that container to receive the GPO settings. The act of creating the link grants the Read and Apply Group Policy permissions for the GPO to the users and computers in the container.

CERTIFICATION READY
Configure security filtering.
Objective 6.1

In actuality, the system grants the permissions to the Authenticated Users special identity, which includes all the users and computers in the container. However, by using a technique called security filtering, you can modify the default permission assignments so that only certain users and computers receive the permissions and, consequently, the settings in the GPO.

To modify the default security filtering configuration for a GPO, select it in the left pane of the Group Policy Management console, as shown in Figure 16-10. In the Security Filtering area, you can use the Add and Remove buttons to replace the Authenticated Users special

Figure 16-10

Security filtering in the Group Policy Management console

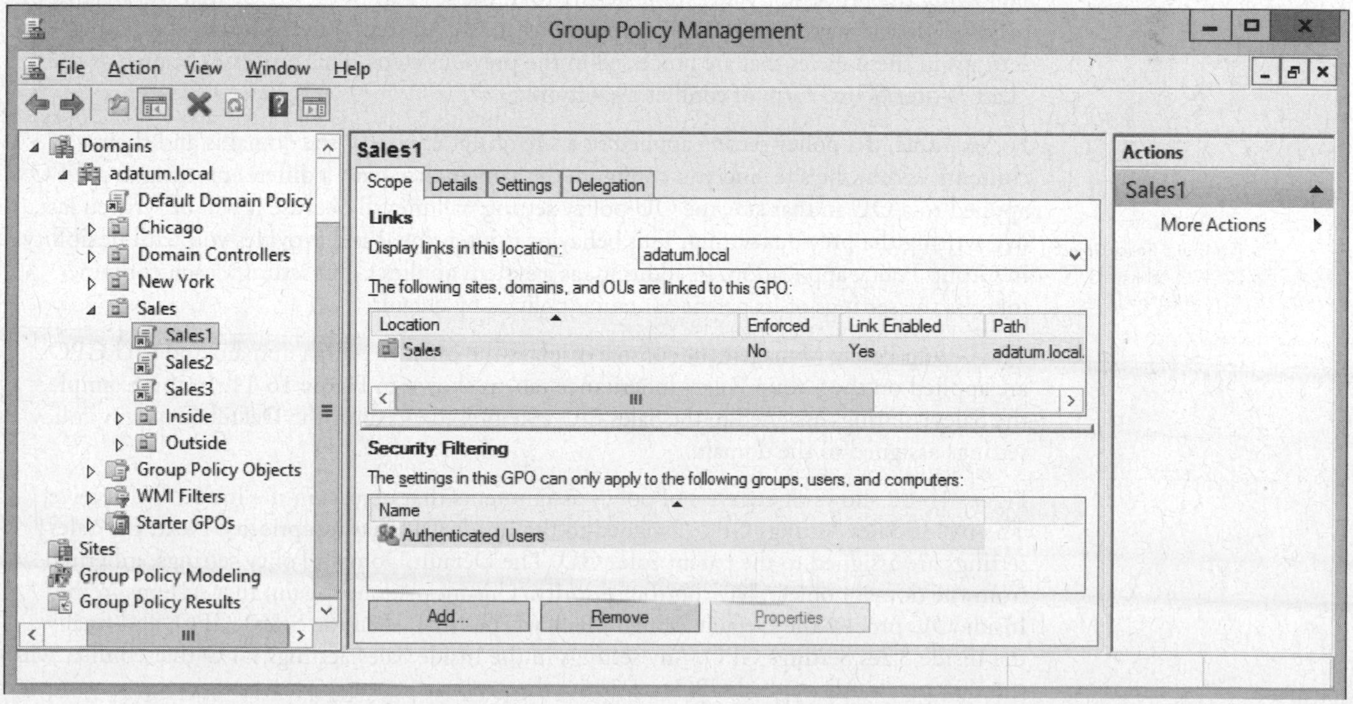

identity with specific user, computer, or group objects. Of the users and computers in the container to which the GPO is linked, only those you select in the Security Filtering pane receive the settings from the GPO.

Understanding Group Policy Processing

As discussed previously, you can have local policies, site policies, domain policies, and OU policies within your domain structure. To learn how to best implement Group Policies to serve the organization, you should understand the order in which Windows systems apply the policies.

You can link GPOs only to AD DS site, domain, or OU objects. You cannot link GPOs to built-in containers, such as the default Users, Builtin, or Computers containers. These containers can receive only policies by inheriting them from GPOs linked to domains or sites above them in the AD DS hierarchy.

GPOs affect the containers to which they are linked in the following ways:

- Site-linked GPOs affect all domains within a site.
- Domain-linked GPOs affect all users and computers within the domain and within any subordinate containers inside the domain. This includes objects in built-in containers, as well as objects within OUs in the domain structure.
- OU-linked GPOs affect all objects within the OU and any subordinate OU structures nested beneath them.

Windows systems receiving GPOs from multiple sources process them in the following order, typically referred to as *LSDOU*:

1. Local policies
2. Site policies
3. Domain policies
4. OU policies

Following the processing order from steps 1 to 4, the settings in the GPOs that the system processes last (that is, those that are assigned to an OU in step 4) override any conflicting settings in the policies that are processed in the previous steps. This process is known as the "Last Writer Wins" form of conflict resolution.

For example, if a policy setting applied to a site object affects all the domains and their contents within the site, and you configure the same policy with a different setting in a GPO applied to a OU in that site, the OU policy setting will prevail because it will be written last, overwriting the previous setting. This behavior is intentional and provides you with flexibility in Group Policy application. In addition, as a system applies GPO settings, each container inherits the settings of its parent container policies by default.

The Group Policy Management console displays the order in which domain and OU GPOs are applied on the Group Policy Inheritance tab, as shown in Figure 16-11. In this example, the Sales1 settings assigned to the Sales OU take precedence over the Default Domain Policy settings assigned to the domain.

Figure 16-12 shows three layers of policy assignments that objects in the Inside OU receive. The Inside Sales Settings GPO, assigned to the Inside OU, has top priority. Next, the Sales1 settings are assigned to the parent Sales OU. The Default Domain Policy settings, inherited from the domain object, have bottom priority. This means, once again, that systems in the Inside OU process the Default Domain Policy GPO first, then the Sales1 GPO, and finally the Inside Sales Settings GPO. Any settings in the Inside Sales Settings GPO that conflict with those in previously applied GPOs overwrite the previous settings.

Figure 16-11

The Group Policy Inheritance tab, showing OU and domain inheritance

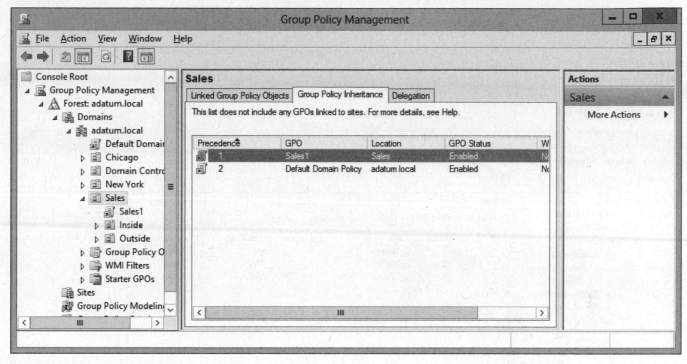

Figure 16-12

The Group Policy Inheritance tab, showing two layers of OU inheritance plus domain inheritance

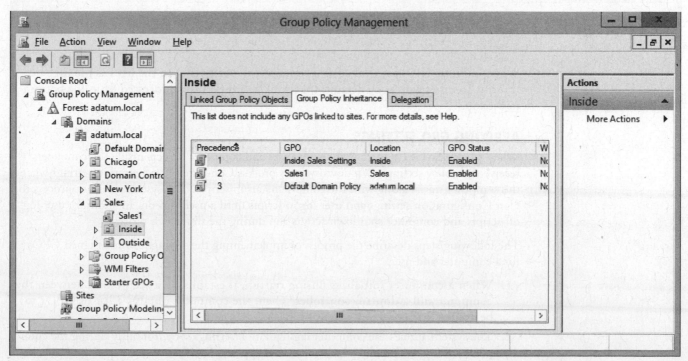

PROCESSING MULTIPLE GPOS

You can link multiple GPOs to domains, sites, and OUs. Many administrators prefer to create individual GPOs for each system configuration task, rather than create one large GPO with a multitude of settings. When multiple GPOs are linked to a single AD DS object, you can control the order in which systems apply the GPO settings, by using the Linked Group Policy Objects tab in the Group Policy Management console.

Figure 16-13 depicts an OU called Sales with three GPOs linked to it, each of which is assigned a link order number. The GPO with link order 1 has the highest priority, which means that of the three GPOs, systems processes it last.

Figure 16-13

The Linked Group Policy Objects tab, with multiple GPOs linked to a single OU

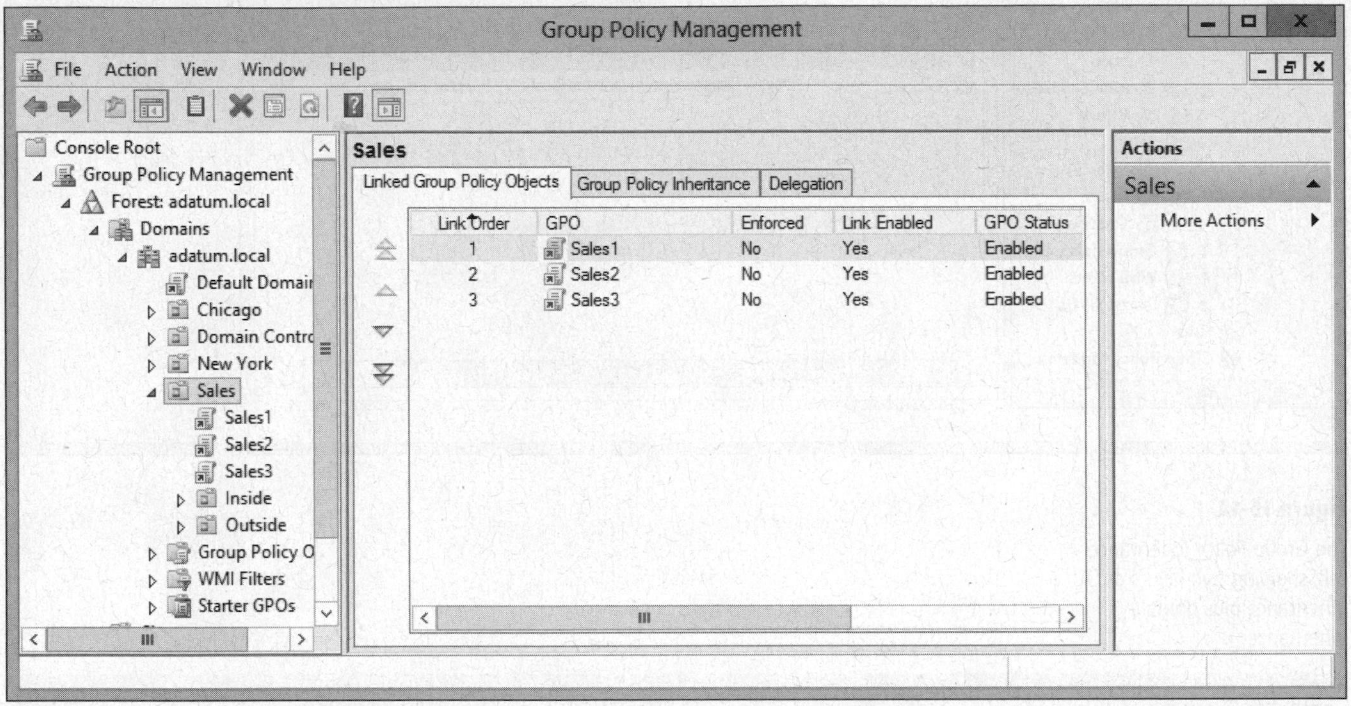

When multiple GPOs are linked to a container, the first GPO in the list has the highest priority. In other words, by default, the list of linked GPOs is processed from the bottom to the top.

APPLYING GPO SETTINGS

When you apply GPOs to containers, the user and computer objects inside the containers receive the policy settings. Windows systems process Computer Configuration settings when the computer starts, along with the computer startup scripts. The system does not process the User Configuration settings and user logon scripts until a user logs on. In addition, user logoff scripts and computer shutdown scripts run during the shutdown process.

The following steps describe the process of implementing the settings of the assigned GPOs for a computer and user:

1. When a computer initializes during startup, it establishes a secure link between the computer and a domain controller. Then, the computer obtains a list of GPOs to be applied.

2. The system applies the computer configuration settings synchronously during the computer startup, before the user logon screen appears. *Synchronous processing* of policies

means that the systems reads and applies each policy completely involving the next one. You can modify this default synchronous behavior, if necessary, but such modification is discouraged. No user interface appears during this process. The system reads and applies the policies in the LSDOU sequence described previously.

3. The system processes any scripts that are set to run during computer startup. These scripts also run synchronously and have a default timeout of 600 seconds (10 minutes) to complete. This process is hidden from the user.

4. After the Computer Configuration settings are applied and the startup scripts completes, the Ctrl+Alt+Del prompt appears to the user.

5. After the user authenticates successfully, the system loads the user profile, based on the Group Policy settings in effect.

6. The system obtains a list of GPOs specific for the user from the domain controller and processes the User Configuration settings in the LSDOU sequence. The GPO processing is again synchronous and transparent to the user.

7. After the system applies the user policies, it runs any logon scripts. These scripts, unlike the startup scripts, run asynchronously by default. *Asynchronous processing* enables multiple scripts to run at the same time, without waiting for the outcome of a previously launched script. However, the user object script runs last.

8. After all policies are applied and all scripts are complete, the user's desktop appears.

CONFIGURING EXCEPTIONS TO GPO PROCESSING

As with most rules, there are usually exceptions, and this is true of Group Policy processing and inheritance. The purpose of having exceptions to the default processing of Group Policy settings is to allow greater flexibility and control over the final settings that are applied.

The exceptions to the default Group Policy processing rules include the following: Enforce, Block Policy Inheritance, and Loopback Processing.

Enforce

Configuring the *Enforce* setting on an individual GPO link forces a particular GPO's settings to flow down through the AD DS hierarchy, without being blocked by child OUs.

As discussed previously, if you assign a GPO policy at a site level, it is inherited by all domains within that site. The inheritance process takes place in the same order that Group Policies are applied. Specifically, this process results in sites obtaining GPO settings from site-linked GPOs; domains inheriting policies from site-linked GPOs and obtaining settings from domain-linked GPOs; OUs inheriting GPO settings from both site-linked and domain-linked GPOs, as well as settings from OU-linked GPOs; and child OUs inheriting settings from all the above. Inheritance then means that all objects within each of these containers inherit the GPO settings from higher up in the hierarchy. Because child container settings can overwrite the settings that were invoked at a parent container, you can assign the Enforce attribute to a GPO link to force a parent setting, preventing it from being overwritten by a conflicting child setting. The Enforce option denies the capability of child objects to apply the Block Policy Inheritance setting.

To enable the Enforce setting, right-click an entry in the Linked Group Policy Objects tab and, from the context men, select Enforced.

Block Policy Inheritance

Configuring the *Block Policy Inheritance* setting on a container object such as a site, domain, or OU blocks all policies from parent containers from flowing to this container. The setting is not policy specific; it applies to all policies that are applied at parent levels. GPO links that are set to Enforce are not affected by this setting; they are still applied. This setting is useful when you want to start a new level of policy inheritance or when you do not want a parent policy to affect objects in a particular container.

To enable this setting, right-click a container object and, from the context menu, select Block Inheritance.

Loopback Processing

Loopback Processing is a Group Policy option that provides an alternative method of obtaining the ordered list of GPOs to be processed for the user. When set to Enabled, this setting has two options: merge and replace.

When a computer starts up, a domain controller supplies a list of GPOs that apply to the computer, which it then processes. Similarly, when a user logs on, the system receives and processes a list of GPOs based on the user object's location in the AD DS hierarchy.

In certain situations, you might not want user-specific settings applied to certain computers. For example, when you log on to a domain controller or member server computer, you probably do not want Group Policy to install software applications associated with your user object that are intended solely for workstation use. Because Windows applies user policies after computer policies, you can alter this situation by using the Loopback Processing capability.

As the name implies, Loopback Processing enables the Group Policy processing order to circle back and reapply the computer policies after all user policies and logon scripts run. When you enable loopback processing, you can choose the Merge option or the Replace option. When you select the Merge option, after all user policies run the system reapplies the computer policy settings, which enables all current GPO settings to merge with the reapplied computer policy settings. In instances where conflicts arise between computer and user settings, the computer policy supersedes the user policy. This occurs before the desktop is presented to the user. The system simply appends the settings to those that were already processed. Merging might not overwrite all the settings implemented by the User Configuration settings.

The Replace option overwrites the GPO list for a user object with the GPO list for the user's logon computer. That is, the computer policy settings remove any conflicting user policy settings.

In addition, the Loopback Processing setting is a valuable tool for managing computers shared by more than one user, as in a kiosk, classroom, or public library. Using the Replace option can greatly reduce the need for you to undo actions, such as application installs and desktop changes, that are implemented by settings associated with a user object.

For example, consider an academic environment in which the user objects for administrative accounts, such as teachers and staff, are placed in a separate Admin OU. All workstation computer objects are located in a Lab OU. In computer labs, anyone can log on to the network. However, when users in the Admin OU log on to lab computers, their User Configuration settings configure the computers to print on printers located in their offices, and install applications on the lab computers intended only for the users' office computers. Teachers complain that they have to walk back to their offices to pick up print jobs that should print on the printers located in the lab. In addition, applications that should not reside on the lab computers are installed there and now must be removed. One solution to this problem is to use the Replace option in Loopback Processing. When you set the Replace option, the system applies only the user settings from the Lab OU applied. This resolves the issue of applying unwanted settings on shared computers from other locations in the AD DS hierarchy.

To enable Loopback Processing, you must configure a Group Policy setting in a GPO and link it to an appropriate object. To find the setting open a GPO, browse to the Computer Configuration\Policies\Administrative Templates\System\Group Policy folder and enable the Configure User Group Policy Loopback Processing Mode policy, as shown in Figure 16-14.

Figure 16-14

The Configure User Group Policy Loopback Processing Mode policy

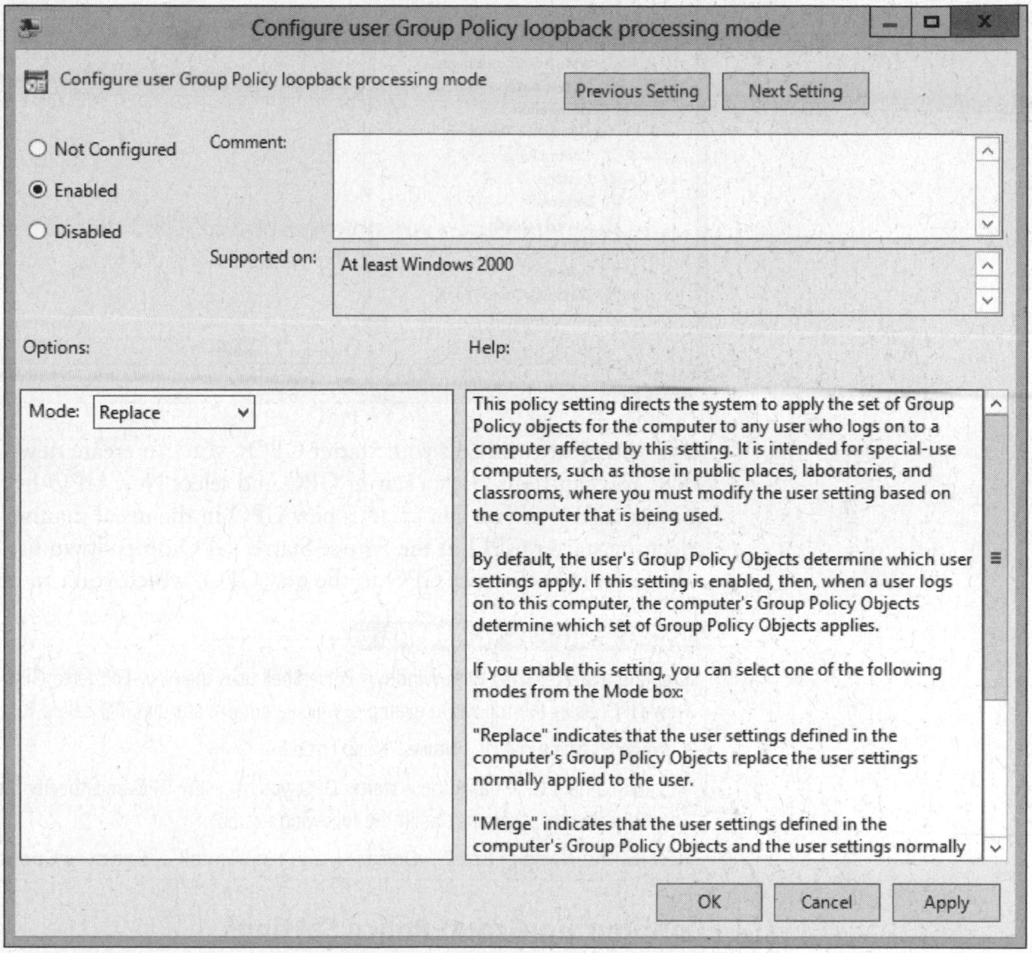

Managing Starter GPOs

Starter GPOs are templates that create multiple GPOs with the same set of baseline Administrative Templates settings.

You create and edit starter GPOs just as you would any other Group Policy object. In the Group Policy Management console, you right-click the Starter GPOs folder and, from the context menu, select New to create a blank starter GPO. You can then open the starter GPO in the Group Policy Management Editor, as shown in Figure 16-15, and configure any settings you want to carry over to the new GPOs you create.

CERTIFICATION READY
Manage starter GPOs.
Objective 6.1

TAKE NOTE* When you view the Starter GPOs node in the Group Policy Management console for the first time, a message appears, prompting you to create the Starter GPOs folder by clicking a button.

Figure 16-15

A starter GPO in the Group
Policy Management Editor

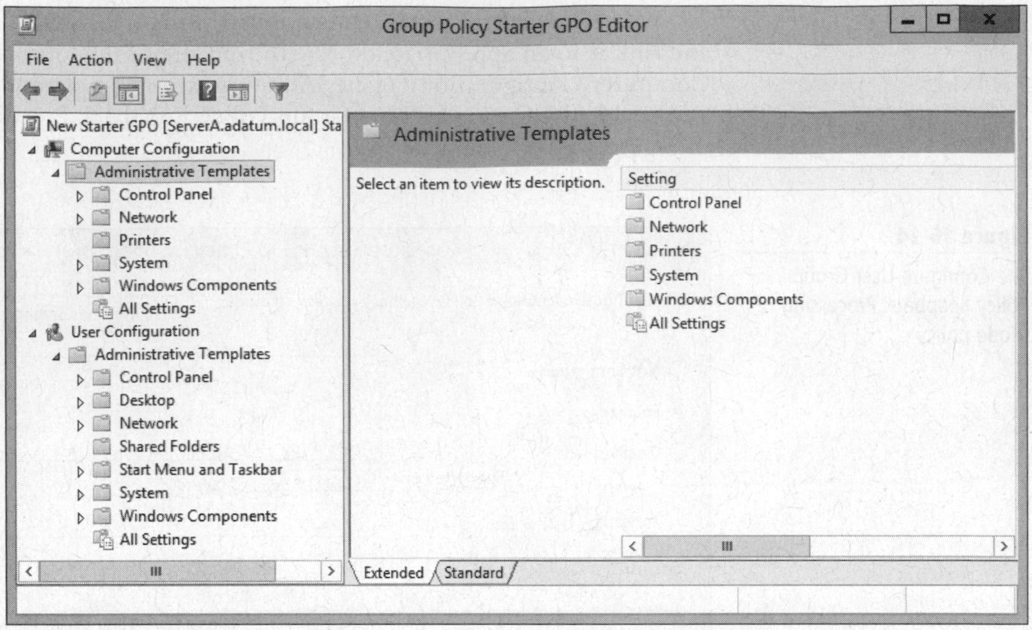

After you create and edit your starter GPOs, you can create new GPOs from them in two
ways. You can right-click a starter GPO and select New GPO from Starter GPO from the
context menu, or you can create a new GPO in the usual manner described previously and
select the starter GPO in the Source Starter GPO drop-down list. This process copies the
settings from the starter GPO to the new GPO, which you can continue to edit from there.

USING WINDOWS POWERSHELL

Creating a starter GPO with Windows PowerShell uses the New-GPStarterGPO cmdlet with the same syntax as
New-GPO, as in the following example, which creates a starter GPO called Template1.

```
New-GPStarterGPO –Name Template1
```

To create a new GPO based on a starter GPO, you use New-GPO and specify the name of the starter GPO in the –
StarterGpoName parameter, as in the following example:

```
New-GPO –Name Test2 –Domain adatum.local –StarterGpoName Template1
```

Configuring Group Policy Settings

Group Policy settings enable you to customize the configuration of a user's desktop,
environment, and security settings. The settings are divided into two subcategories:
Computer Configuration and User Configuration. The subcategories are referred to as
Group Policy nodes. A node is a parent structure that holds all related settings. In this case,
the node is specific to computer configurations and user configurations.

Group Policy nodes provide a way to organize the settings according to where they are applied.
The settings you define in a GPO can be applied to client computers, users, or member servers
and domain controllers. The application of the settings depends on the container to which you
link the GPO. By default, all objects within the container to which you link the GPO are
affected by the GPO's settings.

The Computer Configuration and the User Configuration nodes contain three subnodes, or
extensions, that further organize the available Group Policy settings. Within the Computer
Configuration and User Configuration nodes, the subnodes are as follows:

- **Software Settings:** The Software Settings folder located under the Computer
  Configuration node contains Software Installation settings that apply to all users

who log on to a domain using a specific computer. These settings are applied before any user is allowed to log on. Rather than being computer specific, the Software Settings folder located under the User Configuration node contains Software Installation settings applied to users designated by the Group Policy, regardless of the computer from which they log on.

- **Windows Settings:** The Windows Settings folder located under the Computer Configuration node in the Group Policy Management Editor contains security settings and scripts that apply to all users who log on to Active Directory Domain Services from that specific computer. This means that the settings are computer specific. The Windows Settings folder located under the User Configuration node contains settings related to folder redirection, security settings, and scripts that apply to specific users. The computer from which a user logs on does not affect these policy settings; the policies are applied regardless of the user's log on location.

- **Administrative Templates:** Windows Server 2012 includes thousands of Administrative Template policies, which contain all registry-based policy settings. Administrative Templates are files with the .admx extension. They are used to generate the user interface for the Group Policy settings that you can set by using the Group Policy Management Editor. The Windows Server 2012 .admx files are based on the eXtensible Markup Language (XML), unlike the Windows 2003 .adm files, which are token-based text files.

POLICY EXPLANATIONS

Because Administrative Templates is an area of Group Policy where many commonly used administrative settings reside, you should be familiar with the resources that enable you to determine the function of each policy setting. In the Group Policy Management Editor, you can view descriptions of policy settings by using the Explain tab, as shown in Figure 16-16. This comprehensive help feature describes the function of the policy setting. Additionally, the Group Policy Management Editor console includes a Requirements section for each setting that indicates the minimum operating system revision that supports it.

Figure 16-16

Explanations of Group Policy settings

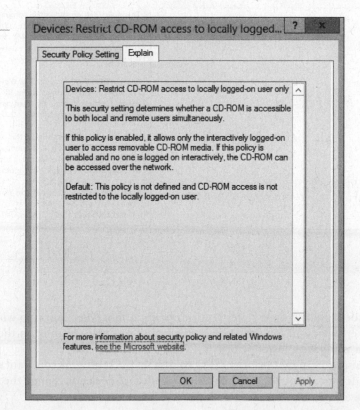

UNDERSTANDING POLICY STATES

To work with Administrative Template settings, you must understand the following three states of each policy setting:

- **Not Configured:** No modification to the registry from its default state occurs as a result of the policy. Not Configured is the default setting for the majority of GPO settings. When a system processes a GPO with a Not Configured setting, the registry key affected by the setting is not modified or overwritten, no matter what its current value might be.
- **Enabled:** The policy function is explicitly activated in the registry, whatever its previous state.
- **Disabled:** The policy function is explicitly deactivated in the registry, whatever its previous state.

Figure 16-17 shows the available options for a typical Group Policy setting.

Figure 16-17

Group Policy states

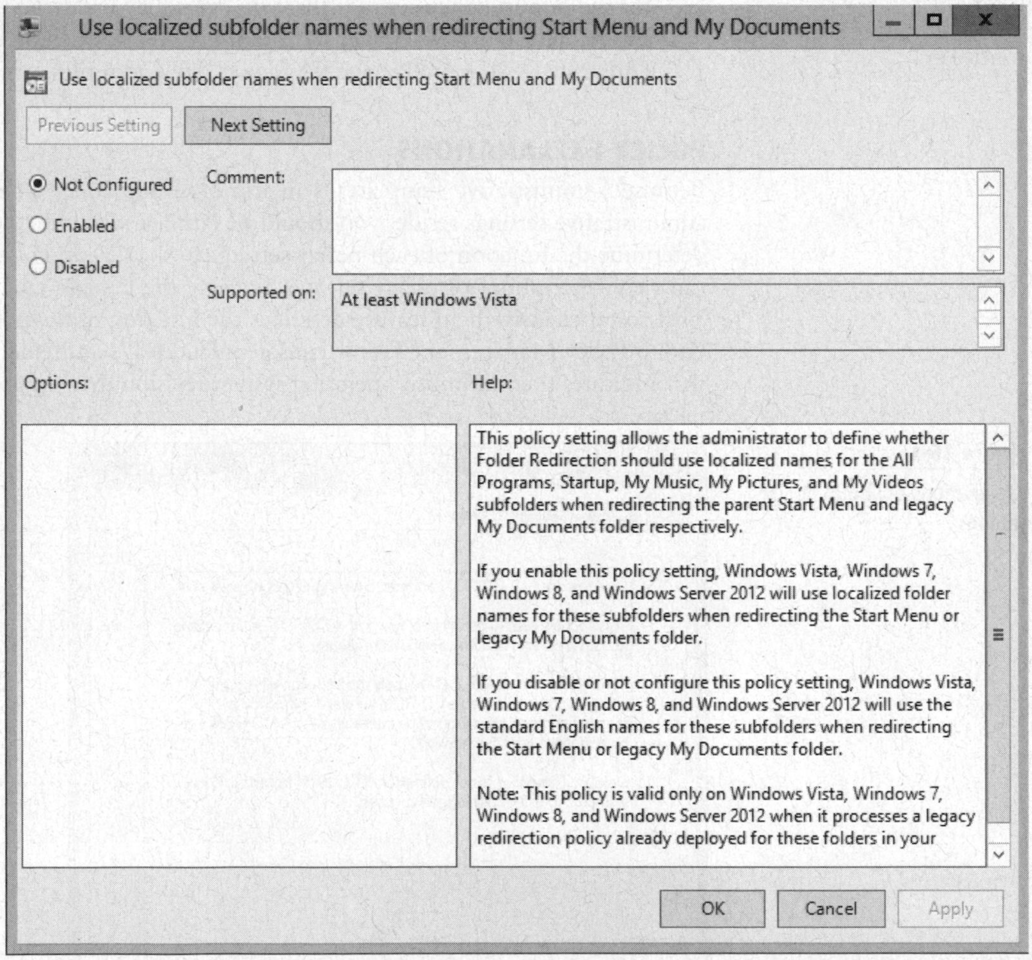

Understanding these states is critically important when working with Group Policy inheritance and multiple GPOs. If a policy setting is disabled in the registry by default, and you have a lower priority GPO that explicitly enables that setting, you must configure a higher priority GPO to disable the setting, if you want to restore it to its default. Applying the Not Configured state does not change the setting, leaving it enabled.

SEARCHING POLICIES

Since Windows Server 2008, you can search for a particular GPO setting under the Administrative Templates folder based on elements such as keywords or the minimum operating system level. This is convenient, because hundreds of settings are available under any number of nodes and subnodes within the Administrative Templates folder.

Figure 16-18 shows the Filter Options dialog box in the Group Policy Management Editor. In addition, each individual Administrative Templates setting includes a Comment tab that enables you to enter a description. You can search against the text in the comments fields by using the Filter Options window. Finally, the All Settings node beneath the Administrative Templates node enables you to browse and sort all available policies alphabetically or by state.

Figure 16-18

The Filter Options dialog box

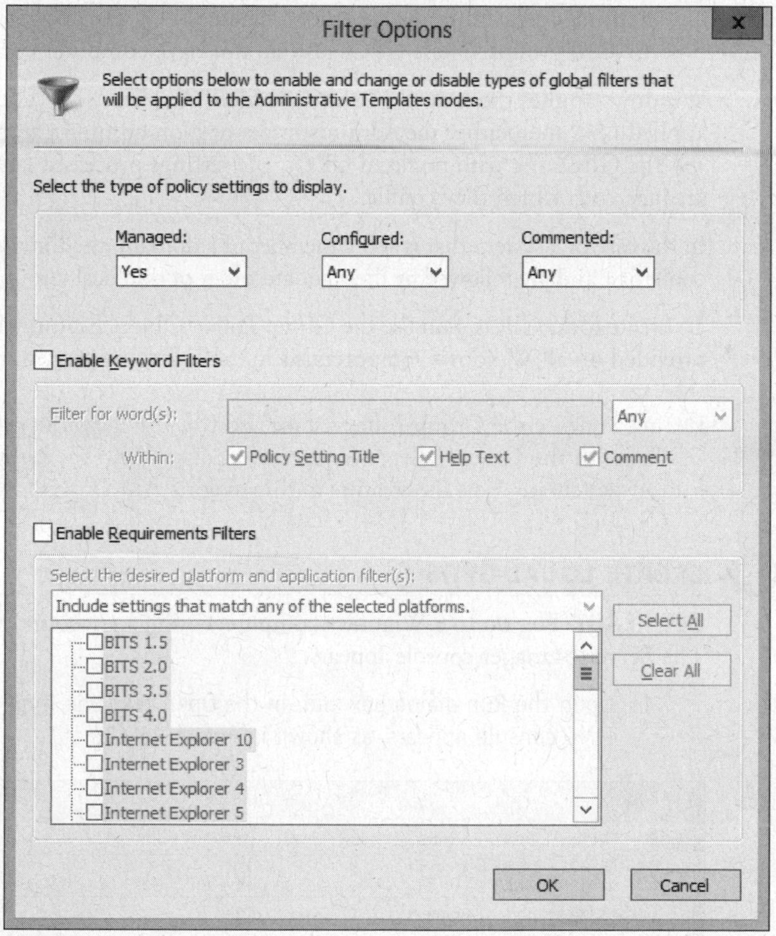

■ Creating Multiple Local GPOs

↓ THE BOTTOM LINE

Computers that are members of an AD DS domain benefit from flexibility when it comes to Group Policy configuration. Standalone (non-AD DS) systems can achieve some of the flexibility, as long as they are running at least Windows Vista or Windows Server 2008 R2. These operating systems enable you to create multiple local GPOs that provide different settings for users, based on their identities.

CERTIFICATION READY
Configure multiple local group policies.
Objective 6.1

Windows systems supporting multiple local GPOs have the following three layers of Group Policy support:

- **Local Group Policy:** Identical to the single local GPO supported by older operating system versions, the Local Group Policy layer consists of both Computer and User settings and applies to all system users, administrative or not. Because this is the only local GPO that includes computer settings, you must use this GPO to apply Computer Configuration policies.
- **Administrators and Non-administrators Group Policy:** This layer consists of two GPOs, one of which applies to members of the local Administrators group and one that applies to all users that are not members of the local Administrators group. This enables you to easily create user settings that distinguish between administrative and non-administrative users. Unlike the Local Group Policy GPO, this layer does not include computer settings.
- **User-specific Group Policy:** This layer consists of GPOs that apply to specific local user accounts created on the computer. These GPOs can apply to individual users only, not to local groups. These GPOs also do not have computer configuration settings.

Windows applies the local GPOs in the order listed here. The Local Group Policy settings are applied first, then either the Administrators or Non-administrators GPO, and finally any user specific GPOs. As with nonlocal GPOs, the settings processed later can overwrite any earlier settings with which they conflict.

In the case of a system that is also a member of a domain, the three layers of local GPO processing come first and are followed by the standard order of nonlocal Group Policy application.

To create local GPOs, you use the Group Policy Object Editor, which is an MMC snap-in provided on all Windows computers, as in the following procedure.

TAKE NOTE* Do not confuse the Group Policy Object Editor, which you use to create and manage local GPOs, with the Group Policy Management console and the Group Policy Management Editor, which are tools for creating and managing AD DS GPOs.

CREATE LOCAL GPOS

GET READY. Log on to a Windows computer, using an account with Administrator privileges. The Server Manager console appears.

1. Open the Run dialog box and, in the Open text box, type mmc and click OK. An empty MMC console appears, as shown in Figure 16-19.

Figure 16-19
An empty MMC console

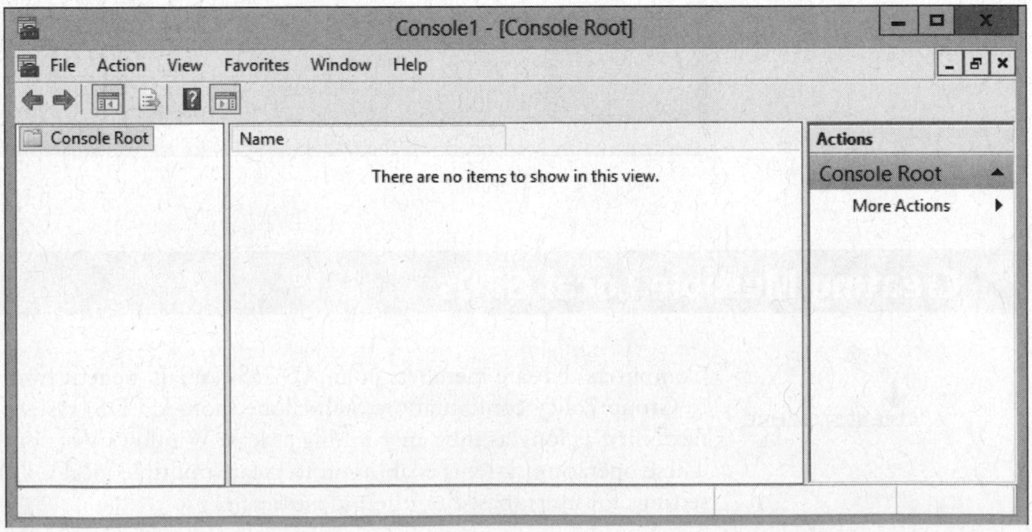

2. Click File > Add/Remove Snap-in. The *Add or Remove Snap-ins* dialog box appears, as shown in Figure 16-20.

Figure 16-20

The *Add or Remove Snap-ins* dialog box.

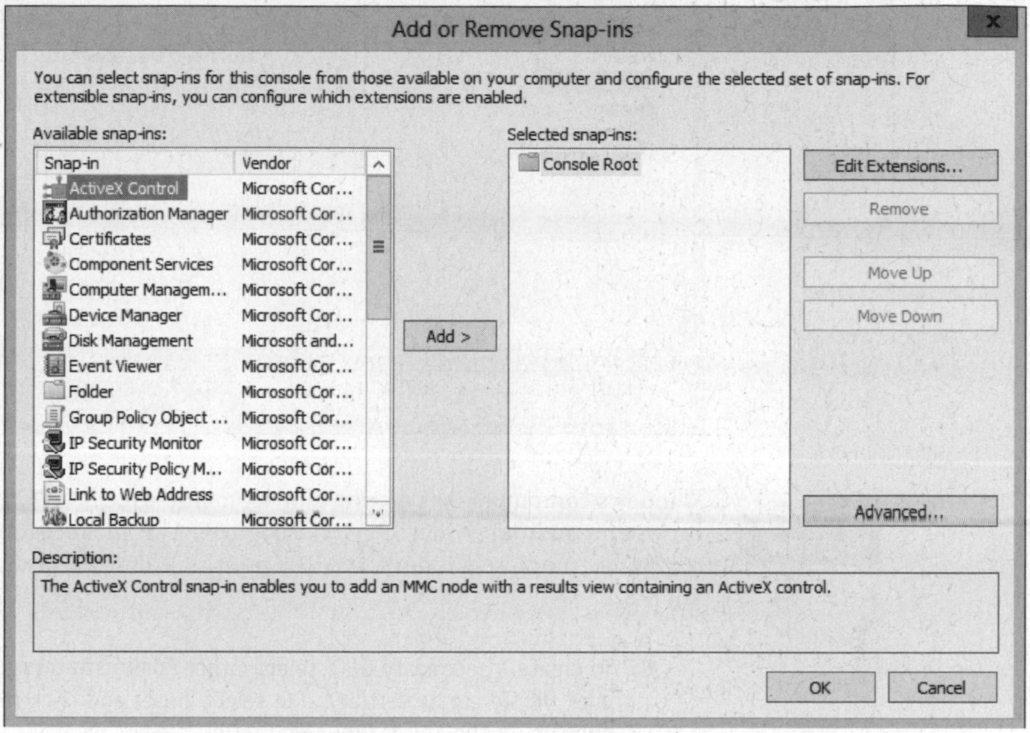

3. Select Group Policy Object Editor from the *Available snap-ins* list and click Add. The *Select Group Policy Object* page appears, as shown in Figure 16-21.

Figure 16-21

The Select Group Policy Object page

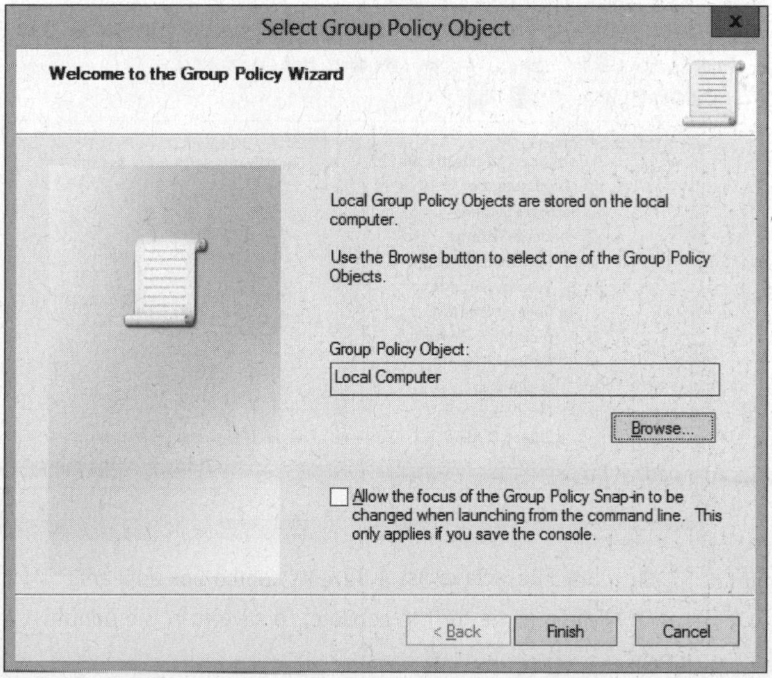

4. To create the Local Group Policy GPO, click Finish. To create a secondary or tertiary GPO, click Browse. The *Browse for a Group Policy Object* dialog box appears.

5. Click the Users tab, as shown in Figure 16-22.

Figure 16-22

The Users tab of the *Browse for a Group Policy Object* dialog box

Browse for a Group Policy Object

Computers | Users

Local Users and Groups compatible with Local Group Policy:

Name	Group Policy Object Exists
Administrator	No
ocox	No
Administrators	No
Non-Administrators	No

OK   Cancel

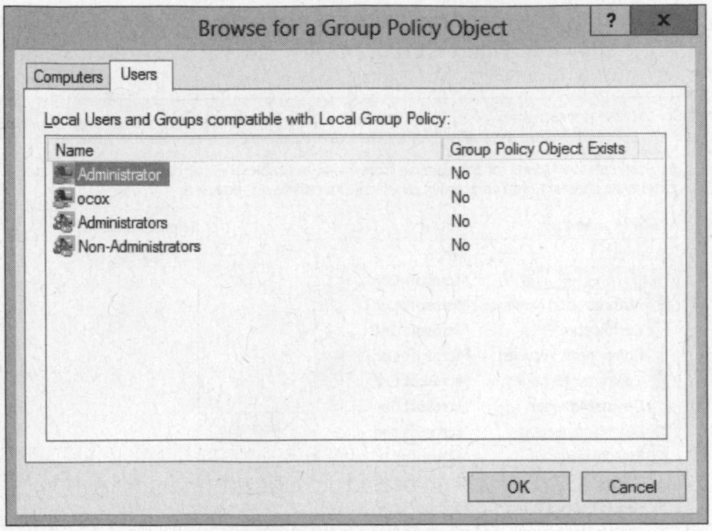

TAKE NOTE* Windows computers that do not support multiple local GPOs lack the Users tab on the Browse for a Group Policy Object dialog box. This includes domain controllers and computers running Windows versions prior to Windows Vista and Windows Server 2008 R2.

6. To create a secondary GPO, select either Administrators or Non-Administrators and click OK. To create tertiary GPO, select a user and click OK. The Group Policy object appears on the *Select Group Policy Object* page.

7. Click Finish. The snap-in appears in the *Add or Remove Snap-ins* dialog box.

8. Click OK. The snap-in appears in the MMC console, as shown in Figure 16-23.

Figure 16-23

A Group Policy Object Editor console

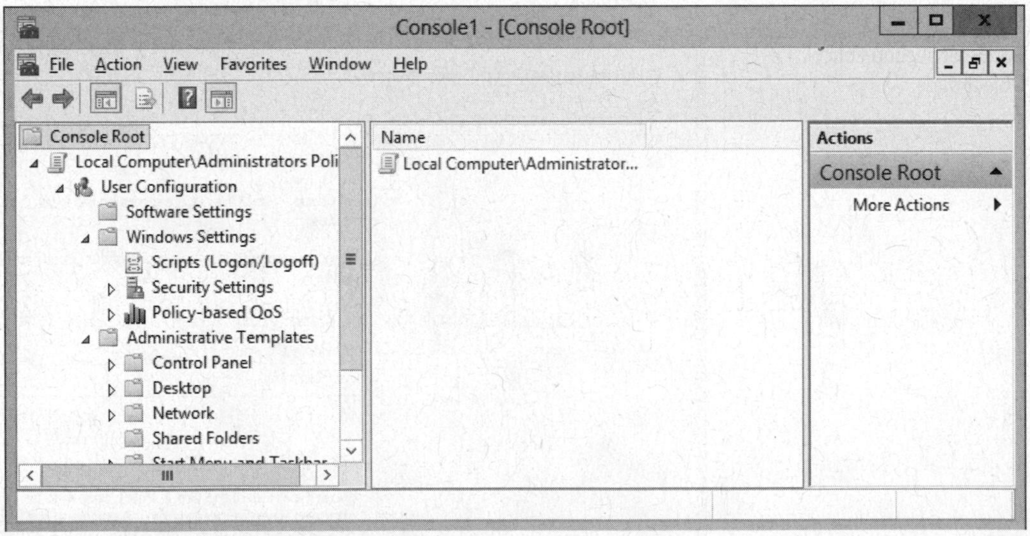

Console1 - [Console Root]

File   Action   View   Favorites   Window   Help

Console Root
  ▲ Local Computer\Administrators Poli
    ▲ User Configuration
      Software Settings
      ▲ Windows Settings
        Scripts (Logon/Logoff)
        ▷ Security Settings
        ▷ Policy-based QoS
      ▲ Administrative Templates
        ▷ Control Panel
        ▷ Desktop
        ▷ Network
        Shared Folders
        Start Menu and Taskbar

Name
  Local Computer\Administrator...

Actions
  Console Root
    More Actions

9. Click File > Save As. A *Save As* combo box appears.

10. Type a name for the console, to save it in the Administrative Tools program group.

CLOSE the MMC console.

You can now open this console to configure the settings in the GPO you created. A Local Group Policy GPO has both Computer Configuration and User Configuration settings, whereas the secondary and tertiary GPOs have only User Configuration settings.

SKILL SUMMARY

IN THIS LESSON, YOU LEARNED:

- Group Policy consists of user and computer settings that can be implemented during computer startup and user logon. These settings customize the user environment, implement security guidelines, and assist in simplifying user and desktop administration. Group Policies benefit users and administrators, because they increase a company's return on investment and decrease the overall total cost of ownership for the network.

- In Active Directory Domain Services, Group Policies can be assigned to sites, domains, and OUs. By default, there is one local policy per computer. Local policy settings are overwritten by Active Directory policy settings.

- Group Policy content is stored in an Active Directory GPC and in a GPT. Whereas the GPC can be seen by using the Advanced Features view in Active Directory Users and Computers, the GPT is a GUID-named folder located in the systemroot\sysvol\SYSVOL*domain_name*\Policies folder.

- The Default Domain Policy and the Default Domain Controller Policy are created by default when AD DS is installed.

- The Group Policy Management console is the tool used to create and modify Group Policy objects and their settings.

- GPO nodes contain three subnodes, including Software Settings, Windows Settings, and Administrative Templates. Administrative templates are XML files with the .admx file extension.

- You can remember the order of Group Policy processing by using the acronym LSDOU: local policies are processed first, followed by site, domain, and, finally, OU policies. This order is an important part of understanding how to implement Group Policies for an object.

- Group Policies applied to parent containers are inherited by all child containers and objects. You can alter inheritance by using the Enforce, Block Policy Inheritance, or Loopback settings.

■ Knowledge Assessment

Multiple Choice

Select one or more correct answers for each of the following questions.

1. Which of the following types of files do Group Policy tools access from a Central Store by default?
   a. ADM files
   b. ADMX files
   c. Group Policy objects
   d. Security templates

2. Which of the following local GPOs takes precedence on a system with multiple local GPOs?
   a. Local Group Policy
   b. Administrators Group Policy
   c. Nonadministrators Group Policy
   d. User-specific Group Policy

3. Which of the following techniques can you use to apply GPO settings to a specific group of users in an OU?
   a. GPO linking
   b. Administrative templates
   c. Security filtering
   d. Starter GPOs

4. Which of the following best describes the function of a starter GPO?
   a. A starter GPO functions as a template for the creation of new GPOs.
   b. A starter GPO is the first GPO applied by all Active Directory clients.
   c. Starter GPOs use a simplified interface for elementary users.
   d. Starter GPOs contain all of the settings found in the default Domain Policy GPO.

5. When you apply a GPO with a value of Not Configured for a particular setting to a system on which that same setting is disabled, what is the result?
   a. The setting remains disabled.
   b. The setting is changed to not configured.
   c. The settings is changed to enabled.
   d. The setting generates a conflict error.

6. Local GPOs are stored _____, whereas Domain GPOs are stored _____.
   a. in Active Directory; in Active Directory
   b. in Active Directory; on the local computer
   c. on the local computer; in Active Directory
   d. on the local computer; on the local computer

7. By default, linking a GPO to a container causes all the users and computers in that container to receive the GPO settings. How can you modify the default permission assignments so that only certain users and computers receive the permissions and, consequently, the settings in the GPO?
   a. You cannot separate or divide permission assignments within the linked container.
   b. You can create and link a different GPO to the applicable objects, overriding the previous GPO.
   c. You remove the applicable objects and place in a new container.
   d. You apply security filtering in the Group Policy Management console.

8. When multiple GPOs are linked to a container, which GPO in the list has the highest priority?
   a. The last
   b. The first
   c. The most permissive
   d. The most restrictive

9. Group Policy settings are divided into two subcategories: User Configuration and Computer Configuration. Each of these two settings is further organized into three subnodes. What are the three subnodes?
   a. Software Settings, Windows Settings, and Delegation Templates
   b. Software Settings, Windows Settings, and Administrative Templates
   c. Security Settings, Windows Settings, and Delegation Templates
   d. Security Settings, Windows Settings, and Administrative Templates

10. What is the order in which Windows systems receive and process multiple GPOs?
    a. LSOUD (local, site, OU, and then domain)
    b. LOUDS (local, OU, domain, and then site)
    c. SLOUD (site, local, OU, and then domain)
    d. LSDOU (local, site, domain, and then OU)

Best Answer

Choose the letter that corresponds to the best answer. More than one answer choice may achieve the goal. Select the BEST answer.

1. What are the different types of Group Policy objects (GPOs)?
   a. Computer, user, and organizational unit
   b. Local, domain, and starter
   c. Local, domain, and universal
   d. Site, domain, and organizational unit

2. Installing Windows Server 2012 Active Directory Domain Services (AD DS) installs two default policies: Default Domain Policy and Default Domain Controller Policy. As an administrator, you need different policy settings than the default. What is the best approach to make those changes?
   a. Add new settings in the default policies as needed.
   b. Create new GPOs to augment or override the existing default settings.
   c. Change existing ones in the default policies as needed.
   d. Link a new GPO using the AD DS role.

3. If creating a local GPO, then a secondary GPO, then a tertiary GPO, what policy settings are included in each GPO?
   a. The first GPO contains both Computer Configuration and User Configuration settings, whereas the secondary and tertiary GPOs contain only Computer Configuration settings.
   b. Each GPO contains both Computer Configuration and User Configuration settings.
   c. All GPOs contain User Configuration settings.
   d. The first GPO contains both Computer Configuration and User Configuration settings, whereas the secondary and tertiary GPOs contain only User Configuration settings.

4. Group Policies applied to parent containers are inherited by all child containers and objects. What are the ways you can alter inheritance?
   a. Using the Enforce, Block Policy Inheritance, or Loopback settings.
   b. Using Active Directory Administrative Center (ADAC) to block inheritance.
   c. Inheritance can be altered by making the applicable registry settings.
   d. Using the Enforce or Block Policy Inheritance settings.

5. You are an administrator in a mixed environment of Windows Server 2012, Server 2008 R2 and desktops running Vista. You need different settings for users, based on their identities. Can you achieve this through multiple local GPOs?
   a. All these operating systems support for multiple local GPOs. However, some servers are standalone (non-AD DS) systems.
   b. Yes, this is achievable through support by all OSs, regardless of whether standalone or whether members of an AD DS domain.
   c. No, this is not achievable given the current environment.
   d. No, this is not achievable until software is added.

Build a List

1. Order the steps to create and link a GPO to an OU.
   a. Right-click the Group Policy Objects folder and, from the context menu, select New. The New GPO dialog box appears.
   b. Expand the forest container and browse to your domain. Expand the domain controller and select the Group Policy Objects folder.
   c. Log on to a domain controller with domain administrator privileges.

  d. Open Active Directory Administrative Center and create an OU called "Halifax" in your domain.

  e. From the Tools menu, select Group Policy Management.

  f. In the left pane, right-click the domain, site, or OU object to which you want to link the new GPO and, from the context menu, select Link an existing GPO. The Select GPO dialog box appears.

  g. In the Name text box, type a name for the new GPO. The new GPO appears in the Contents list.

  h. Select the GPO you want to link to the object and click OK. The GPO appears on the object's Linked Group Policy Objects tab.

2. Order the steps to create local GPOs.

  a. Select Group Policy Object Editor from the Available Snap-ins list, and then click Add.

  b. Log on to a Windows computer, using an account with Administrator privileges.

  c. Open MMC. Click File > Add/Remove Snap-in.

  d. Click File > Save As. A Save As combo box appears. Type a name for the console, to save it in the Administrative Tools program group.

  e. To create the Local Group Policy GPO, click Finish. The snap-in appears in the Add or Remove Snap-ins dialog box.

  f. You can now open this console to configure the settings in the GPO you created.

3. List the order of Group Policy processing, starting with the policies, which are processed first.

  a. Local

  b. Domain

  c. Organizational Unit

  d. Site

■ Business Case Scenarios

Scenario 16-1: Creating Device Restrictions

After a recent incident in which an employee left the company with a substantial amount of confidential data, the IT director has given Alice the task of implementing Group Policy settings that prevent all users except administrators and members of the Executives group from installing any USB devices. Alice creates a GPO called Device Restrictions for this purpose and links it to the company's single domain object. The GPO contains the following settings:

- Allow administrators to override Device Installation Restriction policies—Enabled
- Prevent installation of devices not described by other policy sessions—Enabled

What else must Alice do to satisfy the requirements of her assignment?

Scenario 16-2: Deploying a GPO

Ralph has a number of Group Policy settings that he must deploy to the workstations of his firm's department managers, so they can run a timesheet application for their hourly employees. He has created a GPO containing those settings, and has named it HourlyTime. After linking the GPO to his company domain object in Active Directory Domain Services, Ralph quickly receives a number of trouble tickets referred to him from the help desk. The salaried employees are complaining that the application they use to file their weekly expenses has stopped working. Ralph's testing eventually establishes that it is the settings in the HourlyTime GPO that are causing the expense voucher application to malfunction. How can Ralph deploy the HourlyTiime GPO to the department managers only, without interfering with the other application?

Configuring Security Policies

70-410 EXAM OBJECTIVE

Objective 6.2 – Configure security policies. This objective may include but is not limited to: configure User Rights Assignment; configure Security Options settings; configure Security templates; configure Audit Policy; configure Local Users and Groups; configure User Account Control (UAC).

Lesson Heading	Exam Objective
Configuring Security Policies Using Group Policy	
Defining Local Policies	Configure Audit Policy Configure User Rights Assignment Configure Security Options settings
Customizing Event Log Policies	
Understanding Restricted Groups	
Using Security Templates	Configure Security templates
Maintaining and Optimizing Group Policy	
Configuring Local Users and Groups	Configure Local Users and Groups
Using the User Accounts Control Panel	
Using the Local Users and Groups Snap-In	
Configuring User Account Control	
Performing Administrative Tasks	
Using Secure Desktop	
Configuring User Account Control Settings	Configure User Account Control (UAC)

KEY TERMS

Admin Approval Mode

auditing

credential prompt

elevation prompt

Gpupdate.exe

refresh interval

secure desktop

security template

User Account Control (UAC)

■ Configuring Security Policies Using Group Policy

↓
THE BOTTOM LINE

In Lesson 16, "Creating Group Policy Objects," you learned how to create and deploy Group Policy objects (GPOs) by linking them to Active Directory Domain Services (AD DS) objects. This lesson focuses on configuring the settings in the Group Policy objects themselves, and particularly on the ones that can help secure your network.

It is important for administrators to know the difference between user and computer settings. In addition to learning about these settings and categorizing them based on where you apply them, this lesson also looks at the default Group Policy refresh process and how to invoke a manual refresh of Group Policy objects when necessary.

One of the primary aims of Group Policy is to provide centralized management of security settings for users and computers. Most of the settings that pertain to security are found in the Windows Settings folder within the Computer Configuration node of a GPO. You can use security settings to govern how users are authenticated to the network, the resources they are permitted to use, group membership policies, and events related to user and group actions recorded in the event logs. Table 17-1 briefly describes some of the security settings that you can configure within the Computer Configuration node.

Table 17-1

Computer Configuration Node Security Settings

SETTING	DESCRIPTION
Account Policies	Includes settings for Password Policy, Account Lockout Policy, and Kerberos Policy. A domain-wide policy, such as the Default Domain Policy GPO, also includes Kerberos Policy settings. Prior to Windows Server 2008, you could configure only Password Policy and Account Lockout Policy settings at the domain level. Starting with Windows Server 2008, you can configure Fine-Grained Password Policies that enable you to specify multiple password policies in a single domain.
Local Policies	Contains three subcategories that pertain to the local computer policies: Audit Policy, User Rights Assignment, and Security Options.
Event Log Policy	These settings pertain to Event Viewer logs, their maximum size, retention settings, and accessibility.
Restricted Groups Policy	This setting gives you control over the Members property and the Members Of property for specific security groups.
System Services Policy	These settings can be used to define the startup mode and access permissions for all system services. You can configure each service to be disabled, to start automatically, or to start manually.
Registry and File System Policies	These settings configure access permissions and audit settings for specific registry keys or file system objects.
Wired Network (IEEE 802.3) Policies	Enables you to create policies specifying authentication settings for computers on wired networks running Windows Vista or later.
Windows Firewall with Advanced Security	Enables you to create inbound and outbound firewall filters and distribute them to network computers.
Network List Manager Policies	Specifies whether unidentified networks should be designated as public or private, causing them to receive a specific group of firewall rules.
Wireless Network (IEEE 802.11) Policies	Enables the creation of policies for IEEE 802.11 wireless networks. Settings include preferred networks and authentication types, in addition to other security-related options.

(continued)

Table 17-1

(continued)

SETTING	DESCRIPTION
Public Key Policies	This node includes options to create an Encrypted File System (EFS), automatic certificate request, trusted root certificates, and an enterprise trust list.
Software Restriction Policies	This policy can specify software that you want to run on computers, and that you want to prevent from running, because it might pose a security risk to the computer or organization.
Network Access Protection	Enables you to create policies to configure Network Access Protection clients.
Application Control Policies	Configures access control policies for applications using AppLocker.
IP Security Policies on Active Directory	Includes policy settings that enable you to define mandatory rules applicable to computers on an IP-based network.
Advanced Audit Policy Configuration	Provides more granular audit policy settings than the Audit Policy node found under Local Policies.

Table 17-2

Security Settings Applied in the User Configuration Node

Policy settings in the Computer Configuration node apply to a computer; it does not matter who logs on to it. You can apply more Computer Configuration security settings than settings to a specific user. Table 17-2 describes the security settings that you can apply within the User Configuration node of a Group Policy object.

SETTING	DESCRIPTION
Public Key Policies	Includes the Enterprise Trust policy that enables you to list the trusted sources for certificates. Also, auto-enrollment settings can be specified for the user within this node.
Software Restriction Policies	This policy can be used to specify software that you want to run for the user. Specifically, it can be used to disallow applications that might pose a security risk if run.

Defining Local Policies

Local Policies enable you to set user privileges on the local computer that govern what users can do on the computer and determine whether the system should track them in an event log. Tracking events that take place on the local computer, a process referred to as *auditing*, is another important part of monitoring and managing activities on a computer running Windows Server 2012.

The Local Policies node of a GPO has three subordinate nodes: User Rights Assignment, Security Options, and Audit Policy. As discussed in the following sections, keep in mind that Local Policies are local to a computer. When they are part of a GPO in Active Directory, they affect the local security settings of computer accounts to which the GPO is applied.

PLANNING AND CONFIGURING AN AUDIT POLICY

The Audit Policy section of a GPO enables you to log successful and failed security events, such as logon events, account access, and object access. You can use auditing to track both user activities and system activities. Planning to audit requires that you determine the computers to be audited and the types of events you want to track.

When you consider an event to audit, such as account logon events, you must decide whether to audit successful logon attempts, failed logon attempts, or both. Tracking successful events enables you to determine how often users access network resources. This information can be valuable when planning your resource usage and budgeting for new resources. Tracking failed events can help you determine when security breaches occur or are attempted. For example, if you notice frequent failed logon attempts for a specific user account, you might want to investigate further. The policy settings available for auditing are shown in Figure 17-1.

Figure 17-1

Audit Policies in the Default Domain Policy

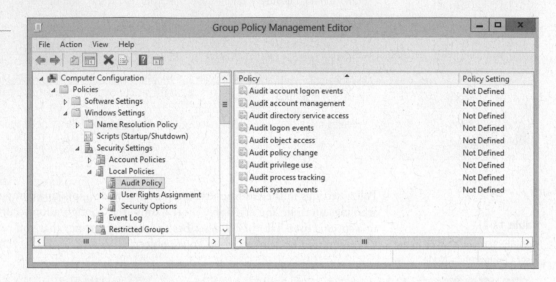

When an audited event occurs, Windows Server 2012 writes an event to the security log on the domain controller or the computer where the event took place. If it is a logon attempt or other Active Directory–related event, the event is written to the domain controller. If it is a computer event, such as a floppy drive access, the event is written to the local computer's event log.

You must decide which computers, resources, and events to audit. You should balance the need for auditing against the potential information overload that would be created if you audited every possible type of event. The following guidelines can help you plan the audit policy:

- **Audit only pertinent items**. Determine the events you want to audit and consider whether it is more important to track successes or failures of these events. You should plan only to audit events that will help you gather network information. When auditing object access, be specific about the type of access you want to track. For example, if you want to audit read access to a file or folder, make sure you audit the read events, not Full Control. Auditing Full Control triggers writes to the log for every action on the file or folder. Auditing uses system resources to process and store events. Therefore, auditing unnecessary events creates overhead on your server and makes it difficult to monitor the logs.

- **Archive security logs to provide a documented history.** Keeping a history of event occurrences can provide you with supporting documentation. You can use this documentation to support the need for additional resources based on the usage of a particular resource. In addition, it provides a history of events that might indicate past security breach attempts. If intruders have administrative privileges, they can clear the log, leaving you without a history of events that document the breach.

- **Configure the size of your security logs carefully.** You need to plan the size of your security logs based on the number of events that you anticipate logging. You can configure Event Log Policy settings under the Computer Configuration\Windows Settings\Security Settings\Event Log node of a GPO.

You can view the security logs by using the Event Viewer console and configure it to monitor any number of event categories, including the following:

- **System events:** Events that trigger a log entry in this category include system startups and shutdowns; system time changes; system event resources exhaustion, such as when an event log is filled and can no longer append entries; security log cleaning; or any event that affects system security or the security log. In the Default Domain Controllers GPO, this setting is set to log successes by default.

- **Policy change events:** By default, this policy is set to audit successes in the Default Domain Controllers GPO. Policy change audit log entries are triggered by events such as user rights assignment changes, establishment or removal of trust relationships, IPsec policy agent changes, and grants or removals of system access privileges.

- **Account management events:** This policy setting is configured to audit successes in the Default Domain Controllers GPO. This setting triggers an event that is written based on changes to account properties and group properties. Log entries written due to this policy setting reflect events related to user or group account creation, deletion, renaming, enabling, or disabling.

- **Logon events:** This setting logs events related to successful user logons on a computer. The events are logged to the Security Log on the computer that processes the request. By default, this setting logs successes in the Default Domain Controllers GPO.

- **Account logon events:** This setting logs events related to successful user logons to a domain. The events are logged to the domain controller that processes the request. By default, this setting logs successes in the Default Domain Controllers GPO.

Implementation of your plan requires awareness of several factors that can affect your audit policy's success. You must be aware of the administrative requirements to create and administer a policy plan. Two main requirements are necessary to set up and administer an Audit Policy. First, you must have the Manage Auditing and Security Log user right for the computer on which you want to configure a policy or review a log. This right is granted by default to the Administrators group. However, to delegate this task to someone else, such as a container administrator, that person must possess the specific right. Second, any files or folders to be audited must be located on NTFS volumes.

Implementation of your plan requires that you specify the categories to be audited and, if necessary, configure objects for auditing. To configure an audit policy, use the following procedure.

➔ CONFIGURE AN AUDIT POLICY

GET READY. Log on to a domain controller running Windows Server 2012, using an account with domain Administrator privileges. The Server Manager console appears.

1. From the Tools menu, select Group Policy Management. The Group Policy Management console appears.
2. Expand the forest container and browse to your domain. Then expand the domain container and select the Group Policy Objects folder. The GPOs that currently exist in the domain appear in the *Contents* tab.
3. Right-click the Default Domain Policy GPO and click Edit. A Group Policy Management Editor window for this policy appears.
4. Browse to the Computer Configuration\Policies\Windows Settings\Security Settings\Local Policies node and select Audit Policy. The audit policy settings appear in the right pane.
5. Double-click the Audit Policy setting you want to modify. The Properties sheet for the policy you chose appears, as shown in Figure 17-2.
6. Select the Define This Policy Setting check box.
7. Select the appropriate check box(es) to audit Success, Failure, or both.

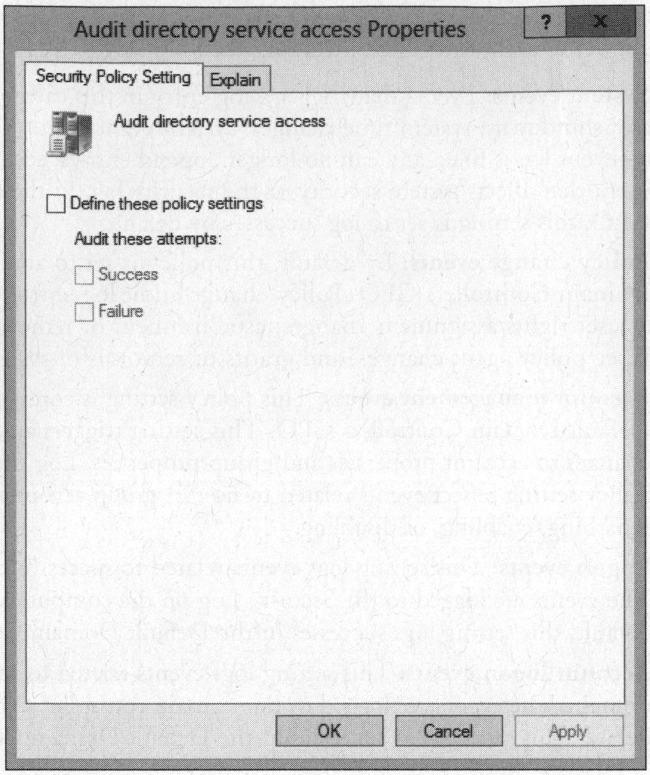

Figure 17-2

The Properties sheet for a policy setting

8. Click OK to close the setting's Properties sheet.

CLOSE the Group Policy Management Editor and the Group Policy Management console.

You now configured an audit policy in the Default Domain Policy GPO, which will be propagated to all the computers in the domain during the next policy refresh.

Configuring objects for auditing is necessary when you configure either of the two following event categories:

- **Audit Directory Service Access:** logs user access to Active Directory objects, such as other user objects or OUs.
- **Audit Object Access:** logs user access to files, folders, registry keys, and printers.

Each of these event categories requires additional setup steps, which are described in the following procedure.

CONFIGURE AN ACTIVE DIRECTORY OBJECT FOR AUDITING

GET READY. Log on to a domain controller running Windows Server 2012, using an account with domain Administrator privileges. The Server Manager console appears.

1. From the Tools menu, select Active Directory Users and Computers. The *Active Directory Users and Computers* console appears.
2. From the View menu, select Advanced Features.
3. Browse to the object that you want to audit. Right-click the object and, from the context menu, select Properties. The object's Properties sheet appears.
4. Click the Security tab, and then click Advanced. The *Advanced Security Settings* dialog box for the object appears.
5. Select the Auditing tab, as shown in Figure 17-3.
6. Click Add. The *Auditing Entry* page for the object appears.

Figure 17-3

The Auditing tab of an object's Advanced Security Settings dialog box

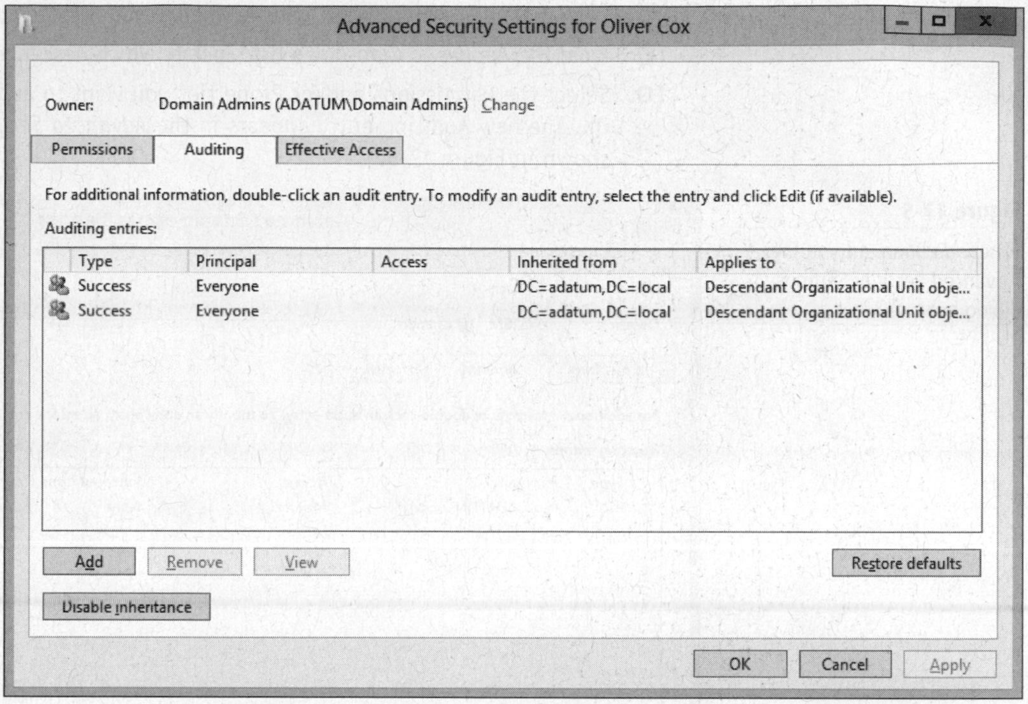

Figure 17-4

The Auditing Entry dialog box for an object

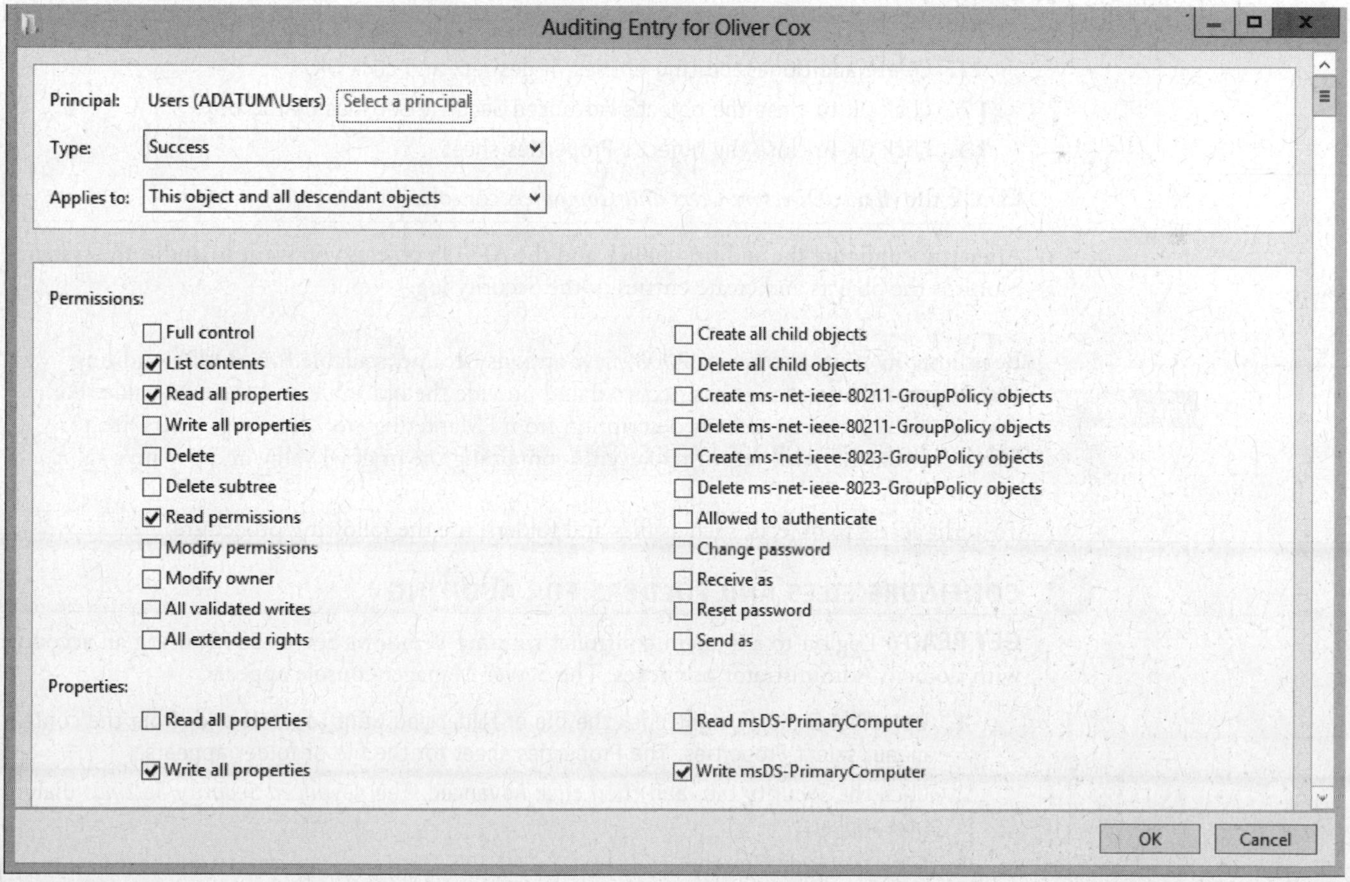

7. Click Select a Principal. The *Select User, Computer, Service Account, or Group* dialog box appears. Select the users or groups to be audited for Active Directory object access and click OK. The users or groups appear in the *Auditing Entry* dialog box for the object, as shown in Figure 17-4.

8. From the *Type* drop-down list, specify whether you want to audit failures, successes, or both.

9. From the *Applies to* drop-down list, specify which descendent objects should be audited.

10. Select the Permissions and/or Properties you want to audit for this object and click OK. The new Auditing entry appears in the *Advanced Security Settings* dialog box, as shown in Figure 17-5.

Figure 17-5

A new auditing entry in the Advanced Security Settings dialog box

	Advanced Security Settings for Users	– □ x

Name: C:\Users

Owner: SYSTEM 🛡 Change

Permissions	Auditing	Effective Access

For additional information, double-click an audit entry. To modify an audit entry, select the entry and click Edit (if available).

Auditing entries:

	Type	Principal	Access	Inherited from	Applies to
	Fail	ocox (ADATUM\ocox)	Modify	None	This folder, subfolders and files

[Add] [Remove] [Edit]

[Disable inheritance]

☐ Replace all child object auditing entries with inheritable auditing entries from this object

[OK] [Cancel] [Apply]

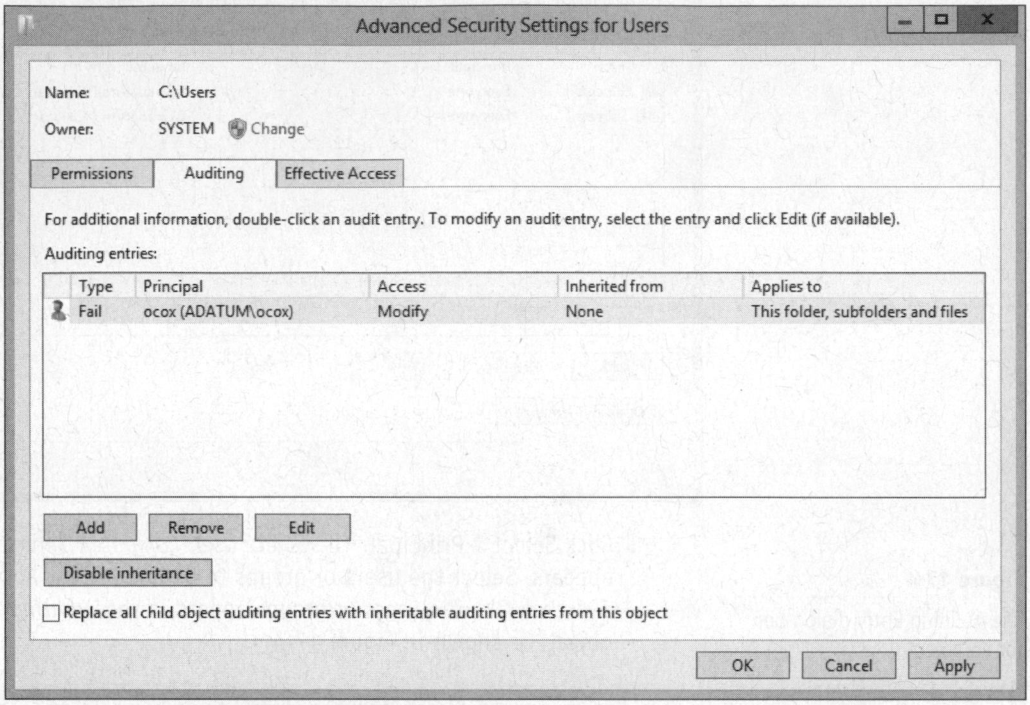

11. Create additional auditing entries, if desired, and click OK.

12. Click OK to close the object's Advanced Security Settings dialog box.

13. Click OK to close the object's Properties sheet.

CLOSE the *Active Directory Users and Computers* console.

After you configure the auditing policy and the AD DS objects you want to audit, the systems monitor the objects and create entries in the Security log.

TAKE NOTE *

Beginning in Windows Server 2008, new options became available for AD DS auditing that indicate that a change has occurred and provide the old value and the new value. For example, if you change a user's description from "Marketing" to "Training," the Directory Services Event Log will record two events containing the original value and the new value.

To audit access to objects, such as files and folders, use the following procedure.

CONFIGURE FILES AND FOLDERS FOR AUDITING

GET READY. Log on to a domain controller running Windows Server 2012, using an account with domain Administrator privileges. The Server Manager console appears.

1. Open File Explorer, right-click the file or folder you want to audit and, from the context menu, select Properties. The Properties sheet for the file or folder appears.

2. Click the Security tab, and then click Advanced. The *Advanced Security Settings* dialog box appears.

3. Click the Auditing tab.

4. Click Add. The *Auditing Entry* page appears.
5. Click Select a Principal. The *Select User, Computer, Service Account, or Group* dialog box appears. Select the users or groups to be audited for Active Directory object access and click OK. The users or groups appear in the *Auditing Entry* dialog box for the object.
6. From the *Type* drop-down list, specify whether you want to audit failures, successes, or both.
7. From the *Applies to* drop-down list, specify which descendent objects should be audited.
8. Select the basic permissions you want to audit for this object and click OK. The new Auditing entry appears in the *Advanced Security Settings* dialog box.
9. Create additional auditing entries, if desired, and click OK.
10. Click OK to close the object's *Advanced Security Settings* dialog box.
11. Click OK to close the object's Properties sheet.

CLOSE the File Explorer window.

You now configured auditing for files and folders within the Windows operating system.

ASSIGNING USER RIGHTS

The User Rights Assignment settings in Windows Server 2012 are extensive and include settings that pertain to rights users need to perform system-related tasks, as shown in Figure 17-6.

Figure 17-6

User rights assignment settings in a Group Policy object

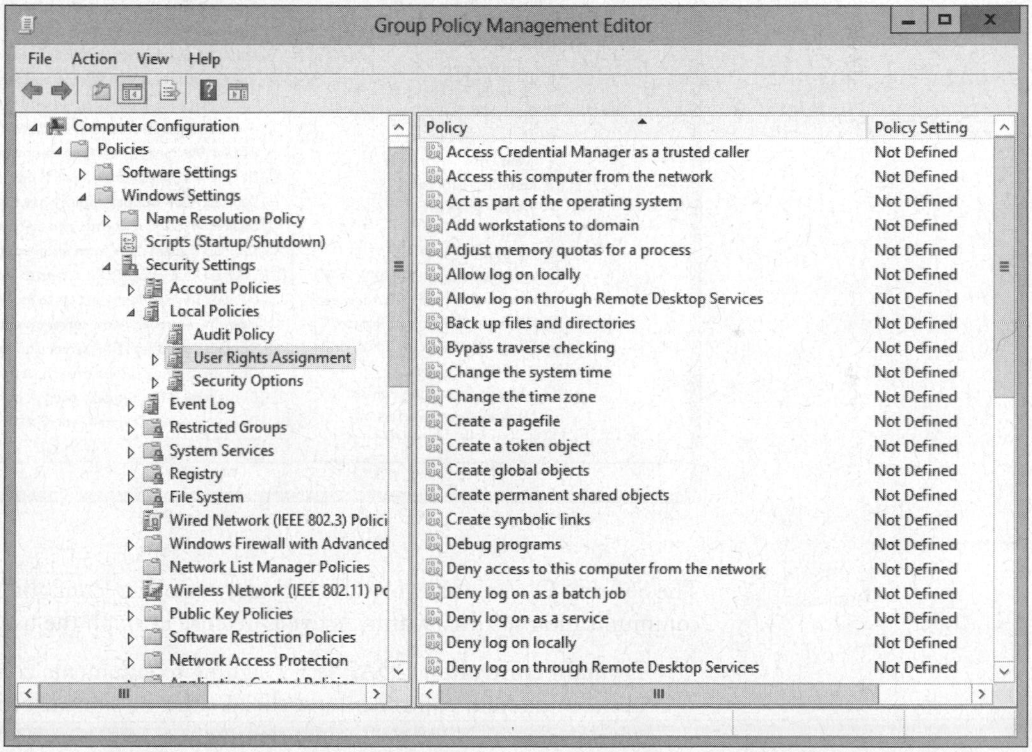

CERTIFICATION READY
Configure User Rights Assignment.
Objective 6.2

For example, a user logging on locally to a domain controller must have the Allow Log On Locally right assigned to his or her account or be a member of one of the following AD DS groups:

- Account Operators
- Administrators
- Backup Operators
- Print Operators
- Server Operators

These group memberships enable users to log on locally because Windows Server 2012 assigns the Allow Log On Locally user right to those groups in the Default Domain Controllers Policy GPO by default.

Other similar settings included in this collection are related to user rights associated with system shutdown, taking ownership privileges of files or objects, restoring files and directories, and synchronizing directory service data.

CERTIFICATION READY
Configure Security
Options settings.
Objective 6.2

CONFIGURING SECURITY OPTIONS

The Security Options node in a GPO, shown in Figure 17-7, includes security settings related to interactive log on, digital signing of data, restrictions for access to floppy and CD-ROM drives, unsigned driver installation behavior, and logon dialog box behavior.

Figure 17-7

The Security Options node in a GPO

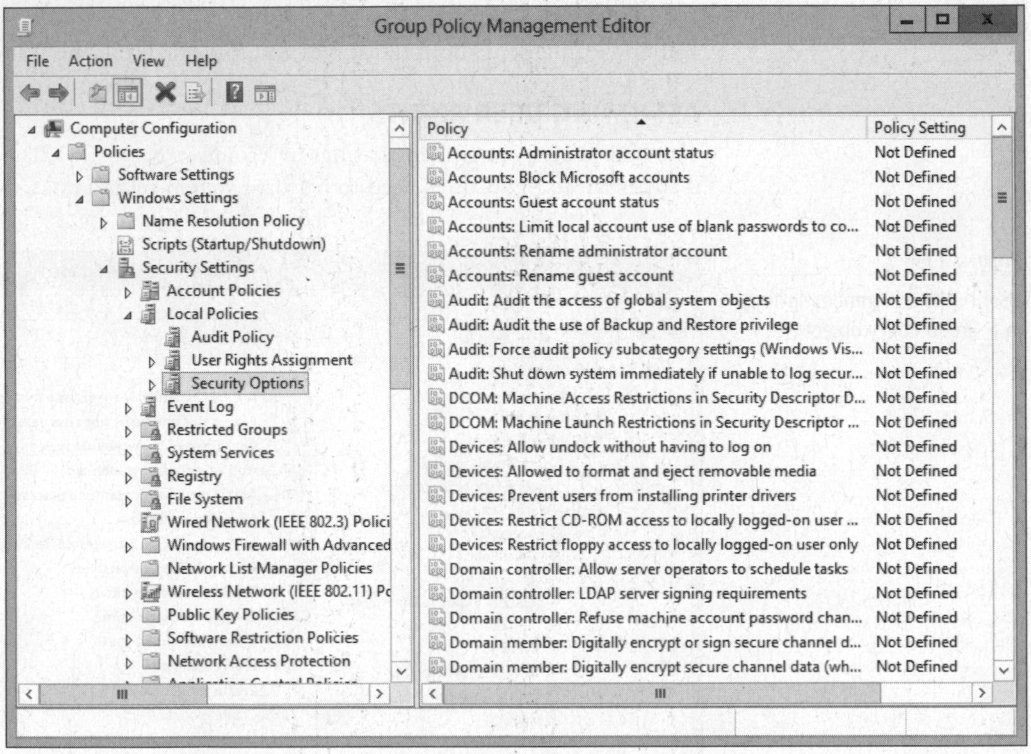

The Security Options category also includes options to configure authentication and communication security within Active Directory through the use of the following settings:

- **Domain controller:** LDAP server signing requirements controls whether LDAP traffic between domain controllers and clients must be signed. This setting can be configured with a value of None or Require signing.

- **Domain member:** Digitally sign or encrypt or sign secure channel data (always) controls whether traffic between domain members and the domain controllers are signed and encrypted at all times.

- **Domain member:** Digitally encrypt secure channel data (when client agrees) indicates that traffic between domain members and the domain controllers is encrypted only if the client workstations are able to do so.

- **Domain member:** Digitally sign secure channel data (when client agrees) indicates that traffic between domain members and the domain controllers is signed only if the client services are able to do so.

- **Microsoft network client:** Digitally sign communications (always) indicates that Server Message Block (SMB) signing is enabled by the SMB signing component of the SMB client at all times.
- **Microsoft network client:** Digitally sign communications (if server agrees) indicates that SMB signing is enabled by the SMB signing component of the SMB client only if the corresponding server service is able to do so.
- **Microsoft network server:** Digitally sign communications (always) indicates that SMB signing is enabled by the SMB signing component of the SMB server at all times.
- **Microsoft network server:** Digitally sign communications (if server agrees) indicates that SMB signing is enabled by the SMB signing component of the SMB server only if the corresponding client service is able to do so.

From this section, you can also enforce the level of NT LAN Manager (NTLM) authentication that is allowed on your network. Although Kerberos is the default authentication protocol in an AD DS network, NTLM authentication is used in certain situations. The original incarnation of NTLM authentication was called LAN Manager (LM) authentication, which is now considered a weak authentication protocol that can easily be decoded by network traffic analyzers. Microsoft has improved NTLM authentication over the years by introducing first NTLM and subsequently NTLMv2.

NTLM authentication levels are controlled by the *Network security: LAN Manager authentication level* security setting, as shown in Figure 17-8, which enables you to select one of the following options:

- Send LM and NTLM responses.
- Send LM and NTLM—use NTLMv2 session security if negotiated.
- Send NTLM response only.
- Send NTLMv2 response only.
- Send NTLMv2 response only. Refuse LM.
- Send NTLMv2 response only. Refuse LM and NTLM.

Figure 17-8

The *Network security: LAN Manager authentication level* security option

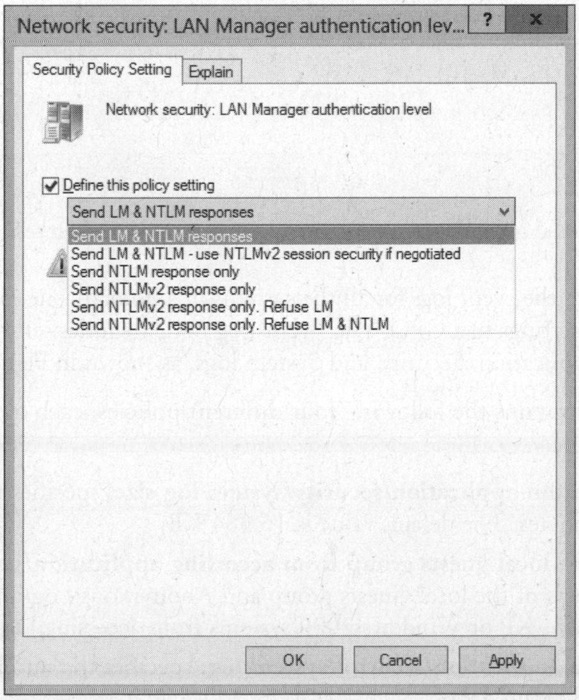

By allowing only the most stringent levels of NTLM authentication on your network, you can improve the overall communications security of Active Directory.

Customizing Event Log Policies

The Event Log node enables you to configure settings that control the maximum log size, retention, and access rights for each log.

Depending on the roles you install, the number of logs on a computer running Windows Server 2012 can vary. For example, if your server is configured as an AD DS domain controller, you will have a Directory Service log that contains Active Directory-related entries. In addition, if your server is configured as a Domain Name System (DNS) server, you will have a DNS Server log that contains entries specifically related to DNS.

To configure event log policies on an individual system, you use the Properties sheets for the logs in the Event Viewer console, as shown in Figure 17-9.

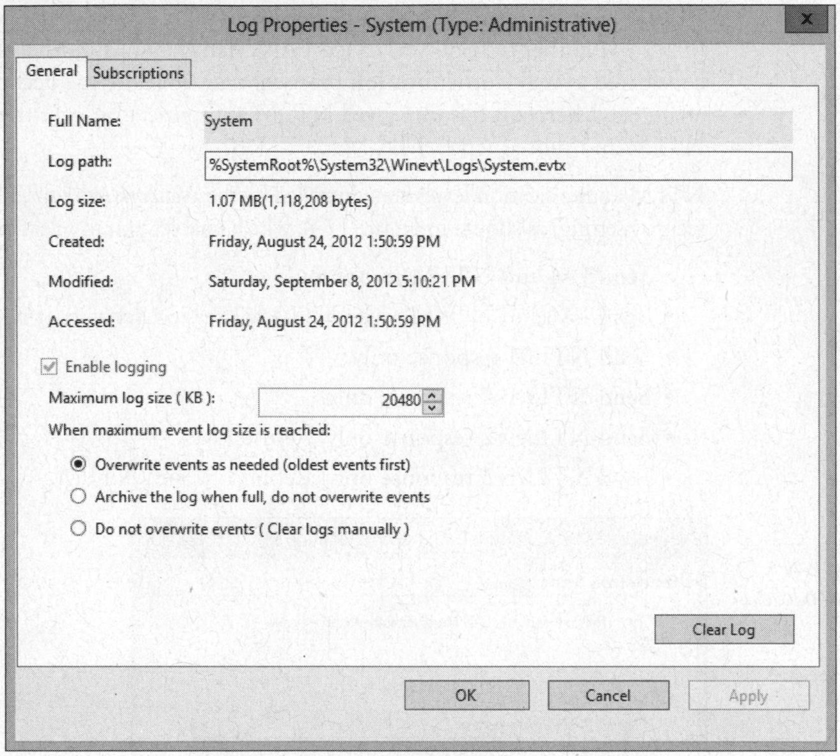

Figure 17-9

The Properties sheet for an event log in the Event Viewer console

To configure the event logs for all the systems in a domain, site, or OU, you can create Event Log policy settings in a GPO. The Event Log node includes settings for the three primary log files: the Application, Security, and System logs, as shown in Figure 17-10.

The node contains the following four different policies, each of which is repeated for the three logs.

- **Maximum application/security/system log size:** specifies the maximum size of the log, in kilobytes. The default value is 16,384 KB.
- **Prevent local guests group from accessing application/security/system log:** prevents members of the local Guests group and Anonymous Login users on computers running Windows XP or Windows 2000 systems from accessing logs.
- **Retain application/security/system log:** specifies the number of days that the log should retain data.
- **Retention method for application/security/system log:** specifies whether logs should purge data by its age, wait until the log is nearly full, or not purge data at all.

Figure 17-10

Policies in the Event Log node of a GPO

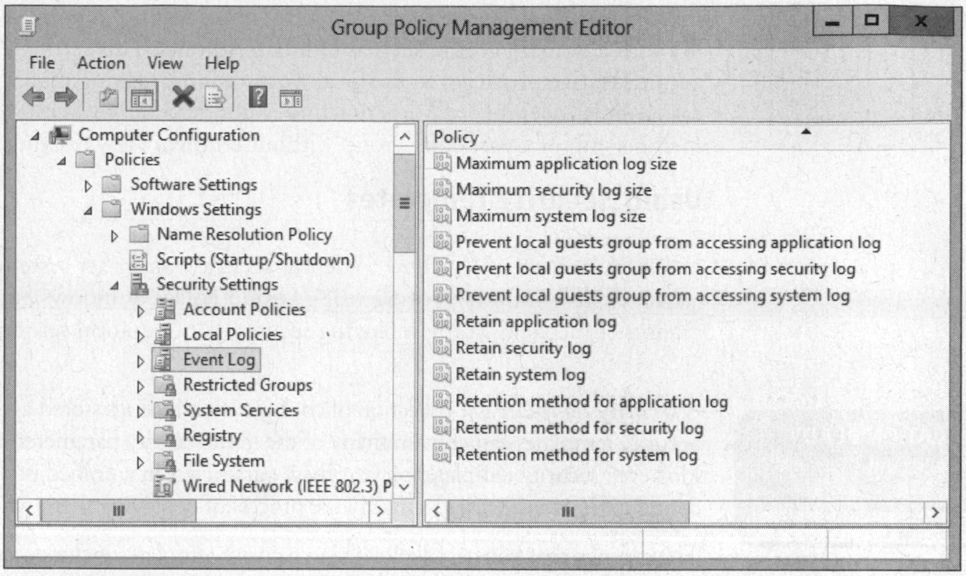

Understanding Restricted Groups

X REF

Refer to "Maintaining and Optimizing Group Policy" later in this lesson for information on the refresh process for restricted groups.

The Restricted Groups policy setting enables you to specify group membership lists. By using this policy setting, you can control membership in important groups, such as the local Administrators and Backup Operators groups.

For example, when you use the Restricted Groups policy to specify the membership of a computer's Administrators group, using the interface shown in Figure 17-11, that membership is enforced every time the computer refreshes its Group Policy settings.

Figure 17-11

Group membership in the Restricted Groups policy

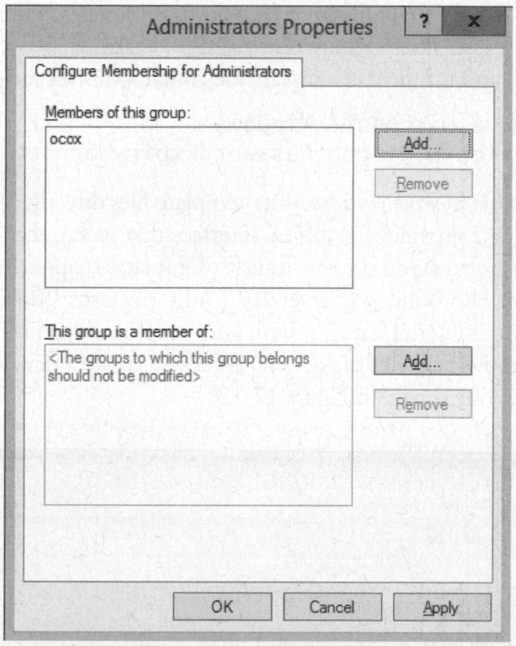

If another user is added to the Administrators group by using Active Directory Users and Computers or any other tool, whether for malicious or other reasons, the manually added user is removed when the Group Policy is reapplied during the refresh cycle. Only those users who are part of the Restricted Group membership list within the policy setting are applied.

In addition, you can use the Restricted Groups setting to populate a local group's membership list with a domain group, such as Domain Admins. This setting enables you to transfer administrative privileges to the local workstations, making management and access to resources easier. This "Member of" functionality is nondestructive, because it adds users or groups to the membership of a particular group without removing any existing group members.

Using Security Templates

You learned previously how to deploy security and other system configuration settings on a Microsoft Windows network using Group Policy. Windows Server 2012 also includes another mechanism for deploying security configuration settings called security templates.

A *security template* is a collection of configuration settings stored as a text file with an .inf extension. Security templates can contain many of the same security parameters as group policy objects. However, security templates present these parameters in a unified interface, enable you to save your configurations as files, and simplify the process of deploying them when and where they are needed.

The settings that you can deploy using security templates include many of the security policies covered in this lesson, including audit policies, user rights assignments, security options, event log policies, restricted groups, and others. By itself, a security template is a convenient way to configure the security of a single system. When you combine it with group policies or scripting, security templates enable you to maintain the security of networks consisting of hundreds or thousands of computers running various Microsoft Windows versions.

Using these tools together, you can create complex security configurations, and mix and match the configurations for each of the various roles computers serve in your organization. When deployed across a network, security templates enable you to implement consistent, scalable, and reproducible security settings throughout the enterprise.

USING THE SECURITY TEMPLATES CONSOLE

Security templates are plain text files that contain security settings in a variety of formats, depending on the nature of the individual settings. For example, many of the security policies are implemented by registry settings, and for these, a template file contains entries such as the following:

```
MACHINE\Software\Microsoft\Windows
NT\CurrentVersion\Winlogon\PasswordExpiryWarning=4,14
```

Although it is possible to work with security template files directly, by using any text editor, Windows Server 2012 provides a graphical interface that makes the job much easier. To create and manage security templates, you use the Security Templates snap-in for Microsoft Management Console. By default, the Windows Server 2012 Administrative Tools menu does not include an MMC console containing the Security Templates snap-in, so you need to create one by using the MMC Add or Remove Snap-ins dialog box. After you create a new template, the console provides an interface like the one shown in Figure 17-12.

Figure 17-12

The Security Templates snap-in

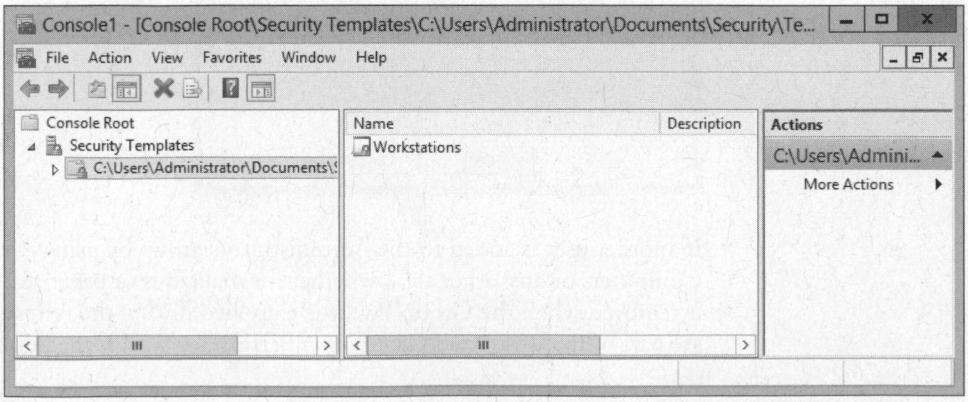

The left pane of the Security Templates snap-in points to a default folder in which the console stores the template files you create by default. The snap-in interprets any file in this folder with an .inf extension as a security template, even though the extensions do not appear in the console.

When you create a new template in the console, you see a hierarchical display of the policies in the template, as well as their current settings. Many of the policies are identical to those in a GPO, both in appearance and function. You can modify the policies in each template just as you would those in a GPO.

PLANNING A SECURITY TEMPLATE STRATEGY

When planning a security template strategy, think in terms of computer roles, rather than individual computers. It is possible to create a separate template for each computer and customize the settings for that particular computer's needs, but that defeats the purpose of creating templates in the first place, because it is just as easy to configure each computer manually. By creating templates for specific roles, you can apply them to multiple computers, using combinations in cases where computers perform multiple roles.

For example, if a domain controller also functions as a file server, you should create separate security templates for the domain controller role and the file server role, and apply both of the templates to that computer. This way, if the organization adds a dedicated domain controller or file server to the network at a later time, you can apply only one security template to the new computer.

In large organizations, different divisions are likely to have different security requirements. This is most evident in government organizations, where material classified at different levels has distinctly different security requirements. In this case, you should first determine which roles are required, and then determine the security levels required by each role. If one organization has a file server that stores only public content, and another organization has a file server that stores highly confidential files, you should create two file server security templates, one with higher security than the other.

CREATING SECURITY TEMPLATES

After the plan for a network's security templates is in place, you can proceed to create the templates. To create a new security template from scratch, use the following procedure.

CREATE A SECURITY TEMPLATE

GET READY. Log on to a Windows computer, using an account with Administrator privileges. The Server Manager console appears.

1. Open the Run dialog box and, in the Open text box, type mmc and click OK. An empty MMC console appears.
2. Click File > Add/Remove Snap-in. The *Add or Remove Snap-ins* dialog box appears.
3. Select Security Templates from the *Available snap-ins* list and click Add. The snap-in appears in the *Add or Remove Snap-ins* dialog box.
4. Click OK. The snap-in appears in the MMC console.
5. Click File > Save As. A *Save As* combo box appears.
6. Type a name for the console, to save it in the Administrative Tools program group.
7. Expand the *Security Templates* node.
8. Right-click the security template search path and, from the context menu, select New Template. A dialog box appears.
9. In the *Template name* field, type a name for the template and click OK. The new template appears in the console, as shown in Figure 17-13.

Figure 17-13

A new template in the Security Templates snap-in

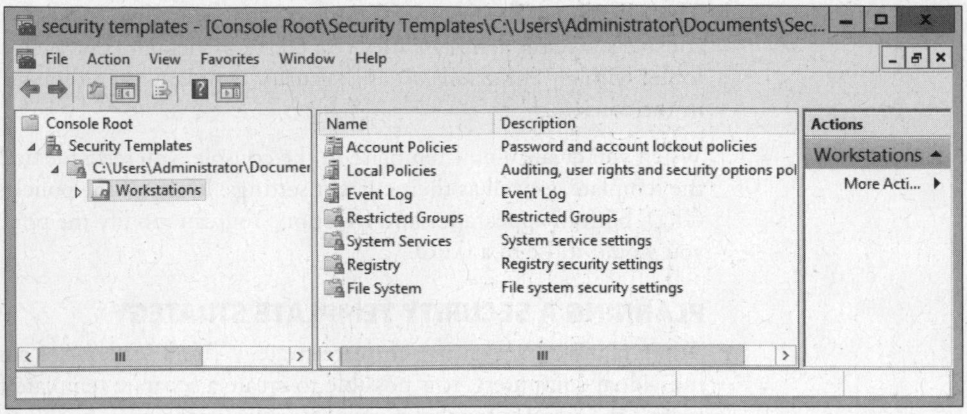

LEAVE the console open.

When you create a blank security template, there are no policies defined in it. Applying the blank template to a computer has no effect on it whatsoever.

WORKING WITH SECURITY TEMPLATE SETTINGS

Security templates contain many of the same settings as group policy objects, so you are already familiar with some of the elements of a template. For example, security templates contain the same local policy settings described previously; the template is just a different way to configure and deploy the policies. Security templates also provide a means for configuring the permissions associated with files, folders, registry entries, and services.

Security templates have more settings than Local Computer Policy, because a template includes options for both standalone computers and computers that participate in a domain.

IMPORTING SECURITY TEMPLATES INTO GPOs

The simplest way to deploy a security template on several computers simultaneously is to import the template into a group policy object. After you import the template, the template settings become part of the GPO, and the network's domain controllers deploy them to all the computers affected by that GPO. As with any group policy deployment, you can link a GPO to any domain, site, or organizational unit (OU) object in the Active Directory tree. The settings in the GPO are then inherited by all the container and leaf objects subordinate to the object you select.

To import a security template into a GPO, use the following procedure.

IMPORT A SECURITY TEMPLATE INTO A GPO

GET READY. Switch to the Security Templates console you created in the previous procedure:

1. From the Tools menu, select Group Policy Management. The Group Policy Management console appears.
2. Expand the forest container and browse to your domain. Then expand the domain container and select the Group Policy Objects folder. The GPOs that currently exist in the domain appear in the *Contents* tab.
3. Right-click the GPO into which you want to import the template and click Edit. A Group Policy Management Editor window for this policy appears.
4. Browse to the Computer Configuration\Policies\Windows Settings\Security Settings node. Right-click the *Security Settings* node and, from the context menu, select Import Policy. The *Import Policy From* dialog box appears, as shown in Figure 17-14.

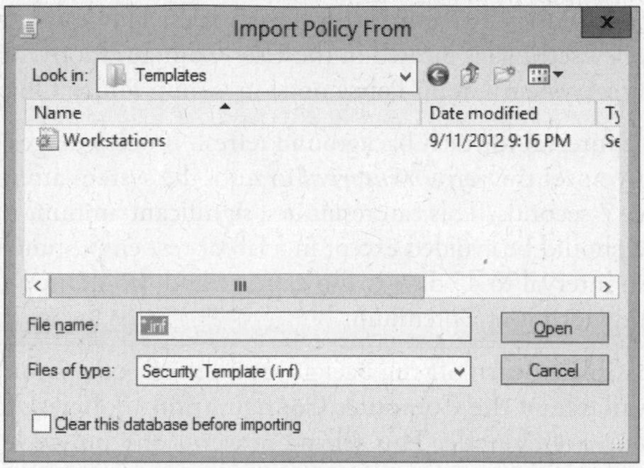

Figure 17-14

The *Import Policy From* dialog box

5. Browse to the security template you want to import and click Open. The policy settings in the template are copied to the GPO.

CLOSE the Group Policy Management Editor and Group Policy Management consoles.

Maintaining and Optimizing Group Policy

Windows applies Computer Configuration policies by default when a computer starts up, and User Configuration policies during the user logon process. Systems also refresh both of these policies at regular intervals, so that any changes you make to Group Policy objects disseminate throughout the network. When Windows performs a Group Policy refresh, it reprocesses all the settings in every GPO that applies to the computer or user.

For example, any settings that were previously enabled and are now set to disabled are overwritten by the new setting. Settings that were previously enabled and are now set to Not Configured are ignored, leaving the registry setting unchanged. Each policy type has a default refresh cycle that runs in the background to ensure that every system receives the most recent policy changes, even if the system is not restarted or the user does not log off and back on.

> **TAKE NOTE***
>
> Although Windows reapplies most Group Policy settings during a refresh, there are some policy settings that process only during an initial startup or during the first user logon. For example, a policy that installs an application might interfere with another application currently running on the computer, which could cause the installation to fail. Therefore, software installation policies are processed only during computer startup. In the same way, Folder Redirection policies are processed only during user logon.

The default refresh periods for the various types of Group Policy settings are as follows:

- **Set Group Policy Refresh Interval for Computers:** The setting for the refresh interval for computers is located in the Computer Configuration\Policies\Administrative Templates\System\Group Policy node in the Group Policy Object Editor window for a GPO. By default, computer policies are updated in the background every 90 minutes, with a random offset of 0 to 30 minutes.
- **Set Group Policy Refresh Interval for Domain Controllers:** The setting for the refresh interval for domain controllers is located in the Computer Configuration\Policies\Administrative Templates\System\Group Policy node in the Group Policy Object Editor. By default, domain controller group policies are updated in the background every 2 minutes.

- **Set Group Policy Refresh Interval for Users:** The setting for the refresh interval for user policy settings is located in the User Configuration\Policies\Administrative Templates\System\Group Policy node in Group Policy Object Editor for a GPO.

The available interval for each background refresh process ranges from 0 to 64,800 minutes (45 days). If you set the *refresh interval* to zero, the system attempts to update the policy settings every 7 seconds. This can result in a significant amount of traffic on a production network and should be avoided except in a lab or test environment. However, setting the policy refresh interval to 45 days is also extreme and should not be implemented unless network bandwidth is at a premium.

It is also possible to turn off the background refresh of a Group Policy entirely. This setting is available in the Computer Configuration \Policies\Administrative Templates\ System\Group Policy node. This setting prevents any policy refreshes, except when a computer is restarted.

MANUALLY REFRESHING GROUP POLICY

When you modify Group Policy settings that you want to be immediately invoked without requiring a restart, a new logon session, or waiting for the next refresh period, you can force a manual refresh by using the *Gpupdate.exe* tool.

An example of the syntax necessary for *gpupdate.exe* to refresh all the user settings affected by the User Configuration node of the Default Domain GPO is as follows:

```
Gpupdate /target:user
```

To refresh the Computer Configuration node policy settings, the syntax is as follows:

```
Gpupdate /target:computer
```

Without the /target switch, the program refreshes both the user and computer configuration policy settings.

OPTIMIZING GROUP POLICY PROCESSING

When you create a GPO that contains computer or user settings, but not both, you can disable the setting area that is not configured for faster processing. For example, to configure a computer policy that applies to all computers within an OU, you should disable the User Configuration node settings so that the policy processing is faster. When one part of the policy is disabled, systems ignore that section and disregard the settings in it.

To partially disable a GPO, use the following procedure.

➔ OPTIMIZE GROUP POLICY PROCESSING

GET READY. Log on to a domain controller running Windows Server 2012, using an account with domain Administrator privileges. The Server Manager console appears.

1. From the Tools menu, select Group Policy Management. The Group Policy Management console appears.
2. Expand the forest container and browse to your domain. Then expand the domain container and select the *Group Policy Objects* folder. The GPOs that currently exist in the domain appear in the *Contents* tab.
3. Right-click the Default Domain Policy GPO, click GPO Status, and select User Configuration Settings Disabled, Computer Configuration Settings Disabled, or All Settings Disabled.

CLOSE the Group Policy Management console.

You now modified a GPO to optimize its performance at computer startup and shutdown or user logon and logoff.

■ Configuring Local Users and Groups

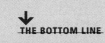

THE BOTTOM LINE

Windows Server 2012 provides two separate interfaces for creating and managing local user accounts: the User Accounts control panel and the Local Users and Groups snap-in for MMC. Both of these interfaces provide access to the same Security Account Manager (SAM) where the user and group information is stored, so any changes you make using one interface will appear in the other.

CERTIFICATION READY
Configure Local Users and Groups.
Objective 6.2

Microsoft designed the User Accounts control panel and the Local Users and Groups snap-in for computer users with different levels of expertise, and they provide different degrees of access to the Security Account Manager, as follows:

- **User Accounts:** Microsoft designed the User Accounts control panel for relatively inexperienced end users; it provides a simplified interface with limited access to user accounts. With this interface, you can create local user accounts and modify their basic attributes, but you cannot create groups or manage group memberships (except for the Administrators group).
- **Local Users and Groups:** Microsoft includes this MMC snap-in as part of the Computer Management console; it provides full access to local users and groups, as well as all their attributes. Designed more for the technical specialist or system administrator, this interface is not difficult to use, but it does provide access to controls that beginning users generally do not need.

Using the User Accounts Control Panel

Windows Server 2012 creates two local user accounts during the operating system installation process, the Administrator and Guest accounts. The setup program prompts the installer for an Administrator password during the installation, whereas the Guest account is disabled by default.

After the installation process is complete, the system restarts. Because only the Administrator account is available, the computer logs on using that account. This account has administrative privileges, so at this point you can create additional user accounts or modify the existing ones.

CREATING A NEW LOCAL USER ACCOUNT

To create a new user account with the User Accounts control panel, use the following procedure.

 CREATE A NEW LOCAL USER ACCOUNT WITH THE CONTROL PANEL

GET READY. Log on to Windows Server 2012, using an account with Administrator privileges. The Server Manager console appears.

TAKE NOTE*

This procedure is valid only on Windows Server 2012 computers that are part of a workgroup. When you join a computer to an AD DS domain, you can create only new local user accounts with the Local Users and Groups snap-in.

1. Open the Control Panel. The Control Panel window appears.
2. Click User Accounts. The User Accounts window appears
3. Click User Accounts. The *Make changes to your user account* window appears, as shown in Figure 17-15.

Figure 17-15

The *Make changes to your user account* window

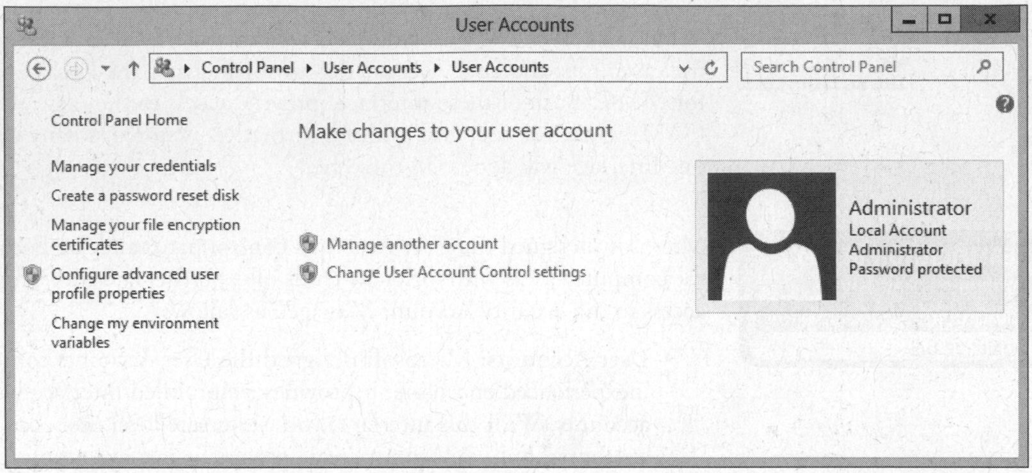

4. Click Manage another account. The *Choose the user you would like to change* page appears.
5. Click Add a user account. The *Add a user* page appears, as shown in Figure 17-16.

Figure 17-16

The *Add a user* page

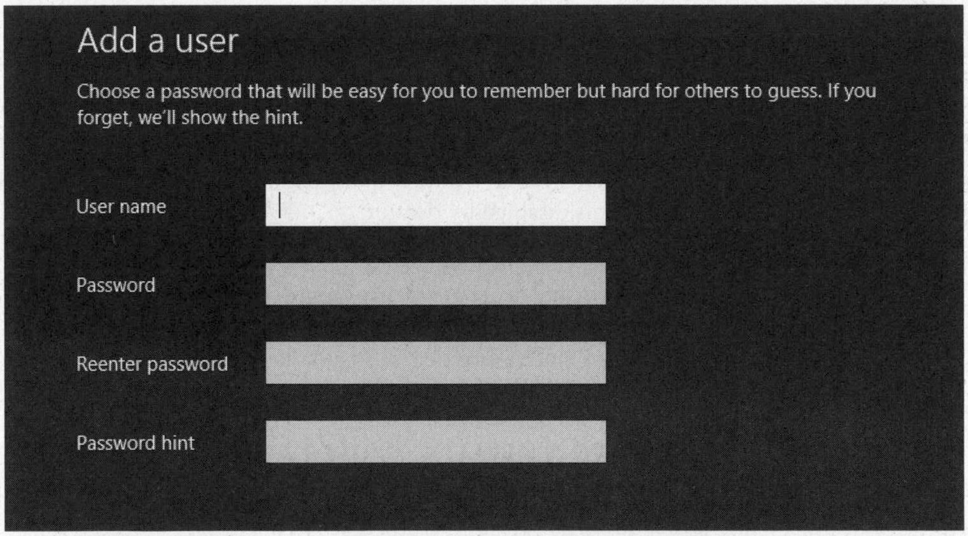

6. Type a name for the new account in the User name text box, and a password for the account in the Password and Reenter password text boxes.
7. Type a phrase in the Password hint text box and click Next. The system creates the account.
8. Click Finish. The new account appears in the Manage Accounts window, as shown in Figure 17-17.

Figure 17-17

The Manage Accounts window

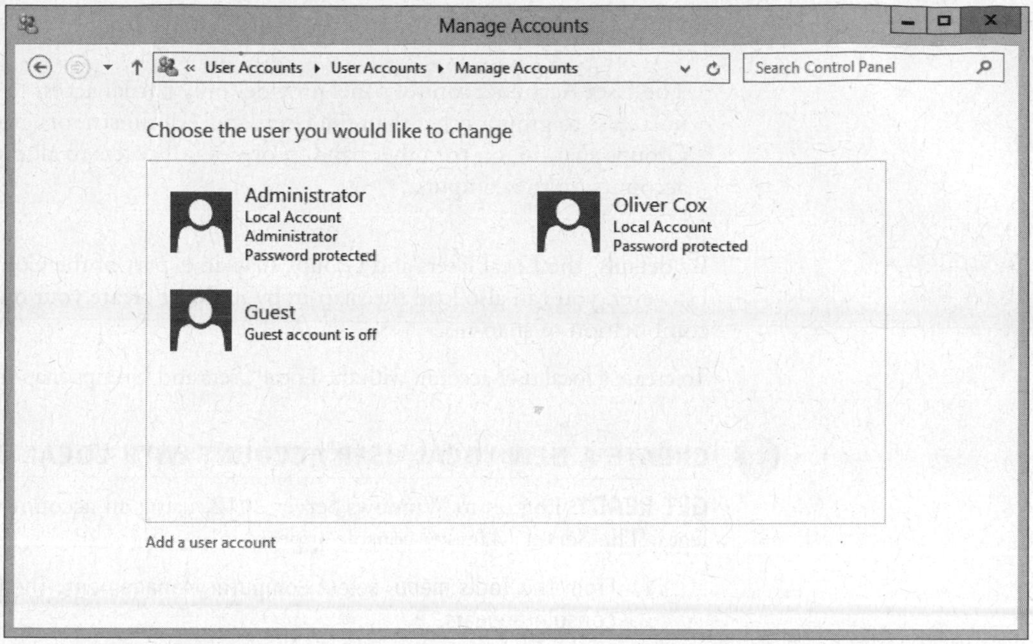

CLOSE the Manage Accounts window.

By default, this procedure creates standard accounts. To grant a local user administrative capabilities, you must change the account type, by using the interface shown in Figure 17-18.

Figure 17-18

The Change Account Type window

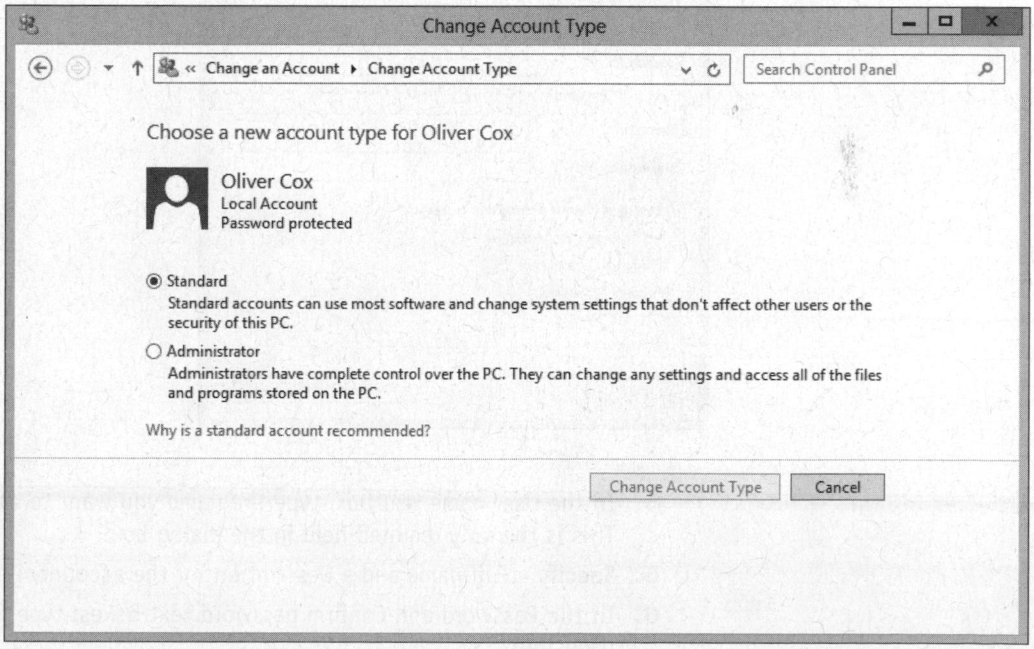

What the User Accounts control panel refers to as an account type is actually a group membership. Selecting the Standard user option adds the user account to the local Users group, whereas selecting the Administrator option adds the account to the Administrators group.

Using the Local Users and Groups Snap-In

The User Accounts control panel provides only partial access to local user accounts, and no access to groups other than the Users and Administrators groups. The Local Users and Groups snap-in, on the other hand, provides full access to all the local user and group accounts on the computer.

By default, the Local Users and Groups snap-in is part of the Computer Management console. However, you can also load the snap-in by itself, or create your own MMC console with any combination of snap-ins.

To create a local user account with the Local Users and Groups snap-in, use the following procedure.

CREATE A NEW LOCAL USER ACCOUNT WITH LOCAL USERS AND GROUPS

GET READY. Log on to Windows Server 2012, using an account with Administrator privileges. The Server Manager console appears.

1. From the Tools menu, select Computer Management. The Computer Management console appears.
2. Expand the Local Users and Groups node and click Users. A list of the current local users appears.
3. Right-click the Users folder and, from the context menu, select New User. The New User dialog box appears, as shown in Figure 17-19.

Figure 17-19

The New User dialog box

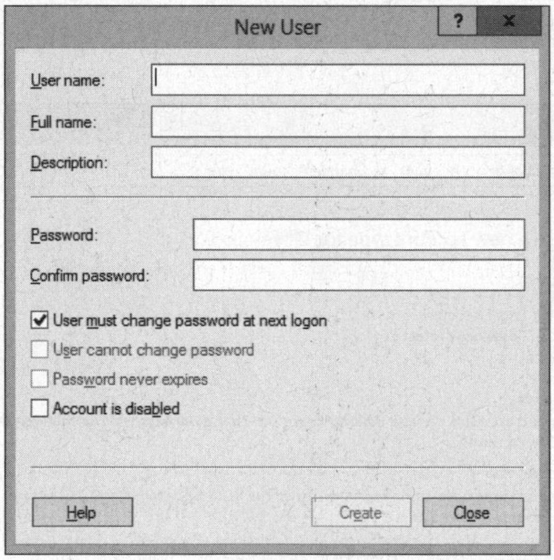

4. In the User name text box, type the name you want to assign to the user account. This is the only required field in the dialog box.
5. Specify a Full name and a Description for the account, if desired.
6. In the Password and Confirm password text boxes, type a password for the account, if desired.
7. Select or clear the four checkboxes to control the following functions:
   - User must change password at next logon: forces the new user to change the password after logging on for the first time. Select this option to assign an initial password and enable users to control their own passwords after the first logon. You cannot select this option if you selected the *Password never expires*

check box. Selecting this option automatically clears the *User cannot change password* check box.

- User cannot change password: prevents the user from changing the account password. Select this option if you want to retain control over the account password, such as when multiple users log on with the same user account. This option is also commonly used to manage service account passwords. You cannot select this option if you selected the *User must change password at next logon* check box.

- Password never expires: prevents the existing password from ever expiring. This option automatically clears the *User must change password at next logon* check box. This option is also commonly used to manage service account passwords.

- Account is disabled: disables the user account, preventing anyone from using it to log on.

8. Click Create. The new account is added to the user list and the console clears the dialog box, leaving it ready for the creation of another user account.

9. Click Close.

CLOSE the Computer Management console.

CREATING A LOCAL GROUP

To create a local group with the Local Users and Groups snap-in, use the following procedure.

CREATE A LOCAL GROUP

GET READY. Log on to Windows Server 2012, using an account with Administrator privileges. The Server Manager console appears.

1. From the Tools menu, select Computer Management. The Computer Management console appears.

2. Expand the Local Users and Groups node and click Groups. A list of local groups appears.

3. Right-click the Groups folder and then, from the context menu, select New Group. The New Group dialog box appears.

4. In the Group name text box, type the name you want to assign to the group. This is the only required field in the dialog box. If desired, specify a Description for the group.

5. Click the Add button. The Select Users dialog box appears.

6. Type the names of the users that you want to add to the group, separated by semicolons, in the text box, and then click OK. The users are added to the Members list. You can also type part of a user name and click Check Names to complete the name or click Advanced to search for users.

7. Click Create to create the group and populate it with the user(s) you specify. The console clears the dialog box, leaving it ready for the creation of another group.

8. Click Close.

CLOSE the Computer Management console.

Local groups have no attributes other than a members list, so you only can add or remove members when you open an existing group. As noted previously, local groups cannot have other local groups as members. If the computer is a member of a Windows domain, a local group can have domain users and domain groups as members.

To add domain objects to a local group, you click the Add button on the group's Properties sheet and, when the Select Users dialog box appears, change the Object Types and Location settings to those of the domain. Then, you can select domain users and groups just as you did local users in the previous procedure.

Configuring User Account Control

↓
THE BOTTOM LINE

One of the most common Windows security problems arises from the fact that many users perform their everyday computing tasks with more system access than they need. Logging on as Administrator or user that is a member of the Administrators group grants the user full access to all areas of the operating system. This degree of system access is not necessary to run many of the applications and perform many of the tasks users require every day; it is needed only for certain administrative functions, such as installing system-wide software or configuring system parameters.

CERTIFICATION READY
Configure User Account
Control (UAC).
Objective 6.2

For most users, logging on with administrative privileges all the time is simply a matter of convenience. Microsoft recommends logging on as a standard user, and to use administrative privileges only when you need them. However, many technical specialists who do this frequently find themselves encountering situations in which they need administrative access. There is a surprisingly large number of common, and even mundane, Windows tasks that require administrative access, and the inability to perform the tasks can negatively affect a user's productivity.

Microsoft addressed this problem by keeping all Windows Server 2012 users from accessing the system using administrative privileges unless the privileges are required to perform the task at hand. The mechanism that does this is called *User Account Control (UAC)*.

Performing Administrative Tasks

When a user logs on to Windows Server 2012, the system issues a token, which indicates the user's access level. Whenever the system authorizes the user to perform a particular activity, it consults the token to determine whether the user has the required privileges.

In versions of Windows prior to Windows Server 2008 and Windows Vista, standard users received standard user tokens and members of the Administrators group received administrative tokens. Every activity performed by an administrative user was authorized using the administrative token, resulting in the problems described previously.

On a computer running Windows Server 2012 with UAC, a standard user still receives a standard user token, but an administrative user receives two tokens: one for standard user access and one for administrative user access. By default, the standard and administrative users both run using the standard user token most of the time.

Despite the introduction of UAC, Microsoft still recommends that Windows users log on with a standard user account, except when they log on for administrative purposes only. UAC simplifies the process by which standard users can gain administrative access, making the use of standard user accounts less frustrating, even for system administrators.

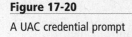

When a standard user attempts to perform a task that requires administrative privileges, the system displays a ***credential prompt***, as shown in Figure 17-20, which is an authentication request that requires the user to supply credentials for an account with administrative privileges.

Figure 17-20

A UAC credential prompt

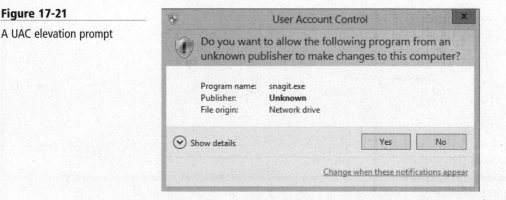

When you attempt to perform a task that requires administrative access, the system switches the account from the standard user token to the administrative token, which is known as ***Admin Approval Mode***.

Before the system permits the user to employ the administrative token, it might require the human user to confirm that he or she is actually trying to perform an administrative task. To do this, the system generates an elevation prompt. An ***elevation prompt*** is the message box shown in Figure 17-21. This confirmation prevents unauthorized processes, such as those initiated by malware, from accessing the system using administrative privileges.

Figure 17-21

A UAC elevation prompt

Using Secure Desktop

By default, whenever Windows Server 2012 displays an elevation prompt or a credential prompt, it does so using the secure desktop.

The ***secure desktop*** is an alternative to the interactive user desktop that Windows normally displays. When Windows Server 2012 generates an elevation or credential prompt, it switches to the secure desktop, by suppressing the operation of all other desktop controls and permitting only Windows processes to interact with the prompt. The object of this is to prevent malware from automating a response to the elevation or credential prompt and bypassing the human reply.

Configuring User Account Control Settings

Windows Server 2012 enables User Account Control by default, but it is possible to configure its properties, or even disable it completely.

In Windows Server 2012, four UAC settings are available through the Control Panel. To configure UAC through the Control Panel, use the following procedure.

CONFIGURE UAC SETTINGS

GET READY. Log on to Windows Server 2012, using an account with Administrator privileges. The Server Manager console appears.

1. Open the Control Panel. The Control Panel window appears.
2. Click System and Security > Action Center. The Action Center window appears.
3. Click Change User Account Control settings. The *User Account Control Settings* dialog box appears, as shown in Figure 17-22.

Figure 17-22

The User Account Control Settings dialog box

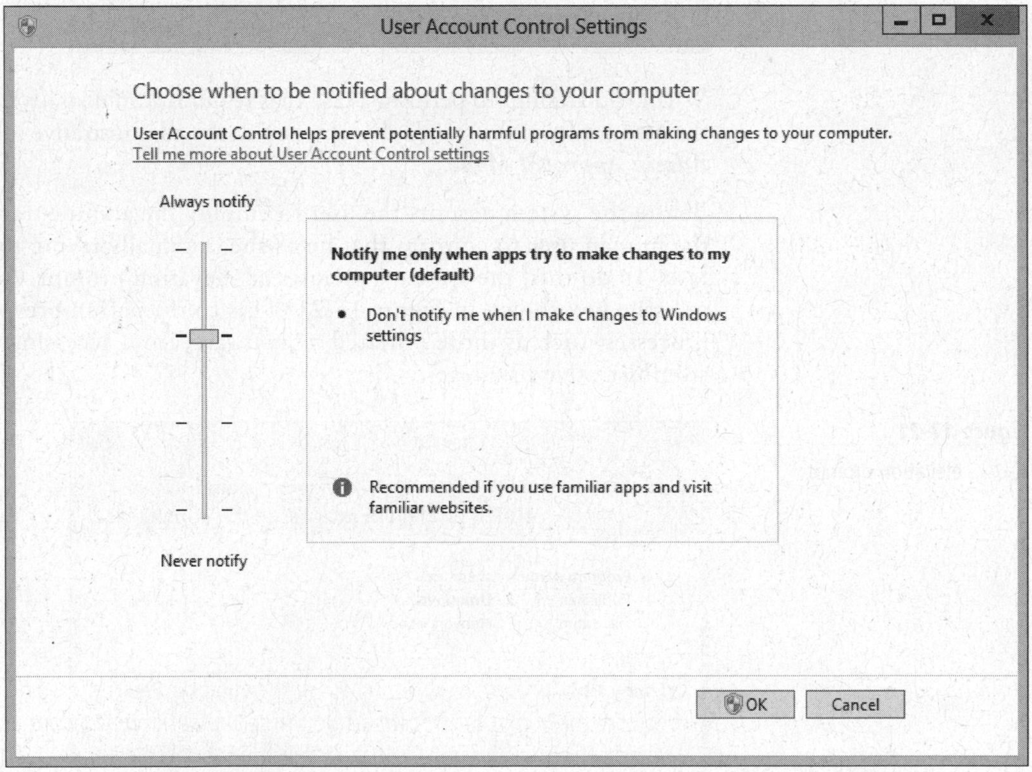

4. Adjust the slider to one of the following settings and click OK.
   - Always notify me
   - Notify me only when programs try to make changes to my computer
   - Notify me only when programs try to make changes to my computer (do not dim my desktop)
   - Never notify me

CLOSE the Action Center window.

Although the Control Panel provides some control over UAC, the most granular control over UAC properties is still through the Security Options node in Group Policy and Local Security Policy. Table 17-3 lists the Security Options policies that provide control over UAC.

Table 17-3

UAC Local Security Policy Settings

POLICY SETTING	VALUES AND FUNCTIONS
User Account Control: Admin Approval Mode for the Built-In Administrator Account	• When enabled, the built-in Administrator account is issued two tokens during logon and runs in Admin Approval mode. This is the default setting, except in cases of upgrades from Windows XP systems in which the built-in Administrator account is the only active member of the Administrators group. • When disabled, the built-in Administrator account receives only an administrative token, and runs with full administrative access at all times.
User Account Control: Allow UIAccess applications to prompt for elevation without using the secure desktop	• When enabled, causes User Interface Accessibility programs to disable the secure desktop when displaying elevation prompts. • When disabled, elevation prompts use the secure desktop, unless the *User Account Control: Switch to the Secure Desktop when Prompting for Elevation* policy is enabled.
User Account Control: Behavior of the Elevation Prompt for Administrators in Admin Approval Mode	• When set to *Elevate without prompting*, administrative users are elevated to the administrative token with no consent or credentials from the human user. This setting, in effect, disables the security provided by UAC and is not recommended. • When set to *Prompt for consent on the secure desktop*, administrative users elevate to the administrative token only after the presentation of an elevation prompt on the secure desktop and the consent of the human user. • When set to *Prompt for credentials on the secure desktop*, administrative users elevate to the administrative token only after the presentation of a credential prompt on the secure desktop, to which the user must supply a valid administrative account name and password, even if he or she is already logged on using such an account. • When set to *Prompt for consent*, administrative users elevate to the administrative token only after the presentation of an elevation prompt and the consent of the human user. This is the default setting. • When set to *Prompt for credentials*, administrative users elevate to the administrative token only after the presentation of a credential prompt, to which the user must supply a valid administrative account name and password, even if he or she is already logged on using such an account.
User Account Control: Behavior of the Elevation Prompt for Standard Users	• When set to *Automatically deny elevation requests*, suppresses the credential prompt and prevents standard users from being elevated to an administrative token. Standard users can perform administrative tasks only by using the Run As program or by logging on using an administrative account. This is the default setting for the Windows 7 Enterprise edition. • When set to *Prompt for credentials on the secure desktop*, standard users attempting to perform an administrative function receive a credential prompt on the secure desktop, to which the user must supply a valid administrative account name and password. • When set to *Prompt for credentials*, standard users attempting to perform an administrative function receive a credential prompt, to which the user must supply a valid administrative account name and password. This is the default setting for the Windows 7 Home Basic, Home Premium, Professional, and Ultimate editions.
User Account Control: Detect Application Installations and Prompt for Elevation	• When enabled, an attempt to install an application causes standard users to receive a credential prompt and administrative users to receive an elevation prompt. The user must supply authentication credentials or consent before the installation can proceed. This is the default setting. • When disabled, elevation and credential prompts are suppressed during application installations, and the installations will fail. This setting is for use on enterprise desktops that use an automated installation technology, such as Microsoft System Center Configuration Manager.

(continued)

Table 17-3

(continued)

POLICY SETTING	VALUES AND FUNCTIONS
User Account Control: Only Elevate Executables that are Signed and Validated	• When enabled, requires successful public key infrastructure (PKI) signature verifications on all interactive applications that request administrative access. Unsigned applications will not run. • When disabled, both signed and unsigned applications run. This is the default setting.
User Account Control: Only Elevate UIAccess Applications that are Installed in Secure Locations	• When enabled, Windows 7 provides access to the protected system user interface only if the executable is located in the Program Files or Windows folder on the system drive. If the executable is not located in one of these folders, access will be denied, despite a positive response to the elevation prompt. This is the default setting. • When disabled, the folder location checks are omitted, so any application can be granted access to the protected system user interface upon successful completion of the elevation prompt.
User Account Control: Run All Administrators in Admin Approval Mode	• When enabled, standard users receive credential prompts and administrative users receive elevation prompts, when either one requests administrative privileges. This policy essentially turns UAC on and off. A change in the value of this policy does not take effect until the system is restarted. This is the default setting. • When disabled, the AIS service is disabled and does not automatically start. This turns UAC off and prevents elevation and credential prompts from appearing. When the system starts, the Windows Security Center warns the user that operating system security is reduced and provides the capability to activate UAC.
User Account Control: Switch to the Secure Desktop when Prompting for Elevation	• When enabled, causes Windows 7 to display all elevation prompts on the secure desktop, which can receive messages only from Windows processes. This is the default setting. • When disabled, causes Windows 7 to display all elevation prompts on the interactive user desktop.
User Account Control: Virtualize File and Registry Write Failures to Per-User Locations	• When enabled, enables non-UAC-compliant applications to run by redirecting write requests to protected locations, such as the Program Files and Windows folders or the HKLM\Software registry key, to alternative locations in the registry and file system. This process is called virtualization. This is the default setting. • When disabled, virtualization is disabled, and non-UAC-compliant applications attempting to write to protected locations fail to run. This setting is recommended only when the system is running UAC-compliant applications exclusively.

SKILL SUMMARY

IN THIS LESSON, YOU LEARNED:

• You can find most security-related settings within the Windows Settings node of the Computer Configuration node of a GPO.

• Local policy settings govern the actions users can perform on a specific computer and determine whether the actions are recorded in an event log.

• Auditing can be configured to audit successes, failures, or both.

• Because audited events are recorded in the appropriate event log, it is necessary to understand the Event Log Policy setting area. This area enables control over maximum log sizes, log retention, and access rights to each log.

- Restrictions on group memberships can be accomplished by using the Group Restriction Policy setting. Implementing this policy removes group members who are not part of the configured group membership list or adds group members according to a preconfigured list.

- You can use security templates to configure local policies, group memberships, event log settings, and other policies.

- Computer configuration group policies refresh every 90 minutes by default. Domain controller group policies refresh every 2 minutes. You can alter these settings based on the frequency in which policy changes occur.

- When a standard user attempts to perform a task that requires administrative privileges, the system displays a credential prompt, requesting that the user supply the name and password for an account with administrative privileges.

- By default, UAC is enabled in all Windows Server 2012 installations, but it is possible to configure its properties, or even disable it completely, by using Group Policy.

■ Knowledge Assessment

Multiple Choice

Select one or more correct answers for each of the following questions.

1. Which of the following tools would you use to deploy the settings in a security template to all of the computers in an Active Directory Domain Services domain?
   a. Active Directory Users and Computers
   b. Security Templates snap-in
   c. Group Policy Object Editor
   d. Group Policy Management console

2. Which of the following are local groups to which you can add users with the Windows Control Panel?
   a. Users
   b. Power Users
   c. Administrators
   d. Nonadministrators

3. Which of the following tools would you use to modify the settings in a security template?
   a. Active Directory Users and Computers
   b. Security Templates snap-in
   c. Group Policy Object Editor
   d. Group Policy Management console

4. The built-in local groups on a server running Windows Server 2012 receive their special capabilities through which of the following mechanisms?
   a. Security options
   b. Windows Firewall rules
   c. NTFS permissions
   d. User rights

5. After configuring and deploying the Audit Directory Service Access policy, what must you do before a computer running Windows Server2012 begins logging Active Directory access attempts?
   a. You must select the Active Directory objects you want to audit in the Active Directory Users and Computer console.
   b. You must wait for the audit policy settings to propagate to all of the domain controllers on the network.
   c. You must open the Audit Directory Service Access Properties sheet and select all of the Active Directory objects you want to audit.
   d. You must add an underscore character to the name of every Active Directory object you want to audit.

6. What is the purpose of the Audit Policy section of a Local Group Policy objects (GPO)?
   a. Administrators can log successful and failed security events, such as logon events, database errors, and system shutdown.
   b. Administrators can log successful and failed security events, such as loss of data, account access, and object access.
   c. Administrators can log successful and failed events, forwarded from other systems.
   d. Administrators can log events related specifically to domain controllers.

7. What are the three primary event logs?
   a. Application, Forwarded, and System
   b. Application, Security, and Setup
   c. Application, Security, and System
   d. Application, System, and Setup

8. After you create a GPO that contains computer or user settings, but not both, what can you do for faster GPO processing?
   a. Set the priority higher for the configured setting area.
   b. Manually refresh the GPO settings.
   c. Disable the setting area that is not configured.
   d. Regardless of whether part or all of a GPO is configured, the GPO is processed at the same speed.

9. What are the two interfaces for creating and managing local user accounts for a computer joined to the domain?
   a. Control Panel and ADAC
   b. User Accounts control panel and the Local Users and Groups snap-in for MMC
   c. ADAC and the Active Directory of Users and Computers snap-in for MMC
   d. Server Manager and PowerShell

10. What did Microsoft introduce in Windows Server 2012 to ensure users with administrative privileges still operate routine tasks as standard users?
    a. New Group Policy and Local Security Policy
    b. Secure desktop·
    c. User Account Control (UAC)
    d. Built-in administrator account

Best Answer

Choose the letter that corresponds to the best answer. More than one answer choice may achieve the goal. Select the BEST answer.

1. When would you need to create a user account through the Control Panel?
   a. You can create users through the Control Panel or with the Local Users and Groups snap-in.

  b. You can create users through the Control Panel when the Windows Server 2012 computer is part of a workgroup.

  c. When you join a computer to an Active Directory Domain Services (AD DS) domain, you can create only new local user accounts with the Local Users and Groups snap-in. Control Panel is while the computer is not a member of an AD DS domain.

  d. Creating users through the Control Panel is not possible.

2. What is the best approach for planning a security template strategy?
   a. Plan according to the needs of individual computers, not users.
   b. Plan according to the needs of computer roles, and also company locations.
   c. Plan according to the needs of computer roles, but not individual computers.
   d. Plan according to the needs of users.

3. What are the key benefits of security templates?
   a. Apply consistent, scalable, and reproducible security settings throughout an enterprise.
   b. Deploy alongside with group policies.
   c. Although a text editor is possible, Windows Server 2012 enables the use of a graphical interface.
   d. Simple deployment as configuration files are text (.inf extension) and uses a graphical and unified interface.

4. How are most Group Policy settings applied or reapplied?
   a. Every time a computer starts up
   b. At the refresh interval
   c. Whenever a user logs on
   d. Whenever the domain controller is restarted

5. What are the two interfaces available for creating and managing user accounts in Windows Server 2012?
   a. Control Panel and the MMC snap-in
   b. Server Manager and Control Panel
   c. Control Panel and Active Directory Users and Computers
   d. User Accounts control panel and the Local Users and Groups snap-in for MMC

Build a List

1. Order the steps to configure files and folders for auditing.
   a. Click Select a Principal. The Select User, Computer, Service Account, or Group dialog box appears. Select the users or groups to be audited for Active Directory object access and click OK.
   b. Open File Explorer, and right-click the file or folder to audit. From the context menu, select Properties. Click the Security tab, and then click Advanced.
   c. Click the Auditing tab. Click Add. The Auditing Entry page appears.
   d. From the Type drop-down list, specify whether you want to audit failures, successes, or both. From the Applies to drop-down list, specify which descendent objects should be audited.
   e. Log on to a domain controller running Windows Server 2012, using an account with domain Administrator privileges.
   f. Select the basic permissions you want to audit for this object and click OK. The new Auditing entry appears in the Advanced Security Settings dialog box.

2. Order the steps to create a security template.
   a. Open MMC. Click File > Add/Remove Snap-in. The Add or Remove Snap-ins dialog box appears.
   b. Expand the Security Templates node. Right-click the security template search path and, from the context menu, select New Template. A dialog box appears.
   c. Select Security Templates from the Available snap-ins list and click Add. The snap-in appears in the Add or Remove Snap-ins dialog box.
   d. Click File > Save As and choose a name for the new console, to be saved in the Administrative Tools program group.
   e. In the Template name field, type a name for the template and click OK. The new template appears in the console.

3. First, switch to the Security Templates console you created in the previous procedure. Order the steps to import the new security template into a GPO.
   a. Browse to the Computer Configuration\Policies\Windows Settings\Security Settings node. Right-click the Security Settings node and, from the context menu, select Import Policy.
   b. Expand the forest container and browse to your domain. Then expand the domain container and select the Group Policy Objects folder. The GPOs that currently exist in the domain appear in the Contents tab.
   c. Right-click the GPO into which you want to import the template and click Edit. A Group Policy Management Editor window for this policy appears.
   d. From the Tools menu, select Group Policy Management. The Group Policy Management console appears.
   e. Browse to the security template you want to import and click Open. The policy settings in the template are copied to the GPO.

4. Order the steps to create a new user account with the Control Panel. This procedure is valid only on Windows Server 2012 computers belonging to a workgroup, not an AD DS domain.
   a. Click Add a user account. The Add a user page appears.
   b. Type a name and a password for the new account. Type a phrase in the Password hint text box and click Next.
   c. Open the Control Panel.
   d. Click User Accounts. The User Accounts window appears. Click User Accounts. The Make changes to your user account window appears.
   e. Click Manage another account. The Choose the user you would like to change page appears.

5. Order the steps to create a new local user account with Local Users and Groups.
   a. In the User name text box, type the name you want to assign to the user account.
   b. If desired, specify a Full name, description for the account. Type and confirm a password.
   c. From Server Manager's Tools menu, select Computer Management. The Computer Management console appears.
   d. Right-click the Users folder and, from the context menu, select New User. The New User dialog box appears.
   e. Expand the Local Users and Groups node and click Users. A list of the current local users appears.
   f. Click Create.

Business Case Scenarios

Scenario 17-1: Understanding Group Policy Planning

You are the administrator for Coho Winery, Inc. a large wine distribution company that has locations in the United States and Canada. In the last six months, Coho Winery, Inc. has purchased several smaller distribution companies. As you integrate them into your forest, you want to allow them to remain autonomous in their management of desktops and security. In the process of making their domains part of your corporate network, you have some policies that you want to become part of their environment, and others that you do not want to implement at this time. As you discuss this with your IT team, your manager asks you to explain which features in Windows Server 2012 enable you to provide the Group Policy flexibility needed by the new Active Directory structure. List several of the features in Windows Server 2012 Group Policy that will enable Coho Winery, Inc. to achieve its postacquisition goals.

Scenario 17-2: Deploying Security Templates

You are a network administrator planning a security template deloyment on a network that consists of 100 workstation. The workstations are all running various versions of Microsoft Windows, broken down as follows:

- Windows 7: 30 workstations
- Windows XP Professional: 40 workstations
- Windows XP Home Edition: 20 workstations
- Windows 2000 Professional: 10 workstations

In the past, some computers on the network have been compromised because end users modified their workstation security configurations. Your task is to deploy your security templates on the workstations in such a way that end users cannot modify them. To accomplish this goal, you decide to use Group Policy to deploy the templates to an Active Directory Domain Services OU object that contains all of the workstations.
Based on the information provided, answer the following questions.

1. How many of the workstations cannot receive their security template settings from a GPO linked to an AD DS container?

2. Which of the following methods can you use to deploy your security templates on the workstations that do not support Group Policy, while still accomplishing your assigned goals?
   a. Upgrade all of the computers that do not support Group Policy to Windows 7.
   b. Run the Security Templates snap-in on each computer and load the appropriate security template.
   c. Create a logon script that uses Secedit.exe to import the security template on each computer.
   d. Run the Security Configuration and Analysis snap-in on each computer and use it to import the appropriate security template.

18 LESSON

Configuring Application Restriction Policies

70-410 EXAM OBJECTIVE

Objective 6.3 – Configure application restriction policies. This objective may include but is not limited to: Configure rule enforcement; configure AppLocker rules; configure Software Restriction Policies.

LESSON HEADING	EXAM OBJECTIVE
Installing Software with Group Policy	
Repackaging Software	
Deploying Software Using Group Policy	
Configuring Software Restriction Policies	Configure Software Restriction Policies
Enforcing Restrictions	
Configuring Software Restriction Rules	
Configuring Software Restriction Properties	Configure rule enforcement
Software Restriction Best Practices	
Using AppLocker	
Understanding Rule Types	
Creating Default Rules	
Creating Rules Automatically	Configure AppLocker rules
Creating Rules Manually	

KEY TERMS

application control policies (AppLocker)
Assign
certificate rule
distribution share
file-activated installation
hash

hash rule
hash value
Install This Application At Logon
.msi file
network zone rule
patch files

path rule
Publish
repackaging
self-healing
.zap file

■ Installing Software with Group Policy

THE BOTTOM LINE

You can use Group Policy to install, upgrade, patch, or remove software applications when a computer starts, when a user logs on to the network, or when a user accesses a file associated with an application that is not currently on the user's computer.

In addition, you can use Group Policy to fix problems associated with applications. For example, if a user inadvertently deletes a file from an application, Group Policy can launch a repair process that will fix the application. To perform these tasks, Group Policy works together with the Windows Installer Service.

Windows Server 2012 uses the Windows Installer with Group Policy to install and manage software that is packaged into Microsoft Installer files, with an .msi extension.

Windows Installer consists of two components: one for the client-side and another for the server-side. The client-side component is called the *Windows Installer Service*. This client-side component is responsible for automating the installation and configuration of the designated software.

The Windows Installer Service requires a package file that contains all the pertinent information about the software. This package file consists of the following information:

- An *.msi file*, which is a relational database file that is copied to the target computer system, with the program files it deploys. In addition to providing installation information, this database file assists in the *self-healing* process for damaged applications and clean application removal.
- External source files that are required for software installation or removal.
- Summary information about the software and the package.
- A reference point to the path where the installation files are located.

To install software by using Group Policy, you must have Windows Installer–enabled applications. An application that has an approval stamp from Microsoft on its packaging, including the Certified for Windows Server 2012 logo, is Windows Installer–enabled by default. This means the application provides support for Group Policy deployments using an .msi file.

At times, you might need to modify Windows Installer files to better suit the needs of your network. Modifications to .msi files require transform files, which have an .mst extension.

For example, corporate network administrators who use .msi files to deploy their desktop applications might have users that require all the Microsoft Office 2010 applications, except for Microsoft Access. The Office 2010 product contains an .msi file that installs all the Office applications. However, because you do not want to install Access, you need to create an .mst file to modify the .msi file by using the *Custom Installation Wizard* included with Office. When you place the .mst file in the same directory as the original .msi file, it customizes the installation by omitting Access from the Office package. In addition, you can create transform files that add new features to the package, such as document templates for Microsoft Word, that are specific to your organization.

Windows Installer files with the .msp extension serve as patch files. You use *patch files* to apply service packs and hotfixes to installed software. Unlike an .msi file, a patch package does not include a complete database. Instead, it contains, at minimum, a database transform procedure that adds patching information to the target installation package database. For this reason, .msp files should be located in the same folder as the original .msi file when you want the patch to be applied as part of the Group Policy software installation.

Repackaging Software

Not all software on the market provides .msi support. Therefore, you might not be able to use Windows Installer with all your enterprise applications. To remedy this, you might consider *repackaging* some software packages to take advantage of the Windows Installer technology.

Several third-party package-creation applications on the market enable you to repackage software products into a Windows Installer-enabled format. However, repackaged software might not support all the features of an original .msi, such as self-healing. For this reason, you should consider the long-term cost of implementing software within your organization that does not conform to the Microsoft Logo program.

In the simplest case, the process of repackaging software for .msi distribution consists of the following steps:

1. Take a snapshot of a clean computer system.
2. Install and configure the application as desired.
3. Take a snapshot of the computer after the application is installed.

By comparing the two snapshots, the software can create a package that takes into account the changes to the registry, system settings, and file system caused by the installation. When you repackage an application, you are creating a relational database that tracks the installation parameters associated with the application. Windows Installer uses the database to find these items at installation time.

Generally, application manufacturers do not support the reengineering of their .msi packages. However, you can use the .mst process to modify manufacturer-supplied .msi packages to reflect the needs of your organization. When repackaging an application is not an option and a Windows Installer file is not available, you can use a .zap file to publish an application. A *.zap file* is a non–Windows Installer package that you can create by using a text editor. A .zap file looks and functions similar to an .ini file. The disadvantages of creating .zap files are as follows:

- They can be published, but not assigned. These two options are discussed in detail later in this lesson.
- Deployments require user intervention, rather than being fully unattended.
- Local administrator permissions might be required to perform the installation.
- They do not support custom installations or automatic repair.
- They do not support the removal of applications that are no longer needed or applications that failed to install properly.

Deploying Software Using Group Policy

Group Policy enables you to deploy required user software when the computer starts, when the user logs on, or on demand, based on file associations. From the user's perspective, applications are available and functional when they need them. From the administrator's perspective, the applications for each user do not need to be installed manually.

You can use the Software Installation extension in Group Policy to deploy software to computers running any NT-based version of Windows, including Windows Server 2012 and Windows 8.

Before deploying software using Group Policy, you must create a *distribution share*. This shared folder, also called a *software distribution point*, is a network location from which users can download the software that they need. In Windows Server 2012, the network location can include software distribution points located in other forests when there are two-way forest trusts established on your network. This shared folder contains any related package files and all the application files that are required for installation. Each application that you want to install should have a separate subfolder in the parent shared folder. Windows Installer uses this directory to locate and copy files to the workstation. Users who receive the Group Policy assignment must have the NTFS Allow Read permission to the folder containing the application and package files.

After you create a software distribution point, you must create a GPO or modify an existing GPO to include the software installation settings. As part of configuring a GPO for software installation, you need to decide whether to use the *Assign* or *Publish* option for deploying the application.

The Assign option is helpful when you are deploying required applications to pertinent users and computers. The Publish option enables users to install the applications that they consider useful to them. If you use the Assign option, you must also decide whether you will assign the application to a computer or a user account.

ASSIGNING AN APPLICATION TO A USER OR COMPUTER

When you assign an application to a user, the application is advertised on the Start menu of the user's workstation. The actual installation is triggered when the user attempts to access it. This enables the software to be installed on demand.

For example, if you need the Sales department to have all users running Microsoft Excel to complete their daily sales reports, you can create Group Policy object, modify its settings to include the assignment of the Excel package file, and link it to the Sales OU. When a user in the Sales OU logs on, Windows Installer adds Excel as a selection on the user's Start menu and changes the registry to associate XLSX files with Excel. When the user attempts to access the program for the first time using the Start menu selection, or when the user tries to open an XLSX file, the installation process begins. You can configure the installation to be automated or to require some user input.

The process of assigning an application using the Computer Configuration\Software Settings\ Software Installation node of Group Policy is somewhat different than assigning it within the User Configuration node. When you use the Computer Configuration node, the systems install the application during startup. This is a safe method, because a minimum number of processes compete for utilization and few, if any, other applications are running that could cause conflicts.

 WARNING As a precautionary step, you should test the available applications to ensure that they can function together if the user opts to install them all. With certain application types, such as multimedia applications, conflicts in the required versions of supporting files might cause a malfunction. It is always prudent to test each application and its compatibility before you distribute to the users. In addition, testing the deployment to be sure that applications are distributed only to the intended recipients is equally important.

PUBLISHING AN APPLICATION

Publishing an application is possible only by using the User Configuration\Software Settings\Software Installation extension. When you publish an application, it is advertised in the Windows Control Panel. A published application does not appear on the Start Menu or on the desktop as it does when you assign an application. Using the Publish option rather than Assign is generally preferable when users are allowed to choose their applications.

For example, a company that has many graphic artists might prefer to accommodate the user's different software preferences. They might determine that three applications will be available and users can install the application they prefer. Publishing a list of available applications enables users to install their preferred application, or they can install all of them, if desired.

Using the Publish method of distributing applications also enables a *file-activated installation* to take place. This functionality is identical to the assigned application functionality discussed previously. When a user opens a file associated with an application that does not currently exist on the user's workstation, the application is installed.

To configure a GPO to assign or publish an application, use the following procedure.

⊙ CONFIGURE SOFTWARE INSTALLATION DEFAULTS

GET READY. Log on to a server running Windows Server 2012, using an account with domain Administrator privileges.

1. From the Tools menu of the *Server Manager* console, select Group Policy Management. The *Group Policy Management* console appears.

2. Expand the forest container and browse to your domain. Then expand the domain container and select the *Group Policy Objects* folder. The GPOs that currently exist in the domain appear in the *Contents* tab.

3. Right-click a GPO and click Edit. A *Group Policy Management Editor* window appears.

4. Browse to the Software Settings folder under Computer Configuration or User Configuration, as shown in Figure 18-1.

Figure 18-1

The Software Settings folder in a GPO

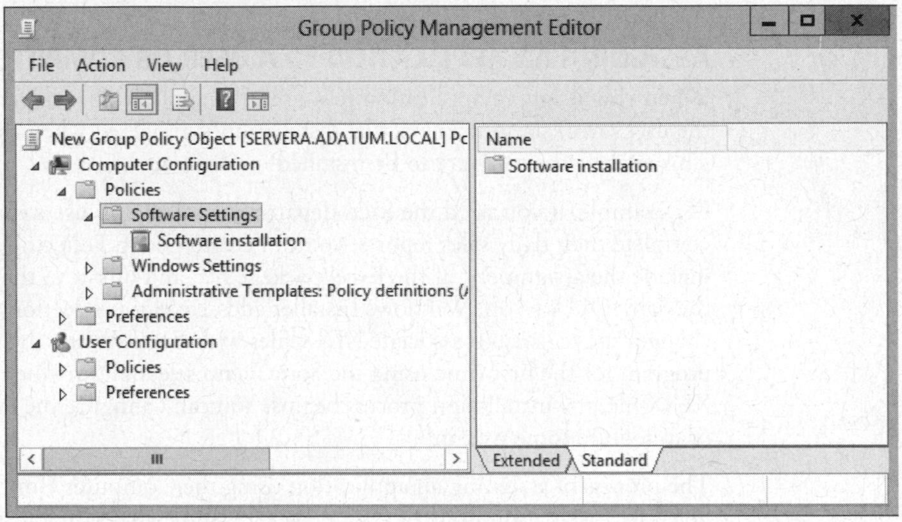

5. Right-click the Software Installation node and, from the context menu, select Properties. The *Software Installation* Properties sheet appears, as shown in Figure 18-2.

Figure 18-2

The Software Installation Properties sheet

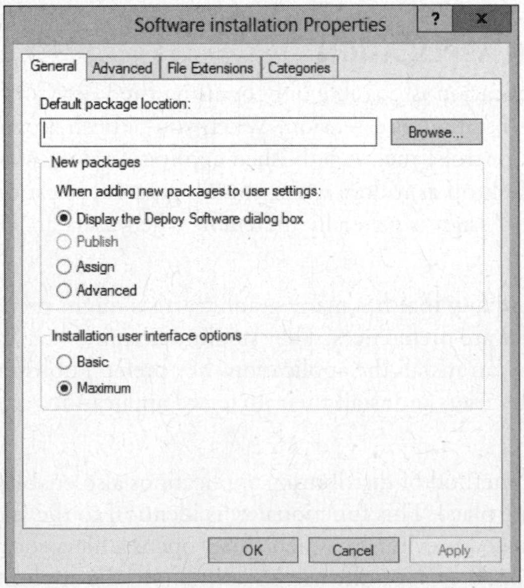

6. On the General tab of the *Software Installation Properties* dialog box, type the Uniform Naming Convention (UNC) path (\\servername\sharename) to the software distribution point for the Windows Installer packages (.msi files) in the Default Package Location box.
7. In the New Packages box, select one of the following options:
   - Display The Deploy Software Dialog Box: Use this option to specify that the Deploy Software dialog box should appear when you add new packages to the GPO, enabling you to choose whether to assign, publish, or configure package properties. This is the default setting.
   - Publish: Use this option to specify that the applications will be published by default with standard package properties when you add new packages to the GPO.
   - Assign: Use this option to specify that the applications will be assigned by default with standard package properties when you add new packages to the GPO. Packages can be assigned to users and computers.
   - Advanced: Use this option to specify that the Properties dialog box for the package will appear when you add new packages to the GPO, enabling you to configure all properties for the package.

TAKE NOTE*

Packages can be published only to users, not computers. If this is an installation under the *Computer Configuration* node of the *Group Policy Object Editor* console, the *Publish* choice is unavailable.

8. In the Installation User Interface Options section, select one of the following options:
   - Basic: Use this option to provide only a basic display for users during all package installations, for example, a progress bar and any applicable error messages.
   - Maximum: Use this option to provide all installation messages and screens for users during the installation of all packages.
9. Click the Advanced tab, as shown in Figure 18-3, and select any of the following options:

Figure 18-3

The Advanced tab of the Software Installation Properties sheet

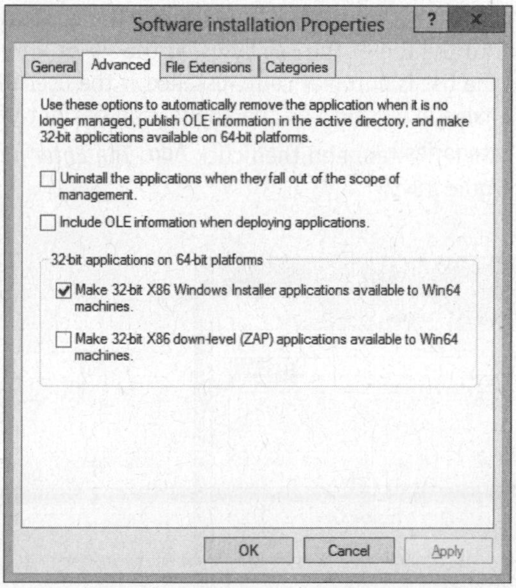

   - Uninstall The Applications When They Fall Out Of The Scope Of Management: Use this option to remove the application when it no longer applies to users or computers.
   - Include OLE Information When Deploying Applications: Use this option to specify whether to deploy information about Component Object Model (COM) components with the package.

- Make 32-Bit X86 Windows Installer Applications Available To Win64 Machines: Use this option to specify whether 32-bit Windows Installer Applications (.msi files) can be assigned or published to 64-bit computers.
- Make 32-Bit X86 Down-Level (ZAP) Applications Available To Win64 Machines: Use this option to specify whether 32-bit application files (.zap files) can be assigned or published to 64-bit computers.

10. Click the File Extensions tab, as shown in Figure 18-4.

Figure 18-4

The File Extensions tab of the Software Installation Properties sheet

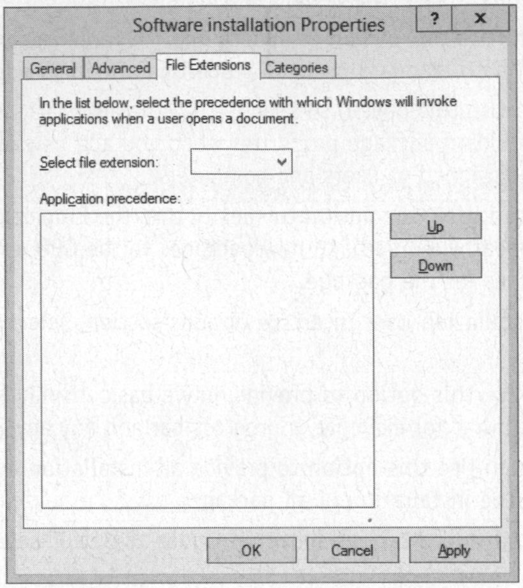

11. In the Application Precedence list box, move the application with the highest precedence to the top of the list by using the Up or Down buttons. The application at the top of the list is automatically installed if the user invokes a document with the related filename extension and the application has not yet been installed.

12. Click the Categories tab, and then click Add. The *Enter new category* tab appears, as shown in Figure 18-5.

Figure 18-5

The Enter new category tab of the Software Installation Properties sheet

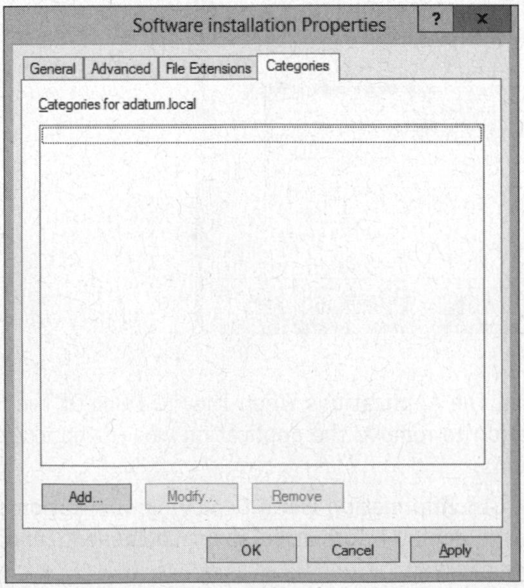

13. Type the name of the application category to be used for the domain in the Category box, and click OK.

TAKE NOTE*

The application categories that you establish are per domain, not per GPO. You need to define them only once for the whole domain, not once for each GPO that you define.

14. Click OK to save your changes.

CLOSE the *Group Policy Management Editor* and the *Group Policy Management* console.

You have now configured default Software Installation settings. To create a new software installation package, use the following procedure.

CREATE A NEW SOFTWARE INSTALLATION PACKAGE

GET READY. Log on to a server running Windows Server 2012, using an account with domain Administrator privileges.

1. From the Tools menu in the *Server Manager* console, select Group Policy Management. The *Group Policy Management* console appears.
2. Expand the forest container and browse to your domain. Then expand the domain container and select the Group Policy Objects folder. The GPOs that currently exist in the domain appear in the *Contents* tab.
3. Right-click a GPO and click Edit. A *Group Policy Management Editor* window appears.
4. Browse to the Software Settings folder under Computer Configuration or User Configuration.
5. Right-click the Software Installation node and, from the context menu, select New > Package. The *Open* combo box appears.
6. In the filename text box, type the UNC path to your software distribution point and the name of the Windows Installer package (.msi file) you want to deploy, and then click Open. The *Deploy Software* dialog box appears, as shown in Figure 18-6.

Figure 18-6

The Deploy Software dialog box

Deploy Software

Select deployment method:

○ Published
● Assigned
○ Advanced

Select this option to Assign the application without modifications.

OK   Cancel

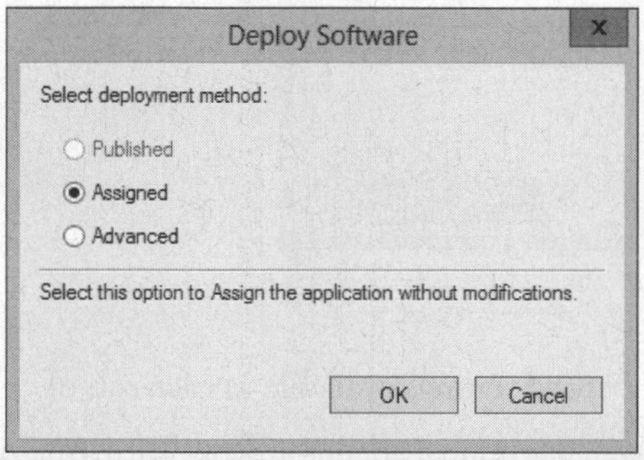

TAKE NOTE*

The UNC path is critical to a successful software deployment. If you do not use a UNC path to the software distribution point, clients will not be able to locate the package files.

7. Select one of the following options:
   • Published: Use this option to publish the Windows Installer package to users, without applying modifications to the package. This option is available only if the policy was configured under the User Configuration node of Group Policy. Publishing cannot occur in a computer-based policy.

- Assigned: Use this option to assign the Windows Installer package to users or computers, without applying modifications to the package.

- Advanced: Use this option to set properties for the Windows Installer package, including published or assigned options and modifications.

8. Click OK. If you selected Published or Assigned, the Windows Installer package is added to the GPO and appears in the console. If you selected Advanced, the Properties sheet for the Windows Installer package appears, enabling you to set properties for the Windows Installer package, including deployment options and modifications. Make the necessary modification and click OK.

CLOSE the *Group Policy Management Editor* and the *Group Policy Management* console.

You have now created a Software Installation package in the GPO.

CUSTOMIZING SOFTWARE INSTALLATION PACKAGES

In the Properties sheet for each Windows Installer package, as shown in Figure 18-7, you can associate additional settings with the package, such as those in modification or transform (.mst) files and upgrade settings. You can also make modifications to the previously assigned deployment settings.

Figure 18-7

The Properties sheet of a Windows Installer package

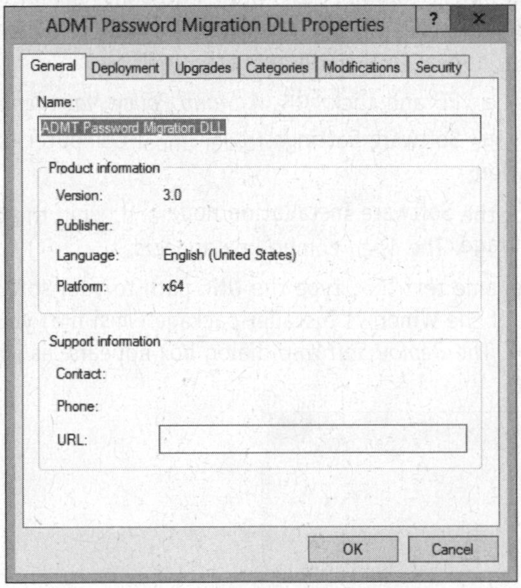

The following list describes the settings available in each tab of a package's Properties sheet:

- **General:** This tab enables you to change the default name of the package. In addition, you can add a Uniform Resource Locator (URL) to point to a support web page. Some packages already contain a URL from the manufacturer of the software.

- **Deployment:** As shown in Figure 18-8, this tab contains all the deployment options discussed previously, including the Deployment Type (Published or Assigned), Deployment Options (Auto-install when the associated document is activated, Uninstall when the application falls out of scope, and Control Panel display selection), and Installation User Interface Options (Basic or Maximum). An Advanced button contains additional deployment information, such as advanced deployment options and diagnostics information.

Figure 18-8

The Deployment tab on a
software installation package's
Properties sheet

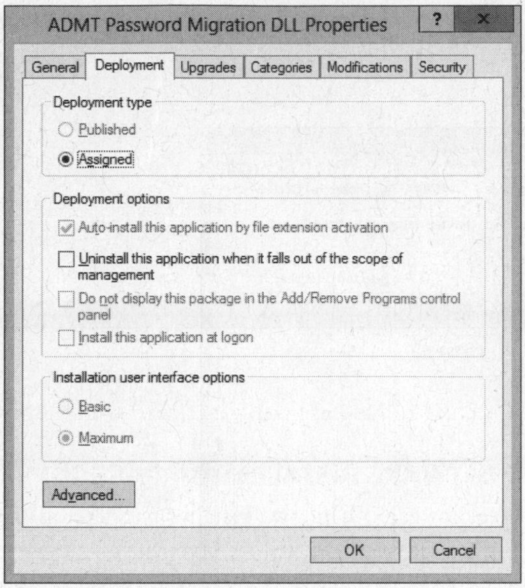

> **TAKE NOTE***
>
> If the package is set to Assigned, the ***Install This Application At Logon*** option is
> available. This option enables the application to be installed immediately, rather than
> advertised on the Start menu. If users have slow links between their workstations and the
> software distribution point, this option should be avoided. Installation can take a lot of
> time when performed using a slow link.

• **Upgrades:** Use this tab, as shown on Figure 18-9, to configure any upgrades that will be
applied to a package. This tab does not appear on .zap package files.

Figure 18-9

The Upgrades tab on a
software installation package's
Properties sheet

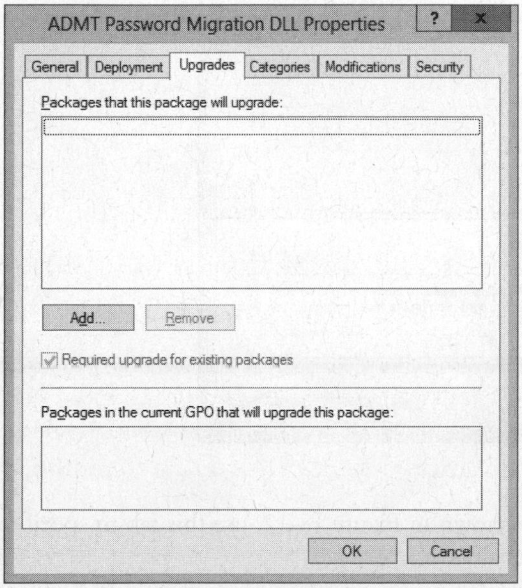

- **Categories:** As shown in Figure 18-10, use this tab to configure software categories in Control Panel.

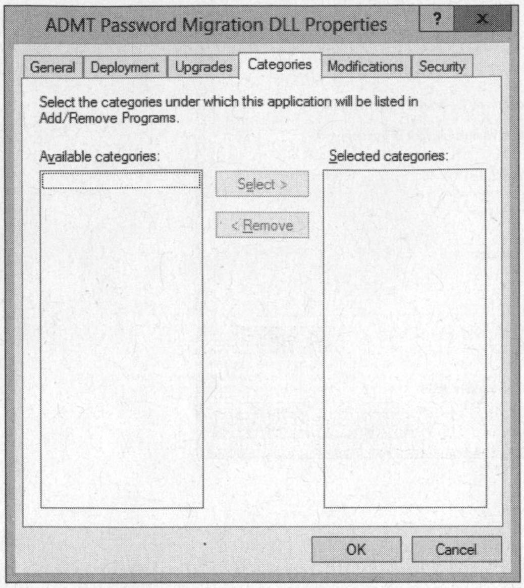

Figure 18-10

The Categories tab on a software installation package's Properties sheet

- **Modifications:** Use this tab, shown in Figure 18-11, to specify the transform (.mst) files or patch (.msp) files that should be applied to the package. You can also modify the order in which systems will apply these files to the package.

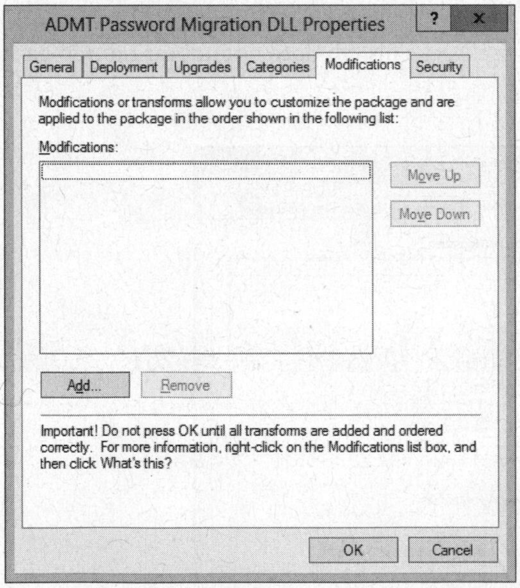

Figure 18-11

The Modifications tab on a software installation package's Properties sheet

WARNING When adding the transform or patch files that you want to apply to an application, be sure that you complete all aspects of this tab before clicking OK. After you select OK, the application is assigned or published immediately. If all the proper configurations have not been made on this tab, you might need to uninstall or upgrade the package to make the proper changes.

- **Security:** As shown in Figure 18-12, use this tab to specify who has permission to install the software using this package.

Figure 18-12

The Security tab on a software installation package's Properties sheet

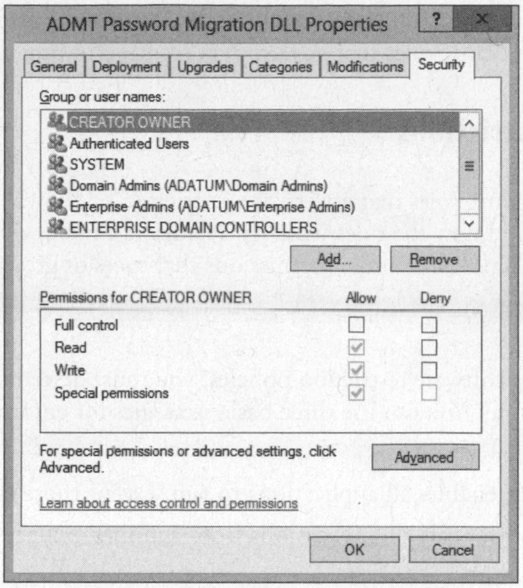

ADMT Password Migration DLL Properties   ?   ×

| General | Deployment | Upgrades | Categories | Modifications | Security |

Group or user names:

- CREATOR OWNER
- Authenticated Users
- SYSTEM
- Domain Admins (ADATUM\Domain Admins)
- Enterprise Admins (ADATUM\Enterprise Admins)
- ENTERPRISE DOMAIN CONTROLLERS

[Add...]   [Remove]

Permissions for CREATOR OWNER   Allow   Deny

Full control	☐	☐
Read	☑	☐
Write	☑	☐
Special permissions	☑	☐

For special permissions or advanced settings, click Advanced.   [Advanced]

Learn about access control and permissions

[OK]   [Cancel]

■ Configuring Software Restriction Policies

↓
THE BOTTOM LINE

The options in the Software Restriction Policies node provide organizations greater control in preventing potentially dangerous applications from running. Software restriction policies are designed to identify software and control its execution. In addition, you can control who is affected by the policies.

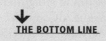

CERTIFICATION READY
Configure Software Restriction Policies.
Objective 6.3

The *Software Restriction Policies* node is found in the *Windows Settings\Security Settings* node of the *User Configuration or the Computer Configuration* node of a Group Policy object. By default, the Software Restriction Policies folder is empty. When you create a new policy, two subfolders appear: Security Levels and Additional Rules, as shown in Figure 18-13. The *Security Levels* folder enables you to define the default behavior from which all rules are created. The criteria for each executable program are defined in the Additional Rules folder.

Figure 18-13

The Software Restriction Policies folder

Group Policy Management Editor   _ □ ×

File   Action   View   Help

▷ Wired Network (IEEE 802.3) Policies
▷ Windows Firewall with Advanced Se
  Network List Manager Policies
▷ Wireless Network (IEEE 802.11) Polic
▷ Public Key Policies
▲ Software Restriction Policies
    Security Levels
    Additional Rules
▷ Network Access Protection
▷ Application Control Policies
▷ IP Security Policies on Active Directe
▷ Advanced Audit Policy Configuratic
▷ Policy-based QoS

Object Type
- Security Levels
- Additional Rules
- Enforcement
- Designated File Types
- Trusted Publishers

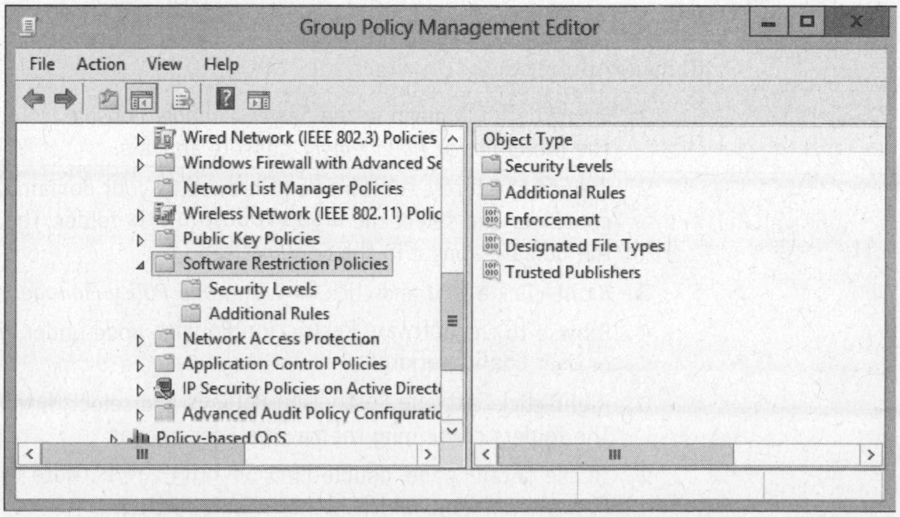

In the following sections, you learn how to set the security level for a software restriction policy and how to define rules that govern the execution of program files.

Enforcing Restrictions

Prior to creating any rules that govern the restriction or allowance of executable files, you should understand how the rules work by default. If a policy does not enforce restrictions, executable files run based on the permissions that users or groups have in the NTFS file system.

When considering software restriction policies, you must determine your approach to enforcing restrictions. You can use three basic strategies for enforcing restrictions, as follows:

- **Unrestricted:** enables all applications to run, except those that are specifically excluded.
- **Disallowed:** prevents all applications from running except those that are specifically allowed.
- **Basic User:** prevents any application from running that requires administrative rights, but enables programs to run that only require resources that are accessible by normal users.

The approach you take depends on the needs of your particular organization. By default, the Software Restriction Policies area has an Unrestricted value in the Default Security Level setting.

For example, you might want to enable only specified applications to run in a high-security environment. In this case, you set the *Default Security Level* to *Disallowed*. By contrast, in a less secure network, you might want to allow all executables to run, unless you have specified otherwise. This option requires you to leave the *Default Security Level* as *Unrestricted*. In this case, you need to create a rule to identify an application before you disable it. You can modify the *Default Security Level* to reflect the *Disallowed* setting. Because the Disallowed setting assumes that all programs will be denied unless a specific rule permits them to run, this setting can cause administrative headaches if not thoroughly tested. You should test all applications you want to run to ensure that they will function properly.

To modify the *Default Security Level* setting to *Disallowed*, use the following procedure.

MODIFY THE DEFAULT SECURITY LEVEL

GET READY. Log on to a server running Windows Server 2012, using an account with domain Administrator privileges.

1. From the Tools menu in the *Server Manager* console, select Group Policy Management. The *Group Policy Management* console appears.

2. Expand the forest container and browse to your domain. Then expand the domain container and select the Group Policy Objects folder. The GPOs that currently exist in the domain appear in the *Contents* tab.

3. Right-click a GPO and click Edit. A *Group Policy Management Editor* window appears.

4. Browse to the Software Restriction Policies node under either Computer Configuration or User Configuration.

5. Right-click Software Restriction Policies and select New Software Restriction Policies. The folders containing the new policies appear.

6. In the details pane, double-click Security Levels. Note the checkmark on the *Unrestricted* icon, which is the default setting.

7. Right-click the Disallowed security level and, from the context menu, select Set As Default. A *Software Restriction Policies* warning message box appears, as shown in Figure 18-14.

Figure 18-14

Setting the Default Security Level of a software restriction policy

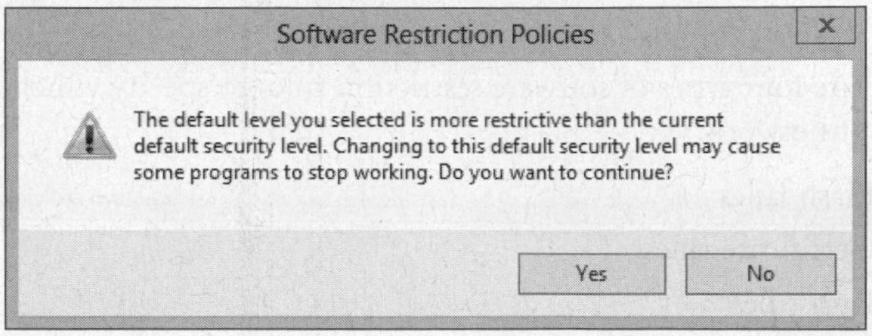

CLOSE the *Group Policy Management Editor* and *Group Policy Management* consoles.

You have now modified the Default Security Level for a software restriction policy.

Configuring Software Restriction Rules

The functionality of software restriction policies depends on the rules that identify software, followed by the rules that govern its usage. When you create a new software restriction policy, the *Additional Rules* subfolder appears. This folder enables you to create rules that specify the conditions under which programs can be executed or denied. These rules can override the Default Security Level setting, when necessary.

You create new rules of your own in the *Additional Rules* folder, using a dialog box like the one shown in Figure 18-15.

Figure 18-15

The New Path Rule dialog box

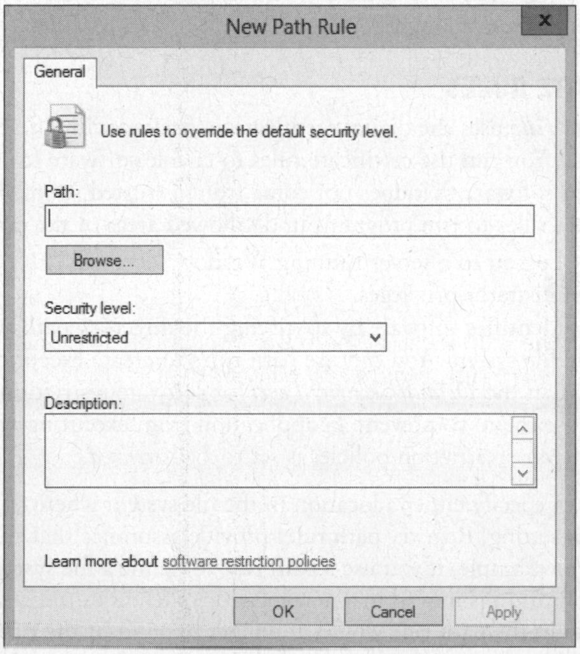

The most common way to implement software restriction policies is through Group Policy objects linked to Active Directory Domain Services containers, so that you can apply their policy settings to several computers simultaneously. However, it is also possible to configure software restriction policies on individual computers by using *Local Security Policy*.

There are four types of software restriction rules to specify which programs can or cannot run on your network:

- Hash rules
- Certificate rules
- Path rules
- Network zone rules

There is also a fifth type of rule—the default rule—which applies when an application does not match any of the other rules you create. To configure the default rule, you select one of the policies in the *Security Levels* folder and click *Set As Default* on its Properties sheet.

The functions of the four rule types are explained in the following sections.

HASH RULES

A *hash* is a series of bytes with a fixed length that uniquely identifies a program or file. A *hash value* is generated by an algorithm that essentially creates a fingerprint of the file, making it nearly impossible for another program to have the same hash. If you create a hash rule and a user attempts to run a program affected by the rule, the system checks the hash value of the executable file and compares with the hash value stored in the software restriction policy. If the two values match, the policy settings will apply. Therefore, creating a *hash rule* for an application executable prevents the application from running if the hash value is not correct. Because the hash value is based on the file itself, you can move the file from one location to another and it will still function. If the executable file is altered in any way, such as if it is modified or replaced by a worm or virus, the hash rule in the software restriction policy prevents the file from running.

CERTIFICATE RULES

A *certificate rule* uses the digital certificate associated with an application to confirm its legitimacy. You can use certificate rules to enable software from a trusted source to run or to prevent software that does not come from a trusted source from running. You can also use certificate rules to run programs in disallowed areas of the operating system.

PATH RULES

A *path rule* identifies software by specifying the directory path where the application is stored in the file system. You can use path rules to create exceptions that enable an application to execute when the *Default Security Level* for software restriction policies is set to *Disallowed* or you can use them to prevent an application from executing when the *Default Security Level* for software restriction policies is set to *Unrestricted*.

Path rules can specify either a location in the file system where application files are located or a registry path setting. Registry path rules provide assurance that the application executables will be found. For example, if you use a path rule to define a file system location for an application, and the application is moved to a new location, such as during a network restructuring, the original path in the path rule would no longer be valid. If the rule specifies that the application should not function, except if it is located in a particular path, the program would not be able to run from its new location. This can cause a significant security breach opportunity if the program references confidential information.

In contrast, if you create a path rule using a registry key location, any change to the location of the application files will not affect the outcome of the rule. When you relocate an application, the registry key that points to the application's files updates automatically.

NETWORK ZONE RULES

Network zone rules apply only to Windows Installer packages that attempt to install from a specified zone, such as a local computer, a local intranet, trusted sites, restricted sites, or the Internet. You can configure this type of rule to enable Windows Installer packages to be installed only if they come from a trusted area of the network. For example, an Internet zone rule can restrict Windows Installer packages from being downloaded and installed from the Internet or other network locations.

USING MULTIPLE RULES

You can define a software restriction policy using multiple rule types to allow and disallow program execution. By using multiple rule types, it is possible to have a variety of security levels. For example, you might want to specify a path rule that prevents programs from running from the \\Server1\Accounting shared folder and a path rule that enables programs to run from the \\Server1\Application shared folder. You can also choose to incorporate certificate rules and hash rules into your policy. When implementing multiple rule types, systems apply the rules in the following order:

1. Hash rules
2. Certificate rules
3. Network zone rules
4. Path rules

When a conflict occurs between rule types, such as between a hash rule and a path rule, the hash rule prevails because it is higher in the order of preference. If a conflict occurs between two rules of the same type and the same identification settings, such as two path rules that identify software from the same directory, the most restrictive setting will apply. In this case, if one of the path rules was set to *Unrestricted* and the other to *Disallowed*, the policy enforces the Disallowed setting.

Configuring Software Restriction Properties

> Within the *Software Restriction Policies* folder, you can configure three specific properties to provide additional settings that apply to all policies when implemented.

These three properties are enforcement, designated file types, and trusted publishers, as described in the following sections.

ENFORCEMENT

As shown in Figure 18-16, Enforcement properties enable you to determine whether the policies apply to all files or whether library files, such as Dynamic Link Library (DLL), are excluded. Excluding DLLs is the default, which is the most practical method of enforcement. For example, if the *Default Security Level* for the policy is set to *Disallowed* and the *Enforcement* properties are set to *All Software Files*, you would need to create a rule that checked every DLL before the program could be allowed or denied. By contrast, excluding DLL files using the default Enforcement property does not require you to define individual rules for each DLL file.

CERTIFICATION READY
Configure rule
enforcement.
Objective 6.3

Figure 18-16

Configuring Enforcement
properties

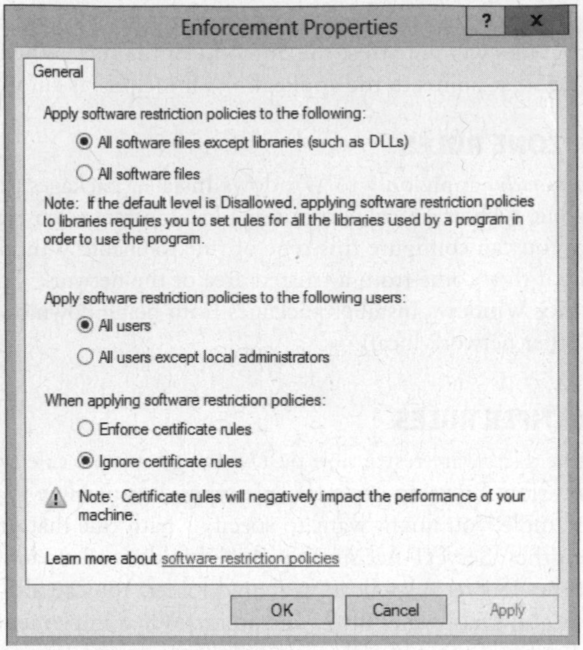

DESIGNATED FILE TYPES

The Designated File Types properties within the Software Restriction Policies folder, as shown in Figure 18-17, specify file types that are executable. File types that are designated as executable or program files are shared by all rules, although you can specify a list for a computer policy that is different from one that is specified for a user policy.

Figure 18-17

Configuring Designated File
Types properties

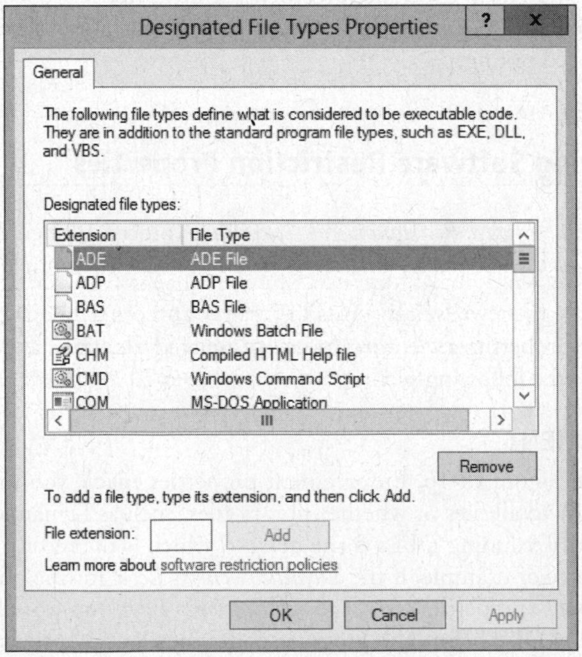

TRUSTED PUBLISHERS

Finally, the Trusted Publishers properties enable you to control how systems handle certificate rules. In the Properties dialog box for Trusted Publishers, as shown in Figure 18-18, the first setting enables you to specify which users are permitted to manage trusted certificate sources. By default, local computer administrators have the right to specify trusted publishers on the local computer and enterprise administrators have the right to specify trusted publishers in an OU. From a security standpoint, in a high-security network, users should not be allowed to determine the sources from which certificates can be obtained.

Figure 18-18

Configuring Trusted Publishers properties

In addition, the Trusted Publisher Properties sheet also lets you verify that a certificate has not been revoked. If a certificate has been revoked, the user should not be permitted access to network resources. You have the option of checking either the *Publisher* or the *Timestamp* of the certificate to determine whether it has been revoked.

> **TAKE NOTE** *
>
> Although software restriction policies can enhance network security, they are not a replacement for firewalls, anti-virus programs, and other standard security measures. Software restriction policies also do not prevent applications from running under the System account. For example, a malicious individual might infect a server with a malicious service that starts under the Local System account, it starts successfully even if there is a software restriction policy configured to restrict it.

Software Restriction Best Practices

> Software restriction policies can be an asset to your organization's security strategy when they are understood and implemented properly. Planning how you want to use software restriction policies is your best defense in preventing problems.

Microsoft has several recommendations that can help you plan and implement software restriction policies, including the following:

- Software restriction policies should be used with standard access control permissions. Combining these two security features enables you to exercise tighter control over program usage.

- The Disallowed Default Security Level should be used cautiously, because all applications are restricted unless explicitly allowed.

- If you accidentally create policies that cause undesirable restrictions on a workstation, reboot the computer in *Safe Mode* to troubleshoot and make changes, because software restriction policies cannot be applied in Safe Mode. Rebooting in Safe Mode is a temporary solution, because the policies remain in effect until they are modified or removed.

- When editing software restriction policies, you should disable them first so that a partially complete policy does not cause undesirable results on a computer. After you complete the policy modifications, you can enable and refresh the policy.

- Creating a separate GPO for software restriction policies enables you to disable or remove them without affecting other policy settings.

- Test all policies before deploying them to the users. Overly restrictive policies can cause problems with files that are required for the operating system to function properly.

■ Using AppLocker

THE BOTTOM LINE

Software restriction policies can be a powerful tool, but they can also require a great deal of administrative overhead. If you elect to disallow all applications except those matching the rules you create, there are a great many programs in Windows Server 2012 that need rules, in addition to the applications you want to install. You must also create the rules manually, which can be an onerous chore.

AppLocker, also known as *application control policies*, is a Windows feature that is essentially an updated version of the concept implemented in software restriction policies. AppLocker also uses rules, which you must manage, but the process of creating the rules is much easier, thanks to a wizard-based interface.

AppLocker is also more flexible than software restriction policies. You can apply AppLocker rules to specific users and groups and also create rules that support all future versions of an application. The primary disadvantage of AppLocker is that you can apply only the policies to computers running Windows 7 and Windows Server 2008 R2 or later.

Understanding Rule Types

The AppLocker settings are located in Group Policy objects in the Computer Configuration\Windows Settings\Security Settings\Application Control Policies\ AppLocker container, as shown in Figure 18-19.

Figure 18-19

The AppLocker container
in a GPO

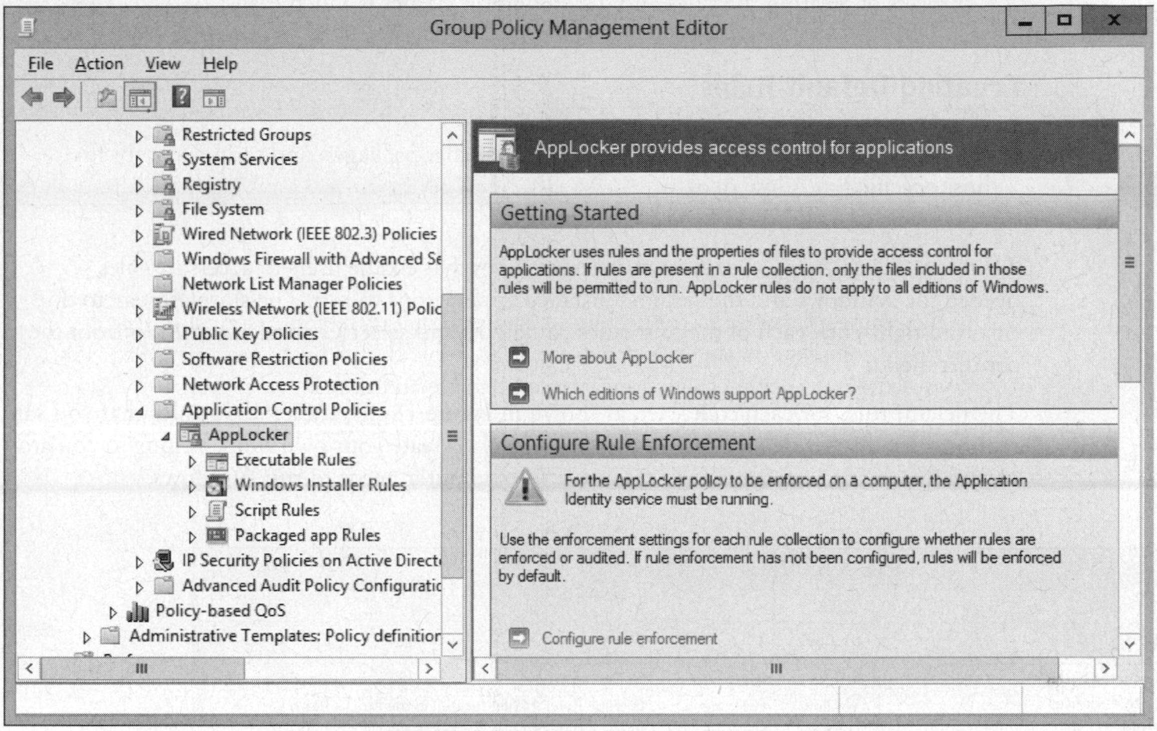

In the AppLocker container, four nodes contain the basic rule types, as follows:

- **Executable Rules:** contains rules that apply to files with .exe and .com extensions.
- **Windows Installer Rules:** contains rules that apply to Windows Installer packages with .msi and .msp extensions.
- **Script Rules:** contains rules that apply to script files with .ps1, .bat, .cmd, .vbs, and .js extensions.
- **Packaged app Rules:** contains rules that apply to applications purchased through the Windows Store.

TAKE NOTE*

You can also configure AppLocker to use DLL rules, which require you to create rules that provide users with access to all the DLLs in an application, as well as the executables. This option, although more secure, can incur a significant performance penalty, because AppLocker must confirm access to each of an application's DLLs before it can load. To configure this option, open the Properties sheet for the AppLocker container, click the Advanced tab, and select the Enable the DLL rule collection checkbox.

Each of the rules you create in each of these containers can allow or block access to specific resources, based on one of the following criteria:

- **Publisher:** identifies code-signed applications by means of a digital signature extracted from an application file. You can also create publisher rules that apply to all future versions of an application.
- **Path:** identifies applications by specifying a file or folder name. The potential vulnerability of this type of rule is that any file can match the rule, as long as it is the correct name or location.

• **File Hash:** identifies applications based on a digital fingerprint that remains valid even when the name or location of the executable file changes. This type of rule functions much like its equivalent in software restriction policies; in AppLocker, however, the process of creating the rules and generating file hashes is much easier.

Creating Default Rules

By default, AppLocker blocks all executables, installer packages, and scripts, except for those specified in Allow rules.

Therefore, to use AppLocker, you must create rules that enable users to access the files needed for Windows and the system's installed applications to run. The simplest way to do this is to right-click each of the four rules containers and select *Create Default Rules* from the context menu.

The default rules for each container, as shown in Figure 18-20, are standard rules that you can replicate, modify, or delete as necessary. You can also create your own rules, as long as you are careful to provide access to all the resources the computer needs to run Windows.

Figure 18-20

The default AppLocker executable rules

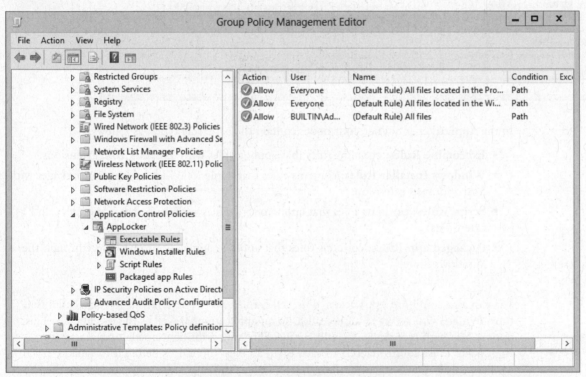

To use AppLocker, Windows Server 2012 requires the Application Identity service to be running. By default, this service uses the manual startup type, so you must start it yourself in the Services console before Windows can apply the AppLocker policies. This behavior is deliberate. With AppLocker, it is relatively easy to inadvertently create a set of rules that omits access to executables or other files that Windows needs to run, thus disabling the operating system. If this should occur, simply restarting the computer causes the operating system to load without the Application Identity service, which prevents AppLocker from loading. Only when you are certain that you have configured your rules properly should you change the startup type for the Application Identity service to automatic.

TAKE NOTE*

Creating Rules Automatically

> The greatest advantage of AppLocker over software restriction policies is the capability to create rules automatically.

CERTIFICATION READY
Configure AppLocker
rules.
Objective 6.3

When you right-click one of the three rules containers and select *Create Rules Automatically* from the context menu, an *Automatically Generate Rules Wizard* appears, as shown in Figure 18-21.

Figure 18-21

The Automatically Generate
Executable Rules Wizard

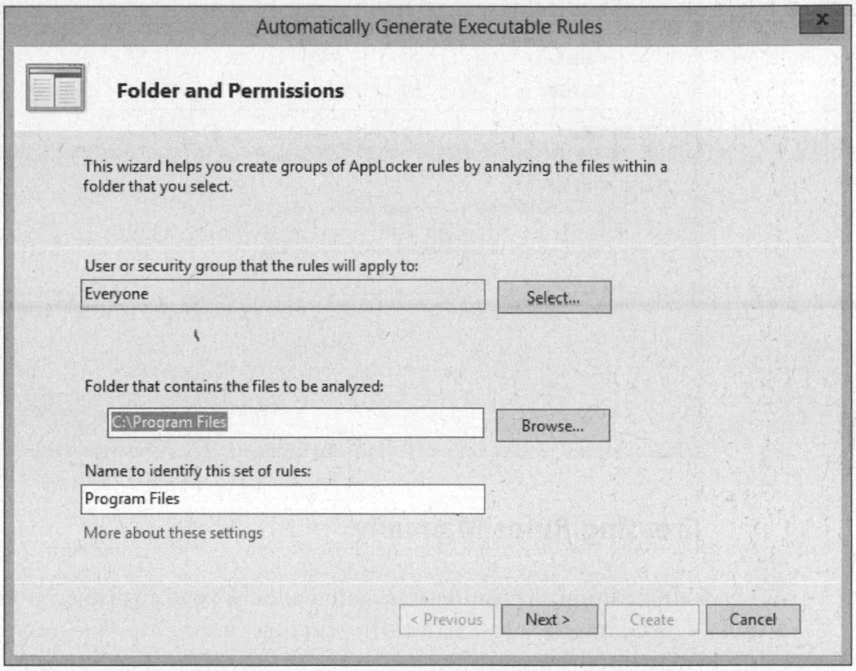

After specifying the folder to be analyzed and the users or groups to which the rules should apply, a *Rule Preferences* page appears, as shown in Figure 18-22, enabling you to specify the types of rules you want to create.

Figure 18-22

The Rule Preferences page of
the Automatically Generate
Executable Rules Wizard

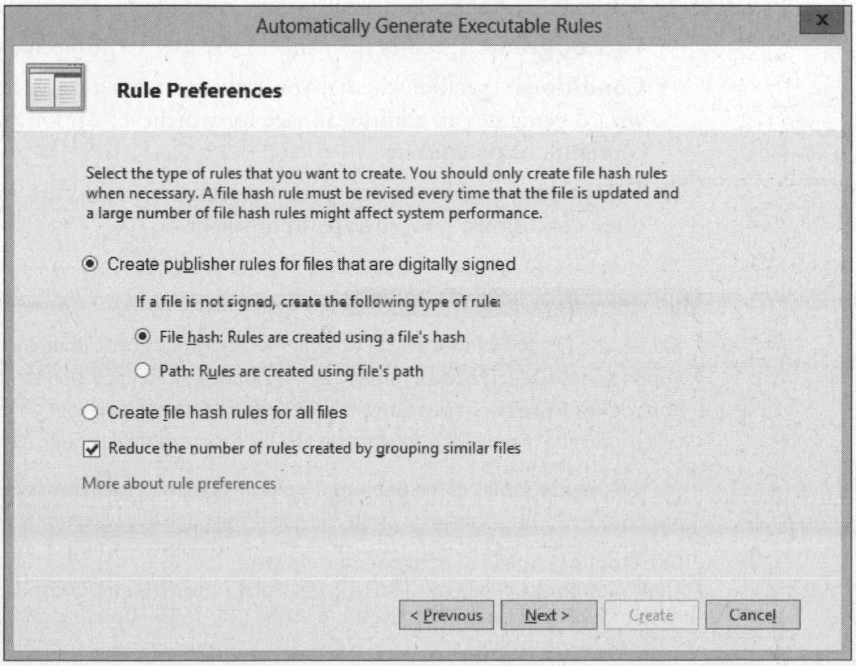

The wizard then displays a summary of its results in the *Review Rules* page, as shown in Figure 18-23, and adds the rules to the container.

Figure 18-23

The Review Rules page of the Automatically Generate Executable Rules Wizard

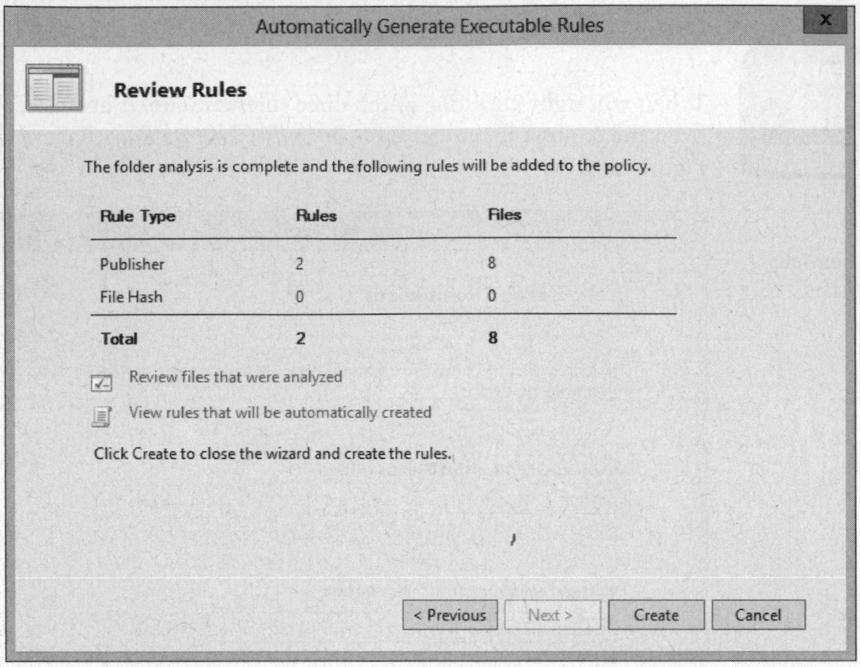

Creating Rules Manually

In addition to creating rules automatically, you can also do it manually, using a wizard-based interface you activate by selecting *Create New Rule* from the context menu for one of the three rule containers.

The wizard prompts you for the following information:

- **Action:** specifies whether you want to allow or deny the user or group access to the resource. In AppLocker, explicit deny rules always override allow rules.
- **User or group:** specifies the name of the user or group to which the policy should apply.
- **Conditions:** specifies whether you want to create a publisher, path, or file hash rule. The wizard generates an additional page for whichever option you select, enabling you to configure its parameters.
- **Exceptions:** enables you to specify exceptions to the rule you create, using any of the three conditions: publisher, path, or file hash.

USING WINDOWS POWERSHELL

You can use Windows PowerShell to create a new AppLocker policy, using a combination of the `Get-AppLockerFileInformation` and `New-AppLockerPolicy` cmdlets. The `Get-AppLockerFileInformation` cmdlet returns the information about a file (or files) needed to create the policy, including the publisher information, the file hash, and the file path, as shown in Figure 18-24.

You can pipe the results of the `Get-AppLockerFileInformation` cmdlet directly to the `New-AppLockerPolicy` cmdlet to create the policy, using the following syntax:

```
Get-AppLockerFileInformation <path>
|New-AppLockerPolicy -RuleType Publisher|Hash|Path
-User <security principal>
```

Figure 18-24

Output of the Get-
AppLockerFileInformation
cmdlet

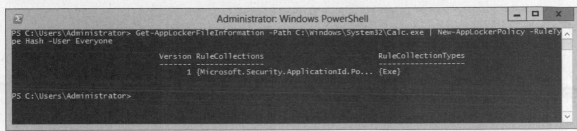

For example, to create a new AppLocker policy for the Windows Calculator application, you can use the following command:

```
Get-AppLockerFileInformation C:\Windows\System32\Calc.exe
|New-AppLockerPolicy -RuleType Hash
 User Everyone
```

SKILL SUMMARY

IN THIS LESSON, YOU LEARNED:

- You can use Group Policy to deploy new software on your network and remove or repair software originally deployed by a GPO from your network.

- The Windows Installer service supports three types of package files: .msi files for standard software installation, .mst files for customized software installation, and .msp files for patching .msi files at the time of deployment.

- You must create a shared folder, called a *software distribution point*, to store application installation and package files to be deployed by using Group Policy.

- Software to be deployed using Group Policy can either be Assigned or Published. Assigning software using the User Configuration node of a Group Policy enables the application to be installed when the user accesses the program using the Start menu or an associated file. Publishing an application enables the application to be available through Control Panel.

- Software restriction policies enable the software's executable code to be identified and either allowed or disallowed on the network.

- The three Default Security Levels within software restriction policies are Unrestricted, which means all applications function based on user permissions; Disallowed, which means all applications are denied execution regardless of the user permissions; and Basic User, which enables only executables to be run that can be run by normal users

- Four rule types can be defined within a software restriction policy. They include, in order of precedence, hash, certificate, network zone, and path rules. The security level set on a specific rule supersedes the Default Security Level of the policy.

- Software restriction policies are Group Policy settings that enable you to specify the programs that are allowed to run on workstations by creating rules of various types.

- AppLocker enables you to create application restriction rules easily.

■ Knowledge Assessment

Multiple Choice

Select one or more correct answers for each of the following questions.

1. Which of the following rule types apply only to Windows Installer packages?
   a. Hash rules
   b. Certificate rules
   c. Internet zone rules
   d. Path rules

2. Which file type is used by Windows Installer?
   a. .inf
   b. .bat
   c. .msf
   d. .msi file

3. Which of the following is not one of the Default Security Levels that can be used with a software restriction policy?
   a. Basic User
   b. Unrestricted
   c. Restricted
   d. Disallowed

4. As part of your efforts to deploy all new applications using Group Policy, you discover that several of the applications you wish to deploy do not include the necessary installer files. What can you use to deploy these applications?
   a. Software restriction policies
   b. .msi files
   c. .mdb files
   d. .zap files

5. Which of the following describes the mathematical equation that creates a digital "fingerprint" of a particular file?
   a. Hash rule
   b. Hash algorithm
   c. Software restriction policy
   d. Path rule

6. Which of the following rules will allow or disallow a script or a Windows Installer file to run on the basis of how the file has been signed?
   a. Path rule
   b. Hash rule
   c. Network zone rule
   d. Certificate rule

7. You want to deploy several software applications using Group Policy, such that the applications can be manually installed by the users from the Add/Remove Programs applet in their local Control Panel. Which installation option should you select?
   a. Assign
   b. Disallowed
   c. Publish
   d. Unrestricted

8. You have assigned several applications using GPOs. Users have complained that there is a delay when they double-click on the application icon, which you know is the result of the application being installed in the background. What option can you use to pre-install assigned applications when users log on or power on their computers?
   a. Uninstall when the application falls out of scope
   b. Install This Application At Logon
   c. Advanced Installation Mode
   d. Path rule

9. Which of the following Default Security Levels in Software Restriction Policies will disallow any executable from running that has not been explicitly enabled by the Active Directory administrator?
   a. Basic User
   b. Restricted
   c. Disallowed
   d. Power User

Best Answer

Choose the letter that corresponds to the best answer. More than one answer choice may achieve the goal. Select the BEST answer.

1. When installing software using Group Policy, what file or files does an administrator use?
   a. Windows Installer package files, or .msi files. Modifications to the package files are transform files, or .mst files. Further, patch files are designated as .msp files.
   b. Any approved software from Microsoft, including the Certified for Windows Server 2012 logo on the packaging.
   c. Windows Installer package files, or .mst files. Modifications to the package files are instruction files, or .msi files.
   d. Windows Installer packages that contain all the information about the software.

2. You want to deploy software using Group Policy. What is necessary before deciding to Assign the software to your user accounts?
   a. You must create a Group Policy object (GPO) or modify an existing GPO. As part of configuring the GPO, you decide whether to Assign or Publish the application.
   b. You create the GPO. Whether to Assign or Publish is decided elsewhere.
   c. You must create a distribution share, also called a software distribution point. Then create the GPO, specifying how to deploy the application.
   d. You decide whether to Assign or Publish the application. If using .zap files, you might need user intervention.

3. If a software package is set as Assigned, the option to Install This Application At Logon is available. This option enables the application to be installed immediately, rather than advertised on the Start menu. However, when should you avoid this method?
   a. If users have slow links between their workstations and the software distribution point
   b. If computers are already under a very strict security policy and computer configuration
   c. If users often take their computer home
   d. If computers require administrative logon for each new package

4. What does file-activated installation mean, and where is it utilized?
   a. When a user opens a file associated with an application that does not currently exist on the user's workstation, the application is installed. It is used for both Publishing and Assigning an application to a user.

b. When a user logs on and the local computer has a file associated with an application that does not exist, the application is installed. It is used when Assigning an application to a user.

c. When a user opens a file associated with an application that does not currently exist on the user's workstation, the application is installed. It is used when Assigning an application to a user.

d. When a user logs on and the local computer has a file associated with an application that does not exist, the application is installed. It is used when Publishing an application to a user.

5. What is the most common way to implement software restriction policies?

a. By configuring software restriction policies on individual computers by using Local Security Policy

b. Through Active Directory Users and Computers

c. Through GPOs linked to Active Directory Domain Services (AD DS) containers, so that you can apply their policy settings to several computers simultaneously

d. By using AppLocker, provided you apply to a computer running Windows 7 and Windows Server 2008 R2 or later

Build a List

1. Order the steps to configure software installation defaults.

a. From the Tools menu of the Server Manager console, select Group Policy Management. The Group Policy Management console appears.

b. Right-click the Software Installation node and, from the context menu, select Properties. The Software Installation Properties sheet appears.

c. Browse to the Software Settings folder under Computer Configuration or User Configuration.

d. Expand the forest container and browse to your domain. Then expand the domain container and select the Group Policy Objects folder. The GPOs that currently exist in the domain appear in the Contents tab.

e. Right-click a GPO and click Edit. A Group Policy Management Editor window appears.

f. Select one of the New Packages options (Display the Deploy Software Dialog Box, Publish, Assign, or Advanced).

g. Select one of the Installation User Interface Options (Basic or Maximum).

h. Click the Categories tab and then click Add. Type the name of the application category to be used for the domain.

2. Order the steps to create a new software installation package.

a. Browse to the Software Settings folder under Computer Configuration or User Configuration.

b. From the Tools menu in the Server Manager console, select Group Policy Management. The Group Policy Management console appears.

c. Expand the forest container and browse to your domain. Then expand the domain container and select the Group Policy Objects folder. The GPOs that currently exist in the domain appear in the Contents tab.

d. Right-click the Software Installation node and, from the context menu, select New > Package. The Open combo box appears.

e. Right-click a GPO and click Edit. A Group Policy Management Editor window appears.

f. In the filename text box, type the UNC path to your software distribution point and the name of the Windows Installer package (.msi file) you want to deploy, and then click Open. The Deploy Software dialog box appears.

g. Select from the following options: Published, Assigned, or Advanced.

3. With regards to enforcing software restriction policies, order the steps to modify the default security level setting to Disallowed.
   a. Expand the forest container and browse to your domain. Then expand the domain container and select the Group Policy Objects folder. The GPOs that currently exist in the domain appear in the Contents tab.
   b. From the Tools menu in the Server Manager console, select Group Policy Management.
   c. Right-click a GPO and click Edit. A Group Policy Management Editor window appears.
   d. Right-click Software Restriction Policies and select New Software Restriction Policies. In the details pane, double-click Security Levels. Note the checkmark on the Unrestricted icon, which is the default setting.
   e. Browse to the Software Restriction Policies node under either Computer Configuration or User Configuration.
   f. Right-click the Disallowed security level and, from the context menu, select Set As Default. A Software Restriction Policies warning message box appears. Close the Group Policy Management Editor and Group Policy Management consoles.

Business Case Scenarios

Scenario 18-1: Planning Group Policy Software Deployments

Your company, a healthcare organization, is currently working toward compliance with new government standards on patient confidentiality. Your IT department has decided that using software restriction policies with standard user access permissions will help to fulfill the necessary security requirements. You are preparing an implementation plan that is based on user needs and security requirements. Users should not be able to access any programs with the exception of those that are pertinent to their jobs. In addition, the user needs within the organization are as follows:

- Users only need access to e-mail and a patient database.
- The patient database has its own built-in security access system that is configured for each user based on the user's needs within the program.
- All user accounts are located in containers based on the user's office location.

In addition, the following points should be considered in your implementation plan:

- Software restriction policy settings should not affect settings that are already in place within existing GPOs. If problems arise with software restriction policies, they should be easy to rectify, without affecting other security areas.
- Administrator accounts should not be affected by software restrictions.
- Other applications should not be affected by any of the restrictions.

List the key points that should be part of your implementation plan based on the information provided here.

Scenario 18-2: Using AppLocker

Sophie is planning on using AppLocker to control access to applications on a new network she has constructed for the Research and Development department at a major aerospace firm. The software developers in the department have recently deployed a new application called Virtual Wind Tunnel, which is based on government project research and is therefore classified. All of the full-time personnel have sufficient clearance to use the application, but the interns in the department do not. Sophie has placed the user accounts for everyone in the department into a security group called ResDev. The interns are also members of a group called RDint.

How can Sophie use AppLocker to provide everyone in the department with access to the Virtual Wind Tunnel application without changing the group memberships and without having to apply policies to individual users?

Configuring Windows Firewall

70-410 EXAM OBJECTIVE

Objective 6.4 – Configure Windows Firewall. This objective may include but is not limited to: Configure rules for multiple profiles using Group Policy; configure connection security rules; configure Windows Firewall to allow or deny applications, scopes, ports, and users; configure authenticated firewall exceptions; import and export settings.

LESSON HEADING	EXAM OBJECTIVE
Building a Firewall	
Understanding Windows Firewall Settings	
Working with Windows Firewall	
Using the Windows Firewall Control Panel	
Customizing Settings	
Allowing Applications	Configure authenticated firewall exceptions
Using the Windows Firewall with Advanced Security Console	
Configuring Profile Settings	
Creating Rules	Configure Windows Firewall to allow or deny applications, scopes, ports, and users
Importing and Exporting Rules	Import and export settings
Creating Rules Using Group Policy	Configure rules for multiple profiles using Group Policy
Using Filters	
Creating Connection Security Rules	Configure connection security rules

KEY TERMS

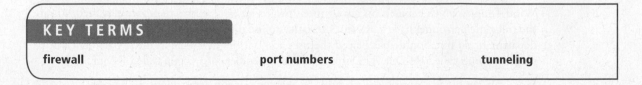

firewall	port numbers	tunneling

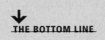

■ Building a Firewall

You may have locked the door to the computer center in which the servers are located, but the computers are still connected to the network. A network is another type of door, or rather a series of doors, which can allow data out or allow it in. To provide services to your users, some of the doors must be open at least some of the time, but server administrators must make sure that only the right doors are left open.

A *firewall* is a software program that protects a computer or a network by allowing certain types of network traffic in and out of the system while blocking others. A firewall is essentially a series of filters that examine the contents of packets and the traffic patterns to and from the network to determine which packets they should allow to pass through the filter.

Some of the hazards that firewalls can protect against are as follows:

- Network scanner applications that probe systems for unguarded ports, which are essentially unlocked doors that attackers can use to gain access to the system.

- Trojan horse applications that open a connection to a computer on the Internet, enabling an attacker on the outside to run programs or store data on the system.

- Attackers that obtain passwords by illicit means, such as social engineering, and then use remote access technologies to log on to a computer from another location and compromise its data and programming.

- Denial of service attacks that use authorized access points to bombard a system with traffic, preventing legitimate traffic from reaching the computer.

The object of a firewall is to permit all the traffic in and out that legitimate users need to perform their assigned tasks, and block everything else. When you work with firewalls, you are not concerned with subjects such as authentication and authorization. These are mechanisms that control who is able to get through the server's open doors. The firewall is all about which doors are left open, and which doors are shut tight.

Understanding Windows Firewall Settings

Windows Server 2012 includes a firewall program called *Windows Firewall*, which is activated by default on all systems.

By default, Windows Firewall blocks most network traffic from entering the computer. Firewalls examine the contents of each packet entering and leaving the computer and comparing the information they find to a series of rules, which specify which packets are allowed to pass through the firewall and which are blocked.

The TCP/IP (Transmission Control Protocol/Internet Protocol) protocols that Windows systems use to communicate function by packaging application data using a series of layered protocols that define where the data comes from and where it is going. The three most important criteria that firewalls can use in their rules are as follows:

- **IP addresses:** identify specific hosts on the network. You can use IP addresses to configure a firewall to allow only traffic from specific computers or networks in and out.

- **Protocol numbers:** specify whether the packet contains TCP or UDP (User Datagram Protocol) traffic. You can filter protocol numbers to block packets containing certain types of traffic. Windows computers typically use UDP for brief message exchanges, such as DNS (Domain Name System) and DHCP (Dynamic Host Configuration Protocol) transactions. TCP packets usually carry larger amounts of data, such as the files exchanged by web, file, and print servers.

- *Port numbers*: identify specific applications running on the computer. The most common firewall rules use port numbers to specify the types of application traffic the computer is allowed to send and receive. For example, a web server usually receives its incoming packets to port number 80. Unless the firewall has a rule opening port 80 to incoming traffic, the web server cannot function in its default configuration.

Firewall rules can function in two ways:

- Admit all traffic, except that which conforms to the applied rules
- Block all traffic, except that which conforms to the applied rules

Generally speaking, blocking all traffic by default is the more secure arrangement. From the server administrator's standpoint, you start with a completely blocked system, and then test your applications. When an application fails to function properly because network access is blocked, you create a rule that opens up the ports the application needs to communicate.

This is the method that Windows Firewall uses by default for incoming network traffic. There are default rules preconfigured into the firewall that are designed to admit the traffic used by standard Windows networking functions, such as file and printer sharing. For outgoing network traffic, Windows Firewall uses the other method, allowing all traffic to pass the firewall except that which conforms to a rule.

Working with Windows Firewall

Windows Firewall is a single program with one set of rules, but there are two distinct interfaces you can use to manage and monitor it.

The Windows Firewall control panel provides a simplified interface that enables you to avoid the details of rules and port numbers. If you just want to turn the firewall on or off (typically for testing or troubleshooting purposes) or work with the firewall settings for a specific Windows role or feature, you can do so simply using the Control Panel. For full access to firewall rules and more sophisticated functions, you must use the Windows Firewall with Advanced Security console, as discussed later in this lesson.

In many cases, you never need to work directly with Windows Firewall. Many of the roles and features included in Windows Server 2012 automatically open the appropriate firewall ports when you install them. In other situations, the system warns you of firewall issues.

For example, the first time you open Windows Explorer and try to access the network, a warning appears, as shown in Figure 19-1, informing you that Network Discovery and File Sharing are turned off, which prevents you from browsing the network.

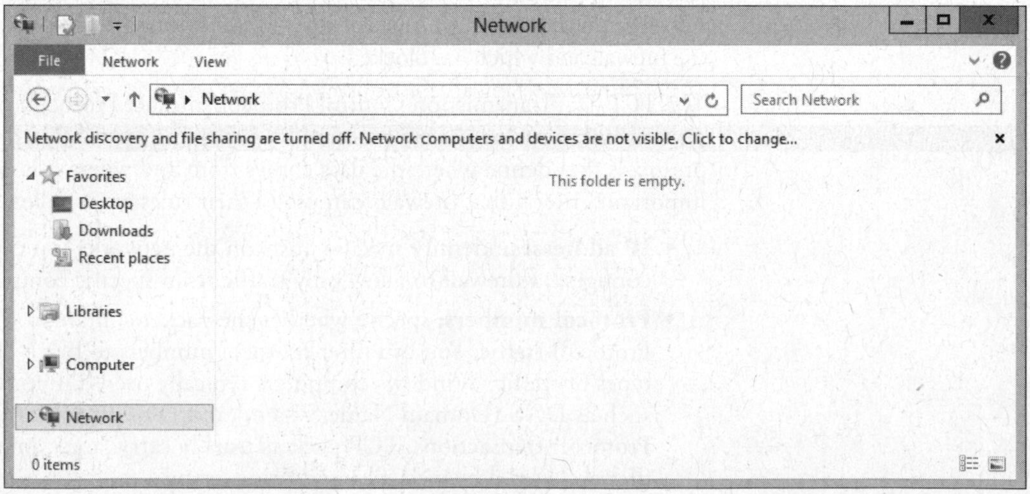

Figure 19-1

Windows Explorer with Network Discovery and File Sharing turned off

Network Discovery is nothing more than a set of firewall rules that regulate the ports Windows uses for network browsing, specifically ports 137, 138, 1900, 2869, 3702, 5355, 5357, and 5358. By default, Windows Server 2012 disables the inbound rules associated with these ports, so the ports are closed, blocking all traffic through them. When you click the warning banner and choose *Turn on network discovery and file sharing* from the context menu, you are in effect activating these firewall rules, thereby opening the ports associated with them.

In addition to the menu command accessible through the warning banner, you can also control the Network Discovery and File Sharing rules in other ways. The Network and Sharing Center control panel, through its Advanced Sharing Settings page, provides options that you can use to turn Network Discovery on and off, as shown in Figure 19-2, as well as File Sharing and other basic networking functions.

Figure 19-2

The Advanced Sharing Setting page of the Network and Sharing Center control panel

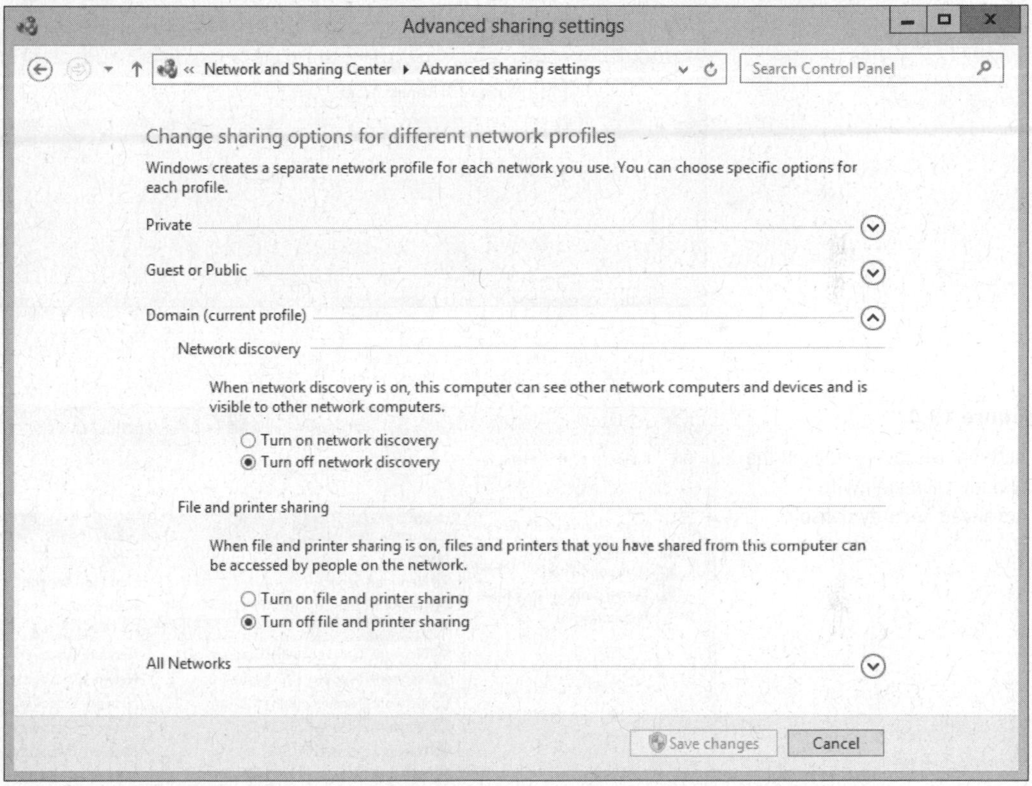

The Windows Firewall control panel has an *Allow an app or feature through Windows Firewall* link, which opens the *Allowed apps* dialog box, as shown in Figure 19-3. The *Network Discovery* check box on this dialog box enables you to control the same set of rules as the Network Discovery control in the Network and Sharing Center.

Finally, you can access the individual Network Discovery rules directly, by using the *Windows Firewall with Advanced Security* console. When you select the *Inbound Rules* node and scroll down in the list, you see nine different Network Discovery rules, as shown in Figure 19-4.

Figure 19-3

The Network Discovery application in the Allowed apps dialog box

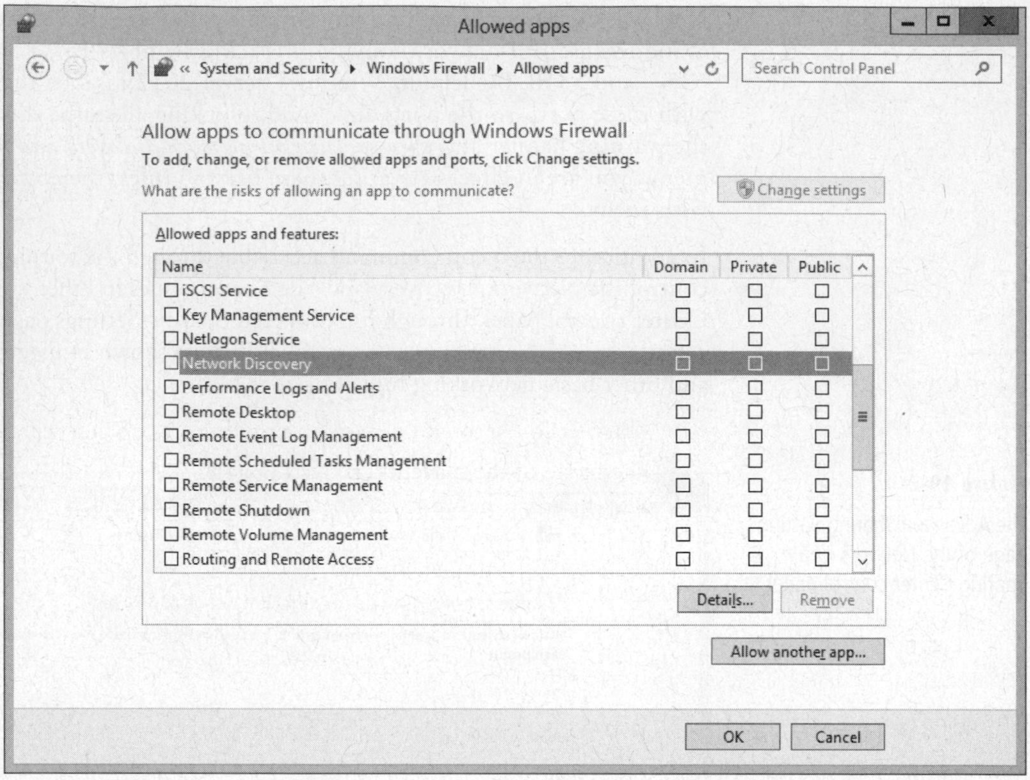

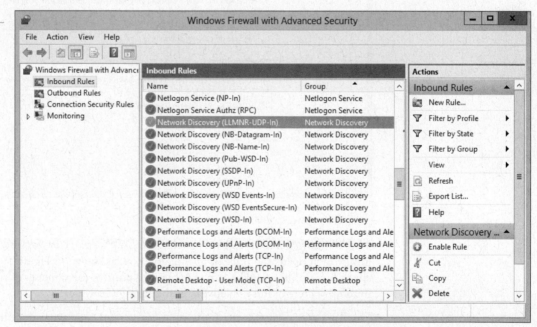

Figure 19-4

Network Discovery rules in the Windows Firewall with Advanced Security console

As you can see by examining the rules in the console, Network Discovery is a complex Windows function that would be difficult to control if you had to determine by trial and error which ports it uses. Therefore, Windows Firewall includes a large collection of rules that regulate the ports that the applications and services included with the operating system need to operate.

Using the Windows Firewall Control Panel

↓
THE BOTTOM LINE

The Windows Firewall control panel provides the easiest and safest access to the firewall controls. These controls are usually sufficient for most server administrators, unless the system has special requirements or you work with custom server applications.

When you open the *Windows Firewall* window from the *Control Panel*, as shown in Figure 19-5, you see the following information:

- Whether the computer is connected to a domain, private, or public network
- Whether the Windows Firewall service is currently turned on or off
- Whether inbound and outbound connections are blocked
- The name of the currently active network
- Whether users are notified when a program is blocked

Figure 19-5

The Windows Firewall control panel window

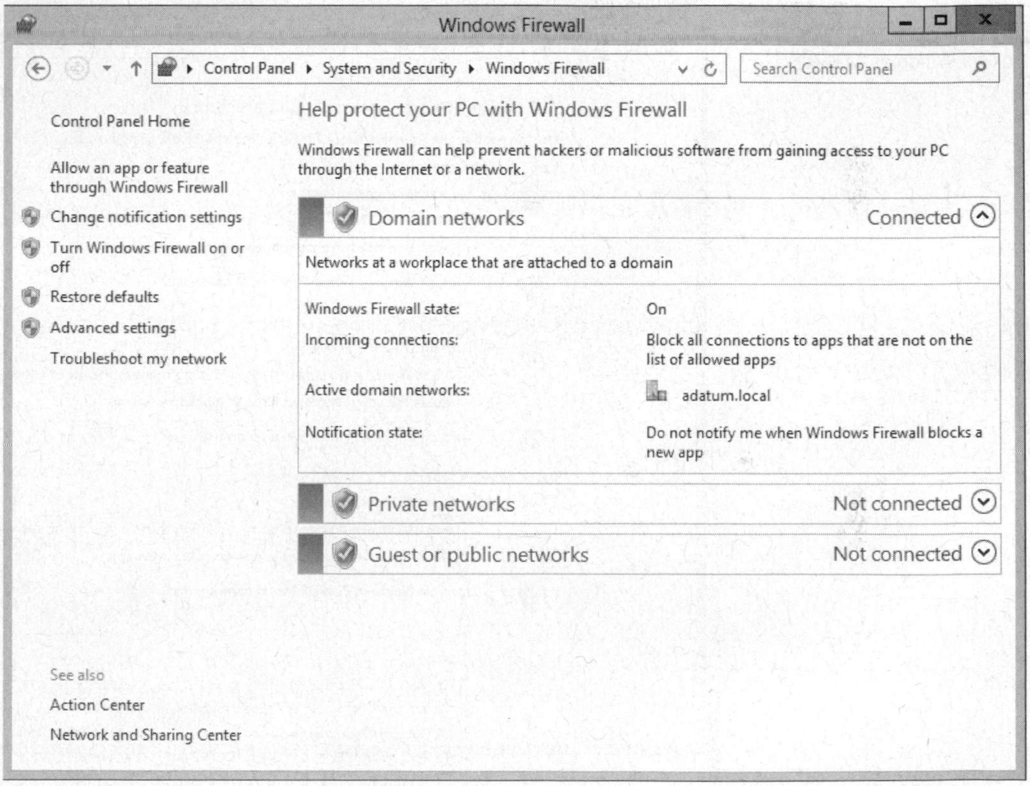

On the left side of the window is a series of links, which provide the following functions:

- **Allow an app or feature through Windows Firewall:** displays the Allowed apps dialog box, in which you can select the applications that can send traffic through the firewall.
- **Change notification settings:** displays the Customize settings dialog box, in which you can adjust the notification settings for each of the three profiles.
- **Turn Windows Firewall on or off:** displays the Customize settings dialog box, in which you can toggle the state of the firewall in each of the three profiles.
- **Restore defaults:** returns all firewall settings to their installation defaults.
- **Advanced settings:** launches the Windows Firewall with Advanced Security console.
- **Troubleshoot my network:** launches the Network and Internet troubleshooter.

Customizing Settings

Several of the links on the Windows Firewall window point to the same place: a Customize Settings dialog box that contains controls for some of the most basic firewall functions.

The Customize Settings dialog box, as shown in Figure 19-6, is broken into three areas, corresponding to the three profiles on a Windows computer. Windows Firewall uses these profiles to represent the type of network to which the server is connected, as follows:

- **Public:** is intended for servers that are accessible to unauthenticated or temporary users, such as computers in an open lab or kiosk.
- **Private:** is intended for a server on an internal network that is not accessible by unauthorized users.
- **Domain:** applies to servers that are members of an Active Directory Domain Services domain, in which all users are identified and authenticated.

Figure 19-6

The Customize Settings dialog box for Windows Firewall

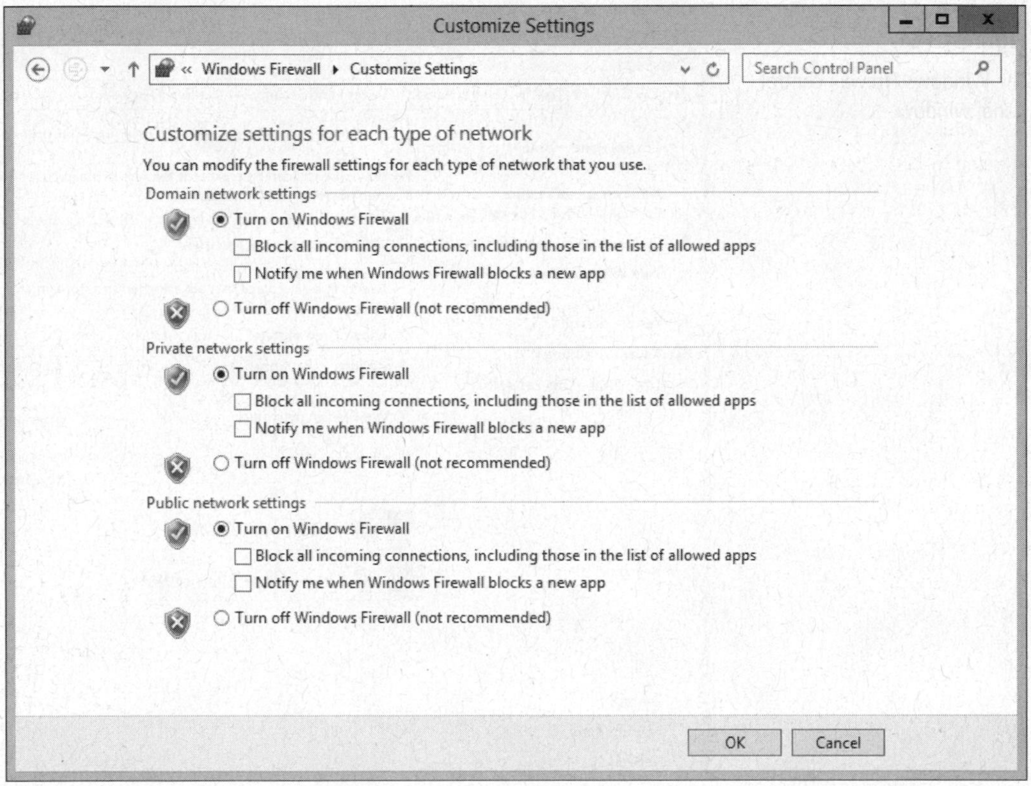

In Windows Firewall, the three profiles are separate sets of rules that apply only to computers connected to the designated network type. You can control the environment for each type of network by configuring separate rules and settings for each profile.

The Customize Settings dialog box has the following controls for each of the three network profiles:

- **Turn on/off Windows Firewall:** toggles the Windows Firewall on and off for the selected profile.
- **Block all incoming connections, including those in the list of allowed apps:** enables you to increase the security of your system by blocking all unsolicited attempts to connect to your computer.
- **Notify me when Windows Firewall blocks a new app:** causes the system to notify the user when an application's attempt to send traffic through the firewall fails.

TAKE NOTE*

Blocking incoming connections does not prevent users from performing common networking tasks, such as accessing websites and sending or receiving e-mails. These activities are not unsolicited connection attempts; they begin with the client contacting the server. When the firewall detects the outgoing traffic from a web browser to a web server on the Internet, for example, it knows that it should admit the incoming response from the server.

Allowing Applications

Sometimes, administrators might be required to modify the firewall settings in other ways, typically because a specific application requires access to a port not anticipated by the firewall's default rules.

CERTIFICATION READY
Configure authenticated firewall exceptions.
Objective 6.4

To do this, you can use the Allowed Apps dialog box in the Windows Firewall control panel, as shown in Figure 19-7.

Figure 19-7

The Allowed Apps dialog box for Windows Firewall

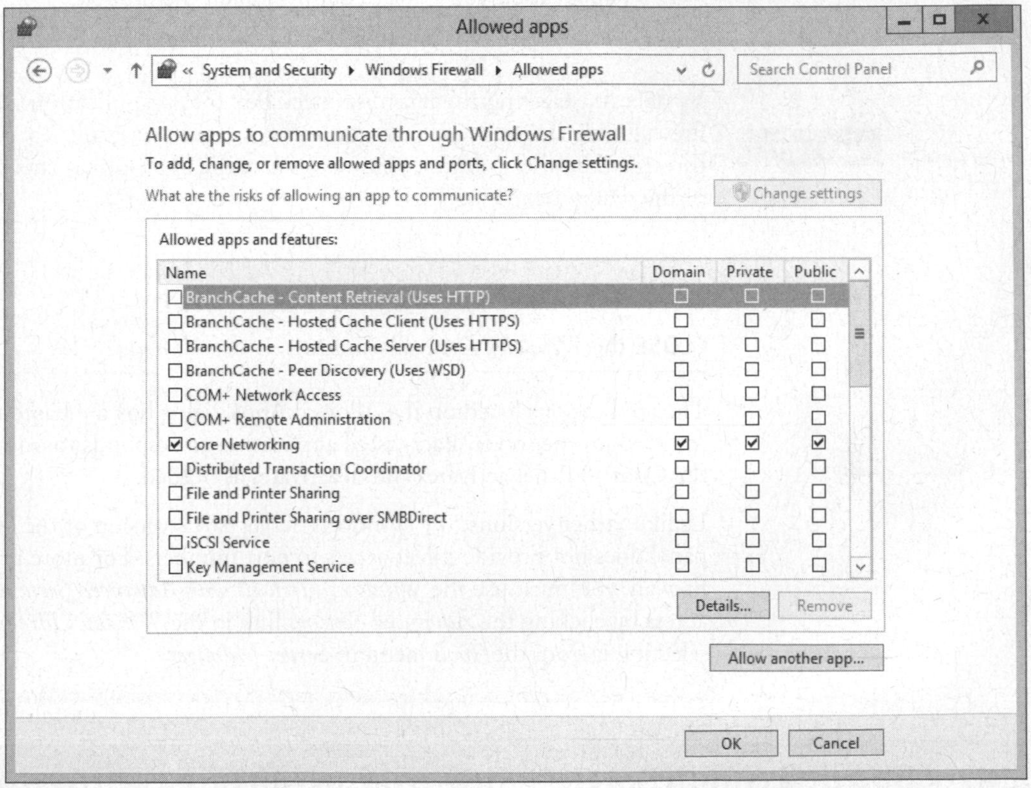

Opening a port in a server's firewall is an inherently dangerous activity. The more open doors you put in a wall, the more opportunities that intruders can exploit to get in. Windows Firewall provides two basic methods for opening a hole in your firewall: opening a port and allowing an application. Both are risky, but the latter of the two is less so. This is because when you open a port by creating a rule in the Windows Firewall with Advanced Security console, the port stays open permanently. When you allow an application through the firewall using the Control Panel, the specified port is open only while the program is running. When you terminate the program, the firewall closes the port.

TAKE NOTE*

Previous versions of Windows refer to allowed applications as *exceptions*, meaning that they are exceptions to the general firewall rules closing off all the computer's ports against intrusion.

To allow an application through the firewall by using Control Panel, use the following procedure.

➔ ALLOW AN APPLICATION

GET READY. Log on to a server running Windows Server 2012, using an account with domain administrator privileges.

1. In the *Server Manager* console, open the Control Panel and click System and Security > Windows Firewall. The *Windows Firewall* window appears.
2. Click Allow an app or feature through Windows Firewall. The *Allowed Apps* dialog box appears.
3. Scroll down in the Allowed apps and features list and select the check box for the application you want to allow through the firewall.

TAKE NOTE*

By default, selecting the leftmost check box for an application allows it through the firewall only in the profile the computer is currently using. To allow the application through the other profiles, you must select the appropriate check boxes on the right side of the dialog box.

4. Click OK to close the *Allowed Apps* dialog box.

CLOSE the *Windows Firewall* window.

The applications listed on the Allowed Apps dialog box are based on the roles and features installed on the server. Each listed application corresponds to one or more firewall rules, which the Control Panel activates and deactivates as needed.

Unlike earlier versions, the Windows Server 2012 version of the Windows Firewall control panel does not provide direct access to port numbers. For more precise control over the firewall, you must use the *Windows Firewall with Advanced Security* console, which you can access by clicking the *Advanced Settings* link in the *Windows Firewall* control panel, or by selecting it from the *Tools* menu in *Server Manager*.

■ Using the Windows Firewall with Advanced Security Console

↓ THE BOTTOM LINE

The Windows Firewall control panel is designed to enable administrators and advanced users to manage basic firewall settings. For full access to the Windows Firewall configuration settings, you must use the *Windows Firewall With Advanced Security* snap-in for the *Microsoft Management* console.

To open the console, open *Server Manager* and, from the *Tools* menu, select *Windows Firewall With Advanced Security*. The *Windows Firewall with Advanced Security* console appears, as shown in Figure 19-8.

Figure 19-8

The *Windows Firewall with Advanced Security* console

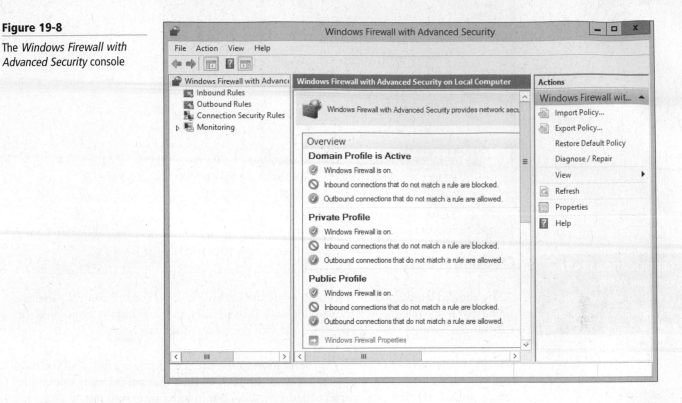

Configuring Profile Settings

At the top of the Windows Firewall With Advanced Security console's middle pane, in the Overview section, are status displays for the computer's three network location profiles. If you connect the computer to a different network (which is admittedly not likely with a server), Windows Firewall can load a different profile and a different set of rules.

The default Windows Firewall configuration calls for the same basic settings for all three profiles, as follows:

- The firewall is turned on.
- Incoming traffic is blocked unless it matches a rule.
- Outgoing traffic is allowed unless it matches a rule.

You can change this default behavior by clicking the *Windows Firewall Properties* link, which displays the *Windows Firewall With Advanced Security On Local Computer* dialog box, as shown in Figure 19-9.

In this dialog box, each of the three network location profile has a tab with identical controls that enables you to modify the default profile settings. You can, for example, configure the firewall to shut down completely when it is connected to a domain network, and turn the firewall on with its most protective settings when you connect the computer to a public network. You can also configure the firewall's notification options, its logging behavior, and how it reacts when rules conflict.

Figure 19-9

The *Windows Firewall with Advanced Security on Local Computer* dialog box

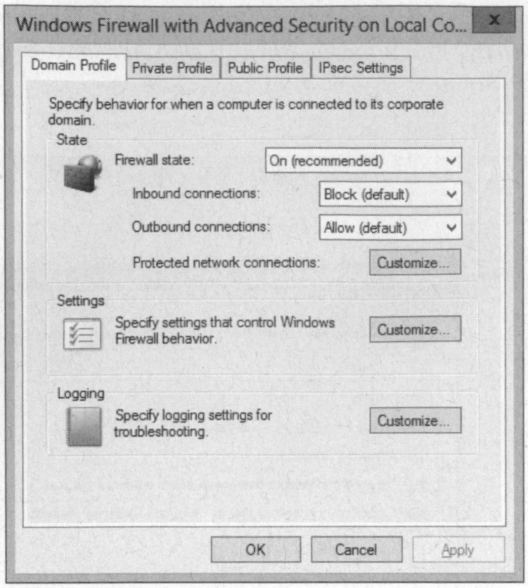

CERTIFICATION READY
Configure Windows Firewall to allow or deny applications, scopes, ports, and users.
Objective 6.4

Creating Rules

The allowed applications that you can configure in the Windows Firewall control panel are a relatively friendly method for working with firewall rules. In the Windows Firewall With Advanced Security console, you can work with the rules in their raw form.

Selecting either *Inbound Rules* or *Outbound Rules* in the left pane displays a list of all the rules operating in that direction, as shown in Figure 19-10. The rules that are currently operational have a check mark in a green circle, whereas the rules not in force are grayed out.

Figure 19-10

The Inbound Rules list in the Windows Firewall with Advanced Security console

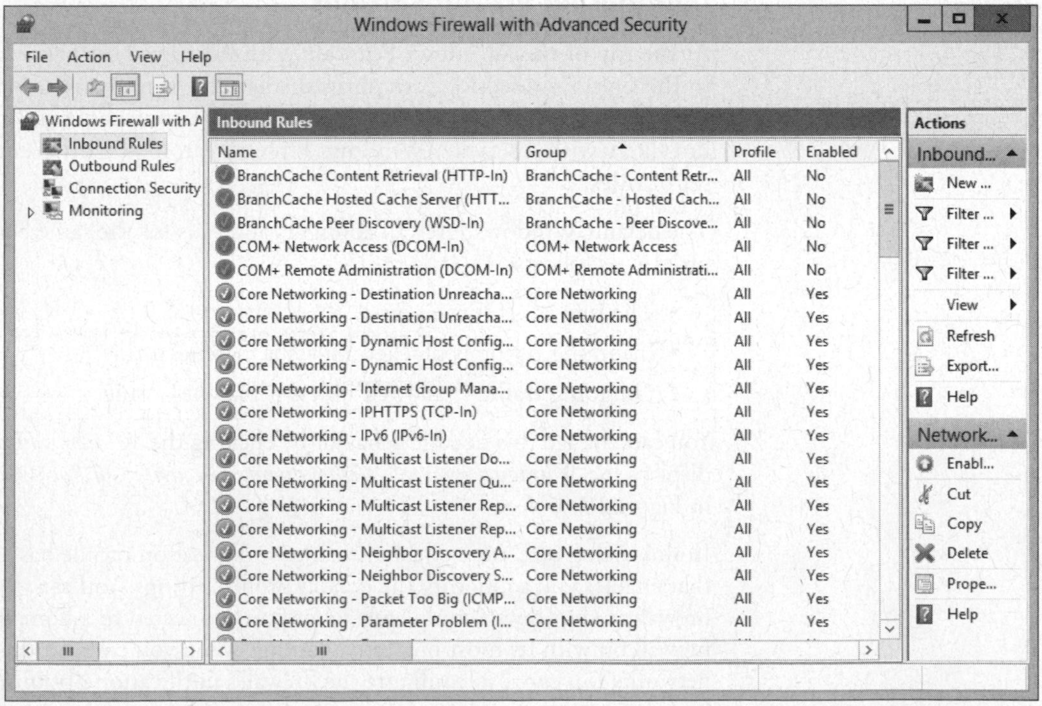

Creating new rules with this interface provides more flexibility than the Windows Firewall control panel. When you right-click the *Inbound Rules* (or *Outbound Rules*) node and select

New Rule from the context menu, the *New Inbound* (or *Outbound*) *Rule Wizard* takes you through the process of configuring the following sets of parameters:

- **Rule Type:** specifies whether you want to create a program rule, a port rule, a variant on one of the predefined rules, or a custom rule, as shown in Figure 19-11. This selection determines which of the following pages the wizard displays.
- **Program:** specifies whether the rule applies to all programs, to one specific program, or to a specific service, as shown in Figure 19-12. This is the equivalent of defining an allowed application in the Windows Firewall control panel, except that you must specify the exact path to the application.

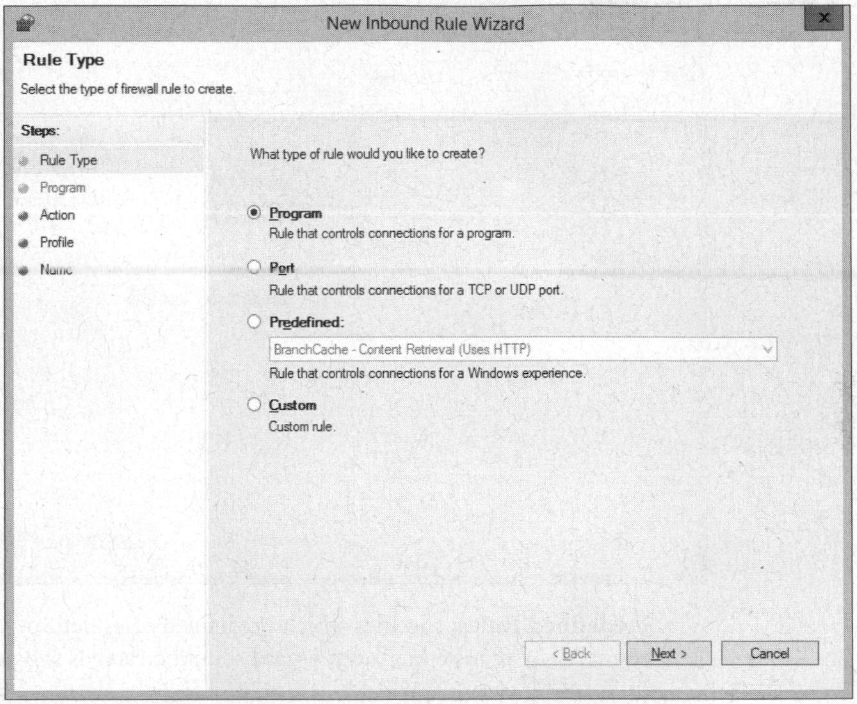

Figure 19-11

The Rule Type page in the New Inbound Rule Wizard

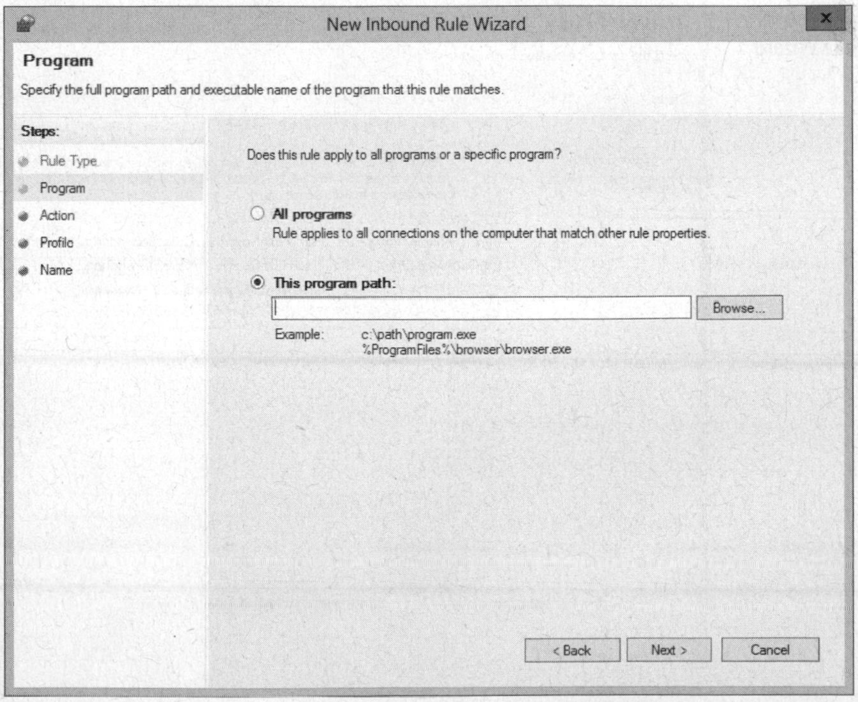

Figure 19-12

The Program page in the New Inbound Rule Wizard

- **Protocol and Ports:** specifies the network or transport layer protocol and the local and remote ports to which the rule applies, as shown in Figure 19-13. This enables you to specify the exact types of traffic that the rule should block or allow. To create rules in this way, you must be familiar with the protocols and ports that an application uses to communicate at both ends of the connection.

Figure 19-13

The Protocols and Ports page in the New Inbound Rule Wizard

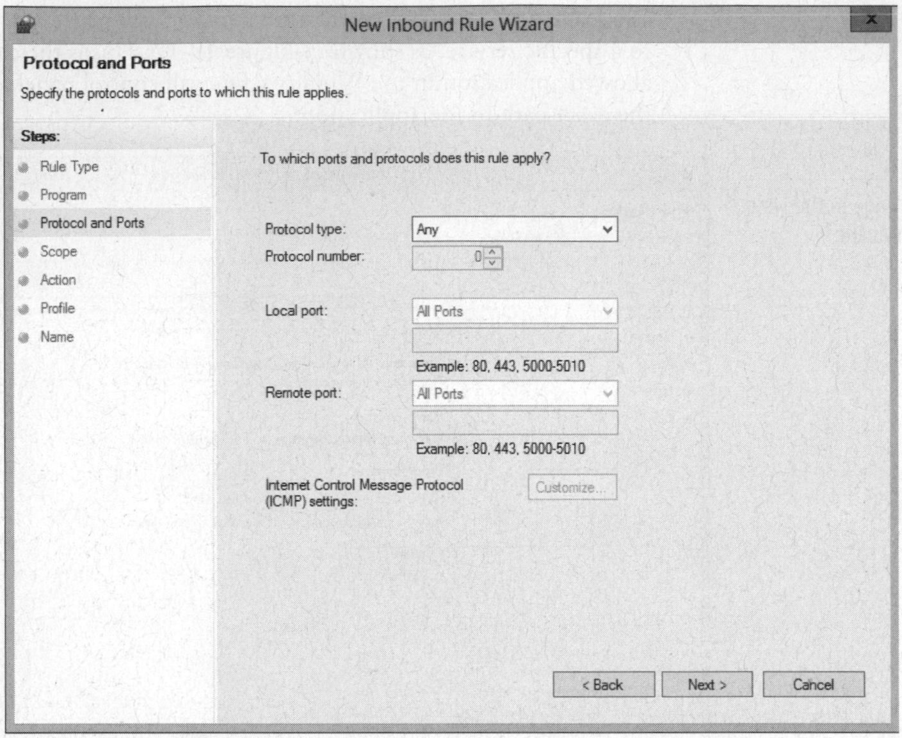

- **Predefined Rules:** specifies which predefined rules defining specific network connectivity requirements the wizard should create, as shown in Figure 19-14.

Figure 19-14

The Predefined Rules page in the New Inbound Rule Wizard

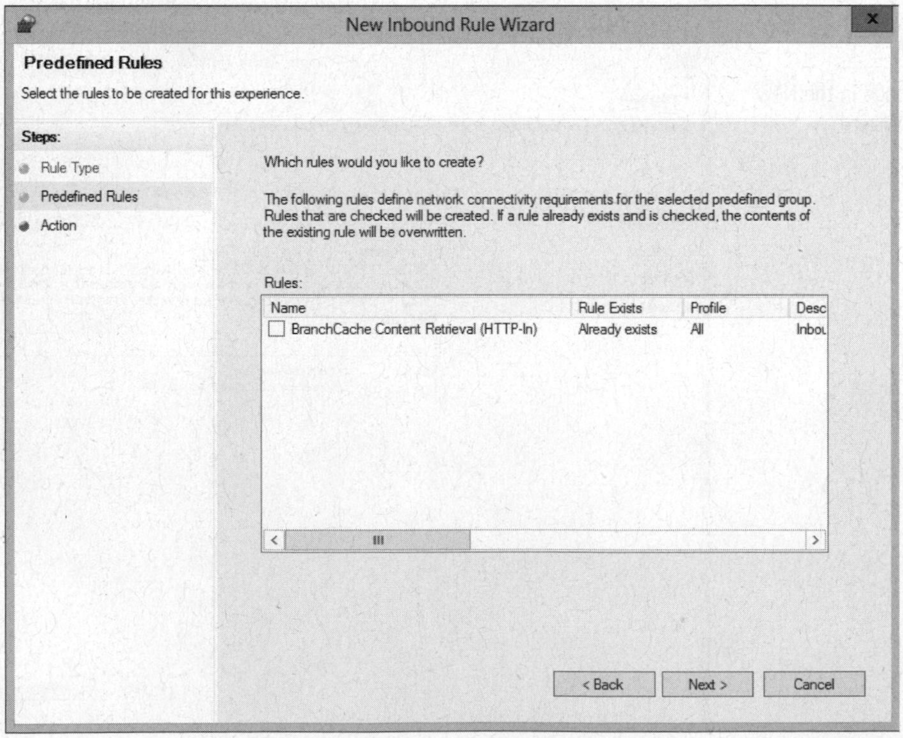

- **Scope:** specifies the IP addresses of the local and remote systems to which the rule applies, as shown in Figure 19-15. This enables you to block or allow traffic between specific computers.

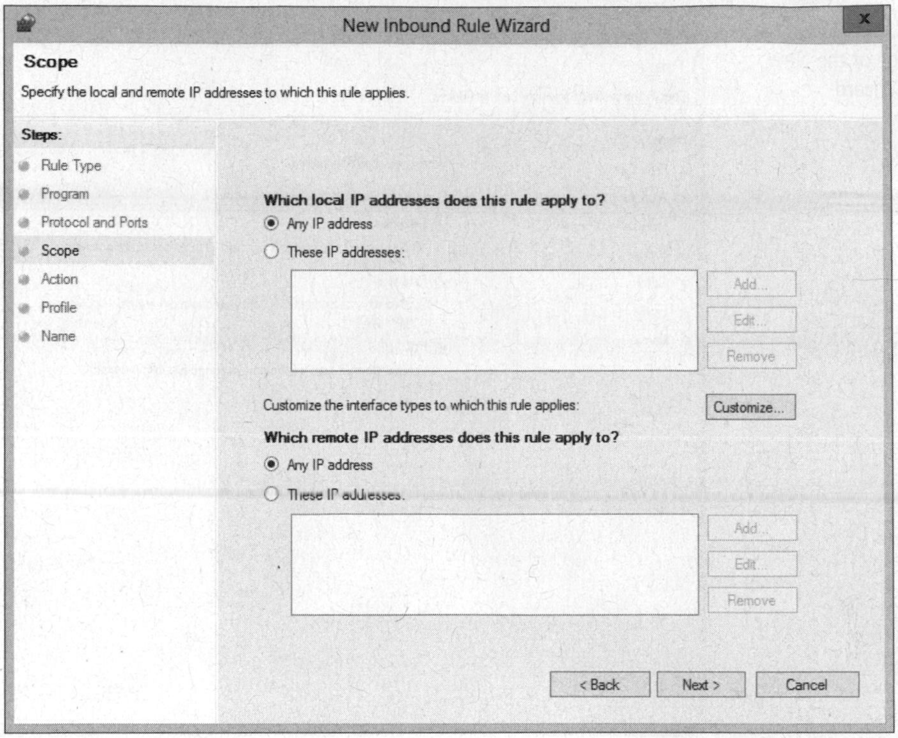

Figure 19-15

The Scope page of the New Inbound Rule Wizard

- **Action:** specifies the action the firewall should take when a packet matches the rule, as shown in Figure 19-16 You configure the rule to allow traffic if it is blocked by default, or block traffic if it is allowed by default. You can also configure the rule to allow traffic only when the connection between the communicating computers is secured using IPsec.

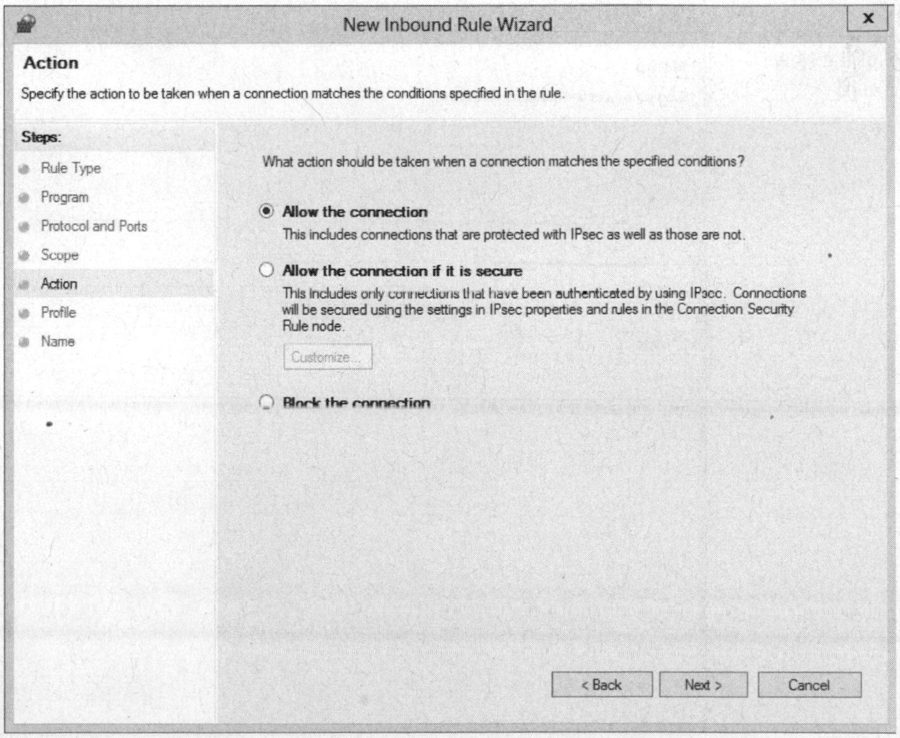

Figure 19-16

The Action page of the New Inbound Rule Wizard

- **Profile:** specifies the profile(s) to which the rule should apply: domain, private, and public, as shown in Figure 19-17.

Figure 19-17

The Profile page of the New
Inbound Rule Wizard

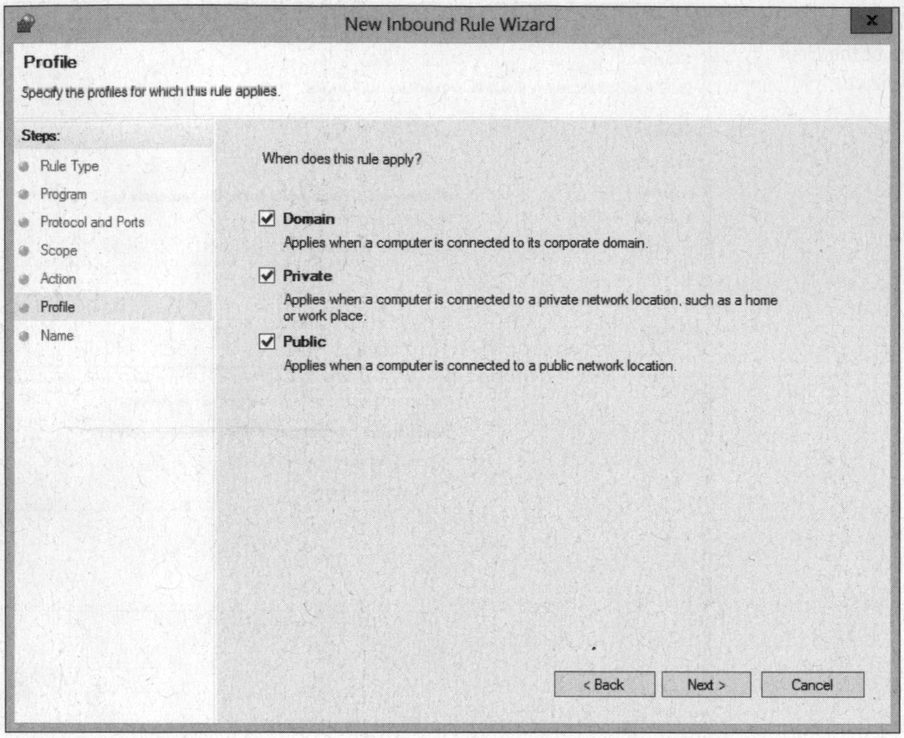

- **Name:** specifies a name and (optionally) a description for the rule, as shown in Figure 19-18.

Figure 19-18

The Name page of the New
Inbound Rule Wizard

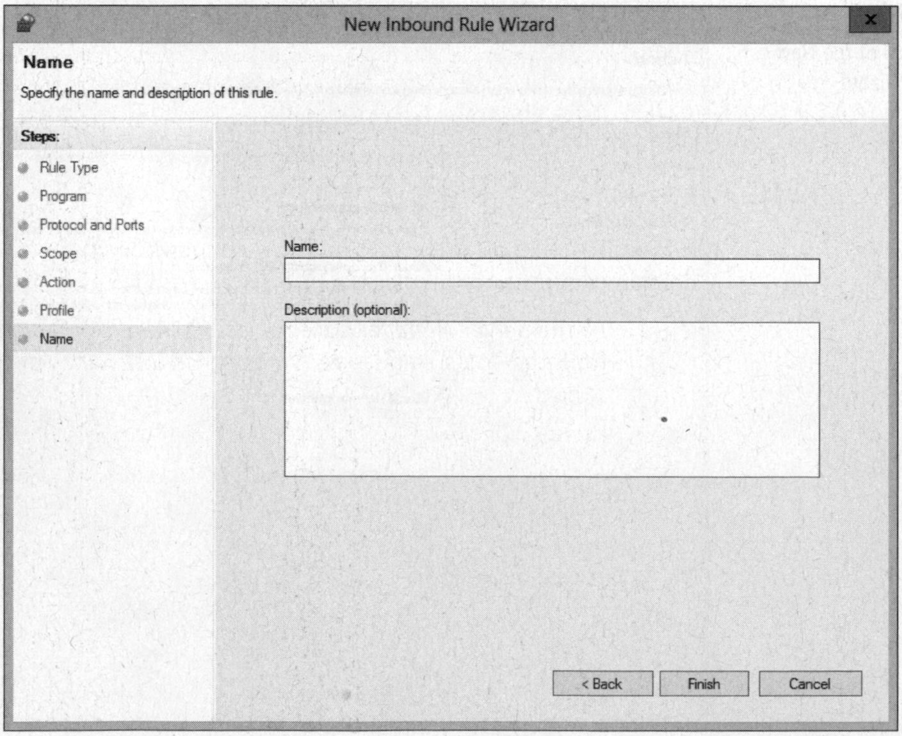

The rules you can create by using the wizards range from simple program rules, just like those you can create in the Windows Firewall control panel, to highly complex and specific rules that block or allow only specific types of traffic between specific computers. The more complicated the rules become, however, the more you need to know about TCP/IP communications in general and the specific behavior of your applications. Modifying the default firewall settings to accommodate some special applications is relatively simple, but creating an entirely new firewall configuration is a formidable task.

USING WINDOWS POWERSHELL

You can create new Windows Firewall rules with Windows PowerShell by using the New-NetFirewallRule cmdlet with the following basic syntax:

```
New-NetFirewallRule -DisplayName <name>
-Direction Inbound|Outbound -Action Block|Allow
-LocalPort <number> -Protocol TCP|UDP -Program <name>
```

For example, to create a rule that blocks all inbound traffic through TCP port 80

```
New-NetFirewallRule -DisplayName "Block 80"
-Direction Inbound -Action Block
-LocalPort 80 -Protocol TCP
```

The New-NetFirewallRule cmdlet has a great many other parameters you can use to create complex rules.

Importing and Exporting Rules

> The process of creating and modifying rules in the Windows Firewall with Advanced Security console can be time-consuming, and repeating the process on multiple computers even more so. Therefore, the console makes it possible for you to save the rules and settings you create by exporting them to a policy file.

A policy file is a file with a .wfw extension that contains all the property settings in a Windows Firewall installation, as well as all of its rules, including the preconfigured rules and the ones you created or modified. To create a policy file, use the following procedure.

⊙ EXPORT WINDOWS FIREWALL RULES

GET READY. Log on to a server running Windows Server 2012, using an account with domain administrator privileges.

1. In the *Server Manager* console, select *Windows Firewall With Advanced Security* from the Tools menu. The *Windows Firewall with Advanced Security* console appears.

2. Modify the inbound or outbound firewall rules or create new rules as needed.

3. In the left pane, select the Windows Firewall with Advanced Security on Local Computer node.

4. From the Action menu, select Export Policy. The Save As combo box appears.

5. In the File Name text box, type a name for the policy file and click Save.

CLOSE the Windows Firewall With Advanced Security console.

CERTIFICATION READY
Import and export settings.
Objective 6.4

You can then duplicate the rules and settings on another computer by copying the file and using the *Import Policy* function to read in the contents, as in the following procedure.

⊖ IMPORT WINDOWS FIREWALL RULES

GET READY. Log on to a server running Windows Server 2012, using an account with domain administrator privileges.

1. In the *Server Manager* console, select *Windows Firewall With Advanced Security* from the Tools menu. The *Windows Firewall with Advanced Security* console appears.
2. From the *Action* menu, select Import Policy. A message box appears, warning that importing a policy file will overwrite all existing firewall rules.
3. Click Yes. An *Open* combo box appears.
4. Locate and select the policy file you want to import and click Open.
5. A message box appears, stating that the policy was successfully imported.
6. Click OK.

CLOSE the Windows Firewall With Advanced Security console.

TAKE NOTE *

When you import policies from a file, the console warns you that all existing rules and settings will be overwritten. You must therefore be careful not to create custom rules on a computer, and then expect to import other rules using a policy file.

Creating Rules Using Group Policy

The Windows Firewall with Advanced Security console makes it possible to create complex firewall configurations, but Windows Firewall is still an application designed to protect a single computer from intrusion. If you have a large number of servers running Windows Server 2012, manually creating a complex firewall configuration on each one can be a lengthy process. Therefore, as with most Windows configuration tasks, administrators can distribute firewall settings to computers throughout the network by using Group Policy.

When you edit a Group Policy object (GPO) and browse to the *Computer Configuration\Policies\ Windows Settings\Security Settings\ Windows Firewall with Advanced Security* node, you see an interface, shown in Figure 19-19, which is similar to the Windows Firewall with Advanced Security console.

Figure 19-19

The *Windows Firewall with Advanced Security* node in a Group Policy object

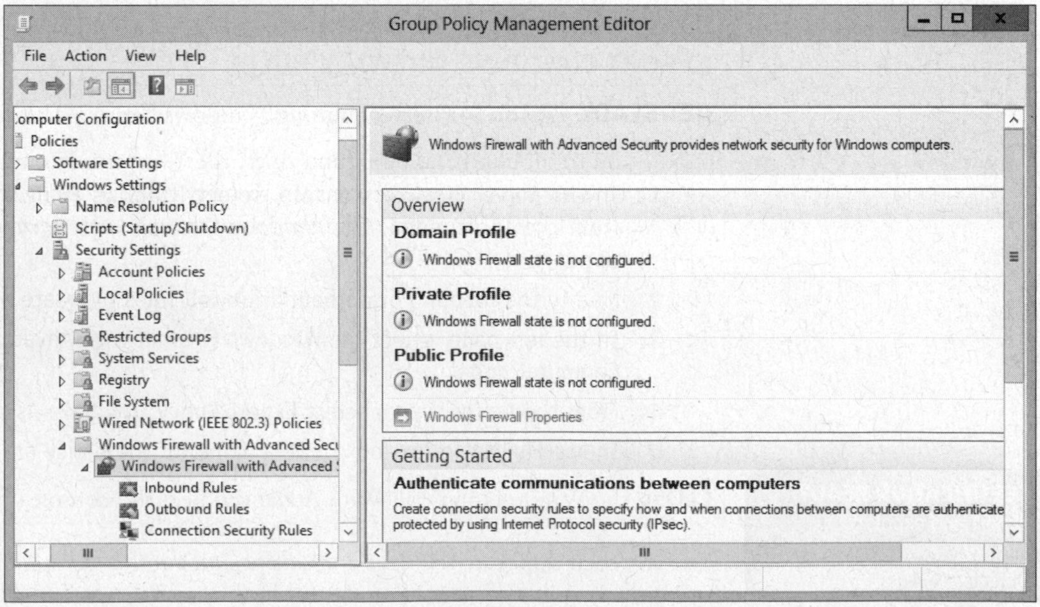

You can configure Windows Firewall properties and create inbound, outbound, and connection security rules, just as you would in the console. The difference is that you can then deploy these settings to computers anywhere on the network by linking the GPO to Active Directory Domain Services object.

When you open a new GPO, the Windows Firewall with Advanced Security node contains no rules at all. The preconfigured rules that you find on every computer running Windows Server 2012 are not there. You can create new rules from scratch to deploy to the network, or you can import settings from a policy file, just as you can in the Windows Firewall with Advanced Security console.

Group Policy does not overwrite the entire Windows Firewall configuration, as importing a policy file does. When you deploy firewall rules and settings by using Group Policy, the rules in the GPO are combined with the existing rules on the target computers. The only exception is when you deploy rules with the same names as existing rules. Then, the GPO settings overwrite these found on the target computers.

Using Filters

Although what a firewall does is sometimes referred to as *packet filtering*, in the Windows Firewall With Advanced Security console, the term filter refers to a feature that enables you to display inbound or outbound rules according to the profile they apply to, their current state, or the group to which they belong.

For example, to display only the rules that apply to the public profile, click *Action > Filter By Profile > Filter By Public Profile*. The display of the Inbound Rules list then changes to show only the rules that apply to the public profile. This can simplify the process of locating specific rules in a long list. In the same way, you can apply a filter that causes the console to display only the rules that are currently turned on, or the rules that belong to a particular group. Click *Action > Clear All Filters* to return to the default display showing all the rules.

Creating Connection Security Rules

Windows Server 2012 also includes a feature that incorporates IPsec data protection into the Windows Firewall. The IP Security (IPsec) standards are a collection of documents that define a method for securing data while it is in transit over a TCP/IP network. IPsec includes a connection establishment routine, during which computers authenticate each other before transmitting data, and a technique called **tunneling**, in which data packets are encapsulated within other packets, for their protection.

In addition to inbound and outbound rules, the Windows Firewall With Advanced Security console enables you to create connection security rules, by using the New Connection Security Rule Wizard. Connection security rules define the type of protection you want to apply to the communications that conform to Windows Firewall rules.

When you right-click the *Connection Security Rules* node and select *New Rule* from the context menu, the *New Connection Security Rule Wizard* takes you through the process of configuring the following sets of parameters:

- **Rule Type:** specifies the basic function of the rule, such as to isolate computers based on authentication criteria, to exempt certain computers (such as infrastructure servers) from authentication, to authenticate two specific computers or groups of computers, or to tunnel communications between two computers, as shown in Figure 19-20. You can also create custom rules combining these functions.

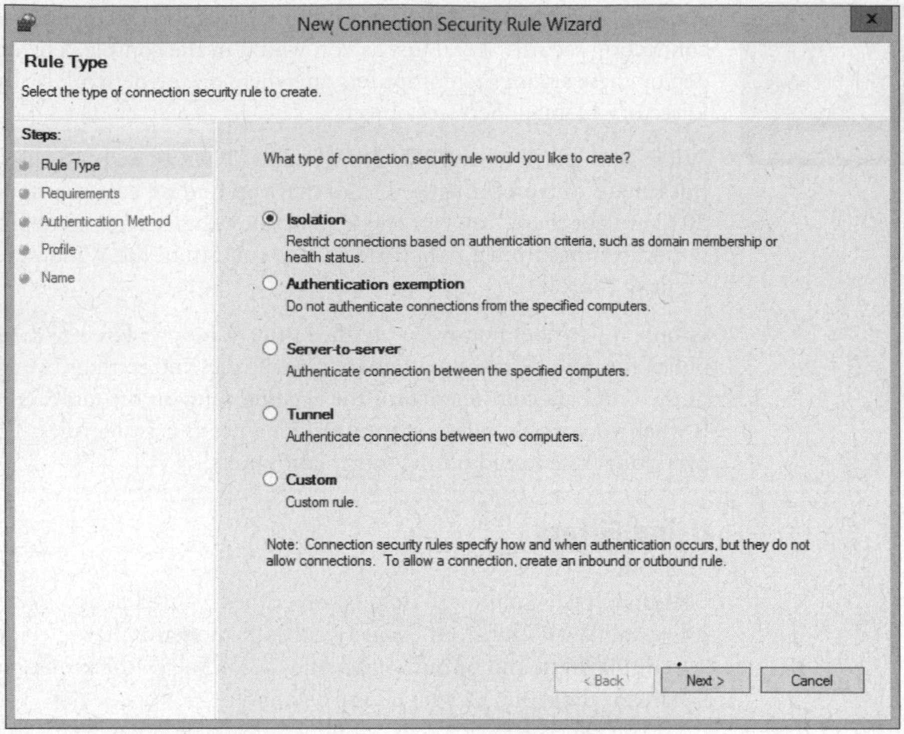

Figure 19-20

The Rule Type page in the
New Connection Security
Rule Wizard

Figure 19-20
The Rule Type page in the New Connection Security Rule Wizard

- **Endpoints:** specifies the IP addresses of the computers that establish a secured connection before transmitting any data, as shown in Figure 19-21.

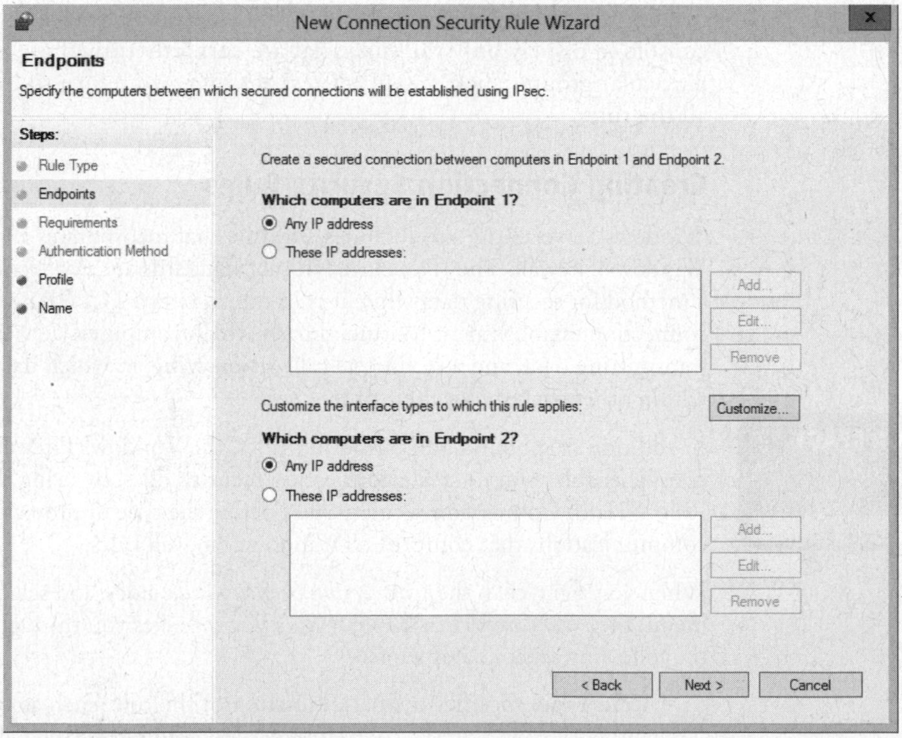

Figure 19-21

The Endpoints page in the
New Connection Security
Rule Wizard

Figure 19-21
The Endpoints page in the New Connection Security Rule Wizard

- **Requirements:** specifies whether authentication between two computers should be requested or required. If required, options include requiring authentication for inbound connections only or for both inbound and outbound connections, as shown in Figure 19-22.

Figure 19-22

The Requirements page in
the New Connection Security
Rule Wizard

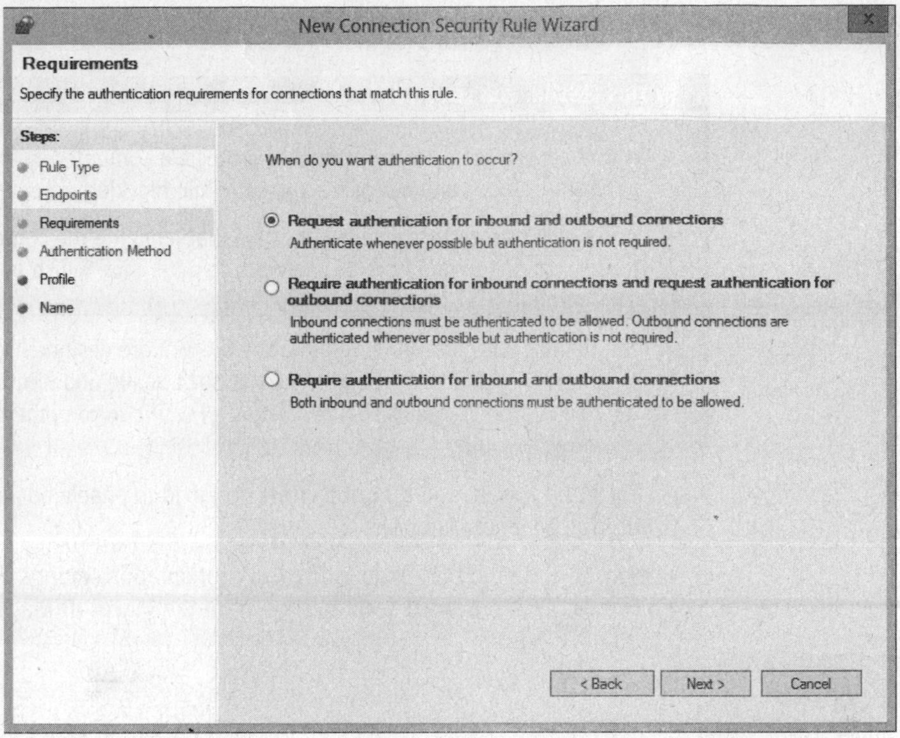

- **Authentication Method:** specifies the type of authentication the computers should use
  when establishing a connection, as shown in Figure 19-23.

Figure 19-23

The Authentication Method
page in the New Connection
Security Rule Wizard

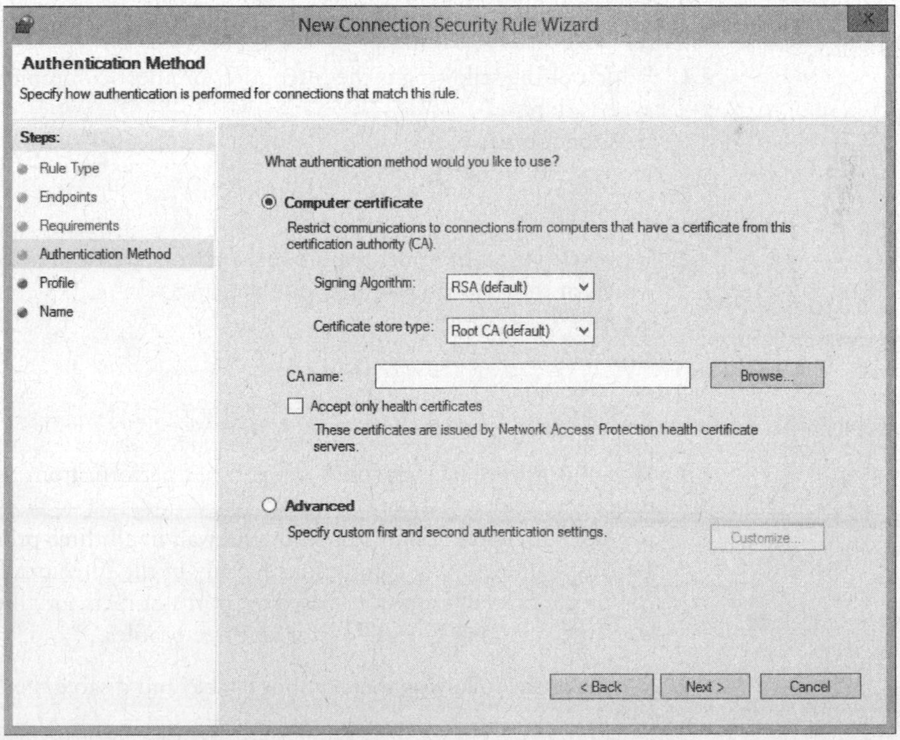

- **Profile:** specifies the profile(s) to which the rule should apply: domain, private, and public.
- **Name:** specifies a name and (optionally) a description for the rule.

SKILL SUMMARY

IN THIS LESSON, YOU LEARNED:

- A firewall is a software program that protects a computer by allowing certain types of network traffic in and out of the system while blocking others.

- A firewall is essentially a series of filters that examine the contents of packets and the traffic patterns to and from the network to determine which packets they should allow to pass through the filter.

- The default rules preconfigured into the firewall are designed to admit the traffic used by standard Windows networking functions, such as file and printer sharing. For outgoing network traffic, Windows Firewall allows all traffic to pass the firewall except that which conforms to a rule.

- The Windows Firewall control panel is designed to enable administrators to perform basic firewall configuration tasks as needed.

- For full access to the Windows Firewall configuration settings, you must use the Windows Firewall With Advanced Security snap-in for the Microsoft Management console.

■ Knowledge Assessment

Multiple Choice

Select one or more correct answers for each of the following questions.

1. Which of the following is the filter criterion most commonly used in firewall rules?
   a. IP addresses
   b. subnet masks
   c. protocol numbers
   d. port numbers

2. Connection security rules require that network traffic allowed through the firewall use which of the following security mechanisms?
   a. EFS
   b. IPsec
   c. UAC
   d. Kerberos

3. Which of the following actions can you not perform from the Windows Firewall control panel?
   a. Allow an application through the firewall in all three profiles.
   b. Block all incoming connections for any of the three profiles.
   c. Create firewall exceptions based on port numbers for all three profiles.
   d. Turn Windows Firewall off for all three profiles.

4. Which of the following tools cannot enable and disable the Network Discovery firewall rules?
   a. File Explorer
   b. Network and Sharing Center
   c. Action Center
   d. Allowed Apps dialog box

5. Which of the following statements about Windows Firewall are true? (Choose all that apply.)
   a. Applying firewall rules with Group Policy overwrites all of the firewall rules on the target computer.
   b. Applying firewall rules with Group Policy combines the newly deployed rules with the ones already there.
   c. Importing firewall rules saved from another computer overwrites all of the rules on the target system.
   d. Importing firewall rules saved from another computer combines both sets of settings.

6. Windows Firewall uses three profiles to represent the type of network to which the server is connected. What are the three profiles?
   a. Private, Temporary, and Authenticated
   b. Public, DMZ, and Private
   c. Internet, Secure, and Private
   d. Domain, Private, and Public

7. When a user attempts to visit an Internet-based e-mail account, what is the response of the Windows Firewall?
   a. Firewall will not permit the user to visit non-corporate website.
   b. Firewall by default will not block client-initiated network traffic.
   c. Firewall will block the webmail account unless the user is already authenticated.
   d. Firewall will block all outbound traffic.

8. In the Windows Firewall With Advanced Security console, while creating a new rule, the Program page specifies whether the _____.
   a. rule applies to all programs, to one specific program
   b. rule applies to all users, to one specific user
   c. rule applies to all systems, to one specific system
   d. rule applies to all programs, to one specific program, or to a specific service

9. By exporting the Windows Firewall policy, you have a file with a .wfw extension that contains _____.
   a. all its rules, including the preconfigured rules and the ones you have created or modified
   b. all the rules you have created or modified
   c. preconfigured rules to be applied to another firewall
   d. firewall settings as specified by the Group Policy settings

Best Answer

Choose the letter that corresponds to the best answer. More than one answer choice may achieve the goal. Select the BEST answer.

1. What is the primary objective of a firewall?
   a. To authenticate and authorize users past the network perimeter
   b. To permit traffic in and out for legitimate users, and to block the rest
   c. To compare traffic information against a list of known valid traffic
   d. To protect a network by allowing certain types of network traffic in and out of the system

2. Windows Firewall Customize Settings contains three profiles (Public, Private and Domain). What differentiates these profiles from each other?
   a. Public is for servers accessible to temporary users. Private is for servers on an internal network. Domain is for servers in which users are all authenticated.

b. Public is for servers accessible to unauthenticated users. Private is for inaccessible servers. Domain is for servers accessible only to authenticated users.

c. Public is for servers accessible to temporary users. Private is for servers on an internal network. Domain is for servers across multiple sites.

d. Public is for servers accessible to unauthenticated users. Private is for servers on a private network. Domain is for servers spanning different domain groups.

3. Windows Firewall allows you to create inbound, outbound, and connection security rules for individual servers or systems. How can you do this for multiple systems?

a. You can delegate to administrators the task of performing the same configuration to their local servers.

b. You can create a new Group Policy object (GPO) and create matching rules to match the desired configuration. Then deploy the GPO to other systems on the network.

c. You can visit individual systems and configure them as you have the initial system.

d. You can create a new GPO and you can import settings from a policy file created earlier. Then deploy the GPO to other systems on the network.

4. What is the primary benefit of configuring it through the Windows Firewall With Advanced Security snap-in for the Microsoft Management console?

a. The Microsoft Management console offers a more familiar interface than the Windows Firewall control panel.

b. The Microsoft Management console snap-in offers full access compared to the Windows Firewall control panel.

c. The Microsoft Management console snap-in applies the rules faster than the Windows Firewall control panel.

d. Compared to the Windows Firewall control panel, the Microsoft Management console can be brought up in fewer clicks.

5. When creating a firewall exception, what is the difference between opening a port and allowing an application?

a. Opening a port is permanent, and thus is less risky than allowing an application.

b. Allowing an application opens the specified port only while the program is running, and thus is less risky.

c. Both options are available in the Windows Firewall with Advanced Security console.

d. There is no functional difference between opening a port and allowing an application.

Build a List

1. Order the steps to allow an application in Windows Firewall.

a. Click Allow an app or feature through Windows Firewall. The Allowed Apps dialog box appears.

b. Scroll down in the Allowed apps and features list and select the check box for the application you want to allow through the firewall.

c. Log on to a server running Windows Server 2012, using an account with domain administrator privileges.

d. Click OK to close the Allowed Apps dialog box.

e. In the Server Manager console, open the Control Panel and click System and Security > Windows Firewall. The Windows Firewall window appears.

2. Order the steps to export Windows Firewall rules.

a. From the Action menu, select Export Policy. The Save As combo box appears.

b. Log on to a server running Windows Server 2012, using an account with domain administrator privileges.

    c. Modify the inbound or outbound firewall rules or create new rules as needed.

    d. In the Server Manager console, select Windows Firewall With Advanced Security from the Tools menu. The Windows Firewall with Advanced Security console appears.

    e. In the left pane, select the Windows Firewall with Advanced Security on Local Computer node.

    f. In the File Name text box, type a name for the policy file and click Save.

3. Order the steps to import Windows Firewall rules.

    a. In the Server Manager console, select Windows Firewall With Advanced Security from the Tools menu. The Windows Firewall with Advanced Security console appears.

    b. A message box appears, stating that the policy was successfully imported.

    c. From the Action menu, select Import Policy. A message box appears warning that importing a policy file will overwrite all existing firewall rules.

    d. Click Yes. An Open combo box appears. Locate and select the policy file you want to import and click Open.

    e. Log on to a server running Windows Server 2012, using an account with domain administrator privileges.

■ Business Case Scenarios

Scenario 19-1: Configuring Windows Firewall

Ralph is a junior network administrator at Wingtip Toys, left in change of the IP department while everyone else is out of town at a conference. Ralph receives a call from the company's best customer, reporting that they are unable to place orders through the company's website. Ralph examines the logs for the Windows web server and notices a huge amount of incoming traffic that began that morning.

Ralph suspects that the server is the target of a denial of service (DoS) attack, but he doesn't have access to the network firewall, nor does he know anything about the firewall configuration his company uses. Ralph does have access to the Windows Firewall running on the web server, however. What temporary modifications can he make to that firewall to block the attack and allow the customer to submit orders as they normally do?

Scenario 19-2: Configuring Firewall Rules to Require IPsec Encryption

Alice is responsible for the file server where all of the company payroll and accounting data is stored, and as a result, security is one of her primary concerns. To prevent potential intruders from intercepting sensitive data in transit over the network, Alice wants to ensure that all of the company bookkeepers and accountants use IPsec to encrypt their traffic as they access the financial spreadsheets stored on the server.

Alice has located the inbound firewall rules on the server that enable users to access files using their spreadsheet application. How can she modify those rules to permit access only under the following conditions:

- The user must be a member of the Accounting group.
- The user must be using a computer on the company subnet.
- The user must connect using IPsec encryption.

Appendix A
Exam 70-410 Installing and Configuring Windows Server 2012

EXAM OBJECTIVE	OBJECTIVE NUMBER	LESSON NUMBER
Install and Configure Servers		
Install servers.	1.1	1
Configure servers.	1.2	2
Configure local storage.	1.3	3
Configure Server Roles and Features		
Configure file and share access.	2.1	4
Configure print and document services.	2.2	5
Configure servers for remote management.	2.3	6
Configure Hyper-V		
Create and configure virtual machine settings.	3.1	7
Create and configure virtual machine storage.	3.2	8
Create and configure virtual networks.	3.3	9
Deploy and Configure Core Network Services		
Configure IPv4 and IPv6 addressing.	4.1	10
Deploy and configure Dynamic Host Configuration Protocol (DHCP) service.	4.2	11
Deploy and configure DNS service.	4.3	12
Install and Administer Active Directory		
Install domain controllers.	5.1	13
Create and manage Active Directory users and computers.	5.2	14
Create and manage Active Directory groups and organizational units (OUs).	5.3	15
Create and Manage Group Policy		
Create Group Policy objects (GPOs).	6.1	16
Configure security policies.	6.2	17
Configure application restriction policies.	6.3	18
Configure Windows Firewall.	6.4	19

Index

Note: Page numbers followed by "f" represent figures and page numbers followed by "t" represent tables.